A History of the Early Church

A History of the Early Church

Hans Lietzmann

with foreword and bibliography
by W.H.C. Frend

Volume 1

James Clarke & Co.
Cambridge

James Clarke & Co. Ltd
P.O. Box 60
Cambridge
CB1 2NT

English Translation © Bertram Lee Woolf, 1951
Foreword and Bibliography © W.H.C. Frend, 1993

British Library Cataloguing-in-Publication Data:
A catalogue record is available for this book from the British Library

ISBN (Vol. 1) 0-227-67925-3
ISBN (Vol. 2) 0-227-67926-1
ISBN (Set) 0-227-67927-X

Printed in Great Britain by
Hillman Printers (Frome) Ltd, Somerset

Contents

Volume 2

Foreword

H ANS LIETZMANN DIED at Locarno on 25 June 1942 before he could
complete the fourth volume of his *Geschichte der Alten Kirche*. The
long chapter on the 'Origins of Monasticism' and chapters on 'Ambrose
and Theodosius' and 'Popular Piety in the Fourth Century' were in
manuscript, and the abbreviated volume of 200 pages was prepared for the
printer by his daughter Sabina, and a brilliant student, Kurt Aland. It was
published in 1944 through the good offices of his friend Walter Eltester.
Long before this time Lietzmann's work had come to be regarded as a
masterpiece, and it is in the conviction of its lasting value that it is now
being republished.

Lietzmann was born in Düsseldorf on 2 March 1875, the son of a
middle-ranking government official. His mother died at his birth and his
father when he was ten. He was brought up by his father's sister, whom
he always regarded as his mother, and by grandparents. The family moved
to Wittenberg and Hans Lietzmann's early years were hard, especially
financially. At school, however, he gave early evidence of an exceptionally enquiring mind that led him toward the natural sciences and, in
particular, astronomy. None the less, he was finally influenced towards
classics by a teacher of genius, and towards theology by another, who
showed him that a strong Lutheran Christianity could be combined with
an equally strong critical sensitivity applied to the Bible. These ideas were
to guide him through his life.

In 1893 he was able to begin a study of classics at the University of
Jena, but the following year moved to Bonn where he added theology to
his curriculum. This proved to be a decisive move, for in 1896 he was
awarded a prize in the Faculty of Theology for his examination of the
concept of the Son of Man in the Gospels. He concluded that the term had
no equivalent in Aramaic and hence was not used by Jesus himself - it was
an attempted Greek rendering of the messianic and apocalyptic use of
anthropos in Daniel 7.13, and was adopted by the early Christians in the
post-Pauline era. The treatment had been radical. But despite some head-
shaking, Lietzmann became Licentiate in Theology at Bonn on 28
November 1896, having in the previous month satisfied the church
authorities in Koblenz of his competence in theology.

A career in the parish ministry was never in his mind, however. His
first appointment was as an assistant to Hermann von Soden on the latter's

critical edition of the New Testament. The insight into textual criticism which this gave him inspired Lietzmann to take up a demanding challenge in Patristic scholarship. In 1896 the *Gesellschaft der Wissenschaften* at Göttingen had offered a prize for the best collation and organisation of the Catena of surviving manuscript fragments of Apollonaris of Laodicea, condemned at the Council of Constantinople in 381 for ostensibly denying the full humanity of Christ. Lietzmann went to work in Paris - where he carried out research on 50 different manuscripts - and also worked sucessfully elsewhere. He was awarded the prize in 1899. Five years later, he produced his first masterpiece, *Apollonaris von Laodicea und seine Schule; Texte und Untersuchungen.*

He was now set firmly on an academic career. Success in the *Staatsexamen*, in which he passed the four philological disciplines of Latin, Greek, history and religion, was followed by *Habilitation* and election to the Faculty of Theology at Bonn on 3 February 1900. Almost immediately he began a major work of scholarly organisation designed to produce texts to be used in University seminars. These *Kleine Texte*, first appearing in 1902, were to become famous. Including texts such as Greek papyri and Pompeian wall graffiti as well as apocryphal Gospels and fragments of some of Origen's *Homilies*, they foreshadowed Lietzmann's concern for interdisciplinary studies, as well as attracting the collaboration of distinguished scholars such as Adolf von Harnack and Hermann von Soden. By 1942 when the series was brought to an end, 170 separate *Texte* had been published.

In 1905 Lietzmann left Bonn to become Associate Professor at the Univeristy of Jena. There he was soon working jointly with colleagues from the classics and theology faculties to produce a massive series of scholarly studies commenting on the books of the New Testament. These were also to have a long life, 23 volumes having appeared by 1941, and Lietzmann's contribution being *Romans* (1906), *I Corinthians* (1907), *II Corinthians*(1909) and *Galatians* (1910). Not surprisingly, in 1908 he was elected *Ordinarius* (University Professor) supported by von Harnack, Loofs and Bonwetsch. He was regarded as a caring man who combined great scholarly potential with firm Lutheran convictions.

Lietzmann had always been interested in archaeology. In 1905 he wrote in his diary, "I soon saw that without an exact knowledge of archaeological sources it was impossible to obtain a clear picture either of secular or church history". One of his seminars in 1911 was devoted to "The Origins of Christian Art". Next year he had the chance to travel to Greece where contact with the German School of Athens convinced him of the great possibilities that lay in archaeological research aimed at unravelling problems in early Christian history. These convictions were reinforced the following year by visits to Italy (in particular Rome), Sicily and Tunisia. Though he never undertook excavations, his seminars in Berlin in the late 1930s emphasised the importance of archaeology for successful research, especially on non-orthodox Christian movements such as Montanism and Donatism.

By 1914 the strain of such activity was beginning to tell. He was becoming something of a scholarly automaton. Since 1896 he had amassed a bibliography of 132 separate pieces of scholarly writing. A letter from his friend Karl Holl of 28 May 1914, discussing the text of an article he had sent Lietzmann for comment, ended: "I hear that archaeology has again swallowed up all your interests. There are other things in life than science. Do please remember this!" (Aland, Letter 299).

Lietzmann was now 39. Bad eyesight, made worse by an over-concentration on manuscript texts, ruled him out for military service. He was, however, beginning to take an active part in public service. In January 1914 he was elected to the City Council (*Stadtgemeinrat*) of Jena, and the following year became deputy chairman of the Red Cross in the city. It was in this work that he met his future wife who was helping as a medical student. Jutta Hoffer and he became friends. They became engaged in December 1918 after the end of the war and married in February 1919.

In the first two years of the war Lietzmann was able to continue to work more or less untroubled. In 1915 he published *Petrus und Paulus in Rom* in which he indicated a belief in the truth of the historical tradition, supported by apocryphal sources, for the deaths of Peter and Paul in Rome. In a second edition published in 1927 he was able to show that the results of the excavations in the San Sebastiano catacomb indicated that, from at least the end of the second century, Christians had believed that the apostles had been buried in Rome. The excavations under the Vatican from 1939 onward and the discovery of the shrine connected with St Peter in the Red Wall have now led scholars to date this belief from as early as c.A.D. 160.

Lietzmann's letters in 1917 and 1918 show his continued dedication to scholarship while receiving increasingly distressed and pessimistic letters from colleagues. His Chair survived the revolutions of 1918-19, and he was able to participate actively in the reorganisation of the Lutheran Church in Thuringia in 1919-20. Though this was to become one of the centres of the 'German Christian' movement which was allied to the Nazis, Lietzmann himself became identified with the conservative nationalism of the *Deutschnational Volkspartei* which he joined in 1919 and to which he remained faithful.

In this second period of his life, which extended from the end of the First World War and his marriage, to Hitler's seizure of power in January 1933, he achieved the position of Germany's premier patristic scholar. In 1921 he became editor of the *Zeitschrift für Neutestamentliche Wissenschaft*, broadening its scope to include the first five centuries of the Church's history. Then, in 1923 he was elected to succeed Adolf von Harnack in the Chair of New Testament and Christian Archaeology at Berlin University. The following year he moved with his growing family - comprising Sabina (1919), Joachim (1921) and Regina (1923) - to Berlin.

The next four years were to be the busiest and most varied in his life. The crisis caused by the Rhineland occupation and the inflation of 1923-24 saw him as a member of the Council of the *Notgemeinschaft deutscher Wissenschaft* (Organisation for Emergency Aid for German Scholarship). Next year he published an autobiography, a curious action for one near, but not quite at, the height of his career, who could expect another 20 years of full activity. In this he hoped he would be able to continue his many varied scholarly activities. However, the attempt to do so over-taxed his strength and nearly led to his early death in 1927.

Interest in the development of Christian liturgy was competing with archaeology, editorial and faculty business, as well as family life. Since 1921 he had been working on the manuscript tradition of the Gregorian Sacramentary, which formed the basis for his classic *Messe und Herrenmahl* published in 1926. The same year, belatedly, he became a member of the *Kirchenväter Kommission*, and in 1927 he was elected to the membership of the Prussian Academy of Sciences. The demands of his inaugural lecture on '*Probleme der Spätantike*' and responsibilities arising from his re-founding of two scholarly periodicals - *Gnomon*, specialising in full-length reviews of studies on the whole range of classical and early Christian antiquity and *Antike*, in the field of classical philology - all proved too much. In the same year Lietzmann suffered a heart attack and, though he recovered completely, was compelled thenceforth to cut his workload. He gave up the Presidency of the *Gesellschaft für Kirchengeschichte* (Church History Society) and spent a year in Istanbul, where he was able to study at first hand the Byzantine walls of Constantinople. Returning via Rome he visited the recent discovery and excavation of the Jewish catacomb in the grounds of the Villa Torlonia, and was associated with H. W. Beyer in the publication of the results in 1930.

This year also saw the 400th anniversary of the Augsburg Confession. Lietzmann was a member of the *Lutherkommission* and was called upon to edit a series of essays setting out the beliefs of the Lutheran Church, under the title *Bekenntnis der Evangelischen Lutheranischen Kirche*. This, and his Academy lecture on the trial of Jesus in 1931 (*'Der Prozeß Jesu'*), aroused considerable public debate because of the author's even-handed apportionment of blame for the Crucifixion on the Jews and on Pilate.

Even-handed assessment was to be the hallmark of the study which Lietzmann was now preparing. He had been working on the *Geschichte der Alten Kirche* since 1928, and Volume I appeared in 1932. Apart from dedications to von Harnack, who had died in 1930, and to Karl Müller, the volume opened without any preliminary introduction. Following a chapter on 'Palestine and the Roman Empire' the story continued through the life and death of Jesus to the Pauline mission and the sub-apostolic period ending, as von Harnack himself would have ended, with Marcion. The second volume, *The Church Universal* appeared in 1936 and the third in 1938, taking the story to the death of Julian (361).

The style was easy, footnotes were kept to a minimum, and the readership for which the author was writing was wider than the normal academic audience. From the outset, critics and members of the public alike asked why, at no point, had the author explained his aims. Lietzmann had in fact planned five volumes recounting the history of the Church to A.D. 600, the period of Pope Gregory the Great. Fate, however, prevented him from reaching the end of the 4th century, leaving the study without a chapter on Augustine. In a long letter to Rudolf Bultmann (Aland, Letter 1096) of 20 May 1939, he explained what he was trying to do.

In Volume I, he wanted to raise questions for discussion without making theological judgements himself. The object was to record what actually happened - as von Ranke had once put it, simply to tell "how it had actually been" and that at times one had only incomplete evidence to deal with. There was no overall plan, but a fitting together of each fragment of a mosaic, so that the former pattern could be reconstructed. It was thus that God's working in history could be discerned; though whatever reality one was able to establish would provoke new and insoluble problems, which had to be left for the theologians to give their verdict.

This is a true assessment of Lietzmann's *History*. He was sparing in his theological judgements. Writing about Jesus' death, Lietzmann ends Chapter 4 with the briefest account of the Crucifixion and the comment:

"The words of the prophet were fulfilled: the shepherd had been struck down and the flocks were scattered. The Messianic dream had ended." The events of Easter and the appearances of Christ to his disciples he records, but declines to offer any comment. Speculation was a matter for theologians and philosophers. The historian must be content to record events.

The successive volumes of the *History of the Early Church* achieved enormous success. The first was written while the Weimar Republic still survived, but the second and third were published when Hitler was in power. At first Lietzmann saw little threat to his position and in 1934 he foresaw ten years work ahead. Like many of his profession and back-ground he was a German nationalist, but with a strong democratic sense derived from his Lutheran convictions. Unfortunately, like many of his colleagues, he also misunderstood and underestimated Hitler's aims. The latter's threat to the Lutheran Church, however, soon became obvious, and it was in defence of his Church that Lietzmann first opposed the regime. Unlike some of his colleagues and friends he rejected the German Christian Movement (*Deutsche Christen*) at once, signing declarations against accepting the 'Aryan Clause' which demanded the exclusion from Church office of any clergy or officials who had married non-Aryans. He gave his allegiance to the Confessing Church in 1934, but was unwilling to sign the Barmen Declaration expressing in theological terms the faith of this Church.

Gradually, opposition in Church matters broadened into opposition to the regime as a whole. Since 1924 Lietzmann had belonged to the 'Wednesday Society' (*Mittwochsgesellschaft*). This was an old and traditional club originating in 1863 which brought together senior civil servants, academics and officers in the armed forces for an informal evening meeting to discuss scholarly and kindred subjects on alternate Wednesdays during the year. The prevailing national/conservative politi-cal outlook of the Society may be gathered from the fact that General Ludwig Beck was Chairman; Johannes Popitz, Finance Minister in the Prussian Government and a survivor in the state service from Weimar, was Treasurer; and Ulrich von Hassell (German Ambassador in Rome), a prominent member. It was through Popitz that Lietzmann was able to bring some influence to bear to secure the release from concentration camp of some Jewish colleagues, such as Paul Friedlander. The Wednes-day Society gradually developed into a centre of anti-Nazi resistance. Popitz himself was involved in the anti-Hitler plot of 20 July 1944, and was arrested and executed the following February. Before illness struck him down, Lietzmann had drafted a scheme for a reform of the German Universities free from Nazi influence.

In the years before the outbreak of the Second World War, Lietzmann continued to receive honours. He was elected Member of the Academy of Science of Athens in 1935, of Stockholm in 1938, and of Vienna 1940; he also became a member of the *Deutsche Archaeologische Institut*, a belated though fitting acknowledgement of his achievement in linking patristic and archaeological studies.

All this time, the work in academy, university and faculty went on. I was privileged to be a *Gasthörer* (visiting student) in Lietzmann's seminar for most of the period 1937-8. Visiting no. 2 Dorotheenstraße, where the seminars were held, was not to be forgotten. Students were expected to be fully acquainted with the relevant *Kleine Texte*. Their contributions were of a very high standard. On occasions the seminar would be treated to the latest on Athanasius from Hans-Georg Opitz, the outstanding scholar whom Lietzmann hoped would succeed him. Accuracy and simplicity were praised; solecisms severely rebuked. An unfortunate *Volksdeutsche* student from the Ukraine dilated learnedly about 'von Mommsen'. Lietzmann listened for a little while and then thundered '*Mommsen war ein Demokrat*'. The class was dumbfounded for a moment and then cheered. In 1938 a formal lecture to the Academy gave him a further chance to make his views public. He chose the subject '*Die Anfänge des Problems Kirche und Staat*' (The Beginnings of the Problem of Church and State). Even today, more than 50 years later, I remember standing at the back of the great *Aula* of the Academy which was packed with a distinguished audience, uniforms in plenty, but none in brown, and listening to Lietzmann's address (repeated at the opening meeting of the *Mittwochsgesellschaft* of 1940/41 in October 1940). The contrast between eastern and western attitudes toward the empire was familiar ground, but the fateful consequences of the eastern emperor's attempts to coerce the Copts and Syrians into accepting the state creed struck a chord. The applause was deafening. A challenge had been issued to the German Christians and also to the Government that strove to impose its own religion on the Church.

To me, an inexperienced member of the seminar with only imperfect German, Lietzmann could not have been kinder. He suggested that my research on the Donatist Church would benefit from a detailed comparison between it and the Montanists in Phrygia since both were basically prophetic movements mainly associated with a single province. He also insisted that I should use to the full my interest in archaeology, and before

I left for Tunisia in March 1938 gave me a warm introduction to Louis Poinssot, the Director of Antiquities at Tunis. This proved to be an essential help in my research in North Africa. On my return to Berlin in June 1938 I saw more of Lietzmann. The translation of a long review of Volume II of *History of the Early Church* was rewarded by two volumes of the great work and a copy of Strack's *Hebraïsche Grammatik*. Before I left Berlin in August 1938 I met his family, and he expressed a fervent desire for Anglo-German co-operation despite the policies of the Nazis.

In retrospect, this was a sad occasion. On 1 September 1939 Germany invaded Poland and began the Second World War. Despite a momentary pride in the successes of German arms in the West in June 1940, Lietzmann regarded the future with foreboding. He had written to Franz Cumont in January 1940 that "once the storm breaks western civilisation will be in the most serious danger" (Aland, Letters 1128), and he did not move from this position. The invasion of Soviet Russia starting on 22 June 1941 justified his fears. Though the German armies swept forward and were sometimes greeted by the local population as liberators from the Communist rule, elsewhere, especially on the central front, resistance was severe. On 9 July 1941 Opitz was killed, followed shortly after by two of his pupils, Ital Gelzer and Karl Holl. Worst of all, on 15 July 1941, Lietzmann's son Joachim, serving in an artillery regiment, fell. At the same time, Nazi pressure on the university theology faculties increased. Lietzmann's health began to decline swiftly and cancer was diagnosed. He gave up his Chair and was allowed to visit a clinic near Locarno where it was hoped he would be able to recuperate. That hope was in vain, and he died on 25 June 1942, his great work on early Christian history unfinished, and the tradition of Harnack-Lietzmann in Berlin University left without an heir.

This new edition of Lietzmann's *magnum opus* is now published as a memorial to a scholar of great distinction. Though written before the major post-war archaeological discoveries, such as the Nag Hammadi library of gnostic works that have altered perceptions of the relations between orthodoxy and non-orthodoxy in the early Christian centuries, Lietzmann's work stands on its own. It was the fruit of forty years' work, by an exceptionally gifted mind, on original sources connected with the progress of the early church. It is also a pioneering work in the interdisciplinary approach to this movement. Though some of Lietzmann's conclusions may now be elaborated in the face of new evidence, very few will be challenged. It remains a work for all students of the early centuries of the Christian era.

The author's text has therefore not been altered, but substantial changes and additions have been made to the bibliographies, both to bring them up to date and to make them more valuable for English-speaking readers. The chronological tables have been re-organised and completed. Similarly, some details have been added to the original translator's otherwise excellent biographical note.

W.H.C.F.
October 1992

Sources

Aland, Kurt, *Glanz und Niedergang der deutschen Universität. 50 Jahre deutsche Wissenschaftsgeschichte in Briefen an und von Hans von Lietzmann (1892-1942)*, Berlin - New York: De Gruyter, 1979 (with introduction by Kurt Aland)

Scholder, Klaus, *The Churches and the Third Reich*, London: S.C.M. Press, 1987

Die Mittwoch-Gesellschaft: Protokolle der geistigen Deutschland 1932-1944, Berlin, 1982.

Andresen, Carl art. 'Lietzmann', *Neue Deutsche Biographie* 14 (1984), 544-547

Part I
The Beginnings of the Christian Church

Chapter One

PALESTINE AND THE ROMAN EMPIRE

IT WAS NOT BY THE PLAN OF SOME TRANSCENDENT GENIUS, but by the compulsion of the political and military situation, that the Roman government was now preparing, in the east, to close the circle of empire round the Mediterranean. Greece and the west of Asia Minor had been conquered by the middle and the end of the second century B.C. respectively. But the daring and the persistence of King Mithradates of Pontus endangered the whole of the eastern conquests again, and compelled the Romans for twenty-five years (88–63 B.C.) to wage a war which finally took on the character of an Asiatic struggle for liberation from the western conquerors who, in their turn, actually found themselves in the position of having to put forth their full strength and use their best men. At the same time Tigranes of Armenia, the son-in-law of Mithradates, not only invaded Media and north-west Mesopotamia but also took possession of Cappadocia and Cilicia, and even made attacks upon the northern half of the Seleucid kingdom in Syria which had long lain in ruins. He made Antioch one of the towns of his official residence, a fact which gave a definite objective to the Roman enemy, whose troops entered Syrian territory. Like an irresistible magnet the victorious general Pompey attracted embassies from all the regions of Syria, where hitherto the different parties had been quarrelling among themselves. Then the intention of Rome began to grow plain. At first it was only tentative and with slight pressure, but towards the end of 64 B.C. Pompey himself came to Syria and acted with decision. A few months later the Roman province of Syria was to be found in place of the remains of the Seleucid heritage. Its means of unifying the administration were of two kinds. Where the Hellenistic cities of the Seleucid period were of the required importance, they were given an aristocratic constitution and declared autonomous, and their city territories were constituted as small administrative districts. On the other hand where there was a region with a predominantly oriental character, a native dynasty was entrusted with control and made responsible for peace, order, and the prompt payment of taxes.

Judea proved to be one of the states of the second kind, and to require handling with special prudence on account of both the spirit and also the political history of its inhabitants. Even in the early centuries, Israel had had painful experience of its unfortunate geographical situation. On the one hand, Palestine was the bridge between the world-empires of the orient and the empire of the Pharaohs, and on the other, it was destined to be continually an apple of discord between the great rivals. Decisive battles were fought upon its soil, and armies marched through its borders. This has remained its lot to the present day, as is shown by the aftermath of two world-wars. As a consequence, it was condemned to continual political dependence upon one of the great neighbouring powers—a feature which all but the latest events have preserved.

The destruction of Jerusalem in 586 B.C. marked the absorption into Babylonia of the southern Kingdom which until then had remained independent of Assyria. When the exiles were sent back by Cyrus, they set up a state under the Persian suzerainty. The country passed from the Persians to Alexander, and was ruled by Macedonian governors. After his death, the Ptolemids and the Seleucids fought for its possession, the former being superior for a century when, in 198 B.C., Antiochus III added it to his great Syrian-Mesopotamian empire. The Egyptian period had been a time of relatively peaceful development and quiet accommodation to the Greek spirit, but the new master quickly brought tempestuous times upon Israel. The political decay of the Seleucid power led to a very large increase in the weight of taxation, and to robbing the temple treasure, while the intrigues and trickery of the city leaders at length occasioned Antiochus IV Epiphanes to pillage Jerusalem with fire and sword (168 B.C.), to raze its walls, and to station a Syrian garrison in its castle. At the same time, efforts were made to suppress the Jewish cult, to hasten the Hellenization of the city population after it had already reached a fairly high level without compulsion, to spread Hellenism throughout the land, and to extend it to the sphere of religion. The response was the insurrection of the religious peasantry under the leadership of the Hasmonæan, Judas Maccabæus, and his brothers who, in the course of a war which endured with varied fortunes for twenty-six years (167–141), not only won religious freedom for their country but, strange to say, also its political freedom. For the first time in more centuries than could be conceived, the people of Israel were free and subject to none. Its High-Priest was a prince and was soon called king by the people: the throne of David was established again. Israel's armies protected and even extended its borders, while the overwhelming empires of the Seleucids and the Ptolemids withdrew into themselves and were powerless. Under Jannæus Alexander (105–78 B.C.), who stamped the title of king in Hebrew and Greek upon his coins, the Jewish kingdom attained its greatest extent and commanded even Greek towns far into Transjordania.

This unusual condition of political freedom had lasted about a century, a period long enough to impress itself upon the memory of the nation for two more centuries as an object of yearning desire. The sons of Jannæus, the indolent Hyrcanus II, and the impassioned Aristobulus II, quarrelled for the crown, and both asked the Romans for help. The Romans came, first Scaurus the legate, who aided Aristobulus, and then Pompey himself. But Aristobulus lost the Roman confidence, and entrenched himself in the temple, when Jerusalem once more became the scene of war. After a three months' siege, the temple hill was stormed by the Romans (63 B.C.), and Pompey outraged the people by entering the Holy of Holies. The dream of Jewish freedom was ended. The conquests of Jannæus were transferred as free cities into the administrative system of the Syrian province, while the Jews received Hyrcanus II as high priest and "ethnarch", and—the Romans as masters.

The following decades saw Julius Cæsar's struggle with Pompey and the senate, and aroused even in the Jewish people and the Hasmonæan princes all sorts of hopes. But Hyrcanus' minister, the crafty Idumæan Antipater, was able to gain Cæsar's favour by certain acts, with the result that Judea was granted freedom from taxes and the obligation of military service. After Cæsar's assassination, Antipater was able to make the rulership of his rivals in Syria favourable to himself—when he was suddenly assassinated. He left behind two sons to whom he had already long entrusted governorships: Phasael in Jerusalem and Herod in Galilee. The first ended his life by a courageous suicide when a Hasmonæan pretender, Antigonus, captured Jerusalem with Parthian help. The second followed the victorious Antony through Egypt to Rome and, on the recommendation of Octavian and Antony, the senate gave him the rank of the Jewish king (40 B.C.).

Meanwhile Antigonus had deposed Hyrcanus and for greater certainty lopped off his ears so that, as a mutilated person, he could never again become High-Priest. At this moment Herod arrived in Palestine supported by Rome. Granted, this meant that Antigonus gained the supporters of Jewish freedom and so strengthened his power of resistance for three years; but in the spring of 37 B.C. Herod besieged Jerusalem, and at the same time gave a sort of dynastic legitimization to his royal title by marrying the Hasmonæan princess, Mariamne, to whom he had long been engaged. After being encircled for five months, the temple hill and the city were stormed, with dreadful bloodshed. From his own pocket, Herod bribed the soldiers to forgo their right to plunder the city. Antigonus was condemned to death by the Roman legate Sosius, and beheaded. The Hasmonæan dynasty disappeared from the stage, and the son of the house-steward assumed the crown.

But being an Idumæan and therefore not native-born, he could not wear the frontlets of the High-Priest; no matter how he might procrastinate or how reluctant he might be, he had to give that honour to the last Hasmonæan, the seventeen-year-old Aristobulus. But at the feast of booths when the jubilation of the people surged up in honour of the young representative of the Maccabæan tradition, the fatal day dawned. Herod caused him to be drowned, and in his place appointed an insignificant puppet of his own choice.

Herod required all his craft and all his good fortune once more when his neighbouring lord and master, Antony, entered into contest with Octavian for a final decision. Antony lost the game. Actium (31 B.C.) was decisive also for his companion, Cleopatra, and for Egypt. The Roman ring was now closed round the Mediterranean, and the Emperor Augustus brought lasting peace to the world. Again Herod found his way into the favour of the victor, and was rewarded with the extension of his rule westward and eastward. Herod owed what he had gained to his own power and skill, and it was attached to him personally, the Jewish people having no part in it. They shared in the outer benefits, and took it in good part when Herod favoured Jewish concerns,[1] but they hated him as a foreign usurper, and as a protégé of the Romans. The extension of his kingdom had nothing at all to do with Israel as a nation. This man ruled nearly forty years, and gave his great military and organizing abilities with relentless energy to building up a state which became a valuable part of the Roman empire. It was a bulwark against the Arab tribes of the wilderness, and it ensured the connection between Syria and Egypt. Moreover, the power and the craftiness of the king could exorcise the dangers which lay in the character of his people. In a chapter which echoes a reluctant but honourable admiration, Josephus[2] tells of his extraordinary activity as a builder: the rebuilding of the temple at Jerusalem, the founding of the city Sebaste on the site of the old Samaria, and the imposing port of Cæsarea—later the capital of the country—numberless castles, palaces, theatres, baths, aqueducts, pillared halls, temples. But the temples were dedicated to pagan gods and to emperor worship, and in their construction was reflected a love for Greek culture which led him even to institute the Olympian games. The heart of the Jewish people responded to all this, not with love, but with furious hatred, not only towards Herod himself, but also his wife, the beautiful Mariamne, whom he killed in a passion of jealousy, but whom he nevertheless could not cease to love.

With the death of Herod "the Great" (4 B.C.), his kingdom was divided to an even greater extent than he had provided in his will. The sons of the first of his ten legal marriages had originally been intended for the succession, but had succumbed to palace intrigues. Alexander and Aristobulus, the sons of Mariamne, who were beloved by the people on account of their Hasmonæan blood, had been strangled by their father's orders, and from his very death-bed he had ordered the

---

[1] Jos., *Ant.*, 16, 27–65   [2] *Bellum*, 1, 401–30

execution of his eldest son, Antipater, on account of his intrigues. Thus there remained three younger sons as heirs mentioned in the will. Philip received the outlying region of Batanea and the neighbouring districts, which lay north and east of Lake Genezareth, and which were mostly populated by pagans. Here he reigned for thirty years and was beloved by his people. Herod Antipas received Galilee and Perea. He built himself a residence, on Lake Genezareth, of a good Hellenistic kind, which he loyally named Tiberias in honour of the emperor. He laid out a fortified town in Perea, which was named after the empress Livia, and later Julia. As far as the people were concerned, he conducted himself as a professing Jew. His evil genius was Herodias whom he alienated from his half-brother, Herod. In order that he could marry her, he set aside his first wife, who was the daughter of his neighbour King Aretas of Nabatea, and whom he had married on good political grounds. This action led to strained relationships, to frontier incidents, and finally to a war in which Antipas suffered defeat, and was compelled to ask Tiberius for help. The emperor died, however, before his help became effective, and Caligula his successor banished Antipas to Lyons instead of giving him the title of king as Herodias desired. He died in exile (A.D. 39) and his rival and accuser, the Jewish king Agrippa, received his tetrarchy.

The principal portion of Herod's territory fell to Archelaos, viz. Samaria, Judea, and Idumea. According to Herod's will, he ought also to have had the royal title, but Augustus withheld it and only named him ethnarch. Almost the whole Herodian family, as well as a deputation from the people, had appeared in Rome, and attempted, in the presence of Augustus, to secure the inheritance for themselves. Meanwhile affairs in Palestine were going from bad to worse. Sabinus, the temporary procurator in Jerusalem, was taken by surprise along with his legion, and the insurrection spread over the countryside, when at least three leaders of insurgent bands had themselves proclaimed as kings of Israel.[1] In the end, Quintilius Varus the Syrian legate intervened; he scattered the rebels, seizing and crucifying 2,000 of them as an example to the rest.[2] Archelaus

---

[1] Jos., *Ant.*, 17, 272, 274, 278   [2] *Ibid.*, 17, 295

arrived, and even began to reign, but he soon showed himself quite incompetent. After he had been tolerated for a few years, a deputation of the leading Jews and Samaritans went to Rome, and appealed for his dethronement. Augustus deposed him (A.D. 6) and banished him to Vienne,[1] placing his lands directly under Roman procurators. These were of equestrian rank, and were loosely subordinated to the Syrian legate upon whom they depended if occasion demanded. They resided in Cæsarea, and had a modest military force of about 3,000 men at their disposal, raised in Palestine itself from the non-Jewish section of the population. The Jews proper, for good reasons, were allowed to remain free from the obligation to military service.[2] One of the Roman cohorts was continually stationed in Jerusalem, their barracks being in the castle of Antonia. The tribune was the chief military authority in the capital. The procurator was responsible for the rates and taxes, but otherwise the internal government and the legal administration were largely left to the Jews. The Jewish central magistracy, the sanhedrin meeting under the presidency of the High Priest, ruled in Judea, and its decisions were of moral authority far beyond these narrow borders, and were voluntarily accepted by the rest of Judaism. In this way, had there been goodwill, harmonious co-operation should have been possible—if misfortune, brutality, and passion had not frequently disturbed the peace. Even such an obviously useful matter as the drawing up of a taxation list, the "census" by Quirinus, the Syrian legate (A.D. 6–7), was bitterly opposed by the population, and almost occasioned open rebellion.[3] Joazar the High-Priest managed to appease the people, but from that time Judas the "Galilean" and Zaddok the priest conceived and preached relentless hostility to Rome, with dreadful consequences.[4] On their side, the procurators in authority only too frequently showed themselves deficient in tact, and they goaded the people sharply. Pontius Pilate was outstanding in this respect, and he frequently showed a ruthlessness which eventually brought him down.[5] This was at the moment when Tiberius died (A.D. 37). Under his successor Caligula, matters grew worse.

[1] *Ibid.*, 17, 342–44   [2] Schürer, i, 458   [3] Schürer, i, 510 ff.
[4] Jos., *Ant.*, 17, 1–10, 23–25   [5] Schürer, i, 488–92

Chapter Two

CONDEMNED TO EXILE BY SARGON IN 722 B.C., THE TEN northern tribes of the Israelitish people had perished, or at any rate had left no historical traces. The inhabitants of the Judaistic southern kingdom, however, reached such a degree of national fixity that they not only survived the catastrophe of 586 B.C., but defied all the succeeding blows of fate; they have preserved their identity to the present day. The basis of this phenomenon lies in the relation of the people to religion. The unique feature was not that the national and the religious communities were identical—that was approximately true, if not quite axiomatic for any ancient people. Had that identity been the basis, the result might have been that Yahweh would have disappeared from history along with his people like the many *baalim*, and, in the end, like Zeus and Jupiter with the whole of Olympus. Rather, the decisive point was that, among this people, religion was an authoritative and urgent power in life in a unique manner. The northern tribes were suppressed at too early a date, and were also too strongly under foreign influences, for the consolidation of religious power among them. The southern kingdom made good use of the four additional generations of independence, and won a faith which as strong enough to gain victory over national death.

The Jew knew that God had chosen his people for Himself since the days of Abraham, and would redeem His promises to them. With the eyes of religion he regarded history as divine rule which, in the end, had to do only with Israel. The preaching of the prophets had lifted him above the primitive forms of such a faith in the future, and above its destruction by political and military calamities. He knew of his own sin and guilt, of God's anger and just punishment for the individual as well as for the people, and he also knew that God was not eternally wrathful with His own, and that His promises would remain undisturbed. This faith held the people together in the stress of exile; it brought them back, and enabled them to bear patiently the following centuries of foreign yoke. And that it did not deceive, had been wonderfully proved in the later course of history. When the time of distress was at its worst, and Antiochus Epiphanes desecrated both God, His law, and His holy temple, freedom was won by the sword of the Maccabees, and God's salvation was visibly poured out over His people. In those days, Daniel saw in nocturnal visions the meaning of history, and he set forth that meaning in the form of a dream revealed to Nebuchadnezzar.

Daniel is the first to have comprehended all earthly history as a great unity which moves towards a final goal according to a divine plan, and his understanding determined the thought and action of mankind for two millenia. The visions which he saw and described originate in Persian mythology,[1] but the explanation owed its origin to the spirit of Jewish religion. Four world empires follow each other in a diminishing order of value; the last is that of the Macedonians and is without inner unity or firm interconnection. Antiochus Epiphanes belongs to it, and he conducts a war of destruction against the "saints of the Most High" and desecrates the temple. But God Himself will intervene and destroy his kingdom. The "Ancient of Days" will ascend the throne, and on the clouds of heaven one will come like a son of man; he will receive power, honour, and royal rank from God, and all nations and tongues will serve him. "The kingdom and the rule and the royal glory under the whole heaven will then be given to the nation of the saints of the Most High, whose kingdom will be eternal and all powers will serve and obey Him." The "Kingdom of God" will be realized as Israel's rule over all the kingdoms of the world, and the Messiah sent by God will be king over His holy people.[2] World history cumulates towards catastrophe reaching its consummation by divine intervention, and issuing in a new kingdom which, in its glorious final end, will bring about the abundant fulfilment of the promises made to Abraham and his people. Thus in the earliest days of the Maccabean rising, the flame of national enthusiasm shot up, fed by unshakable belief in God's undeviating faithfulness, and it illuminated with a flickering light the apocalyptic picture of an earthly paradise.

[1] Ed. Meyer, *Ursprung*, ii, 189 ff.　　[2] Dan., 7: 9, 13, 27

The unsuspected and unaccustomed political freedom of the following century stamped this hope ever more firmly upon the souls of the people and taught them to regard the disillusionments of the Hasmonæan rule and the slavery which came so suddenly in the Roman period, as the prelude to the last fight of all. The strain of the present must instigate the catastrophe which would introduce the revelation of the divine rule in the Messianic kingdom. In the days when Pompey established the Roman authority, new Psalmists arose who gave their people songs in the style and manner of the old "Davidic" psalm-book. We still have these Psalms under the name of Solomon in a Greek translation, and they are an invaluable record of the faith and hope of that period. In them we hear the voice of a devout man who cries to the Lord out of distress and sufferings brought on by war, who is ashamed of the sins and vices of his compatriots, and who recognizes God's judgement as just. All this finds its highest expression in the great Messianic Psalm 17:

Lord, Thou art our king for ever and ever, and our souls shall glory in Thee. What is the span of man's life on earth? All his life long he has his hope. But we hope in God, our Saviour, for the might of our God endures for ever with mercy, and His kingdom extends over the heathen.

Thou, O Lord, hast chosen David to be king over Israel, and sworn to him and his seed for ever, that his kingdom should not cease before Thee. But on account of our sins have sinners risen against us and set up a boastful kingdom on David's throne— i.e. the Hasmonæans—until a foreigner, Pompey, came and brought God's punishment upon them. He has also emptied the land of inhabitants, sent old and young into exile to the far west; he has dealt shamefully with the leaders of the people and treated Jerusalem like a conquered city. For among the people from the highest to the lowest, there was not one who did righteousness and justice, the king in misdeeds, the judges in disobedience, and the people in sin. Like birds frightened out of their nests, the friends of the "devout communities" fled from them and wandered about in the wilderness, in order to save their souls from evil—they were scattered over every country.

Lord, look down and raise up for them their king, the son of David, at the time which Thou hast seen, O God, that he shall rule over Thy servant Israel. Gird him with strength, that he may break in pieces the unjust ruler. Purge Jerusalem of the heathen who have trodden it underfoot. With wisdom and righteousness shall he drive out the sinners from the earth, with his threats he shall terrify them away from his sight, and scold sinners with the voice of their own hearts. And he will gather a holy people in a multitude about himself and rule them in righteousness; he will judge the tribes of the people that the Lord his God has sanctified. And he will not permit injustice to dwell among them any more, and no one shall live among them who knows iniquity. For he knows them, that they are all the sons of their God, and he will divide them by tribes over the land, and no stranger nor foreigner shall again dwell among them.

He will judge the nations and the heathen in the wisdom of his righteousness. And he will submit the heathen to his yoke and they shall serve him, and he will glorify the Lord in the sight of all men, and will purify Jerusalem in holiness, as it was in the beginning, so that the heathen will come from the ends of the earth to see his glory and as gifts will offer his sons who have suffered in a foreign land. They will see the glory of the Lord with which God has clothed it. But he rules over them as a righteous king, instructed by God, and in his days there is no injustice among them, for all of them are holy, and their king is the Messiah of the Lord.

He will not trust in horse and chariot and bow, nor heap up gold and silver as a war chest, and in the day of battle his hope does not depend upon great numbers. The Lord Himself is his king, his strength is that he hopes in God. He will make all the heathen afraid before him. For he will break the earth in pieces with the word of his mouth eternally, he will bless the people of the Lord in wisdom with joy. He is guiltless of sin that he might rule over great peoples, judge the governors, and blot out the sinners with the power of his word. He will not become weak in his days before his God, for God has made him strong through the Holy Spirit, and wise to give good counsel with power and righteousness. The blessing of the Lord is with him in power, and his hope in the Lord will not grow weak. Who can do anything against him? Mighty is he in his work, and powerful in the fear of God; he shepherds the Lord's flock in faithfulness and righteousness, and lets none of them suffer harm in their pasture. He leads them all by a straight path, and there shall be no pride among them for one to oppress another. Thus the king of Israel rules gloriously whom God has planned to set over the house of

Israel to lead it. His words have been purified in fire more than the best and most precious gold, he will direct the tribes of the holy people in the assemblies, his words are like words of saints in the midst of the hosts of the redeemed.

Blessed are they who shall live in those days, for they shall see the salvation of Israel in the assembly of the tribes. May God bring it to pass! O, that God would soon exercise His mercy upon Israel, and save us from the defilement of unclean foes. The Lord Himself is our king now and evermore.

That is the lively Messianic hope of the Roman era clearly and definitely described. The divine promise is to the house of David, the Hasmonæans are unjustified interlopers, and their deeds bear witness against them. Hence, in accordance with God's will Pompey drove them out. But in addition, the people themselves have become wayward, and have been justifiably punished by the Roman invasion. Jerusalem is disgraced, its people scattered in exile; even the devout had to flee into the wilderness from the unholy conditions in the land. If God will hear their prayers, and that at an early date, then the Messiah will arise who will drive the Romans from the country. This does not imply a war of liberation like that of the Maccabees; rather a divine miracle is expected which will sweep away the heathen from before the Messiah. Then Jerusalem will rise up anew in its former glory; the twelve tribes will inhabit Palestine again and have their former boundaries; the scattered people will return from the dispersion,[1] and will be offered as a present to Israel by the heathen who had hitherto oppressed them. And in the reconstituted kingdom, only Israel shall dwell—no heathen, no Greeks, no Samaritans; and this Israel shall not tolerate within itself sinners or half-Greeks. All shall be pure and holy, and live a happy life according to God's will under the righteous and holy Messianic king who has been chosen by Him. In this way, the royal rule of God, the "Kingdom of God" shall be realized in Israel. On the other hand, the heathen shall be subject to Israel and pay tribute to her; they will see in astonishment the glory of Jerusalem but have no share in it. Theirs are not the promises; the idea of a universal salvation was remote from the people of this age.

[1] Cf. Ps. Sol., 11: 2 ff.; 8: 34

The process of imagination had added a good deal in other directions to this kernel, e.g. that Elias or Moses would be the heralds of the Messiah; the glory of the new Jerusalem and the majesty of its future temple are painted in many colours, and the happiness of life in God's kingdom is depicted with pictures of the paradisal wealth of nature and of life. That means little. But there is significance in the question of what the religious communities to which these Psalmists belonged would deem as "holy" and "religious" or "devout".

It is clear that they regarded any intercourse with the heathen as the deadliest sin, and felt that the bulk of the people, and especially the ruling classes, had departed from God in the Hasmonæan epoch, and were now receiving their punishment from the Romans. Immorality, adultery, lying, deceit, and greed are the characteristics of this departure; sacrilege of the temple and disregard of the regulations for worship are the most definite witness of godlessness.[1] On the other hand, the "righteous" man is diligent in observing the law.[2] Sin does not increase in his house, for he is quick upon its tracks and expels it violently. Should an error be made at any time in ignorance, the devout man expiates it with fasting and mortification.[3] Then the Lord blesses him and gladly forgives him. He corrects him without shaming him, and keeps all grievous ill far from him.[4] He grants him definite prosperity, equally remote from grinding poverty and seductive wealth.[5] God has sealed him with His own seal,[6] by which he will be recognized and saved at the Last Judgment. Whereas the godless go to hell, the devout inherit eternal life.[7] The devout experience the righteousness of God towards themselves in the reward which is due to their righteousness; they can see it around them in daily life as well as in the larger course of history[8] where punishment sooner or later falls upon all sinners.

Such is typical "Pharisaic" religion. Even in the older Psalms, we find the circle of the devout who, in quiet inward communion with God, keep aloof from the loud and immoral ways of the daily round, and are repelled by the frivolity of "civilized" life. They have no desire to sit on a bench along with the godless

---

[1] Ps. Sol., 8: 10 f.; 4: 4-14; 2: 3 ff.; 1: 8   [2] 14: 1; 10: 5   [3] 3: 5-10   [4] 9: 12-15; 13: 6-9
[5] 5: 16-20; 16: 12-13   [6] 15: 8; cf. 10   [7] 3: 13-16; 13: 9 f.   [8] 8: 7-31; 9: 3-9

and the scoffers, rather they will meditate day and night upon God's law. In the Maccabean insurrection, these Chasidim, i.e. the devout or religious, occasionally relinquished their aloofness; they took the sword and indeed fought even on the Sabbath day.[1] But when religious freedom had been won, they refused further support to the Hasmonæan dynasty; indeed, after John Hyrcanus, they became fierce and unrelenting opponents.[2] The law was the centre of their thought and practical life and, in continually renewed applications and metaphors, was lauded as Israel's most precious and sacred garment. Indeed, the emphasis veered from its moral to its ceremonial side, for it was the very prescriptions for worship and for cleanness which were felt as defence-works against the burning sea of heathenism round about. But a differentiation was made even within the ceremonial law. The heart of these devout people was not satisfied with the gorgeous temple worship; there were too many critical and sceptical words to be read in prophets and psalms about the value of the outpoured blood of goats. Rather the decisive factor was to be found in personal conduct in fulfilling all the prescriptions of the law. The religion of ritual piety was applied to the individual. Then, however, the strenuous effort to fulfil all the commandments perfectly led to casuistry, and this was continually refined until it spread its crippling net over the whole practical life of a devout person. From the time when he first awoke in the morning till he fell asleep at night, he was continually compelled to remember its prescriptions; his prayers were precisely regulated in wording, time, place, and bodily attitude. Everywhere he was surrounded by prescriptions for cleanness, and they determined the choice and preparation of food; the consecration of the Sabbath by abstaining from work was carried into grotesque consequences in detail. In the time of Jesus, there were two famous rabbis, Shammai and Hillel, and their disciples disputed[3] whether the evening prayer was to be offered in a standing posture or lying in bed; what was the appropriate order for prayers after a meal; whether the

[1] I Macc. 2: 41; Jos., *Ant.*, 12, 276 f.
[2] Jos., *Ant.*, 13, 288–292; Schürer, i, 271 f., ii, 473 f. Some passages *re* the Pharisees in Schürer, ii, 449–75. Billerbeck, iva, 334 ff.
Cf. the passages collected by Schürer, ii, 426, note 38

towel used for drying one's hand was to be placed upon the
table or upon the cushion used as a seat.[1] Granted that on the
Sabbath[2] no food might be cooked, but could one keep warm
the water and food which stood on the hearth where the fire
was still alight on the Sabbath evening? Yes, if it were a gentle
fire of burning stubble, but if the fire was of burning wood, it
must first be covered with ashes, otherwise there is danger that
the food would begin to simmer—this was Hillel's view. In
such cases, Shammai altogether forbade keeping food warm
and only permitted water. Could those foods be put back to
cook which had been taken away from the fire? Hillel said yes,
Shammai, no. Might one eat an egg laid on a holy day by a
hen which did not know the law? Shammai permitted it, Hillel
did not[3]—and so on *ad infinitum* in all the spheres of public and
private life. This mass of prescriptions was handed from one
generation to another, and developed ever more highly until
"tradition" outweighed the kernel of the Mosaic torah. It was
particularly in these spheres that the scribism flourished whose
aim in life was the systematic examination, in reality the
further development, of the law. In so doing, it had created the
material of the "Tradition" which was written down in the
second century A.D. as the "Mishna" and in the fifth as the
"Gemara". The law-book of Judaism known as the "Talmud"
consists of these two sections taken together. The scribes mentioned by name in the present-day text of the Talmud go back
in some cases to the Roman period.

From the end of the second century before Christ, we meet
with the name of Pharisees, i.e. separatists, for the circle of the
Chasidim already mentioned. It cannot be decided whether
the name arose at some time during the Maccabean wars,
because then they "separated" themselves from their former
comrades, or because they help themselves apart from the
masses;[4] perhaps the name was first applied to them by
opponents and afterwards accepted by themselves. At any rate,
the second view aptly describes their attitude in the community.
Their separatism was to be seen on two fronts: against the
socially superior aristocracy of the old priestly families, the

[1] Mishna, *Berachoth*, 1, 1: 8, 1 ff.   [2] M., *Sabbath*, 3, 1
[3] M., *Jom. tob*, 1, 1   [4] E. Meyer, ii, 284. J. Jeremias, *Jerusalem*, ii, 115

Sadducees, and against the uneducated and religiously indifferent mob of the *Am ha-Arez*.

The Sadducees[1] derived their name from a certain Saddok,
and the only question is whether he was the High-Priest of
Solomon whom the Old Testament often mentions[2] and
reveres as the ancestor of an eminent priestly family,[3] or
whether a later Saddok, who was the head of a school, gave
his name to his adherents. The first view is to be preferred, as
the Sadducees were not a school but a caste and, in particular,
they were at home in the priestly families of the capital and
occupied the leading places in the body politic. Their political
activity brought them into contact with the forms of life proper
to the Græco-Roman civilization, and occasioned many accom-
modations of which the Pharisees severely disapproved. In the
Seleucid period, this development went suspiciously far and,
in the earlier Maccabean period, cost them all their influence.
But after the Pharisees broke with John Hyrcanus, they came
into control once more and, except for a short interval, remained there as long as the Jewish state existed. In the
Herodian period, to their chagrin, their adaptability had to
accommodate itself to the requirements of the Pharisees who
were the representatives of public opinion.[4]

Josephus frequently gives himself the pleasure of speaking
about the Jewish "Schools of Philosophers"[5] and in so doing
adduces all sorts of material in regard to Pharisees and Sadducees which smacks of philosophy, but which really renders it
more difficult to understand their real contrast. If the facts can
be reduced to a simple formula, we may say that the Sadducees
held to the traditional form of Judaism as found in the Old
Testament but rejected the new currents which had come in
after the Persian period together with the deductions from them
drawn by the Rabbinic schools. Hence they preferred to ignore
the personal immortality of the soul, and judgment after death,
together with the angels, devils, and intermediate beings of

---

[1] Billerbeck, iva, 335 ff., 348 ff. Schürer, ii, 475 ff.
[2] 1 Kings 2: 35
[3] Ezek. 40: 46; 44: 15; also *Sirach* (Heb.), 51: 12, 9, and in the Damascus
document 6, 1–3; R. H. Charles, *Apocrypha and Pseudepigrapha of the Old Testament*
(1913), ii, 785–834
[4] Jos., *Ant.*, 18, 17; Schürer, ii, 487 f.
[5] Jos., *Bell.*, 2, 119, 160–166; *Ant.*, 13, 171; 18, 11–25

later apocalyptic; hence also they rejected the further development of the law in the tradition of the Pharisees.[1] They remained firm to the old law, and defended themselves against
the Apocryphal books and the Talmud.

In contradistinction to the Sadducees, the Pharisees were at
first, therefore, the vehicles of a freer and more vital religiousness which discovered new forms of expression for the ancient
faith that Israel was the chosen people. But the ever increasing
tendency towards correct fulfilment of the law led to a growing
narrowness and a formalism, which allowed the depth of the
prophetic tradition and the inwardness of the religion of the
Psalms to fall into oblivion, and which conjured up the danger
of arrogant self-righteousness. The frequency with which the
Psalms of Solomon depict the righteous man and his excellence
as recognized and rewarded by God, gives us a plain witness of
it. But this meticulous observance of the law had another consequence, viz. the Rabbis, learned in the Scriptures, became
the leaders of the Pharisaic communities, and determined the
spirit that ruled in them. "Religiousness" became a technique
with ever greater refinement and rested upon learning. One had
to learn painfully how to be "righteous", and the more deeply
a religious man penetrated into the secrets of Talmudic
casuistry, the higher his religious perfection mounted. Religion
became a matter of the trained intellect applied to conduct;
whoever could not scale the ladder of knowledge could not
reach the ideal nor even a tolerable degree of piety. The way
to the righteousness which was acceptable to God, was closed
to him.

From this standpoint, the scribe could only reject and despise
these untrained and uneducated people, and he stigmatized
them as *Am ha-Arez*, i.e. people of the land.[2] People who live
nowadays in some metropolis of culture employ similar
terminology, even if not directly in the religious sphere. Among
the Pharisees, the epithet echoed to some extent their characterization of the heathen, but on the other hand, no aristocrat
of Jerusalem had a charm against this title if he did not fulfil
the requirements of the law. The differentiation went so far that
the faithful Pharisee avoided mixing, or even contact, with the

[1] Jos., *Ant.*, 13, 297   [2] Billerbeck, ii, 494; Schürer, ii, 454, 468

Am ha-Arez, for it was impossible to know, with their defective observance of the law, whether they, or their clothing, or the articles touched by them, were ceremonially clean, or whether the produce which they offered for sale had been correctly "tithed". The devout person had this certainty only in connection with his compeers, his *Chaberim*, i.e. comrades[1] who had bound themselves together for the observance of the ritual and for Levitical correctness in regard to the dues: they and they alone constituted the true Israel in whom God took pleasure. In spite of all its earnestness of endeavour and its undeniable quality of ethical sensitiveness and conduct, this inner separation stamped its characteristic vices upon Pharisaism. That the *Am ha-Arez* responded with fierce hatred to the contempt of the Pharisees would be certain even if we did not possess the witness of the surviving Rabbinic literature.[2]

Besides the Pharisees and Scribes, Josephus mentions the Essenes as a third "School of Philosophers" and praises them for their ideal way of life.[3] Philo describes them in a spirited fashion in one of his Stoic tractates.[4] Otherwise we hear hardly anything about them, especially in the Rabbinic sources. Their name *Chasayya*, i.e. the devout, is Aramaic and corresponds exactly to the Hebrew *Chasidim*, and thus brings them into relation with the same sources as those from which the Pharisees had perhaps sprung. And it is in fact highly probable that we have here another shoot from the same root. The Essenes were a genuine order of monks who had their monasteries in the cities, and more especially in the villages, of Palestine. After the novitiate of one year and a probationary period of a further two years, the candidates judged suitable were accepted as full members, sworn to the manner of life of the society, and bound to keep their writings and teachings secret. Then at length they might share in the sacred meals which were regarded as the central act of worship. Everyone who entered the order, abandoned private property, and handed over his entire possessions to the society, and similarly all his future earnings.

---

[1] Billerbeck, ii, 501, 509 ff.; J. Jeremias, *Jerusalem*, ii, 116 ff.
[2] Billerbeck, ii, 518 f.
[3] Jos., *Bell.*, 2, 119–61
[4] Phil., *omn. prob.*, 75–91 (6, 21–26); also Bousset, *Judentum*, 456; Schürer, ii, 654.
W. Bauer in *Pauly-Wissowa* Supp., iv., 426

In exchange, he received from the order all that he required for an ascetic life, in sickness and in health. Naturally, there were in this society no social differences, no masters and no slaves. The Essenes also withheld from marriage, and no women were admitted to the order; only a special sect among them tolerated marriage for the sake of propagation. Their food was confined to what was entirely necessary for the support of life, and their clothing was of white, i.e. colour of light. The most outstanding commandment of their manner of life was cleanliness and ceremonial washings were the means, employed every day, for avoiding uncleanness. All who abandoned the unclean outer world and entered the order must bathe; the same was required of the fully initiated Essene who had been in contact with a novice or probationer, to say nothing of a non-Essene. Before beginning the midday meal, each washed his body in cold water and then put on a sacred festival garment which, after the meal, was at once exchanged for working clothes. Moses and his law were held by them in the greatest honour, and they observed the Sabbath by strict abstention from work.[1] They rejected animal sacrifices and sent instead sacrificial offerings of money to the temple at Jerusalem:[2] their own sacred customs seemed to them to be better and to be true sacrifices.

They were mainly devoted to cultivating the land, and had no liking for commerce, the sea, or war.[3] They abhorred oaths because they spoke the exact truth without them,[4] and thus they appeared to both Josephus and Philo as patterns of all civic and philosophic virtues—the critical reader will do well to set aside the Greek emendations to both sketches. What remains is the life of a Jewish sect as described above, which had many points of contact with the Pharisees, but which is closer to the old roots. In abnegating sacrifices and emphasizing ethical conduct, they developed that religion of the prophets and of many of the Psalms which was repressed among the Pharisees. The esoteric writings and the names of angels of which Josephus tells us,[5] reveal living relations with popular apocalyptic and

---

[1] Jos., *Bell*, 2, 145; Philo, *omn. prob.*, 80 f. (6, 23). For the readings see Bousset, *Judentum*, 462. note 3
[2] Philo, *op. cit.*, 75 (6, 22). Jos., *Ant.*, 18, 19   [3] Philo, *op. cit.*, 78 (6, 22)
[4] *Ibid.*, 84 (6, 24); Jos., *Bell.*, 2, 135   [5] *Ibid.*, 2, 142

its Persian sources, and these latter are doubtless responsible for the traces of sun-worship which are to be found as isolated characteristics.[1] Baptism and sacred meals are the forms of worship upon which emphasis is laid, although it is doubtful whether they could be called sacraments. But we must remember that also among the Pharisees the ritual washings and the sacred meals of religious societies were greatly insisted upon, and were developed in their ritual. Although at first sight what we learn of the Essenes may seem strange, closer examination shows that they can be readily placed in the course of the religious development of Palestine as already known to us. What were the roots of their monasticism and asceticism is another question which need neither be raised nor answered, for our purposes.

The Essenes afford us an impressive proof that the religious currents of Palestinian Judaism are not exhausted by the artificial constructions which we find in the Rabbinic writings, and which even dominate Josephus's accounts. Only when we are clear as to how far this Essenism was removed from the victorious Pharisaism of the incipient Talmud, and as to the fact that, nevertheless, it enjoyed honourable respect and was widely spread in Palestine—only then are we able to understand the large and various possibilities of religious evolution in the Jewish spirit of that period. Moreover, the constraint of the common origin was more powerful, even in such disparate phenomena, than the wisdom of the schools will usually allow. And a comparison with the foundations of societies in the dispersion, such as we find in "Community of the New Covenant" in Damascus, or the Egyptian "Therapeutæ", deepens the impression of variety in the development of similar germs.

Further witness is borne to the spirit of Palestinian religion by a number of writings which arose in the pre-Christian period, and which enjoyed a more or less apocryphal existence for centuries. Many of them were taken over and edited by Christians, but were then forgotten until modern research brought them to light again from remote corners of eastern libraries. Here we include the books of Enoch, which were the work of several generations of strange prophets from the time

[1] Philo, 2, 128, 148

of the Seleucids to that of Herod. The books show a fantasy diligently at work trimming up and spinning out stories of early Bible times in a manner well known from the Jewish Haggada. Enoch who, according to Gen. 5: 24, had been taken up into heaven, imparted revelations of many hidden things: he had wandered through heaven and hell and reported what he had seen there, and he was able to give detailed information on physics, meteorology, and astronomy. The entire eastern fairy-land is laid under tribute to provide building material for the earth and the heaven which are called into being before our eyes, and the paths become plainly visible which join this product of Palestine to Persia and Babylon.

However, the chief interest of the prophets who wrote the Book of Enoch is in the outcome of this world, the end of time, the Last Judgment, and the future kingdom of God. Their eschatology is quite differently conceived from the Pharisaic nationalism of the Psalms of Solomon. Rather, Enoch joins immediately on to Daniel. He sees in visions the course of world history to its pre-destined end, which is implemented by an all-embracing flood of godlessness. God's anger is revealed in an inversion of the order of nature,[1] and in a judgment of the sword. After a series of miraculous and catastrophic events this æon declines to an end.[2] Accompanied by several thousands of holy angels, God comes to hold judgment;[3] the Messiah, the Son of Man who had been seen by Daniel on the clouds of heaven, will take his seat upon the throne and judge the wicked;[4] the dead will rise, and when the sinners have been destroyed, this world will pass away.[5] A new heaven will receive the "saints, the righteous, and the chosen", with in-effable glory, and they, along with the chorus of angels, will sing "Holy, Holy, Holy" to the Lord of spirits in the endless eternity of the new æon.[6] The Messianic idea and the hope of the promised kingdom are transposed into eschatological and apocalyptic spheres, and shape themselves in a variety of pictures which without inner, and often also without outer, connection with one another, light up and pass before the eyes of the seer in a swirling succession

[1] Enoch 80: 2–6   [2] *Ibid.*, 91, 12–17   [3] 1: 9
[4] 45: 3–46: 8   [5] 51: 1; 91: 14   [6] 91: 16; 39: 5–13

The final aim of this kind of religion is the eternal salvation of the *individual* saint who has been chosen by God; the ancient note of the rulership of the whole chosen people dies away in the distance. The books of Enoch are the deposit of a fanatically religious cast of mind unique in kind, and directed towards the next world. It had much inward power of conversion, but no organizing capacity, and we naturally hear nothing of communities or sects of its adherents. But every attempt is useless to bring the world of ideas of the Enoch literature even into a loosely connected system: everything grows together in rank confusion, as in an oriental magic garden, intoxicating the visitor with varied colours and heavy perfumes.

There are several other similar books, putting now this and again that type of religiousness more definitely in the foreground; in one, ethical instruction is predominant, in another, Haggadic recounting of legend, or apocalyptic speculation on history. Taken one with another, they do us the service of bringing before our eyes the living religious activity of the Jewish people in their homeland before the beginning of our era.

No source, however, informs us of the simple people who, equally removed from scribism and from fanatical apocalyptic, strove well or ill to fulfil the moral requirements of God in the sense of the prophets, and to hope in God's grace after the manner of the Psalmists[1]; people who felt poverty and humble station to be the inheritance which gave them their expectation of God's special protection.[2] For He teaches the afflicted His way[3] and His Messiah will one day, at the Last Judgment, save the poor and the afflicted,[4] who although only a small number of saints, now sigh to Him under the oppression of the godless.[5] Thus in quietness and patience, they waited for the coming of the kingdom of God. They are not to be heard in political affairs, and they do not write books; learning is remote from them, and, as far as the Rabbis are concerned, they are lost in the multitude of the *Am ha-Arez*—who is there to tell of them? And yet it was from their midst that the change in world history took its rise, for Jesus was born and brought up among them.

[1] Mark 15: 43; Luke 2: 25, 38   [2] Ps. Sol. 5: 2, 13; 10: 7; 15:2
[3] Ps. 25: 9   [4] Ps. 72: 2, 4, 12, 13   [5] Ps. 13: 2, 4

Chapter Three

JOHN THE BAPTIST

IN THE DAYS WHEN HEROD ANTIPAS RULED IN GALILEE, (4 B.C.–A.D. 39) a man arose by the name of John. His clothing was woven of rough camel-hair, he had a leathern girdle round his waist, and he lived on locusts and the honey of wild bees. He preached that the kingdom of God was near at hand, and that now was the last opportunity for repentance; whoever repented of his sins and wished to amend his ways, might come to him and receive baptism in Jordan for forgiveness of sins. His call to repentance was very effective, and the crowds streamed out to hear him. He reproved them fiercely: You serpent's brood, who has promised that you shall escape God's threatening anger? Do you think that God will spare you because you are Abraham's children to whom the promises apply? Out of that stone God can create children of Abraham for Himself and present the promised grace to them. Only conversion and repentance will save you, and these must be made plain by your deeds. Already the axe is lying near the root of the tree; if the tree is rotten, the judge will hew it down and throw the timber into the fire. In terror, the people asked John: What are we to do? For answer, he said: Let him who has two coats give to him who has none, and let him who has food do likewise. The tax-collectors also came to him to be baptized, and asked: Master, what must we do? And he said to them: Take no more from the people than is ordered. Also the soldiers asked him: And what shall we do? And he said to them: Do not exercise force and oppression against anyone, and be content with your pay. Now is the time to repent: I am baptizing you with water. After me there is coming the man of authority, whose shoelaces I am not worthy to bend down and unloose: he will destroy you in the fiery baptism of the Last Judgment. The winnowing fan is already in his hand to cleanse his threshing floor. He will gather the wheat into his granary, but burn up the chaff in unquenchable fire.

Thus runs the popular tradition which is preserved in two

different recensions in the synoptic Gospels[1] and, indeed, so
excellently preserved, that very little critical work is required
to remove the few traces of Christian additions. At an early
date, Christian tradition made the attempt to understand John
as a forerunner of Jesus. It made his baptism parallel to the
Christian sacrament—which, as a baptism of the spirit, was
superior to John's baptism of water—and it discovered Jesus to
be the "stronger one" prophesied by John: this had its effect
upon the texts of our gospels. But these re-touchings remained
superficial and left undisturbed everything essential in the
material of tradition.

A clear and definite picture greets our eyes: an ascetic with
the fewest possible needs. Such were not unheard of in Roman
times: Josephus himself lived with one for three years.[2] But
John was a preacher of both repentance and divine judgment.
The Messianic hopes also spoke of a Messianic judgment, but
this judgment was to apply to the heathen, and to set Israel
upon the throne. Since the days of Amos, the prophetic spirit
had been turned against them, and had also threatened punishment to all sinners to be found among God's own people.
Popularly, the faith held to the idea of the advantage of the
chosen descendants of Abraham, who were marked by circumcision as belonging to God: it was against this faith that John's
fiery preaching was directed. What could be read in the
apocalypses, and occasionally heard in earnest Sabbath sermons,
operated with unique force when it echoed through the land
from the mouth of a prophet. For the message proclaimed that
the test was imminent: the Messiah was coming. But nothing
was said about Messianic glory and indescribable happiness;
rather the one who exercised the authority of the Lord, was
coming to hold judgment, he would light a fire for all sinners,
and destroy them. The prophet's preaching made them tremble
in their souls for fear of hell, and then showed them a way to
salvation that still remained open: immediate repentance and
amendment. The gospels and Josephus are unanimous in saying
that the decisive elements in John's message were simple and
complete righteousness in life, and keeping the divine, ethical
commands. According to the gospels, water-baptism indicated

[1] Mark 1: 2–6; Matt. 3: 1–12; Luke 3: 1–18   [2] Jos., *Vita.*, 11–12

forgiveness of sins and a repentant mind, but according to the, perhaps, rather artificial account of Josephus,[1] it did not signify the washing away of any sort of transgressions, but the sanctification of the body after the cleansing of the soul had been completed. In any case, it was to be distinguished from the ceremonial cleansing baths of the Jewish rite, and from the bathings of sects such as the Essenes; it was a single action which signified that the baptized initiate had gone over to the life of righteousness.

The Baptist did not come forward in accordance with any apocalyptic programme whatsoever. It was a new idea that there would be a final opportunity for Israel to repent,[2] and, similarly, that baptism sealed the act of repentance. We may call to mind Isa. 1: 16–17: "Wash you, make you clean, put away your evil doings from before my eyes; cease to do evil: learn to do well; seek judgment, judge the fatherless, plead for the widow." Here we have a baptism linked with ethical requirements which correspond to those of the Baptist, although the apocalyptic perspective is lacking. This may have been derived from Mal. 3, which prophesies of the angel who is to come before the Lord and "purify the sons of Levi, and purge them as gold and silver" (v. 3). Hence God requires conversion,[3] and, thereon, promises His grace. Before the day dawns, which "shall burn like a furnace", God will send the prophet Elias, who "shall turn the heart of the fathers to the children, and the heart of the children to the fathers; lest I come and smite the earth with a curse".[4] The faith in the appearance of Elijah—who is thus equated with the "angel"—as the herald of the Messiah, was entirely popular at this time,[5] and led to the consequence that John was regarded as an Elijah *redivivus*,[6] and Christians regarded this chapter in Malachi as a key for understanding John.[7]

How is this baptism to be understood? Josephus is a poor witness, for he has the obvious tendency of translating Jewish matters into terms of Greek philosophy and ethics, thus making them more to the taste of his readers. On this account, we would

---

[1] Jos., *Ant.*, 18, 117 [2] Cf., say, *Assumption of Moses*, 1, 18, "the day of repentance'
[3] Mal. 3: 7 [4] Mal. 4: 6 [5] Bousset, *Judentum*, p. 232
[6] Mark 6: 15; 8: 28 [7] Matt. 11: 14; 17, 12 f.; Mark 1: 2

be suspicious of his notice of the Baptist's preaching, were it
not in full accord with the gospel tradition, where there is no
question of moralizing tendencies and bias. But the case is
different in regard to the baptism. When Mark characterizes it
as a "baptism of repentance for the forgiveness of sins" (1: 4),
that corresponds with the content of the rest of the tradition,
and, in a certain sense, to the prophetic use of language;
nevertheless, we learn really nothing thereby about the nature
of this baptism. Was the baptism a symbol, as Josephus depicts
it, or was it a sacrament which, when completed, effected a
miraculous operation, and cleansed the sinner—like the
baptism of the Christian church? Was it to be compared with
the baptism of proselytes, which washed away the uncleanness
from the heathen on entering Judaism, and grafted them with
ceremonial purity on to the people of God? This last has been
asserted,[1] and we are then presented with the strange paradox
that John demanded that the Israelite, who was proud of his
nationality, should submit to baptism, and be made clean, just
as the unclean heathen must do, before he could come to God;
which is too paradoxical to be convincing. It scarcely requires
such roundabout arguments before it is comprehensible that
John made his baptism the central action of his work. His
point was by no means to gather his hearers into a new religious
community, but to cleanse and redeem them before Judgment
and the new era came. In this connection, the ceremony of
washing sins away in water had long been customary in Israel,
even more generally than among other peoples. But our sources
make it in no way probable that sacramental ideas were bound
up with John's baptism.

John gathered disciples round himself, and we hear that
they fasted and, in this respect, were in agreement with the
Pharisees.[2] In another passage, we are told that their master
taught them to pray,[3] i.e. that they had received definite forms
of prayer. But what else in this regard was thought, taught, or
done, remains completely hidden from us. We only hear of the
end.

[1] Cf. H. Schaeder in *Gnomon*, 1929, p. 367. J. Leipoldt, *Urchristl. Taufe im Lich d. Religionsgesch.*, 27
[2] Mark 2: 18   [3] Luke 11: 1

The growing power of the prophet over the people un-
settled Antipas, and he feared disturbance. Hence he had John
carried to the bloody prison-castle of Machærus—not far from
the east coast of the Dead Sea—and there secretly executed.[1]
Amongst the people, that graphic but dreadful story was told
which is preserved in Mark's gospel (6: 17–29) for the readers,
poets, and painters of succeeding ages. His school lasted for
some time after his death. This can be deduced from the
indirect polemic of the Fourth Gospel and from the legends of
the Baptist in the gospel message.[2] Quite soon, however, all
trace of them was lost and we hear no more of the disciples of
John.

Is that quite true? The numerous writings of the Mandæans
bear witness to the continued existence of the disciples of John
for several centuries and perhaps the baptist sect in southern
Babylonia at the present time, is the direct heir of John's work
in the days of the Herods. That is asserted nowadays by many
weighty persons, and anyone who regards the Mandæan literature as sources can draw an attractive picture of the spiritual
power which proceeded from John, and which influenced the
religion of Judaism, and especially that of Jesus and His
disciples. John's circle then appears as the nursery of an early
gnosis, which united Babylonian, Persian, and Syrian elements
in a many-coloured mixture on a Jewish background, and
grouped the whole round the ancient Iranian mythology of the
first man, that redeemer who descended from heaven in order
to awaken the soul bound and asleep in the material fetters of
this world, and to open up for it the way to heaven. This is very
intriguing, and gives quite unthought-of perspectives, leading
possibly to a new understanding of primitive Christianity;
nevertheless we must put it firmly and entirely on one side. It
can be shown[3] that the Mandæan literature consists of various
strata which come from widely different periods. And the latest
of these strata, belonging to the Islamic era—i.e. at earliest, in
the seventh century—are those which preserve the notices of
John the Baptist; they are modelled on the basis of the gospel

[1] Jos., *Ant.*, 18, 119
[2] M. Dibelius, *Jungfrauensohn*, 1–11. The notice in *Clem. recog.*, 1, 54, 60, is
valueless; nor do Acts 18: 25, 19: 1 ff. refer to the disciples of John
[3] *Sitzungsber. Akad. Berlin*, 1930, 596–608

records, and distorted till they are grotesque. In the same way, the many sallies against Jesus and Christianity are quite clearly directed against the Byzantine church, and have not the least connection with primitive Christianity. The fragments of the earlier strata belong to a rank oriental gnosis which has run to seed, and have no bearing on the historical John and his disciples.

Chapter Four

JESUS

NOW AFTER THAT JOHN WAS DELIVERED UP, JESUS CAME into Galilee, preaching the Gospel of God, and saying, The time is fulfilled, and the kingdom of God is at hand: repent ye, and believe in the gospel. Thus our earliest record, in Mark 1: 14, tells of Jesus' first appearance; the new era in the history of the world was now beginning.

The question arises whether, and to what extent, the records telling of Jesus are, in fact, historical. Are our sources sufficient to give us a picture of the historical Jesus? Or must we be content with the spiritual conceptions elaborated by the primitive Church, and regard the "historical" Jesus as belonging to the sphere of the unreal, or at least the incomprehensible? That is the precipitate view advanced by some dogmatic radicals today. Both on the side against the Church and on that favouring it, there are several scholars who have wilfully taken the difficulty of the historical problem to be a proof of its impossibility; detesting historical research, they have abandoned it in favour of roaming at will in the fields of pure speculation. But facts have their own importance and demand their rights from serious science; they fight their way through and, in the end, hold the field. It may be granted that our sources containing Jesus' words and deeds have been moulded by the Christian church: we can clearly perceive the work done on them by the earliest Christians, so clearly, indeed, that we can often find therein what is characteristic of the opinions and hopes of this very community. But in spite of all the transformation effected by tradition, we see in every direction the genuine rock of reliable information upon which the historian can build—if only he will deal with the sources of primitive Christianity by the same methods as all other existing sources. That means, however, that he must approach them as an expert and disinterested judge, not as a critic who is sceptical on principle. There is only one historical method; if we hear of special

methods for religion, history, legend, form-criticism, and the
history of worship, we must remember that these are not new
methods, but new standpoints calculated to supplement each
other and to refine the one historical method. Used in isolation,
they can easily do harm.

We obtain our knowledge of Jesus almost entirely from the
first three gospels. Mark's gospel is the earliest of these, and its
author is probably Mark, the disciple of Paul, mentioned in
I Pet. 5: 13, of whom Acts often speaks. The gospel was written
shortly after A.D. 70, but made use of earlier writings; these
however, cannot be restored with precision, and, indeed, are
only sometimes clearly recognizable. Both the other evangelists
used Mark as the basis of their record, and adopted almost the
whole of his material, each of them naturally editing it in his
own way in point of style and material. That the MS. of Mark
of which they made use should show many variations from that
which has come down to us, is not surprising and should not
give occasion for seeking some other hypothesis.

However, both Matthew and Luke have employed another
source which is clearly to be seen in the material they have in
common apart from that of Mark, and which, within limits,
can be reconstructed in these passages.[1] In the form in which it
is available to us, this source also comes from the period after
A.D. 70; it was written in Greek and it contains, in particular,
sayings and speeches of the Lord. For this reason, we call it the
"Sayings Source", and have good grounds for tracing it back
to the apostle Matthew in its earliest Aramaic form. He is
mentioned as the author of some such a piece of writing.[2] It
appears to have been subjected to more definite changes in the
course of its history than the text of Mark, and there is the
difficult question whether the sayings-passages, which are preserved either only in Matthew or only in Luke, are derived
from the document Matthew himself wrote. Luke in particular
is characterized by extensive, valuable, and unique material,
for which we should, perhaps, assume a special source. We
must also reckon with the possibility that, in addition to these
written sources, oral tradition played a part in the same

[1] Cf. Harnack, *Sprüche u. Reden Jesu*, 1907. Eng. trans., *The Sayings of Jesus*, 1910
[2] Euseb., *H.E.*, iii ,39, 16 ,by Papias

period, and added here and there stories separately current.

As a consequence, it appears that the written sources which are immediately accessible, or which can be easily reached by simple critical processes, originated in the seventies of the first century. From them we divine a literature earlier than A.D. 70, and this again rests upon the oral tradition of the first generation of disciples, and therefore appears, in the last analysis, as the foundation upon which all our knowledge of Jesus rests. Such a tradition tends to be a handing down of separate pieces, passed round independently, and put together by collectors who adopt a standpoint altogether foreign to the material itself. How to recognize the origin and understand the growth of this tradition when restored to its original elements, and how to appraise the quality of faithfulness in face of the tendency to transform and to add—these are the particular subjects of discussion to-day. In the records that lie before us, we can observe how the wishes, needs, and theological opinions within the Church added a continuation to a narrative, a saying, or a parable; and sometimes so altered it that the uninitiated did not recognize it again. Indeed, we can see religious fantasy calling some entirely new feature into life, and this, in turn, becomes subject to further development in accordance with the same laws. From what we actually see, we can deduce the early history of the rest of the material by presupposing that the same forces were in operation as at an earlier date; and we can then inquire what these forces may have effected by way of additions to, or transformations of, the history of Jesus in the period not covered by literary sources.[1]

In the course of these studies, analogies from allied spheres are frequently applied in order to gain a sharper focus. The numerous Rabbinic sayings offer a welcome parallel to the sayings of Jesus, for they were passed from mouth to mouth, and school to school, for centuries in the Jewish tradition, and finally they received a fixed written form in the Mishna and Gemara of the Talmud, or in commentaries on the Bible. This analogy is all the more valuable because they were not stored in the memory on account of "historical" interests, but either as

[1] Of fundamental importance is R. Bultmann, *Geschichte der Synopt. Tradition*, 2nd ed., 1931; cf. also Dibelius, *From Tradition to Gospel*, 1934

authoritative references for theological decisions, or as rules for
the lives of the devout. Similar traditions of sayings may be
observed amongst the monks of the fourth century, and these
have been written down in the various collections of
"Apothegms" of the fathers.[1]

The parallels are of value for understanding the tradition of
sayings and speeches. In the same way, the legends of the saints
afford instructive parallels to the way in which the accounts
of the deeds and experiences of Jesus developed their present
form and content. Of course, much skill is required for sorting
out those texts which afford real parallels, i.e. those which
have a sound historical foundation, from the host of merely
imaginary or conventional records. For, here also, we have to
do with an oral tradition which has been reduced to writing,
but cannot be regarded as literature in the ordinary sense;
rather, it corresponds to the style of popular books. This is the
case with the gospels, and, in the shaping of the gospel tradition,
the same laws have operated which usually govern the model-
ling of a popular account of the deeds or miracles of great men
of God. It is useful to adduce examples here from other spheres
of religion. The all-important thing is that the literary critic
should retain a sound judgment of the possibilities, the proba-
bilities, and the actualities, of the subject-matter at a time when
he is absorbed in following the various transformations in the
manner of its literary presentation. There are no infallible
standards on which to base judgments, and all historical
research is essentially an art which, like·every art, depends for
the value of its results on the qualifications of the student himself; but it can be developed by regular cultivation, rich experience, and ever fresh activity in various fields, until an opinion
is reached that must correspond very closely with the facts.

Jesus grew up in·the little Galilean village of Nazareth,
where it is probable that He had been born. Joseph His father
must have died early, for we only hear of Mary His mother. He
had four brothers whose names have come down to us, James,
Joses, Jude, and Simon, and also several sisters. By trade, He
was a carpenter.[2] He was not confined to timber, saws, and

[1] W. Bousset, *Apophthegmata*, 1923   [2] Mark 6: 3

axes, however, for the spirit drove Him forth into the solitude. When the preaching of John the Baptist re-echoed in the land, He went as a pilgrim to the Jordan and had Himself baptized. Thereupon the spirit drove Him into the wilderness, where He wrestled in prayer with God, and strove with the devil. His wonderful personality was watched with many shakings of heads at home, and, in the end, He was pronounced mad. When He began to attract attention and the people crowded round Him, His family set out to take charge of Him, and to bring the disgrace to an end.[1] We find in Him the tragic quality of the lonely soul whom God has laid hold of by force, lifted out of the love and the friendliness of the world, and filled with deep anguish of spirit; but who, nevertheless, courageously confirms the divine imperative. There is the sound of an heroic inversion of all nature in His hard saying:[2] "If any man cometh unto Me, and hateth not his own father, and mother, and wife, and children, and brethren, and sisters, yea, and his own life also, he cannot be My disciple."

When John the Baptist was imprisoned and hidden from public sight, Jesus returned from the wilderness to His Galilean home,[3] and took up the preaching of him who had been silenced. But it sounded different in His mouth. He did not terrify His hearers by threatening them with the fiery flames of impending judgment; rather He spoke of God and the nature of His rule. For Him also, the transmutation of the age was at hand, and men of the present generation would experience the Kingdom coming with power.[4] Then all suffering would be assuaged, all tears wiped away, and he who, for the Kingdom's sake, had sacrified anything dear to himself, would be well rewarded.[5] But it was necessary to prepare oneself properly for this reign of God—and here the simple ethical preaching of John was not sufficient. The Kingdom of God attracted every one's desire to itself, just as treasure hidden in a field delights the lucky discoverer, as a precious pearl the merchant. All mankind must place themselves at the disposal of God's will and obey His call, leaving behind family, friends, and every possession: he who put his hand to the plough and looked back,

[1] Mark 3: 21, 31   [2] Luke 14: 26, modified in Matt. 10: 37   [3] Mark 1: 14
[4] Mark 9: 1   [5] Mark 10: 30

was not suitable for the Kingdom of God.[1] While it is necessary that we should do God's will on earth as it is done in heaven, we must recognize it as a mighty factor which threatens to disrupt every earthly relationship. "Think not that I am come to send peace on earth: I am not come to send peace but a sword." There will be disputes in the family, and enmity in the house—thus He preached;[2] and it was in accordance with His own experience. The people crowded to Him and listened open-mouthed; many ran after Him; a few remained with Him, and became His disciples. The first of these were two pairs of brothers, fishermen of Lake Genesareth, Simon and Andrew, John and James.

But he did more than preach; He also worked miracles, and testified thereby to the divine origin of His mission. The news of His deeds, spreading more rapidly than the content of His preaching, was told far and wide among the people. Cripples, epileptics, and madmen were healed at His command, and evil spirits vanished before the divine power. The lame and the blind, the deaf and the dumb, and even lepers felt His healing power. In one place indeed, He raised from the dead a twelve-year-old girl; in Nain, a young man. It serves no purpose to try, meticulously and pedantically, to determine the "historical kernel" of the various miracle-stories in the gospels, even if here and there it seems possible. No person of judgment to-day can any longer doubt that Jesus possessed miraculous power, and worked "miracles" as understood in the ancient sense; and to the historian, the extant records, just because of their popular character, flash light from very many facets, and are more valuable than dry official reports could be; for from them comes a reflection of His acts and deeds which pierces far into the deeps of human nature.

A prophet mighty in word and deed had arisen, armed with the miraculous powers of Elias—was he not the very Elias who was to be the herald of the Messiah? Or was Jesus the Messiah Himself who was to bestow the Kingdom of God upon His people? No! the other side replied, He is a false prophet, and has made a compact with Beelzebub, the prince of devils; that is why the demons must obey Him. But how could Satan

[1] Luke 9: 62   [2] Matt. 10: 34

destroy his own kingdom? objected Jesus; and if I really do cast
out demons by the finger of God, then take notice thereby that
the Kingdom of God has come to you.[1] In this way it would
seem that His miraculous power was a glorious divine gift and
at the same time a token that His gospel of the Kingdom of
God was true. When in prison, John the Baptist heard of the
deeds of this successor of his, and the popular opinion about
Him, and sent to inquire of Him: Are you He that was to come,
or ought we to look for someone else? For His deeds harmonized
badly with the Baptist's prophecy of a fiery judgment. The
answer resounded the words of Isaiah: The blind see and the
lame walk, lepers become cleansed and the deaf hear, the dead
rise, and the gospel is preached to the poor—the prophesied
signs of the End are here; blessed is the man who takes no
offence in Me.[2] At a later date,[3] Jesus asked His disciples: Who
do men say I am? to which Peter replied: You are the Messiah.
And Jesus knew that he spoke the truth.

The Kingdom of God was not merely knocking at the door;
it was already present. It was like a bit of yeast in a bowl of
dough which would soon leaven the whole batch. It was put
in the earth like a mustard seed which began to sprout and to
grow into a tree. And all this was a great divine miracle: he to
whom God has promised the seed, sows it on the ground; it
sprouts and grows of itself,[4] and brings forth blade and fruit—
finally comes the day of harvest, the Last Judgment and the
glorious End. In the present world, all sorts of weeds are still
growing apace among the wheat, and even this is surely according to God's will; only at the Last Judgment will the chaff be
burnt in the fire. There is no need for you to rise and look
round for the Kingdom of God,[5] or to lie in wait in case some
one says to you: here it is or there it comes; for it is in your
midst. That was a new, astonishing, and estranging message,
the paradox in Jesus' preaching, which would not sink into the
people of His time, nor the scholars of to-day. It is true that
Jesus used the colours of prophetic apocalyptic in preaching the
Kingdom of God and its glory as promising salvation in a

---

[1] Matt. 12: 28; Luke 11: 20. Also Bultmann, *Tradition*, 2nd ed., p. 174
[2] Matt. 11: 2–6; Luke 7: 18–23
[3] Viz. after the death of John the Baptist, Mark 8: 27–29
[4] Mark 4: 26–29   [5] Luke 17: 20–21

future age whose commencement no one could calculate, because the Father had kept that entirely to Himself.[1] But this language was meant to describe the full revelation of the Kingdom, the final phases of which would be preceded by the signs foretold by the prophets; it was the coming of the Kingdom "with power". At this time, the Messiah would also appear on the clouds of the sky and set up His throne in the midst of a renewed Israel. But the Kingdom was coming with no less reality even in the present, and the Messiah was passing unnoticed through the land, illumined only by the splendour of miraculous deeds. He was thereby made recognizable, and He gathered the first subjects of the Kingdom round Himself. The new æon had already begun, before the old had collapsed —the media of time and space fail wherever a genuine prophetic message of divine reality is proclaimed.

Popular imagination took most delight in depicting the splendour and the joys of God's Kingdom on earth, and even Jesus' disciples would gladly have known the answer to the question as to who would sit at the right and the left of the Messiah at the future festival.[2] Jesus had more important matters to publish about the Kingdom of God. In the forefront was the teaching that the legal preciseness which was so keenly watched in Pharisaic circles would not be sufficient for one belonging to it; for God was not satisfied with the outer fulfilment of commands; but required the complete surrender of the heart in its deepest depths. Jesus took up again the Old Testament commandment[3] that we must love God with all our hearts, and our neighbour as ourselves, but He drew out of that commandment the final consequences of making religion an inward matter; the Sermon on the Mount contains a series of classic examples. In the command to love our enemies, He opposed natural feeling, and in the command to look for no reward and no revenge, as well as by prohibiting oaths, and divorce, He opposed the Mosaic law. In so doing, He knew Himself to be proclaiming God's will, and He troubled little about the indignation of the guardians of the Law. Fasting and ritual prayer counted for little with Him: a man must speak

---

[1] Mark 13: 32; this was Jewish teaching
[2] Mark 10: 37   [3] Mark 12: 29–30

with God in solitude. He regarded Sabbath observance as objectionable if it prevented neighbourly actions, or even only the usual eating and drinking. We find here and there many parallels to all this in the surviving sayings of the Rabbis, but they are no more than occasional ripples, which soon die away, and are lost in the sea of legal observances. With Jesus, life with God is like a broad river flooding all the land, and sweeping away every hindrance; there is nothing that would not be covered by its waves. From that life there springs everything which men call righteousness, virtue, good works.

The Jew regarded God as the righteous judge who dealt with men's deeds exactly in accordance with the written code. He also believed in a mercy which God evinced towards His favourites by forgiving their sins; and the Jew hoped that his own good work would receive a just reward, and his sins divine forgiveness. Even Jesus often spoke of reward in a popular, religious sense, and as if the self-denials and sufferings of this world would be recompensed in the Kingdom of God. But when He revealed the final secret of the Kingdom of God, the idea of recompense vanished into nothing. God was like the employer who at different times in the day engaged workpeople for his vineyard,[1] but who gave them all the same wages, and calmly set aside the complaints of the discontented by saying: You who were engaged first, have received what was agreed— are you envious because I have been generous to those engaged last? In the Kingdom of God, all righteousness is simply divine grace. And if you have fulfilled all the commandments, you have only done your duty; you have no claim on any reward, but are unprofitable servants. In the Talmud,[2] we find the answer given by Judaism to this conception of God—we have the same parable but another moral. Here, also, a vine-dresser had worked only two hours, and yet received a full day's pay. But the employer answered those who were discontented with this: This man did more in two hours than you in the whole day. In this instance, everything proceeded according to justice and merit. The contrast is quite clear: on the one hand is the Jewish conception of God with formal righteousness in the

[1] Matt. 20: 1–16
[2] *Jerus. Berachoth*, 2, 8 f., 5c; Billerbeck, iv, 492 ff.

human sense, and on the other, the God of Jesus, and a righteousness whose very nature is grace.

Moreover, it appears that the "righteous" are not those who
are the first to enter the Kingdom of God, but the despised and
the lost, the taxgatherers and the sinners, the poor and the sick.
In the Kingdom of God, there is more joy over one sinner who
repents than over ninety-nine "righteous persons" who, on
account of their very righteousness, never conceive that they
lack the best, i.e. knowledge of the nothingness of every human
being in the sight of the eternal God. The parable of the
Pharisee and the Publican brought that to classic expression
once for all. It was a new thing, and it came with a shock, that
Jesus' preaching of the Kingdom was directed towards sinners.[1]
Even nineteen hundred years later, we find this fact difficult to
grasp, although it was meant for us also.

The Old Testament religion sees God's blessing in riches as a
reward for good conduct upon earth, and is inclined to regard
poverty, illness, and suffering, as the divine punishment for
sin. The obscure and the simple knew better—that God had
promised His salvation to the poor and the pitiable.[2] And now
Jesus came, and blessed not only the poor and the suffering,
but also the sinners—for God is near them and calls them to
Himself. When the guests invited to the wedding feast failed to
respond to the invitation given by the divine host, the messengers went into the streets and lanes and invited the beggars
and the cripples, the lame and the blind.[3] Who is the better
son: The one who says, No! to his father's order, but repents and
does it, or he who says, Yes! and does not do it?[4] Thus the sinner
enters the Kingdom of God if he searches his heart and repents
—the very thing which the righteous man thinks he need not
do. In the same way, the poor man is nearer to the Kingdom
of God, for he is not blinded by the wealth and the cheap self-
righteousness of the giver of charity. He is not bound fast to the
present æon and its values by concern for material possessions,
and he has no treasure on earth, which fills his heart and closes
it to God. The rich young man would gladly have followed
Jesus, but he could not well abandon everything for the sake of

[1] K. Holl, *Ges. Aufs.*, ii, 9 ff.   [2] *Vide supra*, p. 38
[3] Luke 14: 16–24   [4] Matt. 21: 28–31

the Kingdom of God: it would not do; everyone could understand that, but—the pity of it! Hence: blessed are you poor, for
yours is the kingdom of God.

Jesus did not preach like the scribes, but like one authorized
by God—thus Mark[1] expressed the judgment of the hearers.
But for this very reason, i.e. because the accustomed teaching
was held in respect, no one wished to have anything to do with
Him. In Nazareth His home, He said bitterly that a prophet
counted for nothing in his native place; even in the larger
world round Lake Genesareth, He gained no hearing; He pronounced woe upon Chorazin, Bethsaida, and even Caper-
naum.[2] Therefore He avoided the towns and became the
preacher of the *Am ha-Arez*. Galilee was surrounded by pagan
districts, separated by Samaria from the Judaistic centre of
religion, and penetrated with foreign elements. Hence there
was no sympathy here with the strenuous legalism of the
Pharisees.[3] In this region, therefore, a hearing could be found
for a message which proclaimed that the Kingdom of God was
open to pagan or half-pagan taxgatherers, to despised sinners,
and to the poor and the pitiable; but closed to the Pharisees
with their display of righteous correctness, and to the rich
givers of charity. Here Jesus became a popular hero followed
by the masses; Herod Antipas regarded Him with considerable
doubt, and wondered whether He was the Baptist risen from
the dead; and therefore to be rendered harmless.[4] It was the
necessary consequence of His deeds and words that the Pharisees
should hate Him as one who contemned the Law, and should
persecute Him as a false prophet. There was no escaping a
decisive struggle if He was to be really the Messiah, and not be
content with the part of a forerunner.

Our sources speak unanimously of Jesus' Messiahship. Peter's
confession, "Thou art the Messiah", in Mark, harmonizes with
the indirect answer to the direct question of John the Baptist
preserved in "Q".[5] But we have no authentic tradition of a word
of Jesus Himself in which He claims this dignity as His own.[6]

---

[1] Mark 1: 22   [2] Matt. 11: 20–24; Luke 10, 13–15
[3] Cf. Walter Bauer in *Festgabe für Jülicher*, 16–34
[4] Mark 6: 14; cf. 8: 28; Luke 13: 31   [5] Cf. *supra*, p. 51
[6] The confession before the High-Priest (Mark 14: 62) is scarcely historical
cf. *Sitzungsber. Akad. Berlin*, 1931, p. 316

On the other hand our two principal sources have preserved quite a number of sayings in which Jesus describes
Himself as the Son of Man; and it can be clearly seen from the
context in Mark 8: 31 that this was understood in the Messianic
sense. Moreover, other passages show that the enigmatic title
means the future ruler of the Kingdom of God, for, according
to Dan. 7: 13, that ruler would "come on the clouds of heaven
like a son of man". In spite of the fact that no successful solution
has yet been found for the philological problems raised by this
term,[1] the general reliability of the textual tradition is as little
in doubt as the Messianic significance of the phrase. And it is
just as certain that "Son of Man" was not a current term for the
Messiah, for even the earliest Christians no longer understood
it, and avoided using it; thus it has remained a riddle to the
present day. We may take it as a reliable tradition that Jesus
was regarded as the Messiah by His disciples and by various
individuals among the people at large, sick and well, healed
and possessed. So, too, He regarded Himself as the Messiah.
And, just as He had given quite a new sense to the term,
"Kingdom of God", so too, He entirely transformed the meaning of "Messiah". He allowed the apocalyptic conceptions to
remain, and glow on the horizon; but He took the seeds of the
Kingdom, which were replete with divine power, and planted
them in the hearts of those hearers who repented and believed.
Jesus possessed an inner royalty, and was armed with miraculous powers given by His heavenly Father. After He had
received that Father's testimony,[2] He preached the gospel of
the new, divine community, and so brought the long-promised
salvation to His fellows.

Another, new element in the teaching which Jesus gave His
disciples was that the Messiah must die in order to complete
His work. It was most difficult to understand and they simply
did not believe it. No Jew had ever heard of a Messiah who
would have to die by the very nature of His office, and therefore this conception cannot have been applied to Jesus from
the outside. Rather, just as the message of the Kingdom and
the consciousness of His Messiahship received their characteristic nature from Jesus' experience of God, so it came home

[1] G. Dalman, *Worte Jesu*, 2nd edit., 191–219, 383–97   [2] Mark 1: 9–11

to Him, in His own soul, that His death was necessary for the accomplishment of His task; and this, in its nature, was an inner acceptance and affirmation of what His experiences of His opponents led Him to suspect as His personal lot.

We do not know how long Christ's public ministry lasted, for the single year into which Mark compresses his account is only a literary form and was not intended to be historical chronology. The Fourth Gospel quite obviously counts upon three years, but without our being able for this reason to regard it as a more reliable witness. It describes Jesus as attending the Passover in Jerusalem at least twice before He went there for the last time. The synoptics know nothing of this, and the saying from "Q", found in Luke 13: 34, is probably a quotation from the Book of Wisdom mentioned in 11: 49, and has no relevance to this question. Tradition tells of only one journey to Jerusalem, and Mark put His third prophecy of death, like a direction sign, at the head of his account (10: 32–34). Luke wrote down a valuable piece of tradition that had hitherto been circulating freely in the popular memory (13: 31–33): In that hour there came certain Pharisees, saying to him: Get thee out and go hence: for Herod would fain kill thee. And he said to them, Go and say to that fox, Behold, I cast out devils and perform cures to-day and to-morrow, and the third day I must journey; for it cannot be that a prophet perish out of Jerusalem.[1] Both these passages reflect the same sad echo: He is going to the capital to die there, for that is God's will. But Luke's record preserves a note on the historical circumstances. Antipas had sent some Pharisees with the message for Jesus to depart from Galilee. It was possible for Him to go either to Samaria or into gentile regions—but He had no call there. Hence He recognized that His hour had come, and He began the journey that was to prove fatal. His disciples were amazed, and the crowds were troubled about Him, for even they knew into what danger He was running.

The road led through Jericho, where He healed a blind man;[2] then He approached Jerusalem from the east. In the neighbourhood of Olivet, when exhausted by the journey, He appears to

[1] This must be the meaning of the traditional saying in Luke 13; 32–33
[2] Mark 10: 46

have borrowed an ass, an incident out of which later legends developed a Messianic entry into Jerusalem on the basis of Zechariah's prophecy (9: 9) which foretells of the gentle king riding on an ass into Jerusalem. According to the tradition preserved in Mark, Jesus then entered Jerusalem for the very first time, for that is the natural presupposition of the following remark, viz., that in the temple He looked round about upon all things, and then, because it was getting dusk, He went out into Bethany for the night.[1]

As has been the case with many other devout persons in later centuries, so it was with Jesus: His proper, religious feeling was most pronouncedly offended by the more than profane business carried on in the forecourt of the temple. He drove out the dealers with their sacrificial animals, and likewise the money-changers, broke up their stalls, and then closed the forecourt as a thoroughfare; this can only mean that He gathered the people round Himself to take forceful measures against the evil of sacrilege; uttering the denunciations of the prophets of old, He put Himself at their head.

That was a first sign of the storm in Jerusalem: the prophet from Galilee had raised a tumult in the temple, and that must have caused concern to the people in authority. Nevertheless, they did not attempt to overmaster Him by means of the police, but tried by various questions to entrap Him. Mark records a few disputes between Jesus and the Pharisees and Sadducees, which might well be ascribed to this period, the most illuminating being the question as to the payment of tribute money.[2] In Galilee, politics was not a matter of common argument, and the national insurrection in A.D. 66–70 found no echo in that province.[3] Jesus held quite aloof from political hopes, and the national Messianic ideal with its worldly complexion such as we know in the Psalms of Solomon appeared to Him on at least one occasion as a temptation of the devil. Opinion was different in Jerusalem, and liberation from the Roman over-rule was a national as well as a religious desideratum. When Jesus gave an equivocal answer to the question of tribute and showed Himself lukewarm, His standing in the capital was gone. His answer

[1] Mark 11: 11   [2] Mark 12: 13–17, also Jos., *Ant.*, 18, 4, *Bellum J.*, 2, 118
[3] W. Bauer in *Festgabe für Jülicher*, 22 ff.

avoided the trap and dealt with the crucial point of the problem. In effect, He said, "Since you have been obliged to surrender to the Romans the right of minting gold and silver money, it is foolish to ask whether one ought to pay taxes to these same Romans with foreign money." But as soon as the insurrection broke out in A.D. 66, the Jews once more coined silver money.

We have no idea how long Jesus was at odds with the authorities in Jerusalem. Not a syllable in Mark hints that Jesus—possibly in a pilgrim caravan—had come to Jerusalem just for the Passover; and we have already noted the passage in Luke saying that Antipas had banned Him, which makes it indeed unlikely. We may assume, therefore, that Jesus worked for a considerable period in Jerusalem, during which He gained numerous adherents among the people, and many influential enemies among the Pharisees and Sadducees. The members of the sanhedrin eventually decided to get rid of Him; it was to be done without causing a sensation, and before the Passover. Only two days were left.[1]

After He had prayed in a garden on Olivet, Jesus was arrested by night in the midst of His disciples, one belonging to the inner circle having informed the bailiffs of the place where He was accustomed to spend the night. At the arrest, the disciples fled, and only Peter turned back, and slipped after his Master into the courtyard of the High-Priest's official residence. There he mingled with the crowd and, by a couple of lies, managed to escape detection. But it is scarcely probable that we can depend upon his report, for from what we read in Mark about the night-trial before the sanhedrin, all signs indicate that we have a later Christian version here. Mark says that a night-sitting of the sanhedrin was held at once under the presidency of Caiaphas the High-Priest. The first charge was that Jesus had desired to destroy the temple and rebuild it in three days; but the reports of the witnesses did not agree, and Jesus main-tained silence in spite of all the charges. Then the High-Priest put to Him the crucial question, which was one of conscience: Are you the Messiah, the Son of the Most High? And He answered: Yes, and prophesied that He would sit at the right

[1] Mark 14: 1

hand of God, and that He would return as the Son of Man upon the clouds of heaven. Thereupon the High-Priest condemned Him to death for blasphemy. It cannot be proved that this record contains more than a dim memory of the actual events.

But we can say, with some certainty, that the sanhedrin came to no legal condemnation on the count of blasphemy, for then they would have had to execute Jesus on their own authority by stoning. That was prescribed in the Law, and was accordingly carried out, as we see, e.g. in the case of Stephen. It is an error, which the gospels themselves share and have spread, that the Great Sanhedrin did not possess the power to pronounce and carry out capital sentences. Rather the undoubtedly trustworthy report of the course of events shows that the Jewish authorities, probably on quite good grounds, refrained from dealing with this matter in the form of a religious trial, and preferred to hand Jesus over to the Roman authorities as an insurgent.[1] The procurator, Pontius Pilate, is well known to us from other records.[2] He governed as Jewish procurator from A.D. 26–36, and was staying at that moment in Jerusalem, obviously because the people were streaming there for the Passover, and he wished to keep his eyes on the masses. Jesus was denounced to him as the "King of the Jews", which is as much as to say a Messianic agitator in the political sense. After a short hearing, Pilate had Him taken away, scourged, and crucified. That the lot of Jesus was seen in the light of Old Testament prophecy, and was reflected in the hearts of His own people, is shown with moving power in the Passion story of the gospels.

On the thirteenth or the fourteenth of the month of Nisan, in the afternoon in any case before Passover eve,[3] Jesus died on the cross. A devout member of the sanhedrin took the body down from the cross and put it in a tomb hewn in the rock. We hear no further of the disciples. Prophecy had been fulfilled: the shepherd was killed and the sheep were scattered. The Messianic dream was at an end.

[1] This can be plainly seen in Mark 15: 1. For the whole, cf. *Der Prozess Jesu* in *Sitzungsber. Akad. Berlin*, 1931, 313–22
[2] *Prosopographia imp. Rom.*, iii, 84
[3] E. Schwartz, *Z.N.W.*, 7, 23. Wellhausen, *Mark*, pp. 108–10

Chapter Five

THE FIRST CHURCH

THOUGH CRUCIFIED, DEAD, AND BURIED, JESUS DID NOT remain in a state of death. He appeared to His disciples and was seen alive by them. First to Peter, then to the Twelve, then to more than 500 brethren at one time, afterwards to James, and later to all the apostles—that is the record of the oldest and most certain tradition preserved for us by Paul in 1 Cor. 15: 5–7. Mark 16: 7 contains a further clear indication that the first appearance of the Risen Lord to His disciples took place in Galilee: there Peter saw the Master again, there the Twelve came together and were entrusted by the Risen Lord with His mission. Accordingly they went to Jerusalem. Here He appeared to the five hundred, and this led to the founding of the Church,[1] as told in the traditional record of the first Whitsuntide. But Jesus appeared also to His brother James, and thereby gained him for the Church where he at once received an honourable position. Finally, there was a closing appearance to all the leading persons of the Church: it was the ultimate confirmation of their office. Thereupon the Lord went to heaven. Phantasy and apologetics expanded, multiplied, and altered these appearances, added the proof of the empty grave, and brought into existence the later forms of our gospel texts.

Earlier generations of scholars have made strenuous and zealous efforts, either to "explain" the resurrection of Jesus, or else to defend its inexplicable and miraculous character; as if it would be of real advantage if we could see more clearly through the details and the historical connection of the events, or could prove their uniqueness. All the events of history take place in the phenomenal world, and can only be conceived by us in terms of natural causation. But every attempt to comprehend the deepest nature and meaning of history, whether in general, or in individual instances, leads us into regions which lie beyond these boundaries, into the metaphysics of the philosopher and the theologian. Of course it is only in these

---

[1] K. Holl, *Ges. Aufs.*, ii, 47, 49, 53 ff.

deeps that the springs flow from which any interpretation of history draws life and gains value. All criticism of the gospel records, and all attempts to discover the native facts, can only be carried out on the basis of our ordinary experience of the way things happen: and they usually lead to very diverse hypotheses of visions; with which the inquirer must be content. But the verdict on the true nature of the event described as the resurrection of Jesus, an event of immeasurable significance for the history of the world, does not come within the province of historical inquiry into matters of fact; it belongs to the place where the human soul touches the eternal.

The Messiah had to reveal Himself in Jerusalem, for it was here that the Master's death had in fact taken place—hence here also must He return in glory, riding on the clouds of heaven, in order to set up God's kingdom in all its might and splendour. Even in apocalyptic hope, Jerusalem remained, as it had ever been, the central point of divine action, the capital of the new, as of the old, Israel; and from it the disciples must not depart.[1] Here the mother-church of primitive Christianity was constituted of native Jews who were adherents of Jesus, i.e. those who explicitly believed that the promised Messiah had appeared in the person of Jesus of Nazareth and that He had only revealed Himself in humility and died on the cross in fulfilment of the divine will and prophetic foretelling; He would soon come again and bring God's kingdom to the earth.

These believers in Jesus belonged to those quiet, religious people who gladly gave themselves the name of "the poor", as found in the Psalms, and who treasured with faithful hearts the sayings of the Master about the blessedness of the poor. At the same time, however, they knew themselves to be the saints,[2] the faithful who were beloved by God, the remnant of the people separated off for that Last Day of which the prophets and the apocalyptists had spoken. Both names meant the same thing and described those whose hope and expectation was that the existing, sad condition of the lowly and needy would soon end, and that they would be rewarded with overwhelming glory. The eschatological expectation of this original church,

[1] Acts 1: 4
[2] Cf. Lietzmann, *Komm.* on Rom. 15: 25. Excursus

composed of Jews, is reflected in the shining allegories of the Revelation of John.

Its members were Jews: they wished so to be, and so to remain: they attended worship in the temple, and Solomon's portico was their favourite meeting place.[1] They remained faithful to the Law, and zealously insisted that Jesus had not come to end the Law, but to fulfil it; and had warranted that heaven and earth would pass away before a letter, indeed even a fragment of a letter, would pass away, and everything be fulfilled. In addition, they accepted the scribal and Pharisaic exegeses of the scriptures.[2] What differentiated them from the Pharisees was, partly their certainty that the Messiah, whom the remaining Israelites still expected as about come, and partly their faith that He would soon reappear in glory. This conviction and this faith were not mere abstractions, but of vital force. Their experience, when the Risen Lord had appeared to them, still made their hearts throb if they looked with much yearning for His final return, visible to all the world; yet they also knew that He, who had risen from the dead, came close to His own, though invisible, whenever two or three were gathered together in His name.

It was at this point that their table fellowship won its deeper significance.

Whenever the disciples gathered for a meal in accordance with Jewish custom, and one of them pronounced a blessing over the bread, they recalled the happy days when the Master had formerly blessed and broken the bread for them. He returned to them, and they became conscious of His presence. The story of the disciples of Emmaus echoes this sense marvellously. Again, the knowledge of the presence of Jesus and the secret happiness of possessing the highest divine grace made the simplest meal in the rudest hut a foretaste of the heavenly banquet which the Lord would celebrate with His own at the Messianic table. Hence, in the first church, the bread was broken "with gladness and praise",[3] and the yearning prayer "Marana tha", i.e. "Come, O our Lord" alternated with the

[1] Acts 5: 12; 3, 11; cf. John 10: 23
[2] Matt. 5: 17–18; 23: 3
[3] Acts 2: 46 f.

Messianic "Hosanna"; present and future were woven into a single fabric.[1]

In this way the first church was held together by the fact that all its members shared the experience of the presence of the Risen Lord. A rite of initiation was also observed. No account is given of its origin; the first records assume it as well known, and in final form; Matt. 28: 19–20 is a theological explanation, added at a later date. The accounts in Acts as well as the Pauline letters, assume that the Christian is baptized on being received into the Church, whereas the tradition in the gospels does not reflect such a mode of initiation into the circle of Jesus' disciples. The remarks in John 3: 22 and 4: 1 f. are valid and historical reports of Jesus' custom, and perhaps indicate the direction in which we must look for a solution of the problem. Jesus Himself had been baptized by John, and He esteemed John's baptism highly. It appears also as if many of John's disciples had gone over into Jesus' following. Hence John's baptism was taken up into primitive Christianity[2] in its original significance of a washing away of the uncleannesses of the old æon, a cleansing necessary for the entry into the new Messianic world. The recognition that Jesus was the "Coming One" expected by John, was all that one needed to transmute baptism, as practised by John, into a Christian rite of initiation into the Church. Acts[3] records a very instructive story on this point: Paul met a number of Christians in Ephesus who had been baptized with John's baptism. He then taught them that they must be baptized in the name of Jesus; only when they had complied was the Holy Ghost given them, and only then did they receive the gift of prophecy. But they had already been "disciples", i.e. believing Christians (19: 2). In other words, we have here a glimpse of an earlier condition such as we must regard as the first, tentative effort to order the customs of the Church. At a later date, the more exact, liturgical, and definitive formula was added. Simple baptism in the Johannine mode, "for repentance and forgiveness of sins", was no longer sufficient; the name of Jesus must be named over the candidate.[4]

---

[1] Lietzmann, *Messe u. Herrenmahl*, p. 250
[2] Ed. Meyer, iii, pp. 245 ff.   [3] Acts 19: 1–5
[4] Otherwise Acts 8: 16 f. Here even baptism in the name of Jesus is not enough. The apostles must also "lay on" their hands.

These Ephesian Christians were no more disciples of John than was the Apollos who had been mentioned a little earlier;[1] he also had received only the Johannine type of baptism, but his work was that of a Christian missionary impelled by the Spirit.

There is probably some justification, from the gospel texts, for holding that John's following exercised even further influences on the first Christian church. We learn from Luke 11: 1–4 that John taught his disciples to pray,[2] and that, consequently, Jesus' disciples desired similar instruction from their own Master—whereupon Jesus gave them the "Lord's prayer". But we have to recognize that the text of Luke at the beginning of the prayer, as preserved in the principal manuscripts, is very uncertain, and in any case widely different from that in Matt. 6: 9–13, which was adopted for the liturgy of the Church. The most conservative inference from these facts is that, in the earliest tradition, the Lord's Prayer was not repeated in a definite and fixed form of words. This means that Jesus Himself cannot have prescribed and commanded a final and authoritative form; nor has any invariable form been handed down. Rather, it would seem that the original form of the Lord's Prayer consisted of the very simple petitions which underlie the Lukan text. Eschatological petitions for the coming of the Kingdom of God, expressed in phrases influenced by Jewish prayers, have been added. The kernel, which includes the petition that God will forgive us in proportion as we ourselves forgive others, breathes the very spirit of the Sermon on the Mount, the addenda express the Messianic yearning of the Church quite in the mood of the Master's preaching. There is nothing to suggest that the content of the Lord's Prayer[3] had been modelled on the prayers of John's disciples, for these are altogether unknown to us. The fact that a liturgical prayer was authorized and introduced into the Church, however, arose from the desire to do the same as the Baptist's disciples; and this fact is clearly expressed in the gospel tradition.

In addition, the Jewish custom, especially of the Pharisees, of fasting devoutly twice in the week (Luke 18: 12), was observed

[1] Acts 18: 24–28   [2] Cf. Wellhausen, *Comm.*, *ad loc.*
[3] M. Dibelius, *Joh. d. Täufer*, p. 42 ff.

among John's disciples, and was taken over by the first church. The change is explained in Mark 2: 18–20; the joy of the wedding feast was over, for the Bridegroom had been taken from His people.[1] Now was the time for repentance in expectation of the End, and it was well to fast. The Jews fasted on Mondays and Thursdays, so did John's disciples, and so must the Jewish-Christian first church have done. They also observed the Sabbath, as implied by Matt. 24: 20. The prayer to be saved from flight "in winter" as it stands in Mark, is supplemented in Matthew by the addition, "and on the Sabbath". This addition reflects tendencies within the Church, and shows that it observed the Sabbath in the Jewish way, and would not allow it to be desecrated by journeying, even in time of stress. The spirit of freedom as preached by Jesus had obviously suffered, but this was not perceived at the time. The majority had not actually known Him, and they gradually transfigured His impress. Thus it came about that the traditional observance of the Sabbath, doubly holy in Jerusalem, outweighed any memory of Jesus' own attitude. Moreover James, the leader of the church, belonged at bottom to those who were strangers to Jesus, and strove for the ideal of a Jewish "righteousness". One legend, accepted in the Church, which was written down by a Christian of the Antonine period[2] represents James as a devout man held n high respect by the Jews, and as a true, oriental ascetic who, by his lengthy prayers, had grown callouses "like a camel's" on his knees. One of the most trustworthy narratives of Acts[3] depicts the Jewish-Christians in Jerusalem as "all zealous for the law"; four of them had sworn an oath according to the Old Testament rite[4], and Paul had to join them, and undertake to defray the entire cost of the sacrifices necessary to free them from their oath, in order to allay suspicion about his own orthodoxy.

The leader of the first Church was James. He had been gladly given this honour, immediately on joining the Church, obviously because he was Jesus' brother. After James' death, a cousin of Jesus was chosen to be his successor, and, even at a later date, blood relations of Jesus enjoyed special regard in

---

[1] M. Dibelius, *Joh. d. Täufer*, p. 39   [2] Hegesippus in Eus. *H.E.*, ii, 23, 4–18
[3] Acts 21: 20–26   [4] Num. 6: 18–20

the Church.[1] In Acts, "presbyters" are mentioned along with
James at the head of the Church, but we know nothing more
about them.

In Jewish communities, it is customary for a sort of com-
mittee of eminent "elders" to constitute the advisory council.[2]
This was the case even in Old Testament times, and has continued throughout the centuries. Hence it is not surprising to
read of such a council of elders also among Christian believers.
Whether their number was defined—say twenty-four, as in the
Revelation of John—or indefinite, cannot be said.

But what was the position of the original Apostles? May we
still regard them as the real founders and the recognized
authorities of the Church? Most certainly; and their importance is clear enough from the way in which Paul had
to struggle at a later date. They were indeed not only the
guarantors and vehicles of the tradition, but also they had
been appointed to sit on twelve thrones, under the presidency
of the Son of Man, and judge the twelve tribes of Israel in the
Messianic Kingdom (Matt. 19: 28). According to Rev. 21: 14,
John saw their names written upon the twelve foundation
stones of the walls of the heavenly Jerusalem; nevertheless, near
the throne of the Lamb, twenty-four "elders" were seated on
twenty-four thrones.[3] These inconsistencies are the reflection of
opposing tendencies in Jerusalem at an early date.

The Twelve appear to have been a closed circle from which
only Peter and John the son of Zebedee stood out as individuals.
These two, together with James, constituted the "pillars" of the
first Church, as Paul once called them,[4] making use of a title
which he himself had not originated. What they decided ior the
Church was regarded as binding upon the original Christians.
In Acts 3 and 4, Peter and John appear as great miracle-
workers, and are the apologists of the Church. At a later date,
they were sent to Samaria to regularize Philip's missionary
work.[5] That fact makes their outstanding significance quite
clear. But Acts, being written from the opposite standpoint to
that of Revelation, leaves James quite in the background. The

[1] Heges. in Eus. *H.E.*, iii, 11; 20, 1–6; 32, 6. Cf. Julius Africanus, *ibid.*, i, 7, 14
[2] *Z.W.Th.*, 55, 116 ff.   [3] Rev. 21: 14; 4: 4; 5: 8
[4] Gal. 2: 9   [5] Acts 8: 14

differences remained, and often made themselves felt.[1] Eventually, however, the further spread of Christianity, and the destruction of Jerusalem, settled the issue. The Twelve came to be regarded as the founders of the Church universal, while James and his successors were held supreme in the original church and its posterity.

If we look at the circumstances here described, it might appear as if the first Church entered, by force of circumstances, into a Judaizing reaction which would necessarily end with a complete disavowal of the true spirit of the Master. Indeed we shall see that this was the lot which befell a part of it. But other forces remained alive and pressed in the other direction, forces which were grasped by eager and capable men.

We have seen that the Church faithfully retained the Jewish customs of fasting and Sabbath observance. But it was a new departure, and one of special importance, when the Church began to celebrate Sunday as the peculiar day of the new society. It was regarded as "the day of the Lord", and on it believers assembled to break bread, i.e. for the "Lord's Supper". How did the first day of the week come to be called the Lord's Day? The term was used in 1 Cor. 16: 2; Acts 20: 7; Rev. 1: 10, and in the *Didache* (14). The author of the Epistle of Barnabas, writing about A.D. 132, gives as the reason (15: 9) for this celebration of the "eighth day" that the resurrection of the Lord took place then. All this accords with the relevant passages in the gospels.

The choice of this day has been explained by some scholars by parallels from other religions, or they have suggested that it was selected in order to have a special day as a special mark of the Church.[2] But we find few traces of such an interest; rather it seems to have faded away among the churches described above. On this theory, indeed, the observance of Sunday as the Lord's Day would have originated among the Hellenistic Christians, and those who so observed Sunday must have been brought into opposition to James' group. But we do not find the faintest suggestion of that sort, for, apparently from the very beginning, Sunday was the holy day of the week for all Christians alike. If so, the obvious reason is in all probability the

---

[1] Ed. Meyer, *Ursprung*, iii 225   [2] Ed. Meyer, iii, 243

real one, viz. the first appearance of the Risen Lord took place on the first day of the week, hence on a Sunday. It is, in fact, the day on which the church of the Apostles began its new life. We may easily infer that they also expected that the Lord would come again in glory on a Sunday; and if this is so, we have discovered a sufficient reason for the Sunday celebration of the communion of the Lord's Supper, with its Messianic expectations and the "Marana tha". But here, too, was a starting point from which to show that the Church was distinct from Judaism, and for settling on Sunday as the Christian holy day in contradistinction to the Jewish Sabbath. The process began as soon as strict ritualism gave place to a more liberal conception, and as the newness and uniqueness of Christianity came to be more fully understood.

A further differentiation developed readily from this stage. If the Lord had appeared to Peter on a Sunday, it followed that He had risen on a Sunday: the gospel records depict that already. But according to Hos. 6: 2, the resurrection took place "on the third day" after death; hence the death of Jesus must have taken place on a Friday, and it would appear appropriate to respect the day by fasting. The Jewish fast day was Thursday. Thus there seemed to be a parallel shift of a day: the Christian Sunday was observed instead of the Jewish Saturday, and the Christian Friday instead of the Jewish Thursday. Then, by carrying the parallel further, the second Christian fast day would have become Tuesday instead of the Jewish Monday. But the fact that actually Wednesday was chosen is a proof that the displacement was not made for its own sake, but that it was connected with something specifically Christian: in this case, the only reason can have been that Jesus' passion began on a Wednesday, i.e. the day when He was arrested. A Church Order dating from the third century, the *Didascalia*, preserves this basis.[1] Paul did not require his own churches to observe any special days, nor did he even give Sunday a Sabbath character.[2] But the course of evolution was away from this kind of Puritanism, and it brought into being a new division of the week, in which there was a remarkable assertion of

[1] *Didascalia*, c. 21, p. 107, 25 Flemming. Holl, *Ges. Aufs.*, ii, 210
[2] Rom. 14: 5; cf. Col. 2: 16

Christian self-consciousness as distinct from Jewish ceremoni-
alism, and, indeed, the claims of Jewish forms of worship as a
whole. The week was completely rearranged, and this from a
purely Christian standpoint; whoever accepted the new
arrangement could not, in fact, also retain the old one, for
only Tuesday would have remained as an ordinary day. In
theory, perhaps, the Sabbath could have remained as the day
of rest alongside of the Sunday, the day when the Lord's
Supper was celebrated. In fact such was the case for a while,[1]
but gradually the Jewish Sabbath gave place to the Christian
"Lord's Day". Prohibitions dating from the beginning of the
second century betray the last traces[2] of the struggle between
the two kinds of week, but no direct evidence whatever has
survived. It is noteworthy that, in the controversy with gentile
Christians, the question of Sabbath observance played no part.

The record in Acts shows clearly, in spite of all the influence
of literary tendencies, that new elements soon arose alongside
that of the natives of Palestine (the "Hebrews") who constituted
the Judaizing strain in the original church. These elements
brought about an advance, and therefore to some extent a
return, to the historical Jesus. They were the "Hellenes" or
"Hellenists", not merely Jews of Greek speech, but those who
had grown up in the Greek diaspora, and had now settled in
Jerusalem. As a rule they would belong to some corresponding
union or society in their synagogue at Jerusalem, as in Acts 6:
9. These Jews also spoke the Aramaic current in Palestine, as
in the case of Stephen and Paul,[3] and as is assumed in general in
Acts. The carefully edited record in Acts 6: 1–6 shows that
there was a tendency in the first church to regard them as of a
somewhat lower grade, but that they successfully resisted. To
care for their interests, they chose their own council of seven;
significantly enough, all bore Greek names. Their members also
included the proselyte Nicolas of Antioch who had once been
a pagan. It may be that, among other duties, these seven were
made responsible for looking after the Hellenistic widows as
Acts records, but they regarded missionary work as their main

[1] Ebionites in Euseb. *H.E.*, iii, 27, 5, and footnote 2, p. 69, *supra*
[2] Ignat., *Magn.*, 9, 1. *Oxyr. Logion*, 2. *Didache*, 14, 1; 8, 1
[3] Acts 7 and 21: 40

duty.[1] Stephen, their leader, preached a great deal in the diaspora-synagogues of Jerusalem, and gained adherents to the Church. Philip went as a missionary to Samaria, and later evangelized the strip of coast land between Ashdod and Cæsarea. At that time he lived with his four daughters in Cæsarea;[2] finally he went to Hierapolis, where he died.[3]

Acts 6 and 7 records the martyrdom of Stephen in a passage affected by certain literary mannerisms, like all martyrologies, but obviously retaining much historical veracity. It shows, in particular, that the Hellenists held the temple worship in low esteem and disregarded the Jewish, ritual requirements. This led to a charge being preferred before the sanhedrin against Stephen, which ended with a finding of blasphemy. He was stoned to death.

At the same time, however, there was a spontaneous persecution of those who shared his views. Many were imprisoned, the majority fled the city and scattered throughout Judea, where they quietly worked for their Master. The apostles remained in Jerusalem—so the record says.[4] That probably means that the persecution was directed only against the Hellenists, who were hostile to the Mosaic law, whereas the true, Palestinian Jews remained unmolested. The inner division in the Church had now become outwardly visible, and the question arose whether James and the original apostles were able to reclaim the loyalty of those who had become separated.

We are still dealing with the earliest beginnings, where only isolated events can be grasped; and only disconnected, overdrawn records, expanded by legend, are at our disposal. The period is of fundamental importance, but its history cannot be traced authentically. Yet we can recognize the effective forces, and the direction in which they were working.

From the very beginning, the original church was a missionary church; she followed up the preaching of Jesus, and won converts for the Kingdom of God. But she laboured only among the lost sheep of the house of Israel and avoided roads that led to the Gentiles or to the towns of the Samaritans.[5]

[1] E. Schwartz, *Gött. Nachr.*, 1907, 280 f.   [2] Acts 8: 40; 21: 8
[3] Polycrates of Ephesus in Euseb. *H.E.*, iii, 31, 3 (where he is confused with the apostle)
[4] Acts 8: 1   [5] Matt. 10: 5

Perhaps she followed the example set in the lifetime of the Lord,[1] and sent out her missionaries in twos, without money or food, with only one garment, with sandals and staff, as pilgrims always going from place to place. And if any place did not receive them, they shook the dust from off their feet, "as a witness to them", and travelled further. Their hope was high that they would not have come to the last of the towns of Israel before the Son of Man should appear.[2] But we have no further details of the progress of the mission, and only incidentally are we told of churches in Judea, Galilee, and Samaria.[3] The last named had been founded by the Hellenist, Philip, who only later received the approval of the original apostles. Peter is the only one of the Twelve whom we actually see working as a missionary, but, perhaps, even that is to say too much, for we hear of him really only as an inspector of the mission field. Along with John, he visited the churches founded by Philip in Samaria, and later journeyed through the coast land via Lydda, Joppa, and the plain of Sharon, to Cæsarea,[4] i.e. Philip's area over again. Afterwards we meet with him in Antioch and the west. Paul characterizes him[5] emphatically as the apostle entrusted with the mission to the Jews. But the missionary work of the first church was confined to Jewish Palestine. The persecution connected with Stephen, with its far-reaching effect of scattering the Hellenistic section of the church, brought new regions into the Christian orbit for the first time. We have already seen how Philip worked in Samaria and on the coast. Others went to Phœnicia, Cyprus, and Antioch. Acts seems to be correct in asserting that this mission, conducted by the Hellenists, was confined entirely to the Jews. In Antioch, however, a new feature developed. Among the Hellenistic refugees were a few people from Cyprus and Cyrene who did not confine themselves to these limits, but preached to the Gentiles and had astonishing success.[6] The Gentile mission was born, and the confines of the Law were broken.

The church at Jerusalem had maintained the connection with the Hellenistic branch after it had separated off. The inner

---

[1] Mark 6: 7–13; Luke 10: 1–16; cf. E. Meyer, iii, 260   [2] Matt. 10: 23
[3] Acts 8: 5; 9: 31; Gal. 1: 22   [4] Acts 9: 32–10: 1
[5] Gal. 2: 7   [6] Acts 11: 19 f.

contradiction or antithesis, which had certainly existed hitherto, was not strong enough to destroy the feeling of the common bond of faith in the Lord, and this fact was óf decisive significance for the whole history of the Church. Wherever a Hellenistic mission was founded, and new Christian churches were called into being, emissaries of the original church came on the scene to test the quality of the new brethren, and to regulate intercourse with them. In the original Christian consciousness, there was in fact only one single Church of "disciples" of the Lord; its locus was temporarily the earthly Jerusalem, until, at the parousia of the Son of Man, the heavenly Jerusalem would come down and be the dwelling-place of those who belonged to Him. Those who were compelled to live outside Jerusalem belonged equally to the Church at Jerusalem; for all the far-flung hosts of Christians were branches of the one all-embracing central body. All stood under the authority of the apostles to whom the Lord Himself had given the right of pronouncing the final verdict on all questions relating to the proper form of worship.[1] In missionary praxis this meant that Peter, who alone was really active, possessed the highest authority throughout the whole of the daughter churches. The structure of the Church depended upon him in the earliest period,[2] and the grafting of the newly-arisen churches on the total organism depended upon his recognition of them.

There was a second consequence of the central position of Jerusalem. Granted that no communism ruled in the capital such as has been deduced from certain exaggerated expressions in Acts, yet, in the spirit of discipleship to Jesus, there was an appropriate far-reaching mutual readiness to help, which showed itself occasionally in the selling of property for the benefit of the charitable funds.[3] In order to understand this phenomenon there is not the slightest need to suggest that all earthly possessions had lost their value on account of the expectations of the parousia. It was taken for granted in this host of brethren that none should suffer from need. The church was anxious to continue performing these acts of kindness, and soon regarded them as a great privilege. The principle came to be recognized that an itinerant evangelist could claim hospitality

[1] Matt. 18: 18   [2] Matt. 16: 19   [3] Acts 2: 44; 4: 32–35

from the churches as recompense for preaching—that he should reap material things for having sown spiritual things, as Paul expressed it.[1] And, similarly, it came to be generally recognized that the church of the spiritual capital had a right to be supported by her daughter churches. It would be one of Peter's concerns on his journeys of inspection to arrange these financial matters. Thus, perhaps at first only half-consciously, though later systematically arranged, there grew a complete parallel to the temple-tax which was sent to Jerusalem by Jewish communities in the diaspora. By the compulsion of historical development, though without being actually intended, there grew in a few years, from the little group of enthusiasts in Jerusalem, a great fellowship whose links reached as far as the Mediterranean and the capital of Syria, and which was organized in spite of many inner conflicts, as a brotherly unity. James ruled in Jerusalem, but the original church laid claims upon the diaspora, where Peter exercised the headship of the apostolic college, and was the rock on which the Church was built.

[1] 1 Cor. 9: 11

Chapter Six

THE JEWISH DIASPORA

IN THE ELEVATED MOOD OF THE MACCABEAN PERIOD, THE
Hebrew Sibyl, disguised in the dress of Greek prophecy,
foretold the fate of the Jewish people. It bewailed the Babylonian imprisonment, when wife and child languished as slaves
of the enemy, and all possessions were lost; then it continued[1]

> Thou fillest every continent and state;
> And all men learn thy usages to hate.

In the reign of Augustus, Strabo set it down in plain prose
that, by his time, Jews "were to be found in every city, and that
in the whole world it was not easy to find a place where they
had not penetrated and which was not dominated by them".[2]
Documents, literary notices, and excavations agree in support-
ing these statements; and modern reference books contain innumerable passages recording the existence of Jewish colonies
in the late Hellenistic and Roman periods. If, however, we
look more closely, we see indications of a most dreadful
catastrophe. The entire rich culture of Hellenistic Judaism,
which had been carried by many millions through the whole
of the post-classical ancient world and far beyond the eastern
border of Mesopotamia, had been systematically annihilated,
with terrible consequences. Talmudic Jewry destroyed its
Greek-speaking sister, pulled down her buildings, and ploughed
up her sites. What records we possess are due to excavations, or
to accidental finds, e.g. the shattered remains of synagogues and
burial places with a few inscriptions, and occasional scraps of
parchments or papyrus. Besides these, there are certain, disconnected notices in ancient writers. We only possess literary
materials of greater extent in as far as the Christian Church
adopted them, viz. the Old Testament in Greek, Josephus, who
was esteemed as an historian, and Philo, as a model exegete.
In addition, there were all sorts of apocrypha which could be
made to serve their own ends when edited by the Christians.

---

[1] Sibyl, 3, 271   [2] q d Jos., *Ant.*, 14, 115

Of the wealth of their own life, which the lively Jewish spirit must have developed in the many different surroundings; of the development of theological thought and of public worship; of the inner life of the communities of the diaspora, their constitution and their social connection—of all these and many other matters we know practically nothing. Whole centuries of Jewish history have been silenced by their own people. Thereby also our chance of understanding the spread and inner development of Christianity in the first period has been greatly hindered. Our only recourse is to attempt to reconstrue events from the few surviving data, and this in circumstances where even the richest sources would scarcely be sufficient fully to satisfy our inquiries.

From 722 B.C. onwards, great political catastrophes with compulsory transportations of populations continually fell on Palestine, and, in addition, the uncertainty of affairs in their native land, strains and stresses occurring periodically in smaller tidal waves, drove thousands and tens of thousands of Jews to emigration; how many people followed them voluntarily in these circumstances cannot be estimated. But it is certain that, at the beginning of our era, surprisingly large numbers of Jews were to be found throughout the whole ancient civilized world, and also beyond its borders. It is, of course, a gross exaggeration when Philo,[1] on one occasion, asserts that their number was not much less than that of the indigenous population. Nevertheless, a critical examination of figures which have been handed down to us gives an astonishingly high result.[2] In both Egypt and Syria, there may well have been 1,000,000 Jews; in Palestine 500,000; in the rest of the Roman empire at least 1,500,000. If there were 55,000,000 inhabitants in the empire, at least 7 per cent of them must have been Jews. This proportion holds good even if, with other scholars, we raise the absolute figures. Modern records offer no simple comparison, because religious statistics ignore the converted Jews; nevertheless it is very instructive to learn that in Germany about 1 per cent, in Frankfort-on-the-Main 6·3 per cent, of the population, just before the outbreak of the war of 1939–45, were Jews. It is an unsolved enigma how this gigantic growth of Judaism in the

[1] *Leg.*, 214 (6, 195)   [2] Harnack, *Expansion*, i, 9–13. Juster, i, 209–12

diaspora had taken place. Recently an attempt has been made to solve it by supposing that other Semites, and in particular the Phœnicians (who were once very widely spread, and who gradually fade out altogether from the landscape), were to a large extent absorbed by the Jews.[1]

This great multitude of people was not a mere pell-mell of numbers, nor a matter of isolated individuals like (say) Germans to-day in North America, but a national unity with a religious identity, and some general kind of organization.[2] By far the greater majority regarded Jerusalem, not only as their ideal home, but also as the centre of their religion and politics. This was seen in two ways: (1) annually, many thousands of Jews went to Jerusalem for the feast of the Passover, and to offer their sacrifices;[3] (2) much more clearly was it seen in the carefully observed custom that, even in the diaspora, every Jew, of 20 years and upwards, paid annually a double-drachma (about 1s. 6d.) as his temple due. In the various cities, collecting chests were set up with this object, and at specified times correspondingly large sums of money were brought to Jerusalem by delegations sent for the purpose.[4] A number of official regulations are known from the time of Augustus, which guaranteed to the Jews the right to make these collections and transmissions of money.[5] Whether the supreme collegiate council in Jerusalem, the sanhedrin of the seventy, possessed more than a moral authority, to which one could appeal in difficult cases in regard to religious questions and closely connected juristic problems, is a matter that must remain undecided. Positive notices in this respect, about the circumstances in the first century, have simply not come down to us. It is true that Acts 9: 2 says that Saul received full power from the High-Priest to arrest suspected Jews in Damascus and bring them to Jerusalem; all the same, there is scarcely room for doubt that this record is not correctly worded, at least in the juristic sense.[6] There can scarcely have been any jurisdiction of the sanhedrin in the diaspora. Nevertheless, all Jews were conscious of their obedience to the one law, as recorded in the

---

[1] F. Rosen, *Juden u. Phönizier*, 1929   [2] Cf. esp. Philo, *in Flaccum*, 45 f. (6, 128)
[3] Philo, *de spec. leg.*, 1, 69, 76–78 (5, 17 f., 19 f.)   [4] Cicero, *pro Flacco*, 28, 67
[5] Jos., *Ant.*, 16, 163–173. Schürer, ii 314   [6] Juster, ii 145 n. 5

Old Testament and the Tradition, and that law determined the legal relationships of Jews to one another all the world over.

According to ancient law[1] in general, the Jews of the diaspora were "foreigners" everywhere, and enjoyed the usual legal protection of those who were regarded as settlers. This protection also afforded them freedom to regulate their own affairs in their own way. Hence they organized themselves into religious societies centring on the synagogues, and appointed their own officers to settle their legal disputes. The community had a council of elders with "archons" at the head, and an "archisynagogus" as a religious president.[2] It was recognized both as a religious and a political body, and more than one imperial decree confirmed it in due form. In addition there were places, neither few nor insignificant, where the municipal rights of citizenship were granted to Jews. This was particularly the case in Syria, where Seleucus I, in founding his cities, had obviously settled large numbers of Jewish emigrants, and had granted them privileges accordingly.[3] The facts were similar in Asia Minor and Egypt; at least that is what the Jewish writers assert, above all Josephus. But in the case of Alexandria, of which the same statements are made, extant documentary evidence proves them to be false.[4] There, the Jews strove for the rights of citizens, but neither possessed nor obtained them; and we must therefore go cautiously in dealing with the other notices of the same sort.

In any case, they did not cease, when they became citizens, to cling to their own communities with their special status. The idea of fusing themselves with, and melting into their Gentile environment lay quite remote from them. They managed to keep themselves apart from the religious obligations of the Hellenistic citizens, from sharing in the observance of the municipal cultus, and from everything connected with it. Hence the rights of citizenship meant, in their case, an increase in legal protection without the burden of new duties.

The position remained the same when a Jew became a

---

[1] Juster, ii, 1 ff., 111 ff.   [2] Ibid., i, 409–96
[3] Jos., Ant., 12, 119. Schürer, iii, 122. Juster, ii, 2–18, 30–32
[4] H. Idris Bell, Jews and Christians in Egypt (1924), 8–10

Roman citizen. The innumerable freedmen liberated from Pompey's cargoes of prisoners, and the continually reinforced supplies of those who came later, automatically received this honour by the act of enfranchisement. But Roman citizenship was also granted as a genuine honour to single individuals or to entire groups, who had proved amenable to Roman policy. This was not an insignificant matter to a Jew, but it did not therefore alienate him from his people and their legal system if he wished to remain loyal to them. But, in relation to the local authorities, he obtained considerable protection from his citizenship, for he was raised, as a privileged person, above the mass of the population, guarded from dishonourable punishments, and, on a capital charge, was subject only to the imperial court in Rome; in short, he was not liable to the caprice of provincial officers. The Jew obtained this prerogative without being required to share in the corresponding duties in the sphere of the imperial cultus,[1] which would have been inconsistent with his strict monotheism. The Jews sought and found a substitute for that cultus in other forms of expressing loyalty, and went as far as offering daily sacrifice for the emperor in the temple at Jerusalem.[2] The regard paid to their religious scruples was sufficient to have them excused from appearance in a court of justice on the Sabbath; and, in isolated cases, Jewish soldiers were dispensed from military service on this day.[3] Of course they keenly desired general freedom from liability to military service, but this they never attained; in Cæsar's time alone was this privilege occasionally given to those Jews in the province of Asia who possessed Roman citizenship.[4]

Amongst the occupations[5] followed by the Jews of the diaspora, the most important was farming. Strikingly numerous pieces of evidence are extant from Egypt and Asia Minor in regard to Jewish settlements, as well as about property owners, farmers, and day labourers of Jewish nationality. In the west, notices about Jewish farmers are not numerous until the fourth century A.D. On the other hand, commerce is strikingly

[1] Juster, i, 339–53   [2] Jos., c. Ap., 2, 77. Bell., 2, 197, 409
[3] Jos., Ant., 16, 27. 45. 60. 163. 168; 14, 226. Juster, ii, 121; i, 358
[4] Jos., Ant., 14, 227 f., 230, etc. Juster, ii, 265–79   [5] Juster, ii, 294–310, 31–205

small; only in the great city of Alexandria does it seem to
have developed early to any significant extent, and here we also
find great Jewish banks at an early date—and even warnings
against loans from Jews.[1] We hear more frequently of Jewish
industry or trade, and weaving in various branches, especially
in connection with dyeing, which was indeed a Jewish speciality
and remained as such for centuries. We have unfortunately no
available records in regard to the economic rôle of the Jews in
Rome. The epitaphs give scarcely anything of value, and the
rabble of beggars at the *porta capena*, of which Juvenal speaks,[2]
is no more typical of the occupations of Judaism at Rome than
is his doddering, old-woman soothsayer.

Thus Judaism was very closely united within itself, and at
the same time sharply differentiated from the world. Nevertheless, in a remarkable way, it made the greatest efforts to spread
its views, and to gain adherents to its religion from among the
pagans. Jesus and Horace agree in declaring proselytism as a
characteristic of the Jewish nation. "The Pharisees compass sea
and land in order to make even one proselyte" (Matt. 23: 15);
and Horace (1 *Sat.* 4, 142) attacks one who despises poetry and
threatens to overwhelm him with the whole mass of poets, "and
we, like the Jews, will compel you to come over to our side".
How is this to be explained?

From the days of Deutero-Isaiah, the idea had never been
extinguished among the Jews that they were intended to be the
light of the Gentiles, and to proclaim salvation to them; their
conversion would complete the glorious revelation of the Lord.[3]
This idea continued to live in the Psalms and in apocalyptic
literature, and when, in the Hellenistic period, Judaism came
into contact with Greek culture, two things must have become
evident. The first was the ceaselessly progressive decay of "idol
worship"; the second was the relation of Jewish monotheism to
the modern currents in the prevailing religions, together with
the many contacts between Jewish morality and the requirements of the current ethical preaching of the popular philosophers of the Stoic school. Both these features gave educated
Jews the proud conviction that the time had come for

---

[1] U. Wilcken, *Chrestomathie*, n. 55–62   [2] Juv., 3, 14; 6, 543
[3] Isa. 49: 1–6; 60: 1–6

their religion to shine before the Gentiles,[1] and that God would give them the promised success.

From this standpoint we can understand why Hellenistic modes of thought penetrated into Jewish Wisdom-literature. The two streams readily mingled, especially as Hellenistic ethics had already absorbed many elements of the "wisdom" of the orient. Moreover, there arose a Jewish polemical literature against image worship and idolatry, which united arguments, inherited from the distant days of the prophets, with the proofs used by the Greeks since Xenophanes. The essential bases of Jewish religion were felt to be monotheism, a theological axiom; the spiritual quality of worship without images; and law-abidingness in the sense of an ethical attitude in the whole of one's life. Moreover, everything of a ceremonial character, together with the formal acts of worship, was deemed to have been taught by God, and therefore to be worthy of receiving honour. In this way, a process of spiritualization penetrated almost all classes of the relatively small circle of Jews of Greek education in the diaspora, but must have risen only rarely to the height which we find in Philo of Alexandria. Yet in all its phases, it was both the dynamic and the means of propaganda in the Hellenistic world. Judaism overstepped its national confines, and felt itself called to be a universal religion.[2]

The Old Testament was translated in Alexandria into Greek, but this was for use in public worship.[3] It was not a book for an educated public. Hence Hellenistic Jews now appeared who wrote the history of their people in a manner that accorded with prevalent taste. At first, this was done carefully in harmony with the Bible and acknowledged traditions, but after Eupolemus and Artapanus,[4] all the Hellenistic arts were employed in order to give shapeliness, colour, and even unrestricted range to one's own imagination, down to the impudent falsehoods of "Hecatæus".[5] The ultimate aim, in every case, was to show that Moses and his people were the original source

[1] Bertholet, *Die Stellung der Israeliten und der Juden zu den Fremden*, 257–302
[2] Philo, *vita Mosis*, 2, 20 (4, 204). Jos., *c. Ap.*, 2, 280–82
[3] Strack-Billerbeck, iva, 407
[4] Fragments of these writers have been preserved by Alex. Polyhistor, cf. *Fragm. hist. Graec.*, ed. E. Müller, iii, 211–30
[5] Müller, ii, 393–96, but cf. H. Lewy, *Z.N.W.*, 31, 117–32

of all civilization, including the celebrated learning of the Greeks.

No: could the Old Testament scriptures be used forthwith even for purely religious propaganda, for they stood in great need of commentary if they were to be comprehensible to men of the period. At least, only the later Wisdom literature, which bore the names of Solomon and Jesus Sirach, would be immediately appreciated by a Hellenistic mentality. But the writings that were really successful were conceived from the Greek standpoint. A celebrated name as the author of a book would awaken confidence, and the form of the writing must be made to correspond. Thus, in the second century B.C., didactic poems were written in hexameters, and were given out to be the prophecies of a mythical Sibyl. These poems represented a category of literature presumably cultivated by other men of eastern origin. Here Chronus and Zeus, Solomon and Alexander, the Trojan war and the Babylonian captivity, were cleverly conjoined. Homer was condemned as an ancient prevaricator. The history of the world was regarded apocalyptically, and ended in the royal Messianic kingdom of peace in paradise; even the Greeks would be gathered into it. Ancient wisdom was commended under the name of Hystaspes, the Persian, or Orpheus, the Thracian. A modern supplement was added to the praiseworthy didactic poem of Phocylides of Solon's time; and, after the manner of the usual anthologies, a collection of forged quotations was prepared with special skill. These cited the most celebrated writers from Orpheus, Homer, and the dramatists, onwards to the popular, comic poets and the preachers of practical philosophies of life, e.g. Philemon, Menander, and Diphilos, as witnesses to Jewish doctrines.[1] Really, it was propaganda for the Old Testament when, under the name of a certain Greek called Aristeas, a "letter" was published which gave the astonishing information that King Ptolemy Philadelphus had caused the holy book to be officially translated and that an astounding miracle had placed it beyond doubt that God had co-operated in the work.

No estimate is possible as to the value of this kind of activity. It is undeniable that the Jewish mission, as a whole, attained

[1] Schürer, iii, 595–603

a very considerable success, as is plentifully testified by both Jewish and pagan writers.[1] Juvenal[2] describes the development in Hadrian's time, viz. the father rests on the Sabbath day and eats no pork; the son has himself circumcised and becomes a fanatic. Seneca coined the biting epigram[3] during the reign of Nero, that the customs of this accursed people had spread over every country: "The conquered have given their laws to the conquerors." Epitaphs agree with this in mentioning relatively numerous proselytes.[4] Everywhere, the Jews were successful in grouping round their synagogues a circle of "God-fearers", who were attracted by the spiritual excellencies of the Mosaic religion, and turned, with inner conviction, to its monotheism and its ethical teaching. They attended the meetings for worship, and naturally entered into personal association with this or that member of the church. In this way, the Sabbath became to them a sacred day; Jewish table customs and food laws attained practical significance, and became, in effect, a religious usage. After appropriate teaching,[5] even if this did not rise to the very fine distinctions made by Philo's allegory, the religious usage, nevertheless, gained a deeper sense and exerted power over the soul. From this wide circle, there then separated off the small number of those who ventured to take the decisive step, and, by circumcision and the levitical bath of purification, joined themselves completely to the community of Israel; these were the "proselytes" in the strict sense of the word. They took the law upon themselves in its entirety, and thereby became Israelites, and might hope to share in the promises of the chosen people. Of course they could never become "Sons of Abraham"; in prayer[6] they might well address "the God of the fathers of Israel", but not, like the real Jew, "the God of our fathers". Thus they were only later members of the nobility by letters patent, alongside of the old, original aristocracy of the blood, and on occasion they must have felt the difference.

The Roman state was not well-disposed to such conversions, and was not inclined to extend to converted Romans the

---

[1] Schürer, iii, 164 ff.   [2] *Sat.*, xiv, 96–106
[3] Preserved in Augustine, 1 *civ. dei*, vi, 11   [4] E. Diehl, *Inscriptiones*, ii, pp. 497–99
[5] Jos., *Ant.*, 18, 81   [6] Mishna, *Bikkurim*, 1, 4. Schürer, iii, 187

privilege of freedom from religious duties of an official character, such as was granted to born Jews. Hence, at times, there
were punishments on account of "atheism", and we have
isolated notices to the effect that the persons concerned belonged to the Roman nobility.[1] Under Hadrian, circumcision,
which had hitherto been tolerated, was placed under general
prohibition,[2] and at the same time conversion to Judaism was
strictly forbidden. In all such cases the state prosecuted, not
only the guilty proselytes, but also punished the leaders of the
Jewish propaganda.[3]

On a general view, it would therefore seem that the Jews possessed very many more enemies than friends in the world.[4] Even
if they should appear welcome settlers to diadochoi who were
founding cities, and to politicians who were concerned with
economics; and even if they enjoyed imperial favour, nevertheless, the populace could not tolerate them in all the provinces
of the great empire. Just because they did not feel themselves to
be simply a part of the great whole, as did the other peoples,
but separated themselves off, and carefully guarded their special
character, they were everywhere regarded with a mistrust
which developed into hate, a mistrust which the masses, like
children, feel towards anything strange in their midst, if it
seeks to assert itself. However much the Jewish writers might
commend their religion as enlightened philosophy, men in
general, including those of the highest education, were convinced that the Jews prayed to the clouds and the sky, were
committed to a barbarous superstition,[5] and were hostile to
every form of civilized culture. There were many other similar
opinions in Alexandria. They used to tell there of the history of
the Jewish people as a combination of the shameful and the
ridiculous; and also of secret information in regard to their
worship: in the temple at Jerusalem there was a golden ass's
head to which they paid divine honours—or was it a statue of
Moses riding on an ass, and holding the book of the law in his
hand? In any case, the Jews were ass-worshippers,[6] and what

---

[1] Juster, i, 256–59
[2] *vita Hadriani*, 14, 2 (in the *script. hist. Aug.*) also Juster, i, 264, n. 2.
[3] Jos., *Ant.*, 18, 83–84   [4] Heinemann in *Pauly-Wissowa*, suppl., v, 3–43
[5] Cicero, *pro Flacco*, 28, 67 f. Juvenal, xiv, 97. Hecatæus fr. 13, 4 in Müller, *Frag. hist.
Græc.*, ii, 392   [6] Jos., *con. Ap.*, 2, 80. Posidonius fr. in Müller, *op. cit.*, iii, 256

was worse, every year, or at least every seven years, they captured a Greek, killed and sacrificed him in accordance with their ritual. Then they ate his heart, and thereby swore an oath of everlasting hostility to the Greeks.[1] It was self-apparent that such people had to be rendered harmless even when the authorities protected them for some unknown reason. This explains why, when a suitable opportunity occurred, popular feeling against the Jews was unleashed.

At least from the end of the second century B.C., the Greeks in Alexandria lived in hostility towards the Jews who had been granted equal rights by Alexander, and who, in order better to preserve their national characteristics, were segregated, by the Ptolemies, into a special quarter of the town, where they developed their own communal organization.[2] In those days, the Ghetto was a privilege! The latent tension was released violently for the first time[3] after Caligula had come to the throne (A.D. 38); up to this time, Flaccus had been a most excellent prefect, but now being uncertain of the attitude of the new rulership, he did not feel it wise to keep the reins tight. When Agrippa I, the newly appointed king of the Jews passed through, the Alexandrian mob seized a welcome occasion for tumultuous demonstrations, and cunningly demanded also that statues of the emperor should be set up in the synagogues.[4] At the same time, loud complaints were made about the unjustified spread of the Jews in the city: in particular, two of the five quarters were really Jewish, and, even in the other three, there were many Jews. On the other hand, this widespread Jewish population raised a vigorous agitation for recognition as full citizens of Alexandria.[5] Thereupon Flaccus ordered them to be restricted to one quarter, and he also reduced their municipal rights. A riot of the mob ensured the carrying out of the edict; the Jews were driven out of the four quarters, and concentrated in the fifth. But large numbers found no room there, and camped helplessly on the shore and in the cemeteries

[1] Jos., op. cit., 2, 94 f. Damocritus fr. in Müller, op. cit., iv, 377
[2] Claudius in Jos., Ant., 19, 281; Jos., Bell., 2, 487. Bell, Jews and Christians, p. 16 f.
[3] The source is found in Philo, in Flaccum (6, 120 ff.). Bell, Jews and Christians: the letter of Claudius, cf. 16–21
[4] Philo, op. cit., 25, 41 (6, 124. 128)
[5] Bell, op. cit., p. 25: 5, 89; cf. pp. 13. 16

close to the city.[1] Whoever ventured to appear in the cleared quarters of the city was seized and put to death in the most brutal manner. Still further to placate the people, thirty-eight elders of the Jewish community were scourged in the theatre, Jewish houses searched for weapons, and other cunning devices thought out.[2] This, of course, did not help Flaccus; he fell into disgrace, and paid the death penalty. But the Jews who meantime had been reinforced from Egypt and Syria,[3] effected hardly more than an armistice under Pollio, his successor, for the emperor seemed to find in their denial of his divinity an incomprehensible spiritual defect.[4] At length, the emperor Claudius commanded the prefect to bring both parties to peace; at the same time, he re-established the Jews in all the municipal rights they had previously enjoyed, and in their religious liberties.[5] But the antisemites did not give way; a delegation went to Rome and accused King Agrippa, and further disturbances took place at home. Claudius was then enraged. The leaders of the Jew-baiters, the Alexandrian gymnasiarch Isidorus, and Lampon, who had come to Rome as the delegation accusing Agrippa, were executed, and an imperial edict[6] ordered peace in the firmest tones. The Alexandrians, however, honoured these men with pride as martyrs to their well-being and the freedom of the city; and they published the documents of their trial as something to their honour.[7]

Thus hostility remained, and when the outbreak of the Jewish rebellion in Palestine (A.D. 66) greatly inflamed their passions once more, terrible Jewish pogroms took place in Alexandria; 50,000 were killed in the city and 60,000 in the rest of Egypt.[8]

As for Palestine, the Jews in Cæsarea first rose against the Syrians, and the frequent disturbances and local conflicts ended in a general slaughter of the Cæsarean Jews, of whom more than 20,000 were killed at one time.[9] This led to an insurrection in the interior of the country; the Jews broke into Syrian villages

---

[1] Philo, in Flaccum, 54–6 (6, 130) [2] Op. cit., 64–75, 86 (6, 132 f., 136)
[3] Bell, 25, 96. Philo, legum, 129 (6, 179) [4] Phil., op. cit., 367 (6, 222)
[5] Jos., Ant., 19, 280–5. Bell, 25 [6] In the papyrus ed. by Bell, 23–6
[7] Phil., in Flacc., 20; leg., 355 (6, 124; 220). Lietzmann, Greek Pap., 2nd edition (Kleine Texte, No. 14), 21 f.
[8] Jos., Bell., 2, 487–98 [9] Ibid., 2, 266–70, 457

and towns and took their revenge. But the Syrians defended themselves, and then there was more slaughter of Jews in Scythopolis, Ascalon, Ptolemæus, Tyre, Hippo, and Gadara. Josephus is emphatic that peace was maintained only in Antioch, Sidon, and Apamea.[1] But in Antioch, animosity became so sharp that force was used more than once, and the Sabbath rest and obligatory sacrifices were prohibited; and this led to bloodshed. It needed the authority of Titus to put a stop to the angry demands for withdrawing municipal rights from Jews.[2] After Nero, a new wave of hatred for the Jews welled up in the Roman world, and was re-echoed more particularly in Seneca and the satirists. The sketch of Jewish history introduced by Tacitus into his *History*[3] breathes the complete contempt of a cultured Roman for this most despicable of all slave races, a race which hated gods and men, and which was given to an absurd and unclean superstition.

In spite of all the close connections maintained with Jerusalem and all the common feeling, the Judaism of the diaspora had, in the course of time, come to differ in character from that of the people of the native land. The most striking instance was the fact that they had forgotten the language of Palestine, and accepted the Greek of everyday use. The change was due to the history of the Jewish people, who had long abandoned their mother-tongue even in Palestine. When the exiles returned from Babylon, they brought with them the current Aramaic language, and retained it for a millenium. Hebrew remained the sacred language of scholars for religious usage, and the discussions in the Mishna were written down in Hebrew even in the second century A.D. But the Talmuds of the fourth and fifth centuries, being in Aramaic, show that Hebrew was obsolete even in the theological schools.

Valuable documents of the fifth century B.C. belonging to the Egyptian diaspora and written in Aramaic have been found in Elephantine. An interpolation in the text of Isaiah (19: 18) mentions five Egyptian towns in which "the language of Canaan" was spoken. In the Ptolemaic period we still find traces of Aramaic in upper Egypt[4] and in Alexandria;[5] but

---

[1] *Ibid.*, 2, 458, 461, 466, 477–9   [2] *Ibid.*, 7, 43–62, 100–11. *Ant.*, 12, 121
[3] Tacitus, *hist.*, v, 5, 8   [4] Schürer, iii, p. 49   [5] Lidbarski, *Ephem.*, iii, 49

about this time, Greek began to be used by Jews, both as the
language of the administration, and in everyday life. In the
latest period of the Ptolemies, the Jews of Onias not only wrote
Greek epitaphs for their dead, but also bewailed the loss of the
departed in elegiac poems formed on Hellenistic models and
mentioning Hades as well as Moira. In the entire remainder of
the Mediterranean world, the memorial tablets of the Jewish
diaspora are almost exclusively in Greek. Here and there is a
Hebrew phrase, e.g. *shalom*=peace, or *shalom al Israel*=peace
be to Israel, upon a gravestone, but inscriptions genuinely
composed in Hebrew or Aramaic are very rare. The common
opinion that the adjective, "Hebrew", points to communities
speaking Hebrew or Aramaic, is mistaken. The door-post of a
synagogue has been found at Corinth[1] bearing the name of the
congregation: "Synagogue of the Hebrews." But these Hebrews
did not speak Hebrew, for the inscription is in Greek! Outside
Palestine, only the Rabbis knew any Hebrew—but no one
knows how many they were, nor how much they knew. The
remote region of the Crimea is alone in preserving Hebrew
inscriptions of the first to the fourth century A.D.[2]

This change of language, both at home and in the diaspora,
was not without far-reaching effects upon public worship. The
ancient custom of reading the Hebrew scriptures in the
synagogue necessitated a translation into the Aramaic which
the people understood, the original text and the translation
followed one another verse for verse. Dubious passages were not
translated, but read only in Hebrew.[3] Originally the translations were extemporaneous, but naturally they soon assumed
forms fixed by tradition. Out of these forms grew the Aramaic
Targums, which were at last put into writing in the Talmudic
era, i.e. about the fifth century. Moreover the liturgical prayers,
which Jewish prayer books even to-day preserve in their
original Hebrew form, were said by the people in the ver-
nacular. The Mishna[4] expressly permitted it, and a shrewd
Rabbi rightly told an objector that it was better to do so, than
that the people should not pray at all.[5] Nevertheless, this

---

[1] Deissmann, *Licht v. Osten*, 13   [2] P. E. Caspari, *Quellen*, iii, 269
[3] Mishna, *Megilla*, 4, 4, 10   [4] Mishna, *Sota* 7, 1. Schürer, iii, 140 f.
[5] Talm. Jer., *Sota*, 7, 1 f. 21 b

reply seems rather to evade the real point, and Charlemagne gave a better reason for using German in the Lord's Prayer.[1]

An Aramaic targum was current in Palestine, side by side with the original Hebrew, and a Greek translation in the diaspora for public worship in the synagogue.[2] Known and preserved as the Septuagint, or LXX, the latter originated in Alexandria. The first part to be translated was the most important, and it took premier place also in public worship. This was the Pentateuch, the Greek version of which was current as early as the end of the third century B.C. The prophets and the other books followed gradually and by various translators. Soon after 116 B.C., a grandson of Jesus Sirach was familiar with the whole of the Old Testament in Greek.[3] At the time of the early Roman empire, as is shown by the use made of it by Philo and Paul,[4] the LXX was the universally recognized Bible of the diaspora, even for the purposes of divine worship.

In Alexandria,[5] an annual festival was held on the Pharos island, when the people gave thanks for this translation. There seem to have been several translations of isolated books current at the same time,[6] but they disappeared early almost without trace. It was the rivalry of the Christian Church which had made the LXX equally its own, that gave rise, after the second century, to newer and more literal translations for Jewish use. In the nature of the case, it is doubtful whether the original Hebrew was read alongside the translation; possibly custom varied. By the time of the emperor Justinian, greater emphasis was placed on the reading of the original in public worship, and the question was discussed whether any translation at all could be read aloud along with it. These facts show that the influence of the Judaism of the Talmud had grown, but do not prove what was the custom elsewhere in the Empire centuries earlier.

Not only were the Scriptures read in Greek, but also the same language was used for the prayers and the confession of faith, i.e. the "Shema", in the public worship of the synagogue. The sources testify to this fact in regard to Cæsarea, the quasi-gentile capital

---

[1] *Capitulare*, 28, 52   [2] Schürer, iii, 140, 426. Billerbeck, iv, 407
[3] *Sirach*, Prolog. Wilcken, *Archiv. f. Pap.*, iii, 321
[4] Perhaps the headings of the temple-psalms in the LXX also belonged to the Greek synagogue. Cf. Schürer, ii, 351, and Rahlf's edition of the Psalms, 72
[5] Philo, *vita Mosis*, 2, 41 (4, 209)   [6] Cf. *Handbuch* on Gal.; 5, 1

of Palestine,[1] and naturally the same holds good for the diaspora
in general. Only just recently have scholars traced out a little
Greek prayer-book of the Jewish synagogues[2] that dates from
the second century A.D., and that is enshrined in a Christian
liturgy of the fourth century. This discovery is very suggestive.
It is only a drop out of the ocean, but it makes quite clear how
little is really known about worship in the synagogues of the
Greek diaspora. We may take it for granted that this worship,
not only changed in the course of centuries, but also differed
in different places; and moreover that there were many
different degrees of Hellenization.

Besides reading and prayer there were exegesis and preaching, of course in Greek. The collective term, *deuterosis*, was
given to the traditional elements here. The term is a liberal
translation of the Hebrew *Mishna*, i.e. repetition, and it included everything deduced from, or built on the Law or the
historical records of the sacred text: hence the Halakha or
specialized legal casuistic, and the Haggada, the Biblical
legends. Even Augustine testified[3] that this *deuterosis* was
passed on only by word of mouth, not written down—showing
that the diaspora followed the example of Palestine. It follows
that there was a Greek Halakha and a Greek Haggada; or, to
put it otherwise, the diaspora possessed a Greek Midrash and
a Greek Talmud. Traces of both often occur in Paul, Philo,
Josephus, and the Apocrypha—but no actual documents, and
it is scarcely probable that much was written down. Indeed,
everything of this kind disappeared when the Judaism of the
Greek diaspora ceased to be.

Very little evidence has survived affording a true idea of the
cultural life of the Hellenistic diaspora. Most information
refers to Egypt. The LXX translation was made here, and it
was here that Pseudo-Aristeas was at home. III Maccabees,
perhaps IV Maccabees, and the Wisdom of Solomon were
written in Egypt, and here Philo laboured. Other regions afford
little information about Judaism, whereas, in regard to the
contemporary beginnings of Christianity, it is precisely Egypt
that is quite blank. Nevertheless Alexandria distributed its

---

[1] Talm. Jer., *Sota*, 7, 1, 2, 21*b*. Schürer, iii, 141   [2] *Const. Apost.*, 7, 33–8
[3] *C. adv. leg. et proph.*, ii, 1, 2; 8, 580*e* Bened. Philo, *vita Mosis*, 1, 4 (4, 120)

Greek Bible throughout the whole of Judaism, and, except Jerusalem, was apparently the only spiritually productive centre of Israel. This fact makes it possible, within bounds, to generalize the phenomena obtaining there.

The translation of the Bible into Greek opened the door to the Hellenization of the Jewish religion. Greek conceptions inevitably entered, along with the Greek vocabulary, into the sphere of thought of the synagogues, and the philosophical connotations of innumerable terms led to further philosophizing developments of Old Testament trains of thought. Analogous processes took place in regard to religious terminology. It was an unplanned, but unavoidable, consequence of translation from one language to another, and it came forward most prominently in Alexandria. A school of exegetes arose there[1] who approached the Pentateuch from the philosophical standpoint, and who had learned, from the Stoics, the method of allegorical interpretation. These men found philosophical truths expressed in the early stories of the Bible. Thus Adam was understood as *nous*, i.e., reason was the foundation of mankind. His "helpmeet", together with the beasts of the field and the birds of heaven, represent the emotions. Eve was the antithesis to reason and also its necessary sensory complement. The snake was the symbol of desire or love, which brought the two opposite poles together, and effected the unity of man.[2] Sarah and Hagar signify virtue and sound education, but the latter must first be taken to wife, i.e. be united with him who was to have children by the former.[3] When we are told[4] that Jacob fled from Esau to Mesopotamia and entered the house of Bethuel (Gen. 27: 42–28: 5), the meaning is that the upright man ought to plunge into the stream of life, and guard himself there, in a practical way, in order that he may find a quiet harbour in the house of wisdom. The latest researches have succeeded in sorting out from Philo's writings fragments of such teachings of the Alexandrian Jews, and in recognizing an early writing of Philo's about the eternity of the world[5] as the notes

---

[1] W. Bousset, *Schulbetrieb*, 43–56, 74–83
[2] Philo, *leg. all.*, 5–9, 36–8, 71 (1, 91, 97, 104)
[3] Philo, *congr.*, 6, 9–11, 23 (3, 73–7), Bousset 98–100
[4] Philo, *fuga.*, 25–52 (3, 115–21). Bousset, 128 f.
[5] Philo, vol. vi, 72–119. Bousset, 134–37

of a lecture of the kind we have just described. This older tradition appears to be quite intoxicated with the intellectual and spiritual verve, the complete candour of Hellenism, whereas Moses and the Bible are, by contrast, but little emphasized. Jews of this type capitulated completely to the Greeks in the things of the mind—probably without drawing any consequences at all affecting religion in public worship or private life; for they were unaware of having made any real departure from the essence of their own religion. They believed that, with the aid of the newly acquired philosophical means, they were merely enabled to reach a profounder, and therefore a more accurate, conception of the meaning of the Mosaic law. These men felt that it was a point in favour of the new understanding that it harmonized with the teachings of the Greek sages. That the Greeks should have learned from Stoicism how to illumine their own religion in the same way; that the revivified Platonism of the following centuries should have employed the same weapons to defend the Homeric faith, and should have read philosophical wisdom into the Egyptian cults—all this was in accordance with the trend of the times.

Philo of Alexandria was the only one of the Hellenistic Rabbis to give a genuinely literary form to his lectures. Moreover he was in full earnest, and very loyal to Judaism. When the Jewish persecution under Flaccus threatened to outlaw and destroy his people, he regretfully, but nevertheless firmly, sacrificed his contemplative leisure, and joined a diplomatic delegation to the imperial court, although it offered little prospect of success, and might easily have meant death. Obviously the Alexandrian Jews wished to present the most cultured and learned of their number to the emperor. But Philo was a Jew, not only on account of his patriotic feelings, but also by religious conviction. To him, Moses was the source of all truth and wisdom, and the Law was the inexhaustible spring from which he was never tired of drinking. His writings show that "he had meditated upon the Law day and night". And even if he traced deeper secrets beneath the plain meaning of the words, secrets which contained the real sense of the sacred Scripture, he felt that nothing of this detracted, in any way, from the sacred authority of the text, as it actually stood. He warned his readers[1] that none of the customs of the Fathers was to be dropped, "which greater men than ourselves established". Ritual was for the body, just as the deeper sense was for the soul. But, immediately he began to explain the Law, he followed the method of Hellenistic allegory in its entirety. The "great", and "most holy" Plato was, for him, the master whom he cited ever and again; but he referred frequently to Aristotle, Heracleitus, the Pythagoreans, Epicurus, and especially the Stoics, as his authorities. What Moses had taught had been accepted by the Greek philosophers, and explained by them in greater detail; in the last analysis, Greek philosophy was doctrine about God, the world, and man. The Mosaic law was in harmony with the nature of the universe, and he who lived by that law, determined his actions according to the will of nature and was therefore the true citizen of the world: he lived by the same standards as ruled the entire cosmos.[2] In other words, the genuine Jew corresponded to the ideal of the Stoic sage.

In this way, Philo read Plato's theory of ideas, the Pythagorean symbolism of numbers, and the Stoic teleology, into the Biblical story of creation. So also he found that the "unwritten laws", i.e. the fundamental types of virtue,[3] were described in the accounts of the Patriarchs, and he appraised their lives as examples intended to encourage the readers. To him, Enos was the man of hope, Enoch. Translated by God into a better life he represented repentance, amendment, and conversion to the study of philosophy. Noah was the "type" of an "upright man". But these three constituted only an immature striving of mankind, and the three great patriarchs were the first athletes wrestling against hostile passions for the sacred guerdon, with the full strength of grown men.[4] Virtue either sprang from study—as with Abraham, or was innate nature,—as with Isaac,—or the result of practice,—as with Jacob. In this way, the three patriarchs represented the three types of philosophical virtue. Philo's life of Abraham, written from this standpoint, has been preserved. It describes his passage from the astrology of the Chaldæans, through the sphere of sensory knowledge, to

---

[1] *Migr. Abr.*, 89 f. (2, 285 f.)   [2] *Opif. mundi.*, 3, 143 (1, 1, 50)
[3] *Abr.*, 3–5 (4, 2); *decal.*, 1 (4, 296)   [4] *Ibid.*, 48 (4, 12). *Jos.*, 1 (4, 61)

true divine wisdom. The "political man" is added as a fourth type, the sage who undertook the practical realization of the ideal in actual life. The example of this kind of man with his versatility and changeability, was Joseph with his coat of many colours.[1] Then, in another series of books, Philo discussed the details of the Mosaic law, and deduced their general, ethical principles from the Decalogue, which was held as fundamental. He also spiritualized the entire corpus of the ceremonial law, utilizing traditional explanations, and making it philosophically comprehensible.

His biography of Moses is also to be included in the works where he continued to keep in close contact with the literal meaning of his text. Here he showed how the records, when historically understood, and the commandments when genuinely applied, could only be comprehended from a higher standpoint. But in another series of writings he leads us into the temple of his speculations proper. In the *Allegories of the Law* and the appended tractates, all relation to historical event disappears. Adam and Eve, Cain and Abel, Noah, Abraham, Jacob and Esau, Sarah and Hagar, are, for this allegorical interpretation, only "types" of forces in the human soul, and these influence each other by their operation in different directions and by their complementary character. Their reciprocal relationships show the philosopher how to understand the life of the soul, the way to virtue, and communion with God. Even here, Philo, though a Jew, shows that he is in agreement with the spirit of his age, and that, in the end, all philosophy finds its goal in practical life, and its crown in ethics.

He founded this ethic on the Platonic antithesis between spirit and matter, and made much use of Stoic ways of thought, and its ascetic tendencies. God was approached by way of victory over the emotions and conquest of the sensual passions; the freedom of the soul consisted in liberating her from the prison-house of the body which bound her in chains. But at this point other voices were to be heard among doctrines of the philosophic schools. Philo spoke in the tone of a mystagogue to a small group of initiates,[2] when he confided to them the secret

[1] *Jos.*, 31–4 (4, 68)   [2] *Cherub.*, 42–50 (1, 180 f.)

of the immediate divine origin of good in the human soul;
when he urged the soul to leave reason behind, and enter a
Bacchantic frenzy; to get beyond itself and the consciousness of
the ego, and, in "sober intoxication", in the frenzy of heavenly
love, to let itself be lifted up to what truly existed.[1] Here Philo
was no longer a disciple of Greek philosophers, but one of the
Hellenistic mystics, whose esoteric teaching of the God-born
soul languishing in fleshly bonds had penetrated him to the
heart. From those mystics he had also learned that the mystes
could again discover the way to the divine, original spring if he
stripped off what was earthly, and let the divine spirit rule in
him. More than once[2] he calls his readers to make the venture
of flying up to heaven, as he himself had so often been inspired
to do. His idealized description of the order of the Therapeutæ[3]
reached its climax in a nocturnal ceremony which conferred the
rapture of ecstatic enthusiasm upon the ascetic who had been
trained in abstemious living and continual meditation.

His philosophic system provided the basis of this ethic. God
was absolute existence and unity; he could not be comprehended by human organs of perception, and could only be
described with negative predicates. By His nature, He was the
causative principle, and thus active and creative. At the other
pole a passive principle existed in matter, over which He
showed His power when He created the world.[4] Yet the
Highest had no direct contact with unclean matter, but made
use of intermediary and incorporeal powers, called "ideas".[5]
Together, they constituted an intelligible world, an ideal
pattern or model according to which the world of the senses
had been made by the creative activity of these salf-same
powers.[6] The world of ideas might also be understood as a
unity: for it was the logos of God,[7] the original Idea as such,
which united in itself all the various and innumerable ideas.[8]
The logos, the shadow and image of God, His creative organ,[9]
stood between God and the world: not uncreated like God, nor

---

[1] *div. heres.*, 69 f. (3, 16 f.). Bousset, *Judentum*, 450 f. Reitzenstein, *hell. Myst.*,
66 f. *Poimandres*, 204. Hans Lewy, *Sobria ebrietas*, 73 ff.
[2] *Cherub.*, 27 (1, 176); cf. *migr. Abr.*, 35 (275)   [3] *vita contemp.*, 83–9 (6, 69 f.)
[4] *mundi opif.*, 8 f. (1, 2)   [5] *spec. leg.*, 329 (5, 79)   [6] *mundi opif.*, 16 (1, 5)
[7] *Ibid.*, 25 (1, 8), *somn.*, 45 (3, 266)   [8] *sacri. Abel.*, 83 (1, 236)
[9] *leg. alleg.*, 3, 96 (1, 134); *spec. leg.*, 1, 81 (5, 51)

a creature like us.[1] Philo makes use of Biblical terminology in describing the logos as the first-born of God, as the archangel, as wisdom, the high-priest, the advocate who intercedes before God for created beings.[2] Incidentally, he evolved a further system of another five powers, or *dynameis*, which originated from the logos—creative power, royal authority, mercy, commandment, and prohibition.[3] He not infrequently makes brief references to these attributes or powers, although elsewhere he formally enunciates the doctrine that the logos is the union of two prime forces: goodness and authority.[4] It is gratuitous to attempt to find a system in his fanciful speculations on hypostases. The conceptions exist side by side and occasionally intermingle, without losing their peculiar qualities. In particular, the relation of these trains of thought to the theory of ideas is nowhere explained, and this in spite of a few attempts to solve the problem, by suggesting the equation, "The logos equals intelligible world and prime idea." Further on, the innumerable separate *logoi* appear as the Biblical angels,[5] also called dæmons by philosophers. Incorporeal souls inhabit the space between heaven and earth;[6] some descend and become incarnate, others take the opposite direction and fly up to the æther. The best and purest of these souls separate themselves from the rest as the servants and messengers of God, mediating between Him and mankind. But whether, and in what way, these angel-logoi are to be described as ideas, is not explained; both streams of thought remain side by side because they flow from different sources.

It might seem as if the central thought and teaching of Philo could be completely explained from the two roots of Greek philosophy and Hellenistic mysticism; the latter rests upon an oriental foundation, and the Jewish element could then be regarded as its outer form. But this explanation would not penetrate to the final depths. For in spite of all his speculations, ethical deductions, and mystic enthusiasms, Philo remained at bottom a convinced Jew whose lips had been touched by the

---

[1] *div. heres.*, 206 (3, 47)   [2] *Ibid.*, 205 (3, 47); *vita Mosis*, 2, 134 (4, 231)
[3] *fuga.*, 95 (3, 130)   [4] *Cherub.*, 27 (1, 176)
[5] *sobr.*, 65 (2, 228); *conf. ling.*, 28 (2, 235); *migr. Abr.*, 173 (2, 302); *somn.* 1, 115, 148 (3, 229, 236)
[6] *somn.*, 1, 134–41 (3, 234 f.); *gigant*, 6–16 (2, 43 ff.)

God of the Old Testament. He spoke of Him as the Father, in another and more vital manner than did the philosophers; he praised His mercy and grace; he knew that He and all that belonged to Him were holy. He spoke in a tone other than that of the Stoics, about sin and sinners, and he knew the religious significance of repentance. In continually changing phrases, he spoke of the faith which one must offer God as a spotless and most lovely sacrifice, and as exemplified by Abraham.[1] Quite in the Old Testament manner, he felt the nothingness[2] before God of everything human and earthly, and knew Him to be the giver of all good: He had sowed the seeds of good in human souls, and the blessedness of ecstasy was in the end, His highest gift of grace.[3] Philo's God was not the ideal construction of the philosophers, but the Eternal, the Ineffable of the Old Testament and the synagogue; and his logos was, in the last analysis, the personified creative Word of Genesis, and the Wisdom of the writings of Solomon.[4]

Philo was a solitary thinker, and was proud of being such. His writings were intended only for a small circle of readers of a similar degree of culture, and naturally found no echo in the larger circles of the diaspora. They would have disappeared without trace had not the Alexandrine Christians esteemed them, and preserved them in the theological libraries of the following centuries. They are only characteristic of the Judaism of the early empire in as far as they show to what extent philosophical and religious elements of Hellenism could be appropriated by a highly cultivated Jew, without his being conscious of turning aside in any way from his national religion. We must seek other sources for the atmosphere and thought of the Judaism of the Greek diaspora, although these sources usually point to Egypt as their homeland.

The letter of Aristeas is the first writing to catch our eye, and, lately,[5] convincing reasons have been adduced for placing it in the period about 140 B.C. In the form of a letter, it gives a pretty legend in regard to the origin of the Septuagint, the

---

[1] *Cherub.*, 85 (1, 191). *Abr.*, 262–69 (4, 57 ff.). *div. heres.*, 90–5 (3, 21 f.)
[2] *mut. nom.*, 54 (3, 166); *somn.*, 1, 60, 212; 2, 293 (3, 218, 251, 305)
[3] *leg. all.*, 1, 48, 82; 3, 219 (1, 73, 82, 162)
[4] Cf. E. Schwartz, *Gött. Nachr.*, 1908, 537–56
[5] Bickermann, *Z.N.W.*, xxix, 280–98

sacred translation of the Pentateuch. It explains the special
merit of this translation as due to the scholarly interests of
Ptolemy II and his councillor, Demetrios of Phaleron. A
fanciful description of Jerusalem, its temple, and the overawing
nobility of its cultus produces even on the gentile reader a most
charming impression. The "six-times-twelve" translators, who
had been requested to act by Ptolemy, and authorized by the
High-Priest, arrived at the Alexandrian court; here they were
received with high honour and invited to be guests at a banquet. They began to discuss philosophy;[1] the king proposed a
different question to each of the seventy-two elders, and, in
each case, received a sagacious answer. The problems of a
ruler, as well as the various virtues, were discussed philosophically with profit. The religious principle of all Jews, that man
must do everything as in God's sight, echoed, like a refrain, in
every one of their learned answers. God stood as a most
exalted example before human eyes, and He alone could give
the power necessary for every good. The king's legation in
Jerusalem had already been instructed by the High-Priest
himself in regard to the deeper meaning of the Jewish ceremonial law:[2] it was primarily intended to separate the monotheistic Jewish people, by their strict morals, from polytheistic
peoples, in order that they might maintain their own faith in
its purity. But the commandments of purification had a
further, symbolic meaning, and were the embodiment of
ethical teaching. If, however, the question was raised in regard
to the deepest nature of the true worship of God, the sages
answered[3] that one did not truly honour God by gifts and
sacrifices, but by purity of soul and the pious faith that everything was created by Him, and maintained according to His
will.

The religion of the prophets was thus transformed by
Aristeas under Stoic influences into a universal humanism. The
ceremonial law was spiritualized, polytheism repudiated, and
monotheism made fundamental. The essence of religion
appeared to be the recognition of the creative and providential
omnipotence of God and the exercise of the moral virtues. The
typically Jewish element is to be found in the fact that these

[1] *Aristeas epist.*, 187–300   [2] *Arist.*, 128–71   [3] *Ibid.*, 234

virtues could be gained and made operative not by human strength alone, but only by divine aid. We find a similar attitude in the Wisdom of Solomon, which is probably more than a century later, and which linked on to the Hebrew Wisdom-literature of the post-exilic period. Here again we see the idol-worship of polytheists attacked in traditional forms, from a standpoint where the influence of Stoic modes of thought can be traced.[1] In addition, there is a polemic similar to that which is usual in prophetic literature, and which is directed against the godless who oppress the righteous and the religious with brute force.[2] But these wicked men imagined in their hearts that death was the end of all, and, therefore, that it was fitting to enjoy, without restraint, the pleasures of a short life.[3] They deceived themselves, for God had created man for immortality, and death had only entered the world by the devil's envious malice.[4] After death, the righteous were at peace and near God, and would sit in judgment over sinners;[5] the Lord of all would crown and protect them with His right hand. Through the conception of personal immortality, the eschatology of the prophets was developed into a doctrine of recompense which included a theodicy.

A second principal objective of the book now appears in the doctrine of the personified wisdom, the *sophia*. She mediated between God and man,[6] confirmed the rulership of kings, granted all knowledge to man, imparted every virtue to him, and raised him to immortality. She sat on the throne with God, was the reflection of His eternal light, a model of His goodness, a breath of His divine might.[7] She, and she alone, taught how to know the will of God, and led man on the true path to salvation;[8] she also faithfully protected the fathers of Israel.[9] Thus she appeared to be a divine property, but she was still conceived quite personally as a "hypostasis", as an envoy and servant of God and as the good spirit of mankind, exactly as in the earlier wisdom literature of Proverbs[10] and Jesus Sirach.[11] Similarly, approximating to an hypostasis, was the "word" of God, the logos, which saved all, which, like a warrior from the

---

[1] *Sap.*, 13–14   [2] *Ibid.*, 2, 12–20   [3] *Ibid.*, 2, 1–11   [4] *Ibid.*, 2, 23–24; 1, 1 3 f.
[5] *Ibid.*, 3, 1–5, 23   [6] *Ibid.*, 1, 6–11   [7] *Sap.*, 9, 4; 7, 25 f.   [8] *Ibid.*, 9, 13–18
[9] *Ibid.*, 10, 1–21   [10] *Prov.*, 8–9   [11] *Sir.*, 24

throne of the heavenly king, sprang down upon earth and, with
the sword of the commandment of God in his hand, filled the
land of Egypt with death. The parallel is plain when it is said
of God that he created the world by His logos and man by His
sophia.[1] In full analogy, the sophia is also characterized as
the 'spirit (*pneuma*) of God," or made parallel to it: "the
sophia is truly the spirit that is friendly to man;" it is the spirit
of the Lord; it fills the world and searches the hearts of men.[2]
There is no recognizable difference between sophia, logos, and
pneuma. They are only different terms for the same being, a
being which is conceived as a property of God, but which is
separated from God Himself when personification is complete.
Here we see the broad basis upon which Philo erected his
philosophy of hypostases. In the Palestinian literature of the
following period, analogous phenomena are just as evident, and
they appear in ever new forms, owing to the reluctance to
mention God directly, and especially to take His name on one's
lips. In this way, the names of His properties became words
replacing "God". But at the same time, the properties themselves were conceived as active heavenly persons who mediated
the unapproachable and unsearchable being of the Eternal.

IV Maccabees also originated in Egypt. In the form of a Stoic
diatribe with a learned cast, it discusses the thesis that, in a
religious man, reason should control all emotion. After an extraordinary mixture of philosophic phrases and Old Testament
examples, the author passes to his real thesis. He tries to prove
his proposition by the story of the martyrdom of the seven
Maccabean youths and their mother, and he gives a detailed
account of the brave speeches of the martyrs, and the shocking
tortures which they withstood unmoved. In the appropriate
place[3] he points out and emphasizes the conflict between a
confessor's courage, on the one hand, and brotherly or motherly
love, on the other; and declares that even this latter is excelled
by a godly reason. It is a tractate full of warm feeling, and
reflects great national pride in these heroes, and, in spite of the
pedantic logic with which the philosophic point of view is
maintained, it breathes, in essence, the religion of the Judaism

---

[1] *Sap.*, 16, 12; 18, 15; 9, 1, 2   [2] *Ibid.*, 1, 4, 5, 7; 9, 17
[3] 4 Macc. 13: 19–14, 1; 15, 4–24

of the diaspora. The martyrs bravely died and expiated the sins of their race; and they brought to those belonging to them liberation from the stress of persecution. Now they stood near God's throne in the choir of the patriarchs, and had received pure and immortal souls from God.[1]

Jewish legends without philosophical garnishments are recorded in the third book of Maccabees, where reactions to the anti-semitism of the later, Ptolemic period may be clearly recognized.[2] But the High-Priest's prayer[3] is valuable for the study of religion, because obviously it represents the form of prayer used in the synagogue at Alexandria. God is invoked as the King of heaven and the Lord of creation, as the Holy One, the Only, the Almighty who created the world, and who, as righteous ruler, punishes the wicked. Then follow examples from the Old Testament, the giants, the Sodomites, Pharaoh. God had chosen Jerusalem as His holy city, and given it the promise of His special protection. And God was faithful. The stress of the present time—i.e. the pretended desire of Ptolemy Philopater to view the temple—was only the consequence of the Jews' own sins. "Wash away our sins now, and let Thy face again shine upon us." The High-Priest prayed in this fashion for the people, and in this fashion must innumerable prayers have been offered in Greek synagogues in times of persecution. In spite of their Greek dress, these are purely Jewish modes of thought.

If we now consider other prayers, we see at once that an essential part of synagogue worship must have consisted of praising God as the almighty Creator of the world; and also that it was characteristic of Jewish prayers to cite God's ways with His people. We only need to read Psalms 104 and 105, which follow one another because of similarity of content. These Psalms constitute some of the best examples of this way of praising God in the Hebrew synagogue. The conviction that the sins of the people had brought all the misfortunes upon them in the course of their history, is expressed in Psalms 78 and 106 in a great many different ways. And in the midrash contained in the second half of the Wisdom of Solomon,[4] the national and

---

[1] 4 Macc. 17: 18–22; 18: 23   [2] Bickermann in *Pauly-Wissowa*, xiv, 797–800
[3] 3 Macc. 2: 1–20   [4] *Sap.*, 10–19

religious basis of this Jewish philosophy of history becomes clear, for here is a Hellenistic midrash born of a genuinely Palestinian spirit.

The prayers already mentioned[1] are extant in two parallel redactions.[2] They praise God as creator. They reveal the spiritual nature of the Greek synagogue, and enable us to compare it with the older Palestinian mode. For the latter, Psalm 104 is the classical witness. God's mighty acts in creation are hymned in marvellously vivid language: His omnipotence sets boundaries to the sea, His goodness cares for man and beast; He gives life to all, He takes it back and creates new life; His majesty makes the earth tremble, and the devout singer praises the Lord throughout his life. That is simple Old Testament piety with a plain, straightforward way of thinking. On the other hand, the Hellenist offering prayer viewed creation as purposive in structure and arrangement from the beginning. It was created as a cosmos from the start, and the "spirit of life"—a Stoic expression—hovered over the waters. Then the various acts of creation were recounted as in Genesis, but always in such a way as to emphasize the blessings enjoyed by man and beast. Those things which the Psalmist said simply, and for their own sakes, are mentioned in these prayers as examples of a profound principle. God proclaimed the creation of man to His sophia with the words: "Let us make man"; then He created man, the citizen of the world, out of the four elements and with the five senses subordinated to the dominance of reason. When man transgressed the commandment, God did not completely repudiate him, but promised him resurrection after death.

The difference from Psalm 104 is obvious, and comparison immediately brings the Hellenistic elements into the light of day: (a) the Stoic idea of the organized cosmos purposive in all details, and penetrated by the "spirit of life" of the godhead; (b) man as a creature endowed with senses, whom reason rules "as charioteer"; (c) his body consists of four elements; and (d) he is a "citizen of the world". When we add the belief in a resurrection and the hypotasis of sophia, we have all the

---

[1] *Vide supra*, p. 90

[2] *Const. Apost.*, vii, 34 =viii, 12, 9–20; Bousset, *Götting Nachr.*, 1915, 451 ff.

elements characteristic of this kind of prayer. Moreover, nothing here is new, for every trait occurred in the literature of the diaspora already discussed. What we then deduced from the writers is sufficiently confirmed by the prayers of the synagogue. The religion of Greek Judaism is in essence identical with the old religion as found in the tradition of the Fathers, but it is markedly penetrated, and in certain places overwhelmed, by Hellenistic modes of expression and thought.

The remaining prayers in this collection confirm our conclusions. God is worshipped as the Almighty, and as the Saviour.[1] Just as in Philo, He can only be described in negatives:[2] all "rational and holy nature" does Him homage;[2] sophia is His daughter;[3] man is a "citizen of the world",[4] a rational being[5] endowed with a body purposively formed,[6] and with an immortal soul;[7] resurrection is promised to him after death,[8] and therefore he will attain eternal life.[9] His present life is for him a "racecourse of righteousness";[10] only faith, of which Abraham's is the model, can penetrate to heaven; it fills the soul with the hope of rebirth, and precedes knowledge, or "gnosis".[11] These Hellenistic terms are accompanied by the traditional formulas of Biblical religion, and also the typically Jewish view which regards the history of Israel as the revelation of God's choice, discipline, and mercy. What is dealt with in Psalms 105, 106, 78, has parallels, not only in numerous separate passages,[12] but also in the broadly-planned second part[13] of the great prayer, whose first part contains the cosmic hymn of praise on the pattern of Psalm 104. The spirit of the Wisdom of Solomon was active in the Greek synagogue.

---

[1] *Const. Apost.*, vii, 33, 2   [2] *Const. Apost.*, 35, 9   [3] and [4] 35, 10   [4] 34, 6; 39, 2
[5] 34, 6; 38, 5   [6] 38, 4   [7] 38, 5; cf. 33, 3   [8] *loc. cit.*   [9] 39, 3
[10] 33, 3   [11] 33, 3, 4   [12] 33, 4–6; 37, 2–4; 38, 2; 39, 3   [13] viii, 12, 21–26

Chapter Seven

PAUL

As already demonstrated, Acts shows that after the persecution of Stephen, the Hellenists were the first missionaries in the diaspora; and that it was among them that the idea of a mission to the Gentiles became fact. The Syrian metropolis of Antioch is mentioned as the scene of this new departure which was to be so very significant for the history of the world. Further, we said that the first church in Jerusalem heard of it and sent thither, as their trusted representative, a Levite from Cyprus, who bore the Palmyrenian name of Barnabas, and who had already made himself very acceptable to the community.[1] Barnabas rejoiced in the growth of this Hellenistic church and remained with them a whole year as teacher and preacher, after which he sent for an assistant, named Paul, from Tarsus. Thus it was Barnabas who, in fact, introduced Paul, the world-missionary of Christianity, to his life's work. Who was this Paul?

He was born in Tarsus as the son of a Benjaminite Jew who had the distinction of possessing Roman citizenship.[2] We have no information how the father obtained this standing; he may have been the freedman of an eminent Roman, or, already a freedman, he may have earned the interest of the Romans, and so have received the honour of citizenship as a gift. A tradition preserved by Jerome[3] says that his parents belonged originally to Gishala in Northern Galilee, and removed to Tarsus in consequence of warlike disturbances. This tradition is not improbable since Paul on one occasion[4] described himself as a "Hebrew", i.e. probably a man of Palestine. In any case, one may conclude that the boy grew up in a well-to-do household. Besides his Hebrew name, Saul, he bore the honourable Roman cognomen, Paul; it is still undecided whether this name was chosen because of its similarity of sound, or in memory of a former patron of the family.

[1] Acts 4: 36; 11: 22–25   [2] Rom. 11: 1; Phil. 3: 5; Acts 22: 3,28
[3] *Comm. on Philem.*, 23. *Vir. inl.*, 5   [4] Phil. 3: 5

It is certain that the young Paul received a good education and learned some handicraft besides the usual subjects taught at school. He entered into a sort of apprenticeship with a tent-maker.[1] Perhaps even at this stage he had it in mind to follow the calling of a rabbi, which indeed presupposed sources of income from a subsidiary occupation.[2] He appears to have come to Jerusalem at an early age, for, according to Acts, he says he was brought up there, and was a pupil of the celebrated rabbi, Gamaliel, who was an eminent "Tannaite" of the first generation.[3] Paul himself asserts that he was a wholehearted Pharisee, unconditionally faithful to the Law, and, on this account, had hated and persecuted the newly uprising sect of the Christians.

In the Jerusalem church, his active share in the stoning of Stephen was not forgotten,[4] and, according to Acts, he himself told how he had travelled to other towns in order to continue there the persecution of the Christians.[5] He had been commissioned by the sanhedrin to go to Damascus, scarcely in order to bring the Christians, whom he found there, in bonds to Jerusalem—for the sanhedrin were not competent to order this[6]—but in order to encourage the Jews to repel the new danger in the name of the sanhedrin.

On this journey, the hand of God was laid upon him; in broad day the Risen Jesus, whom he was persecuting, appeared to him in a blinding light and called him to be His apostle.[7] Thereupon he went into the wilderness, as behoved a man who had been called of God; the barren steppes of the Arabian kingdom of Nabatea stretched out to the south-east of Damascus. Here he thought out the significance of his experience, and at last turned back to Damascus.[8]

There he began preaching Jesus as Messiah, to the astonishment of the Christians, who were at first dubious; and to the confusion of the Jews, who plotted to kill him. The latter gained for their plans an Arab sheik who was subordinate to the

---

[1] Acts 18: 3   [2] Schürer, ii, 379
[3] Acts 22: 3. Schürer, ii, 429 f. Strack, *Einl. in d. Talmud*, 120
[4] Acts 7: 58–60; cf. 26: 10   [5] Acts 26: 11, 12
[6] Acts 9: 2 = 22: 5. Juster, ii, 145, n. 5
[7] Gal. 1: 16; 1 Cor. 15: 8 f. Acts 26: 13–16; 9: 3–6, 22: 6–10. Hirsch, *Z.N.W.*, 28, 305 ff.
[8] Gal. 1: 17

Nabatæan king, Aretas IV, and who officiated in Damascus as the Nabatæan "ethnarch". They intended to fall upon Paul outside the city, and for this reason kept a close watch on the gates. The Christians heard of the plan and by night lowered Paul in a basket over the walls.[1] He escaped unhurt to Jerusalem at a date fully two years after his conversion.[2] This visit was probably in A.D. 35. In the capital, he desired particularly to make Peter's acquaintance. After doing so, he remained with him for two weeks. At that time he also saw James, but no other apostle, nor did he appear in the church. He must therefore have remained hidden from sight in the greatest secrecy, as is quite comprehensible in the case of a convert in the city where there was still a vivid memory of his work as a persecutor. During this fortnight he had his only opportunity of gaining authentic information about the earthly work and life of Jesus from Peter, his most eminent disciple. Hitherto, he can only have heard accidental and much perverted rumours. Perhaps also he had certain memories of his own, belonging to his previous residence in Jerusalem.

Paul soon left the capital, and went into the regions of Syria and Cilicia, but did not visit the churches of the Jewish Christians, to whom only the rumour of the conversion of their former enemy had penetrated.[3] There now followed thirteen years of missionary work about which we have no further information.

The records of Acts are not clear on this point. They describe details with obvious faithfulness, but give us no picture of the whole. In any case, Barnabas sent for Paul from his home town of Tarsus, whither he had gone from Jerusalem.[4] On Paul's arrival in Antioch, they worked together there for a full year.[5] Accompanied by John Mark a cousin of Barnabas, the two undertook a missionary journey to Pisidia and Lycaonia.[6] The exact period of this journey cannot be determined, and it is possible that other work was done of which we have received no tradition. The only certain fact is, as Paul emphatically declares in Gal. 1: 17–24, that, during all these thirteen years, he never visited Jerusalem.

Meantime, a problem had become acute which had already

[1] Acts 9: 19–26; 2 Cor. 11: 32 f. [2] Gal. 1: 18 [3] Ibid., 1: 21–3
[4] Acts 9: 30 [5] Ibid., 11: 25 f. [6] Ibid., 12: 25–14, 28

existed in germ in the Hellenistic church at Jerusalem, and which had grown to gigantic proportions on account of the mission to the Gentiles, viz. the question as to the operation of the ritual law in the case of new converts who had formerly been Gentiles. As long as the believers in Christ remained, and felt themselves, still to be Jews, the adoption of the ritual law offered no problem; a pagan who had been won for Christ entered the circle of disciples by circumcision and by baptism understood in a Christian sense. But when, under the pressure of the new teaching, the operation of the Law was strongly disputed even amongst Hellenist Jews as is described in Acts,[1] it is not surprising, with the increasing strength of the Hellenistic Gentile mission, and apart from the question of circumcision and other ritual observances, that the observances of further prescriptions for cleanliness in regard to foods should have been felt unnecessary. What was new in Christianity received proportionately fuller recognition, as traditional Judaism necessarily lost significance. Regardless of consequences, Paul had drawn this conclusion for practical life, and had effected the "freedom from the Law" in his missionary churches more logically than was practised in Antioch, the Syrian metropolis. Conflict with the traditionalists at Jerusalem could not be avoided, and it is only astonishing that a dozen years passed before the antitheses compelled an attempt at a solution.

Paul and Barnabas went up to Jerusalem and negotiated with James, Peter, and John, the "pillars" of the first church. They secured recognition of their Gentile mission as free from the Law, i.e. baptized pagans need not be circumcised. The first church, on its side, declared that, as in the past, its mission would be to Jews only. The church at Jerusalem would receive financial support from the Gentile daughter-churches. This was the only obligation laid upon them.[2]

It was with this clear and happy message that the two leaders of the gentile mission returned to Antioch, but it was soon to become evident that a complete solution had not been reached. Obviously the greater majority of the church at Antioch were Gentile Christians; and the standpoint of freedom from the ritual requirements, now recognized even by Jerusalem

---

[1] Acts 6: 11–14; 7: 48, 53   [2] Gal. 2: 1–10 as against Acts 15

as fully justified, was dominant to such an extent that even the Jewish-Christian minority, on occasion, dispensed with the food laws. Especially was this important when it was a question of eating in common with the other brethren, i.e. of celebrating the Lord's Supper. In this way, a friendly agreement was reached in the Pauline sense, and, when Peter appeared in Antioch, he adopted the local custom without more ado.

But other people, commissioned by James, appeared in Antioch and they were not so tolerant. They thoroughly disagreed with the view that born Jews might disregard the Law in any way, and they appealed to the consciences of the local Jewish Christians. Thereupon, Peter himself became doubtful and drew back; and even Barnabas, Paul's former travelling-companion, began to avoid table-fellowship with the "unclean". The logical result was, plainly, that the Lord's Supper could not be observed in common, and the two sections of the church became distinct and separate communities. It was evident to all eyes that the agreement at Jerusalem had not answered the crucial question of the churches of the diaspora, nor settled which section in mixed churches was to have the say. Paul had solved this problem, implicitly, in the gentile-Christian sense; but now the representatives of James came, and gave the opposite answer in no uncertain voice, in so far as they required the gentile Christians to observe the Jewish food requirements before table-fellowship would be permitted. Peter and Barnabas recognized this requirement as justified. Thereupon, Paul rose up in passionate anger on behalf of his contention, and attacked Peter in front of the assembled church. But the other side did not give way, and from that time forward Paul took his own path separately from that of Peter or Barnabas.[1] All this involved Paul in much hatred and strife.

How did this dispute at Antioch arise? The possibility is that, soon after the departure of Paul and Barnabas, the "Apostolic Decree" was drawn up in Jerusalem, and was made known to the most important churches by a circular letter. The text is contained in Acts 15: 23–29, though obviously in an edited form; and Judas and Silas, who are mentioned in it as messengers, must be the representatives of James mentioned by Paul;

[1] Acts 15: 39

their arrival started the dispute. The decree confirmed the view that the gentile Christians were not required to become Jews in all respects; they were required to abjure illicit sexual intercourse in every form, and also to use only *kosher* meat at meals. This was all that was meant by the formal language of the prohibition *re* meat that had been offered to idols, or blood, i.e. meat which had not been drained; or meat from strangled animals, i.e. not ritually killed. This meant, again, that all meat sold in the public market was excluded, and that only a Jewish butcher, or, if he sold nothing to Christians, a Jewish-Christian slaughterer, could be employed for providing meat. This legal requirement was no trivial matter, and there is no room for wonder that Paul should have repudiated it warmly, especially when broadcast in the churches behind his back. Only towards the end of his life, when he again visited Jerusalem, was he given any direct official information. Thus it would seem that he never agreed to this requirement, not even at a later date when it brought his Corinthian church into confusion. He pushed unruffled along the straight road of freedom from the Law.

He now carried his missionary work into the larger world, he alone being the responsible leader. Compared with himself, even the most capable companions appeared to be, at best, only valuable assistants. His sphere was Asia Minor and Greece—but the old questions continually menaced his work. Wherever he went, the "Judaizers" followed. In accordance with the policy of maintaining unity, they explained to the newly converted Gentiles the necessity of eating only kosher meat, according to the Apostolic Decree; and also, contrary to its letter, but quite in accordance with the spirit of Jewish-Christianity, they taught the soteriological significance of circumcision. These emissaries were in continual contact with Jerusalem, and they made it seem credible to the churches that James and the original Apostles stood behind them. Moreover the shadow of Peter was continually falling upon the path of Paul, whose relationship with the original Apostles at last broke down completely; for, when the agreement he had reached at Jerusalem was subsequently revised by the Apostolic Decree with all its consequences, he could not but regard it as a breach

of covenant. Apparently he must have said as much in Antioch
when face to face with Peter, although he says nothing to that
effect in his letters. He did not write a single syllable about the
Apostolic Decree or its authors; and, apart from the passage in
Galatians, he says nothing about his relationship to the original
Apostles. He could not dispute their authority, nor could he
praise their conduct or their attitude towards himself. He therefore had to be content to combat in principle the influences
issuing from Jerusalem, and to rebuke, as firmly as he could,
the emissaries who were ruining his churches. He never wrote
a single word about those who gave them authority; nothing
about James in Jerusalem; nothing about Peter in Corinth and
Rome. He ignored them. But looking more closely, and reading
between the lines of his letters, we perceive behind the "servants
of Satan", the "false apostles", and the "spurious brethren",
the shadows of the great figures in Jerusalem.[1] Paul stood alone
among the Christians whom he had converted, and very
dangerous opponents worked behind his back.

Acts gives us a fairly detailed account of the outer course of
Paul's missionary work. There are indeed larger gaps than the
text itself lets us suspect; nevertheless, the book is of inexpressible value. It records a far-reaching campaign, "the second
missionary journey",[2] which took him through the middle of
Asia Minor, along the Macedonian coast-lands, and into the
heart of Greece. He was not successful in gaining a foothold in
Athens, but he founded a church in Corinth. Here he remained
for eighteen months, when the hostility of the Jews, perhaps in
the summer of A.D. 51, compelled him to return to Antioch. In
spite of many inner difficulties, the Corinthian church remained
faithful, and has maintained an unbroken history until the
present day.

The "third journey",[3] which began soon afterwards, was at
first a renewed visitation of the churches in Asia Minor founded
on the previous occasion. The journey ended in Ephesus, which
Paul made the headquarters of his missionary work for two
complete years. From here he visited Corinth again; and finally,
when he had to leave Ephesus, he added a journey of inspection

[1] 2 Cor. 11: 13–15, 26; Gal. 2: 4   [2] Acts 15: 36–18: 22
[3] Ibid., 18: 23–21: 14

throughout the whole of Greece. But he soon came to the conclusion that he had discharged his task in the east, and he
directed his glance towards Rome, and, indeed, beyond it, to
Spain.

Already, the gospel had penetrated thus far. A gentile
Christian church had been founded in Rome, not by Paul, but,
possibly, by men connected with the church at Antioch. The
danger was that this church, like so many others, would be
manœuvred into opposition to Paul. It is not improbable that
Peter was responsible for this danger, owing to his resentment
at the rebuke he had had to swallow in Antioch. He had visited
Corinth,[1] and gained adherents who made things difficult for
Paul. Quite probably, he had gone thence to Rome and had
persuaded the church to the way he preferred. Paul attempted
to hinder this from Corinth. He wrote powerfully to the
Romans, and made them acquainted with his entire programme. He did this as a preliminary measure because he intended first to go to Jerusalem with the gifts which his churches
had duly collected. Afterwards, he would come himself to
Rome. But things happened otherwise than he hoped, if not
otherwise than he feared.[2] It is true that he attempted to overcome the mistrust of the original church at Jerusalem by correct
observance of the Law, but unfortunately he was recognized in
the temple by certain Jews of Asia Minor, and was at once
accused of having brought into the sacred area a non-Jew
among his companions. For so doing, the penalty was death.[3]

Paul was dragged out of the temple and was in mortal
danger, when the Roman commandant seized and held him in
the hope that he had arrested an Egyptian leader of a band,
who had been diligently sought for. The commandant must
have been astonished to find that the trouble was due to an
uproar among the Jews themselves, and on religious grounds,
and moreover that the prisoner was a Roman citizen. The
further course of events cannot be clearly seen from the only
apparently exact narratives of Acts.[4] In any case, the commandant held Paul in a sort of protective custody, in order that

[1] 1 Cor. 1: 12; 9: 5   [2] Rom. 15: 31
[3] Inscription in Dittenberger, *Or.*, n. 598, Juster, ii, 142 f.
[4] Juster, ii, 143f.

the Jews should not destroy him,[1] and eventually handed him over to the procurator in Cæsarea. Even here no decision was reached; he was neither handed over to the Jewish court, nor set free, nor judged according to Roman law, but kept two years in prison. A decision was only reached when a new procurator appeared in the person of Festus, who suggested to him that he should go before the sanhedrin in Jerusalem. Hitherto Paul had always submitted himself, as a faithful Jew, to the judgment of his own people, and had accepted their verdicts; indeed on five occasions,[2] he had suffered without demur the punishments decreed by them, but now he refused the suggestion and desired to be sent as a Roman citizen to the imperial assize.[3] Thereupon Festus did his duty and dispatched him to Rome.

Paul arrived there after a long and varied journey, and, when he left the ship, was greeted by Christian brethren on Italian soil. He then lived in Rome for two years in relative freedom, though under police supervision, and was able to have unhindered intercourse with the church, and to preach. What happened after that we do not know. It is possible that he was set free, and was able once more to set out on his journeys, and to continue his work. He may have visited Spain, and may also have seen the east again. This may be a legend, but it is certain that he suffered martyrdom in Rome under Nero[4] and was buried on the side of the road to Ostia.

Paul did not initiate missionary work to the Gentiles; even without him, Christianity would have extended round the Mediterranean; but he gave the religion of Jesus the form in which it was capable of conquering the world, without receiving damage to its own soul. He had never sat at the feet of the Master, but nevertheless was the only one amongst the Apostles who really understood Him. Body and soul he was a Jew, but the spirit of the diaspora had extended his horizon. He weighed the meaning of the history of his people, and boldly construed it as issuing in the revelation of the universal religion of the heavenly Lord; the history of the world since then has confirmed his judgment.

---

[1] Acts 23: 12–35; cf. 23: 10   [2] 2 Cor. 11, 24
[3] Acts 25: 10 f.   [4] 1 Clem. 5: 7

To appraise the achievements of Paul's life, we must take yet another fact into account, viz., as far as we can follow his life, he was a sick man. Probably in outward appearance the exact opposite of a handsome figure such as Dürer depicted, he carried a "thorn in the flesh" and "the marks of Christ" in his body.

His work meant that, physically, he "died daily" with Jesus, i.e. he constantly overtaxed his strength in order to be equal to the problems with which his calling faced him. Of recent years, certain "modernists" have made a fanciful attempt to maintain that Paul was an epileptic, but without grounds. However, his nerves were overstrung, and they plagued him with hallucinations which brought bitter suffering to him and others. He did not complain about this, but was proud, even in weakness, to labour for Christ. The Lord Himself had once said to him, "Let yourself be content with My grace, for My power is made perfect in weakness." Thus his theology of the cross[1] was born out of his own experience, and he himself knew what it meant to die with Christ.

Now we must turn to his teaching. How and what Paul had preached to the Gentiles, we can only say in general outlines, for no source depicts Paul as a missionary seeking to win unconverted Jews, or pure pagans. His letters were addressed to churches already in existence, and they assumed that the truths essential to Paul's theology were already known to those churches. And letters, even when they are dictated, give us by no means a reliable idea of the spoken word. Apparently Paul himself had heard on one occasion from his opponents that his personal presence was quite different from his letters[2]—a judgment which may also hold good for his missionary preaching in comparison with what he says in his letters. When we remember, moreover, that the Apostle only took to writing when he had to answer quite definite questions, or to overcome practical difficulties, and never for the purpose of giving a connected account of his teaching, we see further grounds for the manifold uncertainty and defectiveness of our knowledge.

[1] 2 Cor. 12: 7; Gal. 6: 17; 2 Cor. 4: 10. 1 Cor. 9: 27. *Handb.*, excur. on 2 Cor. 12: 10

[2] 2 Cor. 10: 10

There is the further fact that Paul is an individual thinker who
goes his own way and writes in his own highly individual style.
In spite of all his learning, he does not speak "like the Scribes",
but with the rare power of a prophet whose eyes see beyond the
men in front of him, into the deeps of eternity. He understood
human nature in his fellows, without their being able to comprehend him for themselves. None of his hearers and readers
fully understood Paul—and so it is to the present day.

His letters are very revealing, and show his heart while he was
dictating. He discusses a point quietly, calmly, and clearly:
then he tries to draw an elaborate inference. He begins,
becomes entangled in the sequence of his phrases, pursues a
subsidiary line, introduces an incomplete picture, and finally
sticks fast. He begins again, but once more his thoughts, in their
multitude, overwhelm the words which come slowly limping
after, and which get entangled once more in sentences doing
violence to normal construction. The reader guesses what he
means to say, but it is not down on paper. Then finally, though
by no means always, the form is made to suit the content. Yet
it is the same Paul who can fill his words with magic, and let
his feelings stream into the hearts of his readers, or up to the
throne of God. This was the case when he was wrestling for the
souls of the vacillating Galatians, or when, in writing to
the Corinthians, he indited the exalted hymn of love; and to
the Philippians, that of Christ the Lord. Passages like these
exhibit Paul as a master of language who, by the grace of God,
controls the whole register of the human instrument; or, again,
he is like a rare and attractive wild plant growing in the conventional and well-kept garden of contemporary Greek writers.

Let us attempt to draw a picture of his world of ideas. He
knows God by what he learned at home from his parents, at
school, at the synagogue, and from the rabbis; and he has read
God's revelation of Himself in the Old Testament. As a
Hellenist, he knows that even pagans, after earnest meditation
upon the universe, are able to infer the invisible nature of its
Creator,[1] and, from moral promptings in their breasts, to
recognize the will of the divine Law-giver; but he is proud that
only Israel had received the full and direct revelation and the

[1] Rom. 1: 20; 2: 14 f.

written Law, letter for letter.[1] Moreover, it is not sufficient merely to hear and to study this Law, but to practise it, and indeed to keep it in its entirety.[2]

God is righteous—i.e. He punishes the transgressor of His Law, and rewards the obedient or righteous. His wrath against pagans was revealed, similarly, when they departed from the truth. He had turned from them and abandoned them to the greatest moral confusion, which increased to the degree in which the knowledge of God of these idol-worshippers was darkened. But the Jew had reason also for looking at, and testing, his works as to whether he himself really obeyed God better than did the despised pagans, for the Day of Judgment awaited at the end of time. Then God would repay each according to his works, rewarding the doer of good with honour and eternal life, punishing the disobedient with His wrath—Jews as well as Gentiles, without respect of persons. This conception of God went far beyond the prevailing Jewish view, and meant a close approximation to the teaching of the great prophets; but it was a faith which Paul shared with the best of his Jewish fellow-believers. Yet it was understood by them in a totally different way, and this really neutralized it completely, because Paul comprehended the righteousness of God and the meaning of sin from a new standpoint.

The parables of Jesus, as we have already seen,[3] depict the righteousness of God in a way which roused the vigorous opposition of the Talmud. To people who like to draw up a formal account with God, it is provoking if the righteousness characteristic of human ways of thinking be set aside and replaced by a grace which gives freely. Paul, too, understood the divine righteousness in this way, only he expressed it in complicated forms of thought. That it was God's purpose to save men was, for him, the indisputable foundation of all religion. Earthly experience showed him, what he could also prove from the Scriptures, that all men without exception were sinners, and therefore no one, whether Gentile or Jew, could fulfil the Law. None of the children of men is righteous; sin separates them all from God. Therefore, if righteousness, in a legal sense, corresponded with the nature of God, only wrath and punishment

[1] Rom. 2: 27   [2] *Ibid.*, 2: 13; Gal. 5: 3   [3] *Vide supra*, pp. 51 f.

would remain for men. In that case, however, where would be God's redemptive purpose, revealed in the promises of the Old Testament and just as indubitably in His punitive righteousness? Hence God must be able to take sinners to Himself, and yet be righteous in so doing. It follows that His righteousness is different from the human virtue which bears that name; it is revealed when God, of His free grace, accepts the sinner, and "makes him righteous", giving him that characteristic as a gift which he cannot earn by his own achievements.

But there is a condition, viz. the sinner must "believe", i.e. in full recognition of his own insufficiency and helplessness, he must surrender himself entirely to divine grace and, setting aside every doubt, be certain that God makes him righteous, and will give him eternal life. The question arises whether this only means replacing the idea of divine righteousness by that of mercy? Would it not be simpler to say that God is not "righteous" in the human sense, for then no man could escape judgment, but rather that He is merciful? This way of stating the case really meets all the requirements, but Paul would have regarded it as serious blasphemy to deny God the property of righteousness,[1] and so he sought and found a way of uniting his profound, religious experience with a theory of righteousness which satisfied formal logic. God's righteousness must indeed demand punishment and expiation from the sinner; this expiation was made to God when the innocent and sinless Jesus voluntarily bore the punishment of sin, and suffered death. He suffered death as a vicarious, expiatory sacrifice on behalf of sinful mankind. Thereby He reconciled God, satisfied His righteousness, which had demanded expiation, and opened in this manner the way of mercy which can bring to the Christian believer the necessary righteousness. Thus God *is* righteous and *makes* righteous.[2]

The idea of expiatory death for another was crudely expressed in the animal sacrifices of the Old Testament ceremonial law. As we have already seen, Hellenistic Judaism raised the idea to the height of the voluntary sacrificial death of the Maccabean youths for the sins of their people.[3] Paul carried the thought

[1] Rom. 3: 5   [2] Rom. 3: 23–26, 5, 8–9; Gal. 3: 13
[3] *Vide supra*, p. 101

to a sublime height, and used it to reconcile the idea of divine righteousness and that of a sinful mankind.

The supra-mundane and supra-human process involved was, however, not a course of events which takes place in accordance with the inner necessity of the divine nature as Anselm, the Schoolman, teaches, but a free action of God's grace. Paul was well aware that there was no "sufficient ground" for God's action which could offer mankind an excuse for bargaining with God. He knows that he himself was saved by the incomprehensible mercy of God, and he looks shudderingly into the abyss into which His unsearchable will flings the clattering potsherds of the vessels of His wrath.[1] God accepts whom He will and rejects whom He will, and the lot of the babe in the womb is already settled according to God's free choice. As always, where ideas of predestination meet with practical religious needs, these theories did not cramp Paul, but only strengthened his joyous consciousness of the divine election,[2] although his successors, for centuries, were reluctant to discuss the subject. But, even for Paul, the doctrine of divine predestination was not the last word. In the greatest deeps of his soul, he glimpses the holy secret of an all-embracing divine love which would, at last and in the end, redeem the rejected, a love which had concluded all under disobedience in order to have mercy upon all.[3]

For mankind, there was only *one* way to this God and His grace, namely Jesus Christ. This Man had lived His brief life in Palestine as an itinerant teacher, had died, in the end, a criminal's death on the cross. But He had arisen from the dead. He had appeared to His disciples and lastly also to Paul; He still lived and laboured near and with God, and would soon come again. That was the personal message and experience of Paul, but he also sought to explain the secret of His person. He was the Son of God in quite a different sense from any other human being. At one time, He had lived in divine form with His Father,[4] and was equal with God; but then, at the Father's command, He had descended from heaven, and taken human form, in order to redeem mankind. An inescapable fate

---

[1] Rom. 9: 10–29   [2] Rom. 8: 28–39
[3] *Ibid.*, 11: 32   [4] Phil.2: 6–11; cf. Rom. 8: 3

burdened mankind, for in their flesh dwelt the power of an evil dæmon, sin, which was contrary to God, and compelled men to conform to its overpowering will. Even if they should inwardly catch sight of a better self, no matter how much that self might strive and struggle after the good, it was all in vain. One man after another fell as a sacrifice to Death, and was accounted according to God's irrefragable law, as the wages of sin.[1] Then God's son came upon earth, born of the House of David.[2] He took on a body of flesh like ours and one in which sin dwelt and was active.[3] He submitted to the Law which applied to all men,[4] but shattered the power of Sin; He did not do its will, but remained sinless,[5] and thus overcame it in His flesh.[6] Nevertheless, obediently to the will of the Father, He bowed to His human destiny. Being sinless, He was not subject to death, yet He accepted death voluntarily and died like a sinner, indeed like a criminal—and the evil spirits of this world triumphed. But they did not suspect what lay in God's purpose,[7] for the sacrifice was made for the sake of mankind. Sin was conquered on its own ground and therefore death could no longer retain its booty. Jesus, though crucified and buried, rose again to new life.[8] His work had been completed and now God set Him upon the heavenly throne at His right hand, and gave Him the name above every name, the name of *Kyrios*, i.e. the Lord, before whom everything bows whether in heaven, or on earth, or under the earth. This is the cosmic drama of salvation which was carried through by God, Christ, and the heavenly powers against Sin and Death, with all their dæmonic assistants. In spite of all prophecy, the earth below guessed nothing of what was happening there.[9]

Only with the revelation of the risen Christ was redemption proclaimed to man, and the way pointed out by which that redemption could be accepted; for, in the end, the individual man had to be brought into relation with all that had been done in heaven. We have already shown that Paul characterized faith as the means by which man grasps divine grace. In so expressing himself, he formulated the process of salvation from

---

[1] Rom. 7   [2] *Ibid.*, 1: 3   [3] *Ibid.*, 8: 3   [4] Gal. 4: 4
[5] 2 Cor. 5: 21   [6] Rom. 8: 3   [7] 1 Cor. 2: 8   [8] 1 Cor. 15: 3, 4
[9] *Ibid.*, 2: 8; Col. 2: 15

the psychological standpoint. The decisive factor, according to Paul, was the total surrender of self, as distinct from trusting in one's own works; but faith was only the subjective form of perception, viz. the apprehension of an objective process or a positive change which was taking place within the man himself.

The natural man lived in the earthly sphere under the burden of sin and death, in such a way that his "flesh" was predominant. The Lord, however, was a divine being, i.e. He was spirit, pneuma, and He penetrated with this heavenly material each one who trusted himself to Him. A Christian received the spirit and thereby in full reality shared in the Risen Lord. His body became a member of Christ[1] and the sum total of Christians can be described as a single unity, as the body of Christ whose head is the Lord.[2] Hence, he who becomes a Christian enters into a mystical fellowship of the spirit; he is actually "in Christ", as if in a heavenly fluid. This spirit overcomes sin in the flesh. The victorious warfare against sin, which once took place in the person of the historical Jesus, is repeated anew in every Christian to whom the spirit has been given. In effect, every Christian becomes anew a "Christ upon earth". The spirit seizes control in man, breaks the power of the passions of the flesh, and levels the road towards a life according to God's will. The Christian lives "in the spirit" and not "in the flesh". He fulfils the requirements of the divine law,[3] a thing for ever impossible to the natural man. But this fellowship with Christ is also the fellowship of His sufferings. The way of the Lord had led through suffering to resurrection; and, in the same way, the Christian here on earth takes part in the sufferings of Christ in order afterwards to share His glory.[4] From this point of view Christ is the first-born of many brethren whom He will transfigure like Himself.[5] The Christian experiences the divine blessing in the sense of power in the struggle against sin; the proud feeling of freedom from its dæmonic compulsion; the joyful possession of all the virtues well-pleasing to God; the voluntary and victorious bearing of all sufferings in

---

[1] 1 Cor. 6: 15, 12: 13   [2] Rom. 12: 5; 1 Cor. 10: 17; Col. 1: 18, 24
[3] Rom. 8: 3 f., 13: 8
[4] *Ibid.*, 8: 17; 2 Cor. 4: 10, 13: 4; Phil. 3: 10; Gal. 6: 17   [5] Rom. 8: 29

happy consciousness of fellowship with his Lord. On the other
hand, he lives in the hope that complete redemption, i.e. entire
liberation from the body, the joyful experience of heavenly
glory, awaits him in the future.[1]

The process of redemption is therefore something which God
effects in man whereby he is transformed from a being fettered
by earthly conditions, or "of the flesh", into a spiritual,
pneumatic being on the model of Jesus Christ. This process
only ends with the final separation from the body, the entry
into heavenly glory, and the gaining of a transfigured body.
That is redemption in the fullest sense of the word. But we may
ask how it begins, and how the individual sinful man is
brought into this pathway of salvation.

The first step is the preaching of the divine message, the
proclamation of the divine invitation to men[2] to be reconciled
with God, and let themselves be redeemed.[3] They are required
to believe without condition and without limit. This faith, however, is not simply an emotional attitude developed in the deeps
of the soul, but at the same time an impulse of the will which
leads to action, a will which seizes the saving hand of God.
Action must follow decision; the newly converted believer joins
the church of Christ, and is made a Christian by baptism. There
the miracle of a divine mystery is fulfilled in him.[4] He sinks
beneath the water and so dies, yet he dies no ordinary human
death, but the death of Christ. The death once suffered upon
the cross on Golgatha for the sins of the world is accounted to
him; it becomes his own death, a death which he now suffers
for his own sins. Thereby he pays the due price of sin and thus
is set free from it. Through this miracle, God makes him
righteous; he no longer possesses sin. This may be regarded as
the negative side of the process of becoming a Christian, of
being "baptized into Christ", literally, "submerged in Christ".

The positive side is that he "puts Christ on"; he is introduced
into that spiritual body of Christ[5] which is constituted by the
entire Church. In other words, the heavenly substance of the
spirit is granted to him. The sinner dies in baptism: the
Christian who rises from the water is a new creation,[6] "the old

---

[1] Rom. 8: 23, 13: 11   [2] *Ibid.*, 10: 17; Gal. 3: 2   [3] 2 Cor. 5: 20
[4] Rom. 6: 2–11   [5] Gal. 3: 27 f.; 1 Cor. 12: 13   [6] 2 Cor. 5: 17; Rom. 6:4

has passed away, lo! it has become new". He is now "in Christ".

Hence Paul can also say that, just as in baptism we share in the death of Christ, so in coming up from the water we share His resurrection. Paul formulates our experience of sharing in Christ's resurrection, however, in the sense of a goal to be aimed at, i.e. we must now live in the new life, and we are able to do so by the power of the spirit. We are mortified to sin and have suffered death; our new life in the spirit is to be lived in the service of righteousness,[1] and issue in eternal life in the fellowship of the Risen Christ. In this way, baptism brings about the birth of the Christian as a new being free from the natural bonds of earthly life, and united by the spirit with the Risen Lord. The first element is faith, the second is baptism, the third is the spirit. Thereby the man is justified and placed on the pathway to redemption. But the man who is reborn lives, as long as he is in the flesh, by faith and not by sight.[2] Faith is always the attitude of the Christian, and this term is used by Paul to describe the essential character of the Christian state.

Paul's doctrine of baptism contains an explicit, sacramental mysticism which cannot be understood directly on the basis of Hellenistic Judaism, although the latter reveals certain similarities. We shall deal with this subject later; just now it is of decisive importance for understanding Paul that we should determine the ethical level of his theory. This theory depends on his conception of God, and regards redemption as man's liberation from all the powers which prevent our fulfilling God's will, and living according to His commandments, until finally we can abandon the last fetters of the flesh and triumph in fellowship with our Redeemer. For Paul does not regard salvation, *soteria*, as already fully ours; rather it is a promise for the future which faith now seizes upon.[3] At the beginning of this process of salvation, is the decisive act of justification and new birth through the spirit in baptism. The Christian is now righteous, dead to sin, and free from its power.

[1] Rom. 6: 18–23; 8: 9–11   [2] Gal. 2: 20; 2 Cor. 5: 7
[3] Cf. Rom. 8: 24; Eph. 2: 5 8 is the only exception, a fact which is, at the same time, a proof that the letter was by another writer.

If we have followed Paul's theory so far, we shall have understood him to imply that to the Christian, as a new creature, sin is no longer possible. If, in the earlier stage, that of the "old Adam", the dominant factor was sin, now it is the spirit; and if at one time the evil power irresistibly compelled us to sin, now we shall look to the divine power of the spirit, and ascribe to it that sure guidance by which the Christian may attain perfect sinlessness after the example of Christ. We shall see that, in later ages, this conclusion was drawn by many. But Paul did not do so. It is true that he describes the status of a Christian as a new man, justified, sinless, and filled with the spirit—as we have already explained. He strongly insists that the Christian is dead to sin, but nowhere does he say that sin is dead. It is still there, working in the world of unredeemed men with unbroken power, and waiting in ambush for the opportunity of winning back the lost territory. The experiences of life, the battles which the new convert must fight for a moral foundation, showed Paul clearly enough that sin still played an evil rôle in the Christian churches. Deeply pained, he perceived that, in spite of their Christianity, the Corinthians lived in bickerings and strife; to their disgrace, he drew the conclusion that they were still "of the flesh", and deserved censure "as men",[1] and this in spite of the fact that they had not been denied the possession of the spirit.[2] This could only mean that they gave way to the power of sin in the flesh, that they were not successful in the struggle of the spirit against the flesh, as Christ was, but must recognize defeat.

We are now in a position to understand how it is that Paul could describe a Christian's freedom from sin and his spirituality as saving facts and yet, in the same breath, he could urge Christians not to allow sin to rule in them, but to place their bodies at the service of Christ;[3] and how he could discuss the duty of not living according to the will of the flesh.[4] Indeed he exhorts his churches, clearly and unmistakably, to let themselves be led by the spirit of God, and through the spirit to put to death the carnal, i.e. sinful, passions.[5] Sin is not dead in the

---

[1] 1 Cor. 3: 3 f.; cf. Rom. 8: 12 f. [2] 1 Cor. 3: 16; 6: 19, and indeed 5: 5
[3] Rom. 6: 12–14, 19; 1 Cor. 6: 20 [4] Rom. 8: 12
[5] *Ibid.*, 8: 13 f.; Gal. 5: 16 f.; Col. 3: 5–10

flesh any more than it was dead in the body of Jesus when He lived on earth; rather it must be put to death in each individual by the spirit dwelling in him just as it dwelt in the body of Christ. In this way the Christian life, as actually found in the individual, remained only an imperfect copy of the ideal which had been realized in Christ; that life constituted a struggle to be well-pleasing to Christ.[1] All that Paul could say of himself was that he had not yet attained the perfection of the Christian life, but that he was making every effort to reach the prize. Both in the recognition and the conquest of sin, there is a progressive movement from the small to the great, and there are degrees of perfection.[2]

We are now in a position to understand Paul's doctrine of a judgment which all Christians must undergo and which will judge them according to their works.[3] They must show themselves to be free from guilt, and their hearts will be tested as to whether they are able to stand innocent and pure in God's sight.[4] This is not to contradict, but to assume the doctrine of justification by faith alone. The works of the reborn man are done through the spirit, and not by the flesh. From another standpoint, this life in the spirit is to be regarded as the life of faith, i.e. life in faith that we possess the righteousness which comes from God.[5] That is how we must understand the celebrated saying of the Apostle that everything which is not of faith is sin.[6] He could have said, alternatively, that what does not come from the spirit is sin. The Last Judgment decides whether the Christian has really been justified in the spirit by faith, or whether he has remained in the flesh as a sinner. This is not casuistical legalism, not a back-sliding into the Jewish calculation of works, but, in view of the weakness even of the reborn man,[7] it is the final and crucial question as to what dominates the Christian life: spirit or flesh, the life of faith in Christ or the life of man in the world.

Nowhere did Paul discuss fundamentally whether the punishment of a sinful Christian was an absolute rejection or a relative chastisement. Incidental expressions suggest, however,[8]

[1] 2 Cor. 5: 9; cf. 1 Cor. 11: 32; 1 Cor. 9: 23   [2] Phil. 3: 12; 1 Cor. 3: 1
[3] 1 Cor. 3: 14 f.; 2 Cor. 5: 9 f.   [4] 1 Cor. 1: 8; Phil. 1: 10; 1 Thess. 3: 13
[5] Phil. 3: 9   [6] Rom. 14: 23   [7] Gal. 5: 17

that the latter was his view. Indeed the incestuous man of Corinth, while still alive, was to be handed over to Satan who would destroy his flesh—but his Christian spirit would nevertheless be saved at the Last Day.[1] On the other hand, we must not forget that the Apostle threatened sinful Christians with death and therefore with final rejection such as faced every non-Christian.[2] He reckons with the possibility that even a Christian, who has been baptized and endowed with the spirit, can turn once more to the flesh and to sinfulness, in such a way as that God will withdraw His grace and hand him over to damnation. Paul believed, indeed, that God calls and rejects how and whom He will. It was only in the future that an attempt was made to treat the problem of a Christian's sinfulness in a definite and systematic way.

In addition to baptism, Paul speaks of a second sacrament, the Lord's Supper. He did not regard the Supper as a simple table-fellowship with the Risen Lord, as in the first church; rather, it was the fulfilling of an institution founded by the Lord Himself the last time He was with His disciples. Paul had received from the Lord—and this can only have taken place by means of a revelation—and had handed it on to the churches,[3] that this common meal in particular was celebrated in memory of Jesus, and that the death of the Lord was proclaimed by it until He came. Nevertheless, it was more than a mere memorial feast, such as was customary in many places elsewhere in the ancient world. Rather it was similar to a sacrificial meal, since those who took part entered into a mystic fellowship with one another, and also with the Risen Lord in whose honour it was celebrated. The fellowship made them one. The one food, the one bread which they ate, bound them together and made them into *one* body, the pneumatic body of Christ.[4] The mystery of the Lord's Supper, thus understood, is similar to the sacrament of baptism, but the operation is more graphic, for the wine and bread are not common foods, but heavenly nourishment. They are the blood and the body of the Risen Lord, pneumatic substances which enter, with their miraculous powers, into those who share the meal, transforming them into

---

[1] I Cor. 3: 15; 5: 5; 11: 32   [2] Rom. 8: 13; Gal. 5: 21; 6: 7 f.
[3] I Cor. 11: 23   [4] I Cor. 10: 16–21

the spiritual body of Christ. Woe to him who takes these
essentially supermundane elements dishonourably, and as if
they were ordinary food, for they will become poison in his
body, and bring illness and death to such a wicked person.[1]

The possession of the spirit is, therefore, the peculiar characteristic of the Christian. How is it shown? The common opinion
in the churches was that phenomena of exaltation of all kinds
were to be regarded as its signs. There were manifold forms of
religious enthusiasm, including the gift of "prophecy", i.e.
inspired ecstatic speech that might rise to the level of revelations, and issue in heart-stirring searchings of the soul.[2] Among
those who were specially gifted, enthusiasm might develop into
that complete ecstasy which was connected with the apocalyptic vision of the heavenly spheres. Paul himself records, in
awed humility, that, on one occasion, he had been caught up
into the third heaven, had seen Paradise, and there heard
inexpressible words.[3]

The gift of speaking with tongues, or glossolalia, was widespread. He who was thus uplifted by the spirit, uttered meaningless sounds, half-aware, or in complete unconsciousness,
sounds which were regarded as the language of heavenly spirits
and which were interpreted by those who were expert.[4] Paul
had had a rich and personal experience of these utterances of
the spirit, and esteemed them highly,[5] but he does not measure
their value, as the majority did, by their strangeness, but by
their significance for edifying the church. Glossolalia, with its
excitements, was apparently much practised, but Paul would
only tolerate it in the assembly of the church if someone was
present who could interpret the "supernatural" language.
Otherwise he would restrict its use to the private chamber of the
individual concerned.[6] On the other hand, he paid high respect
to the spirit-given words of a prophet delivered during Christian
public worship. Naturally, he praises miracles and healings of
the sick[7] as witnesses of the power of the spirit; but he also
sees the spirit at work in the missionary preaching of itinerant
apostles, in the Scriptural exegesis of the teachers, indeed even

---

[1] 1 Cor. 11: 27–30   [2] *Ibid.*, 12: 8–11; 14: 1–3, 24 f.   [3] 2 Cor. 12: 1–4
[4] 1 Cor. 14: 2, 9–11, 23   [5] *Ibid.*, 14: 1, 18, 39   [6] *Ibid.*, 14: 28
[7] *Ibid.*, 12: 9, 28

in the administering work of the presidents, and of those in the church who looked after the poor.[1] Moreover in the very connection where Paul instructed the Corinthians in this whole matter, and urged them to strive after ever higher gifts of the spirit, he called them to go beyond this kind of spiritual life, and walk in the way of love.[2] One could find the works of the spirit, in the usual sense, in places where the cymbals of the Great Mother re-echoed. There were many mysteries in which the angels spoke, and all sorts of secret wisdom were proclaimed. But where the spirit of Christ was to be found, love was the most valuable fruit.[3] Love gave meaning to all spiritual action and conduct, penetrated and consecrated the entire Christian life. Glossolalia, prophecy, and esoteric wisdom were only partial, vanishing with this present world. When perfection came, they would disappear; but faith, hope, and love would remain, these three—and fhe greatest of these was love. In this way, Paul planted his conception of Christianity among the religions of his time, and yet raised it to that mountain-height where Jesus preached of faith and hope, and that love of God which is fulfilled by loving one's neighbour. Elsewhere, Paul called it faith working itself out through love.[4] That is how the canticle of love, in 1 Cor. 13, was meant to be understood. Love was the purest expression of the spirit; in comparison everything else was of minor importance and without content. In the religious cross-currents of the times, this religion could only go under if it lost its soul.

Paul spoke to his contemporaries in their own language and from their own point of view. He made the gospel of salvation graphic by using the same pattern as the oriental, redemption religions, and he presented Christ in the form traditional for a saviour coming from heaven. Mankind was in bondage to a curse, an evil power, the dæmon of sin. Adam had sinned long ago in the garden of Eden, and the act of the primogenitor brought doom upon the whole of mankind. But, with God in heaven, there lived a "second Adam", the original man,[5] who came down on earth to redeem. He gave mankind a vital power which could loose them from their bonds, and bring them back

---

[1] 1 Cor. 12: 4–11, 28–30   [2] *Ibid.*, 13: 1–13   [3] Cf. Gal. 5: 22
[4] *Ibid.*, 5: 6   [5] 1 Cor. 15: 44–46

to God. This power was heavenly pneuma; it took up its abode in man, drove out the lower beings dominating his soul, and made him divine. Exactly so might an oriental mystagogue have spoken to his disciples, and both Gentile and Jewish hearers would find it easier to follow Paul when he spoke like this, than do twentieth-century students for whom it is difficult even to enter the atmosphere of such ways of thought. Yet we see how well adapted was this form of expression for winning men who were searching for redemption—the yearning desire of the age. It is of vital importance for understanding Paul's thought to notice that, no matter what forms of expression he used, they were never allowed to dominate their content, that content remained intact, and in full operation. In this respect, once more, those who came afterwards were not able to keep in step with the great Apostle. Rather they brought Christendom into the many dangers of which the history of dogma is full.

Although Paul laboured more than any other Apostle to free Christianity from Judaism, yet, in the bottom of his heart he remained faithful to his race and clung to it with profound affection. He found a theological basis for both sides of this attitude. Let us first consider the question of Christian freedom from the Law. The problem had been only half-solved at the convention in Jerusalem, and, as a consequence, the issue pursued him wherever he went. The law of Moses was holy, of divine origin[1] and expressed God's will for the whole of mankind, but it was a mistake to hold that it was fitted to point the way to salvation. Centuries of experience showed that no man was in a position to fulfil it, whereas only unconditional and unfailing obedience could endow man with the required righteousness before God. The tragic element in the history of the Jews was that, owing to a false estimate of the meaning of the Law, they pursued the delusive idea of salvation through their own righteousness. God's purpose in giving the Law was really quite other. Its prohibitions were meant to awaken and excite sin which dwelt in the flesh, compel it to show all its power, and thus make man conscious of his own powerlessness. Then, in doubt of his self-sufficiency, man would look towards God for

[1] Rom. 7: 1

rescue.[1] The Law was not a means of salvation, but had value only as a preparation; it was a "tutor bringing us unto Christ".[2] It left the man who understood its secrets in no manner of doubt about the case, for it prophesied its own abolition. With the appearance of Christ, faith replaced the Law as the genuine principle of salvation. Unlike the Law, faith did not require works upon works, but required the entire personality to yield itself up to the grace of God; it was the new life of the spirit.

Given this universal standpoint, the question could never again be raised whether the ceremonial law was to be separated, e.g. from the moral law, and so, perhaps, be regarded as of no effect. By its very nature, the entire Law was antiquated and had lost all its power over the new man. Its promises still held good, although they no longer applied to "Israel after the flesh", the physical descendants of Abraham, but to the true "Israel of God", i.e. the Christians, who, like Abraham, lived by their faith.[3] Jews and Gentiles, without distinction, were "children of Abraham" and heirs of the promises, in as far as they walked in the footsteps of his faith. With this construction, every national limitation of Christendom was set aside, every prerogative of Judaism was denied, and, at the same time, the Old Testament was claimed for the new universal religion as the sacred book of promises and prophecies.

Nevertheless, Paul could not find it in his heart without more ado to deny his people all pre-eminence, even if in the end they possesed only advantages of honour[4] such as the Holy Scriptures, the promises, the cultus, the name of "son", and the physical genealogy of Christ. Over against this, however, stood the dreadful and undeniable fact that the people of Israel, almost in its entirety, had refused the divine message of the gospel. Ought God to have rejected His people?[5] Paul did not think this conclusion could be drawn, and therefore he proposed a theory in the epistle to the Romans[6] which testified to his unmistakably warm love of his race, a love that was prepared to forgo his own salvation if only his race could be saved.[7] Paul proceeded to argue that God had temporarily hardened his race, and permitted only a small selection to

[1] Rom. 7: 7-25   [2] Gal. 3: 23-25   [3] Ibid., 3: 6-9: 6, 16. Rom. 4: 1-25
[4] Rom. 3: 1-2; 9: 4 f.   [5] Ibid., 11: 1   [6] Ibid., 9-11   [7] Ibid., 9: 3

attain salvation, whereas a multitude of Gentiles had come to Christ. In the end, this would arouse envy in Israel, who would then throw aside their blindness and become subject to Christ. Thus, at last, God's mercy would comprehend all men, and the whole of Israel would be saved. God had concluded all men in disobedience only in order that He might have mercy upon all. Hence behind the life-work of the Apostle to the Gentiles, there lay the undiminished hope of future salvation for his own race also, although for the present he must deny it.

This position in regard to the Law forms the basis of Paul's theology, the foundation for his attitude in missionary praxis, and for his totally refusing any legal requirements from the Gentiles. From this standpoint, moreover, he could require Jewish-Christians to forgo their ritual table-customs when necessary, in order to express the unity of the Christian church, and could sharply oppose Peter in Antioch when he attempted to establish requirements to the contrary. If the Law had no significance as a means of salvation, obedience to it could no longer be made a duty of conscience. In particular, concessions in this regard could easily endanger a true estimation of faith among the Gentiles. Paul's letters show with what stubborn persistence he opposed the many kinds of legal requirement. He found it impossible to differentiate between the ceremonial law which was antiquated and the moral law which still held good unchanged, although such a differentiation characterized the church at a later date; for him the Law was antiquated in its totality just because it was law. The reborn man did not need to read God's will in the book of the Law, for the spirit would lead him into everything good and well-pleasing to God; he need only yield himself to its leading. Naturally, the intimations of the spirit would agree with the Decalogue, but, in place of the Jewish legalism with its concern for details, was the free activity of the Christian character as brought to life by the spirit—this was the vital difference from Judaism. Therefore, in accordance with a saying of Jesus, the Apostle summarized the Decalogue in the commandment to love one's neighbour, and described love as the fulfilment of the Law.[1] He followed the example of the Master in pressing forward

[1] Rom. 13: 9 f.; Gal. 5: 14; cf. Matt. 22: 37-40

from formalism to essence, from the letter to the spirit; for him casuistry was dead. Understanding him in this way, we are in a position to gain a true estimate of his meaning when he occasionally speaks[1] of the "fulfilling of the Law" by those who are reborn. On the other hand, we can see how those who came later found here the backdoor through which they brought the Law into credit again in the churches.

It was no contradiction of his general position that, on occasion, he undertook a vow according to Jewish rite;[2] or that, among Jewish Christians, he subjected himself to the prescriptions of the ceremonial law; or even that he was prepared, on the advice of the original Apostles in Jerusalem, to carry out a ceremonial vow in order to supply mistrustful brethren with a proof of his faithfulness to the Law.[3] Here no confusion of counsel was to be feared, and therefore, in accordance with his fundamental missionary principle, he became a Jew to the Jews, just as, in the outside world, he was free from the Law among those who were free from the Law,[4] in order by one means or another, to save souls.

[1] Rom. 8, 4, 13: 9; Gal. 5: 14, 6: 2; 1 Cor. 9: 21   [2] Acts 18: 18
[3] Ibid., 21: 20–26   [4] 1 Cor. 9: 20

Chapter Eight

THE CHRISTIAN MISSIONARY CHURCHES

PAUL'S ACTIVITY COVERED A GENERATION BEGINNING FROM the death of the Lord and ending in the sixties, in the reign of Nero. This period has been rightly called the Apostolic Age, for in it the missionary labours of the first generation of disciples laid the foundations which were decisive for all the future. If we assemble the scattered notices which have been preserved in incidental records, we can see the broad outlines of the extent of Christendom.[1] On the other hand we have not the slightest information about the size of the churches or the nature of their constitution.

There were churches in Judea outside Jerusalem,[2] and similarly in Galilee and Samaria. Others were to be found in Lydda, and on the Plain of Sharon to the north, as well as in the coastal towns of Ashdod, Joppa, and Cæsarea. All this region was the missionary sphere of Philip "the Hellenist". We know further that the Hellenists, who had fled on account of the persecution of Stephen, carried on missionary work in Phœnicia, Cyprus, and Antioch, the capital of Syria; and that they developed the last named into a centre of Christianity free from the Mosaic law.[3] Here was the centre of the first mission to the Gentiles. It was here, as a consequence, that Christianity became so plainly distinct from Judaism that it was given its own Greek name. From then onwards, those who believed in Christ were called "Christians",[4]—naturally by those outside the movement, whether Jews or Gentiles. In Palestine the Christians were called "Nazorenes",[5] and this nickname was applied even to Jesus Himself, and this, not only by outsiders,[6] but also in the Christian church.[7] What it meant is still not clear in spite of much research on the subject.

We hear mention of Tyre, Sidon, and Ptolemais[8] as Phœnician cities with Christian churches.[9] We learn nothing more

[1] Harnack, *Mission*, ii, pp. 622–26   [2] Gal. 1: 22; Acts 9: 31; 8: 5; 14: 25; 9: 32–36
[3] *Vide supra*, p. 72   [4] Acts 11: 26   [5] *Ibid.*, 24: 5
[6] *Ibid.*, 6: 14; John 18: 5, 7; 19: 19; Luke 18: 37; Matt. 2: 23; 26: 71
[7] Acts 2: 22; 3: 6; 4: 10; 6: 14; 22: 8; 26: 9; Luke 24: 19
[8] Harnack, *Mission*, 1, 412, n. 1   [9] Acts 27: 3; 21: 3, 4, 7

about the work of the missionaries in Cyprus; and when Paul
at a later date visited the towns of Salamis and Paphos, he
began missionary work afresh.[1] Once more, however, nothing
is recorded about the success of the work. It would be helpful
to know more of Paul's activity in Cilicia and Syria, which he
himself mentions,[2] but neither he nor Acts gives us further information. Instead, exact details are given of numerous places
where Paul founded churches on his later missionary journeys.
They were scattered over a wide area. In the south of Asia
Minor, churches arose in Pisidia and Lycaonia, and, further to
the north, in Galatia. Ephesus constituted a new centre whence
Paul's disciples evangelized the Lycus valley, including the
cities of Laodicea, Colossæ, and Hierapolis. Possibly it is in this
period that we must place the beginnings of the churches of
western Asia Minor known to us from the Apocalypse: Pergamon, Thyatira, Sardis, Philadelphia, and Smyrna. Paul's
missionary journeys in Greece gave birth to churches in Philippi,
Thessalonica, Berœa, and Corinth with its port Cenchreæ. We
hear of no church in Athens before the second century, for the
record in Acts 17: 34 shows that the author was informed of
only the smallest beginning in Paul's time, and it is uncertain
whether this did not die out again. We must take it *cum salis*
when the Apostle says, in Rom. 15: 19, "from Jerusalem and
round about unto Illyricum I have fully preached the gospel",
for he means the western border of the orinet, and there is no
need to suppose that he actually went to Dalmatia.

It is surprising that there should have been quite a large
church in Rome even as early as the time when Paul wrote to
it. We have already expressed the view that it may have owed
its foundation to Antioch.[3] Paul's testimony[4] makes it certain
that it was Gentile Christian, a fact which excludes the possibility of its having been founded by Palestinian missionaries.

It is also a matter for surprise that even yet we should not
have the least information about the beginnings of Christianity
in Egypt. It is true that the Apollos of Acts and 1 Corinthians
came from Alexandria,[5] but we do not learn whether he
became a Christian there, or elsewhere. It is only towards the

---

[1] Acts 13: 5–12   [2] Gal. 1: 21; Acts 15: 23   [3] *Vide supra*, p. 111
[4] Rom. 1: 6   [5] Acts 18: 24

end of the second century that we hear of Alexandrian Christianity; by that time there was a large and virile church of whose history we know nothing at all. Records of a later date furnish grounds for supposing that the capital of Egypt received its Christianity from Rome. In the second century, the gnostic movement found very fertile soil in Egypt,[1] and left a deep mark even on the church catholic of Alexandria, but there is no record of events previously.

These numerous separate churches doubtless exhibited a host of differences in outer appearance and inner life. These differences derived not only from the personalities and the customs of their founders, but also from the geographical and ethnographical, the social and religious, conditions of their members. In general, the Christian missionaries made use of the methods which the Jews of the diaspora had adopted for their own communities, and for propagating their religion. Even if Acts here and there presents events as if they happened according to a stereotyped scheme, yet on the whole it undoubtedly reflects the actual procedure when it describes Paul and his companions travelling from one town to another, and beginning as a rule by preaching in the synagogues. What then followed must have been equally stereotyped, viz. sooner or later a conflict arose and the intruding teachers were driven out of the synagogues. Meanwhile they had made some converts, of whom a few were Jews, and more were proselytes. The nucleus of a Christian church was formed. Then contacts were made between proselytes and serious-minded Gentiles who in some places entered the church and became the majority; then they stamped their character upon it. The Christian message was understood, formulated, and then applied in practice, differing in each case according to the spiritual heritage which the believers had brought with them into the new fellowship.

We have already discussed the fundamental characteristics of the Jewish Christianity of the Jerusalem church, and of the Jewish communities which stood in closest connection with it. In regard to the Gentile churches of the Pauline type, we learn many details in the Pauline letters, especially in those to the Corinthians, which refer to many of the problems peculiar to

[1] Harnack, *Mission*, ii, 705 ff.

newly-founded churches. Most of the members of the Corinthian church belonged to the lower class, as Paul reminded them pretty plainly.[1] As there were also many poor people in the church at Jerusalem, there is reason to think that this state of affairs obtained generally. But we must not forget that members of a higher class also belonged to the same churches. In Corinth, Crispus had been the leader of the synagogue,[2] and, along with him, Paul mentions a certain Gaius as an eminent member of the church.[3] Later, Paul lived in his house,[4] just as he had enjoyed the hospitality of Titius Justus on his first visit.[5] These three persons were not poor, any more than the married couple, Aquila and Priscilla, who found work for Paul. Later they removed to Ephesus, where they possessed, or rented, a large house, and still later they gathered a "house-church" round themselves in Rome.[6]

The differences between poor and rich occasionally came to light in an unpleasant manner. Paul vigorously censured the custom[7] that, in the common love-feasts, the well-to-do should get together, and eat the good things they had brought with them, before the church was fully assembled; whereas the poor, who could not come punctually, nor bring well-filled baskets, had to go without. But there was no rooted hostility of the poor towards the prosperous, nothing of a "proletarian movement".

The only question raised was whether a Christian ought to liberate a slave of his who had become a Christian. Paul dealt with the question from the side of the slave, and explained to him that there would be no point in striving after the earthly freedom of a citizen if one lived in the freedom of Christ.[8] Even in writing to Philemon, it never crossed Paul's mind to come to final grips with the problem of slavery; he simply begged Philemon to receive back in a friendly way his runaway slave— who carried the letter—and to regard him no longer as a slave but as a brother, since, in between, he had become a Christian. Philemon could have done so by enfranchisement, or he might have interpreted the report in a purely human, and Christian,

---

[1] 1 Cor. 1: 26–28   [2] Acts 18: 8   [3] 1 Cor. 1: 14   [4] Rom. 16: 23
[5] Acts 18: 7   [6] *Ibid.*, 18: 2–3; 1 Cor. 16: 19; Rom. 16: 3–5
[7] 1 Cor. 11: 21 f.   [8] *Ibid.*, 7: 21–24

and non-juristic manner. In any case, it was Paul's view that
adherence to Christ was not necessarily followed by a change of
status; on the contrary, each was to remain in the condition in
which he was called.[1]

Similarly in regard to the problem of marriage: the married
man was not to think of divorce, nor the unmarried of marriage.[2] In Corinth, the marriage problem had disturbed the
people's minds, and diametrically opposed answers had
obviously been given. Many brought with them into their new
Christianity the attitude of indifference to sexual relations
which was all too characteristic of ancient times; they regarded
intercourse with the opposite sex as the morally indifferent
satisfaction of a natural requirement like eating and drinking.
The traditional Jewish ethic must have already stood out
against this view, but Paul increased the antithesis still further[3]
by maintaining that a Christian's body was no longer at his own
free disposal, but was the body of the Lord, and was profaned
by union with a loose woman: an argument which brings out
clearly the realistic character of his Christ-mysticism.

On the other hand, there were some Christians in Corinth
who regarded all sexual intercourse as improper—even within
marriage. This was an entirely un-Jewish point of view,
although it was frequent in later antiquity as a consequence of
dualistic philosophy. It was to be met among the Essenes, the
Therapeutæ, and also in Hellenistic Judaism. These latter were
influenced by various forms of Philonism. The prescriptions of
sexual abstinence on grounds of cultus, which were to be found
in the native religions, were also in harmony here. In both
cases, the fundamental feeling was that sexual intercourse was
in itself of lower moral value and unclean. It is significant that
Paul completely agreed with this standpoint, and expressed his
conviction, as if it were an axiom, that it was better for a man
not to touch a woman. He emphasized his desire that all should
be like himself, i.e. unmarried.[4] But he perceived that this was
not possible, and therefore he recommended—as a concession
to human weakness[5]—that existing marriages should be maintained; or, if the parties were unmarried, and if necessary for

---

[1] 1 Cor. 7: 20; cf. Col. 4: 1; 1 Tim. 6:   [2] 1 Cor. 7: 27   [3] *Ibid.*, 6: 15
[4] *Ibid.*, 7: 1; 7: 26   [5] *Ibid.*, 7: 6

avoiding irregular intercourse, that marriage should be entered into. It was not sin, but it led to sufferings and cares which were better avoided in those crucial days when the world was ageing and the End drawing nigh.[1] This view of marriage, in which Paul was at one with the most earnest sections of his church, gained the victory, and decided the whole attitude of the Church of the future. It was a question of opposition to "this world" to which marriage really belonged: any idea of uplifting marriage into the spiritual sphere, as among Stoic thinkers, was foreign to the Pauline horizon.

The church at Corinth made an experiment of another kind, one frequently imitated in the church universal of a later date. Granting that sexual life was of lower moral value, "spiritual marriages" were contracted, i.e. a man and a woman lived together in a house in spiritual and religious fellowship, but without sexual intercourse, a form of asceticism which probably often broke down under the pressure of outraged nature. Paul did not prohibit this custom, but advised those whose consciences were suffering, to change the common life into a true and full marriage if nature demanded it, and there would be no sin.[2]

Yet another marriage problem occupied the Corinthian church,—that of divorce, particularly in the case of mixed marriages. Divorce in those days was an extremely frequent, and legally quite a simple, matter; but what Jesus had said about the indissolubility of marriage was remembered in the Christian church, and it was therefore felt that a man who put his wife away, made her an adulteress.[3] Jesus' words were meant by Him to lay a serious charge on the conscience, but the Church treated it as a legal ordinance, and modified it to make it of practical application. Matthew inserted adultery by the wife as an exception which justified divorce.[4] Paul obviously interpreted the Lord's pronouncement quite freely, and with regard to the circumstances. The general rule held good, for him, that a man and his wife ought not to divorce their marriage; if, however, they did so, they must at least not marry anyone else, but rather become reconciled to one another. Even mixed marriages,

[1] 1 Cor. 7: 9, 26–31, 36   [2] *Ibid.*, 7: 25–28
[3] Mark 10: 6–12   [4] Matt. 19: 9; cf. also 5: 32 with Luke 16: 18

i.e. where one of the parties had remained a pagan, were not to be dissolved, at any rate not at the instance of the Christian spouse. In Paul's opinion, the "sanctity" of the latter partner passed over in some way to the other, as is certainly and admittedly the case among the children who belong to both. Thus Paul extended the idea of the mystical body of Christ into the conception of a naturalistic fact similarly to what we have already seen in the Apostle's teachings on the seventh Commandment.[1] But supernatural fellowship with Christ does not operate in a magical way, nor necessarily lead to the salvation of the pagan partner. If he should desire divorce then she need have no hesitation either from respect to the Lord's word, or because there was hope of her husband's conversion: let him go, since God has so ordained it for him![2] That was the Apostle's own view, and he distinguished it plainly from the Master's commandment.[3] These discussions plainly betray a distress of conscience in Paul as a man who has passed from the license of the world into the earnestness of the new æon; they also show Paul's realism as a mystical believer who wished to hold fast to the divine element among all the material circumstances.

Paul's way of handling an isolated case of sheer immorality is of similar import. A member of the church "hath his father's wife"—we are not told if it was an irregular marriage with the step-mother after the father's death, or something else. In any case, the apostle was angered that the church had not already excommunicated the evil-doer. The church must now assemble, Paul would be with them in spirit, and they must consign the sinner to Satan with a solemn curse in the power of Jesus' name. Satan would fall upon him as he did upon Job, as if the man had been a sacrifice dedicated to himself; he would torment him with illness and finally kill him. That will be his bodily punishment, but the spirit of Christ dwelling in the wrong-doer would finally be saved on the Day of the Lord.[4] This instance shows how the Church was beginning to develop its right to punish a sinner. In cases like these of serious transgression of the Christian moral code, the church in full assembly had the duty and the right of excommunication. The punishment

---

[1] 1 Cor. 7: 8–17; cf. 6: 15–16, and *supra*, p. 135   [2] 1 Cor. 7: 15–17
[3] *Ibid.*, 7: 10, 12   [4] *Ibid.*, 5: 1–5

however was not simply a formal, juristic exclusion from the fellowship, but was, at the same time, a sacramental cursing with supernatural effects. Expulsion from the circle of the elect "saints" handed the sinner over to dæmonic powers and grievous punishments, but they did not deprive him of that redemptive nucleus of divine substance which still dwelt in him even when profaned by him, for it was indestructible, and would ultimately regain its due honour. Thus ecclesiastical law had come into existence at this early stage.

A further question that troubled the Corinthians was that of civil law. Even in this young community of Christian brothers, legal dispute arose about money and property: that in itself was bad enough, writes the Apostle,[1] among Christians who should rather suffer wrong than do it. But it was altogether unfitting that the contending parties should resort to secular courts—as if they themselves were pagan. Their past, of course, made it seem natural and unexceptionable to them. Paul, however, was a Jew, and his tradition[2] was to bring cases to the courts of his fellow-countrymen and his fellow-believers, and thus it appeared to him only right that the same custom should be unconditionally required also of self-respecting Christians. He gave the reason for this demand, however, not by referring to the Jewish custom, which would have helped little, but by insisting that the Christian had a higher status on which to act as judge than that of the whole world beside, including the very angels. Everything was subject to the judgment of the "saints". This being so, ought they at any time and for any reason to recognize pagans as judges over them? No! only Christians could judge Christians; and people expert in the particular issue would be found in the church. As a matter of fact, they were so found in the course of time, and the claim to exercise intra-ecclesiastical justice was maintained even in civil cases. But it is significant that a *corpus juris civilis christianum* was never developed, whereas the Jews codified, in the Talmud, a complete system of civil law.

The discussions of the seventh Commandment already mentioned[3] must have been occasioned by the requirements of the

---

[1] i Cor. 6: 7–8   [2] *Vide supra*, pp. 77 f.
[3] *Vide supra*, pp. 136 f.

Apostolic Decree,[1] for it prohibited fornication. The assumption becomes very probable when we also notice that the prohibition of eating sacrificial meat, which occupies the premier place in the Decree,[2] had raised ill-feeling in Corinth. Strictly speaking, all meat offered for public sale was sacrificial meat, for pagans, too, slaughtered "ritually", and dealt with all slaughter-animals as if they were sacrificial. One would have had to buy *kosher* meat from a Jewish slaughterer to be sure of avoiding sacrificial meat, and there is no need to say that that appears to have been impracticable. The idea of having their own slaughter-house would only have occurred to a church which felt itself firmer on the earth than did the first Christians. Hence there would be genuine difficulty if the prohibition were interpreted strictly, and the stronger members of the church would not wish to have anything to do with this narrowness, and would regard it as a piece of formality that ought not to be tolerated. They would feel that there were no "gods" but only the one God, and even if the pagan gods were really believed in as dæmons, still to Christians there was only the one God, the Creator of the world, and the one Lord, Jesus Christ. Such a faith meant that the idea of worshipping idols found no place in one's heart, and thus the eating of meat which happened to come from a sacrificial animal was quite an indifferent matter which it was foolish to forbid. Paul agreed, within limits, and gave practical advice for avoiding the difficulty. A Christian might in good conscience eat anything offered for sale in the meat markets, and could unconcernedly accept the invitation of a pagan friend to a meal in his house. But if this obvious course were disturbed, one should be on guard. If a joint be explicitly described as of sacrificial meat, and if one's attitude were thus being put to the test, then it became a matter of conscience and one must refuse to eat. If this were not necessary for the sake of one's own conscience, then it should be done out of regard for the weaker brethren to whom sacrificial meat was still in the nature of an offering to the old gods, and therefore a dangerous matter with noxious qualities for a Christian.

[1] Acts 15: 29; 21: 25   [2] *Vide supra*, pp. 108 f.; and also Rev. 2: 14, 20 mentions only these two prohibitions since "sacrificial meat" includes the remainder

This fear did not appear to Paul to be altogether groundless, for even he still regarded the gods as actually existent beings of a dæmonic kind. He who sat at their table for a sacrificial meal, entered into their magic circle and gave himself to their fellowship, i.e. would be possessed by them. Similarly, *mutatis mutandis*, a Christian sitting at the table of the Lord and partaking of the holy meal, became a partner of his Master, became indeed His body, and a participator in His spirit, for Christ had taken up His abode in him. Thus the one fellowship excluded the other. Therefore, according to the Apostle's view, the eating of sacrificial meat was never a neutral action when done in cult-form, for thereby the dæmons gained their destructive power. Thus a Christian might in no circumstances accept an invitation to a sacrificial banquet. And in both respects, as permission and as prohibition, this instruction of Paul's became normative for the entire early church.[1]

The problem just discussed brings us once more into the sphere of a realistic kind of mysticism, which comprehended both the pagan and the Christian cultus in a single set of principles. The Lord's Supper appeared as the Christian sacrificial meal and effected a mystic fellowship with Jesus analogous to the fellowship which the pagan theologians deduced from table-fellowship with their gods;[2] for the idea of the sacredness of a sacrificial meal, and its power of making the participators into brethren, derives from the prehistoric roots of nature religion. What Paul says on this subject could count on being understood in the churches because it was born of their own way of thinking. His mystical sacramentalism,[3] in regard to both the Lord's Supper and baptism, was in the closest contact with the belief of the church of these "Hellenists", and would be readily accepted by them, and, indeed, easily degraded into a rude realism. Baptism must surely have appeared to many a Corinthian gentile Christian as an infallible means of purging away sin, and as a guarantee of future salvation: we only need to carry through Paul's expressive parallel of the death and resurrection of Christ. The "old man" sinking in the water dies the death of Christ, and the "new man" rising from the water,

[1] Just., *Dial.*, 34, 8–35, 1. *Didache*, 6, 3
[2] *Handb. z. N.T.*, Excursus on 1 Cor. 10: 21   [3] *Vide supra*, pp. 121 f.

the Christian, receives the resurrection of Christ, and is thereby delivered from all further moral struggle; once for all he is now saved and assured of salvation. This argument accorded quite logically with the system of thought of the ancient mysticism of redemption—and Paul had to wrestle seriously with such arguments. He cited the example of Israel as a warning; they had enjoyed the benefits of baptism in the Red Sea, a heavenly meal of manna, and a miraculous spring in the wilderness. This was not, as it were, a mere symbol, but a pneumatic reality, for the rock out of which Moses struck the water was Christ Himself! Nevertheless the Israelites perished because they sinned against God and, in particular—let the Corinthians take note—by idol sacrifice, immorality, expressing doubts, and murmuring against God. Their sins wiped out the good effect of the sacraments:[1] and the same could happen again even now to every Christian.

The crudely magical way in which the Corinthians conceived the sacrament was shown by a strange custom which Paul mentioned in passing. If a convert died before receiving baptism, another let himself be baptized "for him". We do not know in what form this took place, but we have evidence from a later period in regard to a similar custom. The corpse was baptized, and another person gave the answers to the liturgical questions instead of the dead. In many places, even the Lord's Supper was administered to the dead man.[2] These ideas prevailed in Corinth, and tended to tone Christianity down to a nature religion. In spite of the fact that all his own ways of thinking were rooted in the same type of ideas, Paul defended himself against them with all his might, and strove in the opposite direction.

Probably derived also from pagan usage[3] in the cultus, was the view that the new initiate stood in particularly close mystic union with the missionary who had administered to him the sacrament of baptism. In this way, little personal communities might have arisen in the Corinthian church, who felt themselves linked to their spiritual father by religious bonds, and not merely by those of sentiment—a feature which, of course,

[1] i Cor. 10: 1–12   [2] *Handb. N.T.*, Excursus on i Cor. 15: 29
[3] Reitzenstein, *Hell. Myst.*, 3rd edition, 40

was out of accord with the Pauline doctrine that the whole church was the one mystical body of Christ. Paul attacked this forming of cliques or parties on more than one ground. The point of view, which has just been described, he set aside with the sharp words:[1] "I thank God, I baptized none of you except Crispus and Gaius, so that none of you can say you have been baptized in my name." He had both preached and organized in Corinth—for one and a half years. But he had baptized very few people, and even those only in the very first period: Stephen who was the first convert,[2] Crispus who was the leader of the synagogue,[3] and a certain Gaius with whom later on he lodged;[4] "for Christ did not send me to baptize, but to preach the gospel". That is a crucial assertion for our understanding of Paul's inmost being, for this practical attitude of his chimes with all he had expressed in writing. For him, all sacramental mysticisms, like all pneumatic enthusiasms, were secondary. Even if he valued these things as means of raising moral conduct to a high level, and even if he gave a true explanation of them to his readers, he used them only because they served to give a graphic representation of the nature of the "new creature", as firmly united with God. But he dropped them as soon as they began to endanger this objective. The people in the church conceived the matter in the opposite way, and held readily to a formalistic sacramentarianism. This made the person of the baptizer particularly important to them; and Apollos the learned Alexandrian, as well as Peter, gained adherents from this standpoint during their work in Corinth. It followed that they themselves must have frequently baptized. If Paul did not do so, the question arises: Who then baptized the converts made by him? Possibly Timothy or Silas? Or even Corinthian Christians, and if so, on what authority? Unfortunately no answer is forthcoming, important though it might be for the origins of spiritual offices.

Paul's letters are particularly important in reflecting various details in regard to Christian officials; they are often enumerated by him,[5] and at their head stand apostles, prophets, teachers. These were the original officials of the Christian

---

[1] 1 Cor. 1: 14–17   [2] *Ibid.*, 1: 16; 16: 15   [3] *Ibid.*, 1: 14; Acts 18: 8
[4] 1 Cor. 1: 14; Rom. 16: 23   [5] 1 Cor. 12: 28; Rom. 12: 6–9

church, and they were maintained as such until the beginning of the second century; the Church Order of the *Didache*, which belongs to this period, affords us the best commentary on Paul's words.[1] The apostles or evangelists travelled about in the world, and preached to those who were still unbelievers; they had no permanent place, because their task was inconsistent with their remaining settled. The prophets, however, worked continuously in one place; they were filled with the divine spirit, and preached to the church as messengers of a higher revelation. They prayed for and with them, but also saw visions, prophesied, and read what was in one's secret heart. They were the "priests in charge" of the church, and conducted its worship as the spirit prompted them. Similarly the teachers addressed the church as heralds of the Word, the visionary and ecstatic types of enthusiasm being little practised by them. Their special function was the explanation of the Scriptures on a basis of reasoning, and pedagogical instruction of a theological kind, even if for the most part in a very primitive form. All these three offices required the entire devotion of the whole of a man's strength and left no room for a secular calling. Hence the officers had a claim upon the churches for their livelihood. The *Didache* sketches this picture, and it agrees with much other evidence from the earliest period.[2]

The distinctions between the different officials were not sharply made, and Paul's mode of expression shows clearly that he was entirely unacquainted with any definite system. It is clear, however, that the terminology was borrowed from the Jewish diaspora.[3] Apostles was the name given by the Jews to the official emissaries who brought the commissions of one congregation, especially that in Jerusalem, to another; the term was used occasionally by Paul in this way.[4] Then in earliest Christendom, the emissaries of the gospel, and especially those who went out from Jerusalem, were described in this way as "apostles of the original church". Paul's right to this title was energetically contested because he could not boast of a Jerusalem commission. He therefore boldly called himself an apostle of Jesus Christ, and insisted that he was, indeed, not

---

[1] *Didache*, 11–15. *Z.W.T.*, 55, 108 ff. [2] Harnack, *Mission*, i, 332–79
[3] *Ibid.*, i, 340. *Handb. z. N.T.*, Excursus on Rom. 1: 1 [4] Phil. 2: 25; 2 Cor. 8:

sent by the Jerusalem church, i.e., by human agency, but had received his commission directly from the Lord Himself.[1] He maintained his position; and soon phraseology began to follow the Pauline model, and named as "apostles" only those disciples who had been called by the Lord Himself, including Paul together with the Twelve. Side by side with this usage, for a long time there remained in existence the older custom which continued to designate every missionary as an apostle.

It requires no proof to show that the office of a teacher, with his task of explaining the Scriptures, was taken over from the Jewish synagogue; and that the office inherited from the Jewish community the high honour in which it was held. On the other hand, we know nothing of a Jewish office of prophets[2] in the time of the early empire. To the Jews of those days, the prophets were either the great Biblical figures of the past, or else, at least in the eyes of the people, outstanding men of God in the present. That was how they regarded John the Baptist, or Jesus, or, here and there, someone who proclaimed the future, and knew how to gain the respect of the masses, even if the Scribes took no official notice. Josephus often tells of such prophets, both true and false.[3] They used to arise in a manner which reminds us in every way of those prophets who came from Jerusalem to Antioch, and prophesied to the church there. The most important of them, Agabos, appeared again, years later, in Judea.[4] The connection between the Christian and Jewish prophets of that time is thus quite clear. But there can be no doubt that the character even ·of the Jewish type of prophets was affected by those whose religion was Hellenistic, and this influence must have extended also among the Christian prophets. Pagan religious societies had prophets as leaders of public worship, a custom which became usual among the Christians. We can see the beginning of the process in the Pauline period. The record of Acts[5] in regard to the church in Antioch is very instructive. At the head we find "prophets and teachers", and these, at the command of the Holy Spirit, chose two men from their number to be "apostles". Thus three kinds

[1] Gal. 1: 1   [2] E. Fascher, *Prophetes*, 161 ff.
[3] Jos., *Ant.*, 15, 373 f., 20, 97; *B.*, 1, 78–80 = *Ant.*, 13, 311–13, B., 2, 259-261 = *Ant.*, 20, 167–170, B., 6, 285 f.
[4] Acts 11: 27–30; 21: 10   [5] Acts 13: 1–3

of officers were known before Paul, but the distinctions between them were still fluid. Moreover, these offices were not instituted by men, but by God; they were "charismatic", i.e. dependent upon a special gift of divine grace. He whom God chose by imparting His own spirit was a teacher, prophet, or apostle; and without this "charisma" no one could exercise the office.

In addition to the spiritual officers who served Christendom as a whole, were others who came into place owing to the needs of daily life, and who, in spite of occasional idealization, really resulted from the sociological circumstances of individual churches. Wherever men unite to form a society a means of conducting business must be devised. Outer organization and financial economy require to be dealt with in a practical manner by appropriate persons. Paul frequently speaks of such persons as "helpers", "leaders", "presidents", "servants", and "those who show mercy". In the opening salutation of Philippians (1: 1), are the characteristic titles of certain offices that became normative for the future: "bishops" and "deacons". Their task was to care for the secular business of the individual church, including the prime concern of looking after those in need. We cannot say with certainty how these titles arose, but it appears to be certain that they were not adapted from Jewish usage. Nor do we gain much light from the analogies which have been adduced from mundane spheres or from the religious organizations of the pagan world. The simplest assumption is that the names were freely given on the model of some leading place—one might readily think of Antioch, and that thence they were adopted by the rest of the Gentile-Christian churches. "Bishop" means "overseer" in all the innumerable applications of the term. The business heads of the church, to whom the finances were confided, might easily be named in this way. "Deacon" means "servant", and in particular, one who serves at table, a waiter. Perhaps this gives a hint of the original significance of the office. The deacons served the church at the Lord's Supper,[1] and carried the bread and wine to the homes of those who were absent. These absent ones were mostly, and as a rule, the sick; and thus the deacons combined their special office with that of looking after the sick. In practice

---

[1] Ignat., *Trall.*, 2, 3; cf. Just., *Apol.*, 65, 5, 67, 5

therefore, they became the assistants of the bishops in discharging services of love to all the members of the church who were in need. According to the *Didache*[1] both these offices were conferred by election, and it must have been the same in the times of Paul. Naturally, in the way the choice fell, was seen the verdict of the spirit working in the church. Paul ever and again described, and taught his readers to value these offices of Christian works of love as of a charismatic character, for the help of the divine spirit was needed to carry them out. Nevertheless, there was a difference for the simple observer, in so far as the bishops and deacons could be chosen from amongst the known men of the church, and what was required of them did not go beyond the capacities of an ordinary person. The charismatics, on the other hand, were supermen to whom God had granted miraculous powers. They saw what no human eye was in a condition to see, and they spoke what was higher than any reason; in addition—they worked miracles; healing the sick[2] and exorcizing dæmons were for a long time afterwards the signs of a genuine charismatic gift. Only the charismatics were officers of the church of God which embraced the whole world, the one church of Christ. The bishops and deacons were merely assistants in the service of the local church, i.e. of an accidental institution existing under mundane conditions, with no independent life-force in the Christian sense. These men were of lower status and lesser authority.[3]

Work in the service of the church was not confined to men. Paul calls[4] an obviously well-to-do and philanthropic lady, named Phœbe, a "deacon" of the church at Cenchreæ, the port of Corinth. Even at that time, there had long been women deacons in the Christian church[5] who, when their sex made them specially suitable, came forward and gave signal help in caring for the poor and the sick, and at the baptism of women. But women also shared in the higher gifts of the spirit. Philip the evangelist had four daughters who were prophetesses,[6] and obviously in the Montanist movement of the second century, women prophets appeared again. In reality, they had never died out from the church, but, under other names and without the

---

[1] *Did.*, 15, 1   [2] 1 Cor. 12: 28-30   [3] *Did.*, 15, 2   [4] Rom. 16: 1
[5] Hinschius, *Kirchenrecht.*, i, 8   [6] Acts 21: 9

official character enjoyed in early Christendom, they have continued to the present day. Thus, even in the Corinthian church, there were women who had been seized by the spirit, who prophesied, and led in prayer. Paul did not agree, for although he held in theory that "in Christ, there is neither Jew nor Greek, neither slave nor freeman, neither male nor female",[1] nevertheless, in practice, he held firmly that woman was subject to man by a divine ordinance in creation. He therefore required that a woman prophet should wear a veil as a sign of this condition, and he put forward this requirement as the general custom in the Christian churches.[2] But in another connection, his own view came unreservedly to expression: a woman must maintain complete silence in the assemblies of the church, and if she wished to know anything, she might ask her husband at home; this also was to him the recognized Christian custom.[3] These views agree with each other, for Paul's point was that, in general, a Christian woman in the assemblies for public worship was condemned to an entirely passive rôle, corresponding with the goodly custom among both Gentiles and Jews. But if the prophetic spirit should seize a woman, then no one was empowered to silence her, or rather, the spirit speaking through her. On the other hand, she must at least veil herself in order to satisfy custom.

What then really happened in the assemblies for worship among the missionary churches? Was there a definite liturgical order, and whence did it come? Out of Judaism, or paganism, or was it a complete novelty? Satisfactory answers have not yet been provided for the many questions that have been raised. There is little or no information about the liturgy in the early writers; probably this was because such matters seemed too self-evident to need recording. Nor would Paul have discussed any of these if disorders had not arisen in Corinth causing him to issue exhortations and to give directions. The gifts of the spirit were a prominent feature in this church, and that in their enthusiastic form.[4] Glossolalia was cultivated eagerly and practised without restraint, and this in such a manner that, at times, several persons were simultaneously seized by it. Paul vigorously

[1] Gal. 3: 28   [2] 1 Cor. 11: 3–16   [3] *Ibid.*, 14: 33–35
[4] *Vide supra*, p. 125

attacks this state of affairs;[1] one must take turn after another, and, in one and the same meeting, only two or at most three prophets. The same held good for those who "speak in tongues"; for them there was the further condition that someone must be present who could interpret their utterances. Otherwise glossolalia must not be practised in the church; for the purpose of public worship was to "edify" the church. What did not serve this end, but only furthered private devotions, must now cease. It was from this standpoint that everything was to be judged which an individual might have to offer, whether prophetic speech giving a revelation, didactic instruction, glossolalia with accompanying interpretation, or hymn singing. "And everything should take place in the appropriate form and in order." We are driven to the conclusion that order was not the strong point of the Corinthians, and that their services must have sometimes been quite tumultuous. But we shall do well not to generalize from the circumstances in Corinth. We ought not even to regard the strongly marked over-emphasis on ecstatic enthusiasm as characteristic in this degree of all churches. There must have been very great differences in this respect.

From the hints which Paul lets fall, we may almost gain the impression that there were no fixed orders of public worship, but that prophetic utterance, glossolalia, didactic addresses, prayer, and singing were contributed according as the spirit led individuals. Nothing is said of Scripture-reading in any of the epistles. Thus it is possible that as a matter of fact the actual order of worship by prayers and hymns, in these early churches, was developed independently out of the actual needs of Christian teaching and of general edification. All this would be without fixed forms, but such as were settled each time by the needs of the moment. Attention has been drawn[2] to the fact that the Hebrew synagogues of the period did not sing any of the Psalms, but that, on the other hand, the practices of the synagogues of the Talmud, and the Hellenistic synagogues of the diaspora, differed greatly from each other. In this matter, however, we are in the happy situation of being able to refer to extant writings. There still survive a number of early

---

[1] I Cor. 14: 26–40   [2] W. Bauer, *Wortgottesdienst*, 21, 11

Christian psalms composed on the model of those in the Old Testament, and having direct parallels in the Psalms of Solomon. Three hymns of this character are preserved in Luke's gospel,[1] Mary's hymn of praise, that of Zacharias, and that of Simeon. In the Revelation of John we find a large number of hymns voiced by the heavenly choirs in counterpart to the earthly services of Christian worship. Most of these are not modelled on Jewish exemplars, but genuinely Jewish hymns without any specific Christian characteristics.[2] They cannot be regarded as original Christian compositions; rather, they are apparently hymns used in the Greek synagogue of the diaspora, and taken over by the Christians. Later, following these examples, genuinely Christian hymns were composed such as other passages in Revelation have preserved,[3] the secondary element being readily traceable. Here we can detect contacts with the forms of worship in the Hellenistic synagogue—the one case where texts are at our disposal. If sermons by prophets or teachers had been preserved we should probably have been able to penetrate further into the study of the liturgy.

The Christian churches would seem to have broken new ground, however, when they drew up formulas of a credal nature expressing their beliefs about the Lord and the redemption He had effected. The most impressive are to be found in the great Christological passages in Philippians, 1 Timothy, and 1 Peter.[4] These are only beginnings, followed by important developments finally issuing in the official creeds; and this not only in the "Apostles' Creed", but also in numerous creeds drawn up much more nearly in the form of hymns.[5]

Thus there is at least the possibility of gaining some conception of the "psalms, hymns, and spiritual songs" which were heard in the early churches;[6] they were all very similar to those used in Jewish forms of worship. But where we tread upon gnostic ground, as in the *Acts of Thomas*,[7] the influences of an

---

[1] Luke 1: 46–55, 68–79; 2: 29–32. Gunkel in the *Festgabe für Harnack* (1921), 43–60
[2] Rev. 4: 8, 11; 15: 3–4, and the double choruses in 11: 15, 17–18 and 7: 10, 12 (where only "the Lamb" is interpolated)
[3] Rev. 12: 10–12, 19: 1–2, 5, 6–8
[4] Phil. 2: 5–11; 1 Tim. 3: 16; 1 Pet. 3: 18–32
[5] Lietzmann in the *Festgabe für Harnack* (1921), 226–42
[6] Col. 3: 16; Eph. 5: 19   [7] *Acta Thomæ*, 6–7, 108–13

exotic religion are open to our hand. Christian poetry soon grew to great proportions in this environment, whereas it died away in the normative church catholic.

At any rate, our observation of the further development of the forms of Christian public worship teaches that though the churches were apparently not fettered as to their liturgy, but possessed a freedom conferred by the spirit, yet they did not produce new and peculiarly Christian forms of service; rather they lost all originality. The earliest period was marked by the tempestuous working of the spirit. But, as a rule, the Christian churches soon adopted the forms used by the Hellenistic synagogues, and they constitute the foundation of Christian public worship to the present day. The diets of worship were not only suited for the edification of the church proper, but, similarly to the services of the synagogue, could also be attended by unbelievers who might become converts to the new teaching. Side by side with the diets stood the celebration of the Lord's Supper, as a cultus-act properly so-called, and here, as in the Jewish ceremonial meals, only the members of the church might take part.[1] We have already seen[2] how Paul taught his believers to observe this feast. It was always held in the evening;[3] it was attended as the love-feast of the church; and each one contributed according to his means.

The Lord's Supper commenced with a blessing, followed by the breaking of a loaf, the pieces of which were distributed to be ritually eaten by the participators. All who ate of this bread, which was the body of Christ, became united in one body among themselves, the body of Christ.[4] Then began the meal proper, which ran its course in agreeable fellowship, and due enjoyment of the food and drink. After the meal, the president pronounced a blessing upon a glass of wine, and gave it to them all to drink—they now drank the blood of Christ. From the feast of the Lord's Supper celebrated in this way, many of the greetings must originate that we find in the Pauline letters, or that are preserved in later formularies as their earliest liturgical material; e.g. "Lift up your hearts," cried the liturgist to the church which had sat down to the meal while still burdened by the cares of the day. The exhortation frequently met with in

---

[1] *Did.*, 9, 5   [2] *Vide supra*, pp. 124 f.   [3] 1 Cor. 11:20–34   [4] *Ibid.*, 10:17

the conclusion of the Pauline letters:[1] "Greet one another with the holy kiss", urged the Christians to unite with one another in a conciliatory attitude of mind, as enjoined by Matt. 5: 23 f., and in brotherly love before making the sacrifice.[2] The greeting: "The grace of our Lord, Jesus Christ, and the love of God, and the fellowship of the Holy Spirit be with you all," was well fitted to introduce the sacred ritual proper. The church would then respond: "and with your spirit" as it does to-day. Since we find this formula at the end of 2 Corinthians[3] we may conclude that the letter was intended to be read aloud in a "closed" assembly of the church, and that the celebration of the Lord's Supper was to follow the reading.[4] Presumably, the custom held similarly with regard to the writings addressed to the whole church.

The circumstances reflected in the story of Paul's life, show that there was a marked cleavage in early Christianity. On the one side was the Jewish-Christian church at Jerusalem, conscious of its roots in Judaism, and true to the Law in a way that constantly threatened it with a Pharisaic narrowness. On the other side, was the decided repudiation of Jewish ritual, in accordance with the preaching of the Antiochene Hellenists, and of Paul. We have already shown that the solution reached in the compromise of the Apostolic Decree,[5] was intended to form a basis for bridging the cleavages in the churches of the diaspora. This Decree of the Jerusalem church was known in Corinth about the year A.D. 52. We may well suppose that Peter brought it there, and thus to have occasioned the discussion into which Paul enters in his first epistle. If so, then Peter stood for compromise as far as the Judaizers were concerned.[6] The Decree conceded to the Gentiles freedom from the Law, and burdened them only with a single ritual requirement so as to enable Jewish Christians to enjoy table-fellowship with them. On the other hand, the Pauline requirements went further by demanding full freedom from the Law, and his theory was that Jewish Christians were likewise free. His views were set aside tacitly by the Decree, but, we may suppose,

---

[1] Rom. 16: 16; 1 Cor. 16: 20; 2 Cor. 13: 12; 1 Thess. 5: 26, cf. 1 Pet. 5: 4

[2] *Didache*, 14, 1–3   [3] 2 Cor. 13: 13   [4] Lietzmann, *Messe u. Herrenmahl*, 229

[5] *Vide supra*, pp. 108 f.   [6] Hirsch, *Z.N.W.*, 29, 67 ff.

definitely and clearly so in the course of the negotiations among
the churches. This meant, however, that Paul's apostolic
authority was contested. In the young church at Corinth,
various parties were formed; each adhered to the person of
some leader. Those who were faithful to Paul opposed the
adherents of Peter. The third group mentioned is the Apollos
party, who may be regarded as those having a turn for philosophy, for Apollos was an Alexandrian, and a learned man.[1]
To them, the Pauline theology of the cross was intolerable,[1]
because they sought a rational foundation for the new faith, and
one that would appeal to the Greek spirit. Finally, Paul mentions a fourth party in Corinth. They named themselves "of
Christ", in emphatic distinction from the others, obviously
because they would not allow that Paul and the other leaders
were sufficient authorities, and because they relied upon
alleged revelations given by the Risen Lord. As against this
party, Paul remarked with a certain irony that he himself really
belonged to Christ as much as certain other people, and that he
himself had been blessed in high degree with divine revelations.[2] Thus the most varied tendencies wrestled with each other
in this church: ecstatic enthusiasm, Hellenistic "wisdom", the
Pauline doctrine of freedom, and the Petrine semi-Judaism. The
last was particularly dangerous to Paul's plain requirements,
because its aim was to appease Jerusalem, a policy which
threatened to ruin the success of his life's work. Paul did not
wish merely to keep the Gentiles free from the Law—in
Galatians he had passionately struggled for this and against the
Jewish emissaries—but also to win the Jews over to the new
freedom of the children of God. To him, Christ was nothing
else than the end of the Law, for Jews and Gentiles alike, and
that was what he laid down before the Roman church in his
weightiest epistle.

The Pauline letters afford only incidental glimpses of this
contest between old and new, but they make it possible for us
to surmise with what passion and earnestness the struggles were
being fought everywhere in the numerous churches of the
newly-won Gentile Christians, viz. those founded by Paul, the
missionary churches of Barnabas and the other Hellenists,

[1] 1 Cor. 2: 1–5   [2] *Ibid.*, 10: 7; 12: 1–4

including the important church of Rome. All of these churches had to settle their attitude to the question of the Law, and did so, as the future was to show, in the sense of freedom from it. Jewish radicalism, in the matter of the Gentile churches, had had an isolated success in Galatia and perhaps also at an earlier date in Antioch; but it had no future, and served only to keep Jewish Christians faithful to the Law. As time went on, it was, in practice, more and more confined to the churches in Palestine and its immediate surroundings. In the empire beyond, the Gentile Christians were free, and they attracted Jewish converts to themselves.

Other and smaller questions continued to disturb consciences —about the worthiness and necessity of asceticism of various forms, including abstinence from wine, and vegetarianism,[1] the latter being frequent and regarded as devout among widely differing kinds of people at that time. With the advent of Apollos, arose the question of the attitude of the young religion to Greek philosophy, and educated Christians were always troubled by the problem. Paul's disciple, Epaphroditus, laboured as a missionary in the Lycus valley, and founded churches in Colossæ and Laodicea. There, in Phrygia, spirits rose up out of the ground, and through the swelling clouds of syncretistic speculation, the phantom of gnosticism already showed its enigmatic face, to the wrath of Paul as he lay in prison.[2] The Apostolic Age, with its simple antitheses and its broad outlines, was drawing to an end, and the omens of a new period were visible on the horizon.

[1] Cf. *Handb. z. N.T.*, Excursus on Rom. 14: 1   [2] *Op. cit.*, Excursus on Col. 2: 23

Chapter Nine

THE ROMAN EMPIRE AND ITS RELIGIOUS LIFE

THE BATTLE OF ACTIUM HAD BEEN FOUGHT, THE LEUCADIAN
Apollo had pressed the myrtle of victory upon the brow
of Octavian, and Cleopatra had chosen death. There was an
end to the century-old struggle which the Greek world, in conjunction with the orient, had fought against Roman encircle-
ment. Once for all Rome had conquered, and from mud,
destruction, and blood, arose the miracle of the statecraft of
Augustus, the empire of peace which comprised the whole
world, the Imperium Romanum. Its material foundation was
assured by the army, which had been trained in the ancient
Roman tradition and by the magnificently organized system of
administration. Its soul, however, was the "Latin genius"
which was born in these days. The gift of oratory and a turn
for practical philosophy had been put into swaddling clothes by
Cicero. But a simple conception of life, a healthy understanding
of human nature, a flair for politics and law, a sense of form
and value, were its heritage from ancient times. Livy now
endowed it with a glorious history and a mythology of an
origin from heroes. Horace originated a lyric poetry, which
combined a sunny enjoyment of life with meditation and fine
patriotism. Ovid added to this compound the charming
elements of a graceful eroticism, until bitter experiences drove
him into the arms of a more learned Muse. But Virgil, above
all others, understood the deepest nature of his people when he
sang to them the saga of the Æneid, which the Romans were
never tired of reciting as if inspired, and the images of which
stir the hearts of the Latin races to the present day. It is indeed
the case that the reign of Augustus not only saw Jesus born,
but also that Latin genius which for nineteen centuries has
determined the history of Europe.

But Horace was right. The Greeks, who had been conquered
by the soldiers, had long gained a spiritual victory over the
conquerors; for when the world empire arose, the Latin genius
had not only been suckled with Greek milk, and educated at the

Greek school, but had clothed its native religion in a Greek garment. Elements which were not now at home sank into oblivion. But cultured people in Rome had learned from Greek philosophy how to apply rationalistic criticism fully to traditional religion. When, therefore, the dreadful decades of the Civil War had destroyed all the ethical foundations of public and private life, religious feeling and practice had also suffered very severe damage.

It is a highly valuable testimony to the statesmanlike genius of Augustus that he regarded the restoration of a sound religion as one of his most urgent tasks. And it is characteristic of his practical sense that he did not command sermons to be addressed to the people, but that he reinstated, in large degree, the ancestral religion as a state function. He rebuilt the ruined temples and, by means of ceremonial worship, sought to win the masses of spectators to take some part. In this way, the lost religion was to be given from above to the people. It was the right way, but there would have had to be a genuine religion in the upper circles if it was to penetrate below. This was not the case. The æsthetic mythology of Horace, which was instinct with genuine patriotism, well reflected the mind of the best men who surrounded the emperor. That at best was what his newly appointed augurers and pontifices thought; and the children of the aristocracy, of the year 17 B.C., must have had even less religious feelings when they sang Horace's *Carmen Sæculare* than the choir of a large modern city in rendering one of Reger's Psalms. Hence, the emperor's restoration of religion only availed as an act of imperial policy. It was the incarnation of an æsthetic culture conditioned by patriotism. In this last sense it entered into the being of the Latin genius as a permanent quality. But it was not religion.

The autochthonic ideas and powers of the simplest conceptions of a nature religion were still alive among the masses of the people, as also were the religions of the east which were streaming through numerous channels into the west. Of these, the most important were the Egyptian cults which, already for nearly a century, had carried on a vigorous and successful propaganda. The buildings, pictures, and inscriptions of Pompeii give the necessary information in these matters. After

Pompey had imported them as slaves, the Jews were added to the Egyptians and played a significant part in Rome in the period of Augustus. Under Claudius, the first Christians came to Rome; but they spoke Greek, and appeared at first to be adherents of the Jewish communities, who also used Greek as their mother tongue. It was not until the middle of the third century that the Roman Christians made use of Latin in church worship, and thus at last were culturally at home in Rome. It follows that Christianity was not influenced by the west during the times when its foundations were being laid; it grew up in the east, and arrived ready-made in the west. Therefore, if we wish to examine the conditions under which it was first modelled, we must consider the religious circumstances of the orient in the time of the early empire. But even that is an extremely difficult problem, for the literary sources of this period are almost entirely lacking; the surviving religious writings of the eastern people come from either a definitely older, or a distinctly later, period. Scarcely any contemporary literature is extant, witnessing to the faith which lived in the people, and not the mere sacerdotalism of the priests, or a matter of theological speculation. Thus we have to make the attempt to draw a picture by combining the surviving fragments. The correctness of this picture will, at best, be supported only by its own inner probability.

Antioch, the cradle of Hellenistic Christianity, is hidden from us, inaccessible beneath the dwelling-houses and gardens of the present day Antakie. The second important scene of Paul's activity was in western Asia Minor. This region has been largely explored by the systematic excavation of the most significant towns, and answers have been found for many of the questions important for our purpose. Nowhere in the world do the epigraphs speak so clearly and so frequently of the greatness of Alexander, who used the Greek sword, and carried to the east the might of the Greek spirit. The Hellenistic period began when he founded his empire and when the marshals who succeeded him organized the states into which it was subsequently divided.

A new economic civilization, with a new intellectual outlook, sprang from, and prospered in, the old Greek colonies along the western coasts of Asia Minor. Alexander himself consecrated the majestic temple of the city goddess Athena in Priene. King Lysimachus rebuilt the city of Ephesus by the sea, and protected it with mighty walls. Miletus, which had been destroyed, rose again from its ruins and the royal residence of the Attalids was built upon the city hill of Pergamon. All these achievements of the period of the Diadochoi bring the pride of their Greek nationality visibly to expression. They were conscious of standing under the protection of the Greek gods and they stamped their images and emblems upon their coinage. Numerous dedications found among the inscriptions tell us of their public and private worship. Their temples dominated the city and spoke to the citizens of their faith in the same way as the medieval cathedrals of European cities testify to the religion of the times in which they were built.

Zeus, Athena, and Dionysos lived upon the height of Pergamon. Asklepios had his great temple in the valley below the city. Half-way up the hill, the sanctuaries of Demeter and Hera were to be found. Priene felt itself to be the daughter of Athens, and honoured Athena Polias as its tutelary goddess; her huge temple excelled any other building in the little town, including the area dedicated to Asklepios in the market-place, and the temple of Demeter on the northern declivity. Miletus had preserved its ancient tradition, and the temple of Apollo Delphinios constituted the centre of the cult even for the Hellenistic city. The famous sacred street leading to the shrine of the oracle of Apollo in Didyma gained a new significance when, about 300 B.C., two architects, from Ephesus and Miletus, began to build the marvellous temple whose ruins, even to-day, fill spectators with astonishment and awe.

Ephesus was entirely dominated by the worship of the "Great Artemis". Her ancient temple, which was rebuilt in ever greater dimensions after each destruction, was the most impressive building in the city, one of the seven wonders of the world even after being burnt by Herostratos in 355 B.C. Cheirocrates rebuilt it more magnificently and thus it stood' until it was destroyed by the Goths in A.D. 263.

The Artemis who was worshipped here, however, was not the Greek huntress, the virgin sister of Apollo, although the city coinage, throughout the entire Hellenistic period, represents her in this way. Rather she was the mountain mother-goddess native to Asia Minor, the mistress and protectress of wild animals. In the Roman period the coinage no longer shows the bashful figure of the Hellenistic copy, but faithfully reproduces the original temple idol. According to the evidence of numerous replicas, this idol must have been greatly favoured in the time of the Empire, a partiality which can only be explained by the ever increasing influence of oriental religion upon the civilization as a whole. This image was carved in ebony. It represented a woman standing bolt upright. Her body was bound from head to foot by wrappings between which a number of metal bosses can be seen. At a later period sculptors reproduced these bosses as the numerous breasts of the goddess of fertility. A crescent moon was shown behind her head which was decorated by a mural crown; in her hands, which are stretched out from the body towards the right, she holds long sheaves, or even ears of corn. Lions creep fawningly up to her arms, and deer stand on either side of her. This Asiatic mountain goddess was the mistress of the soil of Ephesus when the Greeks took possession in early times. The colonists gave her a Greek name, a Greek temple, and many Greek forms of worship, but she remained Asiatic, and her worship must have kept alive the native religion. But our sources are not sufficient to give us all the details.

From Ephesus, her worship came to penetrate the Archipelago and the Greek motherland. It also spread far and wide in the interior of Asia Minor. In many cities a closely analogous development took place, for it is this very goddess that is meant by Artemis Leucophryene of Magnesia on the Meander, as is seen both in her character and in the form of her image. In the same way, this Asiatic Artemis is to be found in various places, but with a great variety of epithets.[1] In Ephesus itself at the north-east corner of the Panajir-Dagh, about half a mile from the temple of Artemis, the site of a cultus has been found where the "Mother of the Mountain" was worshipped under the open sky.[2] She was also known as the "Phrygian Mother"

---

[1] *Pauly-W.*, v, 2767. Roscher, *Lex.*, i, 593
[2] J. Keil in *Oesterr. Jahreshefte*, 1926, 256 ff.

On numerous votive tablets she is represented as a woman wearing a mural crown, and standing between two lions, with a shell and a tambourine in her hands, a typical representation of Cybele. Her youthful companion, who is always present, we should call Attis. These Greeks named him Apollo, but this fact shows clearly how all these names were only "echo and smoke". The description of the goddess as the "Mother of the Mountain" is the nearest approach to a definitely religious conception. She was worshipped as Artemis in Ephesus in the great temple, and as the Phrygian goddess on the lower slope of the hill. In both places she was presented in Greek form, but in different ways.

At first the priests of the Ephesian Artemis were eunuchs who had probably emasculated themselves according to Phrygian rite while in ecstasy. The priestesses were virgins. This is what Strabo records on the basis of his sources, but he briefly adds, on the ground of his personal observation about 50 B.C., "Many of the old customs are still followed, many are not".[1] This notice means that the characteristic of the cultus just mentioned may not have been preserved to the time of the apostle Paul. In the days of Alexander, however, this Artemis may have been hymned as the leader of a tumultuous throng of Mænads,[2] and, according to the inscriptions, the mysteries of Artemis must have existed until the third century A.D. In the second century these ceremonies appear to have begun to suffer neglect, for, about A.D. 200,[3] they were newly financed and reinstituted by private subscription. A romantic writer of the third century A.D. describes the great annual festival of Artemis, in which those who took part indulged in the greatest excesses.[4] The *Kuretes* who were connected in some way with the cult of Artemis, brought mystical sacrifices in the grove Ortygia, near the harbour, when they celebrated their feasts.[5] The mysteries of Demeter were regularly celebrated in Ephesus even in the time of the Empire, although in connection with emperor worship: evidences of this have come down to us from the eighties of the first Christian century. A religious society localized outside the city united the mysteries of Demeter with

[1] Strabo, 14, p. 641   [2] Plutarch, *de aud. Poet.*, p. 22a, *de superstit.*, p. 170a
[3] *Ephesuswerk*, iii, 144, no. lix, 156, no. lxxii, 29; cf. C.I.G. 3002, Hicks, *Inscr.*, 596
[4] *Achill. Tat.*, 6, 3   [5] Strabo, 14, p. 640

those of Dionysos.[1] Mystics of Dionysos were still to be found
in Ephesus in the time of the Antonines,[2] and afford a welcome
addition to the large amount of extant evidence in regard to
the cult of Dionysos which was observed in the theatre. The
Dionysian carnival, celebrated at the principal feast of the god,
drew the whole town even in the Roman period.[3] The coinage
is especially instructive as to how strongly the mysteries determined the atmospheres and attitudes of the Hellenistic period.
In 200–55 B.C., not only in Ephesus, but in all the towns of the
entire kingdom of Pergamon and beyond, silver coins known
as *kistofori* were struck as common money. On the obverse was
the mystical kista of Dionysos with a snake in a garland of ivy;
on the reverse, a bow in a carrier—perhaps belonging to
Artemis—between two snakes. Thus both sides reproduce the
symbols of the mystery cult.[4] The inscriptions fully support the
widespread occurrence of the mysteries which we may deduce
from the coinage. Thus, e.g., the cult of Dionysos was held in
high honour in Pergamon. A college of *bukoloi*, i.e. cattlemen,
is often mentioned, and they used to celebrate the mysteries of
the god in the period of the early Empire; an imperial rescript
dealt specially with them.[5] The mysteries of Mētēr Basileia[6]
were still in existence in the early Roman period and the
ancient mysteries of the *Kabeiroi* of Pergamon are lauded by the
orator Aristides, in the Antonine period.[7] A calendar of the
imperial feasts preserved on an inscription, indicates a special
feast for the mysteries in the month of June.[8]

In Pergamon we are now in a position to observe one of the
ways in which, as early as the Hellenistic period, Asiatic religion
penetrated into the Greek world. In the year 189 B.C., King
Eumenes II married the Cappadocian princess Stratonice, and
she brought her home god, Sabazios, into the royal palace of
Pergamon and worshipped him as her special protector. However, he showed himself gracious to the Attalid house as well,
and, indeed, often appeared to their help, so that, in the year

[1] Dittenb., *Syll.*, 2, 820. Hicks, *Inscr.*, nos. 506 n, 595
[2] Hicks, *Inscr.*, nos. 600–602   [3] Plut., *Anton.*, 24. Lucian *de saltat.*, 79
[4] Regling, *Antike Münzen*, 58 f. Head, *Historia Nummorum*, 534, 575
[5] *Inscr. Perg.*, no. 482, 485–87; cf. 248   [6] *Inscr.*, no. 334
[7] Pausanias, i, 4, 6, Inscr., no. 252, 26. Aristides, *or.*, 53, 5; 2, p. 469, Keil
[8] *Inscr.*, no. 374

135 B.C., Attalus II assigned him official worship, both in the temple of Athena Nicephoros, and in her celebrated sacred grove in the valley below the city. Sacrifices were to be offered to him, and processions and mysteries celebrated. He appointed a member of the royal house to be a priest of the god.[1] In this way the cult and its mysteries[2] spread among the Greeks of the kingdom of Pergamon in the most vigorous manner.

The cult of Sabazios, which originated in Phrygia and Lydia, introduced many new elements into the mysteries of Dionysos. The kistophoric coinage bears witness, among other matters, to this fact.[3] But its greatest significance is in its connection with the Judaism of Asia Minor which equated Sabazios Dionysos with Yahweh Sabaoth. This identification was known in Rome as early as 139 B.C., and occurs again in the imperial epoch; for Plutarch uses it for explaining to his readers the meaning of the Sabbath.[4] In the period of the earliest empire, a college of the "Sabbatists", with a "President of the Synagogue" is noted on an inscription on a wall of rock in the neighbourhood of Elæussa in Cilicia.[5] We are probably justified in claiming this as a witness of some such compound of Jewish with Sabazic elements. Clearly recognizable threads lead from this city to the communities which were very widespread in Asia Minor and on the northern shore of the Black Sea. These communities worshipped the *Hypsistos*, the anonymous "highest" god. Such facts clearly show the connection between the two religions which, on the surface, appear so different.[6] One of their memorials, belonging to the second century B.C., has been found in the present-day Panderma, the port of the kingdom of Pergamon on the Sea of Marmora. Hence we may probably regard the Judaization of the cult of Sabazios as a new phenomenon occurring alongside the purely pagan form, both in Pergamon and far beyond its borders, even at such an early date. It is probably an accident that the extant inscriptions in regard to the communities in Pergamon and Miletus

---

[1] *Inscr.*, no. 246, iv; cf. Dittenberger, *or.*, 332   [2] Roscher, *Lex.*, iv, 250
[3] *Ibid.*, *Lex.*, iv., 236
[4] Valer. Max., i, 3, 3. Tacitus, *hist.*, v, 5. Plutarch, *quæst conv.*, p. 671 f.
[5] Dittenberger, *Or. inscr.*, 573
[6] Cumont, *Orient. Rel.* (3rd edit.), 59, 231, n. 60. Roscher, *Lex.*, iv, 238, 263, 266. *Pauly-W.*, ix, 448

date only from the second century A.D.,[1] for the college of Sabbatists of Elæussa, just mentioned, existed very near to Paul's time and was also geographically not far distant from his home town of Tarsus; this fact is important for the study of the history of the Church.

Another form of the penetration of foreign religion into the Greek world is illustrated by an inscription carved about 200 B.C. on the temple of Isis in Priene. The city ordered the regular celebration of the cult of Isis, provided the means for it, regulated the income of the priests, and decreed that only the officially appointed Egyptians could offer the sacrifices exactly according to the rite; and every unofficial person offering a sacrifice was threatened with a fine of a thousand drachmas. This corresponds entirely with the Egyptian conception of the value of the proper forms of the cultus. The Ptolemies zealously spread the cult of Sarapis which they had founded, so that, as early as the third century B.C., it had gained a firm foothold in Greece, a fact which shows an active interest on the side of the Greeks. Obviously, the missionary work of the Egyptian priests met with acceptance, and gained adherents in such numbers and importance that, in the end, the city authorities agreed to support the cultus. Like all the Egyptian temples in Asia Minor, the building dedicated to the cultus was itself of the most modest size, and was probably erected by the private subscriptions of the group concerned.

A similar inscription from the same period has been preserved from the neighbouring town of Magnesia on the Meander,[2] where the priesthood of Sarapis obtained a regular agreement from the city authorities, and salaries were fixed. In this case also the temple is a very small building. It would appear that the Egyptian prophets at first sought and found believers among the lower classes, whence the movement spread to other classes. Only under the Empire did it grow to be the normal thing, to the extent that the Egyptian gods were depicted on the coinage. Specimens have been found in Magnesia and Pergamon. Even in Ephesus in the time of the Empire, evidence is not lacking of the worship of Isis and

[1] *Inscr. Perg.*, nos. 330, 331, Dittenberger, *or.*, nos. 755, 756
[2] *Inscr. Magnesia.*, no. 99

Sarapis;[1] and we may assume with certainty that, in the Hellenistic period, this cultus possessed adherents in the port; but the temples of these gods will have had the same insignificant form as that customary in other places. The mighty temple in the market-place belonging to the middle of the second century A.D., which twentieth century scholars have inclined to regard as a Sarapeum,[2] must be one of the three dedicated to the emperor, which Ephesus proudly regarded as its principal temples beside that of Artemis.[3] Neither Isis nor Sarapis appears on Ephesian coinage.

There is no doubt that, in addition to these religions, of which there is so much evidence, innumerable others pressed their way into western Asia Minor in the period of the early Empire. Of these other religions, the memorials either tell us nothing, or date only from a later period. It is noteworthy that inscriptions never speak about the Jews although, by that time, they had long been very numerous in those cities, and had carried on their missionary work amongst the Greeks with some success. What is known with certainty is sufficient to give us a basis upon which we can carry our inquiries further, for we must assume that the principal views and ideas of these religions were known in the milieu of the growing Christendom of Asia Minor.

We must now go on to take account of a new religion which entered into relation with the manifold complex which we have just described. This new religion can be traced from the days of Alexander in a well-marked line through the centuries. About the beginning of the Christian era, it came forward so definitely that all other expressions of religious life were overshadowed by the various forms of emperor worship.[4] Among the people of the orient, it was traditional to regard the king as an incarnation of the godhead. The conception was also current among the Greeks in such a way that a gifted person, and especially a successful statesman or soldier, was held to be the revelation of a divine being. This belief was frequently expressed in a myth to the effect that he was of divine descent, or

---

[1] *Ephesus*, i, 70, 97, 173, iii, 97. Hicks, *Inscr.*, no. 503
[2] J. Keil, *Oestr. Jahreshefte*, 1926, 266
[3] Cf., the coins of the four Neokorate in Head, *catal. Ionia*, pl. 14, 6
[4] *Pauly-W.* suppl., iv, 806. Wendland, *Kultur*, 2nd edition, 123, 146

⁻lse by canonizing him as a "hero". Alexander's achievements from the Bosphorus to the Indus were so tremendous that other men never hoped to outvie him. Indeed, both in the orient and in Greece, it came to be felt appropriate to pay divine honours to this god in human form. The revelation of actual power is always stronger than dogmatic theories, and therefore, under the impress of this extraordinary personality, even the Greeks went beyond regarding Alexander as a "hero", and worshipped him fully as a god. Political considerations played an additional part in the highest circles, and thus the cult of Alexander was furthered and, indeed, soon obligatory. The Diadochoi had already moved in this direction, to lend additional support to their own power. When they also claimed to be divine kings, they invested the idea in the Greek forms which had been accorded to Alexander.

In that region of Asia Minor over which we have cast our eyes there is a small shrine for Alexander in Priene,[1] an "Attaleion" in Teos,[2] and a temple for Eumenes II in Miletus.[3] Numerous inscriptions record the prevalent practice of emperor worship in the kingdom of Pergamon, the forms of which became ever richer as time went on. The most instructive example comes from an inscription in the little town of Elaia,[4] not far from Pergamon. The last king of the little kingdom, Attalos III (138–133 B.C.), returned from war victoriously into his capital. Thereupon the citizens of Elaia decided to award him the following honours: he should be given a golden garland; a statue five cubits high should be set up in the temple of Dionysos "in order that there he might be a companion of the gods"; and a gilded, equestrian statue should be set up in the market-place near the altar of Zeus, on which "the royal priest" was to burn incense every day. Since he had arrived home on the eighth of the month, the eighth of every month was to be a feast-day, and the anniversary of his return was to be celebrated by an annual procession with appropriate sacrifices. The inscriptions upon the columns of the statues give him the divine predicate "Euergetes", i.e. "the well-doer" or "the beneficent",

---

[1] *Inscr.*, nos. 205, 206, 108, 75
[2] Cf. *Inscr. Perg.*, no. 240. Dittenberger, *or.*, 326, 20
[3] *Sitz. Akad. Berlin*, 1904, 86. *Miletwerk*, i, 9, pp.144 ff.
[4] *Inscr. Perg.*, no. 246. Dittenberger, *or.*, 332

and call him the son of the divine king, Eumenes Soter, i.e. of the "Saviour". Such was the insipid, and hence foolish, excess to which the formerly vital appreciation of the genius of Alexander had descended in the course of two centuries. Only conventional reverence remained when the kingdom passed to the Romans; and it is not surprising that Roman generals and governors were accorded similar fustian.

However, with Roman rule, a somewhat new element entered this Greek world: the cultus of the goddess Roma,[1] i.e. the personified genius of the city which had become a world power. It represented, for the empire as a whole, what the "Tyche" of the Greek towns meant to those towns. It was an abstraction artificially cultivated, and did not spring from the soil of a genuinely religious feeling. It was characteristic of times in which the persons of the ancient gods had become shadows and the indestructible religious feeling of the people endeavoured to conceive the powers of history in new forms.

Cæsar tried to use the state-form of Hellenistic kingship in order to give graphic expression to the essential meaning of Rome's historical development. It was for this reason that the republican ideology, which was already approaching its doom, used its last flickering powers to plunge the dagger into his heart, but that ideology crumbled over his corpse. Octavian Augustus was the heir of Cæsar, of both his power and his conceptions; he became the great monarch who ruled the entire world. Although he still wore the republican toga in the sight of the Romans of the city, yet the world, and especially the east, saw him wearing the purple mantle of Alexander. One does not need to say that the same divine honours were offered to him as had been accorded to the kings of the diadochian dynasties, and which had not been denied to the Roman officials who were their successors. At this stage, however, a new content was given to a form of honour which had sunk into being the mere flattery of the court. The entire Roman world felt it a marvellous experience, when, after a hundred years of distress and bloodshed, there was peace at last; when anarchy gave place to a uniform government, destruction to reconstruction, caprice to law, and confusion to order—and it was

[1] Roscher, *Lex.*, iv., 130. Wissowa, *Relig. u. Kultus d. Römer*, 2nd edition, 341

one man who had brought all this about by his immense power, Augustus. Gigantic upheavals, whether for good or for evil, both in nature and in history, make even the dullest souls feel the shadow of men of higher powers, men who determine the course of world events. Then the imperfect intuitions of the masses proceed to fill the forms of customary religion with new life. This was the case now.

For a long time, the figure of Alexander, glorified with the halo of divinity, had filled the imagination of the peoples. History, mythology, and delight in the fabulous, had created an enchanting picture of his glory and boundless power. In his person, the Hellenistic, divine kingship had come for the first time to a credible actuality. And now the appearance of a kingly god-upon-earth was repeated in still greater dimensions in Augustus; and the world echoed again with his praises. The ancient yearning of the orient was mixed with Greek belief and Etruscan augury when Virgil,[1] at the commencement of the Augustan period, prophesied a saviour who would descend upon earth as a divine child, wipe out the sins of the past, and introduce the golden age; or when, in the years of realization, he depicted the glory of the new epoch with the brilliant colours of the legend of Alexander. His prophetic song found a spirited echo among all the poets of Rome; to them Augustus was a god upon earth, *præsens divus*, the prince of an era similar to paradise.

This was not merely poetic phraseology; it was genuine homage felt by those who could express authentically the feeling of the people; it was an expression of religious feeling in so far as this sceptical upper class was at all capable of religion. At the same time it was the spirit of the east which now celebrated its greatest triumph in Rome. A glance at Asia Minor shows plainly how the Hellenistic form of belief in its kings, which had become outworn, rose again with a power that cast its beams far and wide, owing to the impress of the super-man, Augustus. Even Pompey had been welcomed as the longed-for prince of peace,[2] but in vain. Later, in 48 B.C., the cities of Asia Minor greeted Julius Cæsar as a son of god, a god upon earth, and a universal saviour of human life.[3] Forty years later still,

---

[1] *Eclogues*, 4. *Æneid*, 6, 791 ff.   [2] Dittenberger, *Syll.* (3rd edition), no. 751
[3] *Op. cit.*, no. 760

these hopes were realized, and a well-known calendar, inscribed at Priene,[1] sings ravishing melodies about the good fortune of the Augustan period. "Has the birthday of the divine emperor given us more joy, or more benefit? Is it not rightly to be regarded as equally important with the beginning of the world, if we look, not only at the fact, but also at its meaning? For he has re-established an institution which was crumbling and hurrying to destruction. He has given another outlook to the entire world, a world which otherwise would have much preferred destruction if the universal blessing had not been born for all—the emperor." Hence, in the whole of Asia Minor, his birthday, 23rd September, was in future to be New Year's Day, "For this day was the beginning of the message of peace which was conjoined with his person"—the word used is *euangelia*, at that time lightly spoken, but later to become full of meaning. What the people of Asia Minor meant was really nothing other than what the Church, from the sixth century onward, put in a somewhat different form, viz. the recognition of the fact that the beginning of a new epoch was brought about by the epiphany of God upon earth; it therefore dated a new era from the redemptive birth of the divine child, Jesus. The form of this homage corresponded with a genuine faith felt by people who had been redeemed from misery.

Augustus greeted this attitude with pleasure, and, for all the shrewd reticence which he had to maintain in Rome, he gladly forwarded it in the eastern provinces. He ordered the cult of the emperor there to be combined with the worship of Roma. In Pergamon[2] there quickly arose the first of a large number of temples in Asia Minor to Roma and Augustus. In this religious conception of the Emperor-Saviour, statesmen found the idea which alone was able to unite all parts of the empire into a unity. The outer links were the army and the officials; and the world economy made possible by peace and security. What was it, however, which united the innumerable elements of this highly complex phenomenon? Even the most optimistic person could not speak of an all-embracing national feeling. There was really no civilization in common at this early period among the

---

[1] *Inscr. Priene*, no. 105. Dittenberger, *or.*, 458

[2] Tac., *Ann.*, 4, 37. Dio. Cass., 51, 20, 7, *Inscr. Perg.*, no. 374

many peoples between the Rhine and the Euphrates. Hence belief in the divine mission of the peace-giving, imperial power was graphically expressed in the cult of the God-Emperor; and this effected a community of feeling which passed over the boundaries of the provinces and the differences of race, and created the vitally necessary ideology of the Roman empire.

The imperial cult immediately pressed into the foreground and remained permanently in this position; in the following centuries it adapted itself to the prevailing religious development. It is easy to understand how it would then come about that Christians, who refused to conform, would have to pay with their blood; and why even the privileged Jews themselves were at last shattered by the ensuing conflict. Even to-day the ruins in western Asia Minor teach us that, after the beginning of the imperial epoch, only imperial temples were built. The ancient gods—the health deities excepted—had to be content with what the faith of earlier centuries accorded them, for the active interest of the worship established by the state had centred on the person of the emperor. It was only natural that the experiences of the Hellenistic period were repeated in the worship of the emperor. Yet the high tone of the Augustan period could not endure. In the capital, where, in spite of everything, a critical attitude lived on, the foolish exaggerations of Caligula and of Nero, in giving themselves divine status, caused the cult to decline rapidly into a servile formality. In the eastern provinces the conception of the emperor remained sacred for a longer period, because the personal deficiencies of its representatives remained for a large part concealed, and because they continued to enjoy the benefits of the institution. Nevertheless, even there, decline was unavoidable.

The religious tone of the early empire was characterized, firstly, by the fact that the religion of the ancient Greek gods, i.e. the religion of the official cult, linked with city, race, and family, died away. It was still officially carried on but it lived no longer in the heart. Its place was taken either by irreligious indifference, or by the philosophers' habit of mind. Secondly, religion took possession of the solitary soul of the individual as a question of practical life and hope. Such persons now united

with others of a similar cast of mind and began to form a
community far excelling that of the old Greek cult-societies.
These latter were *ad hoc* unions of men who did not differ in
any way from their fellow-citizens. The new communities were
a unity, an actual organization, and a miraculous superhuman corpus. He who belonged to one felt himself lifted out
of the multitude of his "profane" fellow-citizens, and placed in
a secret relationship with the powers of the godhead. He had
trodden a road which led out of this common world and its
narrow confines, into the sphere of the gods; and which at
times brought the reality of that higher world blissfully to consciousness. This kind of religion had spread in the form of the
mysteries from the east, and at an early date had found its
way into Greece. Mythology had preserved the echoes of the
one time triumphant progress of the Dionysian mysticism.
Although Dionysos had been incorporated among the gods of
the Greeks, and his official cult had been preserved, like that of
the other Olympians, yet in the end he sank into being the
patron of the theatre, and a symbolic figure. Nevertheless, he
still remained the actual god of the Dionysian mysteries in
which the soulof an individual enjoyed, in Bacchantic rapture,
the ecstasy of divine possession; his soul cleansed from everything that disavowed the godhead, or countenanced the influence of evil demons. At long last he had been made divine and
thereby assured of a blessed life after death.

There were solemn rites of initiation with fastings and
ascetisms, baptisms and meals, strange ceremonies of a primitive cult, intoxicating dances with wild songs to the sound of
the flute and the clang of cymbals and tambourines. A confused variety of records, both inscriptions and documents, have
survived, but, as yet, it is impossible to analyse them satisfactorily. They belong to eight different centuries, and to all the
lands of the Roman empire, and it is only by combining data
of the most different origin that we are able to gain any comprehensible idea of the nature of these mysteries.[1] So far, it is
impossible to sketch the evolution of a mystery religion, its
different forms in various places, or its active and passive
relationships with other mysteries. Hence we must be content

[1] Cumont, *Or. Rel.* (3rd edition), 192. J. Leipoldt, *Dionysos* (1931)

with a general outline. What has been said about Dionysos applies to the remaining eastern cults. In the Hellenistic period, the mysteries blossom out and, in the Roman period, adopt still further features from the east. In the second century A.D., the orient flowed in religious triumph towards the west, reaching its culmination in the middle of the third century. Hence we may assume that in the Claudian-Neronian period, the important one for our present purpose, even in Asia Minor these forces flourished and were preparing for the struggle of the next century. If we combine the details of information in extant memorials and documents, with the results of an analysis of the Pauline letters, we are possibly in a position to make deductions as to the presence, and the nature, of certain religious currents in the Pauline period.

Although the world which surrounded early Christianity provided this great variety, it was not characterized by simple joys and undiluted happiness. A burden pressed upon it, and the individual felt, in his deepest soul, that he was miserable and in chains. It might either be the stars, as the Chaldeans taught, which pursued their fateful course in the heavens; or an impersonal fate, which could not be visualized; yet, even if one conceived it pictorially as Ananke, or a heartless and capricious Tyche, it was inescapable, and could not be influenced by the sacrifices or the prayers of a poor mortal. Why so? Because he was of another nature, and could only be the object of the will of a higher power. Had he no soul? Yes, but it lay in the fetters of the body, and could not free itself from all the bonds of this world. Therefore—enjoy the good things of this world as long as you may, for afterwards you will fall into dust and ashes. That was the answer given by many children of this world, and it re-echoes to us from many gravestones.[1] But there was a large number of earnest-minded men who could not easily be satisfied merely by knowing the worthlessness of this world, a worthlessness which, at that time, was universally recognized by all who meditated more profoundly upon the nature of things. In such people was to be found a desire for redemption which the eastern mysteries largely satisfied. The

[1] Examples in Buecheler, *Carm. epigr.*, 185–91, 243–44, 420, 5, 1081, 1082 1495–1500. E. Rohde, *Psyche*, ii, 393–96

soul of man was of divine origin, an ancient wrong having plunged it into what was material, and banished it to the body. But a divine messenger had descended upon earth and shown his disciples the way by which the soul could break the fetters of the body, overcome or outwit the hostile powers, mount up through the seven heavenly spheres, and be reunited with the divine original source. That was wisdom, and, at the same time, knowledge and action, suffering and enjoyment. This was what was meant by gnosis, and its practice was the *mysterium*. To turn toward the godhead set one free from the body, for the body itself belonged to the world which was considered to be of lower value. In the middle of the search for pleasure belonging entirely to the present sensual world, mysticism spread many ascetic customs, abstinence from wine, meat, and sexual intercourse, by those who longed for the other world. They longed to free themselves from the senses and sought to have their lives dominated by the spirit which lived as the divine spark in the soul; the *mysterium* showed them the means. It brought death to them and at the same time a rebirth to a new and true life. It brought the divine to life in their hearts, and let them gaze in ecstasy upon the blessed fields of the divine world; and the man whose lips the god had touched could give heavenly revelations. The community of mystics, when listening to him with devout thoughts in their hearts, regarded such a person as a man no longer, but as the mouthpiece of god, an apotheosized man, a prophet. The religion which he proclaimed, in God's commission, from his own experience was a redemptive religion, and its founder, who brought the *mysterium*, was the saviour of the world. This is the conception whose earthly inflections we have already discussed: the saviour, Augustus, had freed the world which was languishing in distress and fated to shed blood. In the mysteries, however, are laid bare the religious roots of his god-head, and of the prophecy of the birth of a divine child bringing salvation to the world. This explains also what it would sound like in human hearts of the time when Paul wrote to his Galatian churches (4: 4), "But* when the fullness of time came, God sent forth His Son, born of a woman, born under the law, that He might redeem them which were under the law, that we might receive the adoption of sons". This repeated the phraseology of a redemptive religion, and the doctrine of a saviour of the world.

While there is no doubt that the conceptions of "cleanness", and the corresponding prescriptions as found in the mysteries, originally flourished among the purely nature religions, and, consequently, wore an exclusively ritual character, we can recognize equally clearly the ethical elements that began to infiltrate in the course of the later development. As early as in ancient Orphicism, we find the idea of a last judgment on sinners[1], and learn that their evil would require expiation. Fasting and continence were the important means, in numerous cults, whereby the wicked man might win back the grace of the gods; and, as the religion became ever more inward, these means were no longer understood in the old sense of warding off dæmons, but as the education of the soul to inner purity.[2] For example: a temple law of the first century B.C. has been found in Lydian Philadelphia,[3] which on the basis of a revelation of Zeus to Dionysos prescribes a whole moral catechism to the religious community, which they were called upon to observe anew on the occasion of each monthly sacrifice. It is expressly declared that entry into this fellowship was open to men and women, free-born and slaves, without difference. The advance is specially striking when we compare the numerous Phrygian inscriptions[4] with confessions of sins, all in the nature of ritual transgressions. We can also understand whence the change came: the philosophy of the open air preachers had made the people familiar with Stoic ideas of equality as well as Stoic moral principles; and consciences had been aroused.

We must read Epictetus's lectures in Arrian's notes, which date from about A.D. 100, to gain a vivid picture of what constituted popular philosophy in the time of the early empire, and indeed long before. Here the most vivid language, and graphic, frequently pungent, and sweeping, phraseology are used to attack the shallowness of living a day at a time, and to

---

[1] A. Dieterich, *Nekyia*, 126. A. Olivierli, *Lamellae aureae orphicae* (*Kl. Texte*, 133), p. 9, 4, 11, 4
[2] Cumont, *Or. Relig.* (3rd edition), 219
[3] Dittenberger, *Syll.*, 985, cf. 983. K. Latte, *Arch. Rel. Wiss.*, 20, 291 ff.
[4] Cumont, *Or. Relig.* (3rd edition), 219, n. 40. Reitzenstein, *Hellen. Myst.* (3rd edition), 139. Steinleither, *Die Beicht im Zusammenhang mit der antiken Rechtspflege*, 1913, gives a collection of the texts

drive the hearers to turn to their inner selves. Questions are
proposed in regard to the meaning and value of life, and the
common views are subjected to an impressive criticism. One
prejudice after another disappears when it is breathed on by
a philosophy which usually presents itself as robust and sound
common sense. The man himself remains to be taught as man
and as "cosmopolitan", as a citizen of the world, and as neither
Greek nor barbarian, neither free nor slave, neither male nor
female, but only as human,[1] and who, as such, is to practise
"philosophy" i.e. to think and act according to sound ethical
principles.[2] The only thing necessary was to observe nature
with unveiled eyes in order to find the right way of shaping
one's life. The innate instinct of self-preservation, and the
natural desire for happiness, will make plain to anyone who
gives them earnest consideration, what he must do, or leave
undone, in respect of both himself and others. Even if men, for
the most part, do what is wrong, foolish, or harmful, it is only
because they give place in their lives to the feelings, to pain and
pleasure, and these exercise a determinative influence upon
their actions, and thereby confuse clear thinking. If you wrestle
for the peace of your soul, then the pure light of reason will
shine upon you unclouded, and point you the way of virtue,
exercise of which alone means genuine happiness.[3] Thus true
inner freedom arises in the soul,[4] and makes it independent of
all the changing circumstances of the outer world.

This philosopher-evangelist penetrates very deeply. He
teaches that the foundation of all ethical life is the truth that
all of us were created by God, the father of gods and men. We
have a body in common with animals, but understanding and
reason in common with the gods.[5] The creative germ had been
sown in the world by God, and has developed in rational
creatures; hence we men are partakers of a fellowship which
unites men and God; we are related to God, and man may
proudly call himself a son of God. He who has grasped that fact
knows that God is his creator and father and protector; and
never experiences either suffering or fear. He is not anxious
about what he will eat to-morrow, although he must stand in

[1] Epictetus, i, 9; i, 6; ii, 10, 1–3   [2] Chrysippus, *fr.*, 253 f., Arnim
[3] Epictetus, i, 4, 3, 28   [4] *Ibid.*, iv, 1   [5] *Ibid.*, i, 3, 1–3

shame before animals who can be certain of their support.[1]
Even if the prison house of the body may impede the soul conscious of her vital relationship with God, nevertheless she bears
the imprisonment in the serene consciousness of standing in the
service of God, who, as commander, has placed her at a post
which she must defend—until the moment when God sets her
free. It will be only a short while before she will hear the
liberating cry and come to God.[2]

This is no longer the home-made and pedantic pantheism of
the ancient Stoa. Over that dry landscape, the fertilizing rain
of a genuine, religious feeling has fallen, and has caused to
spring, from hidden seeds, a real faith in God which inspired
the Stoic preaching of virtue with new power.

About a century before the birth of Christ, a man on the
island of Rhodes came to exercise a far-reaching influence, a
man who was, above all else, the vehicle of this new tendency
in Stoicism. We refer to Poseidonios[3]—and, since he was born
in the Syrian city of Apamea, oriental religions must have been
prominent and formative in his early years. His works, covering
all fields of knowledge, include, beside treatises dealing with
fate and the art of prophecy, a writing about the gods which
was of the greatest significance for the development of Stoic
theology and which enjoyed a very large circulation. When,
soon after 80 B.C., Cicero was a student in Rhodes, he sat at the
feet of Poseidonios who was held in the greatest respect by the
Roman aristocracy.[4] Cicero began to write on popular philosophy in 44 B.C., the year that Cæsar was assassinated, and
he used Poseidonios's work as the basis of the second book of his
study of the nature of the gods. Two hundred years later,
Poseidonios's book was still held in such high regard that the
sceptic physician, Sextus, felt it to be an authoritative account
of philosophical belief in the gods, and accordingly made
many verbatim quotations from the work.[5]

A century later, in St. Paul's time, another capable writer,
who used the pseudonym of "Aristotle", published a work in-

---

[1] Epictetus, i, 9, 1–9, 16–19   [2] Ibid., i, 9, 16–17, 24–2
[3] P. Wendland, Kultur (2nd edition), 134–6. E. Schwartz Characterköpfe (5th
edition), i, 85–93
[4] Cic., Tusc., 2, 25, 61; cf. ad. Att., 2, i, 2; Hortensius, fr., 44, Müller
[5] Cic., de nat. deor., 2; Sextus Emp., adv. phys., 9, 60–136

tended for the use of the cultured people of his times. It avoided pedantry, and gave an account of the universe,[1] the best passages containing a theology of the cosmos in the style of Poseidonios.

Following the example of the early Stoa, Pseudo-Aristotle discussed the cosmological proof of God with penetrating ardour in these writings. The exalted reason of the creator and governor follows from the order and the teleological construction of the world and all its parts; the many grades of creatures compel the assumption of a highest and perfect being; the fact that the cosmos is an organism proves the existence of a soul, giving life to the material world; i.e. a power which penetrates and activates the whole, and which is recognized by its operations, as the supreme, purposive Reason and guiding Providence. By various transformations of itself, this immanent divine spirit creates the four elements, beginning with the finest, fiery æther, and going on to the grossest, earthly material; and every cosmic event is the consequence of their interaction. In this way the innumerable variety of beings were created, and at their head were those endowed with reason, i.e. men and gods, for whose sake alone this entire world was created as a "state", a community embracing both.[2] Whereas, in the last analysis, we can speak only of *one* god as the prime soul, the evolution of the phenomenal world teaches a plurality of gods, even if only of a secondary nature; these are the shining stars which in abiding peace adorn the highest heaven, or which as planets pursue their heavenly paths in an eternally, unchanging order.[3] But in addition, there are innumerable beings of an æthereal nature between heaven and earth, which are appropriately described as dæmons, and honoured by men as gods.[4] Here we have reminiscences of that early Stoic theology of intermediate beings which was intended to rationalize popular belief.[5]

The most fruitful thought in Poseidonios was his monotheism; it recognized, in the old pantheistic prime-being, the creator and sustainer of the world, and gave to the individual

---

[1] Ps. Aristot., *de mundo*, i, 391–401, ed. Bekker   [2] Cic., *nat. deor.*, 2, 62
[3] *Nat. deor.*, 2, 42, 54. Sext., 9, 86 f.   [4] Cic., *ibid.*, 2, 6. Sext., 9, 87
[5] Cf. (e.g.) Chrysipp., ii, 315–321, Arnim

the certainty of divine providence.[1] This is the source of that faith in God which Epictetus instilled into the souls of his disciples to make them proud and strong; here is the origin of the glowing, poetic inspiration which uses the most varied language to laud the eternal harmony and beauty of the cosmos.

The author of the pseudonymous *Concerning the World* boldly took a further step, and passed from the immanence to the transcendence of God. It appeared to him to be unworthy to find the godhead everywhere in the world; not in its midst, but above in heaven, to which we men lift up our hands in prayer; beyond the utmost limits, and as a pure being in a pure place, above all the confusion of the lower regions, the God of the cosmos sits upon His throne, the Saviour and Creator of all things. Just as the steersman his ship, the driver his waggon, the conductor his choir, the law the state, the general the army, so does He govern the world. Just as the Persian "Great King", unapproachable and invisible, gives out his commands, which are then passed on from the great ones about the throne, to the officials, and so maintains order in his mighty kingdom, so, too, the divine power which preserves all things, operates upon the nearest material world, i.e. the constellations of heaven; it is carried further by them, and brought down to our regions beneath. Naturally it becomes weaker in its benefactions the further the distance; nevertheless it binds the whole in a harmony which proceeds from him and returns to him. He gives the signal. Then the stars and the whole heaven revolve, the sun pursues his double journey, creating day and night and the four seasons of the year; rain falls and the winds blow at their proper time; the streams flow and the sea ebbs and flows; trees become green and fruits ripen; living creatures are born, they grow and pass away, each one according to its own nature.[2] What Goethe's angels sang in praise of the Lord on His heavenly throne was based on the faith of this ancient time. This faith resounded in philosophic disquisitions and in popular wisdom literature, in Jewish and Christian liturgies, throughout the centuries, as the noblest expression of ancient monotheism.

[1] Cic., *nat. deor.*, 2, 164
[2] Ps. Aristot., *de mundo*, 5–6

Chapter Ten

THE FATE OF JEWISH CHRISTIANITY

THE ORIGINAL CHURCH AT JERUSALEM STOOD APART FROM the development of Christianity into a world religion. The free attitude of the Hellenists of Antioch denied the permanent authority of the Law. In the same way, the freedom preached and, in principle, founded by Paul, appeared to it as entirely heretical and to call for definite repudiation. We have already described the conflict of Paul with Peter and the representatives of James in Antioch, and Galatians tells us of Jewish propaganda in the Galatian churches. The propaganda was intended to bring about a complete observance of Jewish ceremonial, including circumcision, among all Gentile Christians. It disallowed any compromise reached in Jerusalem. This aggressive programme had only a restricted and temporary success, if it could claim any at all. In view of missionary work which was making rapid progress among the Gentiles, it was a practical impossibility to fetter the converted multitudes to the entire ritual law, and even the relatively modest requirements of the Apostolic Decree could not be maintained, because the course of evolution had passed over the heads of the people at Jerusalem. From a distance, they were regarded with the highest respect and were recognized as the supreme "apostolic" authorities, nevertheless their views were quickly and entirely disregarded. The only thing that was definitely kept in mind was that they had recognized the Gentile Christian's freedom from the law. They were not able to influence the development of Christianity any further, because the apostolic age was approaching its end in both the east and the west.

As time went on, the relation of the original church to the Jews became more strained. By the favour of his friend Caligula, Agrippa was made king of a great part of Palestine after an adventurous life as a prince. This Agrippa was the relatively unimpressive grandson of Herod the Great, and his life, in both Rome and the east, had landed him into large debts. On becoming king he made himself acceptable by his Pharisaic scrupulousness and his popular behaviour. One of his popular deeds was to imprison James, the son of Zebedee, and Peter, two leading members of the Christians. Subsequently he killed James with the sword, whereas Peter miraculously escaped from prison.[1] But the king only kept his throne for three years (A.D. 41–44) before he died, when the Roman procurator took control of the entire land once more. The Christian church was still threatened. The High-Priest, Chananiah ben Chananiah,[2] dragged James, the leader of the church, before the high court in the year 62, and had him condemned to death, obviously on account of alleged religious wrong-doing, seeing that he was stoned.[3] Although this was disapproved of severely by eminent members of the Pharisaic party, it brought the church to the definite decision to leave Jerusalem. In addition there was growing unrest in the country, and Jewish nationalists believed that their day had come. The apostles received a revelation in regard to coming terrors and therefore the original church left the city and migrated to Pella.[4] This was a Gentile city in Transjordania opposite Samaria, bitterly hated by the Jews,[5] and ravaged by them at the beginning of the war for freedom. But it offered welcome shelter to the Christians.

And now, the tremendous drama of the Jewish war entered upon its first act, after it had already been announced for many years by beacon flame after beacon flame, in various places throughout Palestine. More than one "Messiah" had called the embittered population to arms, and organized bands of the "Sicarii" had wandered, pillaging and murdering not only Gentiles and Samaritans, but also leaders of their own people whom they disliked. In Cæsarea there was, in the end, a conflict between Jews and Greeks which led to bloodshed. On this account Florus the procurator did not meet the wishes of the Jews, although a large bribe had been offered him to that end. On the contrary, he demanded the payment of almost double the sum from the temple treasury of Jerusalem. This caused an insurrection amongst the people, which at first he managed to put down with barbaric methods, but later the rising spread

---

[1] Acts 12: 1–19   [2] Schürer, ii, 273
[3] Jos., *Ant.*, 20, 200. The Christian legend is given by Hegesippus in *Eus.* ii, 23, 4–18
[4] *Eus.*, iii, 5. 2–3   [5] Jos., *B.*, 2, 458

rapidly. King Agrippa II, who controlled a little of eastern and northern Palestine, failed in his efforts to mediate; open rebellion broke loose in an attempt to throw off Roman suzerainty. The symbol of liberation would be that sacrifices for the emperor were brought to an end.

It was in vain that the Jerusalem aristocracy uttered warnings. They followed these warnings by begging Florus and Agrippa to intervene quickly. The king alone acted and sent two thousand men to their aid. These men tried to defend themselves, along with the Roman garrison, in the upper city. It was useless; the castle Antonia and the palace of Herod were stormed by the insurgents and burnt. The garrison was destroyed partly in honourable battle and partly by breach of terms after they had capitulated. About the same time, the Roman garrisons in Masada, Machærus, and Jericho were overpowered. Meanwhile in the Gentile cities and especially in Cæsarea, there was a general slaughter of the Jews, which the Jews repaid in blood wherever they had sufficient power. All this happened in the late summer of A.D. 66, and the procurator let it happen. Then the higher military authorities began to move: the legate of Syria, Cestius Gallus, combined the available auxiliaries with his twelfth legion, marched from the coast into the Jewish region, and pressed to the walls of Jerusalem, but he could do no more. Surprise attacks were unsuccessful, and he had not sufficient force for a regular siege. Therefore he faced about, and, in descending from the Jewish highlands to the lowlands, his army was brought to a stand on the coast, and definitely defeated by the Jews. The first act of the drama ended with victory for the insurgent people. The freedom of Israel was then proclaimed and silver shekels were coined with the proud inscription "Israel's shekel. Year 1", and "Holy Jerusalem", and henceforward the years were numbered on the coins from the "Liberation of Zion". The aristocracy of the city, who had hitherto been in the opposition, now placed themselves àt the disposal of the victorious movement and provided it with leaders.

It is obvious that Rome could not tolerate this weakening of its authority in the east. Nero entrusted one of his best generals, Vespasian, with the task of suppressing the insurrection. The latter carefully prepared the army, and, round a nucleus of three legions, he collected a force of auxiliaries, so that he could march in the spring of A.D. 67 with sixty thousand men into Galilee. The army gathered by the insurgents was at once routed, and the open country of Galilee was soon in Vespasian's hands. But the stubborn enemy drew back into fortified places and offered fierce and stiff resistance to the besiegers, although they were always overcome sooner or later. Even the Samaritans, strangely enough, at this time gathered an armed force on the holy mountain Gerizim, and seemed to threaten the Romans. Therefore a large division attacked and killed them all, eleven thousand six hundred men according to the notice in Josephus:[1] but it is difficult to see what purpose the slaughter really served.

In the spring of A.D. 68, Vespasian successfully began to bring the southern half of the land, as well as Perea, under his control; but Nero's death, and the subsequent frequent change of emperors, caused him to adopt a waiting attitude which lasted to the end of 69, when he put himself forward as a candidate for the throne, and went to Italy. His son, Titus, took over the command of the Jewish campaign after having already held a command under him. Shortly before Easter A.D. 70 Titus marched against Jerusalem where, meanwhile, the great majority of those had gathered who had resolved to fight to the last. The two years of Roman military inactivity had been wasted in bitter quarrelling between various parties who fought it out among themselves. The aristocracy were deprived of power and killed. The Zealots under the Galilean, John of Gishala, held the temple and fought the volunteers of Simon bar Giora, who held the upper city; but the appearance of the Romans rallied them together for common defence. During five long months they fought heroically against the machines and the weapons of Titus, and against the still more terrible power of famine. In July the castle Antonia fell; on August 10th the temple was destroyed in flames; on September 8th the last bulwark of Jerusalem fell in ruins together with the defences of the upper city. Yet it was not until the spring of A.D. 73 that the last sparks of the rebellion were extinguished by the fall of the southern outpost, Masada.

[1] Jos., B., 3, 315

When victory was decided by the capture of the capital, Rome made the full political consequences felt: Judea became a Roman province separate from Syria and subject to a *legatus pro prætore*. It also received a more powerful military garrison, and a whole legion, the tenth,[1] was transferred to Jerusalem, where it camped among the ruins of the city, which had been rendered uninhabitable.[2] The sacrificial system was deservedly destroyed along with the temple. Soon afterwards fugitive Sicarii tried to initiate disturbances in Egypt, and, as a conseqence, the Jewish temple in Leontopolis, which had been in existence at least two centuries, was closed and sacrifices forbidden,[3] in spite of the loyal attitude of the Alexandrian Jews. The sanhedrin was dismissed and the High-Priest deposed at the same time. The Romans were spiteful enough to continue the temple-tax paid by the diaspora, the proceeds being devoted to the temple treasury of Jupiter Capitolinus in Rome. The Jewish national state, and the central religious organization of all Judaism, were thus destroyed.

When, two generations later, Barkochba once more raised the Messianic banner in a fanatical rebellion (A.D. 132–35) the Emperor Hadrian confirmed Vespasian's judgment in a terrible manner. He built on the site of Jerusalem the Roman colony of Ælia Capitolina, and Jews were forbidden to enter under penalty of death.

The Christians of the original church had separated themselves, some years before this catastrophe, from the Jewish people, and so did not share the tragedy. But, by their flight to Pella, they came into contact with Jewish sects of various kinds which had separated themselves at an earlier date, and had prepared places of refuge in the region east of the Jordan as well as east and south of the Dead Sea. Josephus does not mention them, but Christian authors of the second century[4] enumerate many Jewish groups alongside the Pharisees, Sadducees, and Essenes. They bore all sorts of names, mostly meaningless to us nowadays.

Of course the "Samaritans" are familiar enough, they were not Jews in a racial sense but descendants of foreign colonists

---

[1] Ritterling, *Pauly-W.*, xii, 1,671–77   [2] Jos., *B.*, 7, 3
[3] *Ibid.*, 7, 433–36   [4] Justin, *dial.*, 80. Hegesippus in *Eus.*, iv, 22, 7

whom the Assyrians had settled in mid-Palestine. In the course of time they had accepted the Mosaic religion, but held themselves aloof from the temple at Jerusalem and possessed one of their own on Mount Gerizim. They expected the Messiah with a lively hope, and, when the Romans suppressed a Messianic pretender of theirs, they paid the cost with their blood.[1] The baptizing sects, of which several appeared under various names, were undoubtedly genuine Jewish organizations. Their characteristic was the custom, already found amongst the Essenes,[2] of purifying themselves daily by a ceremonial bath, whereas official Judaism employed such lustrations only for special cases of defilement. Only in the fourth century do we find further particulars in Epiphanius,[3] in regard to other Jewish sects. He collected together all sorts of pedantic details about seven "pre-Christian heresies" among the Jews, and examined their effects subsequently on Christianity. Beside the groups known to us from Josephus, he mentions also the baptists and says that the Nasarenes[4] followed them. These lived in Galaaditis and Basanitis, i.e. in the neighbourhood of Pella up to the mountains of Hauran. In general, they observed the Jewish rites, but adopted a somewhat critical attitude towards the Pentateuch; they ate no meat and rejected animal sacrifices—once more reminding us of the Essenes.[5] Apparently the Ossæans,[6] or Sampsæans, who lived in the south in Moab or Nabatea, were closely similar to the Nasarenes, because they agreed with them in their attitude towards sacrificial worship and the Mosaic tradition.

It was into this sphere that the Christians came who had fled to Pella. They had been expelled by the Jews in Jerusalem because, in spite of all their adherence to the ancient traditional basis of their religion and race, they were driven by their religious peculiarities into irreconcilable antagonism. There was much in the earliest traditions of the Christian church which was, perhaps, very similar to the older sects; thus approximations were prepared for, and confirmed occasionally in later times.

The original church disappeared with the migration to Pella

---

[1] Jos., *Ant.*, 18, 85–87   [2] *Vide supra*, pp. 36 f.   [3] Epiph., *haer.*, 14–20
[4] *Ibid.*, 18   [5] *Vide supra*, pp. 35 f.   [6] Epiph., *ibid.*, 19; cf. 53, 1

and the destruction of Jerusalem. At the same time it sank
below the horizon of Gentile Christianity which was in process
of conquering the world and which had thereby become
dominant in Christendom. It was felt that the judgment of God
had fallen on the Holy City, and, to all eyes, it was plainly
His punishment for the crucifixion of the Lord. By the
destruction of the temple and its worship and the abolition of
the Law, Jewish Christianity lacked not only a racial, but also
a religious basis for its former claims, and thus was forgotten in
the church catholic. It sank to oblivion in the lonely deserts of
East Jordan. In later centuries Christian theologians only
occasionally cast curious glances at these remnants of a most
honourable past, and spoke to their own contemporaries about
them as a strange phenomenon. In theological terms, they set
these Jewish Christians down under the rubric of "heretics",
but only very few people can ever have bothered about them,
if only because they lived in such a remote region. But about
A.D. 150 the Apologist, Justin,[1] who had been born in Palestine,
discussed the question whether Christian Jews, who observed
the Law, could be saved. Obviously he knew of such churches,
and was inclined to let them count as Christians if only they did
not require that same observance from others; but he was aware
that many people would not recognize them even then. However, there is ground for assuming that Justin was not discussing
an actual problem, but only a theoretic case. Even the warnings
of Ignatius, which had been written a generation earlier against
Jewish ways, can scarcely have anything to do with the early
Jewish Christians.[2]

Towards the end of the second century, a statement was
drawn up by Irenæus of Lyons[3] which is the source of the
official records of the Church in regard to the Jewish Christians.
He calls them "Ebionites", which is a Biblical Hebrew expression for the "poor", and a term which the Jerusalem church used
of itself.[4] The name bears witness to the connection between the
later Jewish church of Transjordan and the first church in
Jerusalem. Irenæus was aware that Ebionites denied the virgin
birth of Jesus, used only Matthew's gospel, and would have

---

[1] Justin, *dia.*, 47, 1–3   [2] Ign., *Magn.*, 8–10, *Philad.*, 6, 1
[3] Iren., i, 26, 2   [4] *Vide supra*, pp. 62 f.

nothing to do with the apostle Paul. They explained the prophetic writings in their own way, and their manner of life was
quite Jewish, and this to such an extent that they even faced
Jerusalem in prayer as if God dwelt there. Is this statement
based on Irenæus's personal knowledge, or on extraneous information from an older source? It is certain that he himself had
found no Ebionites in Gaul, and it is at least doubtful whether
he had met with them in his home town of Smyrna in Asia
Minor.

Almost throughout the whole of the following two centuries,
we hear nothing more of Jewish Christian churches, except that
the old records are passed on, sometimes with minor additions.
Origen,[1] for example, says that, besides the Ebionites already
mentioned, there were others who accepted the Virgin Birth.
Only isolated and shadowy persons are known to have come
over from that little world into the church catholic. Ariston the
apologist came from Pella and thus perhaps was one of those
Jewish Christians. He tells of the war of Barkochba,[2] but
Barkochba was not a Jewish Christian. Hegesippus, who
laboured in the Antonine period, and who was rightly held by
Eusebius in high esteem, made use of Jewish-Christian sources
in his work and shows himself to be a Christian formerly of the
Jewish faith. Eusebius agrees,[3] but does not say that he belonged
to the sect of Jewish Christians. On the other hand Origen[4]
tells of Symmachus, a translator of the Bible, and says that he
had been an Ebionite. Moreover, Origen knew of writings of his
which criticized Matthew, an item confirmed by a later notice.[5]

Not till the second half of the fourth century are further
details available in regard to the remains of Jewish Christianity, in the writings of two men who had investigated the
problem for themselves. Epiphanius, the historian of the
heretics, is our chief source of information. He came from
Salamis in Cyprus, and about A.D. 370 he collected everything
that had come to him about the "Nazorenes" and the
"Ebionites". He describes the former in the same manner as
the Ebionites of Irenæus, and expressly said that they spoke

---

[1] Orig., c. Cels., 5, 61, cf. 2, 1; 5, 65. Hom. in Jerem., 19, 12, Klost
[2] In Euseb., H.E., iv, 6, 3   [3] Eus., H.E., iv, 22, 8   [4] Orig. in Eus., H.E., vi, 17
[5] Marius Victorinus, Com. on Gal., 1, 19; 2, 26 (Migne lat., viii, 1155, 1162);
cf. in addition Epiph., haer., lii, 1, 8

Hebrew.[1] The Old Testament was read aloud by them in the original text, and their gospel of Matthew was written in Hebrew with Hebrew characters. They dwelt in Pella, in Kokaba in the Hauran, and in Berœa which lay far to the north and east of Antioch. The impression given is that the Hebrew Jewish-Christians of Antioch may, at an early date, have left the entirely Hellenistic church in the great city, and fled to the east—so that Berœa was related to Antioch as Pella to Jerusalem.

Jerome was living about that time in the wilderness of Chalcis, east of Antioch, and he also had found traces of "Nazarenes". He visited them in Berœa and copied their Hebrew gospel of Matthew,[2] asserting that he translated it afterwards into both Greek and Latin; unfortunately nothing has been preserved of these translations except a very few quotations.[3] According to him there was a copy of this Hebrew Matthew in the library at Cæsarea. But this gospel was not, as Jerome thought, the ancient Aramaic original but a translation of our present canonical text into the west-Syrian dialect; it contained not a few legendary glosses. Apparently there was also a Greek retranslation of it for Greek-speaking Jewish Christians, isolated traces of which survive in the Fathers and in critical, marginal notes of New Testament manuscripts.[4]

Of course, these churches of the east, distinct from the church catholic, did not maintain unchanged the traditions of the early period, but, rather, came largely under the influence of the Jewish sects already described, and shared their spiritual life. In Trajan's third year (A.D. 101), a prophet, called Alexis, arose in East Jordan, who was afterwards known by the Syriac form of his name Elxai—Chel-Ksai, meaning "the secret power".[5] He wrote his prophecies in a book which his churches faithfully preserved. The chief historians of the heretics discuss

[1] Epiph., haer., xxix, 7, 4; 9, 4
[2] Jerome, vir. inl., 2, 3, dial. adv. Pelag., 3, 2. Epist, cxx, 8, 2. Epiph., haer., xxix, 9, 4. Euseb., Theophany, 4, 12, p. 183, 29, Gressmann
[3] A. Schmidtke, jüden-christl. Evang. (T.U. 37, 1), 32–41. E. Klostermann, Apokrypha, ii (Kl. Texte, 8)
[4] Ignat., ad Smyrn., 3, 1–2, = Jer., op. cit., 16; the fragment no. 45 in Schmidtke, op. cit., 39 f. proves retranslation from the Syriac. Do nos. 3–5 (Clemens und Origenes, Klosterm. fr., 5, 27) also originate there?
[5] Lidzbarski, H., d. nord sem. Epigr., p. 217 n. and Ephemeris, 2, 198. Epiph., xix, 2, 10

it and preserve fragments.[1] The Jewish basis of religion, including circumcision, ritual ordinances, and Sabbath observance, as well as facing Jerusalem in prayer, is fully maintained by Elxai.[2] The prophet shared with the sects east of the Jordan the non-acceptance of the Prophets and of bloody animal sacrifices,[3] which meanwhile had become impossible on account of the destruction of Jerusalem. He set a high value upon washings, "the baptisms" which he particularly recommends as therapeutics for illness and dæmon possession.[4] Christ was the Son of the "Great and Highest God" and was called the "Great King". He was a pre-existent being of divine power who already in previous ages had been incarnated in various persons, e.g. in Adam. Elxai had seen Him as a giant equal in size to a great mountain whose height could be estimated at ninety-six miles. At His side, and similarly tall, was His sister, Rucha, the Holy Spirit.[5]

Thus Christianity was for him the divine religion and his sacred book was intended for baptized Christians. But he knew better than the Church, since he preached a second baptism for forgiveness of sins a second time. Whoever had sexual sins of any kind upon his conscience, and listened to the words of the book must at once go and let himself be baptized in the name of God and of the Great King, and in particular, as is asserted both here and elsewhere, in his clothes, and not naked as was customary in the Church. Then forgiveness of sins would be imparted to him afresh. But during the performance of the sacred rite, he must call upon the "seven witnesses", heaven, water, the holy spirits, the angels of prayer, oil, salt, the earth; these would guarantee that he neither sins, commits adultery, steals, oppresses, deceives, hates, transgresses, nor finds pleasure in any evil thing.[6]

It was a genuine baptism of repentance for forgiveness of sins, and it necessitated conversion. It offered another opportunity for obtaining salvation before the end of all things, just

---

[1] Hippol., ix, 13–17; x, 29. Epiph., *haer.*, xix, 1–5; xxx, 17 cf. Harnack, *Lit.*, i, 207–29

[2] Hippol., ix, 14, 1; 16, 3. Epiph., xix, 3, 5   [3] Epiph., xix, 3, 6; liii, 1, 7

[4] Hippol., ix, 15, 1; 4–16, 1. Epiph., *haer.*, xxx, 17, 4

[5] Hippol., ix, 13, 1–3. Epiph., xix, 4, 1–2; xxx, 17, 5–7; liii, 1, 8–9

[6] Hippol., ix, 15. Epiph., xix, 1, 6; xxx, 2, 4–5

as had formerly been preached by John, and a conversion quite similar to that preached a generation later by the Shepherd of Hermas to the Roman Christians. He who accepted it, though he were a heretic, would attain "peace and his share with the righteous". Sexual sins are particularly emphasized in this prescription because they appeared to Elxai to press hardest. On this account, he would have nothing to do with sexual asceticism but required early marriage,[1] and in so doing he expressed the popular and universal view of these Judaizing Christians.

The names of the "seven witnesses" testify to the fact that speculations on the elements and their sacramental power, and on the heavenly world of spirits, were not foreign to his sphere of ideas. Fire appeared to him as the element of error and estrangement from God, whereas the sound of water leads along the right road.[2] Moreover astrology supplied him with building material for his system of doctrine. He knew the influence of evil stars and their authority over many days, particularly if the moon entered into conjunction with them. At such times no one might begin any work, baptize either man or woman, but must wait until the moon had left its inauspicious orientation. Of the seven days of the week, the Sabbath was to be kept particularly holy, but also on the third day, i.e. Tuesday, no work might be begun because the number three was the symbol of a universal catastrophe: three years after Trajan's Parthian war (A.D. 114–116), war would break out between the wicked angels of the north.[3] But nothing further is recorded about this unfulfilled prophecy,[4] and we cannot say whether Elxai developed an apocalyptic of his own.

It is not easy to get a clear picture of the essential nature of this prophet from the scattered remarks of his opponents. The Jewish elements of his preaching are clearly recognizable, and are full of a rank imagery with which both the apocalyptic, and the specifically Christian, ideas are decked out. His baptismal ceremonies, and his negation of animal sacrifices and false prophecy, show that he belonged to one of the sects east of Jordan. In addition, his ideas about astronomy and elementary spirits remind us of the polemical discussions in Paul's

[1] Epiph., xix, 1, 7   [2] Epiph., xix, 3, 7; liii, 1, 7
[3] Hippol., ix, 16, 2–4   [4] E. Schwartz, *Z.N.W.*, 31, 195

epistle to the Colossians (2: 9, 16–18). Such ideas had probably already become naturalized in dissenting sects of Judaism. Nothing of this is syncretistic in the proper sense; but we are standing at the cradle of a Judaistic gnosis, and the succeeding ages found in Elxai the "secret power", i.e. the incarnation of the godhead in a superman. This idea occurs elsewhere[1] about A.D. 100. The characterization of fire as an evil element was meant to express antithesis to Persian views.

The *Book of Elxai* seems to have been kept a close secret in accordance with the wish of its author,[2] and would never have been known had not a certain Alcibiades brought it about A.D. 200 from Apamea in Syria to Rome. He claimed to be a prophet of Elxai's, though without much success.[3] His preaching about the forgiveness of sins made Bishop Hippolytus suspicious, for Hippolytus was a rigorous defender of penance. He examined the new apostle and his old book very closely, and wrote a detailed account in his work on heretics, and this work is the source of our knowledge. Elxai had little significance for church history, or for the evolution of Jewish Christianity. His teaching is only a welcome testimony to the strength, and fantastic variety, of the gnosis which was then beginning to appear in Syria or round about.

About A.D. 380 Epiphanius, the zealous bishop of Cyprus, not only read the record of Hippolytus, but apparently also the *Book of Elxai*. He mentions two sisters of the prophet's family who were still alive and who were honoured as saints because they possessed miraculous power.[4] But he then asserts that the book had exercised great influence and had been made much use of in the Clementine writings, which Epiphanius regarded as documents coming from the early Jewish-Christian church. For a long time this misled students; and only quite recently have penetrating researches[5] made it possible to recognize the Clementine writings as fictions without historical basis, and valueless for the study of the early Christian and Judaistic period, and without any connection with Elxai and his church.

Unfortunately, Epiphanius commits many sins of confusion also in the details of his account of the "Nazorenes". In

---

[1] Acts 8: 10   [2] Hippol., ix, 17, 1   [3] *Ibid.*, ix, 13, 1
[4] Epiph., *haer.*, xix, 2, 1 2;liii, 1, 5   [5] E. Schwartz, *Z.N.W.*, 31, 151–199

particular he naïvely introduces here facts which really refer to
the Ebionites. This makes it most difficult to discover the truth.
Perhaps this much can be said: that some "Ebionites" were
living on the island of Cyprus, and therefore in his own diocese;[1]
he owes his more reliable information to them. He was aware
that various apocryphal Acts of the Apostles were in use
amongst them, and he specially emphasizes a "Jacob's Ladder"
which expressed their aversion to sacrificial rites and burnt
offerings, and which calumniated Paul bitterly.[2] He had had
in his hands the gospel which was in use amongst them, and
he quotes numerous passages from it that make their gospel
appear to have been a fantastic redaction of the canonical
Matthew, but making use also of Luke. Vegetarianism seems
to have been favoured in it, and, clearly, it was hostile to
sacrifices.[3] It said that John the Baptist lived on oil-cakes
instead of animal locusts; that Jesus expressly repudiated the
roasted Passover lamb, and that it was His work to abolish
ceremonial sacrifices. Whether this apocryphal gospel had anything to do with the Gospel to the Hebrews, already mentioned,[4]
cannot be determined, because the passages quoted are not
such as to allow any comparisons, and what Epiphanius himself
says[5] is no guarantee of accurate knowledge.

Hence we find in Cyprus the last remains of the separate
Jewish church. It was still living a vegetative sort of life toward
the end of the fourth century, and apparently it was not much
different from the strange church in Berœa and other survivals
in the east. It has been suggested recently[6] that Asia Minor also
had offered a home to fugitive Jewish Christians. True, Philip
the evangelist, who had settled in Cæsarea with his four
prophetic daughters, was claimed towards the end of the
second century by Hierapolis as a local saint. They averred that
he and two of his daughters were buried there, and that a third
daughter's grave was in Ephesus the capital.[7] The Easter-
praxis in Asia Minor, of which we shall have to speak later

---

[1] Epiph., *haer.*, xxx, 18, 1   [2] *Op. cit.*, xxx, 16, 6–9
[3] *Op. cit.*, xxx, 13–14. Extant passages given in E. Klostermann, *Apokrypha*, ii
(2nd edition) (*Kl. Texte*, 8), p. 9–12; fr. 2, 6, 5
[4] *Vide supra*, p. 185.   [5] Epiph., *haer.*, xxx, 3, 7
[6] K. Holl, *Ges. Aufs.*, ii, 66 f. E. Schwartz, *Z.N.W.*, 31, 190 f.
[7] Acts 21: 8, 9. Polycrates' epistle to Victor of Rome in Eus., *H.E.*, iii, 31,3;
cf. Gaius in Eus., *H.E.*, iii, 31, 4

remained closely attached to the Jewish mode as distinct from the custom which obtained in the rest of the church which had departed therefrom. The Apocalypse of John, which was based on Jewish sources, and which was rooted in Jewish feeling, was undoubtedly written in Asia Minor. Its author presupposes that the Apostolic Decree[1] held good in the church at Pergamon, and that it was endangered by the Nicolaitans. Even the polemic of the Fourth Gospel, against the Jews, seems to become more comprehensible if regarded as essentially a reaction against a Jewish Christianity which remained faithful to tradition. It is better to set aside the tradition that John, the son of Zebedee, lived in his old age in Ephesus, and was buried there, because that tradition was unknown to Ignatius about A.D. 117, and probably rests on a false identification. In any case the arguments are not cogent enough for more than a possibility. The Jewish-Christian church died out quietly, and in isolation. The church of the conquering, universal form of Christianity, which was now waxing mightily, took no notice of the decease of her elder sister.

[1] Rev. 2: 14

Chapter Eleven

THE SUB-APOSTOLIC PERIOD

THE APOSTOLIC AGE CLOSED WITH THE DEATH OF THE LAST
apostle of whose decease trustworthy information has been
preserved, viz. Peter. The blood-red glow of the Neronian persecution lit up the end of the period during which the young
religion had gained a firm foundation in history. The Roman
church wrote no chronicle, and the fearful event left no trace
behind in the memory of Christians elsewhere. As a consequence we learn no exact details from church sources about
this first great attack upon the church. Even Eusebius[1] only
touches it in a few words which tell very little. But Tacitus
found material here which he could use for his sketch of Nero's
savagery and he affords us a record which is of immeasurable
value and which shows how the few hints in the epistle of
Clement of Rome are to be understood.[2] In July, A.D. 64, a
tremendous fire, lasting for more than six days, laid the greater
part of the city of Rome in ashes. Nero immediately began to
rebuild energetically, prescribed the style and reconstructed
with the greatest beauty. Then came a rumour that the fire
had been instigated by high authority. In order to root out this
suspicion, the Emperor accused the Christians of responsibility,
and punished them severely. A few confessed themselves
Christians, and were arrested: others began to make the same
confession, and in the end a great number were gathered
together. It is true that examination brought out nothing which
implicated them in the fire, but it was decided that they were
"enemies of the human race". They must therefore die, not by
simple execution, but in various forms of a hideous game: they
were sewed up in animal skins and mauled by bloodhounds;
they were bound on oxen; torn to pieces in the arena; crucified.
Swathed in bindings dipped in pitch, they were burned as
torches in the imperial gardens at the Vatican. It is highly
probable that Peter was crucified in this persecution, as is

[1] Eus., *H.E.*, ii, 25, 1–8
[2] Tac., *Ann.*, 15, 44; cf. Suetonius, *Nero*, 16. 1 *Clem.*, 6, 1–2

testified by a very early witness.[1] His body was buried near to
the Neronian circus on the Via Cornelia. It is probable that
Paul had been executed with the sword some time before and
had been buried on the road to Ostia. Both graves were shown
to sightseers about A.D. 200 in the same places where they are
revered to-day. They lie in sites apart from those of all other
cults of early Christian Rome, so that there can be scarcely any
doubt of their genuineness.[2]

But the glare of this outburst only lights for a brief moment
the darkness which shrouds the early history of the Roman
church. That church disappears from our knowledge, and only
becomes visible again a generation later, and this time in clear
light. It happened in the following manner. A quarrel had
broken out in the church at Corinth. The younger generation
had set itself against the authority of the older, and had deprived of office the bishops and deacons chosen by them,
although no material accusation of any kind could be made.
The motive which caused the whole disturbance must therefore
have been simply the desire for a new distribution of the positions of authority. The formal basis must be sought in parallel
phenomena in ancient confraternities. It was everywhere
customary—for that matter among the Jews also—for the
authorities of religious organizations to be chosen only for a
term, and after the end of their period of office to be replaced
by fresh persons if they were not re-elected. Many members
must have felt that the same custom ought to obtain with the
Church. Action was taken accordingly, and those who had
formerly been chosen[3] by the church were deposed by a new
decision of the church. Of course this did not take place without
opposition, and the noise of the conflict resounded across the
sea as far as Rome.

Then the Roman community, in full consciousness of the
unity of the Church as a whole, felt itself obliged to discharge
a service of love, and so intervened. One of its bishops, Clement
by name,[4] carried out the commission, and wrote a letter to

[1] John 21: 18, 19
[2] Gaius in Eus., *H.E.*, ii, 25, 7; cf. Lietzmann, *Petrus und Paulus in Rom.*, 2nd
edition, 1927
[3] 1 *Clem.*, 44, 3; cf. *Didache*, 15, 1
[4] Dionys. of Corinth in Eus., *H.E.*, iv, 23, 11

Corinth. Feeling himself to be the heir of Paul, he shows clearly both in his words of greeting, and in the whole style of his introduction, that he intended to write a letter in the way that the Apostle was accustomed to write to his churches when in need of earnest exhortation. It feels almost like this: if Clement had not been commissioned by the Roman church, but had written on his own initiative, he would probably have written the author's name as "Paul, the apostle of Jesus Christ", and we should have possessed another pseudo-Pauline letter.

The Roman church had to deplore difficulties of her own: sudden blows of fate had followed one another swiftly and had prevented her intervention in Corinthian affairs until this late date. But she intervened now in full force; the leaders of the rebellion were severely chided, jealousy and envy described as the instigating causes, and then in the style of a sermon the author passes on to deliver to the Corinthians a lengthy address which offers us a good example of contemporary religious oratory, and which concludes at last with an extended liturgical prayer. We gain highly important details in regard to the case itself.[1] We know[2] that the early churches were inclined to hold their bishops and deacons in low esteem as compared with the charismatics who were led by the spirit of God; but we are informed also that these officials, who had been entrusted with their office by election, gradually and to an increasing extent, took over the spiritual duties and liturgical functions properly so called—probably *pari passu* with the growing infrequency of prophets with the charisma. In practice therefore they gradually came to be the normal leaders of public worship without abandoning their technical obligations and competence. This meant, however, that they united spiritual and secular power in their own persons.

As long as they were only the business and financial officials of individual churches they could be regarded as analogous to Jewish or pagan leaders in a similar community, and a temporal limit to their office could be required and applied. By the nature of the case, a charismatic could not be deposed, because he had been appointed by God through the gift of the spirit; and he could only lose office by God's intervention, and

---

[1] I *Clem.*, 40–44   [2] *Vide supra*, p. 146. *Didache*, 15, 2

this at the same time as he lost the gift of the spirit. If now the elected *episcopos* took the place of such a prophet, the next thing was to grant that the former could no more be set aside than the latter—and it is this very point that the epistle of Clement explains to the Corinthians. Of course he does not do so by historical evidence like us, but by arguments which were to become of the greatest importance to the entire church catholic. Time, place, and personnel of the cultus, so he explains, were already prescribed by God in the Old Testament and exact regulations established for all spiritual functions; and to transgress these regulations was a deadly sin. In the same way, the divine revelation that had come to the Church followed a definite order: God sent Christ, Christ the Apostles, and these, on their missionary journeys, installed bishops and deacons, just as had already been explicitly prophesied in Isa. 60: 17. Since the Apostles foresaw future disputes, they prescribed that the offices should be taken over by other approved men only after the death of their first holders. Thus those bishops who stood in the traditional succession, who had been appointed "with the assent of the whole church", and who had exercised their office blamelessly, were not to be deposed on any account, for their status had been legitimized by apostolic authority. Their status differed fundamentally, and by divine will, from that of the laity.[1]

Here is the germ of the doctrine of the divine ordination of the clergy, and of its indelible character. Not unjustly has the writing of this chapter been described as the moment in which Roman Catholic canon law was born. As yet the theory was not formulated quite clearly, for it does not say expressly that a bishop could only be installed in his office by another bishop. The author only speaks of "other respected men" who install bishops, and, in so doing, act in the place of Apostles.[2] But since Clement traces the traditional succession in the other direction emphatically to God, his ideal is undoubtedly the future lengthening of this chain through a whole series of bishops; and from this point of view we have to regard the "respected men" as bishops. Then the doctrine follows logically, viz. that apostolic succession, i.e. the unbroken transference of office from the Apostles, and

---

[1] I *Clem.*, 44, 1–3; 40, 5   [2] I *Clem.*, 44, 3

from one bishop to another, legitimizes the present holder of spiritual power and makes him independent of the local church. Once on a day the church chose its bishops as technical functionaries, but now the bishops chose their successors and the church only possessed the "right of assent". She possesses it, and exercises it, in Rome to the present day, when a newly elected pope shows himself on the loggia of St. Peter's and receives the joyous acclamation of the crowd assembled on the campus.

It is also significant that Clement founded his doctrine on Scripture, i.e. the Old Testament. He regarded it as very obvious that the prescriptions for the cultus in the Holy Book were types of the new Christian ordinations for worship, and he said nothing more about carrying them out in their original sense. From the fact that, in the Old Testament, the forms of public worship were exactly regulated in every respect, and that departure from them was on pain of death, Clement deduced, without more ado, that the same must be the case in the Christian church. And, since he plainly regarded his argument as obvious to the readers of his document, we may draw the conclusion that it was a method of theological thought common to Christians of the day. The Old Testament had, therefore, already been wrested from the Jews and had become the special property of Christians to such an extent that its commandments could be regarded as "types", and used to regulate church life.

But there was more. The entire epistle is dominated in the highest degree by the language of the Greek Bible; moreover, it cites, ever and again, shorter or longer Biblical passages. Its theological proof relies throughout on the Old Testament side by side with two quite isolated passages,[1] where words of Jesus are cited as authoritative bases. God Himself spoke in this Holy Book, as also did Christ[2] through the Holy Spirit, and revealed everything necessary for salvation. Every truth of the knowledge of God, every record of God's commands, of His strictness as a judge, and of His forgiving bounty, were to be found in the Old Testament. This book had led the generations of the past into a better condition of heart, just as it led Christians in the

[1] *Clem.*, 13. 2; 46, 8   [2] *Ibid.*, 22, 1

present in the right way. Thus the teachings of Biblical history, and the experiences of Old Testament men and women, could offer exhortation to, and example for, a right way of life.[1] We must add that the value, which could be placed directly upon the literal word, was extended significantly by discovering allegorical meanings, and concealed prophecies, about Christ;[2] this will enable us fully to understand the central place of the Holy Scriptures in the Christianity of the church at Rome. It was the foundation book of divine revelations, fitted to teach the "chosen people", and to point them the way to salvation. This meant, however, that this people belonged to the host of those who were denoted by the allegorical name of "Israel", and whom God had chosen through Christ out of all the peoples of the world,[3] i.e. the Christians. The literal reference to the Jewish people was no more taken into account than the ritual observance of the ceremonial law.

The content of the divine law consists, above all else, of moral prescriptions formulated in commandments, or illustrated by historical examples; indeed God's joy in His works of creation is put forward as an example for human conduct.[4] It also teaches that God is no pitiless judge, but forgives the repentant sinner who contritely confesses his transgressions, and does not harden his heart. God is gracious to such a man, and brings him back to the way of truth.[5] This way itself, however, consists, first of all and above all, in observing the Jewish-Hellenistic moral doctrines which we have already discussed in connection with the literature of the diaspora described on an earlier page.[6] Dependence upon this Jewish moral theology is so strong that long passages in 1 *Clement* could have been just as well prescribed, or read aloud to the Roman synagogue. If on occasion it speaks of "immortal gnosis", or "deeps of divine gnosis",[7] no conceptions proper to Hellenistic mysticism are implied by these words, in spite of their esoteric sound; but rather a clear knowledge of the divine commands and a right interpretation of God's word in the Old Testament. If we ask about the specifically Christian element of Clement's religion,

---

[1] 1 *Clem.*, 7, 5–7; 9–18; 19, 1, 43; 45, 2; 50, 3; 53, 1–5   [2] *Ibid.*, 12, 7, 16
[3] 1 *Ibid.*, 29, 1–3; 50, 7; 2, 4   [4] *Ibid.*, 33, 1–8
[5] *Ibid.*, 51, 3–52, 4; 7, 5–7; 48, 1; 35, 5   [6] *Vide supra* pp. 81 ff.
[7] 1 *Clem.*, 36, 2; 40, 1

we receive a very wordy answer with frequent mention of the name of Jesus Christ, on many pages of the letter. If, however, we inquire about the contents, it is Christ who, as the very vehicle of the divine revelation, preaches and completes the teachings just depicted. The commandments of God are indeed His commandments, and in their fulfilment is found the essence of Christian love. Clement, like Paul, sang an exalted hymn of the love which brought all the virtues to perfection and lifted men up to God; or Christ showed what that love was. He sacrificed His blood by His love[1] and lighted our way as the pattern of humility.[2] Moses possessed this love in a similar fashion, and portrayed it in perfection. God's elect were[3] also perfected in this love, so that Christ's own loving work excelled that of the earlier age only in the height of its accomplishment, and not in its innate quality.

Christ, and, in particular, the blood of Christ, are then spoken of in another way and in passages which reveal a deep sense of their value: "It was shed for our salvation, and it brought the grace of repentance to the whole world," and "through the blood of the Lord, redemption comes to all those who believe and hope in God";[4]—otherwise, however, Clement says nothing about "redemption", and, according to his explicit teaching, repentance was possible even in the days of the Old Testament. But was not the resurrection of Christ the point of departure of Christianity and thereby an essentially new element as contrasted with Judaism? Assuredly, for it gave a conclusive sense of certainty to the Apostles, and was now the guarantee of the future hope that the Creator of the world, who had raised so much in nature from death to life, would also justify the faithful confidence of His devout servants, and raise them up, just as He had raised Christ, who was the first fruits.[5] The echo of Pauline teachings is clear, but we notice also that Clement is a long way from grasping their proper sense, and does not base the Resurrection on a doctrine of the pneuma.

Hence Clement, indeed, speaks of man's redemption, not by his own wisdom, piety, or works, but through faith. But when

---

[1] 1 *Clem.*, 49–50   [2] *Ibid.*, 16   [3] *Ibid.*, 53, 5; 49, 5, 6; cf. 21, 6
[4] *Ibid.*, 7, 4; 12, 7; 21, 6   [5] 1 *Ibid.*, 42, 3; 24, 1; 26, 1

we hear, further, that from the beginning, God had justified all by faith, we find that the formula as far as the wording goes is Paul's, but it is now filled with a strange meaning; Clement's real view is expressed where he closes his exhortations to holiness and the practice of virtue with the sentence that we "are justified by works and not by words".[1] It is true that, even with him, faith is a comprehensive word for the spiritual quality of the Christian status, but, for the most part, it is only one of the Christian virtues and is put on the same plane as the others. He illustrates its nature by the examples of Noah and Abraham, of Rahab and Esther, as consisting of an unconditional confidence in God.[2] Thus it comes about, in one passage where he inserts a long quotation from Paul's epistle to the Romans, that, in clear contradiction to the Apostle's meaning, Clement actually sums up the Christian life as a ceaseless struggle for God's gifts promised in the future on the basis of gifts which we already possess, viz., life in immortality, joy in righteousness, truth in freedom of mind, faith in trust, and restraint in sanctification.[3]

This is not the only passage in which Paul is cited. Shortly afterwards the readers are expressly urged to take the first Epistle of the Corinthians into their hands, and to notice the warnings against schism in the church; still further on in the exhortation, Clement sings a panegyric of love, clearly dependent on Paul's. The Apostle's parable of the body and its members, as a symbol of the unity of the church, appears also in Clement in a shortened form[4]—only as a figure of speech. The mystical conception of the church as the body of Christ is remote from Clement's way of thought. Equally remote are the meaning of the doctrine of justification, and the cosmic drama of the antithesis of flesh and spirit, sin and grace, Adam and Christ. The only one of all these matters that is alive in him is the conception of the spirit as the most precious possession of Christians, "abundantly poured out upon them"; but the spirit stands in the forefront of his teachings rather as an organ of

---

[1] 1 *Clem.*, 30, 3; 32, 4
[2] *Ibid.*, 1, 2; 3, 4; 5, 6; 6, 2. Examples are 9, 4; 10, 7; 12, 1; 55, 6; cf. 26, 1; 35, 2
[3] 1 *Clem.*, 35, 1–6 of which 5–6 comes from Rom. 1: 29–32; cf. 62, 2, 64
[4] *Ibid.*, 47, 1–3; 49, 5 from 1 Cor., 13: 4–7; the parable of the body, 37, 5–38 1; cf. 1 Cor. 12: 12–31, 46, 7; cf. also 1 Cor. 1: 13

revelation in the Old Testament and in the apostolic period. We hear nothing more of the pneumatic enthusiasm of the early church, although the incorporation of the spirit into the Trinity is proclaimed in the confessional formula:[1] "We have one God, and one Christ, and one Spirit of Grace poured upon us, and one calling through Christ."

Apart from the Old Testament, a few sayings of the Lord, and the Pauline epistles, a final source is cited which leads to an unexpected disclosure, the Roman liturgy. Not only at the end of the letter where Clement turns to prayer, but in three places earlier, phrases, which are unmistakably formed in a liturgical manner, strike the ear, and must have come from the formula used in public worship by the church at Rome.[2] They show that this church had borrowed its liturgy from the synagogue; that is the origin of the "Holy, holy, holy"; the song of praise at the orderly creation of the world and the benevolent purpose of the Creator of man; and the prayer of praise, petition, and intercession, which concludes the whole. The Christian changes and interpolations are recognizable, but the Jewish character of all the rest of the text is just as certain. And since this congregational prayer fits perfectly into the rest of the letter, it follows that a conclusion based on this letter is valid for the Roman church. It reproduces, not some special liturgy, perhaps drawn up by Clement, but the practice of Roman Christians at the end of the first century, and therefore leads to an important inference.

This church was not born of the Pauline tradition, but had only a remote and outer contact with it. It grew directly out of the Greek-speaking synagogue, and represented a conception of Christianity such as we must assume was held in those circles of proselytes who were converted by the Christian preachers, and who accepted the new gospel. In other words: just as the external considerations, with which we have already dealt, made it probable that the Roman church was founded by missionaries from Antioch, so this, the earliest document of its inner life, confirms that hypothesis in every way. Christianity to this church was the religion of the moral code commanded

[1] i *Clem.*, 2, 2; 46, 6; for the Trinity 46, 6; 58, 2
[2] i *Clem.*, 33, 2–6; 34, 5–8; 38, 3–4; 59, 2–61, 3

by God, written down in the Old Testament, and finally revealed by the last and the greatest of the prophets, Jesus, who was the personal vehicle of the Holy Spirit. To be a Christian meant to follow these ethical commands, and, if in spite of honest desire, it was not possible to fulfil them completely, the sincere confession of sin, together with a genuine desire to do better would gain the forgiveness of a merciful God. Nevertheless the fundamental proposition stood firmly, viz. that works were all important. That had been the case from the beginning of the world, and would remain so until the Day of Judgment.

The specific kind of Christianity found in the church at Rome did not recognize the authority of the ceremonial law of the Old Testament, and can never have done so. Its religion was that of the Hellenistic proselytes, who, on their Jewish side, had adopted the specific ethic of Judaism, while spiritualizing its ritual by allegory. In churches where freedom from the Law was really maintained, as can be proved of even the earliest pre-Pauline church at Antioch, Christianity must have been conceived as the direct continuation, the fulfilment, of the religion of Jewish ideals such as had already been preached to proselytes everywhere. This conception did not hinder their taking over cult-forms and liturgical prayers from the synagogue. That is what had happened, too, in the Roman church.

We know too little of Peter to be able to say what influence he exercised on the Roman church's way of thinking. But Paul had been known personally to some of Clement's generation; to these he was the celebrated world-apostle and, like Peter, the model of a martyr. Over and above that, he was the author of letters which were held in the highest honour, and were, even then, known far and wide in Christendom; copies were current throughout the world, but had already suffered the first sign of literary corruptions on being transcribed, even in Rome.[1] They were fine examples of a Christian epistolary style, their well-defined formulas, exhortations, and teachings, influenced the church's manner of speaking, but the Roman Christian had not felt the least breath of the Pauline spirit. It is not an eviscerated Paulinism, but a purely Hellenistic proselyte

---

[1] 1 *Clem.*, 35, 6, cites according to the Western text Rom. 1: 32

Christianity, that we meet with here in Rome, an independent growth from a root in the first church, and of importance for the future. The Roman church could trace its descent back to the Hellenistic circle of Stephen.

The next document of the church at Rome may date from a generation later. It is known to us by the name of the second Epistle of Clement, but it faithfully preserves the same spirit. This pseudepigraphic writing is a sermon which a presbyter had delivered to the church,[1] and which we may place in Rome on account of its relations with 1 *Clement*. The Christian life is depicted as a continual struggle with the world and its wiles, a struggle to maintain the purity gained in baptism.[2] To live according to Christ, according to God's commandments, is the genuine confession of the Lord;[3] and the attitude required of the Christian is that of repentance, of hatred toward this world and its brief but destructive pleasures.[4] "Let us do righteously in order that we may be saved at the end; and even if we must suffer pains for a short while in this world, we shall reap the immortal fruit of the resurrection." This struggle, however, is not easy, and even the preacher knows himself to be altogether a sinner;[5] but, although all cannot win the crown, all must strive to come as near to it as possible. God rewards honest striving, the active repentance that is shown in prayer, fasting, and especially alms-giving. He rewards the "righteous" with the glory of the coming kingdom, and He casts sinners into hell.[6] Reward and punishment are the motives of the Christian life.

In this writing also, the Old Testament is the inexhaustible source of revelation, and, side by side with it, the words of Jesus appear as the words of God;[7] but, just as in 1 *Clement*, a certain carelessness in citing the words of the Lord is unmistakable, so also we find, in 2 *Clement*, such a rank growth of fantastic extensions and confabrications of sayings[8] that we see, quite clearly, the freedom with which men of this generation handled the most worthy traditions of the original church. A

---

[1] 2 *Clem.*, 19, 1; cf. 17, 3   [2] *Ibid.*, 6, 9; 7, 1–6; 8, 4–6   [3] *Ibid.*, 3, 4; 4, 2
[4] *Ibid.*, 5, 1–7; 6, 3; 8, 2; 19, 3   [5] *Ibid.*, 18, 2
[6] *Ibid.*, 16, 4; for the Kingdom: 5, 5; 9, 6; 11, 7; 12, 1; for Hell: 6, 7; 17, 7; 18, 2
[7] *Ibid.*, 13, 4   [8] *Ibid.*, 4, 5; 5, 1–4; 12, 2; 13, 2

generation later, gnostic caprice, which outgrew everything else in this sphere, had made the Church ripe for a careful sifting of tradition, a fact which was of importance for its own welfare, and for ours.

The letter which bears the name of James breathes the same spirit, viz., a Christian faith which has been nurtured in the Greek synagogue. On account of the pseudonym which its author uses, this letter was included in the New Testament canon. It appears to have been known at an early date in Rome, but the place in which it was written cannot even be guessed, although such information would be valuable. Like 1 *Clement*, it stands in literary dependence upon Paul, but it goes beyond him in so far as it is not intended for a single church, but presents its greetings to the whole of Christendom in the entire Roman empire, for that alone is what is meant by the "twelve tribes of the diaspora". This term, which for many centuries had no longer corresponded to any racial entity, was now the symbol of the "true Israel" of the Biblical promises, and thus of the Christian people. In this form, which finally denied all Jewish claims, it could have been coined only in the Gentile church. This Gentile church, however, was not Pauline; on the contrary, it regarded James as the leader of the first, Jerusalem, church. Taking him as the supreme authority, it now issued the epistle of James to exhort the entire Church, and to utter warnings against the characteristic language of Paul. It was not true, e.g., that a man was justified by faith apart from works; rather we must say that a man was justified by works, and not by faith alone. Even the examples of Abraham and of Rahab, adduced in Romans and in Hebrews as a proof, spoke, on closer examination, against the Pauline theory of faith.[1] This is a definite and conscious polemic against the teaching of Paul.

But when the author carries the discussion further, and understands by "works" the exercise of all the Christian virtues; and when faith is for him the rational acceptance of a proposition,[2] it becomes clear that he had not the least understanding of Paul. The reason was that the opposition to the

[1] Jas. 2: 14–26; for verse 23, cf. Rom. 4: 3; for verses 21 and 25, cf. Heb. 11: 17, 31
[2] Jas. 2: 19

Pauline thesis had no longer any reality. The Jewish legal righteousness and its "works" had disappeared and been forgotten, together with all the obligatory rites. The vital thing, the perfect, royal law of freedom, was expressed in the commandment to love one's neighbour,[1] and this, when applied, issued in a number of ethical commandments corresponding to the Jewish catechism for proselytes. What is adduced by James as Christian exhortation is so entirely Jewish that many of its details show how possible it is that the epistle was, originally, a product of the Greek synagogue, made Christian by a few additions where necessary. The name of Jesus Christ is, in fact, only mentioned twice,[2] and in purely formal phrases. Nothing is said that distinguishes Christian feeling—so near had this non-Pauline Gentile Christianity of the succeeding age returned to missionary Judaism.

It was from a church of this kind that the oldest Church Order arose. By a fortunate discovery, this Order became known, in the year 1883, to the world of scholars, and since then it has enriched and established our knowledge of the growth of the ancient church in an unforeseen manner. It bears the title: *Teaching of the Twelve Apostles*, and is usually cited, by its Greek name, as the *Didache*. It combines in the shortest form all the principal prescriptions for the regulation of church life. It begins with directions for giving instruction to catechumens. There follow prescriptions for baptism, fasting, prayer, and the Lord's Supper. Then it deals with the officials who were the vehicles of the spirit, i.e. apostles, prophets, and teachers; and a short discussion is added about observing Sunday. Then it goes on to deal with bishops and deacons; and the little book concludes with an urgent admonition to shape the Christian life with reference to the imminent parousia of the Lord, the omens and accompanying phenomena being described. Everything is in the briefest form and the most sober language.

It is particularly significant that the teaching given to the candidates for baptism should be built upon the Jewish plan of the "Two Ways" as used in the Hellenistic synagogue for instructing proselytes, and of which the roots were buried deep

[1] Jas. 2: 8; cf. Matt. 22: 40   [2] Jas. 1: 1–2: 1

in the past. It begins with the Jewish confession of faith (Deut. 6: 4–5) and the Decalogue, and then develops, in several variations, the principle of a pure ethic, free from all ritual elements. The Christians of the *Didache* now added the commandment of love of one's neighbour as prescribed by Jesus,[1] and as found, similarly, in the Old Testament, followed by the rule: "Nothing that you do not desire to happen to yourself, must you do to any other." It is significant that the Golden Rule is given in the negative form, otherwise usual, and not in the positive redaction in which Jesus laid it down.[2] Then a series of sayings of the Lord are placed before the next section of the Jewish text, sayings which demand love of one's enemy, self-sacrifice, and generosity. We see clearly that the question of the giving, and the right acceptance, of alms caused the writer anxiety. That is understandable, because earthly possessions were to be employed by a Christian as a means of redemption from his sins.[3] The way of life was an ethical struggle for an exalted goal, and flagellation of one's self was a valuable means of attaining it, but which, of course, not everyone could employ. Thus, near the end, we read the comforting words:[4] "If thou art able to take the whole yoke of the Lord upon thyself, thou shalt be perfect. But if thou canst not do it, then thou shalt do as much as thou canst."

Its asceticism extended to food, and we are reminded of the vegetarians, who had already been mentioned by Paul,[5] when the exhortation proceeds: "In regard to food be as abstemious as you are able. But withhold unconditionally from meat offered to idols, for that is worship of dead gods." Hence, in this church, the prescriptions of the Apostolic Decree were binding upon everyone. But already a differential ethic had been developed: the "perfect" take upon themselves the entire yoke, including obligatory asceticism; the great majority do as much as they are able, according to their ability. Sins appeared scarcely avoidable, but they could be annulled by the consistent giving of alms, and by public confession before the assembled church.[6] Fasting was practised in the Jewish mode but, as distinct from the "hypocrites", i.e. the Jews, it is to be

---

[1] Mark 12: 28–31   [2] Matt. 7: 12; Luke 6: 31   [3] *Did.*, 4, 6; cf. *Barn.*, 19, 10
[4] *Did.*, 6, 2–3; cf. 11, 11   [5] Rom. 14: 2   [6] *Did.*, 4, 6; 14, 1

on two other week-days; it was also prescribed as an express preparation for receiving baptism. The Lord's Supper is accompanied by prayers based on Jewish models. In these prayers, the church gives thanks for the divine gifts of life and knowledge brought to them through Jesus, and for spiritual food and drink; and it prays that Christians scattered throughout the entire world should be united in the Messianic Kingdom for which it earnestly longs. Neither here nor elsewhere in the *Didache* is anything said about the death and resurrection of Jesus, about His Cross and the meaning of His sacrificial death, about sin and the redemption of mankind, nor even about the divinity, pre-existence, and ascension, of Jesus.

The *Didache* gives the clearest possible outline of a type of Christianity entirely free from the Mosaic law. It has grown out of the earliest Christian mission as sent out by the Hellenistic, proselyte church. The document lauds Jesus as the teacher of a higher ethic and as victor over Judaism. Its Christian life depends on the operation of the spirit in the Church, and it looks forward to the coming of the Lord and His glorious kingdom. All the efforts of the Christian, all striving for steadfastness and perfection, are dedicated to this goal. The entire period of faith will have no value if, at the last moment, the Christian does not bravely withstand the threatening dangers, and reach perfection.[1] The Christian way of life does not consist in a consecrated endurance, but in straining all powers to full stretch, in the midst of a world which is tottering to ruin more markedly every day. The Christian is always on pilgrimage and he must hasten to meet a bright future, which comes down from heaven as a gift of God, but which must be striven for in a hard, self-denying struggle against one's self, and against the distractions and allurements of the present age.

An entirely different atmosphere blows over the fields into which the life-work of Paul had struck root and borne vigorous fruit. Of course, we find the characteristics of epigonism here too. This is not surprising, for in comparison with such an exceedingly creative person, all who come after him must necessarily appear less forceful. But in contradistinction from the dilute, ethical religion of the theologians and their churches,

[1] *Did.*, 16, 2

which we have already considered, the Christianity of the disciples of Paul was of far greater power.

As an addendum to the series of the Pauline epistles, a writing has been preserved which was provided by the librarians of the church with the title, "To the Hebrews", in accordance with the content. It is a religious tract intended to edify and instruct Christians. Using general phraseology it combines a retrospect on the most recent past with hints about the anxieties of the present.[1] At the end and quite intentionally, it makes use of one of Paul's own concluding formulas.[2] This fact shows that, even although the author belonged to the sub-apostolic period,[3] he meant to write in the spirit of the great Apostle, and to be heard with corresponding respect. Hebrews is remarkable from the literary standpoint: it begins as a theological tractate, is continued as such, although interspersed with digressions in the manner of a sermon, but ends as a pseudo-Pauline letter. This has not diminished its value to its readers in either ancient or modern times; only to scholars has it been the cause of much useless and fruitless speculation.

Hebrews has *one* great theme: Christ. Everything revolves round Him from the first word to the last; yet not round the Jesus of gospel tradition, but the Son of God preached by Paul. He was before all time, and had created the world, including everything of both higher or lower nature; He became man, died on the Cross for us, ascended to the right hand of God, and would soon appear again to those Christians who steadfastly yearned for Him.[4] But the author was not a mere imitator or expounder of Paul; rather he had an independent mind able to carry Paul's ideas further and enrich them from his own thought.

In place of the brief, almost reticent, phraseology with which Paul[5] speaks of the pre-existent Christ, we find here[6] the method of statement which became basic for future theological developments, viz. that the Son is the reflection of the divine glory and the impress of His being (His "hypostasis"). These expressions come from the language employed by Hellenistic

---

[1] Heb. 10: 32–34   [2] *Ibid.*, 13: 18–25   [3] *Ibid.*, 2, 3
[4] *Ibid.*, 9: 28, 10: 25   [5] Phil. 2: 6; *vide supra*, pp. 117 f.
[6] Heb. 1: 3; cf. Windisch, *ad loc.*

Jews in their theology; the terminology has a philosophic sound and points the way to future dogma. Since the Son was higher than all angels, higher also than Moses, so also His word, preached by the apostles, confirmed by signs and wonders, and testified by the outpouring of the Holy Spirit, was more powerful than the Law proclaimed by angels and served by Moses.[1] Just as John at a later date, so also now, Hebrews expanded Paul's thought, and stressed the "cosmic" significance of the incarnation of the Son of God:[2] God sends Him "into the world", and He "comes into the world". Then Hebrews comes to the cosmic drama, to which Paul had devoted very few words, and describes it fully in his own way, whilst owing almost every trait to Paul himself. Christ became our brother, similar to us in every respect, clothed in flesh and blood. He experienced human weakness, was tempted like us; this had taught Him sympathy with us, and enabled Him to help us in the danger of temptation.[3] To the Pauline phrase about the Redeemer who was obedient unto death,[4] he adds the gospel picture of the Jesus who struggled in Gethsemane,[5] "who in the days of His flesh, having offered up prayers and supplications with strong crying and tears unto Him that was able to save Him from death, and not having been heard for His godly fear, yet learned He obedience by the things which He suffered; and having been made perfect, He became unto all them that obey Him the author of eternal salvation."

While such passages show a psychological deepening of the Pauline *motif* of obedience, their elaboration of the contemplation of the Passion should be regarded as the principal theme of the entire tractate. The author describes the objective soteriological significance of the death of Jesus, in so far as he conceives it, not only as a sacrificial death as such, but as the ideal celebration of the high priestly sacrifice; and he supports this view by the kind of Biblical exegesis used by Hellenistic Jews. The king and priest Melchisedek, who mysteriously enters history without father and without mother, is the allegorical anti-type of the Son of God; and when he takes tithes

---

[1] Heb. 1: 4, 2: 1–4, 3: 1–5   [2] *Ibid.*, 1: 6, 10: 5   [3] *Ibid.*, 2: 11–18; 4: 15
[4] Phil. 2: 8
[5] Heb. 5: 7–9: the "not" has fallen out of our text; cf. Harnack, *Studien*, i, 249

from Abraham, the tribal father of the Israelite people, and blesses him, he shows thereby his higher worth. This in turn proves that the high-priesthood of Christ is higher than the Old Testament priesthood that goes back to Aaron, Levi, and Abraham.[1] It proves also that the new covenant (the new "testament"), whose mediator was Christ, was superior to the earlier covenant concluded with Abraham which is regarded as "antiquated" according to definite expressions of the epistle.[2] But no testament is valid apart from a death, no priestly, expiatory sacrifice is effective without blood.[3] This is exemplified in the Old Testament ritual, and expressed through the annual sacrifice of blood by the High-Priest in the Holy of Holies; but the full reality was brought about only by Christ when He, the sinless One, offered His body as an expiatory sacrifice for our sins and, once for all, made with His own blood an eternal expiation of the guilt of sin. Thus He became the true High-Priest after the order of Melchisedek, and His work made an end of every earlier priesthood. He preceded us into the Holy of Holies of heaven, where He sits on the throne at the right hand of God.[4]

To a man of this standpoint, Judaism is no longer a problem for the Church itself as it was in Paul's day. Rather it is the antiquated forerunner of the true, new religion; a subject to be discussed theologically, not because it represents a threatening danger, but because a full examination of the essential difference makes it possible to gain a deep understanding of the Christian position. Judaism and Christianity are fitted by Hebrews into an old antithetic scheme, which Jewish thinkers had previously used to contrast the heavenly world of perfection and the earthly world of weakness and sin. Thus, by contrast, the Levitical worship of sacrifices now appears as shadow and imitation as distinct from the heavenly truth of Christianity, the law given from Mount Sinai as distinct from the heavenly Jerusalem and its church of the first-born. But towards the end of the epistle,[5] the eschatological attitude of a Christian, who is a stranger upon this earth, is nevertheless expressed in a similar metaphor: "We have here no abiding city, but we seek

[1] Heb. 7: 1–19   [2] *Ibid.*, 7: 22; 8: 6–13; 9: 15; 12: 24   [3] *Ibid.*, 9: 7, 16–18, 22
[4] *Ibid.*, 8: 5; 9: 23; 11: 10; 12: 18–23; 6: 20; 8: 1, 2   [5] *Ibid.*, 13: 14

one to come." That is the heavenly Jerusalem as the goal of Christian hope.

In this way, the scriptural testimony to the sacrificial death of Christ becomes at the same time for the author a means for proving that Judaism had served its day. His purpose is not apologetic; rather he seeks to deal with the problems actually facing the Church; and how strongly his thoughts are conditioned by the needs and distresses of the Church is shown by the numerous digressions of his speculations and exhortations which he keeps introducing. For him also the Christian life is a warfare, a voluntary denial of happiness, and a bearing of suffering after the example of Christ: it is a wrestling even unto death against sin in the knowledge that God's fatherly love is revealed even in painful chastisement.[1] Patience is paired with faith in the reality of the things hoped for, and hope lightens the burden of the struggling Christian so that he can hold out to the end.[2] Paul had expressed himself similarly, but our author has his own answer to the question of a Christian's sinfulness, and this shows clearly how far he was removed from the pneumatic enthusiasm of the first period, and how largely he was influenced by the experience of the Church. That a Christian does not live an entirely sinless life was known to him as well as it was to Paul, and hence he too encourages his readers to fight against sin. In this way the sins which are actually committed appear as manifestations of human weakness and as involuntary transgressions. But if we sin deliberately after we know the truth, then no further expiatory sacrifice is available for us. Judgment waits for us because we have trodden the Son of God under foot and despised His blood, and—it is a terrible thing to fall into the hands of the living God. In another passage he declares it impossible that a baptized Christian who has fallen into sin could repent again because he has crucified the Son of God by his deed and brought Him into contempt.[3]

It is clear that under this "fall" a genuine denial of Christ and His teaching was understood, and that "deliberate" sin must have consisted in a gross transgression of the Christian

[1] Heb. 12: 1–11   [2] *Ibid.*, 12: 2; 10: 36–11: 1; 3: 6, 14; 6: 11
[3] *Ibid.*, 10: 26–31; 6: 4–6

moral law. In the same way, the immoral and the adulterers were expressly consigned to the divine judgment, and the possibility of repentance was refused to "immoral" Esau.[1] Thus even at this early date a distinction was made between "venial" and "mortal" sins. It dominated the entire practice of the Church from this time forward,[2] as it attempted to realize the Pauline ideal of a Christianity free from sin, but in this modified sense. Moreover in place of the cautious reticence of Paul[3] we have a clear pronouncement as to the lot of those who commit mortal sin. This whole doctrine, however, had only become possible because the absoluteness of the Pauline conception of sin had been surrendered and a relative toleration had taken its place. This was of course a step backward to a Judaizing moralism which however we must regard as an attempt to translate the genuine paradox of the Pauline teaching of justification and sanctification into something rational, and so make practicable what had been found impossible. This turning aside from the definiteness of genuine Paulinism is to be found elsewhere in our author—or rather in the whole trend of the succeeding period. He praises faith frankly, and also cites the saying about the righteous man who lives by his faith: but for Hebrews, faith means the firm conviction that the Christian hopes had already been realized, i.e. the inherent expectation of the heavenly Jerusalem which was founded upon the certainty that God is, and that He had created the world and would reward His own.[4] When we compare the deductions of Hebrews with the very similar words of Clement of Rome[5] it is obvious that the former possess a greater reality and a more specifically Christian quality; measured by Paul, however, they still sound weak. With the narrowing down of the Pauline conception of faith, the doctrine of justification retreated into the background because the presuppositions necessary for its understanding, which were difficult enough to grasp in themselves, completely disappeared when Jewish Christianity became a separate entity. The extent to which this separation had taken place is shown by the comfort which the author offers to his readers[6]: he says that God would not be so unjust as to forget

---

[1] Heb. 13: 4; 12: 16-17   [2] 1 John 5: 16   [3] *Vide supra*, p. 124
[4] Heb. 10: 38; 11: 1, 6, 10, 16   [5] 1 *Clem.*, 9, 4-12, 8   [6] Heb. 6: 10

their work and their loving deeds which they had done to His honour at an earlier date, and were now doing in ministering to the "saints".

We do not know where Hebrews was written, and no attempts to guess the author have reached a convincing conclusion. Not even the assertion made about A.D. 200 in the west[1] to the effect that the letter was written by Barnabas, can be regarded as an ancient tradition. It is a pure guess and, when examined critically, it seems far from probable. Since the concluding phrases are consciously modelled on Paul's lines, they might have been written by someone outside his circle altogether,—if only on account of their literary pseudonymity. Otherwise the Italians, who sent their greetings (13: 24), could quite well be conceived as members of the church at Rome, and this might be taken to mean that the epistle was written there. It was certainly known at an early date in that city, for 1 *Clement*[2] unmistakably quoted and imitated it. But it gives us no reflection of the religious and theological position of the Roman church, such as we gain from anything which we have discussed so far. If the author had written in Rome, he must have been a newly-arrived, or an itinerant teacher, who had received his education in Jewish, Hellenistic circles, and his Christian faith from Paul. The question may be raised whether after Paul's activity in Rome there were disciples of his who preserved his ideas, and on occasion expressed them forcefully in contradistinction from other views. Further, one may ask whether the warning against various strange teachings, with special emphasis on food restrictions,[3] had reference to the prohibitions in regard to meat, as contained in the Apostolic Decree, or to after-effects of Roman vegetarianism with which Paul had himself already dealt. Such questions may be raised, but there is no hope of a satisfying answer.

The writing which bears the name of Peter and which was taken up into the New Testament canon as 1 Peter breathes the same Pauline atmosphere. It deals comprehensively with the subject of a Christian's rebirth, by the word of God and by faith, and leading to a hope of salvation. It may well have been

---

[1] Tertullian ,*de pudic.*, 20   [2] 1 *Clem.*, 36; cf. 17, 1; 9, 3-12, 8
[3] Heb. 13: 9; cf. Rom. 14: 2

a sermon addressed to newly baptized persons, and adapted to form a circular letter. At least this would account for the fact that it attempts to discuss all the principal heads of the Christian doctrine of salvation. Redemption had been planned by God before the foundations of the world were laid, but had been revealed now when the present age declines towards its end. In previous ages the prophets had already foreseen it, but now the evangelists carried the eternal word of God throughout the world, viz. that Christ had redeemed us from a vain life and had died for our sins.[1] A sacrificial lamb, He had accepted suffering and death, and had borne our sins upon the cross in order to set us free from them.[2] Then He had descended into hell in order to preach there to the spirits in prison and to offer them the opportunity of hearing the gospel.[3] After that, He rose from the dead, ascended to heaven, where He now sat at the right hand of God as ruler over all spiritual powers, whence we await His coming as the judge of the living and the dead.[4]

The theme is not developed systematically, but, formulated in various ways; it passes to and fro through many homiletic discussions and digressions, the Pauline evangel being the foundation of the Christian faith, both in the author and of his hearers and readers. This evangel is expanded somewhat further, as in the teaching of Christ's descent into hell, and, to some extent, handed on in a formal fashion, as in its theory of sacrifice and propitiation (a theory which Hebrews had developed in its own way): the principle of salvation "through faith" is maintained, but it is no longer conceived vitally. Nothing is said about justification or the righteousness of God. Christians are just "the believers" and faith is either faith in God, or else the confident expectation of the future revelation of the Christ who is still invisible.[5] The hope of the parousia is still alive, and the conviction of the near approach of the End is a motive for the exhortation to be sober and constant in prayer.[6]

The profound, mystical idea of a Christian's fellowship with the sufferings of his Lord,[7] a fellowship which had been brought

---

[1] 1 Pet. 1: 18–20, 10–12, 23–25; 3: 18   [2] *Ibid.*, 1: 19; 2: 24
[3] *Ibid.*, 3: 19, 20; 4: 6   [4] *Ibid.*, 1: 3; 3: 21–22; 4: 5–7
[5] *Ibid.*, 1: 5, 9, 21; 2: 7; 1: 8   [6] *Ibid.*, 4: 7, 8   [7] *Vide supra*, pp. 119 f.

about by the spirit, was by this time no longer comprehensible; but suffering for Christ's sake had become a terrible reality for Christians throughout the world. It was felt as a temptation, a testing of the genuineness of faith; and the Pauline phrase about "sharing the sufferings of Christ" was understood in the sense of following His example. Thus there arose the conception that the very suffering of a Christian had propitiatory power in itself; it set him free from sin and led him along the path of fulfilling the will of God.[1] The presupposition of this conception was that a man was "reborn" through Christ, and "like a new-born child" began his life afresh with a longing for purer, spiritual milk.[2] Here we have a metaphor drawn from Hellenistic mysticism, and, at an early date, it may have been employed at baptismal services in the Christian churches, after being taken over from the initiatory ceremony of some mystery or another. When Paul speaks of a new life effected by baptism,[3] he presupposes this conception, in the last analysis. But what followed for our author was, not mystical excesses or dreams of a sacramental certainty of salvation, but a conception of Christians as the temple of God, a temple built on Christ as the foundation stone and governed by the spirit; a "holy people" who feel themselves strange in this world, and contend with the devil and the lusts of the flesh in order to do the will of God.[4]

References to the Christian life, exhortations to persons of different status in the form of family regulations, warnings against the snares of the world and the wiles of the devil, constitute the practical kernel of this writing, and indicate the way of "purifying the soul in obedience to the truth".[5] The author's ethic, like his dogmatic, bears a Pauline stamp; but it is a diluted Paulinism, because it has lost the final and, for religion, the deepest motives of the genuine Paul.

This writing is another that can be conceived as originating in Rome, for the city "of Babylon", whose church sends greetings at the end, can only be the capital "of this world" described by its apocalyptic name, i.e. Rome; and the companions of the writer, Silvanus and Mark, belong to the Pauline circle, the

[1] I Pet. 5: 9, 4, 12–13; 1: 6–7; 2: 21; 4: 1–2   [2] *Ibid.*, 1: 3, 23; 2: 2; 3: 14
[3] Rom. 6: 4   [4] I Pet. 2: 5–15; 5: 8   [5] *Ibid.*, 1: 22

latter in particular during the Roman imprisonment.[1] The pseudonymous author in this case is not Paul, but Peter; and that he could be put forward as the author of such an entirely Pauline document was only conceivable at a time, and probably also in a place, which were at a considerable distance from the scene of the last historical activity of both Apostles. Once the author settled on Peter as the patron of his epistle, he had decided the place from which it should be written, and the circle from which a few secondary figures should be chosen. But what acceptance could a Roman writer expect in addressing persons in the missionary regions of northern and western Asia Minor? Hence, the hypothesis at once arises that the letter was really intended for these churches, and, consequently that it was written in one of the original Pauline churches in the province of Asia. Here no one would dream of anything else than that Peter, while in Rome, had been converted by Paul to his teaching.

A few pages earlier, we showed that Paul's mystical ways of thought, together with his metaphors familiar in Hellenistic religion, had not led to some sort of nature religion, but were expanded in the opposite direction into an ethic which the Church could apply—a feature which entirely corresponded to the Apostle's own leaning. The same holds good to an even greater extent in Ephesians, which, at a considerably earlier date, was modelled on Paul's letter to the Colossians. In the latter, Paul defines his attitude towards an incipient gnosticism —we shall have to deal with this later—and in so doing develops ideas which can only be understood as intentionally contrasted with the doctrines he is refuting; in fact, Paul outlined a kind of cosmic mysticism. Ephesians, however, uses the same words, but without reference to views current in the Christian church. Like other Pauline conceptions they have many ethical implications.[2]

The expression *pleroma* ("the fullness" of God), used without explanation in Colossians is used frequently in Ephesians, although not to characterize the cosmic significance of Christ. Rather, it refers to the Church[3] which is filled by the spirit of

[1] Col. 4: 10. Philem. 24; cf. also 2 Tim. 4: 11
[2] Dibelius, *Handb*. on Eph. 4: 16   [3] Eph. 1: 23; 3: 19; 4: 13

Christ. It is true that Paul often[1] named the Church as the "body of Christ", and in Colossians he extended this metaphor to the whole of the spiritual beings, whether above or beneath the world, who serve Christ, or whose head is Christ. In Ephesians[2] the same passage is stripped of its higher meaning and used to describe the Church. Occasionally, Paul employed[3] the metaphor that a Christian was a temple of God in which the spirit had its dwelling; we now meet the same metaphor, but with the express meaning that the Church as a whole, "is built on the foundation of the apostles and the prophets, Christ being the corner stone"—just as 1 Peter also employed it.[4] The relation of Christ to the Church is exemplified for the author[5] by marriage, as in the Old Testament figure; and he characterizes this relationship with the word "mystery", a term which had been of great importance in Paul, but in another sense. The conversion of the Gentiles to Christ appears to him[6] as a revelation of a long-hidden, divine mystery confided to "His holy apostles and prophets", whereas what was said in the passage from Colossians, copied here, meant the gospel in its full extent, the gospel that was proclaimed to "His Saints" as such, i.e. to the Christians. It is therefore plain that Ephesians is the work of a writer of the sub-apostolic period.

The Church with its numerous individual congregations constituted the object of the author's spiritual care in the so-called Pastoral Epistles, i.e. the two letters to Timothy and the one to Titus. Here the Church found itself under a necessity of adopting a definite constitution because it must reckon with the possibility of an extended existence. The second coming of the Lord was still expected, but that expectation no longer furnished a criterion for testing the value of one's work and life: the Lord would indeed come but[7] "only at His own time". The world lived now in its last period and the apocalyptic "final times" were here. Thus prophecy was fulfilled, as the Church was finding to its cost, the prophecy[8] of the appearance of heretical persons and Satanic seducers who confuse doctrine

---

[1] *Vide supra*, p. 119   [2] Col. 2: 19; Eph. 4: 16; 5: 30
[3] 1 Cor. 3: 16–17; 6: 19; 2 Cor. 6: 16
[4] Eph. 2: 20–22; 1 Pet. 2: 5; cf. *Hermas, Vis.*, iii, 3, 3. *Sim.*, ix, 13, 1
[5] Eph. 5: 31–32   [6] Eph. 3: 4–6; cf. Col. 1: 24–26   [7] 1 Tim. 6: 15
[8] *Ibid.*, 4: 1

and morals. The Pastoral Epistles were meant to deal with this case inasmuch as they insist on the apostolic ordination of the church officers (including the presbyters, as well as the bishops and deacons), who had been commanded to care for "sound teaching" and the moral life of the Church. Hence in these writings we find a large number of ethical exhortations, some of which are introduced as detached injunctions, quite in the Pauline manner. Others are fitted into the favourite category of the family regulations, and extended, by the addition of relevant sections, into genuine regulations for the Church.

Numberless efforts have been made to gain a clear and unbroken picture of the opponents who were attacked, but the effort fails ever and again on account of the shadowy character of the records. "The heretics" were concerned with myths and endless genealogies, and these myths were "old wives' tales", and of Jewish origin; both they and the genealogies were bound up with foolish questions, with disputes and discussions "about the law":[1] they were concerned with "clean" and "unclean", with abstaining from certain foods, and also the prohibition of marriage; and finally the assertion was made that the Resurrection had already taken place[2]—this could only mean that, when a Christian received the gift of the spirit, he was *ipso facto* granted victory over death.[3] Whether they deduced therefrom that the true Christian did not die, or that bodily death was an indifferent matter, whether they, like the Corinthians whom Paul attacked,[4] denied the Jewish idea of the resurrection, cannot be determined more exactly. But since their teaching is expressly described[5] as "gnosis falsely so-called", we have every right to say that it was Jewish gnostics that were attacked in the Pastoral Epistles in the references to the office and the doctrine of the Church; only we are unfortunately not in the happy position of being able to complete their picture from other sources, or to connect them with gnostic schools otherwise known.

The Pastoral Epistles are the earliest documents in which we may see how the Church had to contend with heretics. The

---

[1] 1 Tim. 1: 4; 4: 7; 2 Tim. 4: 4; Tit. 1: 14; 3: 9; *re* Jewish, 1 Tim. 1: 7; Tit. 1: 10, 14; 3: 9
[2] *Ibid.*, 1: 15; 1 Tim. 4: 3; 2 Tim. 2: 18   [3] *Vide infra*, p. 231
[4] 1 Cor. 15: 12   [5] 1 Tim. 6: 20

first traces of gnosticism were to be found in Paul's time in the Lycus valley,[1] and by the time of these letters, it had adopted a Jewish dress, crept into the churches, and brought about confusion. It was then attacked in accordance with the literary models which the Apostle himself had formerly employed in Colossians, and the Pauline style of letter was of service to our author for making his writings effective in developing the authority of tradition. The very language of the author is modelled on the Pauline letters, and his theological formulas, which occur from time to time, have been derived from the same sources. The letters appear to have originated in Asia Minor, a region which is expressly[2] mentioned as the home of the heresies that they attacked; they undoubtedly arose in a church of Pauline tradition, and the praise given to Onesiphorus of Ephesus[3] makes it likely that this city was the author's home.

We must take notice in this connection of another writing current under the name of Barnabas. A greeting by way of preface endows it with the epistolary form which by now had become customary. Apart from this there is no literary artifice, for it is a straightforward, theological tractate. The author frequently says with emphasis that he does not speak "like a teacher", but rather that he desires to be regarded as a member of the church.[4] Apparently he had really been a "teacher", of a kind known to us as Christian officers in the *Didache*. He was a learned manikin, more than a little proud of his dexterity, and, on account of this, he wishes to make the results of his inquiries available to Christian people in general in the form of a pamphlet. Apparently he had made the acquaintance of Christianity in the shape depicted in the *Didache*: he regarded the catechism, contained in the Teaching of the Two Ways as of fundamental significance; and he pressed home the necessity for standing firm in the stress of the final woes, by suggesting that otherwise the entire period of one's life and faith would be of no value.[5] However, he knew of the Pauline teaching in the form, and with the kind of understanding, which it enjoyed in the sub-apostolic period—a kind of superstructure on a foundation of Jewish ethic. Thus we find in him a similar attitude to

---

[1] *Vide supra*, pp. 195 f.   [2] 2 Tim. 1: 15   [3] *Ibid.*, 1: 16, 18
[4] *Barn.*, 1, 8; 4, 6–9; 6, 5   [5] *Barn.*, 18–20; 4, 9; cf. *Did.*, 16, 2

that which we saw in Clement of Rome, except that now Paulinism is emphasized much more markedly; it is felt to be an essential element in Christian theology, and is presented as such. Faith, love, hope, are the characteristics of a Christian, and righteousness is now added.[1] Christ is the pre-existent Son of God, and the Father, at the creation of the world, spoke to Him the word:[2] "Let us make man." Hence Christ co-operated at creation. Although He was Lord of the entire world, He nevertheless decided to appear on earth in the flesh, to preach to Israel's deaf ears, and so complete the heinousness of the sins of this people who killed the prophets. The Pauline *motif* of stiff-neckedness is thus presented without any reconciliation at the conclusion.[3] Therefore He accepted death upon the cross for our sakes, in order that He might bring us forgiveness of sins through His blood, and that we might thus be created anew.[4] He had vanquished death, and revealed resurrection from the dead; and, at the last day, He would come to judge both the living and the dead.[5]

Those are the principal heads of his theology;[6] they re-echo throughout the epistle and they provide him with the most important individual points of his argument. The purpose of his work is everywhere to prove that the whole of Christianity had been prophesied beforehand by the prophets in the Old Testament.[7] Strings of quotations, apparently derived from the tradition of some catechumen school, serve this purpose. Over and above this, however, he strains his exegetical ingenuity to the utmost, in order to buttress his proofs down into the smallest details, using allegorical artificialities, and tracking out unsuspected relations. He is still following the customary paths, however, when he interprets the food-laws of the Old Testament spiritually, e.g. the prohibition to eat pork was, according to him, not intended to be carried out literally but only to warn against intercourse with men who are similar to pigs; and, from this standpoint, he finds it possible to draw comparisons between other forbidden animals and certain types of human sins.[8] His symbolism of the cross cannot have been un-

---

[1] *Barn.*, 1, 4, 6   [2] *Ibid.*, 5, 5; 6, 12; 14, 5   [3] *Vide supra*, p. 128
[4] *Barn.*, 5, 1; 6, 11   [5] *Ibid.*, 5, 6; 7, 2, 9   [6] Cf. especially *Barn.*, 5, 1–14
[7] *Barn.*, 1, 7   [8] *Ibid.*, 10, 1–8

known to the Church: he finds the cross foreshadowed by the outstretched hands of Moses in prayer, and by the brazen serpent which Moses lifted up in the wilderness.[1]

It is not surprising that, in Old Testament passages which speak of living water and the like, he sees evidence of baptismal water. It is more forced when he explains the "tree (wood), planted on the water-brooks" by Paul's doctrine of baptismal death:[2] "In confidence in the wood of the cross do the baptismal candidates go down into the water." The scapegoat, which is sent away into the wilderness, in acordance with Lev. 16: 7–10, is for him, of course, Jesus; but in this connection he also explains the later rite, which had come to him through some Jewish source. According to this rite, the animal was spat upon, and stabbed; a strip of red woollen cloth was then bound on its horns and afterwards laid upon a thorn-bush in the wilderness. Barnabas regarded the lot of the scapegoat as reflecting the sufferings of Christ even in detail, and the strip of red cloth reappears at the Parousia as the purple mantle of the Lord when He returns to act as judge.[3] Naturally circumcision was not to be regarded as a bodily operation but to be understood as circumcision of the ears and heart. When we are told that Abraham circumcised his three hundred and eighteen servants, this is to be regarded as a particularly subtle reference to the death of Jesus on the cross: for the number eighteen is written in Greek with the letters I and H (=a long Greek "e"), i.e. the first two letters of the name Jesus, and the letter representing the number three hundred is the Greek T, i.e. the cross.[4]

By this method, he seeks to prove everything that appears to him worth proving, including chiliasm: a thousand years are like a day in the eyes of God. Hence the six days of creation mean a period of six thousand years after which the present evil time will be destroyed, and the Son of God will come again and judge the world. Then will dawn the Sabbath of the millennial kingdom in a world which has been transformed into a thing of beauty. Then will follow a new world, which will apparently be reckoned as an eighth millennium, since its symbol was Sunday the eighth day as solemnized by Christians.[5]

[1] *Barn.*, 12, 1–7; cf. John 3: 14   [2] *Barn.*, 11, 1–8, following Ps. 1: 3
[3] *Barn.*, 7, 6–10   [4] *Ibid.*, 9, 1–9   [5] *Ibid.*, 15, 1–9

The author describes this extraordinary learning with the exalted name of "gnosis". He intended his readers to gain from his book "perfect knowledge" as well as faith,[1] the final result being that the relevance of the Old Testament is altogether denied to the Jewish people. He declares, in spite of the fact that many teachers assert the contrary, that we must deny outright that God had concluded a covenant with Israel which now applies to the Christians. The covenant which God offered Moses, was never accepted by Israel, for Israel had immediately taken to idol-worship and thus refused it. Therefore God had suspended the covenant for the sake of us Christians and revealed it through Jesus in order that we might be loosed from darkness, and, as a holy people, receive the heritage promised to the patriarchs.[2] Similar propositions in Hebrews were not based on genuine discussions with Jews or Jewish Christians,[3] and that is equally the case with Barnabas. But the recent erection of the temple of Capitoline Jupiter on the ancient holy site of the temple in Jerusalem (A.D. 123), an event which brought about the war of Barkochba, is regarded by him as the fulfilment of the prophetic saying Isa. 49: 17, and referred to the second destruction of the city, the people, and the temple.[4] This affords us at the same time a hint that the writing originated shortly after this insurrection which ended (A.D. 135) in the last years of Hadrian's reign. We can say nothing with any probability of accuracy as to the place in which it was written.

Our survey of the writings of the sub-apostolic period shows that, after the early separation of Jewish Christianity, two streams began to flow in the church mixing in varying ways and degrees. The first was the mission of the Hellenists, who were free from the Law. These worked in large areas round about themselves, especially among the proselytes of the Greek synagogues, to whom they offered the gospel as a teaching of purified morality on a monotheistic basis, as it had been preached and deepened by Jesus. They took over from Judaism not only the Old Testament, but also, to a large extent, its liturgy and mode of worship; and they successfully used its

[1] *Barn.*, 1, 5; 5, 4; 6, 9 (9, 8; 10, 10), 13, 7; 18, 1   [2] *Ibid.*, 4, 6–8; 14, 1–9
[3] *Vide supra*, p. 208   [4] *Barn.*, 16, 3–4

Hellenized learning and its propaganda writings for their own purposes. Side by side with this stream, was that of the Pauline churches with their proud heritage of the letters of the great Apostle. Thus its theology was rejuvenated ever afresh, a theology which comprehended heaven and earth, and probed the profundities of the Godhead. The Pauline churches stressed his doctrine of redemption through Christ and His death, as well as the pneumatic, and personal character of Paul's Christ-mysticism. For the practical purposes of everyday life there resulted, here again, a refined, ethical doctrine built and Christianized on a Jewish basis, and corresponding, in essence, to the views of the other group. Concurrently with the decay of understanding of the original power of the Pauline thoughts, and with the rise of the necessity for the moral education of the churches, the differences gradually smoothed themselves out. In the days of Trajan and Hadrian, early Catholicism began to show its face. It had taken over from Judaism its moralism and its liturgy; from Hellenism its popular sacramental theology and various forms of pneumatic mysticism; from the Pauline world of thought his theology as a doctrine of God and Christ, of redemption through the blood of Christ, and of sanctification through the spirit.

Chapter Twelve

JOHN

AT THE BEGINNING OF THE SECOND CENTURY THERE WAS in Asia Minor a group of five writings, which were inter-related in many respects, and which were regarded as the work of a single author. His name was John, and, in the tradition of the church in the succeeding age, he was looked upon as the son of Zebedee and the disciple of Jesus. The first part of the book of Revelation includes seven letters to churches in Asia Minor. The letters had been dictated to John by divine revelation, and he had received them on the island of Patmos in the open sea off the bay of Miletus;[1] but there is no hint in the book whether this John was the apostle or not. Nevertheless, it is clear that the author was familiar with a number of ideas and phrases characteristic of the other writings in the Johannine corpus. This is more markedly the case in the two short letters, 2 John, addressed to an unnamed church, and 3 John, to a certain Gaius. The language is restricted to Johannine phraseology,[2] viz. knowledge of the truth, walking in the truth, the commandment of brotherly love that is not new but old, the perfect joy, to be from God, to see God, the testimony. Indeed one phrase at the end of the third epistle recurs word for word at the end of the gospel,[3] and the beginning of the first epistle is unmistakably related to the commencement and the conclusion of the gospel.[4] Even should the Apocalypse be set in a place apart, if only on account of its linguistic peculiarities, the identity in authorship of the letters and the gospel is obvious, both in theological ideas and in idiom. This assumption, however, does not immediately settle the Johannine problem, but rather makes it more urgent; the main difficulty lies in the gospel.

The paradoxical character of many of its expressions has always been a puzzle to expositors. In attempting an exact

[1] Rev. 1: 9   [2] 2 John 1: 4, 5, 12; 3 John 3: 4, 6, 11, 12
[3] *Ibid.*, 12; John 21: 24   [4] 1 John 1: 1–2; cf. John 1: 1–4; 20: 25–27

exegesis, commentators become involved in intolerable contradictions, which cannot be understood nowadays as due to
literary style, or to the absent-minded unconcern of a capricious
or careless writer. They are only comprehensible by assuming
far-reaching interpolations of an editor, or, perhaps, that the
original form has been re-arranged in several places. But it
would be useless to attempt to separate old sources and later
additions completely from one another: everything is so firmly
interconnected that, although we may be able to point out the
different elements here and there, yet we cannot unravel the
threads. And since it was the author of the letters who was
responsible for the definitive redaction, then, in spite of all
contradictions in detail, nothing will ever affect the final
result. There will always be a single, harmonious, religious
and theological attitude throughout the entire "Johannine"
literature, of which the gospel constitutes the main part. And
the gospel has the appearance of belonging to an epoch, and of
trying to present a message, which are very remote from the
traditions and purposes of the synoptists. Of course, even the
latter plainly and abundantly show that the churches influenced
the form into which the gospel-material was cast; but, in their
case, the re-casting of the tradition, or the transformation of
legendary elements, took place in a naïve and obvious manner,
and indeed, to some extent, entirely unconsciously. The Fourth
Gospel, however, is the free and bold, creative work of a man
who, starting from his knowledge of Christ, depicts the earthly
forms of revelation of the incarnate logos, and only employs
tradition to add detail and graphic quality. On the whole, however, in the free exercise of his fantasy, he goes far beyond the
old limitations in presenting, and in meaning to present, not
history but theology.

The synoptic tradition relates miracles of the Saviour with
great restraint; He performed them owing to His sympathy
with suffering and need; but for our author, the miracles are
cogent proofs of a god-like power; they are not done for the
sake of the person concerned, but to reveal the glory of God
and His only-begotten Son.[1] For these reasons, they go beyond
all human power to grasp: Lazarus's body had already begun

[1] John 11: 4, 15; 9: 3; 2: 11

to decompose when he was raised again to life; and, instead of
the healing of the blind beggar told simply by the synoptists,
John records the healing of a man born blind, "since the world
began it was never heard that anyone opened the eyes of a man
born blind" (9: 32). At the marriage in Cana, the needs of the
guests were not serious, but as a proof of His glory, Jesus worked
a Dionysian miracle and changed the water in six large vessels
into wine of the finest flavour. Thus He did sign after sign for
men to see and believe that the Father had sent Him. But
alongside the mere performance of these miracles stands their
spiritual value: they are miracles in themselves, and also
symbols of final truth. When Jesus had fed the five thousand
with five loaves and two fishes, He proceeded to speak on the
theme: "I am the bread of life" and drew to a conclusion with
a doctrine of the Lord's Supper:[1] "Except ye eat the flesh of the
Son of man and drink his blood, ye have no life in yourselves.
He that eateth My flesh and drinketh My blood hath eternal
life; and I will raise him up at the last day." He introduced the
healing of the man born blind with the words:[2] "When I am
in the world, I am the light of the world"; and before the
raising of Lazarus He said to Martha:[3] "I am the resurrection
and the life: he that believeth on Me, though he die, yet shall
he live: and whosoever liveth and believeth on Me shall never
die."

The Christ of this gospel is free from all the burdens of earth
from the outset. The world may take offence at Him because,
after all, He is the son of Joseph and Mary, and has come from
Nazareth whence no good thing can come[4]—the evangelist
never thinks of speaking about the virginity of Mary nor of
saying that Jesus was born in Bethlehem, as prophesied. He is
in a position to give a higher message: "In the beginning was
the word, and the word was with God, and the word was God.
All things were made by him; and without him was not anything made that hath been made. And the word became flesh
and dwelt among us and we beheld his glory, as of the only-
begotten from the Father, full of grace and truth." Christ is the
earthly epiphany of the divine logos in human form: he had been
in heaven with God before time began, and now He had

---

[1] John 6: 53, 54   [2] *Ibid.*, 9: 5   [3] *Ibid.*, 11: 25, 26   [4] *Ibid.*, 1: 45; 6: 42

returned to the Father, where He abides in glory.[1] The hypostatization of the divine functions is boldly taken from the Jewish
sphere of ideas,[2] and used as the key to the secret of Jesus. In
the book of Proverbs, the word for wisdom, *sophia*, is of the
feminine gender. John rejected both the Hebrew and the Greek
form, in favour of a term of fairly similar meaning, but masculine gender, viz. the logos. This was a term that Philo, too, had
used instead of *sophia* as the subject of his speculations,[3] because
it could be linked with the logos of the Greek philosophers. And
since the author uses these ideas, not only in the formal expressions of the prologue, but really also throughout the whole
gospel, he is in a position to separate the life of Jesus from
history, and, in a way, to free Him from temporal conditions.

What Jesus says in this gospel is not derived from tradition—
there are only rare echoes of synoptic sayings of Jesus. Rather,
he gives a supra-temporal, eternal revelation of God to His
own, i.e. to the world, in as far as it accepts the word of God.
Only in appearance does Christ speak to the persons whom the
evangelist has ranged around Him; in reality, His words, un-
conditioned by time, sound in the ears of the Church and bring
it to the knowledge of the truth, bring light and life to it.
Nicodemus comes to the Master by night desiring to learn
from Him. Jesus takes up the conversation, and soon begins to
speak of re-birth in baptism, His ascension, His death on the
cross, the soteriological meaning of His incarnation, and the
division between believers and unbelievers. Nothing further is
recorded about Nicodemus; he has disappeared.[4] He would not
have been able to understand a word of what Jesus said—he
had served the evangelist only as the voice uttering the key-
word which starts the address to the Church of the succeeding
age. Similarly in the case of the Greeks who desired to see
Jesus, and therefore applied to Philip: he and Andrew go to
Jesus, and announce the inquirers, but Jesus responds with a
prophecy of His death, into which are interwoven certain
strands from the synoptic account of Gethsemane. A voice from
heaven announces the coming, glorious transfiguration. "And
the people, who stood nearby and heard it, said: it thundered;

---

[1] John 8: 38, 58; 3: 13; 6: 62; 12: 16   [2] *Vide supra*, pp. 99 f.
[3] *Vide supra*, pp. 95 f.   [4] John 3: 1–22

others opined: an angel spoke with Him." Jesus continued His speech[1]—but we do not learn whether the Greeks ever did get to see Jesus; they vanish, like Nicodemus, as soon as they have served the technique of the narrator.

In regard to another matter, we grant that the evangelist takes great pains to give the impression that he is keeping close to his facts. He gives not only many notes about the time,[2] and indeed the hour, of an event, but also numerous data about place.[3] He goes far beyond all the synoptic traditions and phraseology, and produces the impression of a most exact acquaintance with the locality. The details are not always clear, and cannot always be checked; but if they turn out to be geographically correct, they prove the author's knowledge of the Holy Land. There is something to be said for the supposition that he had travelled in Palestine, and become acquainted with the local legends alive in the churches there.[4] In any case, he was familiar with Jewish customs and points of view,[5] naturally of his own times, however. He knows so little of the period before the destruction of Jerusalem that he assumes, quite naïvely, that the Jewish high-priest was changed and installed each year, just like a provincial high-priest among the Hellenists.[6] All these matters are employed to give colour to the record, colour and life which could only be attained by concrete touches. For John's subject matter is really always the same, and the speeches deal with only a few, main, ever-recurring ideas.

The use of another literary device of the same character makes the hearers appear constantly to misunderstand. The device is used to introduce another and opposite consideration into the course of the speech, and give a new starting point for its continuation. At the same time, it offers the opportunity for using language with two meanings, concealing ultimate truths in the most trivial guises. Thus, the Jews misunderstand the saying about rebuilding the temple in three days;[7] Nicodemus is perplexed by the new birth;[8] the disciples by the secret food;[9]

[1] John 12: 20–36   [2] *Ibid.*, 1: 39; 4: 6; 6:4; 13: 30; 19: 14
[3] *Ibid.*, 1: 28; 3: 23; 4: 5; 5: 2; 6: 59; 8: 20; 9: 7; 10: 23; 11: 18, 54; 18: 1, 2; 19: 13; cf. 6: 19; 21: 8; also 2: 20
[4] K. Kundsin, *Topologische Ueberlieferungsstoffe im Johannesevangelium*, 1925
[5] John 7: 22, 27, 37, 41, 52; 10: 22; 18: 28; 19: 40
[6] *Ibid.*, 11: 49, 51; 18: 13   [7] *Ibid.*, 2: 20   [8] *Ibid.*, 3: 4   [9] *Ibid.*, 4: 33

the Jews by the bread from heaven, and the saying about freedom.[1] Thus the saying that Lazarus was sleeping deceived the
disciples just as that about his resurrection deceived Martha.[2]
The fearsome command to Judas, "What thou doest, do
quickly", appears quite harmless to the other disciples;[3] and,
in the parting speeches, neither Thomas nor Philip understand
simple words of the Lord, any more than the Jews earlier on had
grasped similar phraseology.[4] But the Christian who read the
gospel seized the meaning, and perceived clearly throughout
that, in the revelation which was being made to him, were included the solution of all enigmas, and the eternal truth; and
that was the aim of the evangelist's literary devices.

Therefore, just as the figure of the Master reflects not past
history but present faith, so also His surroundings are depicted
out of the experience of the evangelist. The strong emphasis
upon the subordinate rank of the forerunner, John the Baptist,[5]
may of course be a purely literary modification of the synoptic
presentation. But the possibility cannot be excluded that our
author was acquainted with churches of John's followers, to
which churches he tried to assign the true place. On the other
hand, it is quite obvious that the struggles of the Apostle Paul
lay behind him, and what he had won was by now held without
question by the church. Judaism and its issues had vanished,
and if the unbelief of Israel had offered a painful problem to
Paul it was an uncontested dogma for our evangelist.

"The Jews" stand as a compact group hostile to the Lord, to
whom of a truth He preaches, but who never once believe, will
not believe, and cannot believe.[6] Jesus never accommodates
Himself to their company as a fellow-countryman, but stresses
His distance from them. Moses gave "you" the Law, "you"
circumcision; in "your" law it is written—that is how He speaks
to them,[7] and Moses is set in opposition to the Lord not only
in the mouth of the Jews,[8] but also in the language Jesus Himself uses.[9] In the prologue is the epigrammatic saying:[10] The
law was given by Moses; grace and truth came by Jesus Christ.
For Christians the Old Testament had been set aside as Law;

[1] John 6, 34; 8, 33   [2] Ibid., 11: 12, 24   [3] Ibid., 13: 29   [4] Ibid., 14: 5, 8; 8: 22
[5] Ibid., 1: 6–8, 15, 19–34; 3: 22–36; 5: 33   [6] Ibid., 12, 37–40
[7] Ibid., 7: 19, 22; 8: 17   [8] Ibid., 9: 28   [9] Ibid., 6: 32   [10] Ibid., 1: 17

it had meaning and abiding significance only as a book of prophecy pointing to Christ.[1] Jesus had as little to do with the Law as with the Jews; He did not appear in order to be "under the Law", but to be free from, and above it. To the Samaritan woman at the well, He spoke of the coming time when men would pray to the Father, neither on Gerizim nor in Jerusalem, i.e., when the old cult, together with its holy places, would have passed away, and the Christian churches, grown out of Judaism, would pray in spirit and in truth;[2] blind Judaism had died in its sins.[3] That is how a Christian saw the course of history after A.D. 70.

Of course the only implication was that, for the religion of the church of Christ, Judaism had been completely overcome in principle. In the life of the outside world, hatred towards the infant church was constantly and spitefully expressed by the Jewish people, who were still powerful even after their collapse as a nation; there are various echoes of this fact in the words of the gospel. But it was not only the Jews that adopted a hostile attitude to Christ and His church: "the world" outside the Church took up arms against the Christians, with hate and persecution.[4] The world had not recognized the logos, nor had His own people accepted Him,[5] for their nature was contrary to God and their prince was the devil.[6] The kingdom of Christ[7] was not of "this world"—that is the harsh formula which the persecuted church employed to express its sense of hostility to the surrounding world, its aims, and its entire civilization. Elsewhere the tension between the new and the old was expressed by speaking of the antithesis of the new æon to the old; but the Johannine writings contrasts "this world" and the kingdom of God, the sphere of Christ and the Father. The former is "below" on earth, the latter is "above" in heaven, whence the logos had descended and whither he had returned.[8]

Like Paul, our evangelist speaks of a divinely ordained obstinacy, and predestination. He who belongs to this world, i.e. who, like the Jews, has the devil for his father, *cannot* accept

---

[1] John 2: 17, 22; 5: 39, 46; 12: 16; 19: 34, 36, 37, and frequently
[2] *Ibid.*, 4: 21–23   [3] *Ibid.*, 8: 24; 9: 41
[4] *Ibid.*, 7: 7; 14: 17; 15: 18–19; 16: 2, 33; 17: 14
[5] *Ibid.*, 1: 10–11   [6] *Ibid.*, 12: 31; 14: 30; 16: 11. 1 John 2: 16; 4: 4–5; 5: 19
[7] John 18: 36   [8] *Ibid.*, 8: 23; 3: 31; 13: 3; 16: 28

Jesus' word for no one can come to the Father unless permitted by the Father.[1] Christians are not of this world, but chosen from it, and given by God to their Lord as His own.[2] They are "born of God", not "of the flesh" but "of the spirit", as it is expressed in a Paul-like antithesis;[3] and are thereby true children of God.[4] The speech to Nicodemus teaches that this divine birth is effected through baptism as a rebirth by water and spirit.[5] He who has received it is endowed with the Holy Spirit, and sends out its effects like streams of living water. Such a child of God has faith in Christ, and believes, not only on account of the signs and miracles that he sees, but also on account of the message of the gospel that he hears.[6]

What then is the meaning of "faith"? Firstly, the grasping of a religious truth—viz. that "Christ is the Son of God", who comes into the world as "the saviour of the world"; he who makes that confession, believes on Him, on "His name", and thereby, at the same time, on God who has sent Him; he who sees Him has seen the Father.[7] God is invisible and no one can see Him;[8] thus the Son is His phenomenal form, and in Him are revealed to mankind God's being, power, and glory. "I and the Father are one" says the Lord, and "you shall know that the Father is in Me and I in the Father."[9] A further development of the Pauline mysticism of Christ and the church is added to this series of ideas, which have been woven out of the logos theology of Jewish Hellenism, when it is said that: "the glory, which Thou hast given Me I have given unto them; that they may be one, even as we are one; I in them, and Thou in Me, that they may be perfected into one. Abide ye in Me as I in you.[10] As the Father hath loved Me, so I love you, abide in My love. If ye keep My commandments, ye shall abide in My love, as I have kept the Father's commandments and abide in His love." Since God is love, the truth can be stated thus: "God is love, and who abides in love, abides in God and God

[1] John 8: 43, 47; 6: 37, 65. 1 John 3: 8, 10 [2] John 15: 16, 19; 17: 6
[3] *Ibid.*, 3: 6; cf. 6: 63
[4] *Ibid.*, 1: 12, 13. 1 John 2: 29; 3: 1, 2, 9, 10; 4: 4, 6, 7; 5: 1, 4, 18
[5] John 3: 3–8 [6] *Ibid.*, 20: 29
[7] *Ibid.*, 11: 27; 20: 31; 4: 42. 1 John 4: 15; 5: 5; 2: 23. John 12: 44–45; 14: 9–11
[8] *Ibid.*, 1: 18; 5: 37 [9] *Ibid.*, 10: 30, 38
[10] *Ibid.*, 17: 22–23, 26; 15: 3–7

in him."[1] Thus, through the commandment of love, Christ-mysticism leads to God-mysticism. But the love of God and of Christ is not fanatical feeling nor ecstatic rapture; rather, as in Paul's hymn in 1 Cor. 13, it is the active power of God, and is seen in the Christian as practical work in the church. This love is due to a Christian brother as a member of a supra-mundane community; it is not neighbourly love *per se*, such as the Samaritan exercised in the Synoptic parable. Rather, it is the sum of all the commandments: to love Christ means to keep His commandments, and to love the brethren. It is a "new commandment" because it came into the world only with ᴄhristianity, but it is an "old commandment" because it derives from God's being and is eternal.[2]

Like love, so also other great forces flow out from God; they determine Christ's nature,[3] and are conveyed by Him into the church: truth, glory, light, life, spirit. But only one of them is described as of God's nature: the Lord says to the Samaritan woman:[4] "God is a spirit." Even the formula "God is love" occurs only once, in the first epistle.[4] It is more frequently said of Christ that He is "the light" or "the life"; once He also calls Himself "the truth", a term which elsewhere is applied particularly to the spirit.[5] Thus these predicates are not far removed from a genuine personification, and the author might even have begun his gospel with the words: "In the beginning was the truth", or "the light". He did not do so because these terms lacked the history which gave force to the term logos. All the other concepts arose at a later stage. They were current in Paul's world of thought, and occasionally we can observe how, in the post-Pauline literature and the language of the liturgies, they approximate[6] to the usage of the Johannine writings.

In discussing the miracles, we have already remarked that two opposite tendencies are combined in the gospel record: the crude realism of miraculous acts in a most exaggerated form

[1] John 15: 9–10. 1 John 4: 16
[2] John 14: 15, 21, 23; 15: 10; 13: 34–35; 15: 26. 1 John 2: 7–10, and oft
[3] John 5: 26   [4] *Ibid.*, 4: 24. 1 John 4: 16
[5] Light: John 1: 4, 9; 8: 12; 9: 5; 12: 46. Life: John 11: 25; 14: 6; 1 John 5: 20. Truth: John 14: 6. Spirit and truth: 1 John 5: 6; cf. John 14: 17; 15: 26; 16: 13
[6] Life: Col. 3: 4; *Didache*, 9, 3. Light: 1 Thes. 5: 5; Eph. 5: 8; Jas. 1: 11; 1 *Clem.*, 59, 2

and, on the other hand, their symbolical interpretation. Similar contrasts recur in the way in which expectation of the End is formulated. The hope of the near return of Christ seems much emphasized both in the Fourth Gospel and 1 John; indeed the latter holds that now is the "last hour", and 2 John characterizes doubt about the coming of the Lord "in the flesh" as a heresy of the Antichrist, and, in so doing, the epistle stands on common Christian ground.[1] The fact that the Apocalypse undoubtedly belongs to the Johannine circle illustrates most clearly the liveliness of the expectation of the parousia, and the way in which it was painted by religious fantasy.

This idea was fully neutralized in the gospel when it declared that, after the Ascension, the "spirit of truth" would be given to comfort the Church, to supply the place of the Christ who had gone from earth and to complete His revelation. It would be sent from the Father as a second "paraclete"—the first was Jesus Himself[2]—in order to abide with Christians, and to be in them for ever.[3] Here the Pauline doctrine of the pneuma is raised to a higher theological stage, and enriched by the Church's experience of further pneumatic revelations. Even the characterization of the spirit as "paraclete"—which always means "advocate" and never "comforter"—must have been customary in the Church, and may well be explained from the Pauline conception of the spirit who intercedes for us in prayer with God.[4] And if this indwelling of the spirit in Christians is equated with the one-ness of the Church with Christ, the presupposition for so doing is in Paul's doctrine of the pneuma which on occasion is brought to its climax by saying that the Lord is the spirit.[5]

In addition to the parousia, other scenes of the final drama shimmer with a double light in the Fourth Gospel. There was, in the Church, a current teaching taken over from Judaism, to the effect that, at the last day, all the dead would be awakened, judged and awarded either damnation or salvation; and the resurrection to eternal life is, in one passage, connected with partaking in the Lord's supper as elsewhere in the New

[1] 1 John 2: 18, 28; John 14: 3; 2 John 7 like *Barn.*, 6, 9
[2] 1 John 2: 1; cf. John 16: 26   [3] John 14: 15–17; 16: 7–15
[4] Rom. 8: 26; similarly Mark 13: 11
[5] John 14: 16–17, 18–20; cf. 2 Cor. 3: 17

Testament.[1] But, on the whole, the gospel teaches that death and judgment have no relevance to those who believe in Christ. Already, i.e. with the preaching of the incarnate logos, judgment has come on the world: he who decides for Jesus, is risen from the dead; he has passed through death to life, and does not come to judgment; but he who denies faith in the Lord, is already judged, because he has not believed on the only-begotten Son of God. He who keeps the word of Jesus will never see death.[2]

While it is undoubtedly part of the literary art of the evangelist to employ certain metaphors and ideas in a double sense, it is nevertheless improbable that, on this basis alone, we can explain these sharply opposed antitheses. Rather there must have been various strata of theological conception which were neither reconciled, nor reconcilable, as the writings of different authors succeeded one another, and this fact complicates still further the problem of authorship, which is already complicated enough.

The opinion of the Church, from the end of the second century,[3] tended to regard the Apostle John, the son of Zebedee, as the author of the whole body of writings: he was held to have lived in Ephesus until Trajan's time, and to have composed the gospel when a very old man. Possibly this legend of the John of Ephesus is hinted at in the appendix to the Gospel, 21: 22. It was not yet known to Ignatius,[4] since he revered the Ephesians only as "members of Paul's church", and the legend of John is proved unhistorical by the additional fact of an ancient record,[5] according to which the two sons of Zebedee were killed by the Jews. This record is confirmed by the extremely ancient prophecy of martyrdom preserved in the gospel tradition,[6] and is in harmony with a fast day of the martyrdom of the sons of Zebedee observed in the Eastern Church; the one difficulty is that the memorial day itself, 27th December, was settled on theoretic grounds only towards the end of the fourth century.[7] The martyrdom of James is recorded

---

[1] John 5: 28; 6: 39, 40, 44; 12: 48; Lord's Supper: John 6: 54
[2] John 3: 18, 19; 5: 22–27; 9: 39; 12: 31; 8: 51
[3] *Iren.*, iii, 1, 2; 3, 4; cf. Polycrates of Ephesus in Euseb., *H.E.*, v, 24, 3
[4] Ign., *Eph.*, 12, 2
[5] Papias in *Philippus Sidetes*; de Boor, *Texte u. Unters*, vol. 5, 2, p. 170
[6] Mark 10: 39   [7] Lietzmann, *Petrus und Paulus* (2nd edition), pp. 134 f.

in Acts,[1] but we are not told when, or where, his brother John
met his end. There is probably no room for doubt about the
fact itself. The Fourth Gospel, like the others, does not mention
its author by name; it is true that a "disciple that Jesus loved"
plays an important part, but his name is not given. From
general considerations, it is usual to assume that the author intended this mysterious figure to be John the son of Zebedee,
whom he places explicitly and definitely at the side of, and
indeed above, Peter.[2] That view is possible, but cannot be
regarded as certain, since it is remarkable that the sons of
Zebedee are nowhere mentioned as such in the gospel proper.
Only the appendix, chapter 21, names the sons of Zebedee,[3]
and appears to be drawing on the legend of the very aged
John. Quite at the end of the appendix, yet another writer[4]
describes him, too, as the author of the gospel. But here again
the text and its applications are a subject of dispute; thus it is
still impossible to arrive at assured conclusions. The only things
that come to light from the gospel itself are (i) that the Beloved
Disciple is not a historical figure, and is not so intended. Rather
he is the ideal bearer of the apostolic testimony that flows from
the heart of Jesus to those of the hearers; and (ii) that the
author was not an eyewitness of an historical event, but the
God-inspired interpreter of a supra-historical process.

The part this group of writings played in the history of
religion, however, offers a problem that attracts present-day
scholars to a still greater extent than that of authorship. We
can see clearly enough how Pauline thought has been adopted
to a large degree, and then extended and developed in a completely independent manner; and this in a direction of which
there are also occasional traces in other writings belonging to
the sub-apostolic period. But it is not less significant that this
was no mere private evolution of thought within Christian
circles, but that a large rôle has been played by influences from
the world surrounding this youthful movement. Paul had
gathered together all the elements that seemed of service to
him from Hellenistic Judaism and the religious currents of the

---

[1] Acts 12: 2   [2] John 13: 24; 18: 15; 19: 26 f.; 20: 4; 21: 20–22
[3] *Ibid.*, 21: 2; scarcely 1: 41, where the reading should be "as the first"
[4] *Ibid.*, 21: 24

awakening east, constraining them to illumine his experience of Christ; in the same way, his disciples and successors lived in continual contact with the world that they wished to convert, and learned from it how to shape their own ideas in ever new forms: and the greatest among these successors was "John".

Although, in Paul's old-age, gnosis had appeared in the distance and as an incongruous factor, and although the Pastoral Epistles had disowned it as a purely foreign element, it was operative in full force in Asia Minor when the Johannine writings were produced in that region. It was not repelled now in an unreasoning fashion, but greeted as a new form of the affirmation of God, and valued for purposes of rounding out and re-shaping the inherited tradition of Christianity. This is the source of many changes in the traditional presentation of the gospel story: the heightened glory of the figure of Jesus, the increase of the miraculous element,[1] the evolution of Pauline Christ-mysticism into God-mysticism, the tendency to advance conceptions like truth, love, light, life to the point of personification, and especially the introduction of the formula "to see God" and "to know God"; including also the ceremonial, "hieratic" style of the gospel with the striking monotony of its speeches, the "meandering" turns of its course of thought, and the "I am" pronouncements of the Son of God.[2]

However, as soon as we attempt to pass from these general observations to questions of detail, strong doubts arise about the results of much recent research. For the gnostic material which can be used for comparison, either dates almost throughout from a considerably later time, or has been influenced by, and to some extent makes use of, the Fourth Gospel; or else it lives in a world having a totally different point of view. On the other hand, we can understand the Johannine theology, as a whole and in detail, simply from the tradition of the Church, from Paul, and from Hellenistic Judaism. Gnosis operated as a condition and as a formative power, but never beyond a certain limit, a limit that was set up very early. The epistles of John tell of gnostics, and characterize and attack them as anti-Christ, but do not enable us to recognize their teachings clearly: "They

---

[1] E. Norden, *Agnostos Theos.*, 177–239

[2] P. Wendland, *Kultur* (2nd edition), 310 f.

deny that Jesus is the Christ", i.e. perhaps, they repudiated the Jewish idea of the Messiah, as of inferior value, because they would have nothing to do with a second coming of the Lord in the flesh. Moreover, "they do not confess Jesus", or they "annul him" (R.V. Marg.). They certainly asserted that they possessed knowledge of Christ, and yet at the same time set themselves above His commandments.[1] However, the author of the letters preaches that knowledge of Christ was proved by keeping His commandments. The love of God was perfected by observing the words of the Lord: "Thereby we know that we are in Him; he who says he abides in Him must live as He lived."[2] The antithesis to gnostic mysticism, thus expressed, has a gnostic sound, but in content it consists of a re-assertion of a pure Christian ethic.

Johannine Christianity stands firmly within the tradition of a Church whose lines had been settled by Paul. It had meanwhile received powerful impulses from a gnosis whose tide was flowing strongly. But an eminent thinker, "John", gathered the elements into a unity, and that unity sheds its light in the Fourth Gospel. Although there was no one in the succeeding age who rightly understood the master mind of Paul, yet here was a man who comprehended the Pauline thought authoritatively, both in its cosmic breadth, and equally in its religious depth; and clarified its stormy passion into a deep-souled, godly religion of the spirit. He saw in the gospel story the incarnation of the divine logos; for him Christianity was, in very truth, heaven upon earth.

[1] 1 John 2: 22; 2 John 7; 1 John 4: 2–3; 1 John 2: 4; 3 John 11
[2] 1 John 2: 3–6

Chapter Thirteen

IGNATIUS

AFTER ALL THE SHADOWY FIGURES OF UNKNOWN WRITERS belonging to the sub-apostolic period, we meet at last, at the beginning of the second century, a personality who is plainly described: Ignatius. The ancient list of bishops[1] enters him as the second bishop of Antioch and the successor of Euodius. Eusebius informs us, in his *Chronicle*,[2] that he was martyred under Trajan. Unfortunately we are not in a position to make sure whether this dating rests on an old tradition, or whether it owes its origin to a schematic reconstruction of Eusebius himself. But we have seven letters from Ignatius's own hand which afford most valuable information, not only of his death and theology, but also of his own church and of the churches of Asia Minor. These letters were written consciously in imitation of the Pauline epistles, and they were soon taken to heart by eastern Christendom. Polycarp, the bishop of Smyrna, collected them—possibly soon after the author's death —and we still possess the letter with which he forwarded the small corpus to the church at Philippi.[3] It was much read in the following period, and was also translated into other languages. In the fourth century Polycarp's text was extended in Antioch by considerable interpolations, and by the addition of spurious epistles. Elsewhere, the text contains only three letters, much abbreviated. About the middle of the nineteenth century there was much discussion as to the relationship of the three variants of text to one another, and as to the authenticity of any of the letters. This discussion may now be regarded as ended: the seven letters in the redaction which stands midway between extension and abbreviation may be regarded as the genuine work of Ignatius. He wrote them when on his way to meet his death. They are real letters, intended for the churches and are on the Pauline model: the first four were written from Smyrna,

[1] Eus., *H.E.*, iii, 22; cf. Ign., *Rom.*, 2, 2
[2] Eus., *Chron. Ol.*, 221, 3 f., p. 194, Helm, cf. *H.E.*, iii, 36, 2-3
[3] Pol., *ad Phil.*, 13, 2; cf. 3, 2; P. N. Harrison, *Polycarp's Two Letters*

the rest directed to Philadelphia and Smyrna; a typical pastoral letter sent from Troas to Bishop Polycarp, concludes the whole.

Ignatius had been arrested as the head of the church, and condemned to death by the Roman authorities, just as happened a generation later to his younger friend Polycarp. But he was not executed in Antioch because the governor expected to gain prestige by putting the bishop of the Syrian Christians on show in the capital. Hence he consigned him to the wild beasts in the arena at Rome, and sent him with a squad of ten soldiers across Asia Minor, where they made halts in Smyrna and Troas, and then brought him to Naples. From there he must have been transferred to Rome and put to death, although we have no exact information. The different *martyria* of Ignatius, contained in the collections, are documents of a later time, and without value as sources. Since he stayed in Smyrna on August 25 of that year,[1] it is not improbable that the liturgical tradition[2] of Antioch, where his memory was celebrated in the fourth century on October 17, has preserved rightly on that day the memory of his death in Rome. Unfortunately the liturgy had no interest in giving the year in which it occurred.

A very special interest attaches to these letters because they are the earliest original documents of the church which, above all others, must be regarded as the cradle of Gentile Christianity, in which also Paul had laboured for a long time, and which we have reason for calling the mother church of Rome. It is here that that proselyte Christianity which was free from the law must have blossomed, and was very clearly represented in the west, in the capital of the empire; here also Hellenistic influences of all kinds may have found entry into Christianity, influences which, either apart from the great Pauline stream, alongside of it, or perhaps even before it, made themselves felt in the churches, and are still recognizable in occasional traces.

Ignatius was much too impulsive a person to be regarded as merely an echo of the average opinion of the church. Very much in contrast to the epistle of Clement of Rome, his letters

---

[1] Ign., *Rom.*, 10, 3

[2] *Martyr. Syriac.*, of A.D. 411 on October 17; confirmed by J. Chrys., *Homil. in St. Ign.*, i, 2, 592a (Montfaucon); J. H. Lightfoot, *Apostolic Fathers*, Vol. II (2nd edit.), p. 419; H. Lietzmann, *Die drei aeltesten Martyriolgien* (K.T.), p. 14

bear everywhere the stamp of his own spiritual quality. He was very strongly influenced by Paul, and to some extent also by John, and his letters express his dependence, even in face of all the other signs of originality which continually appear, in the way he forms his ideas, as well as in the numerous re-echoes of passages which he almost quotes. But we should always be right in assuming that he is expressing the views of the church in passages where the mystical inclination of the author to spiritualize everything, causes him to make use of metaphors which apparently owe their origin to the cruder realism of the religious thought of the time.

The services for public worship are described by the term "assembly", which was already current and even customary in Paul,[1] although we must note that occasionally he uses the Jewish term "synagogue."[2] Moreover it is obvious that a typological valuation of the Old Testament cultus had become customary: the place of assembly was described as the "place of sacrifice" (*thysiasterion*),[3] and the allusions of Ignatius make it very probable that the conception of the Lord's Supper as "Eucharist", i.e. as the thankoffering of the church, had caused this name to be applied to the hall where it was celebrated.

In this sacred ceremony, the Christian partook of the flesh and blood of Christ or, as it is sometimes called, the bread of God, and as a consequence received a pledge of resurrection, a "medicine of immortality", an antidote against death guaranteeing to him eternal life.[4] His body became interpenetrated with the eternal substance of Christ's body, could withstand dissolution, and so experience a resurrection like the Lord's. Already on earth the Christian bears the "flesh of the Lord" in his body. In the Pauline period, this implied that continence was a duty in the sense of avoiding every kind of immorality,[5] but in Ignatius, complete sexual abstinence is the worthy way of honouring the flesh of the Lord, even if that way were not possible for every Christian.[6] However, it was an unconditional

---

[1] 1 Cor. 11: 20; 14: 23; cf. Acts 1: 15; 2: 1, 44; 3: 1; 4: 26. Ign., *Eph.*, 5, 3; cf. 13: 1. *Magn.*, 7, 1
[2] Ign., *ad Pol.*, 4, 2; cf. *James*, 2, 2. *Hermas. Mand.*, 11, 9, 13, 14.
[3] Ign., *Eph.*, 5, 2. *Trall.*, 7, 2. *Magn.*, 7, 2. *Philad.*, 4; cf. *Rom.* 4: 2
[4] Ign., *Eph.*, 20, 2. *Trall.*, 2, 1; 8, 1. *Rom.* 7: 3. *Philad.*, tit. *Smyrna*, 1, 1; 6, 1; 7, 1; 12, 2
[5] *Vide supra*, pp. 135 f.   [6] Ign., *ad Pol.*, 5, 2

duty for everyone in all circumstances to maintain his flesh as the "temple of God", pure from all the sexual vices of the pagan world.[1] Christianity was the doctrine of immortality, the gospel its realization, and the life of a Christian a struggle for the proffered reward of immortality and of eternal life.[2]

All these sequences of thought existed in germ in the Pauline churches of the early period. They had grown up on soil where religion had a Hellenistic cast, and they had attracted the pagan world in a high degree. Such teachings were grasped even by simple people, and were accepted and passed on by them with a naïve realism. A theology was developing in the local church which was soon to become a great force in the church universal. It led the pagan critic,[3] Lucian, to say scornfully that these contemptible Christian f aternities imagine that they have become immortal and live for ever. They despised death itself and frequently surrendered themselves to execution voluntarily. We have also seen how Paul erected a structure of thought on this foundation, which rose to the heights of an entirely spiritual Christ-mysticism. We can observe a similar effort in Ignatius, except that in him all the lines are extended further, all the motives more strongly emphasized, and all the Pauline limits, which are of classic elegance, are exceeded.

The Christians' confidence, which overcame death and at which Lucian scoffed, comes to expression most attractively in Paul's epistle to the Philippians:[4] he is weary, and desires to depart and be with Christ, for that is far better; but he must still abide in the flesh because he must still labour for the Church. Thus he quietly awaits the day of martyrdom. As distinct from this, the soul of Ignatius burns in flaming desire for a martyr's death. He is obsessed only by fear that the Roman church will procure his freedom and so prevent his death. He desires to be torn by the teeth of the beasts, to be entirely eaten up by them; and he expresses the horrid event in religious metaphors. The teeth of the animals must grind him like corn in a mill, for then he will be "the pure bread of Christ"; by this means he will be offered as a sacrifice to God—the altar is prepared for

[1] Ign., *Philad.*, 7, 2; cf. 2 *Clem.*, 14, 3; also Rev. 14: 4, but without this basis
[2] Ign., *Magnes.*, 6, 2. Eph. 17: 1. *Philad.*, 9, 2. *ad Pol.*, 2, 3
[3] Lucian, *de morte peregrini*, 13   [4] Phil. 1: 23

him, and this death is his liberation effected through Christ; in Him he will attain the resurrection, and the bonds which now fetter his hands and feet will then adorn him as with a spiritual link of pearls.[1] These are not expressions which a great man would use calmly, as, e.g., Paul, but the temperamental voice of one whose "enthusiasm" has grown beyond human measure, a man who felt he would become a man in the highest sense only by martyrdom, and thus a genuine disciple of Christ. He believes himself filled with the Holy Spirit, which cannot err, and which places words of divine truth upon his lips. Now that he is in bonds and awaiting martyrdom, he feels himself blessed with a higher knowledge: he knows of heavenly things, including the different orders of angels, and the groups of spiritual beings. He knows of things visible and invisible,[2] but he expects perfection only with death.

Fellowship with Christ is for him the essence of Christianity: he desires "to be found in Jesus Christ" in order that he might truly live, and he often uses the Pauline formula, "in Christ". But he also puts the matter the other way round, and says that believers have Jesus Christ in themselves. Further, since Christ is God, he calls them not only vehicles of Christ (*christophoroi*), but also vehicles of God (*theophoroi*), just as he had given himself the eponym Theophorus. Really this was only another application of the metaphor of the temple of God which is also to be found in his writings, and which the Christian exemplifies.[3] In the same way, he exhorts his readers to be imitators of the Lord, imitators of God, and, accordingly, he himself strives to imitate in martyrdom the sufferings of Christ.[4] Further, just like Paul, he deduces from this union with the Lord the necessity of following His commandments, "Those who are in the flesh cannot perform what is spiritual, and those who are spiritual cannot perform what is carnal; but what you do even in the flesh, i.e. in the life of the body, is spiritual, for you do everything in fellowship with Jesus Christ." He who has once confessed the faith, does not sin, and he who possesseth love, hateth not.[5]

[1] Ign., *Rom.*, 1, 2; 2, 1–2; 4, 1–3. *Eph.*, 11, 2
[2] Ign., *Philad.*, 7, 1; *Rom.*, 6, 2; 5, 3. *Trall.*, 5, 2
[3] Ign., *Eph.*, 11, 1. *Magn.*, 12. *Eph.*, 9, 2; 15, 3
[4] *Ibid.*, 10, 3. *Trall.*, 1, 2. *Rom.*, 6, 3   [5] Ign., *Eph.*, 8, 2; 9, 2; 14, 2

Faith and love—here is a second formula summarizing the Christian life: "Faith the beginning, love the end or perfection, and these two are a unity, i.e. God"—which is as much as to say: whoever unites these perfectly in himself, lives in full communion with God.[1] Starting from the idea of mystical unity, he equates the flesh of the Lord partaken at the Lord's Supper with faith, the blood of Jesus Christ with love, and he greets the church at Philadelphia with the words, "in the communion of the blood of Jesus Christ", i.e., in the communion of the love of the Lord.[2] For the Lord's Supper unites one with the Lord who is divine love. John says: "God is love, and he that abideth in love abideth in God, and God abideth in him"; and the high-priestly prayer concludes with the words: "I made known unto them Thy Name and will make it known; that the love wherewith Thou lovest Me may be in them and I in them." The two passages give the foundation of the Ignatian thought although the simile of the Lord's Supper is new. Here again, however, John offers the exemplar: "He that eateth My flesh and drinketh My blood abideth in Me and I in him."[3] Add the three quotations together, and Ignatius' formula is the result.

The Christology of Ignatius became of the utmost significance for the theology of the future. He was not content with the Pauline allusions, nor with the solemn sound of the Johannine phraseology, but proceeded to express his thought in theological formulas. The Church was already busy with drawing up a confession, partly in short sentences, and partly in hymnlike periods; a creed frequently varied by Ignatius.[4] Even in the early stages of the tradition, all sorts of more or less definite formularies kept crystallizing out. Ignatius's own Christology rests upon a Pauline foundation enriched from John, and he boldly proceeds further upon the road they indicated. Before all the æons, Jesus Christ was with the Father, and had appeared at the end of the times upon earth.[5] He was the vehicle of divine revelation, the mouthpiece which did not deceive, the one through whom the Father had truly spoken,

---

[1] Ign., *Eph.*, 14, 1; 9, 1; 20, 1; *Smyrn.*, 6, 1
[2] Ign. *Trall.*, 8, 1. *Rom.*, 7, 3. *Philad.*, tit. *Smyrn.*, 1, 1
[3] 1 John 4: 16. John 17: 26; 6: 56
[4] Ign., *Eph.*, 7, 2; 18, 2; 20, 2. *Magn.*, 11. *Trall.*, 9, 1–2. *Smyrn.*, 1, 1–2
[5] Ign., *Magn.*, 6, 1

the expression of the will of the Father or—making forceful and
clearer use of the Johannine formula—the word, the logos of
God, who broke through the silence.[1] Thus in Ignatius, more
clearly than in John, the roots of the logos conception are
plain. In the Wisdom of Solomon, the Hellenistic author had
sung:

> For while all things were in calm silence,
> And night in the midst of her swift course:
> Thine Almighty Word leaped from heaven, Thy royal throne,
> As a fierce man of war into a doomed land.

His intention was to describe how Yahweh walked in Egypt
on the night of the Passover in order to destroy the firstborn;
but in place of the name of God he personified His activity in
revelation, and, to the active "Word" of God, he appropriately
opposes His meditative silence, out of which action was born.
That is how Ignatius understood the passage, and he is not
likely to have been the first to say that the active "Word"
sprang from Silence. That idea must have been familiar to every
Hellenistic rabbi: and Ignatius could have got it from Greek
Judaism even if he had not hit upon it independently. In any
case he employs the idea freely, in his own way, and without
secondary, gnostic pedantry when, in another passage, he
equates the Godhead with "Silence".[2] It is true, however, that
he carries further the idea, which had been suggested tenta-
tively by Paul, and formulated by John in the prologue of the
Gospel, that the logos was God by nature. At last, he characterizes[3] Jesus Christ as "our God", or simply "God"; this he
does frequently and by preference. John preached that the
logos had become flesh, but Ignatius goes further and says
without hesitation that God had come in the flesh or had
appeared as man, and this characterization of Christ as divine,
leads him, in the end, actually to speak of the sufferings of God,
and the blood of God.

Nevertheless the person of the Son is clearly distinguished
from that of the Father, and this not only in the numerous

[1] Ign., *Rom.*, 8, 2; *Eph.*, 3, 3. (17, 2); *Magn.*, 8, 2; cf. Wisd. Sol., 18: 14–15

[2] Ign., *Eph.*, 19, 1; cf. Paul's Rom. 16: 25. Schlier, *Religionsgesch. Unters.*, 38 f.

[3] Paul's Phil. 2: 6. John 1: 1. Ign., *Eph. tit.*, 18, 2, *Romans tit.*, 3, 3; 6, 3. *ad Pol.*,
8, 3; *Trall.*, 7, 1. *Smyrna*, 1, 1; 10, 1

passages where Pauline formulas and turns of speech, or creed-
like expressions of the church, are reproduced or varied, but
also in new and well-considered judgments. Thus, for example,
he restates a frequent Johannine thought, and says that Jesus
Christ proceeded from *one* Father, was one with Him, and
returned to Him; or, further, he describes the Risen Lord as
spiritually united with the Father in spite of the fact that He
had a real, physical body.[1] The difference between the Father
and the Son becomes still more evident when the subordination
and the exemplary obedience of the Son are emphasized;[2] the
idea is of course Pauline, but the application and, in particular,
the parallel relationship of God to Christ, on the one hand,
and the bishop to the Church, on the other, or the bishop to
the deacons, carries the characteristic signs of the genuine
Ignatian mode of thought. The fact that, although the unity
is maintained, yet the distinction persists, even after the earthly
life of the Lord, is seen in the parallel found in the words: "The
Church is united with Jesus Christ as Jesus Christ with the
Father, in order that everything might harmonize in a unity."
Both in the abstractions of theology, and in the concrete religion
of Ignatius, the Risen Lord is a person clearly separated from
the Father, the one God of his monotheism.[3] The difficulties
which arise, on further consideration, from the juxtaposition of
the two antithetic spheres of thought, never rose to consciousness in Ignatius with his rich spiritual resources. Theologians of
the succeeding centuries felt the difficulties most strongly, and
groaned not a little over the saintly man who had to be respected as an authority from a revered past, and nevertheless
explained in an orthodox manner.

With all his naïvety, he deals with Christology speculatively.
At the side of this trait is another which is rooted in the religion
of the Church, but which borrows its ideas really from
mythological schemes. At the end of his letter to the Ephesians,
Ignatius proceeds to develop, with obvious earnestness, a
theology of redemption which mixes new ingredients with the
Pauline and Johannine elements already discussed, and which

[1] Ign., *Magn.*, 7, 2. *Smyrna*, 3, 3
[2] Ign., *Magn.*, 7, 1; 8, 2; *Smyr.*, 8, 1. *Trall.*, 3, 1. *Magn.*, 6, 1. *Eph.*, 5, 1
[3] Ign., *Magn.*, 8, 2

appears to be so important to the writer that he proposes to send to the Ephesians a second letter dealing with this theme. Unfortunately this letter was never written. He first of all teaches that by God's ordinance, "our God", Jesus Christ, was born of Mary through the agency of the Holy Ghost; in passing, he remarks that His baptism implied that the water was "purified" for the future baptism of Christians. Thus he seems to be presenting the conceptions of a Jewish Hellenism which were active in the Church, and which had been written down by Matthew and Luke.[1] The work of redemption began with the birth of Christ; the devil never suspected what was happening; he knew nothing of Mary's virginity, nothing of the birth, nothing of the meaning of the death of the Lord. Yet these were three great secrets which God had prepared in secret and silence, and had brought into effect; they were now patent to all. But how was the secret made known to the æons?

A star lighted up in the sky with a new and unheard of light, and outshone all the stars as well as the sun and moon. These heavenly bodies all crowded round it, wondering and fearful, and then followed in its train. Magic now lost its power to bind, every fetter of wickedness fell away, ignorance was vanquished, and the old kingdom of evil destroyed; God had appeared as man, and introduced a new and eternal life. Then was begun what had already been perfected in the councils of God: the universe shuddered, for now death had been destroyed.[2]

Here we have mythological ideas in poetic language. Lately attempts have often been made to reconstruct the "mythology which lies at its basis". The effort could only be successful if we were able to introduce into the text elements which it does not contain. At the beginning of the chapter, Ignatius is working with a thought which is also to be found in Paul.[3] It is that God had kept a plan of salvation secret, and this enabled Him successfully to deceive the devil and his dæmons. Then follows a new conception which, however, leaves it very much of an open question whether Ignatius means an event in heaven

---

[1] Cf. M. Dibelius, *Jungfrauensohn und Krippenkind*, 1932
[2] Ign., *Eph.*, 18–20, quoted in *Exc. ex Theod.*, 74, 2
[3] Paul's 1 Cor. 2: 6–8. Col. 1: 26. Eph. 3: 9–10. Rom. 16: 25

following the birth of Christ; or a mythological event in the cosmic empire of the spirits, which is accessible only to one who has been blessed by God, although no human eye has seen it; or whether he is giving a parable in a mythological form. In all probability the last assumption is correct, for the radiant star is not the same as that which, in the tradition of the Church, stood over the inn in Bethlehem on the night when Jesus was born. Rather it is a similar legend. For Ignatius, the shining host of sun, moon, and stars is the sum-total of the powers which had hitherto ruled the world. The stars determine the lot of everyone with a necessity which cannot be avoided, and only the wicked art of magic is able to interweave their cosmic powers with human desires. Paganism is regarded as an astral religion and as the servitude of mankind to dæmonic rulers. At length, a certain star grew in brilliance, outshone all the other starry powers, and made them subject to its own will as its obedient satellites: i.e. the power of paganism and its dæmonic gods was broken; God himself had appeared as man, had overcome the doom of death and set in its place an ascent to a new and eternal life; a new æon under the lordship of Christ had begun. The stars and their cosmic power, magic, and the pagan belief in dæmons, were real to Ignatius, and not merely metaphors: and their conquest by the power of God in Christ was for him another real thing. But he consciously describes it in a metaphorical analogy which he only chose because it expressed graphically the victory of the Lord over the evil spirits. The entire work of redemption, at the end of which was Christ's journey to hell to visit the prophets who were expecting Him,[1] was now described by Ignatius as a divine "plan of salvation (*œconomia*) based upon the new man, Jesus Christ". This plan was to be carried out in the Passion and the Resurrection in faith and love, because in Jesus as the incarnate God a new man had appeared and presented mankind with new life. The idea of a rejuvenescence of man, and of a new man, Jesus, is known to us from the Pauline discussions of the second Adam. The author of Ephesians had already given the name *œconomia*[2] to God's plan of salvation, and this he discussed in a way which showed he was quite master of the Pauline scheme

---

[1] Ign., *Mag.*, 9, 2. *Philad.*, 5, 2; cf. 9, 1   [2] Paul's Eph. 1: 10; 3: 9

of thought. Thus even in this connection Ignatius was only a pupil of the great master.

It is clear that, with the conception of Christ as the incarnate God, His humanity was in danger of becoming a mere mask: we shall have plenty of opportunity to pursue this subject further in the life of early Christianity. Ignatius already knew of communities in which the idea was at home, and he strove energetically against it. What appeared particularly objectionable to the latter was the idea that the incarnate God could really suffer, for suffering was simply irreconcilable with the Greek conception of God. For this reason, Ignatius placed all the greater emphasis on the reality of the sufferings of a Christ who was truly incarnate; and this again led to the thesis, which would have been impossible for Paul, that the Lord was "in the flesh" even after the resurrection. He derived this deduction from John;[1] probably beyond John's intention, even if it corresponded to the naïve view of the Church: yet a deduction that Ignatius defends in this passage. For him, Jesus Christ was "perfect" man; the divine pneuma and the human flesh were united both in His life on earth and after His resurrection. Therefore Ignatius, obviously enamoured of the paradox they contained, formulated the pair of antitheses which, from this time onwards, resound through Christian dogma: One is our physician; He is of both the flesh and the spirit, begotten and unbegotten, God in the flesh, true life in death, from Mary and from God; first suffering, and then without suffering, Jesus Christ our Lord.[2] He does not give a theological proof for this statement of the case, the traditional faith of the Church being his guide. That faith postulated the resurrection of Christ in the flesh because of the hope, formed on Jewish models, of one's own resurrection. The Pauline doctrine of redemption[3] presupposed that, while on earth, Jesus was a genuine man of flesh and blood, and that, as such, He waged war to the knife against sin. When Ignatius twice asserts[4] that his own sufferings would only have meaning if Christ had really suffered in the flesh, we are brought near to this line of thought.

[1] John 20; 20, 27; 21: 5, 12, where we should note that it does not say that Jesus ate with them
[2] Ign., *Smyrn.*, 2–5. *Trall.*, 10 *Eph.*, 7, 2   [3] *Vide supra*, pp. 117 f.
[4] Ign., *Trall.*, 10. *Smyrn.*, 4, 2

Whether those whom he attacked can really be called gnostics, is a question which cannot be answered. In any case, Ignatius gives warnings against people who assert that they have more knowledge (gnosis) than the bishop, and he exhorts the Church to lay hold of "the knowledge (gnosis) of God, that is Jesus Christ".[1] On another occasion he describes the teachings which he attacks as false opinions and old myths of a Jewish kind, and adherence to them as "Judaizing". Perhaps the enemy celebrated the Sabbath instead of Sunday; they certainly made a great deal both of the Old Testament and its authority as against the gospel message, and also of the eminence of the O.T. priesthood. Thus Ignatius insisted on the decisive and independent significance of the gospel, and the superiority of the high-priesthood of Jesus[2]—we are reminded of the thesis of Hebrews. However, the opponents were not Jews but uncircumcised persons, and even though he says that they deny the soteriological significance of the death of Jesus, they are nevertheless the same persons as all the other passages repudiate. It is noteworthy that they do not call themselves "Christians",[3] but obviously had a name for their own sect. Not sufficient is known for a more exact description of these heretics.

Those who had been redeemed by Christ constituted a single great spiritual unity of saints: that was undoubtedly a doctrine obvious in itself and essential to Ignatius;[4] and all the letters which he wrote rest on this dogma.

Meantime, another unity has become of importance, a unity which covered not only his human and official, but also his theological interests: it is that of the individual church and, in particular, the church as an organism governed by a threefold order of clergy. At the head of the church stands *one* bishop, under him the college of presbyters; the deacons occupy the third rank. The unity of the church is personified in the bishop; he is in the place of God, and the presbyters are to be compared with the college of Apostles. He is the highest authority for doctrine, commissioned by Jesus Christ, just as Jesus was commissioned by the Father and was of one mind with Him; thus

[1] Ign., *ad Poly.*, 5, 2. *Eph.*, 17, 2
[2] Ign., *Magn.*, 8, 1, 9–10. *Philad.*, 6, 1; 9, 1; 8, 2
[3] Ign., *Magn.*, 10, 1   [4] Ign., *Philad.*, 5, 2; cf. catholic church, *Smyrn.*, 8, 2

the bishop must be looked up to as to the Lord himself.[1] All the functions of the church are subject to his oversight; nothing can take place apart from him, neither baptism nor agape nor celebration of the Lord's Supper.[2] The command of subjection to him applies without exception to every member of the church, including presbyters and deacons.[3] If the church keeps to that pattern, she will be protected in all the attacks of hostile heretics. It is to be hoped that these latter will one day repent, return to the unity of the church, and submit themselves to the bishop.[4] In Clement of Rome, we found the first beginnings of the doctrine of the divine appointment of the offices of bishops and deacons; but, in Ignatius, we find the completed monarchical episcopate, and the custom was regarded as authoritative in both Syria and Asia Minor. As distinct from Clement, Ignatius built up no theory in regard to the necessity of this institution, or its accordance with scripture; rather he started from it, and was simply concerned with continually pressing home the out and out divine authority of the bishop as the spiritual monarch of the individual church. This institution would be an impregnable bastion against all attacks from without and all dangers of schism within. In so doing he became the classical authority for the Roman Catholic doctrine of bishops.

[1] Ign., *Magn.*, 6, 1. *Trall.*, 3, 1
[2] Ign., *ad Pol.*, 5, 2. *Eph.*, 3, 2; 6, 1. *Magn.*, 3, 2. *Smyrn.*, 8, 1–2
[3] Ign., *Eph.*, 4, 1. *Magn.*, 3, 1. *Trall.*, 12, 2. *Magn.*, 2
[4] Ign., *Magn.*, 6, 1–7, 2; 13, 1–2. *Trall.*, 7. *Philad.*, 3, 2; 8, 1. *Smyrn.*, 5, 3; 9, 1; cf. *Eph.*, 10, 1–2

Chapter Fourteen

MARCION

WHEN THE CHRISTIAN CHURCH HAD GROWN CONSCIOUS OF possessing a life of its own, it began to interpret the Old Testament in the form of types and allegories. The result was to deny the book to the Jews and to claim it as the text-book of the Church. Christians, as the spiritual Israel, recognized only one method of interpretation, which they called spiritual, but which was, in fact, allegorical. This method of interpretation really transformed the sacred book. It began with the prophecies of Christ and the Church, and then tried to wring secrets from the text by the free play of ideas. The literal understanding of the Old Testament was set aside and branded as Jewish error. But if a teacher had come forward, and refused to let himself be blinded by the shimmering gleams of this "spiritual" ingenuity, and had looked the Old Testament plainly and simply in the face, in spite of all cries that he was Judaizing, a catastrophe would have happened. The book would have slipped out of the hands of the Christians again into those of the Jews. If such a teacher had read, and firmly grasped, Paul's doctrine of the abrogation of the Law through Christ, he would have seen how the problem of the Old Testament was to be solved. He would of necessity have come to an understanding of Christianity that would lead him far from the paths hitherto taken by theologians. This possibility became actuality in Marcion.

Marcion belonged to Sinope in Pontus, the present-day Sinope on the Black Sea, where his father was bishop.[1] His family was well-to-do, and he himself is frequently described[2] as a shipowner. This shows that he belonged to the highest social class of the important port and commercial city, but he did not remain in peace at his home; apparently his father excommunicated him from the church on theological grounds. Later, perhaps, he struggled for recognition in Smyrna on the west coast, and was cast out by Polycarp. It is certain that,

[1] *Epiph.*, xl, 1, 3–8 (2, 94 f., Holl), Harnack, *Marcion* (TU, 45), 24*, 24*–28*
[2] *Rhodon und Tertullian* in Harnack, 16* f.

in full manhood he came to Rome in the reign of Antoninus Pius, sought and gained influence in the church there, until bitter quarrels broke out once more. In July, A.D. 144, he separated himself from the church catholic, founded his own fraternity, which spread with astonishing rapidity "over the whole of mankind", as Justin bears witness scarcely ten years later. Marcion died possibly about A.D. 160.[1]

He wrote only a single work which he called *Antitheses* where he brought his teaching together. It has not been preserved, as can easily be understood in regard to a writing which was so subversive to the Church. We have to content ourselves with deducing the content from the notices contained in the writings of opponents, particularly in Tertullian's five volumes against Marcion.[2] Literal quotation only very rarely occurs, so that we can form no idea of the literary quality of this extraordinary man. But the notices about his teachings are so detailed, and agree in so many essential points, that it is possible for us to describe his doctrine with considerable confidence. What, however, we cannot do is to give, on the basis of written sources, a sketch of the development of his religious ideas. What came first and what came second, on what point definitive offence was taken, we are nowhere told; we can only reconstruct subjectively the course and the inner connection of his doctrines. Nor can we give a clear answer to the question of his relation to the Syrian gnostic Cerdon. Irenæus and, following him, Hippolytus assert that Marcion was dependent on him, but, at the bottom, this assertion is due to the prevailing tendency to trace genealogical connections between different heresies. No available material gives clear information about the work and teaching of Cerdon, and the Marcionite tradition never mentions him.[3] This much is certain however: that the Syrian's influence, if he be historical at all, can only have been oɟ secondary importance; for Marcion's teaching is in every way the expression of a self-consistent religious experience, and this is rooted in the one person.

The basic thing that he rejected was allegory in all its forms.[4] In so doing, he fell foul of the whole of theology hitherto, as we

---

[1] Harnack, 6*, 16*–20*   [2] Assembled by Harnack, 256*–313*
[3] Harnack, 31*–39*   [4] *Ibid.* 259* f.

have already said, and of its understanding of the Old Testament. He boldly and forthrightly attacked the learned intricacies of the exegetes, and read the straightforward and plain meaning of the Old Testament with a direct mind. This meaning was often only too clear, and what he found offended him in the highest degree. It is possible that, by his very nature, he was suspicious of all sham learning—he would not have anything to do even with philosophy;[1]—it is also possible that he was affected by anti-Semitic influences, possible also that the gospel had sharpened his understanding. In any case, he recognized with extraordinary clarity the incongruity between the spirit of these ancient Jewish books and the spirit of Christ. The moral elevation of the prophets, the religion of the Psalms, he never saw: but he was antagonized by the anthropomorphic traits of the God of the Old Testament. He saw a God who had created a world full of the most deplorable imperfections; a God who created men, and drove them to fall into sin; who frequently repented of what He had done, and who overlooked the most serious sins in His favourites, although He punished them cruelly in others.

With his views of the Bible, he intermingles his own experience of life: why did God create snakes, scorpions, crocodiles, and all the creeping things? Why must propagation and birth be accomplished in a way that is nothing else than a sum total of dirty and disgusting processes?[2] Here we find a natural and, in certain respects, even a pathological depreciation of the world at large such as had not grown out of Christianity, but must be regarded as due to Marcion's social background. With eyes darkened in this fashion, he read the Old Testament and its naturalism, and saw in the God of the sacred book the same God of imperfection, cruelty, and repulsiveness of whom life preached to him every day.

The proof was plain that the Old Testament was right in proclaiming its God as the creator of the world. It was true—but both were worthy of one another, this God and this world! Yet this God was not therefore absolutely evil. He was not a "wicked principle"; rather He was simply of inferior worth.[3]

---

[1] According to his emendation of the text: Col. 2: 8; cf. Harnack, 51, 122*
[2] Harnack, 268*–273*   [3] *Ibid.*, 269*–274*

What He was able to do fell short of His plan and intention; He strove for perfection with insufficient means and thereby wrought mischief upon mischief. He had pointed out to men the foundation of morality in His "law"; in this respect, the Law was rightly to be regarded as "holy, righteous, and good", indeed as "spiritual".[1] But He wished to enforce His commandments by a system of punishments which rested upon the idea of retaliation. Its principle was an eye for an eye, a tooth for a tooth, blood for blood, and this made Him an unmerciful judge who punished the sins of the fathers on the children down to the fourth generation.[2] His ideal was "righteousness", and therefore He might be called the "righteous God". His chosen people, the Jews, had acknowledged this righteousness and striven after it: but it was a righteousness which caused one to shudder on account of its fearful cruelty.

That was the first strand of Marcion's thought. The second began from the Christian point of view that this Jewish and Old Testament righteousness had been most definitely rejected by Christ, and replaced by something better. Jesus had replaced the Old Testament law of retaliation with the new commandment of patience and forgiveness, and instead of the bloody cruelty of the Jewish God, Christ showed gentleness and compassion: the Sermon on the Mount abrogated the Law.[3] The essence of Marcion's proof consists in working out the contrast between the Old Testament and the gospel's message, and it was buttressed both by him and his disciples who kept bringing forward new series of antitheses, for a final decision rested upon correct understanding in this issue. If he was right—and Marcion had no doubt about it—then Christ had nothing at all to do with the Creator of the world, His book, His people, or His religion; rather He proclaimed another God hitherto strange and unknown, the God of love, kindness, and compassion, who was to be understood as the genuine and true God, supreme above all else. Yet complete reality was to be ascribed even to the Creator of this world, the God of the Old Testament; this was proved by the Old Testament itself whose truthfulness Marcion never for a moment doubted, and the

---

[1] Harnack, 108*, 263*   [2] *Ibid.*, 280* f., 271* f.
[3] *Ibid.*, 280* f., 262*

sum total of the facts of experience of daily life and of history added further proofs.

Thus there were two gods—a lower and a higher, a "righteous" and a "good", one known and proclaimed by Moses and the Prophets, and the other an unknown, strange god. The latter had first been revealed in Christ, who delivered us from the power and the law of the other god, and raised us to a new sphere of life. Incisive logic had led Marcion to his doctrine of two gods, and neither the theological dogma of monotheism, nor dubious philosophical considerations, caused him to shrink back from the last consequences of his position. Whether he was acquainted with the dualistic conceptions of Persia, or gnostic modes of thought of a similar kind, and whether these had facilitated his system is an enigma. It is certain that they were not his starting point, nor in any way the inspiration of his thesis. His main contention is clear enough, and does not require the help of such assumptions. Men of that period were accustomed to find a multitude of intermediate beings between God and man, including both the devil and the divine logos.[1] Moreover Marcion's teaching was in reality neither dualistic in its starting point, nor in the way in which it was worked out.

Was it not clear to Marcion, however, that by this teaching he was contradicting the whole of primitive Christian tradition? No. Rather with the same thoroughgoing heedlessness of the consequences of this thought, he found in Paul the apostolic justification of his system: in him, and in him alone, the true teaching of Jesus had been grasped, unambiguously expressed, formulated in multitudinous ways, and made safe against false opinions. None of the other apostles had understood their Master: they had held Him to be the Messiah of the Jewish God, had understood and misinterpreted His words from that standpoint. The warnings and exhortations of Jesus had not borne fruit.

In spite of beginning sometimes to understand the gospel rightly, in the end they had gone aside into error, and become the protagonists of Old Testament legality. Therefore Christ had revealed the truth once again, and had called Paul as its herald; he alone had maintained it in its purity. It was for this

[1] Cf. Marcion on 1 Cor. 8: 5. Harnack, 307*

reason that he had opposed the original Apostles; he had
rebuked Peter because he did not "walk uprightly according
to the gospel of truth" (Gal. 2: 14); he had fought against the
"false brethren privily brought in", against the "false apostles"
(Gal. 2: 4; 2 Cor. 11: 13), and had accused the apostles of
falsifying the word of God (2 Cor. 2: 17).[1]

For him, Galatians was the fundamental polemic against a
Jewish form of Christianity: here at the very beginning every
"other gospel" was explicitly rejected, the attitude of the first
Apostles was censured, and then it was demonstrated that the
Law was entirely set aside by Christ who taught the one fundamental truth as definitely as possible. Moreover the difference
between the two gods had been clearly expounded in the
Pauline epistles: it was only necessary to read them with unveiled eyes. In 2 Cor. (4: 4) the Apostle said: "The god of this
world hath blinded the minds of the unbelieving, that the light
of the gospel of the glory of Christ, who is the image of God,
should not dawn upon them." Thus the God whose image and
revelation was Christ was opposed to the god of this world who
would protect his own, i.e. "the unbelieving" from knowledge
of the true God, and had therefore blinded them—just as he
had frequently done, according to the testimony of the Old
Testament.[2] Moreover, he whose eyes had been opened by this
passage of Paul's, would have no difficulty in finding the teaching about the two gods in numerous other passages in the
Pauline letters, and therefore none in recognizing Paul as the
apostle of truth and the servant of the good God. Regarded in
this way, his epistles have complete authority, and become the
fundamental sources of Christian knowledge. They give the
criteria by which the gospel tradition of the Church was to be
judged; for the first Apostles' lack of understanding, and the
Judaizing zeal of the false brethren, had brought about a far-
reaching displacement, indeed falsification, of the genuine
evangelical tradition. Whereas Paul had expressly asserted
(Gal. 2: 6; Rom. 1: 16) that there could, and must, only be one
gospel,[3] viz. his own, the Church had made it into four gospels
which always, but wrongly claimed apostolic origin for themselves, in spite of the fact that the Apostles never wrote any-

---

[1] Harnack, 257*–9*   [2] *Ibid.*, 308*   [3] *Ibid.*, 306*, 309*

thing. Rather, these gospels had been falsified throughout in a Judaizing sense, and were therefore, of course, fitted to recommend that the Church, which was walking in evil ways, should submit to the authority of the Old Testament and be deluded by the creator of the world.

Hence Marcion set himself boldly to the task of restoring what he held to be the genuine and true gospel, i.e. that preached by Paul. He began with one of the traditional gospels, viz. Luke. We cannot say with certainty why he made this choice. Perhaps the reason was that he regarded the author, Luke, as a disciple of Paul, and believed him to be more faithful to tradition than the other evangelists. For a remark of Tertullian can be understood to mean that, first, Paul, and through him, Luke, had been illumined by the original evangel; but to understand his remark in this way ignores the fact that, immediately beforehand, Tertullian had recorded Marcion's attack upon the traditional names of the evangelists.[1] We may also surmise that Luke's gospel had long been in use in Sinope, and had therefore been particularly well known to, and highly appreciated by, Marcion from his youth. At any rate he took it as his raw material, and began to carry out a critical sifting of Luke's text.[2] It was a purely "subjective" criticism that he exercised. The kernel and essence of the evangelical message remained fixed for him in the sense and scope already described, and Paul supplied him with further hints. He began boldly to remove the Judaizing interpolations from the gospel, and to restore the spoiled passages by altering the text. That his work could not be applied in every detail, nor brought to an end once for all, he never concealed from himself; both he and his school kept on wrestling with the problem, and the Marcionite text of the gospel went through many changes.[3]

The same problem faced him, as was unavoidable, in the Pauline letters. Many passages did not agree with the fundamental teaching of the Apostle as recognized by Marcion, and gave the impression that Paul had recognized the Old Testament as coming from the most-high God, and recording a

[1] Harnack, 358*   [2] A reconstruction of the gospel in Harnack, 177*–255*
[3] Harnack, 43

revelation that pointed towards Christ. Such passages could
only be Judaizing interpolations introduced by forgers belonging to the church; he who desired to read Paul in a pure form
must first of all remove these foreign passages, and restore the
text where it had been spoiled. Marcion attempted even this
task and he carried it through with a high hand and much self-
confidence.[1] He did this to a larger extent than, but always with
the same good conscience as, that with which many a critic of
the nineteenth century started from his own system of
"Paulinism", excised anti-pathetic verses, and changed words
which he disliked. Marcion let imagination run riot, but we
still have every reason to remark the logic of his thought, and
marvel at his self-confident, unwavering boldness; even in this
respect he was an extraordinary person.

The result of his critical work was a canon of Scripture which
united the genuine, and alone authoritative, gospel with the
Pauline epistles. This combination was rooted in necessity,
and was not the product of the accident of a particular tradition. Neither of the two parts was intelligible without the other;
each guaranteed the sense and meaning of the other. Paul was
the authority for the essential thought and the broad outline
of the gospel. He taught its soteriological significance and the
way in which it was to be accepted. He also showed that the
Christian message had been misunderstood and falsified at an
early date, and likewise what were the dangers of Judaistic
side-tracks. Paul was thus the guardian and the expounder of
the gospel. The gospel text itself gave the record about Jesus,
His works and preaching, His death and resurrection; in short
everything that Paul presupposed as known, and that he used
as the basis of his instruction. Thus the two parts of the Marcionite canon constituted a genuine unity, whose significance
was still further increased by the fact that the Old Testament
was no longer regarded as sacred Scripture. That meant, however, that Marcion set on one side the Biblical canon which had
hitherto been recognized by Christendom, and replaced it with
a new one. He was the first really to proclaim, on a theological
basis, the existence of a New Testament as a collection of
writings, and to put it, not alongside, but in the place, of the

[1] Reconstruction of the Pauline text in Harnack, 40*–176*

Old Testament. Thereby, acting on his own initiative, and relying entirely on his own resources, he carried out an enterprise which was only in its beginnings in the church catholic, and was faced with all sorts of hindrances. The reactions of Marcion's achievement soon made themselves felt. We shall have to speak of them in another connection. What is important for us to notice, at the moment, is that Marcion had now an authoritative written source at hand, out of which he could draw further ideas for the building up and the extension of his teaching.

First of all, we note that Marcion himself exercised a noteworthy reticence, and everywhere avoided fantastic speculations; it was always more important for him to strengthen the foundations than to decorate the superimposed structure. Secondly, after his negative criticism directed against the creator of the world and his book, he taught the resplendent glory of the good God and His gospel. Marcion was no doctrinaire theorist but sought God with earnestness and a warm heart, and he seized on the profoundest meaning brought out by his researches. In particular he believed that he was really proclaiming a new understanding of God to Christian people who were in danger of backsliding into the commonplace thoughts of the past.

His *Antitheses* began with the words:[1] "Oh fullness of wealth, folly, might, and ecstasy, that no one can say or think anything beyond it [the gospel], or compare anything to it!" What Paul said in Rom. 11: 33 of the depth of the wealth, in 1 Cor. 1: 18–23, of the foolishness and power, of the preaching of the cross; and Luke, in 5: 26, of the wondering astonishment which fell upon all those who witnessed the miraculous power of Jesus—all this was comprehended in Marcion's exclamation. It is an attempt to describe the complete newness of the divine message, far beyond all human thought and power of conception. Marcion is never weary of teaching that, before the coming of Christ, mankind knew nothing of this God; that He was fully unknown and unknowable because no bonds of any kind united Him with the world and humanity; He dwelt as a "stranger" in His third heaven (2 Cor. 12: 2) far from the alien

---

[1] Harnack, 256*, corrected by Burkitt, *Journ. Th. Stud.*, 30, 279 f.

world: "No one knows the Father except the Son and he to whom the Son will reveal Him." It was the Jewish god who had created the world out of material substance; he had also created Adam, weak in body and soul, and then, assailed by the wiles of the devil through the Law, he had brought sin and death upon mankind.[1]

Then came to pass what is incomprehensible and overwhelming: the pity of the good God was excited by the lot of mankind, though they were strange and even hostile to Him; from pure compassion, He decided to redeem them from their distress.[2] He sent His Son into the world, the perfect revelation of the Father. He appeared as Jesus Christ in the fifteenth year of Tiberius (A.D. 28–29) and preached the gospel. He was neither "born of a woman", nor "subject to the Law"—these words, says Marcion, were interpolated in Gal. 4: 4 by Judaizers, as also was the story of the nativity in the gospel. How could the pure Son of the most-high God have defiled Himself with the filthiness of human birth! He clothed Himself with nothing earthly, originating from what was material; nor with flesh which had been formed by the Creator of the world: rather He appeared "in the likeness of man" (Phil. 2: 7) in an apparent body, a "phantasma", such as the angels wear.[3] He preached the gospel of the unknown God, taught gentleness and patience instead of cruelty and wrath, love of enemies and forgiveness instead of hate and retribution, compassionate kindness instead of a calculating righteousness. He taught these things as the will of God and showed them forth in both word and deed. He came to abrogate and not to fulfil the Law, and not the contrary, as the spurious verse, Matt. 5: 17, asserts.[4]

He had shown His divine kindness and patience even towards the creator and frequently had regard for his laws. Jesus had never attacked him directly or characterized him as a liar, but had so clearly expressed the pure divine teaching that the intelligent hearer could draw for himself the inevitable conclusion. In the parables, He had unmistakably described the essential content of that teaching. No man can serve two masters; an evil tree cannot bring forth good fruit nor a good

---

[1] Harnack, 264*–7*, 271*, 274*–7*   [2] *Ibid.*, 122, 264*, 284*, 292*, 295*
[3] Harnack, 283*–7*, 74*   [4] *Ibid.*, 252*, 262*

tree bring forth evil fruit; no one should put new wine into old skins, nor new patches upon an old garment—was that not clear enough? Moreover, wealth, happiness, and earthly show had hitherto passed as signs of divine favour: and rightly so, for this was in accordance with the law and regulation of the creator. But Christ blessed the poor, the hungry, those that wept, those who were abused and persecuted; and He pronounced woes upon the rich, the full, and those who laughed. He turned away from the righteous and the Pharisees, and visited publicans and sinners.[1] Thus the gospel re-assesses all previous values. Jesus' gospel of salvation is for all who need help in the whole of the wide world, and not only for the subjects of a chosen people as the Messianic promises of the Jewish god declares.[2]

That is how Jesus taught; then on the cross, He died the death accursed by the creator god (Gal. 3: 13), but which Jesus paid as ransom-money and thus redeemed us, "the strangers", from our previous thralldom and gained us for the good God.[3] He redeemed not only those who were then living or who should live, but also the dead; for He descended into hell, and liberated all the sinners: Cain, the company of Korah, Dathan and Abiram, Esau and the whole multitude of heathen who suffered in the fiery wrath of the revenging god. But the righteous persons of the Old Testament: Abel and Enoch, Noah and the Patriarchs, besides David and Solomon, remained below in the place of their promised reward, in a kind of blessedness which their god had been able to provide for them. They could not be redeemed, because they were bewitched by communion with their own god, and lacked faith:[4] thus they did not dare to *believe* the unheard of and the new, and that was what mattered and would matter. Faith was complete and total self-surrender to the highest God. This meant at the same time the denial of the creator-god and his earthly plan of salvation as found in the Old Testament.[5] The first was the Redeemer, the second was the Judge; love was due to the first, fear to the second. The decision was exclusive, because— you cannot serve two masters.

---

[1] Harnack, 127, 260* f., 265*, 292*–94*   [2] *Ibid.*, 289*
[3] *Ibid.*, 288*   [4] *Ibid.*, 294* f.   [5] *Ibid.*, 296*

Redemption won in this way worked itself out only in the future for it concerned only the soul; as long as a man was still in the flesh, he belonged bodily to this world and its Lord, and must bear its oppression and persecution: true Christians had also to bear the same distress and the same hatred.[1] They defended themselves as well as they could, not with force or by showing resentment, but by turning aside and withholding themselves from everything that would further the objects of the creator-god. The body as a material element was their enemy and thus they mortified it by fasting. Meat-eating was entirely forbidden, and wine belonged to the prohibited things: Paul had given directions by way of example in Rom. 4: 21 and 1 Cor. 8: 13. All sexual intercourse furthered the aims of the god of this world, and therefore was prohibited by Marcion to his disciples: the true disciples of Christ did not marry, and if they were already married when they came to know the truth they separated from their spouses.[2] This Christian church of Marcion's only propagated itself spiritually, and it spread far and wide in the world, and lasted for centuries. The Church Fathers tell us nothing further about his principles for the conduct of life, a fact which proves that at least they had nothing to find fault with there. Marcion's disciples obviously lived quietly and in retirement, and constituted churches with close inner bonds, churches which had much of the earnest strenuousness and decided other-worldliness of early Christianity; thereby they made a great impression on those belonging to the church catholic. A remarkable number of them died as martyrs: a fact which proved attractive to many.

The Marcionite movement flamed up rapidly and, after it separated from the church universal, became a powerful and successful antagonist of early Catholicism which was at that time first taking shape. The pagan philosopher, Celsus, dealt with the Marcionites in A.D. 180, in his polemic against the Christians; he regarded them as a second and equally important branch of the Christian movement.[3] That they permeated the whole world was the testimony of Tertullian of Carthage about A.D. 200, just as it was that of Justin of Rome about A.D. 150.[4]

---

[1] Harnack, 295* f.   [2] Ibid., 149 f., 307*, 311*, 277* f.   [3] Ibid., 325*
Tetr., c. Marcion, 5, 19. Justin, apol., 26, 5. Harnack, 152, 6*

The large number of hostile writings belonging to the second century of which we hear, shows how acute was the danger for the church catholic, and in what regions it existed; for, in addition to western Asia Minor, we find mention of Corinth and Crete; the three world capitals, Antioch, Alexandria, and Rome; besides Carthage and Lyons.[1] In the east, the Marcionite church extended still further and was firmly rooted particularly in the region where Syriac was spoken. Here it was still a danger even in the fourth century, and the Fathers had to issue earnest warnings against it; whereas by that time its power in the west had been completely broken. The strict carrying out of the imperial laws against heretics at last drove the Marcionites out of the towns into the villages, where, in the fifth century, they were oppressed by active bishops, and compelled to receive conversion. Their last remains survived in remote corners of the orient for centuries, although many had been absorbed by Manichæism.[2]

We have no information about the inner life, the constitution, and the evolution of the church. Those who attacked the heresy never troubled themselves about anything except its doctrines. The Marcionites' constant criticism of church doctrine, and the polemic of the church Fathers, naturally brought about a large theological evolution of the former. We can observe manifold differences in the reports about Marcion's Bible and teaching, reports which can be explained as further developments carried out by pupils, as distinct from the earlier theses of the master; a few leaders of the Marcionite schools are known to us by name. Wherever they are dealing with additions of secondary importance or with corrections, we always find that they smooth down the crudities of the original teaching. Thus in addition to the body and animal soul which man owes to the creator-god and which is destined to perish, another "spirit" was also ascribed to him as an original gift of the most high God. This gift at last makes him man in the full sense, and it is this spirit which the God-sent Jesus saves, because it belonged to God even although it had fallen into enemy hands. This was of course a very illuminating thought of a genuine gnostic character, but it destroyed Marcion's fundamental idea of God's

[1] Harnack, 152, 314*–327*   [2] *Ibid.*, 156–160

absolute remoteness from the world and from mankind, and of
how He saved man out of purest love, although he was a complete stranger to Him.[1] Others made the devil into the evil
principle and a third god; thus the god of the Old Testament
became "the mediator" and so was conceived on a considerably
higher plane. On the other hand, the regions which had come
under Manichæan influence held firmly to the two gods, and
they set the creator-god, as the evil god of darkness, in contrast
to the good god of light: and this resulted in a modified kind
of Manichæan theology.

Only one of all these disciples, Apelles, attained any large
and independent significance. He had heard Marcion in Rome,
had afterwards gone to Alexandria, and then returned to Rome
as an enemy of Mani and his dualism. In Rome he exhibited
much literary and propagandist activity. He worked with
Marcion's system of ideas and even with his New Testament,
but he introduced an element of enthusiasm which was entirely
remote from Marcion, in that he gave credit to the visions of a
prophetess, Philumene by name, and regarded them as sources
of revelation.[2] But he then separated the creator of the world
from the Old Testament, and denied Marcion's radical pessi-
mism. This world, he said, was created by an angel of the most
high God, indeed to His honour, and after the model of His
own higher world: but it remained incomplete and bore "the
sting of repentance" until, at the request of the sorrowful
creator, Jesus Christ the Son of God was sent down at the end
of the æon to heal the world. The Old Testament was a lying
book of the god of the Jews, i.e. one of the angels of fire who
had fallen away from God, and become evil. He was the same
as had decoyed human souls to come down from the heavenly
heights, and had clothed them with the sinful flesh of an earthly
body.[3] Origen has preserved a number of passages from a work
of Apelles, entitled the *Syllogisms*, which is devoted to proving
the inferior value of the Old Testament.[4]

An orthodox writer towards the end of the second century,
Rhodon by name, had a discussion with Apelles then growing
old. Fragments of his report of this discussion have been pre-

---

[1] Harnack, 165   [2] *Ibid.*, 404*–412*
[3] *Ibid.*, 406*–409*, 417*   [4] *Ibid.*, 413*–16*

served.[1] We are told strange things. Apelles was of the opinion that doctrine ought not to be criticized, but that everyone should retain the one in which he believed. Then those would be saved who set their hope upon the crucified Lord, but they must of course be "full of good works". The Pauline theology of the cross, and his exhortation to have a faith active through love, are expressed with an uncouthness which must have appeared unheard-of. But worse things were to come. In praiseworthy contrast to Marcion, Apelles recognized only *one* principle, but he immediately added that the question of the Godhead was the darkest of all problems. Although there was only one principle, he grasped it, "not by way of knowledge, but by an inner feeling". And when conjured by his opponent, he again answered and swore: "In very truth he did not *know* how there could be an uncreated God, but he *believed* it." Rhodon then laughed outright and scoffed at a teacher who could not prove his teaching; but, at the same time, and with genuine astonishment, we recognize a spirit in Apelles which was independent of the outlook of his period, which had grasped a great truth, and which had even expressed it almost in modern terms, viz. that the religious idea of God does not belong to the sphere of logic, but to that of "emotional" thought.

Marcion had not actually said that, but it was of the essence of his spirit; for his great aim was to liberate theology from all forms of logical systematization; the intuitive knowledge of God as "entirely other" and quite unattainable from the standpoint of the world; the denial of everything creaturely, and thereby also of every form of natural and historical knowledge of God; the estimate of redemption as a miracle of love which could not be thought out. Here Jesus' genuine message of God, and Paul's real experience, were put into vivid words, even if one-sidedly, boisterously, and with such reckless passion that all the other, and frequently not less significant, values of the Christian religion went to pieces. But is not a prophet always one-sided when seized by the spirit?

[1] Harnack, 404*

Chapter Fifteen

GNOSTICISM

SHORTLY AFTER THE TURN OF THE FIRST CENTURY AND IN the time of Trajan, Dion of Brussa delivered an address to his fellow-citizens which has since become famous.[1] Being proscribed, he moved to and fro in the world as a wandering philosopher in voluntary poverty, but later on he became again a highly respected and wealthy patron of his home town. He says that in Olbia, near to the mouth of the River Dnieper, he had once delivered an address in Greek to the inhabitants, and had dealt with the conception of a well-ordered *polis*, i.e. a state; he reproduces the sequence of thought in detail. From the state and its constitution by man, he proceeds to treat of the divine cosmos and, after he has spoken first of all as a philosopher about gods and men and their fellowship, he gives a myth[2] which "is sung in a marvellous way at the secret ceremonies of initiation of the Magi"; and the myth had been communicated to them as the teaching of the wise and upright Zoroastor.

Like a divinely guided span of four noble horses, the world revolves ceaselessly in a gigantic orbit in an endless succession of periods of time. The outermost horse is the strongest and the most beautiful of all, and runs in the longest path: it is of a light colour shining with pure brilliance and with the glowing splendour of sun, moon, and stars—the heavenly æther, worshipped as Zeus. The second horse bears the name of Hera, and is black in colour: but where illuminated by the sun it is light coloured—the air. The third is sacred to Poseidon and is known to the Greeks as Pegasus—the sea. The fourth, called after Hestia, stands fixed and immovable, bound by steel reins, and constitutes the centre of the whole movement—the earth. Thus the glorious span of horses run amicably together until, after a long time, the fiery snorting of the outside horse ignites the others, sets the mane of the innermost in flames, and so burns up the entire cosmos. The Greeks call it the burning of Phæton. On a second occasion, and after many years, the horse of Poseidon shied and flooded its neighbour with sweat; and that

[1] Dio Chrys., *Or.*, 36, v. Arnim   [2] *Or.*, 36, 39–61

was the universal flood of Deucalion. To men, these appear to be meaningless catastrophes, whereas they are controlled by the firm reins of the chief governor, and brought to a good end.

Now, however, the metaphor changes: the leading horse overpowers the others, and takes them upon itself, just as one wax figure is made out of four. After a short time, which, only according to human ideas appears infinitely long, it stands in glorious beauty as the victor. The world that had been destroyed in the flaming æther, has become a new and higher existence. Then the Lord God perceived a void and was seized by desire of driving the chariot and, yearning for the various kinds of natures, began to create the present world. A flash of lightning shone out and changed the bright flame to a gentle fire. Then the moist element penetrated the whole, as the seed which had been given life by the divine spirit, and created all things: this is what the sages of the mysteries laud as the "holy marriage" of Zeus and Hera. Thus comes into being a new world, young, and of shining beauty, just as it proceeds from the hands of the Creator, more glorious than any human mind can conceive and any tongue can worthily describe: only the Muses and Apollo themselves would be able to do it in the divine rhythm of purest harmonies.

For a long time, this myth of Dion's was regarded as the airy imagery of a speculative theology, that was intended to put his Stoic theories into a many-coloured garment. But the happy discovery of a monument to Mithra and its skilful elucidation, have recently shown that Dion was really speaking the truth:[1] he was giving the contents of a hymn of the "Magi", i.e. those Persian missionaries who laboured in Asia Minor, who mingled the ancient Persian theology of Mithra with astral elements of Babylonian origin, and who Hellenized the whole by assimilating it to Stoic doctrines. Dion's oration was delivered at the time of a flourishing syncretism which mingled the religious ideas of all peoples and put their gods on an equal footing with each other. In Dion only the names of Greek gods appear, but, under this disguise, Persian gods are concealed according to that broadminded way of conceiving things[2] which had formally

[1] F. Cumont in the *Revue de l'histoire des religions*, vol. 103 (1931), pp. 33–44
[2] H. Usener, *Götternamen*, 341

identified the Roman Jupiter with Zeus, Hera with Juno, and which allowed Tacitus[1] to discover Mars, Mercury, and Isis among the Germans.

This syncretism of the gods is one of the most significant phenomena which accompanied the growth of Græco-Roman world civilization. It levelled the way for monotheistic currents of thought, and, in both a negative and a positive sense, constituted a precondition for the rise of world-religions. Dion's oration shows us how an oriental, esoteric doctrine compounded of various elements—in regard to the nature of the world, its end in fire, and the new creation of a more beautiful heaven and a better earth, i.e. a typical eschatology—when clothed in Stoic ideas became a cosmogonic myth unveiling the purpose, and the divine constitution of this world. It was Trajan's time, and Dion, for all his training in logic, and his Greek cast of mind, felt that philosophy alone no longer satisfied. In the present oration, however, he was trying to meet the needs of a new time, and he spices his oration with the mysterious echoes of oriental religion in order to satisfy the yearnings of a large circle of educated people.

It was no accident that Plutarch about the same time wrote a monograph on Isis and Osiris[2] in which Egyptian myths, helped by allegorical interpretation, are made to chime with Greek thought, orientated philosophically. In so doing, Plutarch was not merely a confessed Platonist, but one by conviction. Yet he was also a worshipper and a priest of the Delphic Apollo. He dedicated the monograph to the Delphic priestess Clea, who had been consecrated by her parents to the mysteries of Osiris. Egyptian elements had long been accepted in Hellenism. Persian and Babylonian elements were now added. All these gods began, as it were, to speak Greek and to philosophize, and so became acceptable in every sense. The orient began to conquer the Hellenic world, and even to vanquish the occident. For a while the reawakened Greek consciousness, in its best representatives of the Antonine period, offered resistance; but afterwards the oriental tide flowed irresistibly over the whole empire.

We shall now turn our attention to another stratum of society.

[1] Tac., *Germ.*, 9   [2] Plutarch, *de Iside et Osir.*, p. 364 e., 369 e., 370 c

In the museum at Leyden there is a magical papyrus written about A.D. 350 which proudly bears the title of the *Eighth Book of Moses* or the *Book of Unity*. Among a multitude of most trivial recipes designed to meet the superstitious needs of the lowest class of people, it has preserved an old and valuable gem of the history of religion.[1] This consists of a prayer, in two different recensions, which beseeches the most-high God to come down from heaven; it is really the cult-prayer of some early gnostic church, and it contains a myth of the creation of the world.

God must be praised in every language and every tongue, just as the first and highest beings had once praised Him: first Helios, who had been installed and entrusted with all power by Him, and who had put the stars in their place and founded the world by means of a beam of light that was filled with God. He praised the most-high God in the language of the hieroglyphics, after having mounted up to heaven in the ship of the sun, which is like a round shield. With him went the dog-headed ape, which pronounced the secret numeral for the year, *abrasax*,[2] and the sparrow hawk which croaked with its greedy beak. God was also praised by the first angel who is responsible for punishments, i.e. the judge of the dead, Osiris, and by the "Nine-fold", the sacred nonad of the gods of Heliopolis.[3] This last clapped three times with his hands, and God laughed; seven times His "Ha ha" resounded, and seven gods arose from His laughter.

On the first occasion, light appeared and shone through the universe, and became the god of the cosmos and of fire. Everything was still water; but when God laughed the second time, earth heard the echo, cried aloud, rose up, and separated the water into three parts—the ocean above, upon, and under the earth. A god appeared and was set over the deep; the rise and fall of the tides was due to him. On the third occasion, God laughed grimly, and Nous, understanding, appeared with a heart in his hand, and received the name Hermes. At the fourth laugh, Genna appeared, the goddess of propagation. At the fifth laugh, God's face darkened, and then Moira, the goddess

---

[1] A. Dieterich, *Abraxas*, 16–20, now with a translation in K. Preisendanz, *Papyri Graecæ magicæ*, ii, 93–7 and 109–114

[2] *Vide infra*, p. 284   [3] A. Erman, *Aegypt. Religion*, 30

of fate appeared with a balance, the symbol of Justice. Hermes quarrelled with her because he claimed justice for himself. The most-high God decided that justice should proceed from both, but he gave Moira the sceptre of world dominion. Then he laughed for the sixth time and was glad; Kairos appeared, the god of the fortunate moment, carrying the royal sceptre which he handed to the most-high God. The glancing crown of the god of light was put upon his head, and he was granted the power to rule over everything; a queen wearing a crown of light was placed by his side. Its light, however, was borrowed, it waxed and waned; she was the moon-goddess and the mistress of growth and decay.

God now laughed for the seventh time and groaned deeply; Psyche appeared and everything began to move. God said to her: "Thou shalt move everything, and everything shall be joyful, if Hermes leads thee." Then everything was set in motion and at once filled with the breath of life. God saw it and clicked with His tongue; then Phobos, armed terror, appeared. When God bent towards the earth and whistled aloud, the earth re-echoed, and bore the Pythian dragon which knew everything in advance, because it originated from sounds made by God. The earth reared itself up and threatened to break into heaven, but God said: "Iao" and all stood still.[1] The greatest god then appeared, he who had ordered the past and future of the world, and no longer was anything out of order in the kingdom of the heights. Even Phobos, who, as the elder, wished to resist him, must give place to him at the command of the most-high God. As compensation, he was granted permission to precede the divine Ninehood and have equal power and honour with it.

The writing breaks off at this point for no discernible purpose or reason. It had satisfied the magician so far: but he now conjures up the god, addresses him, chatters, clicks his tongue, whistles, and continues with his hocus-pocus. It is clear enough that some genuine, ancient tradition has preserved here a popular, gnostic cosmology, and one which gives, at the same time, a graphic illustration of the structure of all these systems. There is a most-high God without name and without properties;

[1] *Vide infra*, pp. 269, 290

the only thing said about Him is that He "comprises the whole", and that He is the last source of all power, and of all that comes into being. From Him all the gods originate whom men know and distinguish: they arise from the laughter, the tongue-clickings, and the whistlings of the most-high God. In other systems, it is the laughter and weeping and fear, the out-cries and glances, which give life to creatures;[1] but the fundamental idea is the same. A group of gods appears, but the particular order of succession is meaningless to us. At best we should be justified in regarding Helios as the first. Then others appear, they strive among themselves, and are clothed with power—but it remains a question how the different "world rulers" are related to each other. It is as if the mystagogue's glance could only take in a small bit at once.

At first, we have Egyptian images: the barge of the sun with the shield of the sun, the praying dog-headed apes, the sparrow-hawk, are all universally-known images of the Egyptian cult; and Osiris, the judge of the dead, as well as the divine Ninehood are unmistakable even if they are only shadowy forms. At this point, however, the Egyptian source seems to have ceased. Only at the end do we find the Ninehood again unmistakably. What now follows comes from a Jewish source: first of all light is created, then the wastes of water; then dry land rises and separates the waters. And the last god who originates from the whistling is no other than Yahweh, and thus as in the Old Testament, he is described as the organizer of the whole world, and as "the greatest of great gods". The other gods appear to be Greek, even if more than once a doubt arises whether their Greek character would stand close examination. It has even been suggested that they were modelled upon Iranian deities.[2] In any case they have been affected by Greek philosophy: Hermes is the nous or logos; his struggle with Moira reflects the problem, which was frequently discussed by Stoics, whether reason or blind necessity determined the course of the world.[3] The Pythian dragon which knew everything in advance is still the ancient dæmonic oracle. An arbitrary mixture of most

[1] Dieterich, 24–8
[2] R. Reitzenstein, *Die Göttin Psyche*, 33–44. *Hellen. Mysterienrelig.*, 3rd edition, 359 f.
[3] Dieterich, 75

various elements, syncretism in its purest expression, characterizes the fragment. This medley of religion is modified by
ideas drawn from contemporary philosophy, and its purpose is
to introduce a higher wisdom; and it presents a genuine
cosmogony, like the myth of Dion. In addition there is here a
large and varied number of divine figures, behind which, in the
last analysis, is the great One from whom everything arises
that possesses power and life. Even this strange doctrine is a
form of gnosticism, but the thought is that of untrained minds.

It is not easy to come to close terms with the systems of
gnosticism which the church writers, from the second to the
fourth century, are never tired of recording. These writers are
never objective, and never try to be so. Rather, they pick out
and emphasize anything strange or repellent, and coarsen it,
if they get the chance. We never get a real glimpse into the
teaching and life of a gnostic church; and, in view of the incredibly large number of systems, and the ceaseless flow of the
movement, every description must be regarded only as a snap-
shot of one particular form. Hence we must attempt to get as
close as possible to the original sources, i.e. to the writings
which belonged to the sects themselves; and this can be done
in a few cases.

Hippolytus of Rome, in his *Book of Heretics*, gives records
about the "Naassenes", who used to call themselves after the
Hebrew name for snake (*naash*). At a later date, they described
themselves as gnostics who alone plumbed the deeps of the
godhead. A tractate belonging to this sect had come into the
hands of Hippolytus[1] and he gives his readers a very ample
selection from it—it is possible that only this selection had
come into his hands, and not the complete original. This was
a learned theological monograph based upon a short hymn
addressed to Attis. The hymn was regarded as scripture, and
now explained in a gnostic fashion. It was sometimes sung as a
solo in the theatre. It hails Attis, whom the Assyrians call
Adonis; the Egyptians, Osiris; the Greeks, the Horn of the
Moon; among the Samothracians he is called Adamnas; among
the Thessalians, Karybas; among the Phrygians, Papas; and he

[1] Hippol., *Refut.*, v, 6, 3; 7, 3–9, 9; reconstructed by Reitzenstein, *Poimandres*,
83–98 and reviewed in Reitzenstein und Schaeder, *Studien zum antiken Synkretismus*
(1926), pp. 161–173

is called by still other names. Thus the hymn, which may have originated in Hadrian's time, is a witness to syncretistic "pantheism"; it honours Attis as the god worshipped by every race.

The gnostic preacher found in this hymn the teaching of "important mysteries", and he now proceeded to give wordy and pedantically overloaded descriptions of the myth of the first man, as the solution of the riddle of the universe. As in the legends of all races, man, as we know him, arose out of the ground, but was modelled on the form of the heavenly, original man. At first, he lay motionless and without breath, until a soul was given to him; and this it was that brought suffering and servitude for both the original man and his replica. What is the soul and whence does it come? Passing along roundabout ways which twist and turn in every direction through a multitude of mythologies, we are at last given to understand that the soul which dwells not only in man, but in the entire world of life, is the original man himself and is both male and female. Being a fertilizing germ, he brings everything into being; he is the motionless pole in the flux of cosmic appearances, the logos and the pneuma through which those who are born again are made like him in essence. But the whole account is so sketchy that it is not possible to work it out definitely and clearly. The myth of the original man occurs in innumerable gnostic systems in very varied contexts,[1] and the sermon of the Naassenes gives us a reflection of this variety. It is very ancient teaching, perhaps of Iranian origin, which had regained vitality in this restless period. It attained to some significance within Judaism, and it gave an impulse to the idea of the Messianic Son of Man as found in Daniel. We can trace it also in Philo, and behind the Pauline theory of the first and second man,[2] but only in gnosticism did it attain its full development and effectiveness; and here it remained active for several centuries.

The Naassene sermon is instructive also on other grounds. Similarly to the Leyden cosmogony, in its oldest recension it mingles Jewish elements with a multitude of pagan ideas—this epithet is the simplest. So doing, it betrays a tendency, which

---

[1] W. Bousset, *Hauptprobleme der Gnosis*, 160–233
[2] Reitzenstein, *Poimandres*, 109 ff.

we have already discussed in another connection,[1] to adopt
Jewish ideas and deal with them syncretistically, whereas the
sacred text of the hymn to Attis has no trace of this sort of thing.
The reason is that this form of gnosticism had come into contact
with Christianity, had frequently introduced New Testament
quotations into its text-book, and had interpolated Christian
phrases, but, fortunately, so superficially, and sometimes so
clumsily, that these interpolations can be sorted out again
without difficulty. This work, however, reflects, on the literary
plain, the concrete religious evolution of many of these sects
and, taken on the whole, that of gnosticism as such.

Hippolytus, however, supplies us with still further and, in
this case, more fruitful material. The gnostic Justin wrote a
book called Baruch as the "Scripture" of his church, and this he
surrounded with great secrecy; no one was to talk about it
outside. Hippolytus gained acquaintance with this writing and
he reproduces *verbatim* a chapter from it.[2]

Herodotus tells us that when Heracles was searching for the
cattle of Geryones he met a girl who was half human and half
snake: he united with her in love and she bore three sons. The
girl is a symbol of the origin of the world. At the beginning of
all things were three "unbegotten" principles: two male and
one female: the good God who possesses no other name and
who is omniscient; the father of all creation, who is invisible
but not omniscient and whose name is Elohim; and the woman
Eden who possesses two forms and is moved by passions, and
who is also known as Israel. Elohim unites with her, and in
mutual love, they beget twenty-four angels: twelve take after
the father and are called Michael, Amen, Baruch, Gabriel,
Esaddaios, and so on; twelve take after the mother: Babel,
Achamoth, Naash, Bel, Belias, Satan, and so on. The whole
multitude of angels is Paradise, the single angels are named
allegorically the trees of Paradise; "the tree of life" is the third
father-angel, Baruch; "the tree of knowledge" the third
Eden-angel, Naash. But Mother-Eden is nothing else than the
earth itself: the twelve angels of Elohim take material from her
upper, human part and create the man, Adam, with his earthly
soul; Elohim breathes into him the spirit, pneuma. Thus Adam

is the product of an agreement of Eden and Elohim to work in partnership, and is the seal of their marriage; and in the same way, Eve is created after him. The animals arise from the animal part of Eden.

The picture now changes, and Eden becomes the enemy of the human race. She gives her twelve angels power to bring evil into the world. They divide into four groups—typified in the Bible by the four streams of Paradise—and, in allotted periods and distances, they wander in circular paths: the place where they are at any particular time, determines the strength of their influence upon the earth. Why should Eden be so wrathful? Because at one time Elohim wished to mount into the higher regions of heaven in order to see if he could still improve the world. He took his angels with him, but left Eden behind; she could not follow her husband because she was burdened with the earth. From above, he saw the supramundane light, the doors of heaven opened, and he stood before the "Good", who invited him to sit at his right hand. Then he cried in fear: "Lord let me destroy the world that I have created: for my spirit is in prison in man, and I wish to receive it back again." The Good prevented him from doing evil, and advised him to remain above, and to leave the world to Eden; and this is what he did.

Then Eden grieved because her husband had abandoned her, and she decided to avenge herself on Elohim's spirit that dwelt in man. Her angels become the agents of her hostility. Babel, i.e. Aphrodite, brought immorality and divorce among men, and Naash tormented them in other ways.

Now, however, Elohim sends his third angel, Baruch, to give help. He warns men not to eat of the tree of knowledge, i.e. to learn from Naash. They may eat from any other trees (Gen. 2: 16), for the eleven other angels have passions, but are not hostile to the law, Naash alone being an exception. He seduces Eve to adultery, and Adam to perverse immorality. Then Evil and Good work upon mankind, both coming ultimately from the father, Elohim: his ascent to the "Good" shows the way to man when he is endeavouring to rise, but the betrayal of Eden causes all evils to break in upon the spirit which dwells in man. Baruch came again to Moses and summoned the children of Israel to turn to the "Good", but once again Naash excited the passions of the soul, which was born in Eden, against the spirit, and he successfully contested Baruch's warnings, although they had been preached by the prophets.

At last Elohim turned to the heathen and chose Heracles as a prophet. He fought and vanquished the twelve angels, a deed which the myth honours as the twelve labours of Heracles, but finally succumbed to the power of Omphale's love, who was no other than Babel or Aphrodite. She took his strength from him, i.e. she made him forget Baruch's commandments and covered him with her clothes, viz. the powers of Eden. His mission was in vain.

At last in the days of Herod, Baruch was sent to Nazareth, to Jesus the son of Joseph and Mary when he was minding the sheep as a twelve year old boy. "Preach the word to men—thus he was commanded—and proclaim to them the father, Elohim, and the 'Good', and then mount up to the 'Good' and there take your seat by Elohim, the father of us all." Jesus fulfilled the commandment, and Naash was not able to deceive Him: so he brought Him to the cross. But Jesus abandoned His body to mother Eden: "Woman, behold, thy son." (John 19: 26), He cried to her, and handed over to her His psychic, earthly part, but committed His spirit to the hands of the Father, and departed to the "Good". That is how this myth ends. Hippolytus says that it explained other Greek myths and words from the Bible, and he does not hesitate either to tell us the oath of the sect, or to record how they drank from the water of life and were baptized in this heavenly spring. Even Elohim did this, and the rite blotted out all repentance, whereas earthly men and psychics are baptized in earthly water.

This artificial myth contains a number of conceptions characteristic of gnostic thought, which considerably extend our previous horizon. First of all we observe the preference for a base in Holy Scripture. The actual words are treated allegorically, and so give shape to the dogmas in many respects. Besides Greek myths, Old Testament passages are used in the main, and the Mosaic story of creation supplies the data for depicting the beginnings of things and the tragedy of human corruption. The names of the persons who take active part are borrowed from the Old Testament. Echoes from the New Testament are very rare, and are marked only when Jesus appears in the concluding act: it is not by chance that John is the gospel cited.

As far as the contents are concerned we see that the theology of redemption is the basis of the whole.[1] Man consists of a lower and a higher element; his spirit is of divine origin, but he is exiled in a body endowed with a "psychic" soul and he suffers in this world. A divine messenger comes to redeem him, points him the way to God, and precedes him. We have already discussed the same things in different forms in the Naassene doctrine of the first man. Although it must certainly have been in the other parts of Baruch's book, no extant reference explains how to obtain the redemption which had been brought about by Baruch and Jesus. According to all analogies, it is not likely to have been effected by a simple intellectual acceptance of the theories. Rather, redemption must have been effected by a mystic and sacramental communion with the spirit of the redeemer, and by a way of life intended to liberate the soul that dwelt in man from the earthly passions which were active in his body and soul, i.e. from the falsehood and deceit of Eden.

We have shown that this system of redemption lay behind the Pauline theology. There is a crucial difference, however, in that for Paul, redemption is a pure and incomprehensible act of God's love on behalf of guilty and hostile mankind. Marcion grasped that fact in a certain sense, and carried it to extremes. Moreover, in Paul, the spirit of Christ is not a natural element of man given in creation, but a heavenly gift which brings redemption. In the book of Baruch, on the other hand, the human spirit is itself of divine origin. What it suffers is not connected, in the Pauline sense, with its own sin and guilt, but is the effect of a divine tragedy: and even then the concept of guilt is artificially balanced between the two protagonists. Thus redemption is a necessity for the father, Elohim, a matter which he must bring about for his own sake. Indeed, it is a liberation of himself, for it is his own spirit which he rescues from the fetters of the earthly. Redemption takes place in the form of an ascent to God, and this sect must have been told of the

---

[1] *Vide supra*, pp. 120 f.

"heavenly journey of the soul", or, rather, "of the spirit", as
they express it. The idea of God is the same as we have already
discussed.[1] The One, Great, Good, Almighty, remains in the
background as the final source. The active gods are of lower
rank, and are both male and female: the higher qualities are
ascribed to the male gods. Their mutual antipathies give rise to
the drama of the mystery of redemption. Astral theology plays
a certain part: the twelve angels of Eden run their course and,
in turn, rule over events on the earth because they are the signs
of the zodiac. It is expressly said that the third angel acts as the
herald of both Elohim and Eden, and conveys their will.
Whether this idea is linked with the "third messenger" of
Mani,[2] and whether it comes directly from Baruch or in a
roundabout way through Iranic ideas, must remain an open
question.

If we test the relationship between this gnostic system and
Christianity, the case will be somewhat different from that of
the Naassenes. First of all, we note that the Jewish elements
are more marked everywhere. It is not without purpose that
the redeeming messenger of God is called Baruch, and we can
confidently describe this gnosis as Jewish at bottom, i.e. we can
assume that the Old Testament elements were from the beginning the components out of which the system was built up. The
case is different with the Christian passages. Jesus appears only
at the end, unexpectedly, and when the act of redemption is
taking place; and it is rather strange to hear of Him after we
were expressly assured that Baruch had gone from the Jews,
and had "finally" chosen Heracles. It is striking that he should
then come back regretfully to the Jews, and turn—once more
"finally"—to Jesus of Nazareth. Obviously Jesus was lacking in
the original, and Heracles was himself the Redeemer after he
had freed himself from Omphale's toils, thereby giving mankind
a saviour. The Heracles of Greek mythology does not remain
in the woman's bonds, but goes to heaven and is accepted
among the gods. In this case, there is a formal and final rounding off, in so far as the figure of Heracles constitutes both the

---

[1] *Vide supra*, p. 268
[2] Bousset, *Hauptprob. der Gnosis*, 74 f. H. H. Schaeder, *Urform. u. Fortbildung d.
manichäischen Systems* (1927), p. 102

starting point and the final aim of the myth. The figure of Jesus is brought in only at a later date. His death on the cross is explained in the usual way from the hostility of the lords of this world, in this case of Eden, and His death is understood as a separating of His divine and mundane components; this view, together with the perverting of the last words on the cross, corresponds to the gnostic conception elsewhere. What we have here was borrowed from some other system that had already been Christianized.

The examples that we have cited so far show that gnosis arose apart from any Christian influence. Indeed, it is older than Christianity, and is a phenomenon of pagan syncretism, which mingled Greek and oriental religion in the greatest variety of forms, filled them out with mystical traits, and, at the same time, combined them with philosophical ideas and modes of thought. Thanks to its aggressive propaganda, Judaism shared to a considerable extent in the development of gnosticism. But in its critical early period, Christianity was practically untouched by gnosticism which, at that time, was itself obviously only just showing signs of beginning. First in Colossians, do we find Paul called on to repel an influence which had arisen in the Lycus valley. This influence had gnostic elements and, as a consequence, Paul himself made some positive use of his opponents' forms of thought and expression. After this, similar, mutual reactions are continually occurring: we have discussed them more fully in the case of the Johannine writings. But only in the period that we have now reached, and after we have examined a few typical examples of gnosticism in its simplest form, are we able to deal intelligently with the question as to the effects of such teachings on the Christian church.

What could these systems contribute to the Christian standpoint, when they were so remote from Christianity itself? So long as they were purely pagan and syncretistic, nothing of importance. The matter of greatest moment, the theology of redemption, Paul had already put into a classical form which, at best, could only have been worked out a little further. Enthusiasm, prophecy, and sacramental mysticism might have been able to gain stimuli from gnostic fraternities. Astrology was almost ineradicable at that period, and could have been developed further, along with such observances of certain days as are dependent on it; ascetic tendencies, which were already present and in a certain sense sanctioned by Paul, found new occasions and forms. In other words, gnostics of the earlier type were in a position to send isolated impulses into the Christian church. They made themselves felt in peculiarities of cult, of ethics, or of speculation, some being tolerated and others attacked. Most of the influences up to the end of the first century were of this character.

The situation was different as soon as ever a strongly Judaized gnosis appeared on the horizon of the Christian churches, and opened their eyes to a new way of regarding the Old Testament. Allegorization of the Scriptures had been adopted as a matter of course amongst the Christians, and now the same method was applied with greater boldness and with astonishing new results. The consequence was that the gulf separating Christians from orthodox Judaism widened, and this was felt as pure gain. At the same time numerous questions and doubts were settled, if only the creation and the defects of this world; the Fall and all the evil impulses of the body, as well as all the dubious stories of men of God in the Old Testament, were no longer brought into connection with God, the Father of the Lord Jesus Christ, but were ascribed to an intermediate divine being. If Jesus was regarded as some such revelation of a divine being, i.e. as the logos or the spirit, why should one not find another godhead of more or less secondary character in the God of the Old Testament, and thereby gain a clear understanding of God, and not one oppressed by ethical doubt? Moreover, did not the glimpse of the secrets of supra-mundane happenings attract the unhealthy curiosity even of the simple Christian? To the present day, he is ever and again eager to fathom what Paul condemned no less sharply than Jesus, as belonging not to the sphere of religion, but to that of "carnal wisdom" and unseemly curiosity?

However, if one had gone so far, the next step was almost inevitable. One must be on the look-out to give the person to Christ a place in the system of new knowledge. In this respect there were not a few points of contact for speculative construction. We have made the acquaintance of one of the simplest and therefore one of the most instructive forms, in the book of Baruch. This gnostic myth, in its Christianized form, could have been given out as a legitimate further development of early Christian teachings, and have gathered a church round about itself. These people would believe themselves on a higher level than the masses who moved on the lower grounds of the tradition of the church catholic; and so would regard themselves as the genuine Christians endowed with full insight. So long as such new systems put forward pagan elements strongly and in crude form, and regarded Christ only as one messenger of God among others, they had little power of attraction for normal Christians. Gnosis only became dangerous when it developed systems which placed Christ in the centre of world events and which paid court to any disaffections on the part of the orthodox. A struggle with such gnostics flamed up in the middle of the second century and the church bears the marks of it to the present day.

It is not part of our task to trace the evolution of gnosticism in greater detail, or to describe the exceedingly numerous systems. As a significant phenomenon belonging to the beginning of the declining period of the ancient world, gnosticism is a movement in itself. It must be discussed within the framework of the general history of religion belonging to that period, and its branches stretch out in both space and time, beyond the borders of our account of church history. For our purpose it only comes under observation as far as Christianity was attacked by it, and as the development of the church was influenced by controversy with it. Hence we are not only permitted but required to limit ourselves to the characteristic types: and we ought to deal only with the two most mature gnostic systems out of the overwhelming mass. This means that we must deal with those which come nearest to traditional Christianity, which most strongly influenced the churches, and which, correspondingly, had to withstand the sharpest opposition on the part of the Church: the doctrines of Basilides and Valentine. At the same time, however, we are dealing with those which alone can claim higher significance in the spiritual warfare of ancient times. Apart from the advent of Christianity the whole of gnosticism would have been just as unobserved and obscure as all the other mystical and magical phantoms of the period. Moreover, the gnostics never became of literary significance in the field of spiritual life in general. Literary men occasionally accepted samples of the fare it offered, as we have seen in the case of Dion, but never thought of regarding it as literature proper. Nevertheless influences proceeded from gnosticism, which enabled churchmen to put forth works of higher literary value although that happened only generations later.

As soon as we come to the task of giving an account of the teachings of Basilides, a difficulty arises that is characteristic of the entire movement, a difficulty at which we have already hinted. All these systems were in a state of continual and rapid evolution, and the polemic writers of the church naturally had no interest in antiquarian researches, but attacked the teaching in the form in which it influenced the church of their time. This is particularly striking in the case of Basilides. Clement of Alexandria took the trouble to look up the original writings of Basilides, which he cited, as also what was said by his disciples.[1] Irenæus of Lyons[2] about A.D. 180 described the system, which apparently showed several further developments; the same holds true of the various notices in Hippolytus.[3] But the points with which we are concerned are clear enough.

Basilides lived in the time of Hadrian and Antoninus Pius (A.D. 117–161) in Egypt, particularly in Alexandria, although he made missionary journeys through the nomes of the delta.[4] He wrote a considerable work under the title of *Exegetica*, which, in practice, amounted to a commentary on the gospel. A few fragments have been preserved. The thirteenth book[5] dealt with the parable of the rich man and Lazarus, and found therein hints of the doctrine that the origin of nature was without root in time or space—if we rightly understand his enigmatic words. Our authority, Hegemonius, quotes from this book a report about the dualism of the "barbarians", i.e. the Persians. The passages describe the war of light with darkness

---

[1] Harnack, *Altchristl. Literatur*, i, 157–161; Hilgenfeld, *Ketzergesch. d. Urchristentums*, 207–217, cf. E. de Faye, *Gnostique et Gnosticisme* (2nd edition), 39–56
[2] Iren., i, 24, 3–6 (i, 198–203, ed. Harvey)
[3] Hippol., *Ref.*, vii, 14–27, and in the *Syntagma* ap. Epiph., 24 (i, 256–267), Holl
[4] Clem., *Strom.*, vii, 17, 106, 4; Epiph., xxiv, 1, 1
[5] Hegemonius, *Acta Archelai.*, 67, 4–11, ed. Beeson

and the resulting peculiar character of what was created. But we are not told what attitude Basilides himself took to this theory. Clement of Alexandria,[1] too, quotes several passages from the twenty-third book. Basilides is there dealing with the problem how God could permit the innocent sufferings of the martyrs. His answer is that there are no such things as innocent sufferings, because that would contradict the righteousness of God. The martyrs suffer in punishment of their sins, otherwise secret. And if they really had none—a rare case—their sufferings were to be set on a level with those of infant children. Even these had a predisposition for sin, and it was not their merit that this impulse had not come to effect in practice. The will for evil was present in any case; this, and not merely the accomplished act was wicked and deserved punishment: there is an unmistakable reference to the Sermon on the Mount, with its attitude to adultery and murder.

Thus the formal, philosophically conceived, righteousness of God is for Basilides a fundamental postulate of his system, and this he carries through logically regardless of the contradictions in practical experience. His idea of sin is, in a sense, earnest and profound, corresponding to Paul's doctrines and the Sermon on the Mount. Thus, all suffering is, for him, a just punishment for sin; to that extent, it is good. It may be punishment for sin committed in an earlier life. For he takes the Old Testament principle of punishment to the third and fourth generation, and explains it from the standpoint of metempsychosis; and, only on this assumption, can he understand the Pauline saying: "I was alive apart from the Law once" (Rom. 7: 9). That could not apply to human existence, for this was always subject to some law; it must have been said about a life in another, perhaps an animal body.[2]

The soul which has been destined and chosen for redemption, is of a supra-mundane nature, foreign to the earth. Its knowledge of God proceeds from this nature, and faith is not one of its functions, but self-subsistent; it is the most glorious ornament of the soul. Thus the redeemed have received three things

---

[1] Clem., *Strom.*, iv, 12, 81, 1–88, 5

[2] *Ibid.*, iv, 12, 83, 2; *Exc. ex. Theod.*, 28. Origen in *Epist. ad Rom.*, v; Vol. 6, p. 336. Lommatzsch

by the will of God: (*a*) the power to find everything acceptable
in order that the logos of each may be saved for the All. (*b*) To
have no desires, and (*c*) to have no hatred. Thus, even in the
most inward part, they remain untouched by the attacks of this
world: "Suffering and fear belong to material things, like rust
to iron." Thus also sins committed in ignorance or involuntarily
are forgiven, i.e. simply washed away. We may add: only when
sins are born of the will and thereby have contact with substance must they be atoned by suffering. If we say, in addition,
that Basilides personifies righteousness and, together with its
daughter Irene, i.e. peace, numbered it with the highest ogdoad,
we shall have dealt with the authentic passages from his writings.[1] They do not give a complete picture, but a few points
which other passages help to connect up, and fill out. Thus
they make it possible for us to get an idea of Basilides's way of
thought.

Besides these literal extracts from the writings of the master
himself, our best sources afford not a few notices in regard to
the opinions of the "Basilidians", particularly in the writings
of his son, Isidoros. He also had written a book called *Exegetica*
in which he expounded the words of a prophet, Parchor by
name. Moreover, Basilides himself had his own apocryphal
authorities: a certain Glaucias, a person described as a translator of Peter; and Matthias, of whose tradition we hear elsewhere; further names of prophets are mentioned,[2] Barkoph
and Barkabbas "and other imaginary figures". For Isidor, and
obviously also for Basilides, prophetic talent was a special gift
of God to the elect; and if the Athenians had ascribed a clar-
voyant dæmon to Socrates, and similarly Aristotle to all men,
this was done only in recognition of a theological truth preached
by the prophets. The philosophers just mentioned had not
themselves discovered, but only accepted, it. Thus Isidor in
his commentary on Parchor.[3]

On another occasion, we hear[4] that the Basilidians described
the passions as "addenda", as spirits which had laid hold of the
rational soul only on the occasion of some primeval rebellion;

[1] Clement, *Strom.*, iv, 12, 88, 5 (unlike ii, 3, 10, 1–3). v, 1, 3, 2. iv, 12, 86, 1;
88, 5; 24, 153, 3; 25, 162, 1
[2] *Ibid.*, vii, 17, 106, 4; 108, 1. Agrippa Castor in Euseb., *H.E.*, iv, 7, 7
[3] Clem., *Strom.*, vi, 6, 53, 2–5   [4] *Ibid.*, ii, 20, 112, 1–114, 1

at a later date these spirits had been joined by all sorts of animal and plant spirits which induced the soul to imitate their own "properties" with the help of imagination. Isidor clearly recognized the danger of this conception for moral conduct, and in writing *Of the Twofold Soul,* would not permit reference to the power of these "appended" forces to be regarded as excuses for sin. "The rational part of us must remain master and overcome our lower nature." We have just seen how Basilides himself, by using the metaphor of rust on iron, explains the relationship of the passions to the soul: here we have a further development of the theory.

A fragment, preserved by Clement, gives us the attitude of the school to marriage.[1] The word of Jesus about the three kinds of eunuchs (Matt. 19: 12) is expounded quite correctly, and the "eunuchs for the sake of the kingdom of Heaven" is explained as referring to those who avoid marriage on account of its being bound up with earthly cares—which agrees fairly well with Paul's personal opinion. But "to marry is better than to burn" says the apostle: he who must be always on his guard in order to keep himself pure, lives in a divided hope: he would do better to marry. But he who for any reason does not wish to marry, and yet is afraid of sin, should not separate himself from the brethren. In the holy fellowship nothing could attack him, and their laying on of hands would bring him help. He need only desire to do the good, and he would then be successful. In human life there are things which were natural and necessary, and others which were only natural. To dress oneself was natural and necessary; sexual intercourse was natural but not necessary. It is more than doubtful whether the sexual practices of a gnostic sect which were apparently observed by Epiphanius some two hundred years later[2] reflect any of the theories of Basilides. There is one important notice[3] to the effect that the Basilidians observed a feast of the baptism of Christ by a nocturnal ceremony which preceded the day itself. It was observed on either the 10th or the 6th of January, i.e. in connection with an ancient Egyptian feast of Osiris at which holy water was drawn by all from the Nile during the night.

---

[1] Clem., *Strom.,* iii, 1, 1–3 2 (= Epiph., *haer.,* xxxii, 4, 4–9)
[2] Epiph., *haer.,* xxvi, 4–5; cf. xxvi, 17, 4–9
[3] Clem., *Strom.,* i, 21, 146, 1–2; cf. K. Holl, *Ges. Aufsätze,* ii, pp. 143, 152–4

To these details which have come down to us by the accident of tradition, we now add the sketch of the system of Basilides with which Irenæus presents us.[1] The "unborn and nameless Father" is exalted and alone. He first begot Nous, the understanding; the logos was begotten by Nous and then a series of emanations from Phronesis, Sophia, Dynamis—reason, wisdom, power—to the great powers and archangels who dwell in the first heaven, which they themselves had created. A new emanation of spiritual powers then took place. They created for themselves a second heaven, and so on, until the holy number of three hundred and sixty-five heavens was reached. That this was a holy number was proved by the magic word *abrasax*, 365 being the sum of the numerical values of its Greek letters. The lowest of these heavens was the one which we see, and its inhabitants were those which had created our earth and which shared its rule among themselves. The highest of these was the god of the Jews who wished to subject all other people to his elect, but thereby set the other angels and their nations against himself and his people.

When the anonymous Father saw the distress of mankind, He sent His first-born, Nous, as Christ, in order to redeem those who should believe on Him, from the rule of the creator of the world. He therefore appeared upon earth as man, revealed Himself to the nations, and worked miracles. But He bore human form only in appearance, because, really, He was an incorporeal being. Thus He did not really suffer on the cross. On the *Via Dolorosa*, He handed the cross over to Simon of Cyrene, to whom He lent His own figure, and who was killed as if he were Jesus, while the true Jesus Christ in the figure of Simon stood near by, and laughed at His enemies. Then, invisible to all hostile powers, He ascended to the Father.

He who knows this secret is liberated from the power of the creator of the world: he must confess Him who came in human form, who is regarded as crucified, whose name is Jesus, and who was sent from the Father in order to destroy the works of the creator of the world according to the Father's plan of salvation (*œconomia*). But he who confesses Jesus the crucified

[1] Iren., i, 24

is still a slave, and under the authority of the angels which created our bodies.

Salvation has to do only with the soul, for the body is by nature corruptible. Prophesyings originate from the creators of the world and, in particular, the Law comes from their overlord who had fetched from Egypt his own people, the Jews. Among the Basilidians no one troubled about the prohibition of sacrificial flesh and other matters, and there were no problems in the sexual sphere. They used magic, images, exorcisms, and other forms of witchcraft. They named the angels, and distributed them among their three hundred and sixty-five heavens. In the same way, the Saviour, when descending and ascending through the empires of the spirits, was called Qawlaqaw—a pedantic Hebrew reminiscence coming from Isa. 28: 10, and occurring among the Naassenes as the name of the original man.[1] He who knows all these matters in their proper connections, and the names of the angels, will be invisible to all the angels and spiritual powers, and incomprehensible to them, like Qawlaqaw; he will pass unrecognized through all the heavenly regions. Naturally these are secrets which are only possible for the few and which must be guarded by initiates in the strictest confidence. Thus Irenæus.

His account does not mention the basic doctrine, although it is proved by the separate passages already discussed, viz. that the human soul is of heavenly origin and is related to the son of the most-high God, the redeemer Nous. That is why Nous descends to the earth—also taught in the book of Baruch—and raises to life again the divine power of the human soul. Everyone reached and convinced by this message is transformed to a copy of the original model. He receives the powers and the capacities of the redeemer, so that he himself can now find his way back unrecognized and unhindered to his heavenly home, where the God, who is perfectly good and absolutely righteous, sits on His throne unapproachably distant and majestic.

Here we have the gnostic idea of God, gnostic doctrine of redemption, gnostic cosmogony with the incorporation of the God of the Jews as a spirit of lower rank, gnostic anthropology—including a marked leaning to magic and all sorts of esoteric

[1] Hippol., *Ref.*, v, 7, 41, 4

teachings—and yet one thing is certain: Basilides maintained
he was a Christian. In his system, Christ is not one dæmon
among many, but the only begotten Son of the most-high God,
His only and perfect revelation; through Him everything else
had been created. He is the redeemer of mankind and brings
the elect of all nations back to God.

We have seen that gnostic literature usually took the form of
expositions of sacred books. Basilides was the first to expound
a Christian book, and indeed nothing less than "the gospel".
We cannot say whether one of our four gospels, or a selection,
prepared by Basilides himself, of a gospel-harmony, constituted
the text. That it was not apocryphal is shown by all the extant
citations of the gospel which the Basilidians quoted. The most
significant fact is that this book, written to expound gnostic
doctrine, is the very first commentary on a gospel. No Christian,
who was a member of the church catholic, had, up to that
time, made a gospel the subject of a continuous exegesis; and
it was still to be a long time before Papias wrote his expositions
of the sayings of the Lord, and Theophilus of Antioch (about
A.D. 180) his commentary on the gospels. Further, Basilides
dealt with the gospel as sacred scripture, and therefore explained it allegorically, in exactly the same way as the Church
was accustomed to explain the Old Testament. On this point,
the Church had not yet gone so far as to put the gospels on a
similar level to the traditional book, i.e. the Old Testament,
and so treat it as itself Holy Scripture; the New Testament
canon was still at the prenatal stage. In this respect, again,
gnosticism stimulated the Church and called forth new activity
just because it had gone on ahead.

If we consider the teachings of Basilides, we have no difficulty
in understanding how seductive they must have seemed to many
orthodox Christians. There was no trace of that syncretistic
paganism which had always been felt objectionable; instead of
that, Christ stood clearly and gloriously in the foreground as
the Son of God, in a vigorous monotheism. That there was an
endless number of angels was also the opinion in the Church.
Basilides taught their names and their mutual relationships,
and much about the origin of heaven and earth; that was surely
not forbidden? And when he spoke of the divine origin of the

soul, and founded his doctrine of redemption upon it, what was he doing differently from the author of Acts, who, indeed (17: 23, 28) tells that the Apostle Paul preached about the "unknown God" and quoted Aratos: "For we are His offspring." This is but what Basilides said, and indeed more exactly and clearly. The only objectionable thing was that he did not accept the Old Testament in its entirety. He thought little of the prophecies, and nothing of the Law; nor did he recognize the children of Israel as the elect of God. It is true that the orthodox teachers preached otherwise, but was it so very certain that they were right? Paul himself had said (Gal. 3: 19) that the Law was given by the angels, and such an authority as the author of Hebrews (2: 2) had expressly repeated it. Basilides made exactly the same assertions, but proceeded logically to liberate Christian thought from all the troublesome problems which the old book of the Jews offered to the moral sensibility of a Christian, and indeed, to his idea of God. He replaced the Old Testament, and gave the gospel, as scripture, all the greater reverence in the central position of Christian teaching.

All this and much more was true, and was often said; and he who was completely convinced went over, together with others of like mind, to a schismatic church of the new teachers, and became a sectarian. But much greater was the number of those who remained faithful to the church and who regarded such opinions as quite in keeping with the old doctrine: they opened the doors of the church to gnosticism and unwittingly brought the church into a danger which would soon require all her powers to ward off: the danger of being overrun by the power of gnosis and being drawn into mortal combat with ancient religion.

The most comprehensive and effective system of Christian gnosis goes back to Valentine. He came from Egypt to Rome where he laboured for a lengthy period, about A.D. 160–170, and indeed hoped to become bishop. Later he appears to have left Rome and gone to Cyprus.[1] The various branches of his teaching and school of thought struggled most vigorously with the Church and were most definitely repudiated. Loud

[1] Epiph., *haer.*, xxxi, 7, 1–2; *Iren.*, iii, 4, 3 (2, 17 H.); Tert., *adv. Valent.*, 4

complaints have come down to us from the orthodox,[1] that the
Valentinians preached in the churches, making full use of the
customary phrases and deceiving the simple. Then the seducers
took offence because they were repudiated as heretics, although
they were saying and teaching exactly the same thing as the
orthodox. But that was precisely why they were regarded as the
most dangerous opponents of the Church; and such they were
in fact. They were honourably concerned to do her justice, and
to recognize her as the first stage to perfect knowledge.

Thus the sources are particularly rich in regard to Valentine's
form of gnosticism. Besides reliable reports we possess a not inconsiderable number of quotations from Valentine himself and
his school, even if no complete documents.[2] Of course the
methodological limitations which we had to assume in the study
of Basilides hold good in this case also, but by comparing
various sources, it is possible to begin with the notices of
Irenæus in regard to the Ptolemaic School, and work out details
of an older form,[3] which we may possibly ascribe to Valentine: it
can scarcely have undergone serious changes by the editing of
his disciples.

Above the universe, on invisible and ineffable heights, dwells
the prime Father who is also called Bythos and Chaos. He is
invisible, incomprehensible, superior to time, unbegotten, and
dwells in eternal peace. At His side is His Ennœa also called
Sigē, or Charis, i.e. God's thought, silence, and grace. Personification of divine properties is by now quite familiar to us: it
is a new thing, however, that the prime God should have a
consort. That belongs to the nature of the system, for according
to Valentine all the divine emanations proceed forth in duality;
the mystery of marriage (Eph. 5: 32) is predominant even in
the world of the gods. The first two gods give birth to Nous or
Monogenes, the only-begotten, together with Aletheia, truth,
the latter two produce Logos and Zoē, word and life; and from
these proceed as the final pair of the higher ogdoad, Anthropos

[1] *Iren.*, iii, 15, 2 (2, 79 H.); de Faye *Gnostiques*, 57–141, pp. 251–67
[2] Harnack, *Ges. d. Altchr. Lit.*, i, 174–184; Hilgenfeld, *Ketzerges.*, pp. 293–308,
Ptolemaeus, pp. 345–368, Marcus, pp. 369–383, Herakleon, pp. 472–505, Eastern
School, pp. 505–22
[3] *Iren.*, i, 1–8; cf. Hippol., *Ref.*, vi, 21–55 and Ps-Tertullian, *adv. omn. haer.*, 4.
Exc. ex. Theod., 43–65. Cf. K. Müller, *Götting. Nachr.*, 1920, pp. 205–241. Ed.
Schwartz, *ibid.*, 1908, p. 128, pp. 134–9

and Ecclesia, man and church. Almost all these names are chosen with good conscience from the Biblical sources, including the "chaos" of Genesis and the silence from which according to the Wisdom of Solomon the word of God arises.[1] The germs of hypostatization, recognizable[2] even in John, now attain to full development.

From Logos and Zoē proceed a further decad of five pairs of gods, from Anthropos and Ecclesia a series of six pairs, so that the "pleroma", i.e. the "fullness of the Godhead",[3] consists of thirty "æons", which are conceived, in reality, only as rays of the one ineffable Godhead, but the differences between them express the descent from the highest to the lowest divinity. Among all these beings, the only-begotten Nous alone possesses the possibility of perfect knowledge of the highest God, and gives information to the others about Him. He alone is the divine principle of revelation. His preaching awakens in all a yearning for God, which yearning, however, is a silent desire.

Only the last of the thirty æons, Sophia, lets her desires grow into an unbridled passion, and tries to grasp the nature of the Father. But she would have been overcome by the sweet rapture of her feelings, and have dissolved into the All, had not Horos, the guardian of the borders of the pleroma, held her back, supported her, and brought her back to her senses. Now she understood that the Father was incomprehensible, and so she cast away her former desires and passions;[4] thus she was able to remain in the pleroma. But now at the command of the prime Father, Monogenes brings forth a new pair, Christ and the Holy Spirit, in order that the latter might restore order to the pleroma which had been disturbed by Sophia's action. Christ teaches the æons that they owe their origin to the Father, but their form to Nous, whereas the spirit teaches them how to agree with one another, how to thank God, and thus how to attain genuine peace. This they now do, and all become similar to one another in form and sense. They sing, in chorus, the praises of the prime Father, and then produce Jesus the Saviour as the perfect fruit of the pleroma. He is also

---

[1] *Vide supra*, pp. 242 f.   [2] *Vide supra*, p. 230   [3] *Vide supra*, p. 214
[4] *Iren.*, i, 1, 1–2, 3 (vol. i, pp. 8–16, ed. Harvey)

called Christ or Logos, after the one who begot Him, and He is surrounded by a host of angels as His satellites.[1]

The yearning cast out from Sophia and the pleroma is known as "Enthymesis", and it becomes the first being in the hitherto lifeless void. It is a pneumatic substance still without form, until it is shaped by Christ, and receives a personal nature: it is the lower Sophia, or, using the Hebrew name, Achamoth. Like her mother, she possesses heavenly yearning, and experiences similar suffering. The guardian of the border opposes her urge for the pleroma, and frightens her back by using the name, Iao, which has magic power. She now suffers in the highest degree the pains of all the passions, whence there arises the original model of the world: from her love for the Giver of life, everything that possesses a soul; from her passion, everything that is material; in particular, moisture comes from her tears, out of her laughter comes light, out of her sorrow and anguish, the elements.[2]

At the supplication of the higher Sophia, Christ takes pity upon her and sends to her aid the Saviour or Paraclete, who heals her and "gives form to her knowledge". As a result she rejoices in the sight of the angels which acccompany Him, and so gives birth to a pneumatic substance. The world is now formed of these three elements, matter, psyche, pneuma. In particular, it is created by the demi-urge, the creator of the world with his six angels, and he himself is created by Achamoth out of psychic substance. Thus there arises a new and lower "ogdoad" of Achamoth with seven angelic figures. The demi-urge creates the seven heavens for himself and his angels, and out of the world of dæmons and earthly elements creatures are called into being on the model previously set by Achamoth. His own form and likeness are used when he creates man out of matter and psyche, body and soul. But without his suspecting it, Achamoth sows the pneumatic substance, born of herself, into the human soul, and therefore prepares it for the reception of the perfect logos in the future. The redemption of mankind means, therefore the liberation of his pneuma, which longs for God, from union with lower substances.[3] Thus there is repeated

[1] *Iren.*, i, 2, 4*b*–6 (pp. 18–23 H.)   [2] *Ibid.*, i, 4, 1–2 (pp. 31–36 H.)
[3] Valentine in Clem., *Strom.*, ii, 20, 114, 4

once more the drama which has already been played twice in this world—by the higher Sophia and by Achamoth.

The Saviour descends to the yearning spirit of man. As the firstborn of those whom He is to redeem, He has already accepted from Achamoth the pneumatic element, and from the demi-urge, the "psychic Christ". Matter is not capable of redemption, and thus the Saviour has no earthly, material body. The way of redemption is the same for mankind as it had been for Sophia, the "shaping of gnosis": i.e. the full knowledge of God and of Achamoth, by initiation into the mysteries. This perfection is, however, only granted to the "pneumatics", who carry within themselves the divine seed, which is sown ever afresh by Achamoth. When all the pneuma scattered in the world is perfected in gnosis, then redemption is completed, then Sophia-Achamoth enters into the highest pleroma, and becomes the bride of the Saviour; the pneumatics lay aside their souls, and, unhindered and unseen by all the heavenly powers, they ascend to the pleroma in order to be married as pure spirits with the Saviour's angels.

But also the "psychics", who have not been reached by pneuma, are promised a redemption. The demi-urge, who is entirely without inkling until the arrival of the Saviour, had not shut himself up from the teaching of the redeemer; and so even he labours, according to his power in perfecting the world, and shows particular care for the prosperity of the Church.[1] The latter preserves the divine revelation in its holy scriptures, although most of its members are not able to understand them completely in their spiritual sense, because they themselves lack the pneuma, and are bound to this world. Thus they strive valiantly, in faith and by good works, to reach the goal prepared for them: in the end, the souls of the righteous, together with the demi-urges, will enter into the middle space, between heaven and pleroma, where Achamoth still dwells, and where they will find rest. The earthly world will be destroyed with fire, and will exist no longer.[2]

The whole, exceedingly complicated system is transformed

---

[1] *Iren.*, i, 7, 4–5 (pp. 63–4 H.)

[2] *Ibid.*, i, 4, 4–6, 2;6, 4–7, 2 (pp. 38–55; 57–60 H.), also *Exc. ex. Theod.*, pp. 43–65

further and rebuilt in the various schools; it is also buttressed by a detailed scriptural proof,[1] which relies almost entirely on the Gospels and the Pauline epistles, and only uses the Old Testament in a few quotations from Genesis and Psalms. The method of interpretation is of course allegorical; accordingly, the wandering sheep is Sophia; Simon, who sings the hymn of greeting to the child Jesus, is the demi-urge who rejoices in the Saviour; the prophetess Hannah, who awaits the redemption in the temple (Luke 2: 36), is Achamoth awaiting the re-ascent of the Saviour. The parable of the tares amongst the wheat shows the existence of the spiritual seed side by side with psychic elements in a pneumatic man. The daughter of Jairus is the symbol of Achamoth, who is awakened to knowledge by the Saviour, and the words of Jesus, when suffering on the cross, express the pains of Achamoth.[2]

Valentine's disciple, Heracleon, wrote, probably after the middle of the second century, a detailed commentary on John, of which Origen has preserved many excerpts.[3] Here allegorization is complete; e.g. the demi-urge speaks through the Baptist, and the woman of Samaria is a type of the pneumatic woman who is dissatisfied with the Jacob's Well of the Old Testament, who therefore turns to the living water of gnosis, and who longs for her future spouse in the pleroma.[4] This method was exactly the same as that customary in the Church, and neither its application nor the tendency of its exegesis was out of harmony with the spirit of the Fourth Gospel. In the end, it was the re-examination of the whole presuppositions of gnosticism and its denial of validity to the Old Testament, which created a feeling of doubt among readers within the Church.

A thorough discussion of the Old Testament by another of Valentine's disciples, Ptolemy, has been preserved.[5] Writing an

---

[1] *Iren.*, i, 3, 1–6; 8, 2–5 (pp. 24–31; 68–80 H.), *Exc. ex. Theod. passim*; Hipp., *Ref.*, vi, 34–5, etc. Cf. Carola Barth., *Interp. d. N.T. in der Valent. Gnosis*, 1911 (*T.U.*, 37, 3)

[2] *Iren.*, i, 8, 2–4 (pp. 68–73 H.), *Exc. ex. Theod.*, 53

[3] Origen's, *Commentary of John*, ed. by E. Preuschen, p. cii. Brooke, *The Fragments of Heracleon* (Texts and Studies, i, 4). Hilgenfeld, *Ketzergeschichte*, 472–498

[4] On John 1: 26 (Orig., vi, 200) and on 4, 12 ff. (Orig., xiii, 57; lxiii, 68); W. v. Löwenich, *Johannesverständnis im 2. Jh.*, pp. 82 ff.

[5] Epiph., *haer.*, xxxiii, 3–7; cf. Harnack, *Berl Sitzungsberichte*, 1902, pp. 507–545; Edition in *Kleine Texte*, No. 9

open letter to an eminent lady, Flora by name, he subjects the five books of Moses to religious criticism, and displays keen understanding. First of all he distinguishes the three parts of the Law: the first is from God, the second is from Moses—as Jesus explicitly declares, e.g. in regard to permission for divorce (Matt. 19: 8)—the third from the Jewish "elders", to whose tradition Jesus ascribes a commandment such as the privilege of what is given to God (Matt. 15: 5–6). Even the part which goes back to God is not a unity, but itself falls into three stages. The first stage is the pure commandment of God, in which no foreign element is mixed, and which Jesus did not wish to abrogate, but to fulfil: the Ten Commandments. The second consists of the commandments which have been adulterated with injustice, such as that of retaliation where one wrong act is repaid by a second. The third are the ceremonial laws, which possess only symbolic and typological meaning.

This raises the question: Who was the divine originator of this Law? It is not perfect, and therefore does not come from the perfect God, the unbegotten One; still less does it come from the devil since it contains what is truly good. Thus the Law is the work of an intermediate god, who proclaims righteousness as he understands it. The lady now asks how the lower beings, belonging to this middle position, and especially how the nothingness of the devil, could arise from the "One original principle recognized and confessed by us"—for the goodness of nature only begets things similar and equal to itself. In answer, she is directed toward future teaching, which will tell her of "the apostolic tradition which we have accepted from hand to hand, together with the proof of all the sayings from the teaching of the Saviour". Thus she was to be initiated into the system, and introduced to its scriptural proof; and she would be convinced that this gnosis was truly Christian.

At this point we pause. Much more could be said about Valentine and his school, about gnosis and the other systems. Later on, we shall have the opportunity of filling out the picture which we have just sketched, but these few examples must suffice for us to understand the evolution of the Church in the second century. In particular, the last examples clearly express, by their explicitly Christian character, the decided antithesis, indeed the strangeness and danger of gnosis to which the Church was fully alive. The danger was not to be found in the subjective character of the Biblical exegesis; nor in the unlimited freedom in transforming, or in fabricating gospels; nor in the docetic Christology which makes a mask in one way or another out of the humanity of Jesus; nor in the number of dæmonic or divine figures. More dubious and, when carried through logically, quite intolerable is the denial of the Old Testament: but the *Epistle of Ptolemy* contains so many concessions that, in this case, there seems a possibility of coming to a mutual understanding.

The decisive thing always is the conception of God, with all its consequences. For Christianity, the fundamental principle is the supra-rational fact that the same God, who commands and judges, also redeems the helpless sinner by pure compassion: that is what Jesus put into simple words, and Paul, into the forms of a searching dialectic. Gnosis solves the problem by dividing the Godhead into two, and placing the two halves on different levels; but in so doing it surrenders the profoundest depths of ethical urgency in our experience of God. The miraculous now becomes comprehensible and the unthinkable can be understood: God becomes a philosophic abstraction of the kind beloved by mystics.

The drama which takes place in Valentine's pleroma shows most clearly the sense of this "Divine Comedy" of redemption. It is the self-unfolding and self-understanding of the Godhead. Everything that is begotten flows from the natural necessity of the divine nature, and, in its progress from the one to the many, leads to a differentiation and a continually increasing manifoldness, to an ever more strongly marked diminution of the divine nature. But, with the same inevitability, what is divine, having found one of its forms even in man, turns back to its original source, overcomes the differences step by step, and finally disappears in the One-Whole, the formless and indefinable "fullness of the Godhead", which no longer possesses individuality or personality.

That might have been said also by a philosopher; and pantheism from the days of the Stoa to those of Hegel has really given a series of new forms to this idea of God. But in gnosticism, the mysticism of the orient is added to philosophical pantheism. The path of the individual, in its ascent to the divine Nirvana, is not only to be found by pure thought, but also by magical formulas and actions, and by the control of superhuman powers. This feature is to be found in all gnostic circles and is unmistakable in Valentine,[1] in spite of the high level of his thinking.

Gnosis has been described as the "acute Hellenization of Christianity":[2] we must recognize in addition an equally acute "re-orientalization". But it was not the many colourful figures of the Greek and oriental heaven which threatened Christianity. These were easily overcome. But among the gnostics, the god of oriental mysticism rose up in power and might to contend with the Father in Heaven to whom Jesus had taught His disciples to pray.

[1] Cf. K. Müller, *Gött. Nachr.*, 1920, pp. 188–200
[2] Harnack, *Lehrb. d. Dogmenges.*, 4th edition, i, 250; cf. also F. C. Burkitt, *Church and Gnosis*, 1932

Part II
The Founding of the Church Universal

Chapter One

THE WORLD EMPIRE OF ROME IN THE SECOND AND THIRD CENTURIES

THE EMPIRE OF AUGUSTUS AIMED AT ENSURING PEACE in the whole civilized world; its title to fame was its success in reaching this objective, and the principal task of all the emperors was to maintain the peace thus achieved. The thousand peoples and tribes bordering on the Mediterranean were so closely bound together by the advantages of this state of affairs, that no rebellions from within could endanger the unity of the empire. In the year of the three emperors following on Nero's death, there were only local disturbances, and these were quickly over. The flames of the Gallic insurrection on the Batavian border were due to special circumstances, and Vespasian extinguished them firmly in the same manner as he put an end to the Jewish attempt to gain freedom. The real danger to the Empire lay in wait beyond the borders. On the Rhine and on the Danube, Germanic and, to some extent, Slavonic tribes were driven by elemental forces from the stage of primitive existence into the sphere of history; on the Euphrates, the Iranians of the Near East pressed forward to the Syrian coast. Taught by its experiences under Augustus, the Empire, for almost a century, had maintained its borders in the west defensively, and had only pushed them forward in isolated and safe places, and with the greatest caution. The conquest of Britain, begun under Claudius and completed under Domitian, was the most significant event during this period. Under the Flavian emperors, the defensive character of the maintenance of the frontiers was even more definitely emphasized by placing great fortifications along the boundary in order to protect the border country, on the upper Rhine and on the Danube, against hostile attacks. These fortifications consisted of wooden towers and wattle-work fences; and the progress of this method of defence can be traced from Vespasian to Domitian by the fragmentary remains that still survive.

Trajan recognized that the dangers could not be fully disposed of in this manner, and so he turned back to the modes of thought familiar to the military minds of early Rome. He marched into the land of that enemy which for the time being seemed the most threatening, and fought two severe and bloody wars (A.D. 101–6) against the Dacians, who inhabited the present-day Roumania. In the end, this region was completely incorporated into the empire as the province of Dacia. Trajan's column in Rome still gives us vivid records of the famous deeds of these wars.

Before Dacia was completely conquered, Trajan prepared further measures for the safety of the Empire on the eastern border. The legate of Syria was ordered to put an end to the remaining semi-independence of the tribes of Bedouin who were united in the kingdom of Nabatea. In this way the new province of Arabia arose contiguous to Palestine on the eastern and southern borders. Water conduits, barracks, and roads were built; these ensured the economic life of the new province, and, at the same time, drew a line between the Roman empire and the vast Arabian wilderness inhabited by free Bedouin. The really dangerous zone lay, not here, but on the Euphrates boundary. In that region, the empire of the Iranian Parthians had threatened the Roman empire with war from the very beginning, and the fact that the peace concluded by Augustus had lasted so long depended on the inner circumstances of the Parthian empire rather than on the Romans. Hence the emperor felt that active measures to ensure the safety of the frontier were inevitable in this region. War was waged for three years (A.D. 114–16), and not only the Parthians but also the Armenians, who were allied with them, were vanquished; three new provinces, Armenia, Assyria, and Mesopotamia, were established. By this time a series of new provinces lay beyond the earlier boundaries of the empire, and extended from the river Theiss to the Black Sea, from the Caucasus to the Persian Gulf, and from the Euphrates to the Sinaitic peninsula. This was an extremely generous protective region, and it had been quickly conquered by overpowering forces. It now required an extended period of quiet gestation in order to grow into organic union with the Roman empire, and really to afford the protection which its creator expected from it.

It was questionable whether the Empire possessed the power for solving this problem, and when Trajan died in A.D. 117, after having completed his work, his successor denied it immediately on commencing his reign. A warning sign was given in A.D. 115, when Jews in Egypt, probably in conjunction with the fellahin, who were terribly oppressed, conspired an insurrection which extended to Cyprus and Cyrenaica. Only after two years was the Emperor able to supply the troops necessary to suppress it. Even in other regions, everything was not as peaceful as it ought to have been. Hadrian therefore drew the inevitable but inglorious conclusion, viz. to abandon Armenia, Assyria, and Mesopotamia. It was decided to keep Arabia and Dacia, in spite of a certain hesitation in regard to the latter, and these provinces were in fact retained. It was clear that Rome was no longer in a position to make high-handed conquests, but only to defend its former possessions; this was the task upon which Hadrian concentrated his entire military concern. The fortifications along the borders were pushed forward in many places, and they cut long straight lines through the country. Their principal element now consisted of a mighty palisade which ran from the Neuwied basin to the neighbourhood of Regensburg. In Britain, a wall was built across the island from Solway Firth to the mouth of the Tyne.

Hadrian did not possess the military genius of Trajan, and therefore sought to establish a condition of the Empire which did not demand from the emperor the virtues of a field-marshal; but he was an excellent administrator and had a genius for organization, a fact which was also of advantage to the army. The latter faithfully fulfilled his requirements: for almost half a century it protected the peace of the Empire. Battles for maintaining the safety of the frontier never quite ceased, but they seldom exceeded the ability of the frontier guards. Antoninus Pius used the Trajan model when he erected a pillar to his own honour on the Field of Mars, but he had no occasion to decorate its shaft with a ribbon of martial reliefs. That was reserved for his successor, Marcus Aurelius, whom the necessities of the empire dragged from his quiet meditations into a stern war for its existence. A philosophic sense of duty was strong enough to enable him, although without military inclination or genius, to solve a problem severer than that which had faced the soldier Trajan.

The first danger threatened on the eastern frontier, where the Parthians were once more on the point of extending their rule over the Armenians; already they had destroyed the Roman legions marching to prevent them. Large masses of troops had to be withdrawn from the Germanic frontier in order to provide the forces necessary to conduct the war which now became inevitable. After four years' fighting, the goal was reached. The Roman empire confirmed its military position in Armenia, and pressed its frontier to the left bank of the Euphrates. The ancient Macedonian fortress of Dura received a Roman garrison in A.D. 167, and became the sally-port for future invasions into Parthia. Hardly had this war come to an end when a new and greater danger broke over the Empire.

For a long time unrest had flickered in and out on the western frontier. In Britain and on the upper Rhine, the frontier defences had been broken through, and it had required hard fighting to restore them. Then, all at once, the Marcomanni and the Quadi, from Bohemia and Moravia, swarmed irresistibly over the Danube into the Empire; they crossed the Alps and besieged Aquileia. Plague which had begun during the Parthian war raged in the whole of the Empire, carried off an immense number of people, and was particularly active amongst the crowded masses of troops. Food was short, and the state-coffers were empty: collapse seemed imminent. Marcus Aurelius mastered this danger. He brought armies together, making use of those who were capable of carrying weapons wherever he could find them. He was successful in warding off the invasion: he himself marched into the enemy's country, overthrew all the allied tribes, German and Sarmatian, in a continuous series of invasions, and took possession of their country. The war lasted fourteen years, and then ended finally. The Emperor, in victory as in peace-time, wished to follow Trajan's example, and to push the Roman frontier over the Danube. Bohemia, Moravia, and the land between the Danube and the Theiss, were to become the Roman provinces of Marcomannia and Sarmatia; but Marcus Aurelius died in A.D. 180 at his headquarters in Vienna before his project could be realized.

Commodus, son and successor, had no hesitation in abandoning his father's plans; he vacated the occupied regions and granted the enemy favourable conditions; and this, not owing to keen insight as was formerly the case with Hadrian, but for the sake of convenience. Nevertheless his father's victories did not remain without result. The various enemies were permanently injured, and did not again endanger the Empire. Peace reigned on the Danube frontier for two generations. Even on the Rhine all was quiet for a long time, until, in A.D. 213 under Caracalla, a thrust of the Chatti and the Alemanni opened a period of continuous border warfare, which only issued in an era of peace after more than twenty years. During these years of insecurity the *limes* was strengthened: on the Rhine, a broad trench and a rampart were added to the palisades, and on the Danube, a wall ten feet high was built along the entire frontier.

The cautious placing of the frontier on the Euphrates could not be maintained in the long run. In A.D. 198 Septimius Severus marched forward and made Nisibis the capital of the transformed province of Mesopotamia, a province which now extended to the Tigris and was so strongly protected, from a military point of view, that even weaker emperors were able to defend it. Meanwhile the Parthian dynasty came to an end after being weakened by continuous struggles for the throne. The ancient royal family of the Sassanids spread its power out from Persopolis, and, in A.D. 226, Ardashir I became the ruler of a new Persian kingdom which set aside the Parthian dominion; the king announced his programme of restoring the frontiers[1] of Cyrus and Darius. The Parthians had been very uncomfortable neighbours for the Romans, but the Persians became their embittered and unappeasable enemies. For them, pressure towards the west was a historical duty, and they drew the sword against Rome in order to avenge the blood of Darius on the heirs of Alexander the Great.[2] In other words, they felt themselves to be the protagonists of the suppressed

[1] Herodian, *hist.*, 6,2,2. 6,4,5   [2] Nöldeke, *Tabari*, p. 3

peoples of Asia against Europe, and they worked at this task
for four centuries, with increasing success, until their place
was taken by the surging peoples of Islam who finally broke the
opposition of Europe.

The wars in Mesopotamia began *c*. A.D. 230. Ten years
later, the province was in Persian hands, and five years later
again, the Romans once more stationed their troops between
the Euphrates and the Tigris, and then concluded a bad peace
with Shapur I. About the same time, the leading tribe of the
Germanic movement of peoples, viz. the Goths, appeared on
the lower Danube. They broke into the Roman province
and laid Thrace waste as far as the vicinity of Salonica. The
emperor Decius lost his life in A.D. 251 fighting on the defensive,
and his successor purchased an armistice with money. The
province of Dacia was lost. At the same time, plague broke out
again. Various emperors who enjoyed but a short rule, either
in succession or contemporaneously, defended themselves,
though with hesitation, against Germanic and eastern invaders.
When seventy years of age, in A.D. 260, the emperor Valerian
fell into the hands of the Persians, and died in prison while the
Goths marched plundering through Asia Minor. His son
Gallienus strove manfully with all the dangers, and was
continually threatened by mutinous troops and the opposition
emperors that they set up. He was compelled to suffer the
rise of a buffer state with its own army in Palmyra, because it
served as a bulwark against the Persians. The Roman empire
had never seemed so near to complete collapse as during the
seventh decade of the third century.

.   .   .   .   .

The period of 150 years, which rolled by between Trajan
and Decius, shows us clearly the progressive decay of the Roman
empire and its power. The tension between the military requirements for protecting the frontier, and, on the other hand, the
financial and economic resources of the Empire became ever
greater; at last this brought about an inner decomposition.[1]
That the wars of Trajan had overstrained the resources of the
Empire was immediately apparent in the necessity for debasing

[1] Of fundamental importance, M. Rostovtzeff, *Social and Economic History of
the Roman Empire*

the coinage; the silver denarius which under Augustus had had an intrinsic value of about eightpence, and which fell to about sevenpence when Nero reduced the size of the coins, was now debased, by an admixture of 20 per cent copper, to a value of less than sixpence;[1] prices rose correspondingly. Hadrian knew why he liquidated the policy of his predecessors: it could only be carried out at the expense of the inner health of the state, and this the Emperor wished to preserve at all costs. Events justified his policy for half a century.

From Trajan to Marcus Aurelius there was a period of high culture and a secure development of commerce and industry. On all hands this came to expression in magnificent buildings whose remains can be seen even to-day. The cities became the centres of life. The well-to-do middle class and the great capitalists were responsible for an economic prosperity which comprehended all the provinces, and the educated classes frankly expressed their gratitude for the enlightened reigns of Hadrian and the Antonines. But the inner dangers could only be postponed, not abolished. The pre-eminence of Italy diminished irretrievably as regards politics, military strength, and economic well-being. The old nobility were either destroyed by assassination, or else had no descendants. The populace degenerated by the incoming of endless hosts of barbarian freedmen, and, on this account, as well as because of political aspirations, had little military value. From as early as Vespasian, the legions recruited no soldiers in Italy.[2] Moreover, the prospering provinces made themselves so independent of Italian goods that the emperors were compelled to institute artificial devices for saving the economic condition of the ancient central state.

The provinces were now in every respect the Empire's sources of power: even the army had been recruited from provincials since Hadrian's time. These men received Roman citizenship immediately on entering military service, and were intended to be the defenders of their immediate homeland. But this made an exchange of legions between east and west extraordinarily difficult. Hadrian spent half of his reign on

---

[1] M. Bernhart, *Handbuch Z. Münzkunde*, pp. 20 f.
[2] Mommsen, *Ges. Schriften*, 6,38

journeys through the provinces, and, throughout the east, was unwearied in forwarding the glory of Greek culture. This must not be understood as mere restlessness and romance, but as earnest concern for the security, progress, and cultural advance of wide regions of the Empire upon which the stability of the whole depended now more than formerly.

The course of development is clearly reflected in the wearers of the purple; the first emperors were all Romans. Vespasian and his sons were at least Italian. The families of Trajan and the Antonines descended from the early nobility of Spain and Gaul with a Roman culture; Septimius Severus came from the same class in Africa. But through his consort, the Syrian priestess Julia Domna, the element of barbarian provincialism mounted the throne, and affected the immediately succeeding generations, until the time of the Illyrian soldier-emperors. The provinces first conquered Italy, then the provinces languished, until at length there remained nothing but the soldiers.

It came about in the following manner. The economic prosperity of the Antonine period had no firm foundation. The necessities of the wars of Marcus Aurelius, and the depopulation of the Empire by the plague, brought the good fortune of the period to an end. The misgovernment of Commodus and the confusions following upon his assassination formed a melancholy conclusion to this era. Septimius Severus decided on a policy of severity, and therefore erected a purely military dictatorship. All the auxiliary resources of the state were stretched to the utmost extent in order to maintain the armies, which were now quite indispensable for protecting the frontier. Even the state officials were recruited more and more from the army; and, from the hosts of deserving underofficers, there grew a new nobility of officials, who could not be really regarded, however, as cultured persons. The first half of the third century was the crucial period of the economic collapse. Values fell continually through the debasement of money. Under Marcus Aurelius, the denarius sank to about fourpence-halfpenny; c. A.D. 200 it had still a silver content of about threepence, but after A.D. 260 it was only of impure copper and had a compulsory circulation similar to paper money; even this official circulation went down to about one farthing by A.D. 290.

The army ate up all the fruits of labour, and the imperial policy, finding it impossible to open up new sources of power, contented itself with ruthlessly pumping out those which it already possessed. Caracalla[1] put it drily when he said: "No man except me needs to have money, and I need it in order to pay the soldiers." The propertied bourgeoisie was destroyed. To a large extent, great possessions were commandeered by confiscation after a sham legal process. All others were burdened with intolerable loads. The propertied inhabitants of the cities could be mulcted for everything: for the prompt payment of taxes to meet the entire sums demanded of the city and its surrounding region; for every extra requirement ordered by troops passing through; or demanded by some official on any excuse whatsoever. In addition to this, all the members of the "ruling" public bodies were obliged to provide what was necessary for the prosperity of the city an dthe pleasure of the people. To be freed from the duty of accepting municipal office became a much desired privilege. That last and most painful resort of self-defence, abandonment of all personal possessions, was not rare: but it is significant that, by an imperial edict, those who took this course were explicitly declared to be inculpable; nevertheless they were in fact by no means protected from harsh treatment.[2] In such circumstances business and social life were in bonds. Money ceased to circulate, and the economics of barter entered once more into its inalienable rights. The legions who were fighting on the frontiers could no longer prevent the armies of the barbarians from falling upon wide stretches of land, to say nothing of the fact that the legions were unable to deal with the innumerable bands who took to piracy and brigandage. Moreover the "peaceful" passage of troops through the country, as well as the struggles with one another of pretenders to the throne, had effects which suspiciously resembled those of hostile attacks.

The only class upon which all the concern of the Emperor

---

[1] *Dio Cass.* 77,10,4

[2] Rostovtzeff, *Social and Economic History*, 2,194. 328 n. 42. 344 n. 44. 368 n. 49. Wilcken, *Chrestomathie*, n. 402. Apparently Philostratus, *Vita Apoll.*, 7,23

concentrated was that of the soldiers and, at times also, that of the small cultivators from whom the soldiers were drawn. Even Septimius Severus recognized the marriages contracted by soldiers on active service, and he permitted married soldiers to live outside the camps. In time, this led to farm settlements on the part of the forces, and the foundation of military farm colonies in fortified places. But this development did not help to increase soldierly virtues, or to forward the warlikeness of the army. In the second half of the third century, it became necessary, as a consequence, to hire warlike and unencumbered barbarian tribes: and that led to further results in the succeeding period. Military and economic necessities were inevitably interwoven, and they drew all the other elements of civilization in the empire after themselves in their downward path.

·   ·   ·   ·   ·

Tacitus must be read if we are to grasp fully the change in the spiritual structure of the Roman people effected by Domitian's fifteen year massacre of mental life. Already in his forties, he seemed to be prematurely old, and, at the beginning of a new period of activity, he regretfully observed that it was easier to suppress spiritual life than to re-awaken it.[1] But Trajan was the herald of a new period of freedom: from all sides we hear echoes of the thanks expressed by those who were set free, and Tacitus was able to attain the full extent of his greatness under Trajan's enlightened régime. His *Historiae* and *Annales* are the finest historical works which Rome presented to the world. Darkened by a gloomy seriousness and heroic resignation, his outlook on the future is not optimistic but full of grievous anxiety and tragic fear. Nevertheless only a century had passed from the happy days of Livy, and Trajan's sun was still radiating its life-giving rays over the Empire. But Tacitus was a unique man and, along with the highest gifts of genius, he had also received the disturbing talent of being able to see farther into the future than any of his fellows.

His friend Pliny was entirely happy, and felt himself the heir of an age of spiritual bloom to which he bore witness in letters written in a polished and rhetorical style. Within his narrower circle of vision, he was right in this respect, even if

[1] Tacitus, *Agricola*, 3

one allows for his excessive appreciation of the literary dilettantism which surrounded him.[1] This dilettantism was neither
more nor less than the expression of a genuine love for the
mental refinements of life, and an active acceptance of the
classical traditions from Cicero's time. Of these ways, Quin-
tilian had been the prophet, and he had died only shortly
before. Among Pliny's circle of friends was the young Suetonius,
who fulfilled, under Hadrian, the hopes which had been set on
him. The satirist Juvenal accomplished his best performances
during Trajan's time. None of these three men had a mind of
the first quality, but they used their gifts so excellently that their
influence can still be traced on the world's literature. After
their death, the Latin muse was dumb in the city of Rome:
with Trajan, the genuine literary tradition of Rome came to an
end. The reliefs on Trajan's pillar show how much of its
artistic creative power was still alive. The round *clipei* which
have been preserved on Constantine's arch, and the marble
barriers of the speaker's platform in the forum, show the same
thing.

A new period began with Hadrian; it was dominated by
inspiration drawn from Greece, and men began to pay homage
to the past. The tendency which was now arising is known as
"archaism". Just as the Greeks, oblivious to the speech of the
living present, imitated the Attic classics when they produced
literature, so now, in the Latin sphere, it became the fashion to
go back over Cicero to the early Latin style. Fronto the
African was the great protagonist of this tendency. The world
has rightly forgotten him and his compeers with the exception
of Apuleius, whose numerous writings reached their climax
in the romance of the *Golden Ass*. Here a splendid narrative
style has banished the contemporary dilettantism. Towards
the end, the pure swelling music of a mystic religiosity gives us
a powerful impression of what had developed in the Antonine
period out of the religious romanticism of the Hadrian era.
With Apuleius, ancient Latin literature came to an end: only
in the fourth century did there suddenly appear, in solitary
greatness, "without father, mother, or descent," the remarkable
historian, Ammianus Marcellinus.

[1] Pliny, *Epist.*, 1,17. 3,1,7. 4,3. 8,4. 9,22; very significant are 4,8 and 7,4

Rhetoric dominated decadent Latin literature. Even Tacitus gave way to its seductions; and it was responsible for the fact that Latin authors were still writing after they had nothing of value to say. Greek literature lived on rhetoric to at least an equal extent, and indeed, after Vespasian, developed new blossoms in this art often described as that of the "second sophists". A number of men who were great in their day were brought forward by the movement; the zeal of eminent patrons, some being of the highest rank, founded, in many places, professorships in rather academic subjects, and heaped honours upon the most prominent sophists. Their most splendid representative was the Athenian, Herod Atticus, who used his enormous wealth to erect majestic buildings on the classical sites of Greece; meanwhile, assisted by the favour of Hadrian and the Antonines, he largely dominated literary life; but his buildings have withstood the passage of the centuries better than his speeches. In Trajan's time there were the sermons of Epictetus the Stoic addressed to the educated, and the popular and sometimes sentimental speeches of Dio Chrysostom. These men were opposites, but both possessed a profound spiritual earnestness, and strove in different ways but, in the end, to the same noble goal of improving mankind by philosophic education. Epictetus, who came from the slave class, was by far the greater, because his ethical interest seems to be quite unalloyed, and to have required no earthly ornament. Moreover he recognized no subsidiary aims.

Both Dio and Epictetus came from the north-west of Asia Minor. About the same time, Greece was worthily represented by Plutarch, who conjured an ideal Greece from the mighty past of his nation, and, in his finely constituted soul, brought his efforts to practical effect. His biographies and moral tractates have aroused admiration in every age; and, in his writings of a religious and philosophical character, there is a tragic echo of an honourable but hopeless attempt to rescue dying gods, which fact also makes him winsome. He wrote a series of parallel lives of great Greeks and Romans, quite in the spirit prevalent in Trajan's times. The Emperor Hadrian himself, however, was the one who proclaimed the primacy of Greek culture. He had travelled through all the provinces, but had always held up Greece and its spiritual heritage before the eyes of others: acting as Zeus Olympios, he travelled about the world and built temples which did homage to his imperial divinity under this the highest of Greek names. No city received more kindly concern than Athens, where even to-day the gate of Hadrian separates "the old city of Theseus" from the "city of Hadrian and not of Theseus" which he had newly founded.[1] It was a just recognition of genuine values: the powers of the Empire, which still survived and which could be used for the spiritual unification of the provinces among themselves, rested upon what was Greek; moreover, the Greeks were indispensable mediators in effecting the amalgamation of the oriental countries. The seed which had been sowed by Hadrian brought forth abundantly in the Antonine period. Alongside a fairly large number of genuine specialist scholars and a swarm of mere babblers, we now discover men of Greek tongue who may well claim to be of literary importance, whereas Rome's own power diminished.

Persons of smaller importance were Arrian, who has preserved for us copies of Epictetus's lectures, and who, in his mature years, acted as a new Xenophon by writing the history of Alexander the Great; and Appian, whose Roman history has lasting value. At the end of the Antonine period, Pausanias wrote a traveller's guide for curious visitors to Hellas which was now officially recognized as a classical country. This guide is not only an invaluable symposium of ancient material, but also reflects, in general terms, the taste of the period for archæology and religious interests of a romantic character. The most eminent representative of the spirit of the times was the orator Aristides of Smyrna, a pupil of the Herod Atticus already mentioned. The intellectual values which it was possible at that time to introduce into his carefully composed speeches, he did introduce, and his panegyric of Rome is an ideal picture of the last days of the bloom of the Empire, and is painted in colours drawn from life. His contemporaries, including the Emperor, esteemed him highly, and he himself thought it not inappropriate to claim a place above Demosthenes and Plato, and to ascribe to his life's work as an orator

[1] G. Kaibel, *Epigrammata Graeca*, n. 1045

a value equal to the military deeds of Alexander the Great.[1] If, however, we study the celebrated "sacrèd speeches", and read how often, and with what consequences, the famous man suffered bodily pain; what drastic cures the god Asklepios ordered for him by means of visions in dreams, and how at last, after sixteen years, he was cured by the god's miraculous power; and if we remark that nothing of this is raised into a higher sphere, or ennobled by faith like that, say, in Brentano's accounts of Katherina Emmerich; but that he writes with nothing more than the complete banality of an hysterical hypochondriac: then the veil is torn aside. We see that even the best scholars of the period disguised a mere inner poverty in the shining tinsel of the stage, and, through the goodwill of the applauding public, were taken to rival those heroes of the brilliant past whom they pretended to describe. For these people and their public, the real life and force to be found in history lay beyond the literary stage which constituted their world.

The Syrian writer, Lucian, was a man who knew it and who, as a consequence, could not take his own period seriously, nor any of its great men, himself included. He pulled in pieces whatever came his way, and especially those things which claimed to be of the highest eminence, religion and philosophy. He did everything, however, in a brilliant fashion, and with a wonderfully keen sight for the weak places and the humorous traits of his opponents. The old gods of Homer and the new figures of the orient, 'epic demigods and heroes of modern romances, religious prophets and preachers of Cynic ethics, pedantic professors and loose girls, all this sort of thing whirls in a mad carnival about the reader of Lucian's writings, amuses him for a time until the taste palls, and the man with the cap and bells finally surfeits him. The others had good intentions but they were weaklings playing the part of the strong. Lucian believed in nothing except his own advantage and, with a Mephistophelian self-satisfaction, he calumniated everything that was holy to others, and did so just because it was holy. In this way he was the prime ancestor of a type of journalist who only came fully into his own in the nineteenth century.

[1] Aristides, *Orations*, 50,19. 20. 48. 49: p. 430. 438. Keil

The emperor Marcus Aurelius stood apart from all this literary activity. It had done him no harm that Fronto and Herod Atticus should have instructed him in fashionable rhetoric in Latin and Greek. When a Stoic put Epictetus's lectures into his hands, the course of his spiritual life was decided; the Roman emperor became the respectful disciple of the Phrygian slave. In the most difficult period of his life, while with his army in the field against the Marcomanni, he kept a private diary, not sentimentally like the men of the eighteenth century, but for the purpose of severe self-examination and criticism of all earthly values. He pitilessly destroyed every kindly pretence, every attractive trait. Man was but a mortal frame called into existence for a brief span: then his body would fall into decay, and all-ruling nature mould his remains into new forms, the soul would be scattered in the air, and everything changed. Nothing was stable, and even fame died with posterity. How long you lived was indifferent: it was only necessary that you do your duty, i.e. that you offered the gods a pure soul and showed kindness to mankind. Do not hope for thanks, nor let yourself be embittered by thanklessness. Depart from this world in an agreeable mood when nature calls you from the stage; for what she does is good. Many thousands using this diary for their meditations have drawn strength from it. Frederick the Great read it in his tent when the Seven Years' War was depressing him: but he added contempt for man, a feature which was foreign to Marcus Aurelius's nature.

· · · · ·

Philosophy was religion for the best people of this period: she and she alone showed the way to the next world, and to the recognition of a higher power. The old gods of Hellas and Rome were dead, and did not come to life again; in this respect, even interest in the archaic changed nothing, although it had dominated the educated class from the time of Hadrian. Aristides the orator composed a whole series of prose hymns to the gods: one after the other was celebrated in resounding words, but, if we look more closely, we find Stoic monotheism was the genuine kernel of his belief in the gods, and the separate divine figures appear as personifications of cosmic powers which streamed from the original source in the Father of All. This is expressed with special clearness in the speeches to Zeus and to Sarapis, which for him are only two different terms for the unity which comprehends the world. This is the theme which re-echoes in all the speeches, and is produced in ever renewed variations, the motives being furnished by the traditional mythology. Nothing is said about religion, about a personal comprehension of the divine in an overwhelming, and at the same time emancipating, experience. Aristides maintains a calm attitude towards the world of the gods: he preaches of it but does not live with it, or at least in it. Yet he makes an exception: Asklepios was for him a genuine and powerful healer, and had a personal form. He had even appeared to Aristides numberless times in dreams, and had concerned himself with a thousand details of his life. In nature, he was that one universal godhead whom we also call Zeus;[1] but Aristides had experienced him as a personal helper and as an active god; he depended upon Asklepios with all his soul —without however deducing therefrom any further consequences. Plutarch was much nearer to the ancient faith when he explained the practice of resorting to oracles by an elaborate doctrine of daemons, and when he himself filled a priestly office in Delphi with a clear conscience. For him Apollo was the universal god of his monotheistic faith, but, in a different fashion from Aristides, he believed in an active intervention of God in history; with Plato he believed in the immortality of the soul, and in a compensating retribution on an ethical basis.[2]

Philostratos was another writer who likewise conceived religion from the standpoint of philosophy. He belonged to the circle of scholars in Julia Domna's court, and was also in favour with Caracalla. At the instance of the empress, he wrote a biography of Apollonius of Tyana, who was celebrated under Domitian as the itinerant prophet of a neo-Pythagoreanism. He sketched Apollonius, however, only to suit the taste of the third century: as a saviour of a philosophic and religious kind who, by his preaching and miracles, proved that he was in association with the godheads to a degree exceeding human

[1] Aristides, *Orations*, 42. 4. p. 335. Keil
[2] Cf. Wilamowitz, *Glaube der Hellenen*, 2,497–508

capacity, and who revealed the mystic way to apotheosis by asceticism and contemplation. In accordance with the trend of the times, the orient was regarded as the original source of wisdom, and India was placed high above the Egypt which had once been much celebrated in this regard. Yet Apollonius was at bottom Hellene, and, in spite of all his enthusiasm for the orient, claimed the absolute pre-eminence of Greece for mankind. By making extensive use of geographical handbooks, he spun out the biography into a discursive travel romance, and by cleverly pretending to have reliable sources of information,[1] he enjoys many credulous readers to the present day.

In the course of time, criticism of Homer's gods raised doubts as to the historical faithfulness of that poet, and the educated world discussed the problem of the historical existence of Homeric heroes and the reality of the mythological tradition as to their fate. We are reminded of the beginnings of apologetic attacks on Biblical criticism in the period of the Enlightenment, when we see Philostratos proving the trustworthiness of Homer: in a burial mound in Aia a skeleton of eleven ells had come to light: Hadrian had had it buried afresh. The bones of Orestes dug up in Nemea measured seven ells. Moreover, fifty years earlier, people had gone on pilgrimage in crowds to the promontory of Sigeion where the remains had been discovered of a giant twenty-two ells long, who had been killed by Apollo.[2] This and others of a similar kind were the proofs on which he proceeded to build another kind of world. The heroes still lived, appeared at times to their friends, and did so in the prescribed size of ten to twelve ells.[3] The heroes spoke with them in a friendly manner, and readily gave information about the Trojan war, with all sorts of details not to be found in Homer. Obviously the public interest was great as regards these matters, in spite of scepticism otherwise. Moreover, the heroes afforded assistance in all sorts of cases of need. They blessed the fields, but avenged themselves cruelly if proper respect was denied them. Anyone who wished to be convinced of their existence need only go to the Black Sea and, on the west from the Bosphorus, look for the island of Leuke.[4] The livered

---

[1] Ed. Meyer in *Hermes* 52,409 ff.   [2] Philostratos, *Heroicus*, pp. 668 ff.
[3] Philostr., *vita Apoll.*, 4,16. *Heroicus*, p. 673   [4] Philostr. *Heroicus*, pp. 745 f.

Achilles and Helen, and sailors had frequently taken them by surprise.

It is only a step from such records to creepy ghost stories with witches and magic: Lucian has preserved for us a splendid collection of the kind, and many parts of his mimic travel-romance might have stood, with small alteration, in Philostratos's book of heroes.[1] Philostratos scarcely believed the nonsense which he served up so abundantly to his readers; but it is significant that the general, educated public of his time desired such reading material. It could combine philosophical scepticism with crass superstition, and the remains of conceptions based on a nature religion with pantheistic and Platonistic mysticism; and it listened with quiet expectation to the Pythagorean preaching of metempsychosis, even when crudely emended for the worse. It was in this atmosphere, also, that the romance was written about the youth who had been bewitched and changed into an ass; it was composed by an otherwise unknown Lucius of Patræ. Lucian had entertained his readers with a pretended extract from it, whereas Apuleius retained the substance and atmosphere, extending the whole considerably, and furnishing it richly with additional passages of a similar coloration. His purpose, like that of the original author, was to offer his readers serious food for thought of a moral and religious nature, a fact which does not lead to very flattering conclusions as to the mental quality of those readers.[2]

We have already observed that, in the first century, oriental influence made itself felt on the religion of the Greek world.[3] During the second century, the influence pressed towards the west and had marked effects; in the third century, it reached its peak. The figures of the old national gods gradually paled. It is true that, as at an earlier date, they still appeared on the imperial coinage, but, to an increasing extent, they were replaced by the personifications of abstract ideas:[4] Concord, Fortune, Faithfulness, Freedom, Peace, Salvation, Victory,

---

[1] Lucian, *Philopseudes: Verae Historiae*, 2,6–36
[2] Photius, *Bibl. Cod.*, 129; Lucian, *Lucius*, Apuleius, *Metamorphoses*; cf. R. Reitzenstein, *Hellenist. Wundergesch.*, pp. 32–34
[3] Cf. vol. 1, pp. 154 ff.
[4] Vivid sketch in Gnecchi, *Monete romane* (3rd edit.), pp. 290–99. This kind of personification became considerable under Vespasian and only ended with the triumph of Christianity. Bernhart, *Handbuch*, 1,8,102

Ability—or the "genius" of the Empire, the emperor, or the city. Indeed, state temples were erected in honour of these names[1]—clearly a retreat from the concrete, ancestral religion into the abstract world of the philosophers. On the other hand, the oriental gods, who were popular amongst the masses, and exercised much power, were not added to the figures stamped officially on the imperial coinage. Isis and Sarapis were an exception after Vespasian had accorded them special honour,[2] similarly Cybele from the time of Hadrian. When Septimius Severus the African mounted the throne, he occasionally stamped the Punic "goddess of heaven", and even Eshmun, as saviour, on such coins as he wished should be used specially in Carthage. Elagabalus caused the sacred stone, fetched from Emesa, to be likewise depicted.[3] These were temporary fancies however, and, on the whole, oriental figures of this character were at variance with what was usually stamped on the coins.

The official buildings of the Roman state temples spoke a clearer language.[4] When Augustus's restoration had faded, temples were only built to the ancient gods if there was some special dynastic interest to be served. This held in the case of the temple of Venus and Roma which Hadrian built, and really also of the two temples of Minerva built by Domitian, who ordered himself to be described as Minerva's son.[5] On the other hand, during this period seven temples were erected to the abstract godheads, and five to the deified emperors.[6] Granted that Marcus Aurelius consecrated a temple to Mercury as an expression of thanks for a miraculous gift of rain which saved his troops from dying of thirst during the Quadian war; when we read, however, that an Egyptian sorcerer, Arnufis by name, induced this miracle by invoking "Hermes of the air", it is clear that Mercury was only the Latin name covering the Egyptian Thot;[7] and the temple was therefore really dedicated to an

---

[1] Temples of Concordia, Felicitas, Bonus Eventus, Justitia, Pax, Fortuna, Indulgentia, were built from the time of Augustus to Marcus Aurelius: Wissowa, *Religion*, 2nd edit., pp. 596 f.

[2] Bernhart, *Handbuch*, 1,63 f. Jos., *Bell.*, 7,123

[3] Bernhart, *Handbuch*, 1,59. 106. 2, plate 49,5 (Elagabalus); Gnecchi, *Medaglioni romani*, 3 p. 39; plates of Dea Caelestis in J. Hirsch, *Auktionskatalog*, 31 plate 32, no. 1534; R. Ball, *Auktionskat.*, 6 plate 45, no. 1795

[4] A list is given in Wissowa, *Religion*, 2nd edit., 594–97

[5] Philostr., *vita Apoll.*, 7,24   [6] *Supra*, note 1   [7] *Dio Cass.* 71,8,4

oriental god. At least from the beginning of the empire, Isis enjoyed an increasing number of temples in the city,[1] and, under Caligula or Claudius, a state temple on the field of Mars was dedicated to her along with Sarapis. The Antonines remained tardy towards worshipping other gods. Only when Septimius Severus commenced his reign did a new period begin. He himself built a temple to the gods of his birthplace, Leptis Magna, and gave them the Latin names of Liber and Hercules. He dedicated another to Bellona Pulvinensis who is only a variant of Cybele.[2] Jupiter Dolichenus the war-god of Commagene received a state temple on the Aventine.[3] This dynasty broke with the original Roman tradition which gave to foreign gods a place outside the Pomerium, the ancient sacred boundaries of the city. Caracalla erected an immense temple to Sarapis on the Quirinal[4]—and also, in order to create new hosts of worshippers for the most sacred gods, he abolished all the restrictions of Roman citizenship in the entire Empire, and gave this honour freely to the millions.[5]

There was a conscious purpose in thus setting aside the peculiar prerogatives of what Rome stood for. Septimius Severus was African, but his consort, Julia Domna, was the daughter of the high priest of Baal of Emesa. Her sister's grandson, Bassianus, was brought up for the same priestly office, but at 14 years of age, he mounted the throne and gave himself the honourable name of Marcus Aurelius Antoninus, and, along with this, still bore the title of a high priest of the god Elagabalus. He made this god of his into the ruler of the entire Pantheon. He ordered the sacred fetish stone to be brought from Emesa to Rome. He erected a handsome temple for it on the Palatine, close to the imperial palaces; here were gathered together any holy stones and celebrated fetishes that could be seized, as well as the vestal fire. The Syrian god celebrated a sacred marriage with the Carthaginian Tanit, goddess of heaven,[6] at the same time as the emperor acted the

---

[1] List given in Kiepert-Huelsen, *Formae urbis Romae*, 2nd edit., p. 17; cf Wissowa, *ibid.*, 352 f.

[2] Wissowa, *ibid.*, 349 f.; cf. Dessau, *inscr.*, n. 4180–2   [3] Wissowa, *ibid.*, 362

[4] Jordan-Huelsen, *Topographie der Stadt Rom.*, I. 3, p. 423

[5] Mitteis-Wilcken, *Chrestomathie*, II, 2, n. 377; also Cumont, *Oriental Relig.*, p. 84

[6] *Script. hist. Aug. Heliogab.* 1,6. 3,4. 7,1–5. Herodian, *Hist.*, 5,5–6. Cumont in Pauly-Wissowa, 5,2220 ff.

earthly counterpart by his marriage with the vestal Aquilia Severa.[1] Even as emperor he continued to be the Syrian priest of the sun, and bore himself accordingly until the soldiers killed him, along with his grandmother, who had been the real ruler. His name became accursed, and the fetish was sent back to Emesa; but what had taken place had effects in the succeeding period, because, although in form it was a foolish freak of the emperor, in fact, it was a pointer with a historical foundation, viz. the oriental sun god was really destined to be the final lord in the heaven believed in by this decadent world. When he was deposed he handed down to his successor both his name and also his birthday on December 25: Christ then ruled the world as "the true sun of righteousness".

In the cult of the sun, a certain process reached its climax, a development which was of increasing moment during the Hellenistic period: religious thought, fertilized from the orient, comprehended various gods as merely different forms of the appearance of a single great godhead. In this way we find Zeus, Helios, and Sarapis worshipped as a unity; similarly the images of the universal god, "Pantheos", heaped the characteristics of half a dozen gods on one figure; or else a single god, Jupiter, or Sarapis, or Silvanus, or even Priapus, was described as Pantheos. The idea is clearly expressed by Apuleius in describing what happened when he was permitted to see Isis:[2] "Lo I am here, called up by your prayers: mother of nature, ruler of all the elements, first-born of eternity, highest of the gods, queen of the departed, first of the heavenly beings, the single form of the gods and goddesses. The shining façade of the sky, the health-giving winds of the sea, the silence of the dead—all this do I govern by my nod. The whole circle of the earth worships my sole godhead under various forms, with changing customs and with many names: Phrygians as the mother of the gods, Athenians as Athena, Cypriots as Aphrodite, Cretans as Artemis-Dictynna, Sicilians as Persephone, Eleusinians as Demeter, others as Hera, or Bellona, or Hecate, or Nemesis. The Ethiopians, who are lighted by the rays of the rising sun,

---

[1] *Prosopogr. imp. Rom.* 2,225. n.

[2] Apuleius, *metam.*, 11,5. For the whole cf. H. Usener, *Götternamen*, p. 341–49 Roscher, *Myth. Lex.*, 3,1555

the Aryans, and the Egyptians who possess a most ancient wisdom, worship me with observances proper to me, and name me with my real name: Queen Isis." The fading religions of the ancient world were moving, under oriental leadership, towards the monotheism of a nature religion.

The oriental cults were brought to Rome by the masses of imported slaves and also by merchants and soldiers, and were there celebrated by societies composed of fellow countrymen.[1] They found patrons here and there in the leading circles and finally in the court; thereby their propagandist power was strengthened. These influences then streamed from Rome into the western provinces and were maintained at first by the same nationals as had brought them to Rome. Afterwards they seized on the indigenous population, this last, naturally, in very varied degrees.[2] The whole movement has been described in a masterly fashion[3] and does not require to be depicted again here. It will be enough to sketch the religious development by giving a few examples.

If we travel from Rome to the port of Ostia, which has now been to a large extent excavated, we shall at once discover valuable data illuminating our problem. The old city god was Volcanus: his priest stood at the head of the spiritual aristocracy, and exercised a kind of oversight over all the sacred premises. His temple has not yet been discovered; the forum, which was laid out in Claudius's time, had first of all a "Capitol", i.e. a temple dedicated to the Capitoline triad of Jupiter, Juno, and Minerva: as was appropriate in a "colony" that enjoyed Roman citizenship. Opposite lay a temple of Roma and Augustus, i.e. a fane for the worship of the emperor and the Empire. In a minor street behind the principal street, there were four other small temples dating from the last years of the republic. They may possibly be the temples of Venus, Fortuna, Ceres, and Spes, which were erected by a wealthy citizen named Gamala.[4] In front of them stood a small temple

[1] G. La Piana, *Foreign Groups in Rome during the First Centuries of the Empire*, 1927 (from *Harvard Theol. Review*)
[2] Plentiful material in J. Toutain, *Les cultes païens dans l'empire romain*, vol. 2, Paris, 1911
[3] F. Cumont, *Oriental Religions in Roman Paganism*. Engl. trans., 1911
[4] *CIL.* 14 n. 375 = Dessau, *inscr. lat.*, no. 6147, also O. Seeck, *Untergang*, f. 2,156 with note on pp. 523 f. Calza, *Ostia*, pp. 117 f.

of Jupiter, belonging to the first century. It is not known
to whom the large temple was dedicated, which occupied the
middle place in the Marine Exchange. Moreover, in the second
century, we hear of the restoration of a temple of Castor
and Pollux,[1] and with that our knowledge comes to an end
about the temples of the ancient Roman gods. The colony,
which was rebuilt by Claudius as a modern port, worshipped
the new gods of the Empire, together with those of the
orient.

Silvanus was the god of gardens and had no place amongst
the great gods, but it is important to note that he was much
worshipped in Ostia as a beneficent nature daemon; even in
the Antonine period he was connected not only with the *lares*
but also with Isis and Sarapis.[2] In the third century, a small
chapel of Silvanus was decorated with wall paintings, and
contained figures of the *lares* and of Isis, as well as Augustus,
Fortuna, Liberalitas, and Alexander the Great.[3] Hence it is
indubitable that there was also a temple to the Egyptian gods,
although it has not yet been discovered. On the other hand,
a chapel to the Great Mother, Cybele, has been discovered on
the city wall. A cult grotto of Sabazius lay quite close to
the principal street; at least five temples were dedicated to
Mithra, of which the earliest was built *circa* A.D. 140.[4] The
sacrifice of bulls and goats formed a constituent part in the
cult of the Great Mother, and was conjoined with the blood
bath of the one offering the sacrifice (taurobolium and
kriobolium). This sacrifice was diligently observed in Ostia,
from the days of Marcus Aurelius, "for the health of the
emperor and the well-being of the whole imperial house";[5]
the same custom was observed in the western provinces. This
fearful practice appears to have been brought there from the
Roman site of the cult at the Vatican;[6] and, in Rome itself,
evidences have been discovered that it was practised to the end
of the fourth century. No other eastern cult struck so firm a
root in the whole of the west, or penetrated so deeply into all

[1] *CIL*. 14 n. 376   [2] *CIL*. 14, no. 20   [3] Calza, *Ostia*, 19. 133 f.
[4] *Op cit.*, pp. 119. 134. 165. 169 f., cf. the plans, p. 17. Sabazius, p. 92. Cybele,
p. 168; datum: *CIL*. 14, no. 33. 67
[5] *CIL*. 14, nos. 40–43. 4301–6
[6] Dessau *op. cit.*, no. 4131; Wissowa, *op. cit.*, 322–25. Cumont, *op. cit.*, 66 f.

strata of the population, as did the worship of Cybele, the
Great Mother of the Mountain.[1]

In the remainder of the west there are in general no cities
which have been excavated to such an extent that we can gain a
really comprehensive insight into the attitude taken up by
their inhabitants towards religion. The discoveries made in
western Asia Minor can only be rivalled in Northern Africa.

In A.D. 100, the commandants of the third legion,[2] which
had been in Africa since the time of Augustus, settled a troop
of veterans in Timgad. This place immediately became a
highly developed military colony. It blossomed rapidly, and
existed for hundreds of years, until it was destroyed in the sixth
century.[3] Three temples met the religious needs of the old
soldiers, and the two largest of these buildings stood outside the
city walls; even to-day the pillars of the Capitol rise impressively
towards the sky. As in Ostia, the Capitol indicated the existence
of a colony of citizens, and was dedicated to the triad Jupiter,
Juno, and Minerva. In A.D. 151, the temple of the genius of
Timgad was built at the western gate, and its cultus was
conjoined both with the worship of the triad of the Capitol
and also with that of Bacchus, Silvanus, and Mars. The
worship of city genii was particularly widespread in the
provinces of Africa and Spain with their numerous towns.[4]
A special form of the conception of the genius occurred very
frequently in the period of the Empire, a form under which it
was customary to worship some nameless being as the divine
protector of a place, a building, or an association. That was an
early Roman custom, but at this late period it signified that
religion had grown more pantheistic.

Among the soldiers of the third legion, a special form of
worship was offered to Silvanus, although we do not know why
this should be so. No wonder that the veterans of Timgad should
have associated him with the genius of the city; and the same
principle held good in regard to the worship of Mars, which
was very usual amongst soldiers.[5] Father Bacchus, or rather

[1] Toutain, *op. cit.*, 2,111–19
[2] Dessau, *op. cit.*, 6841. Ritterling, *Pauly-W.* 12,1493–1505
[3] Plan and description in Baedeker, *Mittelmeer*, pp. 302–10. *CIL.* 8,2340–43.
10738–43. Suppl. 2, p. 1693, no. 17811; p. 1712, no. 17939
[4] Toutain, *op. cit.*, 1,450 f.   [5] *Op. cit.*, 1,253· 262

"Liber", as he was now usually called, had many adherents in Africa, who paid him homage for the gift of wine. The adherents were drawn more from the local citizens than from the military.[1] In the case of Timgad, there is no means of deciding to what extent the Græco-Roman god had become the heir of an indigenous Punic god of wine, although a similar assertion can be made definitely in regard to other places. The third temple of the little town stood in the market place behind the forum. The fact suggests that it served some official cult, but unfortunately no name is mentioned. The inscriptions introduce no important new characteristics into the picture. The old soldiers, with their successors and heirs, observed the official religion of the Empire, and worshipped such gods of the Roman heaven as tradition conveyed to them. Here and there it is possible that Punic religion exercised a slight influence, but it was of little significance in Timgad, where the atmosphere was Roman, indeed, more purely Roman than in Rome.

The circumstances were different in regard to Dougga. This once significant place lay to the south-west of Carthage, and had worked itself up from what was originally a Berber settlement to a Roman citizen-colony.[2] The elegant Capitol overlooked the forum; its pediment represented the heavenly ascension of the deified emperor, and, according to the dedicatory inscription, was built under Marcus Aurelius *circa* A.D. 168.[3] The building was used for the official worship of the Roman triad. On the heights above the town, stood the magnificent temple of Saturn which, under Severus, in A.D. 195, took the place of an earlier temple.[4] Although this Saturn was worshipped in both temples, he was not a Roman god, but the Punic Baal.[1] His consort, the Dea Caelestis, i.e. Tanit the queen of heaven,[5] had her temple to the west, where it is still to be found slumbering among the olives, in a good state of preservation, and surrounded by a semi-orbicular wall of gleaming marble. This building also dates from the time of the African dynasty, having been erected under Alexander Severus,

---

[1] *Op. cit.*, 1,361–4

[2] Baedeker, *op cit.*, 371–73; Cagnet, *Carthage, Timgad Tebessa*, 3rd edit., p. 67 gives a plan

[3] *CIL.* 8,1471 = Suppl. 1, no. 15513

[4] *Op. cit.*, 8, suppl. 4, no. 26498   [5] Toutain, *op. cit.*, 3,15 ff.

i.e. *c.* A.D. 230.[1] There can be no doubt in this case, however, but that it replaced an earlier temple. The great African divine couple Baal and Tanit drew to themselves for centuries all the religious feelings of the inhabitants of Dougga. Finally, there was a temple of Mercury complete with two inner rooms, a pillared hall, and apses; inscriptions say, indeed, that the site for the temple of Mercury was presented by the city.[2] Even this god was not Roman, but an indigenous being whose cult was practiced in the small, African country towns round about— but unfortunately it has been as yet impossible to discover the god's name.[3]

Timgad and Dougga were representatives of two opposed types of religious life, their common feature being the almost[4] complete lack of anything imported from the orient. In a certain sense, this is characteristic of the African provinces in general. The autochthonous religions met the needs of the native population even as late as the time of the Empire, and, in Latin transformation, they adapted themselves to the higher culture of the period. Only the mysteries of the Great Mother, together with the taurobolium, were adopted and diligently practised among the citizens.[5] The other eastern cults, i.e. the worship of Egyptian and Syrian gods, had sites in the great garrisons, especially in Lambaesis.[6] Soldiers of all ranks, and provincial officials who followed them, were the people mainly responsible for furthering the religion of Mithra, but, alongside them, oriental slaves effectively proclaimed the new faith, and this even penetrated Africa after the end of the second century.[7]

We do not gain the same impression from the memorials and inscriptions found on the Germanic frontier provinces on the Rhine.[8] Here Roman soldiers of Italian origin met with

---

[1] *CIL.* 8, suppl. 4, nos. 26457–26463   [2] *Loc. cit.*, 26478–26482
[3] Toutain, *op. cit.*, 1,299–307
[4] A Mithraic Dadophor has been found in Timgad (Toutain, 2,147, n. 1), and there is evidence of a Dendrophor in Dougga, *CIL.*, 8, suppl. 1, no. 15527
[5] Toutain, 2,101 ff. Taurobolium and kriobolium: Dessau, *inscr. lat.*, 4136. 4142
[6] Toutain, 2,18 ff. 56 ff.
[7] Toutain, 2,146 ff. 163 ff.; cf. the chart in Cumont, *Mysterien des Mithra*, 2nd edit., 1911
[8] H. Lehner, *Mysterien Kulte im römischen Rheinland*, Bonner Jahrb., 129 (1924), pp. 36–91

others from different provinces of the empire; orientals came into the country, mostly as soldiers, but in isolated cases as merchants or slaves. The provinces themselves reflected their varied history in the jumble of the population which consisted of Celtic, Gallic, and Germanic elements. The varied character of the religion corresponded to this miscellany of people. In the great garrisons, the official worship of the Roman gods and the emperor took the first place, but, in addition and certainly much more vitally operative in the hearts of the populace, was the worship of Jupiter Dolichenus, and especially Mithra, both of whom, in the second and third centuries, were genuinely popular amongst the soldiers.

The native population served their ancestral gods, built temples, and erected sacred statues inscribed in Latin with a corresponding transformation of the divine names—as Cæsar and Tacitus inform us.[1] It follows that when we find the names of Mercury, Mars, or Hercules, we know that Roman appellations have been given to Celtic or Germanic gods; indeed, not infrequently, the identity is made explicit by an additional name.[2] Side by side with these high gods, there was a host of gods of a lower status, or even only local worship, for whom there was no corresponding Roman label. These are recorded under their real names, e.g. Rosmerta, Visuna, Abnoba, and sometimes as statues. This was particularly the case with Epona the guardian of horses, riding sideways on her steed, or the three "matrons" with their immense hoods and baskets of fruit in their laps; also the water-god, Tarvos, in the form of an animal, or Esus, the god of business, who felled trees.

In Altbachtal near Trèves there has lately been excavated a temple space which enables us to read the local religious history of the half-Roman and half-Germanic capital from the first, to within the fourth, century, for here are the remains of more than thirty temples.[3] Everything is either Celtic or Germanic—but once on a day a certain Martius Martialis built a large house in the midst of these temples, and also erected a Mithraeum for the private devotions of himself and

---

[1] Cæsar, *Bell. Gall.*, 6,17. Tacitus, *Germ.*, 9
[2] Wissowa in *Arch. f. Religionswiss.* 19,8 ff. Material has been collected by A. Riese, *Das rheinische Germanien in den antiken Inschriften*, pp. 289–366
[3] S. Loeschcke, *Die Erforschung des Tempelbezirks im Altbachtale zu Trier 1928*

his friends; and this was certainly not the only one in Trèves.[1] The cult of Mithra in Germany was not confined to the troops on the frontier, but had adherents in the native population in the middle of the country. In these regions, moreover, worship was frequently offered to the Egyptian gods and homage was paid to the Great Mother of Phrygia, together with the practice of the taurobolium.[2] Again, numerous stones to the diurnal gods, with representations of the seven planets, show that oriental astrology was not lacking. With progressive Romanization, the educated classes of the population adopted many elements of the religions practised in the eastern civilizations of the Empire, and passed them on to other classes.

The common feature of all these oriental cults was that they had overflowed their original national limits, and tended towards universalism. Most of them took on the form of mystery cults, the meetings and doctrines being strictly reserved for converts and initiates.[3] The myth of the death and resurrection of Osiris was the centre of the mysteries of Isis, round which were grouped numerous rites of an Egyptian and would-be Egyptian character. The anniversary of the death of Osiris was celebrated at the end of October; the weeping congregation cried aloud, and accompanied the high goddess when she searched in despair. In the end, the corpse was found in separate pieces, the parts were reunited, and the happy multitude greeted the re-vivified god with frenzied exultation—he was the guarantor of immortality for each individual among his believers.

Those who wished to enter into this holy fellowship had to submit to a long technical preparation, and undergo a ceremony of dedication. As Apuleius[4] himself tells confidentially, the ceremony brought the candidate to the boundary of the kingdom of the dead, and let him tread upon Proserpine's threshold, finally bringing him back past all the elements. "In the middle of the night I saw the sun sending forth a blinding light, I visited the gods in hell and heaven, and prayed to them face to face." The mystes, or initiate, suffered

[1] Lehner, op. cit., 87, nos. 263–67
[2] CIL. 13, no. 11352. Riese, Rhein. Germ., p. 457, no. 3068b
[3] Cf. Vol. 1, pp. 168 ff.   [4] Apuleius, Metam., 11,23 f.

death in order to return from the kingdom of the dead, guarded by the power of Isis; revitalized in this way, he was made into an immortal god by virtue of having seen god. Clothed in a heavenly garment, his head surrounded by a nimbus, the new initiate showed himself to the congregation in the form of the sun-god.

The mythical content of the principal feast of Cybele, the Great Mother of the Mountain, was sorrow for the death, and joy for the resurrection of the god: on the "day of blood" the mystics practised a whirling dance which put them into a mazed condition, and, staggering without control of the senses, they cut themselves until the blood flowed; or else in a state of complete ecstasy they copied Attis and emasculated themselves; afterwards, the blood spurted at least out of the gashed arms of the dancing priests. But the day of mourning was followed at once by the glad festival of the "Hilaria", on March 25, when the coming of spring was celebrated as the resurrection of Attis.[1] In this religion also, an initiation of a special kind was developed, evidences of which are numerous after the middle of the second century, and which was found here and there, from Rome to the western provinces of the Empire. A ceremonial sacrifice of bulls and goats is described as a taurobolium and kriobolium, and was customarily offered as a solemn part of the cultus "for the health of the Emperor". Certainly in the third century, perhaps even at its beginning, there was associated with this ceremony a blood bath of the one who made the offering. The man was concealed in a hole in the ground beneath the animal, and the blood was allowed to flow over him; afterwards he was greeted by the believers with prayers of homage.[2] By this baptism, he was believed to have been "born again"—in one passage it says "forever"—but elsewhere we read of the repetition of the blood bath after twenty or perhaps twenty-eight years.[3] The ceremony was certainly not the normal mode of initiating new converts, if only because bulls were too dear, but a special act on the part of eminent members on special occasions.

[1] Marquardt, *Röm. Staatsverw*, 3 (2nd edit.), 372 f. and Wissowa, *op. cit.*, 320 ff.
[2] Description in Prudentius, *Peristephanon*, 10,1011–1050
[3] Dessau, *op. cit.*, 4152. 4154. cf. 4150 and Lagrange in *Revue biblique*, 36,561–6. Wissowa, *op. cit.*, 322 ff.

The cult of Mithra, the Persian god of light, was apparently confined to males; in the course of the second century it extended vastly in the west of the Empire, though in a form compounded of various elements very well adapted for missionary purposes; the soldiers carried it in every direction. Its importance increased further in the third century. It seized even non-military sections of the population, and, in the end, was further promoted by being united with the official worship of the sun. Worship of Mithra gripped the hearts of the people most strongly, perhaps because it exemplified in broadest fashion the quality of a mystery cult.[1] The separate congregations did not consist of many members: all the temples were small rooms in which a hundred men would scarcely find accommodation. In this way a close fellowship of comrades might be built up, amongst whom nevertheless the usual military differences of rank persisted. The holy band was divided into seven grades, and a man passed from one to the other only after severe tests which demanded self-control and fearlessness. We read of baptisms and of holy meals amongst the members of the cult; of immortality, and of heavenly reward; and also of Mithra's moral commandments which had an ascetic character.[2] It is clear that an initiate of Mithra was to be a warrior for the god of light, of purity, and of truth, against the kingdom of darkness and falsehood. A strong masculine morality was built on the Persian dualism;[3] it was probably apt to win soldiers' hearts, and to give a firm foothold to their contemporaries who were restless with uncertainty at a time of cultural crisis. This religion, however, was not burdened with philosophical hair-splitting. It spread in ever wider circles in Greece and Asia Minor, finally bringing destruction on itself, for it was in these very regions that Christianity first began to spread.

About this time, Judaism began gradually to lose significance. The people themselves had done nothing to preserve the memory of their own experiences, and other historians ceased to trouble much about Israel. The long series of Jewish

[1] Cumont, *Or. Relig.*, 142 ff.; *Myst. d. Mithra*, 125 ff.
[2] Justin, *Apol.*, 66,4. Tert., *Praescr. haer.*, 40. Porphyrius, *de abstin.*, 4,16. Julian, *Caesares*, near the end
[3] Cumont, *Or. Relig.*, 135 ff.

insurrections under Trajan and Hadrian,[1] with their dreadful barbarities, were expiated even more terribly, and the total of oriental Jews was catastrophically diminished. Many "tens of thousands" were slaughtered in punitive expeditions,[2] and a Roman historian gives the actual figures. Hadrian's war destroyed in Judea, apart from Jerusalem, fifty fortified places and 985 villages; 580,000 Jews fell in battle, and there were immeasurable losses through famine, illness, and fire. The figures are remarkably precise, and perhaps come from an official report of the war: this does not mean that they are literally correct, but they do give an idea of the impression which the public mind received of the course of the war. Whole provinces, Palestine, Mesopotamia, Libya, and Cyprus, were, in fact, emptied of Jewish population.

The insurrection under Hadrian was occasioned by a general prohibition of circumcision.[3] This was so intolerable for the Jews that, even under Antoninus Pius, they again rebelled, and were eventually successful in obtaining permission once more to observe this religious rite. On the other hand, circumcision of non-Jews was once more prohibited with very severe penalties.[4] This law became permanent as it made proselytization impossible in practice, and thus the Jewish missionary activity was suppressed. Of course, one person continued to influence another, and we hear for centuries of a quiet Jewish propaganda: but the time of great accessions, and the hope of a religious conquest of the world, were passed. Instead, Judaism exercised an increasing influence on the syncretistic religions, affecting, in particular, mysticism and magic. The Hermetic writings, of which we shall have to speak in the sequel,[5] are as strongly marked by Judaistic influences as are the magical papyri and the magic gems. In this sphere one can follow esoteric Jewish Wisdom step by step.

The position of the Jews, in the eyes of public law, was not changed in spite of bloody insurrections; and when Caracalla gave Roman citizenship to the whole Empire, Jews were included.[6] Even the religious central organization, which the

---

[1] *Supra*, p. 17   [2] Euseb., *H.E.*, 4,2,4   [3] Spartian, *Hadr.*, 14,2
[4] Julius Capitol, *Ant. Pius*, 5,4. Modestinus in the *Digests*, 48,8,11 p.r.
[5] Vol. 3, chap. 1   [6] Juster, *Les Juifs*, 2,23

people had founded after the destruction of Jerusalem, was recognized. The "patriarch" was the leader of Jewish life, and, by means of his "apostles", gathered a special tax from the Jews—the earlier Temple tax was now paid into the Roman state treasury—and he exercised authority in Palestine to the extent that even his death penalties were upheld.[1] Naturally, the Sanhedrin in its old form had disappeared. In its place there was a kind of rabbinic academy in Jabneh, and later in Tiberias, as a superior court of theology and law.[2] We are now entering into the period when the tradition of the Law became fixed in writing in the form known as the "Mishna", and so afforded the normative basis for the further development of oriental Judaism. Further developments took place on this basis in Tiberias in the third and fourth centuries; what is known as the Palestinian Talmud bears witness to the results. Meanwhile the centre of gravity of Judaism had moved eastwards, and in the fifth century the Jews of Babylon put together the writings which were to be normative for the future, and which were known as the Babylon Talmud after the place of origin. On the whole, as Hellenistic Jews declined in numbers and influence in the Roman empire, Judaism of a purely oriental stamp increased in power, and finally came to exercise sole control among the people.

The latest excavations at Dura, a fortress on the Euphrates, have thrown much light on the circumstances during this intermediate period. Here, beyond the frontiers of the Empire, but in close association with Palmyra on the one hand, and with Parthia and Persia on the other, there was a wealthy Jewish colony possessing a definite life of its own, and speaking Aramaic, Parthic, and Greek. The colony followed its own devices in regard to the legal prescriptions against making pictorial representations of living things, and the walls of their synagogue were painted by good artists, from top to bottom, with a series of representations of Biblical history. These included the destruction of the statue of Dagon in the Philistine temple, and the carrying off of the ark of the covenant (1 Sam. 5, 6);[3] but, instead of Dagon, there lay on the ground

[1] Origen, *Epist. ad Afric.*, 14 (17,44 f. Lo.)
[2] Schürer, *Gesch.*, 2,247. Juster, *op. cit.*, 1,401
[3] *Illustrated London News*, 1933, July 29, p. 190

the fragments of the principal Palmyrene gods worshipped in Dura. This community of Jews felt itself to stand heavens high above its surroundings; and, as yet, it had not adopted the type of thought found in the Talmud. Israel's future, however, was decided. She separated finally from the spirit of Hellenism just about the same time as Christianity became indivisibly wedded to it.

Chapter Two

THE CHURCH

STORY-WRITING IS A VERY ANCIENT ART, BUT THE GREEKS were the first to write history. Herodotus described the heroic struggles of the Persian wars out of which blossomed the might and glory of the Periclean age in which he lived; he did so because he understood those wars as the final, crucial phase of an ancient struggle between the "barbarian" peoples of the orient and the Greeks; for this reason he spread out the panorama of the whole history of this mighty event. As a consequence, he regarded the very great variety of individual events as a series governed by a single idea, events which meant the expiry of an authority controlling the entire orient. He also inquired after the laws which at bottom shaped history and gave it significance; he found his answer in religion. But his faith in the gods had already broken, and so was unable to give him a unified point of view:[1] he tells us of guilt and expiation, of the victory of right over wrong, but also of the gods' envy, the inevitable oscillation between happiness and unhappiness, and, finally, the "necessity" which even the gods cannot change. All this makes history comprehensible only within certain bounds; in the last analysis, it is a tragic enigma, just like the lot of many an individual in the course of his life.

Thucydides liberated the writing of history from theological considerations, limited it to the present world of experience and its presuppositions, and thereby gave it a scientific character; at the same time, he defined its material bounds quite strictly, and prevented it from running off into a series of disconnected sketches. For a long time after him, no one had the temerity to write history: the comprehensive work of Ephoros, which was completed before Alexander the Great commenced his reign, was nothing more than a collection of materials without a governing idea.[2]

[1] Wiliamowitz, *Glaube der Hellenen*, 2,206. Jacoby in Pauly-W., supplement 2,479–483
[2] E. Schwartz in Pauly-W, 6,7 f.

Polybius was the first to re-establish large-scale, historical research when he began his masterly history of Rome. He raised the question of how it came about that, in the fifty-three years between 220 B.C. and 168 B.C., almost the entire world fell under the lordship of Rome. History could show no parallel; all the earlier dynasties, Persian, Lacedæmonian, Macedonian, had only effected a temporary and partial rule; the Romans alone gained possession of most of the inhabited world, thus achieving what could not be surpassed in the future. Before 200 B.C. there were only separate histories; but, from this period in time, history became an organic growth which spanned the world and drove it towards one and the same goal.[1] This means neither more nor less than that Polybius had clearly recognized the immense significance of events within his own experience, and saw, in the Roman empire, the climax of a whole process of evolution: in this opinion he was right for the next six centuries—in a certain sense, indeed, for 2,000 years. For Polybius, history began in 200 B.C. Having a strictly matter-of-fact turn of mind, he looked for driving forces among known causes in the present world, and made no sorties into regions not subject to examination: except that, in the proper place, he made due allowance for the irrational fact of Tyche, which, in his case, meant "accident".

Diodorus was the next to write a universal history at the beginning of the Roman empire; but his spirit was not scientific and his object was only to provide the public with a handy book of reference, in which they could conveniently find what was worth knowing about all periods and peoples. This had nothing to do with history in the proper sense, but, even to writers of this kind, it was clear that the Roman empire summed up history.

The Israelitish people had received far-reaching practical instruction in history at the hands of Syrians and Assyrians, Egyptians and Babylonians, and this so frequently that their eyes were accustomed to look towards the far horizon, and to take in a broad landscape. Moreover, the religious foundation of their thought moved them at an early date to an interpretation of history which started from a conception of God.

[1] Polyb., *Hist.*, 1,1–4

God had chosen Israel alone for Himself from amongst all the peoples of the earth, in order that they might be a means of blessing for the whole world. No matter how war and exile might even yet chastise the people with distress and suffering, nevertheless the day would come when Israel would bring the true knowledge of God, and hence salvation, to all peoples. Then would God establish His glory in Zion, and all the world would make a pilgrimage to His holy mountain in order to worship there. There were many variations of the hope that this kingdom of God would signify the political subjection of all nations under Israel. From that point, the road led to the apocalyptic conception of the miraculous Messianic kingdom of peace, a conception which, from the days of Isaiah,[1] ever and again enflamed the religious imagination of the prophets.

About the same time as Polybius came to his conception of history as centring on Rome, Daniel presented his revelations to the Jewish people during the Maccabean wars: here, in two passages, chapter two and chapter seven, he laid bare the meaning of history. The empires of Babylon, Media, Persia, and Macedonia followed one another: this last, i.e. Alexander's empire, was already crumbling, would soon fall to pieces, and be replaced by a new empire that God Himself would establish. In this empire, the Son of Man sent from heaven, who, in this case, was only a symbol of a nation consisting of the saints of the Most High, would rule the entire world forever.[2] It would therefore appear that the history of the world issued according to divine plan in the Messianic kingdom of God, as Isaiah has already prophesied. We have already seen how this idea developed in late Judaism, and we have described its various forms.[3] In the Maccabean period, hopes were re-confirmed that all earthly powers would be transformed by a great miracle, and, under the oppression of Roman rule, those hopes grew and supplied the inner power in various rebellions, until the catastrophe of the year A.D. 70, and the final desperate struggle which Barkochba fought in Hadrian's time.

The Christian church entered into the heritage of Jewish eschatology, and from apocalypticism learned to regard the

---

[1] Cf. Isa. 11: 6–9   [2] Dan. 2: 44, 7: 13, 18, 27; cf. Vol. 1, pp. 28 f.
[3] Vol. 1, pp. 28, 37 f.

history of the world as the way of approach to the kingdom of God. The Revelation of John shows how a Christian seer regarded the end of the present world and the glory of the new kingdom, after all Rome's glory and might had broken to pieces, following upon certain fearful signs of the divine anger, and after Satan had been bound and flung into the abyss. A new heaven and a new earth would then be erected upon the ruins of the world, and the heavenly Jerusalem would shine as the capital of a holy people, subject to God and the Lamb, and walking in His light for ever and ever.

There were, of course, a thousand variations; but, in this way, or something like it, the earliest Christians conceived the course of the world's history. Fixed and firm, and far removed from any doubt, was, to them, the fact that the great empires of this world, including the Imperium Romanum, had reached their last and highest form. Now catastrophe threatened the latter, and its place would be taken by the promised kingdom of God, and introduced by the second advent of Christ. The dynasties of the Roman emperors would be brought to an end by Christ, the King of kings. He and His kingdom constituted the goal and the final meaning of history.

All of this had been prophesied from ancient times, and described in the Old Testament; and the promises applied, as Paul had shown,[1] not to the Jews, but to the "spiritual Israel", i.e. the Christians. The young, religious society, the Church, had an astonishingly clear consciousness of its own significance as a completely new element that had entered history, and had destroyed the old criteria. The national limitation of former religions did not operate among Christians. A new people[2] were coming forward who could no longer be called Jewish, Greek, Scythian, or barbarian,[3] but were indeed altogether new, "a third race" at the side of Gentiles and Jews,[4] "an elect race, a royal priesthood, a holy nation, a people for God's own possession".[5] All the peoples who had

---

[1] Gal. 3: 6–9, 6: 16; Rom. 4: 1–25; Phil. 3: 3; cf. Vol. 1, 127 f.

[2] Barn. 5,7. 7,5. Or. Sibyll. 1,383; cf. Harnack, Mission, 4th edit., 1,262 ff.

[3] Col. 3: 11; Gal. 3: 28; cf. Rom. 10: 12. 1 Cor. 12: 13

[4] Kerygma Petri, f. 2. p. 15,8. Klostermann, 2nd edit. (Kl. Texte 3). Aristides, Apol., 2. Harnack, op. cit., 1,259–289

[5] Pet. 2: 9

appeared in the world hitherto, were conditioned by flesh and blood, and possessed their own peculiar qualities; Christian people alone were born of the spirit, by the sacrament of baptism in particular. This sacrament united Christians chosen out of all nations, and made them into a new, supramundane organism which Paul described as the body of Christ, and of which, therefore, Christ was the head.[1]

From an early date this body of Christians, united into one in Christ through the spirit, was called *ecclesia*, church. This was the name used by preference in the Septuagint for the assembly of the children of Israel. When the Christians applied this title to their own society, they expressed thereby their consciousness of being the chosen people of God, the people in the Old Testament who had received the promises; they believed themselves to be the spiritual Israel. The sum total of Christian people, who lived in many places in the earth, was called *ecclesia*; every single church, however, was also called by the same name: for where two or three were gathered in the name of the Lord, there was he in their midst, there the body of Christ was visible, there was the "Church".

The author of 1 *Clement* used stiff and formal phraseology, —itself valuable source-material. He began with the words:[2] "The church of God which sojourns in Rome greets the church of God which sojourns in Corinth." The one church of God dwelt on earth as a diaspora; she had been scattered "to all the four winds", and to the ends of the world.[3] She only sojourned on earth, a stranger, because "our home, in which we have citizen rights, is in heaven"; Christians were fellow-citizens of the saints above, and belonged to the household of God.[4] The real home of Christians was the heavenly Jerusalem, in which the living God ruled eternally in the midst of unnumbered angelic hosts, and the Church of the elect and the righteous.[5] The future city towards which we were striving lay there, the "kingdom of God" that united the church scattered over the earth.[6]

[1] Cor. 12: 13, 10: 17; Rom. 12: 5; Col. 1: 18, 24; Eph. 2: 11–19, 5: 23; 1 Pet. 2: 5. *Herm. Vis.* 3,3,3–5; cf. Vol. 1, 119 ff., 214 ff.
[2] 1 *Clem.* 1 title; cf Pol., *ad Phil.*, title, *Mart. Pol.* title
[3] *Didache* 10,5. 9,4; cf. Jas. 1: 1
[4] Phil. 3: 20; Eph. 2: 19; cf. 1. Pet. 1: 1, 2: 11. *Herm. Sim.* 1,1
[5] Heb. 12: 22–24; Rev. 21: 9 f.; cf. 19: 7
[6] Heb. 15: 4; *Did.* 4,4. 10,5; R. Frick, *Gesch. d. Reich-Gottes-Gedankens*, 29 ff.

The *ecclesia* is not the sum of the single communities on earth, but a supra-mundane entity comprising everything that belongs to Christ, and is, indeed, an organ of his body which comprises the high angels and the serving spirits, the saints who have been already perfected, martyrs and confessors, and the Christians who are still striving and struggling here below.[1] Christ loves the Church as his bride; she is His wife, one with Him, like man and wife according to the Scriptures: Adam and Eve in the Garden of Eden show forth the relation of Christ to the Church. Christ's spirit, pneuma, is spiritual and eternal, and so, too, is the Church: she was created by God before the whole world, before the sun and moon.[2] Thus the Church is the origin and goal of all earthly phenomena; but this does not mean that she exists in this world, and, still less, by this world; rather, the world was created for her sake and has no independent purpose. The Church has her own organism and her own laws; the world has other laws: both stand over against each other as two fundamentally different states.[3] The idea of an antithesis between the divine and the earthly state, to which Augustine's most important work gave classical expression, belongs to the original essence of Christian self-consciousness within the Church.

Any cool observer who will consider the lack of proportion between the immensity of the Imperium Romanum, indeed of the whole world throughout six millennia, on the one hand, and the small, scattered, minor community which made up Christianity, on the other; and let it come home vividly to his mind that this handful of people set themselves, aloof and proud, over against the Roman empire, and asserted that the entire history of the world ran its course for their sakes—he will be in a position to understand the criticisms made by Celsus, who was a Greek.[4] Celsus speaks indignantly of these "worms" who assert that "they came directly after God, and had become fully like Him; that all was subject to them, earth, and water,

---

[1] Cf. Col. 2,9–12. 19; and *supra*, p. 52, note 5

[2] Eph. 5: 29–32; 2 *Clem.* 14: 1–5; cf. Ign., *ad. Pol.*, 5,1. *ad.* Eph. 5: 1. Rev. 19:7, 21: 9, 22: 17; Mark 2: 19 = Matt. 25: 1–13. John 3: 29; 2 Cor. 11: 2; pre-existence: 2 *Clem.* 14: 1; *Herm. Vis.* 1,3,4. 2,4,1

[3] *Herm. Vis.* 1,1,6. 2,4,1. *Sim.* 1,1–5

[4] Celsus in Orig., *c. Cels.*, 4,23

and air, and stars; and that everything existed,[1] and had been ordained, for the purpose of serving them". Celsus was quite right; that was the way in which only fanatics would speak, and Christians were commonly "fools". Sometimes, however, although very, very rarely, a fanatic is a genius, and a fanatical community the vehicle of a world-conquering power. In such a case, the historian's reckoning, which depends upon analogy, ceases to be valid. Without knowing it, he is really looking straight through the levels of normal events into the abyss from which those final powers spring that cannot be comprehended on the basis of rational knowledge. In a case like this, faith rightly speaks of miracle.

The essence of the church is the spirit. In discussing the earliest periods, we have already seen how the pneuma made itself known among the Christians, and now we need only to remark, for the sake of completeness, that the enthusiastic operations of the spirit, so vividly portrayed by Paul, showed themselves powerful even in the second century. Missionaries still wandered through the various countries, and the voice of the prophets was to be heard offering prayer and thanks, but also exhorting, giving revelations, and uttering prophecies in the assembly rooms of Christian congregations, sometimes no doubt also in the open air in the squares and streets. The spiritual office won great respect, honour, and outer advantage, for those who possessed it. This fact, on occasion, attracted very unspiritual elements, and brought about deceitful conduct. As early as the Church Order recorded in the *Didache*,[2] we find directions for testing the prophets who possessed the spirit: if their enthusiastic speeches ended in demanding good food, or money, by way of reward, the church was to cast them out as deceivers.

A pagan writer, of the time of the Antonines,[3] sketched an obviously faithful picture of such an adventurer. After various failures in different spheres of life, he became a Christian and set up as a prophet; he conducted public worship, expounded the Bible, wrote his own tracts, and was greatly respected in the churches. In the end, however, he was thrown into prison, a

---

[1] Cf. say Justin, *Ap.* 7,1. Aristides, *Apol.*, 16,6   [2] *Did.* 11,7–12
[3] Lucian, *de morte Peregrini*, 11–16

fact which served further to increase his prestige, and ensured his livelihood after being set free—until he was caught in an offence against the customs of church worship, an offence which immediately brought his prophetic status to an ignoble end.

A few years later, another enemy of Christians, the Celsus[1] whom we have already mentioned, tells us of his own experiences of Christian prophets whom he had heard, as he assures us, in Phœnicia and Syria. They busied themselves in large numbers, inside and outside the temples; visited, and begged in, the cities and camps; and preached as follows: "I am God, or the Son of God, or the Holy Ghost. I am coming. The world is passing away, and you people are going to destruction on account of your sins. I will save you. You will see me returning with heavenly power. Blessed is he who now serves me; but on all the others I will cause eternal fire to rain down on the cities and the countryside. It will be useless for mankind, unaware of its due punishments, to repent and groan; but those who believe on me will I preserve for ever." These observations are made by Celsus in a hostile spirit, but they are keen-sighted: actually the spirit of Jesus Himself was speaking in the prophet in the first person singular, proclaiming the parousia, and frightening citizens with terrible threats. When Celsus adds that the speech ran out into incomprehensible and crazy sounds, which conveyed no meaning, and which were, nevertheless, expounded by a man who could only have been a fraud, the case was obviously an example of the familiar glossolalia with subsequent interpretation.[2] No one can be surprised if Celsus took it all for deception, and if he believed that he was justified in this opinion by the confessions of such prophets; even Christians themselves were not certain what attitude to adopt in regard to deceivers of that kind. Taken on the whole, however, Celsus has given us a true picture of a genuine, pneumatic ecstatic. Of course, it should be added that the classical period of Christian prophecy had already passed, and what Celsus had seen were small fry on the geographical and spiritual periphery of the Church, men who were living on the remains of the prestige of characteristics which were dying out.

[1] Origen 7,9–11   [2] Vol. 1, pp. 125 f.

For a long time the normative sections of the church had been more than mistrustful of all spiritual phenomena of this kind, and people such as these were closely examined to see if they observed a manner of life which corresponded to the commandments of the Lord.[1] The Pauline epistles expressly pointed out the way which all forms of pneumatic activity should take, and that way lay in the direction of giving expression to the Christian virtues; moreover, Paul's canticle of the love which remained when all prophecy and glossolalia had passed away, was not forgotten. The moral principles and habits, taken over from the proselytes of the synagogue, exercised a similar effect. So, too, the words of the Sermon on the Mount found their way ever afresh to the hearts of the faithful, and shaped their conceptions of the Christian life. The opening chapters of the *Didache* show how the words of the Lord combined into a unity with the Old Testament commandments, and we have every ground for assuming that the way of life of the great majority of Christians was governed by these teachings. The pneumatics had to walk on this level, a fact that damped considerably their arbitrary ways, and also gave protection against the fundamental moral libertinism which, in many gnostic circles, was the consequence of pneumatic endowment.[2]

The pneumatics were also vehicles of revelation; their words were identified as those of the same divine spirit as formerly had spoken in the prophets of the Old Covenant, and as had become flesh in Jesus Christ. This identity gave the pneumatics the same ultimate authority. But how could one prove that the spirit speaking in any particular prophet was really divine and not the voice of an evil and misleading spirit? The revelations could have been tested by the Old Testament—if only the allegorical method had not permitted every inconvenient phrase to be readily explained away, or perverted to give any required meaning. The question might be asked whether the Pauline epistles were not a touchstone, and the answer would be that pneumatics of the grand style believed themselves to possess an authority equal to Paul's own. What could be said, however, about the words of the Lord? These undoubtedly

[1] *Did.* 11,8. 10   [2] e.g. Vol. 1, p. 285

enjoyed unconditional authority, but even they were sometimes explained allegorically. But, of even greater importance was the fact that, from the secret darkness of gnostic information there came forth, ever afresh, words of the Lord and secret revelations of the Master to trusted disciples—words which, it is true, the majority of the Church were unfamiliar with, but which in case of necessity could be quoted and used in support of strange prophetic revelations. There was no definite criterion that separated genuine from false, or that could make plain the truth, or the lie, in a pneumatic's mouth.

Even in the early period, the Church suffered not a little from this uncertainty, a fact which kept the door open to all sorts of strange speculations: the later epistles of the New Testament give us a reflection of the earliest struggles against various heresies. At length gnosis bloomed out into full glamour, and reached its greatest influence. Valentine, as well as a thousand others with similar ideas, proclaimed the superiority of a pneumatic, who had received gnostic illumination, as contrasted with the Church's commonplace writings which thought and spoke on the level of everyday life, and were bound to traditions and literal forms.[1] When this happened the Church was in very great danger, and was compelled to take effective measures of self-protection if her unity and purity were not to fade into a mere ideal. The danger of dissolution into conventicles of a more or less syncretistic character was never greater than in the second century, when wide areas of the orient were under the influence of a gnosis then pressing forward victoriously.

The Church prepared a three-fold defence against the pneumatic and gnostic danger. She fixed the sources of the normative tradition in the canon of Scripture, laid the foundations of theological teaching in the Creed, and especially did she set the ecclesiastical office of the bishop as a higher authority than that due to the unbridled exercise of pneumatic gifts. Thus it came about that, not merely books and doctrines, but living guardians, faced living antagonists. The battle was fought out man against man, and, in the end, that was the most important factor.

[1] See Vol. I, pp. 291 f.

Towards the end of the first century, the offices of bishop and deacon, which were originally of a purely technical nature,[1] were described by a Roman writer as the Christian counterpart of the Old Testament priests, and traced back to apostolic institution. The bishops were already portrayed as the appointed leaders of the cultus. They offered a blameless and holy sacrifice.[2] This completed the transition which is hinted at in the Church Order of the *Didache*.[3] In particular, side by side with the gradual decline of the pneumatics, the bishops and deacons added to their previous functions that of leading public worship as priests; thereby, in fact, they united in themselves the entire leadership of the Church.

Shortly afterwards, Ignatius of Antioch wrote about the monarchical episcopacy;[4] he praised and recommended it highly, and knowing it as it existed in Ephesus, Magnesia, Tralles, Philadelphia, and Smyrna; Rome and Philippi, however, had not yet adopted this form of leadership. In Philippi, a college of presbyters and deacons stood at the head of the church,[5] and the case seems to have been similar in Rome.

It is many decades since scholars first began to advance theories to explain the rise of the monarchical episcopacy from an original college of church leaders. The only clear fact, however, is that, by about the end of the first century, in Antioch and certain of the larger cities of Asia Minor, leadership was no longer in the hands of several persons, but full authority had been transferred to a single bishop. The college of presbyters had become an advisory council subject to him; the deacons still consisted of several persons who, on account of their duties in distributing the charities of the church, were in particularly close contact with the person of the bishop. If we inquire for the reason of the change, the simplest answer would probably be the most appropriate: it was recognized that in difficult times—and a state of war now existed against gnosticism—the concentration of power in the hands of a single person offered the surest guarantee of good leadership; the policy of the Church was shaped accordingly.[6] Results showed

---

[1] Vol. 1, pp. 143–146. 192–95   [2] 1 *Clem.* 44: 4   [3] *Did.* 15,1 f.
[4] Vol. 1, pp. 247 f.   [5] Pol. *ad. Phil.*, 5,3. 6,1
[6] W. Bauer, *Rechtgläubigkeit u. Ketzerei*, pp. 65–74

the wisdom of the step in other respects, and hence the monarchical episcopacy spread gradually throughout the whole
Church; in a later time, we find, here and there, a double episcopacy as a noteworthy remnant of a past age.[1] There is also the
possibility that liturgical requirements had suggested the idea of
a single bishop after the centralization of public worship in a
single church for all the members[2] in contrast to the house by
house meetings for prayer.

According to Ignatius, who was the first to discuss the
problem, the bishop was the leader of an individual church;
he was not merely high-priest and leader, but, more than
anything else, the authority on doctrine: he stood before the
church in the place of God, and must be respected like the Lord
himself. Anyone whose knowledge pretended to go beyond the
limits set by the bishop was lost.[3] In other words, the official
pneumatic, in the person of the bishop, was now distinguished
from the earlier prophet who had held no regular office; the
bishop united in himself all authority, and gave a final decision
on all disputed questions. In the early period each separate
church could describe itself as an *ecclesia*, i.e. God's chosen
people, because God's people were always present where the
spirit bore sway: we now find this thought developed with
very important consequences. The spirit no longer held free
sway, nor seized first one and then another. Of course, individual members possessed it from the time of their baptism,
and this fact united them in the one body of Christ. The spirit
revealed himself now, however, in a special manner; not as
formerly in prophets and those who spoke with tongues, but in
the bishop and the clergy whom the bishop led: the bishop was
the head of this spiritual body. In this way, from the saying
"the Church is where the spirit is", the struggle with gnosticism
led to the new thesis: "the Church is where the bishop is." This
thesis triumphed over enthusiasm and gnosticism, and has
remained the fundamental dogma of Roman Catholicism to
the present day.

It is extremely difficult, and, ultimately impossible, to
describe the development of the earliest constitution of the

---

[1] H. Koch, *ZNW.*, 19,81–85   [2] K. Müller, *ZNW.*, 28,295
[3] Ign., *Trall.*, 3,1. Eph. 6: 1 *ad. Pol.*, 5,2; cf. Vol. 1, pp. 247 f.

Church, because our literary sources only rarely give an answer to the many questions which we propose to them. In the early period, these appeared as outer matters, and unworthy of discussion; when they began to be of theological importance, the observers' outlook was influenced by theory. For the period covered by the first century, the leadership of the Church was almost without exception in the hands of a synod—special conditions surrounded the first church in Jerusalem.[1] The members of this synod were called *presbyteroi* wherever Jewish influence was decisive, i.e. not only in churches of Jewish Christians, but also in Gentile Christian churches which had grown out of Hellenistic synagogues. It comprised not only all who possessed an office, charismatics as well as technical officials, but also other revered persons, in particular the martyrs,[2] and occasionally indeed women.[3] In other places, particularly in the Pauline churches, bishops and deacons were spoken of as officials of the church, and a distinction was made between them and the charismatic apostles, prophets, and teachers, as leaders of worship. We have already seen how these different sides developed, and how the functions of the pneumatics were transferred to bishops and deacons. At an early date, however, the term "presbyter", which was sanctified by the Old Testament, and therefore regarded with greater respect, was transferred to the group of leading men in churches to whom this title was really quite unknown.

At any rate we find the college of presbyters in Rome *c.* A.D. 140 at the head of the church, whereas the bishops and deacons are mentioned as special officers entrusted in particular with the care of the poor, the widows, and the orphans.[4] But they were of equal rank with the apostles and teachers of the earlier period; hence they exercised spiritual and liturgical functions,[5] and undoubtedly belonged to the circle of presbyters. The presbyter who conducted worship was the *episcopos*, and he received the gifts destined for the care of the needy.[6] Thus the process was already well-advanced which is described in a preliminary fashion in 1 *Clement*, and in the *Didache*, and by which spiritual

---

[1] Vol. 1, pp. 66 ff.   [2] Hermas, *Vis.*, 3,1,9. Hippolyt. *Church Order*, 34

[3] Müller, *ibid.*, 275   [4] *ZWT.* 55,136–140

[5] Herm. *Vis.*, 3,5,1. *Sim.*, 9,26 f.   [6] Justin, *Apol.*, 67,6

offices were transferred to the bishops. In general, the pneumatics had disappeared and only rarely did a prophet maintain a hopeless struggle for recognition.[1] The development within the college of presbyters, however, had not come to an end, and struggles for position and honour were not lacking;[2] the monarchical episcopacy prepared itself for, and naturally found opposition in, the college which was defending its traditional rights. Towards the end of the century, the victory was gained: the single bishop stood unchallenged at the head of the Roman church, no matter how often one found it convenient to change the title used in the course of a discussion. We hear of the presbyter who led the church, when probably the bishop was meant; and the latter retained for centuries the polite custom of describing the members of the synod as "colleagues", and himself as their "fellow presbyter".[3] After the middle of the century, i.e. after Anicetus and Soter, there can be no further doubt as to the monarchical character of this episcopate.

A special status was given to the Roman bishop in outer matters *c.* A.D 240: the church began to celebrate the anniversary of his entry into office by a liturgical festival, and, in what is known to-day as the catacomb of Callistus, a burial vault was decorated artistically, in which were buried the bodies of departed bishops from Pontianus who died in A.D. 235 to Eutychianus who died in A.D. 282. Moreover, from that time onwards, an official "list of popes" was drawn up giving the day and year of consecration as bishop and of death, and along with it the older list was preserved which had contained no dates, but only the names of the Roman bishops.[4] Irenæus gives us the first of such lists, *c.* A.D. 180.[5] It contains a series of sixteen names which, after mentioning the apostles Peter and Paul, begins with two unknown persons, Linus and Anencletus, and mentions in the third place the Clement who is known to us as the author of the letter to the Corinthians, and who is mentioned also elsewhere.[6]

---

[1] Herm., *Mand.*, 11   [2] Herm., *Vis.*, 3,9,7–10. *Sim.*, 8,7,4–6
[3] Iren. 3,2,2. 3,1 ff. 4,26,2 f. 27,1. Letter to Victor of Rome in Eus., *H.E.*, 5,24,14–16; cf. *ZWT.* 55,146 f. K. Müller, *ZNW.*, 28,274–78
[4] Lietzmann, *Petrus u. Paulus*, 2nd edit., 7–28
[5] Iren. 3,3,3   [6] Cf. Vol. 1, p. 192 f. Herm., *Vis.*, 2,4,3

The list reaches back, therefore, to the apostolic period and may rest on sound, historical tradition as far as the names are concerned; the reservation must be made, however, for the earliest period, that names were preserved of prominent members of the college of presbyters who did not officiate in strict succession, but, frequently, side by side, sharing in the leadership of the church. When the list came to be given in the form handed down by Irenæus, it had to mention the names of the successive bearers of the apostolic tradition,[1] and guarantee that the living bishop of Rome, who stood at the end of the series for the time being, was the genuine heir of the apostolic doctrine, and thereby also the one who could make authoritative pronouncements about it. The theory which Clement had laid down as to the apostolic institution of the episcopal office, and as to the necessity of recognizing apostolic succession,[2] actively developed still further in Rome, and Irenæus[3] insisted on it because it helped to defend the theology of the bishops against the gnostics: what the bishop taught was thereby legitimized as apostolic, without further debate.

From Rome, the doctrine penetrated into the west and contributed more than a little to increasing the respect in which the Roman church was held: for, in the west, Rome was the only church which could trace back its list of bishops to the apostolic period. Tertullian of Africa, writing c. A.D. 200, called Rome happy because the apostles, Peter, Paul, and John, had laboured there as martyrs, and had poured forth both their blood and also the entire volume of their teaching. In this way, Rome, with its bishop as the vehicle of its tradition, became the apostolic authority of the west at an early date. Moreover no place in the entire occident, except Rome, had taken the trouble to make out a list of bishops or a chain of tradition reaching back to the beginnings; neither Carthage, nor the anciently famous church of Lyons, troubled themselves seriously about their early history—if, indeed, they had had such a history.

It is true that, in the east, Ignatius taught the superior authority of the bishop as regards doctrine; Ignatius's teaching was not based on apostolic succession, however, but was simply

---

[1] E. Caspar, *Die älteste röm. Bischofsliste* (1926), 436–72   [2] Cf. Vol. I, pp. 194 f.
[3] K. Müller, *ZNW.*, 23,216–222. Hegesippus who taught this doctrine lived in Rome; cf. Eus., *H.E.*, 4,22,3

asserted.[1] Of course, in this case again, apostolic tradition had been mentioned, and the "elders", the "presbyters", who had been personal disciples of the apostles, played an important part as vehicles of this tradition;[2] but we hear nothing of the view that the bishop, in virtue of the succession of his office, handed down apostolic doctrine. This explains also why the greatest majority of the places founded by Apostles preserved no list of bishops nor any chain of tradition, to say nothing of handing word down. Only three cities had lists of this kind: Alexandria and Antioch, which were the two cosmopolitan cities competing with Rome,[3] and Jerusalem the ancient centre of Christendom. These are the places which, in the course of the history of the Church, grew to be patriarchates, and at an early stage took dominating positions in the life of the Church: their bishops made use of a list of predecessors after they had learnt its meaning and value from Rome. This fact enables us to test the Jerusalem list, and to show, indeed, that, during the whole of the second century, this leading church of Christendom did not possess a monarchical episcopacy with a life-tenure: otherwise fifteen bishops could not have held office in the period between A.D. 134 and the beginning of the third century.[4] But, if so, we are in a position to draw the further inference, viz. a similar state of affairs existed in other places in the east; and still further, that the institution of the monarchical episcopate took a considerably longer time to develop in the interior than we might at first be led to suppose from the circumstances asserted by Ignatius as existing in the leading cities on the coast.

We have no information about the evolution of the episcopate in the occident, apart from Rome. We hear only from Lyons that, in the great persecution there, Bishop Potheinos suffered martyrdom when more than ninety years old, and that Irenæus was his successor; the date must have been approximately A.D. 178; and, since Irenæus was certainly a monarchical bishop, it is likely that his predecessor held a similar status.[5] In saying that, however, we have reached the limits both of our knowledge and our inferences.

---

[1] Vol. I, pp. 247 f. [2] Papias in Eus., *H.E.*, 3,39,3 f. [3] E. Caspar, *op. cit.*, 347f. 368.
[4] E. Schwartz in the large edit. Eus.; *H.E.*, 3, ccxxvi f. [5] Eus., *H.E.*,, 1,29. 5,5,8.

The course of events in Alexandria was parallel to that in Rome; here, remarkably enough, we have exact information which, although coming from a later period, will stand critical examination.[1] Granted that the origins of the Alexandrian church are obscure, and that nothing is extant about the beginning of the episcopacy in this metropolitan city, except the suspiciously conventional list of names already mentioned; nevertheless, in this church, an earlier arrangement held good and was unchanged even at a later period. At any rate, in the third century the Alexandrian church consisted of a number of independent, separate communions, each of which was grouped round its own church-building, and led by a presbyter; moreover this condition of affairs lasted till the beginning of the following century. The presbyters chose one of their number to be bishop,[2] and to take charge of "the Alexandrian churches".[3] Alexander was the first to widen the circle of persons from whom the bishop could be chosen, and he then nominated a deacon, Athanasius, to be his successor (A.D. 328).

We learn of still another and, on the surface, a very remarkable piece of news from Egypt.[4] At first the Alexandrian bishop was the only bishop anywhere in the whole of Egypt. Bishop Demetrius (A.D. 189–232) was the first to institute three others, and his successor Heraklas (A.D. 232–47) instituted twenty others; in the course of the century the number was very considerably increased. It follows that the cities and villages of Egypt were under the leadership of presbyters—a title which was very frequent in secular life as applied to presidents of groups or committees[5]—indeed, whole groups of villages were placed under a single presbyter.[6] This evolution may have been accompanied by the circumstance that, from the legal point of view, Alexandria was for a long time the only "city" of Egypt; and only in A.D. 202, i.e. in the time of Demetrius, did large administrative districts receive a new constitution from

[1] K. Müller, ZNW., 28,278–296

[2] Jerome, Epist., 146,1,6. Severus Antioch., Sixth Book of the Selected Letters, 113, ed. Brooks; Eutychius, Annales (Arab.) Corp. Script. Or. 50,95, ed. Cheikho

[3] Eus., H.E., 5,9,22. 6,2,2. 35. 9,6,2

[4] Eutychius, op. cit., p. 96, Cheikho (Migne Gr., CXI, 982)

[5] H. Hauschildt, ZNW., 4,235 ff.

[6] Athan., Apol. c. Arian., 85; cf. ZWT. 55,150 ff.

Septimius Severus.[1] It is obvious that the Egyptian bishops owed their existence to the bishop of Alexandria, and consequently that he was their head, all of them being subject to him: in the course of the history of the church, that kind of thing occurred frequently and widely. The Alexandrian patriarch always had behind him a troop of bishops who were extraordinarily united and militant.

Only recently have we come to pay close attention to the early stages of the history of the episcopal office;[2] but these observations have sharpened our eyes and illuminated our conceptions of the course of events. What happened in Egypt went by no means beyond the limits of events in the churches elsewhere, in spite of first appearances. Christianity took root always in the towns first of all, and indeed as a rule in the larger towns, and thence spread through the country. In this way, it is obvious that the newly planted country churches would remain under the leadership of the urban bishop and that he would send presbyters and deacons to them; possibly he ordained these clergy and, acting as the superior authority, intervened when necessary. Moreover it was not merely the country churches which were subject in this way to the bishop of a capital city: cities both smaller and greater became spiritually dependent in a similar manner.

About A.D. 200, we see that Serapion, bishop of Antioch, was in charge of Rhossos nearby,[3] and probably of other towns. Many districts in Pontus were grouped, each group under one bishop. Armenia c. A.D. 250 had only one bishop. In Crete it would appear that the two bishops of Gortyn and Knossos, about A.D. 170, shared the spiritual oversight of the whole island.[4] In Gaul, Irenæus of Lyons was described as "the bishop of Gaul", and the neighbouring town of Vienne was certainly subject to his predecessor Potheinos.[5] Even in the time of the fully-developed metropolitan system, such circumstances may still be frequently observed in remoter regions.

If it now came about that a bishop of the centre was no

[1] U. Wilcken, *Grundz. u. Chresto. d. Pap.*, 1a,41
[2] Duchesne, *Fast. Episc. de l'Anc. Gaule*, 1,37 ff. K. Müller, *Beiträge z. Gesch. d. Verf. d. alten Kirche = Abh. Akad. Berlin*, 1922, no. 3, p. 5 ff.
[3] Eus., *H.E.*, 6,12; cf. Ign., *ad Rom.*, 2,2. "Bishop of Syria"
[4] Eus., *H.E.*, 4,23,5. 7   [5] *Op. cit.*, 5,23,5. Duchesne, *ibid.*, 1,40-43

longer able to exercise sole oversight of the districts dependent upon him, he appointed as many bishops as were necessary at the time, and did so in a similar fashion to the way in which the bishop of Alexandria acted in Egypt, i.e. as the number of vigorous churches increased so did the number of bishops. But the relationship of daughter to mother church was retained, and was expressed in the subordination of the newly-instituted episcopal chair to the earlier one; the bishop of the principal town retained for an indefinite period the right of instituting and consecrating the other. Even in the third century, the great centres of Christendom would enjoy an obvious, visible, and superior status over areas of a considerable breadth. In this way also we can explain the rights of Carthage, as principal city, over all Africa, and, similarly, of Rome, over large portions of Italy. Moreover, the close relations between Rome and many regions of southern Gaul and Spain must be due to the same cause. Still further: Carthage itself was clearly conscious, *c.* A.D. 200, of its dependence on Rome:[1] it had received, first, Christianity and, later, the monarchical episcopacy from that city.

In particular, the quite unique relation between the Alexandrian and the Roman church can be explained in the simplest manner from this standpoint. For, after the Egyptian capital had begun to play a part in church history at the beginning of the third century and until the catastrophe of Ephesus (A.D. 449) and Chalcedon (A.D. 451), the closest relations existed between Alexandria and Rome; we shall give many instances in the course of the present work. In the struggles of the fourth century, indeed, Julius of Rome[2] declared, in all seriousness, that it was contrary to the custom of the Church to depose the bishop of Alexandria without the agreement of Rome. We may add that, not only bishop Dionysios of Alexandria, but also several of his successors, including indeed the most eminent, Athanasius and Cyril, subordinated themselves to Rome in a manner which at first bewilders us. In so doing, they acted in a manner very contrary to the traditional attitude of other

[1] Tert., *de Praescr.*, 36
[2] Julius of Rome, *Epist. Danium Flacillum*, 22, p 385*b* Coustant (from Athan., *Apol. c. Arian*, 35)

eastern princes of the Church. This fact brings the conclusion near that Alexandria was founded as a daughter church to Rome and endowed by Rome with episcopal authority. The legend that Mark, the disciple of Peter, was the founder and first bishop of this church,[1] is a deduction based on knowledge as to the historical relationship between the two churches. We see, indeed, that the roots of the Roman primacy extend deeply into the early history of Christianity.

As regards the relationships of the patriarchates, the Church of the first century shows no signs of any wider organic connections. Moreover the whole Church, conceived as a unity, was, and for a long time remained, an invisible entity fully comprehensible only as an idea. It is true that the churches from one end of the world to the other were inspired by the same spirit and bound together by a thousand bonds of mutual aid in either material or spiritual necessity, but there was no outer form which made this unity concrete as an earthly organization also. Yet in difficult times the bishops of the regions concerned came together for mutual counsel. Such synods took place even in the second century in Asia Minor, and served to ward off Montanism and to determine the attitude to the question of Easter, but they were unofficial assemblies, and lacked definite legal competence. It is true that their conclusions were given by the Holy Spirit, and to that extent were normative for the whole Church. In practice, however, that held good only for the churches which, in fact, recognized the conclusions because they agreed with them. In other districts, where a different opinion was held, as in Rome in regard to the question of Easter, the conclusions were not recognized, and it remained uncertain who was in the right. Rome's attempt to claim a superior voice was denied, at that time, on all hands.[2]

Even the synods of the third century bore this character. They made unofficial pronouncements whose weight was the greater according as more bishops took part, i.e. greater according to their geographic basis: and the rightness of the content, together with the appropriateness of their conclusions,

---

[1] Monarch. Prologue to St. Mark (*Kl. Texte*, 1, 2nd edit., p. 16, 16), Eus., *H.E.*, 2,16,1. Similarly the legend of Trophimus *re* Arles; cf. Caspar, *Gesch. d. Papsttums*, 1,347
[2] Eus., *H.E.*, 5,24,10 f., and esp., Cyprian, pp. 235 f., and pp. 254 f. *infra*

gained for many such pronouncements the recognition of the whole Church. But they were not of themselves a higher authority, by spiritual right, in such a way as to be superior to that of the individual bishop. Every bishop was, and continued to be, in possession of complete apostolic authority in doctrine and discipline: the synods were only more powerful because they were able to assert or apply the combined authority of the episcopacy. The principle held good that the Holy Spirit led the Church through the bishops: and the Church was a unity although it was embodied in thousands of churches and hundreds of bishops.

Chapter Three

THE NEW TESTAMENT

AT THE TIME OF JESUS, IT WAS A PREVAILING CUSTOM AMONGST the Jews to give an authoritative decision on theological and religious disputes by quoting the words of celebrated teachers. The whole of the Talmud is constructed of such rabbinic sayings dealing with these discussions; the sayings were diligently collected, learnt by heart, and handed on as a sacred authority from generation to generation. One collection of teachings of human and divine wisdom, which was put together from the words of the earliest Rabbis, bears the name *The Sayings of the Fathers,* and is to be found to-day in every Jewish Prayer book. From this standpoint we can easily understand, if any explanation is necessary, that the disciples of Jesus stored the sayings of their Master faithfully in their memory; they collected, and finally wrote them down, in order that the second generation, and the churches of other regions, might always have this precious material in front of them. Paul's letters are a direct testimony to the significance of the sayings of Jesus for deciding disputed questions,[1] although in the case of Paul, who became a disciple only after the Master's death, references to the historical Jesus are very few. Throughout the whole of the first century and a large part of the second, Christian writings constantly make use of the phrase, "the Lord said", in order to introduce an authoritative quotation.

For early Christendom there were two sources of divine revelation, "Scripture", i.e. the Old Testament, and "the Lord" in His words as handed down. A third source, viz. the Spirit speaking through an ecstatic prophet, was regarded, as we have seen, with ever-increasing mistrust in comparison with the two other sources, and finally it became silent. Hence arose a practical necessity to give a written form to the tradition of the words of the Lord, which we mentioned in the second place, in order that it should be available at all times and everywhere: that is how it came about that the words of Jesus were

[1] 1 Cor. 7: 10, 9: 14, 11: 23; 1 Thess. 4: 15; cf. *Handb. zu Röm.* 12,14

written down in the form which we have already discussed, and which, as the "sayings source", goes back to Matthew.[1] In the case of the Rabbis in the Talmud, many a saying was inseparably connected with some incident; so also was the case with Jesus, and indeed to a much higher degree. In this way, many accounts of the deeds and miracles of the Lord were introduced into the collection of sayings. The preaching about Jesus the Christ gave the hearers doctrine as well as the Master's teachings, for He Himself was the subject of faith; the fulfilment of Old Testament predictions in His life, suffering, and death proved Him, even to opponents, to be the Messiah, and the saviour of the world. Thus, gradually, the record of the Lord's work on earth took shape as a unity, beginning with the Baptism and ending with the Resurrection. This story has actively affected mankind for nineteen centuries, and has constantly gained new disciples for the Master ever afresh.

The earliest form of the record, and the one to which we have immediate access, is Mark's gospel. The gospels of Matthew and Luke are new editions which have been enlarged and improved by incorporating the "sayings source", together with other traditions. The two earliest gospels are typical of popular books without literary claims; on the other hand, Luke, who had made use of other valuable sources, intended his writing for a more educated class: he dedicated his work to a man named Theophilus, who had some eminence owing to his rank or his wealth;[2] and Luke was explicitly, and not unsuccessfully, concerned to write a genuine, historical book, but without robbing his work of its popular character.

These three gospels contain by no means all the genuine, current tradition about Jesus: but almost everything else has been lost to us, and we can rarely lay hold of a saying of Jesus that appears to go back to sound tradition. A few have been introduced here and there in the manuscripts of our gospels: e.g. the *Pericope Adulterae*, which many manuscripts, and hence also our English versions, give as John 7: 53–8: 11, in spite of the fact that it is missing from all good manuscripts of the gospel. The style and vocabulary of the passage help to prove that it is an interpolation.

[1] See Vol. 1, p. 46   [2] Cf. Ed. Meyer, *Ursprung u. Anfänge*, 1,6 f.

Certain manuscripts introduce after Matt. 20: 28 a completely independent parallel to Luke 14: 8–10; and a completely new saying is to be found appended to Luke 6: 4: "on the same day He saw a man working on the Sabbath and said to him: Man, if you know what you are doing you are blessed, but if you do not know, you are accursed and a transgressor of the law."

Other sayings are to be found quoted occasionally in ancient Christian writings, without its being possible for us to trace them back to any particular gospel: nevertheless, they may come from sound tradition current outside, since such tradition did not die out even after the gospels had been composed. As late as the second century, a man like Papias emphasized the fact that he did not think it so valuable to make use of the books as of oral tradition. Some such a tradition is represented in Acts 20: 35: "Remember the words of the Lord Jesus, how he himself said it is better to give than to receive." Such sayings are called "agrapha", and have been carefully collected;[1] but, in spite of excellent work in the past, many questions still remain unanswered. For when the gospels were written down, the process which we have already described,[2] and in which the tradition of Jesus was transformed and reconstructed, did not stand still but, at first unconsciously and then to an increasing extent consciously, brought forth further fruits. We may take an example of the first case. When Clement of Rome wrote to Corinth he said:[3] "The Lord Jesus spoke as follows:

> Be merciful in order that you may receive mercy.
> Forgive in order that you may be forgiven.
> As you do, so will it be done to you.
> As you give, so will it be given to you.
> As you judge, so will you be judged.
> *As you show kindness, so will you be shown kindness.*
> With what measure you mete, it shall be measured to you."

Many scholars have believed this quotation to come from an ancient source, e.g. from a lost gospel or possibly a collection of

[1] A. Resch, *Agrapha* (= *T.U. NF.* 15,3–4, 1906); E. Klostermann, *Kl. Texte*, 11, 2nd edit., 1911; M. R. James, *Apocryphal New Testament*, pp. 33 *seq.*; cf. W. Bauer, *Leben Jesu im Zeitalter*, etc., 377–415
[2] Vol. 1, pp. 47 f. [3] 1 Clem. 13: 2

sayings, and they have pointed particularly to the new saying of Jesus which I have printed above in italics. The fact is, however, that here we have something created by Clement himself; he was putting familiar sayings together, and transforming the style of protasis and apodosis so as to make them similar. The actual sources are to be found in Luke 6: 36; Matt. 6: 14, 15; Luke 6: 31 = Matt. 7: 12; further, Luke 6: 37 = Matt. 7: 1 f.; Luke 6: 38 = Matt. 7: 2. Alternatively, and more simply, we may say that Clement combined certain sayings from Luke 6: 31-38 with Matt. 6: 14 f. There remains the word of Jesus about showing kindness; it was composed freely by Clement himself in order to bring the number of sayings up to seven; and the fact that the word for "showing kindness" is very rare in Greek, but frequently used elsewhere by Clement, proves the correctness of this theory. This is an instance which enables us to understand how such a saying came to be attributed to Jesus. We can see how it was newly created, without any special purpose, half unconsciously, on the basis of rhetoric and style, and by a writer who paid attention to literary considerations.

Other sayings were created with a distinct tendency, and were clearly meant to throw the authority of Jesus into the scale on the side of this or that doctrinal opinion. We have already discussed such transformations of traditional sayings when we dealt with the Jewish-Christian gospels.[1] In addition, the more we learn of gnosticism, the more evident does this practice become, and the more untrammelled and capriciously does theological invention operate. Most of the fragments of papyrus which contain new sayings of Jesus,[2] spring from this way of inventing them when they would accord with the purposes of gnosticism; genuine and spurious were frequently intermingled in order to strengthen the impression of historical trustworthiness.

After the invention of single sayings, the next step was the writing of new gospels; these, however, always followed the earlier Synoptic gospels and used them as foundations. But the

[1] Vol. 1, pp. 185, 188 f.
[2] E. Klostermann, *Kl. Texte*, 8, 2nd edit., p. 16–21; *ibid.*, 11, 2nd edit., pp. 26; H. B. Swete, *ibid.*, 31,4 f.; also H. I. Bell's *Fragments of an unknown Gospel* (1935), are relevant here

new evangelists rejected all the restraints which kept the Fourth Gospel within the bounds of the type of thought characteristic of the Church, and invented freely, the boundless world of speculation being unrestricted by any historical tradition or doctrinal authority. This fact can be clearly seen in the large fragment of the *Gospel of Peter*[1] which was discovered in 1886: building materials are borrowed from all four evangelists, and put together to form a record of the Passion; everywhere we can observe how imagination has added to the historical events. In the description of the Resurrection, the gnostic Christ appears as a giant as high as the sky, carried by two men whose heads reach to the clouds, and behind him hovers the cross in motion: "And I heard a voice saying out of heaven: Hast thou preached to those that sleep? and the answer rang from the cross: Yes."

The forms of what is known as the *Gospel of the Hebrews*,[2] which was current in Jewish-Christian circles, were affected by similar fantasies. Isolated reports of, and quotations from, other gospels of this kind have been preserved,[3] e.g. the gospel of the *Egyptians*, of *Thomas*, *of Matthias*, and others; there can be no question as to the gnostic character of these writings.

The gospels of the Infancy constitute a special category. At an early date, many Christians wanted to know something of the Lord's early history, and since there was no historical tradition, legend took its place. Hence arose the birth stories which we find in Matthew and Luke, and also the story of Jesus at twelve years of age in the temple, Luke 2: 41–52. In order to study the difference between an uncontaminated and genuine legend on the one hand, and on the other, a mere fantasy designed to satisfy curiosity, we need only consider, from this standpoint, the later stories of Christ's childhood. These arose during the second century, but developed further, adopted a new literary form, and persist in substance to the present day in various shapes in devotional books or in apocryphal lumber rooms. Among them are the narratives of *Thomas*[4] of which Irenæus

---

[1] E. Klostermann, *Kl. Texte*, 3, 2nd edit., *Apokrypha I*; English translation in M. R. James, *Apocryphal New Testament*, p. 13
[2] Vol. 1, pp. 185, 189
[3] E. Klostermann, *Apokr. II* (*Kl. Texte*, 8) and M. R. James, *op. cit.*
[4] *Evangelia apocrypha*, Tischendorf, 2nd edit., 140–209

had heard before A.D. 200[1] and of which we possess several expanded forms dating from a later period. Here the child Jesus has been transformed, by an imagination proper to a primitive nature religion, into a little man full of mana and taboo. His playmates, who annoy or strike him, fall dead; and the same happens to a schoolmaster who boxes his ear for an impolite answer. Three teachers attempt, without success, to deal with the miracle-working child:[2] to the first, who was to instruct him in the alphabet, he gave a lecture on the allegorical significance of the letter A; the second he killed; to the third he immediately read a passage from the Bible, and then preached to the people about the Law. But he also worked positive miracles: he shaped sparrows out of clay and made them fly away alive; when his pitcher broke, he carried the water home in the lap of his shirt; he stretched a plank to the required length for his father; he healed wounds, raised the dead, and finally brought back to life again all those he had put to death in his annoyance. In this way the narrative comes to a "happy end"; it concludes with the story of Jesus at twelve years of age in the temple, and thus effects a junction with the Synoptics.

Even in Matthew and in Luke we can see that some believers attempted to give a graphic account of Christ's human origin. This kind of effort continued and brought it about that the story of Mary was depicted in ever richer detail. We find all the basic elements in what is known as the *Proto-evangel of James*[3] which was composed in its present form somewhere in the fourth century from earlier constituents: separate parts were known even in the second and third centuries. First there is the legend of Mary. The Holy Virgin's parents were Joachim and Anna: she was born by an angel's promise to her mother, who had long been childless, and was consecrated to God: she therefore lived from her third to her twelfth year under priestly ward in the temple. Then, in consequence of an oracle, she was entrusted as a consecrated virgin by the priests to the old carpenter Joseph who had long been a widower and who already had grown-up sons. Once when she was drawing water

---

[1] Irenæus, 1,20,1; cf. also *Epist. apost.*, 4 (15)

[2] M. R. James, *op. cit.*, pp. 49ff.

[3] *Evangel. apocr.*, ed. Tischendorf, 1–50. Harnack, *Chronol. I*, 598–603. M. R. James, *op. cit.*, pp. 38 *seq*.

and again, at home, when she was spinning purple for the temple curtain, an angel announced to her that she would conceive a son by the word of God. Just as Luke tells us, she visited her friend Elizabeth and remained there three months. When Joseph returned home after a considerable absence working as a builder, he discovered that she was pregnant but was reassured by an angelic vision, just as Matthew records. A divine judgment by means of testing waters absolved both from the accusations of the priests and scribes. Then the birth of the child Jesus took place in Bethlehem, and, in fact, in a cave: at the same time Mary's physical virginity was confirmed by two midwives as unbroken even after the birth. Magi came from the east, and Herod ordered the slaughter of the infants at Bethlehem. Mary placed Jesus in a cattle manger, whereas little John and his mother disappeared into a mountain which opened automatically. Since Herod was particularly suspicious of John, but could not find him, he killed his father, Zachariah, near the altar in the temple, as is recorded in Matt. 23: 35.

Similarly, imagination got to work on the Passion story, particular attention being paid to the person of Pontius Pilate. To an increasing extent, the Christian church endeavoured to absolve him from the capital guilt of his unjust judgment, and to lay the sole responsibility on the Jews. According to Matthew, Pilate's wife bore witness to Jesus's innocence, and warned her husband. Thereupon he ceremonially washed his hands and refused responsibility for the death of Jesus. The way in which Pilate was later on depicted added further details of this type, as a kind of apologetic; until it came to pass that, about A.D. 200, Tertullian[1] referred his pagan opponents to a report which Pilate, already a Christian by conviction, had himself given to the Emperor Tiberius about Christ. Fifty years earlier, Justin Martyr in similar circumstances had often[2] quoted the *Acts of Pilate* to prove the correctness of his items of information about Jesus. This fact bears witness that the spurious *Letter of Pilate* was known to both of these church Fathers; and it has been preserved in various recensions in later documents.[3] It contains a short account of the Jewish Messianic faith, the miracles of

[1] *Apolog.* 21   [2] Justin, *Apol.*, 35,9. 48,3; cf. 38,7
[3] Conveniently in Harnack, *Chronologie*, 1,605

Jesus, his rejection and crucifixion by the Jews, the sentinels at
the grave, and the Resurrection; it concludes with the words:
"I have reported this to Your Majesty in order that no man may
deceive you otherwise, and lest you think you must believe the
lies of the Jews." Here we see that what the centurion said
at the foot of the Cross (Mark 15: 39) is far surpassed by the
comprehensive and clear testimony of his eminent superior.
In the course of time this kind of writing gave rise to many
others on the subject of Pilate,[1] included a legend of Nicodemus, and another of Veronica, followed by an account of
Christ's descent into hell. We must take note of the fact that the
other side had not been idle, but had fabricated and published the *Acts of Pilate* which was conceived in terms hostile to
Christianity and of which we have no other information than
is given in the indignant protests of Eusebius.[2]

Veronica is the legendary name of the woman with the issue
who was healed by Christ (Mark 5: 25): Eusebius[3] says that a
bronze group erected in her native town of Cæsarea Philippi
represented the miracle. We read of gnostics, as early as the
time of Irenæus,[4] who revered a statue of Christ which had
been made "at the instance of Pilate". It follows that, at an
early date, legend said that statues of Christ had been made.
But the sentimental impulse to produce portraits of the Lord
came to full activity only in the Byzantine period, the most
famous examples of the inventions to which it gave rise being
Veronica's handkerchief, and Abgar's statue in Edessa. On the
other hand, the record of the correspondence between Jesus and
Abgar of Edessa is early, and arose perhaps in the third century:
its kernel was an autograph letter of Jesus to this king, and
Eusebius preserves a Greek text.[5] It is not difficult to understand
how it came to pass that copies of this precious letter were
carried about for several centuries in the orient as protection
against all forms of evil, or were chiselled into houses and city
walls, into gates and doors. A description of Jesus's appearance,
dating from the early middle-ages, and given in the letter of

[1] Epiphan., *hær.*, 50,1,5. Tischendorf, *op. cit.*, 210–486
[2] Eus., *H.E.*, 1,9,3. 9,5,1. 9,7,1
[3] Eus., *H.E.*, 7,18
[4] Irenæus 1,25,6 (1,210, Harvey)
[5] Eus., *H.E.*, 1,13,6–10. Aufhauser, *Kl. Texte*, 126, 2nd edit., 22–38

Lentulus to the emperor Tiberius,[1] is still accepted by many enthusiastic believers; similarly, too, the portrait sketched in accordance with it.

The apostles of Jesus were the vehicles of the authoritative tradition about him: hence it is quite logical that Luke should continue his gospel with a second book, the Acts of the Apostles, which was intended to record how the disciples preached the gospel in Jerusalem, and in all Judea, and Samaria, and to the ends of the world.[2] In this book, the speeches of the apostles give a graphic and authoritative description of the content of the gospel. Not long ago the historical value of the book of Acts was held in very low esteem, and, in consequence of the criticism of the Tübingen school, was regarded as the product of a tendentious reconstruction of history. Meanwhile opinion has changed fundamentally, and we now know that the author carefully collected what was accessible to him, and that he reproduced his sources with commendable faithfulness, including such as were only fragmentary. We need only to separate the fragments of the sources carefully from the historical reconstruction due to the author's mind. The long speeches are, of course, free compositions, and the author used them to place his own conceptions on the lips of the apostles; but he exercised little originality, and so these speeches trustworthily reproduce the average opinion of his time and environment.

The book is not a history of all the apostles. It describes the original church at Jerusalem; it already lay behind the author, its history transfigured in the shimmering light of the past. On that background, Acts tells of the first persecutions and of the spread of the mission, to which they gave rise, as far as the metropolitan city of Antioch. Peter stands in the forefront of events; John is sometimes present as companion, but does not speak. In addition, there are Philip and Stephen as Hellenistic missionaries. The second part of the book is given over to Paul's activities, and reproduces a considerable amount of most valuable tradition deriving from valid, if often only fragmentary, sources; from chapter twenty onwards, the narrative continues in the first person plural, and therefore

[1] Aufhauser, *op. cit.*, 43   [2] Acts 1: 8

comes, in some way, from a travelling companion of the Apostle, probably the author of the book, viz. Luke the physician. This makes it all the more striking that nowhere is there any trace of acquaintance with the Pauline correspondence. Hence the author must have taken up the pen at a very early date, and he must have been firmly convinced of the trustworthiness of his own knowledge; and this to such an extent that in these matters he did not think it worth while to seek further sources, although these would certainly have been readily accessible to him. Such an attitude, however, is readily conceivable in a man like Luke who had been in very close association with the Apostle. On the other hand, the abrupt conclusion and the lack of record of the martyrdom of both great apostles, Peter and Paul, can only be satisfactorily explained by saying that the author died before the work was completed.

In spite of every honest endeavour on the part of the writer, the book of Acts is not a historical work in the strict sense: neither its sources nor the talents of the author were sufficient for such a purpose. It provides us with a good narrative book of a popular kind describing its heroes in traditional style, and traditional conventions are for that very reason continually operative. Luke took over, developed in detail, and put together the sketches of the apostles in the form which was current in the tradition of the Church: in this way a series of separate stories came to be written down. They are, at times, quite loosely interconnected, and do not give the historical contexts; rather, they are concerned, above all else, with depicting the greatness of the Apostles. The Apostles, however, are not individually distinct from one another: each thinks and acts like his fellow, and, even in the case of Peter, the Judaism which marked him at first passes, after the incident of Cornelius, into the universality of Paul. Moreover, their progress is accompanied by miracles which go far beyond the restrained records in the Synoptics; and it is not by accident that we now find a broad similarity to the miraculous acts of the Hellenistic prophets.[1] On two occasions, the author brings his heroes face to face with pagan sorcerers of this latter kind: Peter repels the

[1] R. Reitzenstein, *Hellenist. Wundererz.* (1906), pp. 53 ff., 121 f.

presumption of Simon the Samaritan sorcerer (8: 20), and Paul blinds Bar-Jesus, the Cyprian magician (13: 11). The acts of the apostles do not differ outwardly from those of their miracle-working contemporaries; they are done, however, in the name of Jesus, which fact gives them their special tone and, in case of conflict, their superior power. Finally in Ephesus, both Jewish and Greek magicians are compelled to bow to Paul (19: 11–20). The reader not only enjoyed reading the narrative, but obtained an impressive proof of the veracity of apostolic preaching; in this way Luke, the popular story-teller, became, at the same time, a preacher whose popular phraseology has subsequently served as a basis for theological thought.

The writing of popular books describing the "acts" of the apostles was not brought to a conclusion with this first work. Just as in the case of the gospels, the same impulse continued to operate and produce new examples of the same category; the only difference being that the authentic material in this case was exhausted more rapidly than with the gospels, and imagination had to take its place. Everywhere we can detect that the canonical book of Acts formed the starting-point of the new efforts: it was either supplemented, or else it provided a more or less elastic framework for the new writings.

In the east, the only additional information about Peter was that he had gone to Rome, and had been crucified there: a clear trace of this has been preserved in John's gospel (21:18). The apocryphal *Acts of Peter*[1] fill out the spaces with the free imagination of an oriental who had never seen Rome, but who knew from hearsay that there was a Forum Julium there through which ran a Sacra Via[2]—which is not quite correct —that the little town of Aricia was near, and that somewhat farther off lay Terracina.[3] The canonical Acts had said (21: 13) that one could come by ship to Puteoli,[4] and then continue the journey by land to Rome. There is no trace, however, of genuine local knowledge, nor of a local Roman tradition. Instead, inventive power operated the more energetically. The conflict of Peter with the Samaritan sorcerer

---

[1] *Acta Petri = Actus Petri cum Simone* in Lipsius-Bonnet 1, 45–103
[2] *Op. cit.* 15,32   [3] *Ibid.* 4. 32   [4] *Ibid.* 6

Simon, given in Acts 8: 9–24, was spun out further, and provided the basis of the entire narrative; this is all of a piece with the fact that Simon played a noteworthy part in the later history of gnosticism, and in any case was regarded as the author of gnostic systems.[1] In the *Acts of Peter*, he appears as an anti-Christian prophet in Rome as soon as Paul commenced his long planned journey to Spain[2] and left Rome. Instigated by a vision seen in a dream, Peter now leaves Jerusalem as quickly as possible in order to contend in Rome with the enemy of Christianity. The contest develops into the form of a competition of miracles in the grand style, in which Peter is always the victor. Simon is then compelled to listen pitiably to a long reproof from his own household dog, and a suckling child of seven months orders him out of the city and challenges him to a duel on the Saturday.[3] It is scarcely worth remarking that, in the course of the story, several blind persons are cured, and dead people are raised: but Peter causes a dried sardine, which had been hanging at a window, to swim about happily again in the water;[4] with a word, too, he repairs a broken statue of the emperor.[5]

In comparison Simon's efforts at competition remain poor; but at last, and in front of all the people, he flies triumphantly up to the sky over the Sacra Via, yet, when Peter prays, he crashes down and breaks a leg: as a consequence of this misfortune he dies shortly after.[6] Peter, however, was not able to enjoy his success for long. His sermon on the necessity of chastity in the Christian life caused a considerable number of eminent Roman ladies to withhold from conjugal intercourse. The enraged husbands lay in wait for Peter, whose first intention, on the advice of friends, was to flee; but before he reached the gate he was put to shame by the Lord, and made to turn back. He was now arrested, condemned, and crucified upside down; he then delivered a speech, with marked gnostic qualities, on the symbolism of the Cross, as well as on being crucified upside down.[7] After his death, Nero intended to begin a persecution of Christians but was turned aside by a dream. We may remark in passing that the Neronian persecution was regarded by the author as only an untrustworthy rumour.[8]

---

[1] Pauly-W 2. Reihe 3,180   [2] Rom. 15: 24, 28; cf. 1 *Clem.* 5: 7   [3] *Acta Petri* 9. 12. 15
[4] *Ibid.* 13   [5] *Ibid.* 11   [6] *Ibid.* 32   [7] *Ibid.* 38 f.   [8] Vol. 1, p. 191 f.

The *Acts of Paul* not only provides the record, lacking in the canonical Acts, that his work ended in martyrdom, but, building on a few hints from that source, it constructs a record of extensive missionary journeys on the part of the Apostle which to some extent afford parallels, and to some extent supplements, to the canonical account. The work has not been preserved in its entirety, and we have to attempt to reconstruct it provisionally from various traditions and fragments.[1] In them we meet with Paul, first of all, in Pisidian Antioch (Acts 13: 14), then in Iconium (Acts 13: 51), where the virgin Thecla is strongly impressed by his preaching. She now refuses marriage to her fiancé, and, when he makes complaint, she is condemned by the pro-consul to be burnt, while Paul is to be horse-whipped. But rain puts out the fire, and, having obtained her freedom, she once more seeks out the Apostle and follows him when he returns to Antioch. Here again she is sought in marriage, and when she refuses, is once more condemned to death, this time in the arena. There, however, a lioness protects her at the sacrifice of its own life. In the greatest of danger, she baptizes herself by leaping into a moat, and afterwards encounters other serious dangers. In the end she is again set free. Protected by man's clothes, she once more follows Paul, till finally she dies in Seleucia.

Paul stays first of all in Myra, and from there makes his journey, with many adventures, to Sidon and Tyre. In Ephesus he gets into trouble with the goldsmiths (Acts 19: 24), and is condemned to the arena (1 Cor. 15: 32). Thereupon a large lion lays himself at his feet, and the Apostle recognizes it as an old acquaintance: he had once preached the gospel to the animal in the wilderness at its earnest request, and had baptized it; it is now showing its gratitude. A terrible storm ends the narrative; the hail kills the other beasts, and liberates Paul and the lion. In Philippi, Paul receives a letter from the Corinthians who are being disturbed by gnostic heretics, and who beg for confirmation of their faith. He sends them a reassuring answer—put together from fragments of genuine Pauline letters. By way of Miletus and Corinth he makes his

[1] *Acta Pauli et Theclae* in Lipsius-Bonnet 1,235–269. *Mart. Pauli ib.* 104–17. Carl Schmidt, *Acta Pauli*, 2nd edit., 1905. M. R. James, *op. cit.*, 270 ff.

journey to Rome, and the story is re-told about Peter's meeting the Lord on the way to His second crucifixion. Paul hires a shed in Rome and preaches, until finally Nero steps in and burns so many Christians that the people are sated. Paul himself is beheaded, but appears afterwards to Nero and threatens him with divine punishment, whereupon the latter liberates the remaining prisoners.

The book of the *Acts of Paul* was widely read and much discussed, and the correspondence with the Corinthians stood throughout the Middle Ages in an appendix to church Bibles. The miracle stories are not quite so rank as in the *Acts of Peter*; and the legend of Thecla, with the treasure of her virginity, and the ideal picture of her spiritual love for the Apostle, were extremely acceptable, and were worked out even further.[1] Her grave near Seleucia became an important holy place, and kept her fame constantly alive.[2] As is only rarely the case, we have some information about the author of these *Acts*. About A.D. 200, Tertullian[3] informed his readers that the book was composed by a presbyter of Asia Minor: the man had acknowledged his authorship and defended himself by pleading his love for Paul; nevertheless he had been deposed. It follows that, in the second half of the second century, such kinds of writing displeased the officials of the Church, but, amongst the ordinary members, they nevertheless enjoyed great acceptance.

The apocryphal books of Acts have been described as Christian romances, and the description is justified so long as their character as popular books is not forgotten. They make use of the same *motifs*, and aim at the same effects, as are well-known in the artificial romances of the Greek sophists; at the same time they make use of ideas and metaphors employed in those biographies of ancient prophets and miracle-workers which were written for a definite purpose and which are usually called aretalogies.[4] The proportions of the elements naturally vary. The *Acts of Peter* is really made up of miracle-stories of the rankest kind. The *Acts of Paul* is based on the

---

[1] *Acta* in Lipsius-B. 1, pp. 271 f.
[2] Delehaye, *Origines du culte des martyrs*, 2nd edit., 161 f.
[3] Tertullian, *de baptismo*, 17
[4] Cf. Rosa Söder, *Die apok. Apostel-geschichten und die romanhafte Literatur der Antike* (1932)

motif of journeyings typical of romances, but links this as far as possible to the records contained in the canonical book of Acts. Even the erotic element, which is only faintly echoed in the *Acts of Peter*, occurs much more definitely in the *Acts of Paul*, and passes from the negative attitude of condemnation into the positive attitude of spiritual love.

The *Acts of John* represents a third type.[1] Miracles are greatly increased: the Apostle frequently permits them to be performed by other persons,[2] and a test by means of poison is used as a normal procedure in the case of one transgressor. This man proves the genuineness of the poison in that he dies of it. The Apostle had previously taken the poison without hurt and after the successful test on the subject of the experiment, John now brings him back to life.[3] Side by side, there is the humorous popular story[4] of the way in which John, staying in an inn, turns all the bugs out of doors during the night; they wait obediently until morning breaks and the Apostle permits them to inhabit again their accustomed cracks in the bedstead. The second peculiarity of the *Acts of John* is its marked rhetorical character; it comes out in the narratives, but especially in the Apostle's numerous addresses and sermons.

The content is relatively simple. Domitian had been incited by the Jews against the Christians; John, who was highly revered by them, he exiled to Patmos, although Domitian held him in esteem on account of his virtue and miraculous power. There John saw the revelation which he wrote down. Set free under Trajan, he journeyed by way of Miletus back to Ephesus. Here he restored to life the strategos, Lycomedes, and his wife; he gathered all the old women of the city into the theatre, and healed them of their illnesses; by means of prayer he split the altar and temple of Artemis in two, whereupon the populace destroyed the remains of the temple. The story of Drusiana constitutes the climax, and it works out a *motif* typical of romances. A libertine digs into the grave of a lady who had died of heart trouble on account of his misdeeds; he attempts to reach the body which had been denied him while she was alive. But a snake protects the dead person, kills the wicked man's

---

[1] *Acta Joh.* in Lipsius-B. 2, I, 151–216. M. R. James, pp. 228 ff.
[2] *Op. cit.*, 24. 47. 83   [3] *Ibid.* 9–11   [4] *Ibid.* 60 f.

assistant, and roots the man himself to the spot. John arrives
with the husband, brings back the dead woman to life, and
converts the scoundrel; when the assistant is called back to life
he remains unrepentant, and so goes to the devil.

A theological section follows in which John explains both the
various forms of Jesus's appearances as Risen Lord, and also
His apparent body. In this connection he recites a hymn[1]
which, before being taken prisoner, the Master had sung to his
disciples while they danced round Him in a circle and responded "Amen". Then it records a last revelation of the Lord,
who did not really suffer on the Cross, but who, through the
gnostic mystery of the cross of light, had pointed the way to
knowledge of the redeeming logos and to a higher superhuman existence. The Apostle's own end is introduced by long
speeches and prayers, and a celebration of the Eucharist:
finally he lies down in the grave, and gives up the ghost with
rejoicing.

The three *Acts of the Apostles* mentioned thus far probably
date from *c.* A.D. 200, and consciously connect up with the
earlier tradition of the Church, even if they then proceed to
develop their material quite freely. But Christian people
did not limit their interest to the Apostles of whom genuine
information was to hand, but were concerned also with others
who were nothing but names, and regarded them as welcome
starting points for new fantasies. The *Acts of Andrew* has only
been preserved in fragments[2] but it applies the familiar methods
in delineating an Apostle of whom there was no historical
information. The fragments which can be understood at all
show an ascetic attitude towards marriage, and also contain
observations on the mystery of the cross.[3] The Apostle dies a
martyr's death in Patrae hanging on the cross, similarly to his
brother Peter.

The *Acts of Thomas* are the best preserved examples of these
popular writings which have no historical basis, but best
preserved because they enjoyed the widest circulation. They
originated in the atmosphere of Edessa the east-Syrian capital,

[1] *Acta Joh.* 94–6
[2] *Acta apost. apocr.*, ed. Lipsius-B. *Loc. sit.* pp. 38–45 and 1–37. M. R. James
op. cit., pp. 337 ff.
[3] *Passio Andreae*, chap. 5–10

and were originally in Syriac, but soon translated freely into Greek. They had a wide circle of readers in both languages, and were therefore subject to all sorts of changes. The basis of the narrative is the Apostle's missionary itinerary to India: in the first part, this thread is used for stringing together a number of adventures which conclude with the conversion of an eminent lady, Mygdonia; through her, Christianity enters the court of King Misdaios; and the description of all the resultant complications fills the second part of the *Acts*, and naturally concludes with the Apostle's martyrdom.

It contains the usual apparatus of miracles, but enriched by a few delightful traits. An envious dragon is compelled to suck back again the poison which he had squirted into his opponent,[1] and he dies as a consequence. The foal of an ass addresses a long speech to Thomas, asks him to mount the saddle, and, in response to the Apostle's question, declares itself to be a descendant of Balaam's ass, and related to the one on which Christ rode into Jerusalem.[2] Having rendered its service, the animal dies—similarly to the speaking dog in the *Acts of Peter*; that indeed is typical of such animal fables.[3] Shortly afterwards, a whole drove of wild asses come and show themselves ready to help, and they present the apostle with a span of animals for his waggon; the most gifted of them exorcizes daemons, exhorts Thomas to perform miracles, and itself preaches to the people.[4] There is also a miracle similar to that in the *Acts of John* where a dead person is raised through the instrumentality of an intermediary.[5] We are told what a dead person had seen in heaven, and a woman, restored to life, tells of her journey through hell.[6] Revelations in dreams are frequent everywhere, but here a dream is recorded which foretells the fate of the royal house, and which is an exact reproduction of an ancient Indian myth.[7] Closer examination shows that a multitude of allegorized, mythological motives shape the stories contained in these *Acts*, and also that the large numbers of speeches have been enriched by elements drawn from ideas rooted in a

[1] *Acta Thom.* 30–3   [2] *Ibid.* 39–40
[3] *Ibid.* 41. *Acta Petra* 12. Kerenyi, *Die groech.-orient. Roman-literatur* (1927), p. 255
[4] *Acta Thom.* 68–79   [5] *Supra*, p. 83. *Acta Thom.* 54   [6] *Ibid.* 22. 55–57
[7] *Ibid.* 91. G. Bornkamm, *Mythos u. Legende in den apokr. Thomasakten*, p. 61. This book contains further details on the gnostic character of the Acts

gnosticism which can be traced back with confidence to the
Syrian gnostic Bardesanes, and which provided not a little
material for the Manichean view of the universe. Many passages
can be described as direct quotations, because the author has
been more or less skilful in introducing into his context hymns
or prayers which he found already complete:[1] the celebrated
Hymn of the Pearl depicts Mani's mission mythologically,
and accordingly was incorporated subsequently into the *Acts*
which enjoyed a lasting popularity among the Manicheans.

The early Church possessed no *Acts of the Apostles* in addition
to those already discussed, and at an early date these were
brought together into a unified corpus, which passed as the
work of a certain Leukios Charinos, and of which in the ninth
century the patriarch Photios possessed a copy.[2] While they
were, of course, by different authors, they were written at times
not too widely separated from one another, and all arose in the
orient. What gives them an inner unity is not the general
romantic character, or the world of fable and miracle with
typical sketches and constantly repeated motives, but rather
the similarity of their conception of Christianity. The religion
preached by their apostles emphasizes continence above all
other virtues, and that indeed in the sense of a complete sexual
abstinence which condemns even conjugal intercourse as
sinful. Indeed even a reference to the possibility of the procreation of children is repudiated with outright asperity, indeed with contempt.[3] This attitude is not to be understood as
a romantic or mythical trait in a mystic heavenly eroticism, if
on occasion such motives undoubtedly play a part; rather it is
determined by an ascetic conception of Christianity such as
spread at an early date in the orient and, in its crassest forms,
required celibacy from all baptized persons. In the fourth
century, that was the ideal[4] in Syria. Alternatively, only the
ascetics were regarded as Christian in the full sense. At bottom
this was the view of the hermits and monks of the whole world

---

[1] *Acta Thom.* 6–7 Hymn of the Virgin of Light, 27.50 Epicleses, 108–13 the
Hymn of the Pearl (Syriac, *ZNW.*, 4, 273–309)

[2] *Photios cod.* 114: also Harnack, *Gesch. d. altchr. Lit.*, 1,116–123

[3] *Acta Thom.* 12

[4] Cf. Vol. 4, chap 6; Rev. 14: 4; cf. Aphrahat, *Homilies*, 7,20, p. 345. Parisot., cf. also
Hom. 6,3–4, pp. 256 ff. Parisot.; Burkitt, *Early Eastern Christianity*, pp. 136 ff., etc.

in ancient times, and their writings give unmistakable expression to this standpoint.

The second characteristic of all these *Acts* is their impregnation with gnostic ideas, as is obvious in every story, every speech, every prayer, and every revelation. In particular, Christ is depicted, not only as transformed into the miraculous and superhuman, but into the magical and ghostly. Christ is invisibly present,[1] sometimes bodily, sometimes without body;[2] He appears as a boy, grown man, old man,[3] as the Apostle's double,[4] actually visible then suddenly disappearing,[5] finally as revealing His nature in the form of a cross of light; as the divine logos who is simultaneously Father, Son, and Holy Spirit, and who in ultimate reality had never hung on the wooden cross.[6] All this breathes the spirit of gnosticism.

For these reasons, most of such books were formerly regarded by scholars as productions of a gnosticism outside of, and opposed to, the Church. It was felt, too, that they had come to us edited to a greater or less extent in a catholic sense. This opinion was supported by the existence of later redactions in which the offensive gnostic elements were, as a matter of fact, to a large extent wanting. No trace however has been found of the supposed gnostic original forms, in spite of the numerous new discoveries in recent decades; meanwhile other evidence has shown that it is impossible to draw a sharp line between church and gnosis. Hence it now seems justifiable to regard these books as valuable, popular testimonies to the penetration of gnostic ideas into orthodox churches. It was writings of this very kind which required to be adorned with the fanciful imagery and esoteric language of a superhuman prophecy, if they were to satisfy properly the curiosity which ranged beyond the customary literature provided by the Church, and which longed for secret information of a historical and theological nature. In a case like this, gnosticism acted as an inexhaustible spring, and provided, in a thousand, varicoloured pictures, the things for which hearts yearned. The tendency which comes plainly to the light of day in the

---

[1] *Acta Thom.* 34. 154 f. 165   [2] *Acta Joh.* 93   [3] *Ibid.* 87–92. *Acta Petri* 21
[4] *Acta Thom.* 11. 152 f. *Acta Pauli* 21   [5] *Acta Thom.* 34. 155
[6] *Acta Joh.* 98–101. *Acta Petri* 38

apocryphal gospels, and which might make the reader somewhat distrustful, was here in the happy situation of being able to play its part decked in the mantle of romantic confabulation.

Thus it comes about that all these *Acts* contain gnostic points of view and gnostic doctrines, and these are brought forward naïvely as if obvious, till it is easy to see how readily readers accepted this kind of literature. Here we see one of the means by which gnosticism, regarded as a whole, obtained influence in the churches of the second and third centuries: at the same time the writings themselves are proof of the extent to which gnosis had already been successful. For, at least in the case of the *Acts of Thomas*, it is possible to think of a gnostic sectary as the author: the other *Acts* can scarcely have been introduced into the Church from outside, but originated in the midst of congregations which felt themselves to be faithful members of the church catholic. This, however, plainly indicates the danger of which the early fathers had spoken so earnestly.

Later Judaism, instigated by the Book of Daniel, carried to a further stage, and practised very industriously, the writing of apocalyptic literature. The authors wrote under some name in high esteem, and dated their work back into a much earlier period. At times, they set out from personal experiences, and began with visions and revelations which they described and explained. Alternatively they simply presented holy authorities such as Enoch,[1] Moses, Baruch, or the Sibyls, and let them talk about everything which theological and political curiosity might wish to know in regard to the past, the present, and the future. Among the early Christians in the first period, the question as to the time and manner of setting up the Messianic kingdom was the subject of yearning enquiry, and the negative answer with which the Master refused to inform his disciples[2] gave no sufficient satisfaction to the Church. But the portents of the great event, graphic pictures of stress on earth and terrors in heaven, could be at least inferred from the Lord's last speeches as recorded in the Synoptic gospels.[3] Here the imagination of the prophets flamed up and attempted to

[1] Vol. 1, pp. 37 ff.   [2] Mark 13: 32 and parallels
[3] Mark 13: 5–37 = Matt. 24: 4–36 = Luke 21: 8–36

see in advance what they supposed to be the secrets of the End.

So far as we know, the first work of this kind was the Book of Revelation, sponsored in the Johannine circle. It is the work of quite a great artist who, seized by the Spirit, broke open the doors of eternity by the strength of his feelings. The material was drawn by him from the many coloured world of late-Jewish conceptions of the beyond, and enriched by mythical pictures belonging to ancient oriental and Hellenistic belief. He transformed it afresh, however, and grouped it till it had a sevenfold rhythm, which echoes ever and again, and issues in the tremendous finale of the last vision.

The exiled Apostle is living on Patmos: it is Sunday. Then the Lord calls to him, and he looks around and sees the Son of Man in heavenly glory. He falls prostrate and hears the words: "Fear not, I am the first and the last, and have the keys of death and Hades. Write the things which thou sawest, and the things which are, and the things which shall come to pass hereafter." The prophet has received his call. His first act is one of apostolic admonition. Seven letters are sent to the seven churches of Asia Minor, for the most part uttering warnings and threats, but heartfelt praise about two of them. That ends the prelude. Now the gates of heaven open, the seer mounts upwards, and beholds God on His throne surrounded by twenty-four elders and hosts of angels singing "Holy, Holy, Holy". There lies the book with seven seals, on the throne sits the Lamb, and, surrounded by the loud singing of hymns of jubilation, the Lamb solemnly breaks one seal after another.

The four apocalyptic horsemen now ride into the world; the earth quakes and the sun is darkened. The souls of the martyrs cry aloud for revenge, the angels of God seal the faithful who are to receive salvation. Then the seventh seal is broken: seven angels appear and blow on seven trumpets. A dreadful revelation follows on every blast. The seventh trumpet introduces heavenly visions, the Messiah is born and the dragon attacked. Michael flings the monster to the ground, but already hostile beasts are coming up out of the deep, and making mankind subject to themselves to the point of worship; secret signs and numbers contain the clue for understanding their nature.

And lo: the Lamb now stands triumphantly on Mount Zion surrounded by those faithful to him; angel voices proclaim that Babylon the Great is fallen, and that all idol worshippers shall suffer punishment. The sickle reaps God's bloody harvest. Seven basins of wrath are emptied over the earth, and once more Babylon's condemnation passes in front of the seer's eyes. A heavenly hallelujah pays homage to the King of kings and the Lord of lords, the devil is flung into the prison of the deep, and Christ rules with his own on this earth, for a thousand years.

Then once more hell opens its gates: the devil gets free and, with all the powers hostile to God, makes an attack on the Holy City. But fire falls from heaven and destroys the evil creatures, the devil and his own are flung into the pit of hell to be eternally tortured, and the dead rise. The Last Judgment begins, and each one is judged according to his works. That is the end. "And I saw a new heaven and a new earth: for the first heaven and the first earth are passed away and the sea is no more. And I saw the Holy City, new Jerusalem coming down out of heaven from God, made ready as a bride adorned for her husband." Now the seer comprehends all the magnificence and glory of the heavenly Jerusalem, and his tongue declares in happy jubilation: "And I John am he that heard and saw these things." He then falls down in worship: the heavenly tumult fades, and only disconnected utterances still sound in his ear. Thereupon he writes down what has been revealed to him, and he adjures every one who copies out this book of prophecy, as he values his salvation, to add nothing and subtract nothing. Then he concludes with the yearning sigh: "Yea, I come quickly. Amen: come, Lord Jesus."

Modern research agrees with the ancient church in ascribing the composition of this book to the reign of Domitian, and indeed towards the end of that reign; Domitian died in A.D. 96. The author makes use of earlier ideas and introduces them into his scheme, unaware that the incongruities would show up when modern exegetes examined it; our author was confident of the overpowering, total effect of his composition. Owing to the commanding authority of his personality even the old material shines in the new light of the Christian view of eternity.

This higher perspective transfigures also the hatred against the Roman empire, intended by the reference to Babylon, into a prophetic preaching of judgment by a prophet working with final and absolute standards.

We pass from the workshop of a creative artist into the modest little room of a humble hand-worker when we turn to the second apocalypse belonging to ancient Christianity. Shortly before the middle of the second century in Rome, Hermas, the brother of bishop Pius, wrote a work in three parts which is known by the title *The Shepherd*. It is impossible to determine with certainty to what extent it gives merely a literary form to actual experiences on the part of Hermas: ever and again, however, throughout the whole writing, it is clear that he depends upon elements derived from books, and the obvious attempt of the author to knit together the formless material, which is continually growing under his hands, fosters the impression in the reader that the author is not working independently, even where he asserts that he is giving his own matter. This book is an apocalypse, because it records visions and awaits the divine Judgment. The visions, however, are really allegories which have been artificially worked out while the writer was pen in hand; and the coming plagues, together with the Last Judgment, are not actually seen and depicted as in the case of John, but only worked out in order to serve the main purpose of the book.

The particular object of the whole is to preach repentance to Christendom, and, in continually changing similes, proclaims its teaching that a Christian who has fallen into serious sin has the privilege of again cleansing away his sins by remorse and penitence—but let it be noted carefully that it is only once after baptism: in this way a brief opportunity is still afforded the church. Those who take the prophet's words to heart will make use of this opportunity before it passes, and the Last Judgment begins. The purpose of the book, with its metaphors and its long-winded, moral observations, is to give the reader a deepened understanding of sin and of the true Christian way of life. The teachings are given in the first instance by a revered old lady, who personifies the Church, and by an angel in the form of a shepherd who is strikingly similar to the usual vehicle of revelation in Hellenistic mysticism.[1] Work on behalf of the church is twice symbolized[2] with the metaphor of building a tower, and the metaphor of the shepherd is repeated,[3] and then surrounded by rambling allegories of trees.[4] The parable of the two cities, only one of which can be the true Christian home,[5] reproduces a universal Christian viewpoint.

On the other hand the *Apocalypse of Peter*,[6] which belongs probably to the same period as Hermas, is a worthy representative of its class. Here the Lord addresses His disciples on the Mount of Olives, and, at their request, gives them the portents of His second advent, and of the end of the world. In doing so he makes much use of Synoptic passages, but greatly elaborates the ideas found there. A description of the Last Judgment and the punishment of sinners constitutes the bridge to a detailed description of Hell where the different kinds of wrongdoers are tortured with punishments corresponding to their earthly deeds. The righteous, however, enter the Elysian fields of Acherusia. The disciples ask to be permitted to see a righteous person from that life, and two of the blessed appear in their shining glory; thereupon heaven opens, and the whole splendour of paradise is unveiled to the apostles' eyes. Nevertheless, the author's imagination is able to give but little about heaven, whereas his visions of Hell are numerous and manifold, and compounded of all the images which the orient and Greece had long ago brought together.[7] This difference, it may be said, can also be clearly traced in Dante, the greatest of the successors of our author; but, if we compare the arid description of heaven in this writing of Peter's with the Johannine blessedness of the heavenly Jerusalem, we gain a strong impression of the great difference in the quality of these two works.

An apocalypse in the form of a revelation of the Lord has only lately come to light in the *Epistula Apostolorum*.[8] Here it is the Risen Lord who gathers his own round about himself, and instructs them in heavenly matters: his descent to earth, his

---

[1] Cf. R. Reitzenstein, *Poimandres* (1904)   [2] *Vis.* 3; *Sim.* 9
[3] *Vis.* 5; *Sim.* 6   [4] *Sim.* 2–4. 8; cf. also 5   [5] *Sim.* 1
[6] The entire tradition has been assembled by H. Weinel and Hennecke, *op. cit.*, 314–27
[7] A. Dieterich, *Nekyia* (1893)
[8] Carl Schmidt, *Gespräche Jesu* (*TU.* 43), 1919. H. Duensing, *Epistula Apostolorum*, 1925 (*Kl. Texte* 152). M. R. James, *op. cit.*, pp. 485 ff.

incarnation, his relation to the Father, the resurrection of the dead as well as the signs and sufferings of the final age, the missionary task of the disciples, and the duty of bold, admonitory preaching and faithful confession. On all hands we see that the author was concerned to bring out the New Testament bases of his discussions. But what he gives us over and above bears not only the well-known characteristics of orthodox church opinion, but is also enriched by gnostic ways of thought. On the one hand, admittedly, the bodily character of the Risen Lord is expressly asserted; but on the other hand the deity of the logos is fully equated with that of the Father. The Father is in the logos with His form, power, perfection, light, dimension, and voice.[1] When the logos descended to earth, he put on the wisdom and power of the Father, and in each heaven he clothed himself in the form of the angels domiciled there, so that he remained unknown. Consequently he appeared to the Virgin Mary as Gabriel, and then entered her body and became flesh.[2] On earth, Christ preached salvation, carried the preaching into the underworld, and enabled human flesh to become imperishable by taking it on Himself.[3] He freed mankind from the power of the archons, and brought man to heavenly peace.[4] At bottom, all these are good orthodox ideas although clothed in forms of gnostic origin.

The *Epistula* dates from the period c. A.D. 140 or A.D. 170,[5] and was probably written in Egypt. It is the earliest known example of apocalyptic writings which pretend to be based on speeches of the Risen Lord. This form of writing was frequent among the gnostics, and even in the third century gave rise to such a considerable work as the *Pistis Sophia*. We can readily understand that literature of this kind rapidly became suspect to the Church. But it was not rooted out, and universal human curiosity, which longs to see behind the curtain of the beyond, entered into an alliance with the gnostic type of speculation and, in one century after another, continually produced new apocalypses; these never lacked plenty of readers in spite of the opposition of the Church.

Christian epistolary literature was founded by the apostle

---

[1] *Epist. Apost.* 17 (28)   [2] *Ibid.* 13 f. (24 f.)   [3] *Ibid.* 21 (32)
[4] *Ibid.* 28 (39)   [5] *ZNW.* 20, 173–76

Paul, although he never for a moment thought of writing anything of a literary character. To him his letters were simply the means which served the purpose of his apostolic labours, and, had he been able to deal with everything orally, he would never have written a single line. When he requests the church at Colossæ[1] to read the letter which he had addressed to Laodicea, and to allow the Laodiceans to read the letter he had sent to themselves, he takes this course because it saves time, for he has no need to write the same thing twice. But because his powerful personality is very evident in these letters, they have become genuine literature of the highest kind, and were quickly recognized as such by the churches. The exchange of letters between Colossæ and Laodicea was surely not the first, nor did it remain the only, case.

At an early date the Apostle's letters began to be collected in Corinth, Ephesus, and Philippi;[2] and towards the end of the first century, when someone set about gathering all Paul's letters, copies of nine letters addressed to churches were available, together with that to Philemon. This collection formed the foundation of the extant corpus of letters. What could not be brought together at that time has been lost—this includes, e.g., two letters to the Corinthians, of which one was written before and the other after the canonical 1 Corinthians. Even in the early church, no one had further knowledge of any letter of Paul's outside the collection we possess. Meanwhile these had become widespread throughout the entire church and frequently copied. Even Ignatius and Polycarp were acquainted with them in the time of Trajan. At an early date, a definite order of the letters was established, based broadly on the purely outer principle of their length. The longest letter, i.e. that to the Romans, comes first, the shortest last; nevertheless letters addressed to the same church remain together. In the second century another principle of arrangement existed in which the letters to the Corinthians came first;[3] and Marcion made the attempt[4] of arranging them chronologically. We give this as a

[1] Col. 4: 16
[2] Cf. Dobschütz in *Die evang. Theol.*, 2 (1927), p. 9 Goodspeed, *Introduction to N.T.*, 1937, pp. 210 ff.
[3] *Handbuch* on *Röm.*, 4th edit., pp. 1–4
[4] Cf. Vol. 1, p. 255

deduction from various hints, for all the surviving manuscripts
have Romans at the head of the collection.

Even at this early date the collection contained an unauthen-
tic letter, viz. Ephesians. The *Pastoral Epistles* were soon added:
Polycarp quoted from them[1] and consequently he probably
found them in his Pauline codex. Our canon places them before
that to Philemon so as to give a group of letters to individuals
after those to churches. Probably about the middle of the second
century and somewhere in the east, perhaps in Egypt, the
Epistle to the Hebrews was then declared to be Pauline, and
accordingly introduced into the collection. Its varied situation
in the manuscripts shows even to-day that it was only introduced at a later period: sometimes it comes at the end of the
entire corpus, sometimes after the letters to the churches, sometimes in their midst before or after the letters to the Corinthians,
or between Colossians and Galatians. As early a person as a
teacher of Clement of Alexandria[2] described it as a Pauline
letter, but was already greatly puzzled by the difficulties which
then arose. This cannot have been long after A.D. 150. But the
copies of the earlier Pauline corpus were by that time so widely
dispersed throughout the entire Church that only rarely was
Hebrews added. In the east it was fairly fortunate, but the west
declined Hebrews as non-Pauline, and was only willing to
accept it in the fourth century in consequence of theological
arguments conditioned by ecclesiastical policy.

As we have already said, the Pauline letters became the
model of all the other early Christian epistolary literature.
Because Paul's letters were to be found in all the churches of
Christendom, it came to be thought that they were written with
that object; and his example was imitated by others, who then
wrote tractates intended for the entire church, and gave them
conventional titles: they are called the letters of James, Peter,
Jude and Barnabas, or, as in the case of 1 John and Hebrews,
they preserved, at least to some extent, the form of a letter.
The genuine ancient Christian letters were written in imitation
of Paul; we have already discussed the letter written by Clement
of Rome, the seven by Ignatius, and Polycarp's covering letter.
Other didactic and admonitory letters occur as interpolations

---

[1] *Pol. Epist.* 4,1. 5,2. 9,2. 11,4   [2] Eus., *H.E.*, 6,14,4

in larger works: the seven letters of the Apocalypse, the correspondence with Corinth in the *Acts of Paul*,[1] the exchange of letters between Clement and James at the beginning of the *Clementine Homilies*. Worthless fabrications include the correspondence between Paul and Seneca, which was produced probably in the fourth century,[2] as well as the apocryphal letter to Laodicea[3] which was intended to fill the place of the Pauline letter mentioned in Col. 4: 16. We have already dealt with the imaginary *Letter of the Apostles* which contains an apocalypse.[4]

The whole of this voluminous literature was intended directly or indirectly to give the Church authoritative instruction, and it was largely successful in this object. But the richer the theological speculation and the creative power of imagination, the stronger became the contradictions within this type of literature, and hence also the antitheses between the new teachings and the long-familiar traditions of the Church. The fertile source of new writings was the spirit of gnosis, and we have already seen how strongly it penetrated into orthodox communities. The Church was compelled to search for a trustworthy safeguard, and she found it in limiting the recognized and authoritative teaching to what was apostolic. The Apostles were the last and also the only authorities: so ran the canonical principle which expressed the Church's belief as to the nature of their essence. In the earliest period, until the middle of the second century, "The Lord" was quoted as the highest authority. This referred, of course, to what He had said while on earth. The speaker or writer did not usually say whence he derived the saying of "the Lord", nor at bottom was that fact of importance as long as the validity of the quotation was not subject to doubt. It was assumed, without question, that the quotation had come from the usual sources, and, if a source was an oral tradition, it was not felt to be less trustworthy on that account. This naïve condition of affairs could not be maintained intact when the influence of gnosticism made itself felt. Sayings of Jesus, which had a strange sound, and were full

---

[1] *Supra*, p. 82   [2] Jerome, *vir. inl.*, 12
[3] Published by Harnack, *Kl. Texte*, 12 cf. M. R. James, *op. cit.*, pp. 478
[4] *Supra*, p. 92

of unusual doctrines, began to be put on His lips, as in the new gospels which we have already discussed. It was not the fact that they were new that made the Church mistrustful—even Matthew and Luke were new once on a day, yet without offence—but that they recorded new teachings and unaccustomed theology as spoken by Jesus.

Even the gospel of John had met with opponents in Asia Minor, to whom its logos doctrine was a subject of suspicion, and who rejected it on account of its inconsistencies with the record contained in the Synoptic gospels:[1] nevertheless John's gospel maintained its place. When now the gnostic gospels and apocalypses came forward and made the same claims, the Church sought an unambiguous criterion, and found it in the requirement of apostolic authorship. The Apostles alone were the unexceptionable vehicles of the tradition of the Lord, and as a consequence only those gospels which were composed by Apostles held good in the Church. In this way, the gospels of Matthew and of John assumed canonical authority, and the objection felt in Asia Minor against the Fourth Gospel, on account of its new teachings, was significantly enough combined with the assertion that it was not by John the apostle, but by Cerinthus a heretic.[2] In the case of Mark and Luke, refuge was taken in the declaration that these two persons were disciples of apostles, and accordingly that the former wrote under Peter's authority and the latter under Paul's.[3] Thereby these four books were really canonized, for the reference to their apostolic authority, which can only appear to us as a reminder of sound historical bases, had the deeper meaning that this particular tradition of Jesus—and this alone—had been established and guaranteed by the Holy Spirit working authoritatively in the Church.

The Apostles were recognized in the Church as the only unconditionally legitimate vehicles of the spirit. Everything else which claimed to be the working of the spirit was tested by their messages. In this way their writings were regarded as inspired by the spirit, and were, therefore, of final, divine

[1] Epiph., *Haer.*, 51,3–4 *et seq.*   [2] *Ibid.* 51,3,6
[3] Justin, *Dial.*, 103,8 *Iren.* 3,1,1 f. *Fragm. Murat.* 1–34, and *Mon. Prolog.* (*Kl. Texte* 1, 2nd edit., p. 5, 12–16)

authority. They came to be regarded as equal in origin to the documents of the Old Testament, or, to speak more accurately, as a necessary complement at its side and bringing it to a completion; they, too, were "Holy Scripture". A New Testament came to stand alongside the Old Testament, and it became customary to appeal to it by using the form of words, "it is written", in a way similar to that which, at an earlier date, had been applied only to the Old Testament. And now, when the words of Jesus were quoted, it was not as if they had merely been spoken in the past, but rather in the present: "The Lord says", for He now spoke out of the Sacred Books as if always present to His Church. The process by which the gospels became canonical may be clearly observed in its preliminary stages in Justin[1] shortly after A.D. 150, and it was completed at the time of Irenæus,[2] i.e. a generation later.

It must be admitted that occasionally one detects a certain amount of hesitation. The church at Rhossos in Syria made use of the *Gospel of Peter*,[3] and Serapion the bishop of Antioch had allowed himself to be committed by the presence of the apostolic name to recognize this custom. In so doing, he acted correctly in accordance with the principle of apostolic authority. But when he examined the text more closely, and detected docetic heresy, he forbade the book. In other words, he tested the genuineness of the apostolic title by comparing the teaching of the book with orthodox doctrine, and, since he discovered crucial differences, he declared—conformably to the facts—that the name was spurious and that the authority founded upon it was void. The Church dealt in the same way with the remaining pseudo-apostolic gospels, and thus came to the generally accepted view that there were not more than four gospels, and indeed could not be more—a fact which Irenæus had already demonstrated theoretically and symbolically.[4]

The fact of there being four gospels, however, had its disadvantages. As far as the Church was concerned, there was only *one* gospel, only one message of God to mankind, and the question arose as to why it was divided up among four books. Further, why were there so many repetitions, and also

---

[1] Justin, *Dial.*, 49. 100. 101. 104–07   [2] *Iren.* 3,11,8. 2,22,3. 2,30,2
[3] Eus., *H.E.*, 6,12,2–6   [4] *Iren.* 3,11,8

incompatibilities and apparent contradictions, in the various gospels? Surely the ideal state of affairs would be *one* gospel in *one* book. That was perhaps the case in the earliest period when the Synoptic gospels were confined, each to different regions, some using one gospel and some another. Marcion had permitted only one gospel book to be used in his church. About A.D. 180 two men commenced a practice which the Church employs to-day, whenever popular preachers attempt to revitalize religion by teaching "Bible history"; out of the four records, they make a single text. The first to do this was bishop Theophilus of Antioch; his work has disappeared without trace.[1] On the other hand, the second enjoyed great success: he was Tatian, a pupil of Justin. His gospel harmony "of the Four", known as the *Diatessaron*, arranges sections of all four gospels as a continuous gospel story; this book was accepted in the Syrian church for official use even in divine worship, and only in the course of the fifth century[2] was it displaced by the canonical four gospels. Tatian's work was in common use elsewhere for a long time afterwards, and the surviving translations suggest that Romans as well as Teutons learned the gospel from it; even an Arabic edition has survived. The original has disappeared, and it is a question whether it was first put together in Greek or Syriac: quite lately a Greek fragment has been excavated on the Euphrates.[3]

Nevertheless the Church on the whole refused to accept any such abbreviation of the gospel texts. The struggle against the arbitrariness of Marcion and gnosticism had shown her the value of a tradition founded on a good historical basis, a tradition which was now respected and guarded and recognized as the written word of God, and as something which could not be arbitrarily made shorter. The four gospels were thus kept intact. Nevertheless it is worth while to make the point that the Christians never came to use the small comb after the fashion of the Jewish Masoretes in regard to the Talmud. With all their respect for the word of God, the copyists, even in the later centuries, did

[1] Jerome, *Epist.*, 121,6,15
[2] Theodoret, *Haer. fab.*, 1,20 (4,312 Schulze) Burkitt, *Evangelion da mepharreshe*, 2,173 ff.
[3] Excavation in Dura: C. H. Kraeling, *A Greek Fragment of Tatian's Diatessaron* (*Studies and Documents III*), 1935

not hesitate to "correct" the text here and there in detail, by harmonizings, or by accepting variants, from other manuscripts. The consequence was that a whole forest of variant readings, additions, and omissions came to stand side by side. The same fate overtook the manuscripts of translations of the New Testament, and, as a result, it is the textual criticism of the Sacred Scriptures which offer the most difficult problems in this department of study. Only in Syria were the codices of the official translation of the Bible copied out with an obviously religious care which went far beyond the usual, and which therefore protected the text from distortions.

In regard to their authority as divine revelation, Marcion was the first to put the Pauline letters on the same level as the gospels,[1] a result which necessarily followed from his theology. The orthodox church indeed prized these letters from the beginning; as soon as the Apostles came to be regarded as the unique vehicles of revelation, in the manner described above, their letters had to be regarded as the inspired pronouncements of the Holy Spirit, and so were added to the germ of the New Testament. The process can be traced in the works of the writers who, towards the end of the second century, placed the apostolic letters side by side with the gospels,[2] and then gradually came to quote them with the solemn formula of "Scripture";[3] but this use of language was only gradually adopted. The Pauline corpus constituted the nucleus of the collection of apostolic letters, and Marcion had no other such writings in his canon. The ancient Syrian church also limited its canonical epistles to Paul's.[4]

In the course of the fourth century, the Syrian Fathers recognized the three large, general epistles: James, 1 Peter, 1 John, and the official Bible of the Syrian churches, known as the *Peshitto*, included them, c. A.D. 400 in the New Testament. This "canon of three epistles" held good also in the sphere of the church of Antioch, and the great preachers and theologians who belonged to this province or lived under its influence recognized no other general epistles. In the west it is possible

[1] Cf. Vol. 1, p. 256
[2] *Iren.* 1,3,6 (1,31 Harvey); *Acts* as "Scripture" 3,12,5. 9. (2,57,65 Harvey)
[3] Clem., *Strom.*, 1,87,7 f. 7,84,2 f.; cf. 7,95,3   [4] W. Bauer, *Apost. der Syrer*, 34

to trace an evolution which begins with the two letters, viz.
1 Peter and 1 John, already known to Polycarp of Smyrna
c. A.D. 115; James is never mentioned. These two letters constitute
the foundation to which, after the second century drew to a
close, the four shorter general epistles, 2 Peter, 2 and 3 John,
and Jude, were joined in all possible orders; the Latin lists of the
canon still extant reveal graphically the varied character of the
church's judgments about this part of the New Testament.

The Alexandrian church showed forth her connection with
Rome in the fact that even she made use of the western canon:
Clement of Alexandria quoted 1 Peter, 1 and 2 John, and Jude,
and, in the *Hypotyposes*, wrote a consecutive commentary on
these documents.[1] Alexandria, however, was hospitable. Here
the epistle of *Barnabas* was reckoned in this group,[2] and its
author was called an apostle;[3] even the epistle of Clement of
Rome was regarded as apostolic,[4] and the *Didache* was quoted
as Holy Scripture.[5] We catch glimpses of the same attitude here
and there even in the writings of Origen who, it should be
remembered, was an expert literary critic. The same attitude,
indeed, has left its traces in the great Bible codices which have
come down to us from the fifth century. Both the Codex
Sinaiticus and the Alexandrinus place an appendix at the end
of the New Testament, in which the former includes *Barnabas*
and the *Shepherd of Hermas*, whereas the latter includes the two
epistles of Clement of Rome. This fact shows how strongly
Christians in Egypt felt it was necessary to include these
writings in their Bibles.

If we now combine the canon of all the epistles as recognized
in the west with the canon of Antioch, we get a canon of seven
General Epistles, opening with James, followed by 1 and 2
Peter, 1 and 2 and 3 John, and Jude. The sequence was definite
in the east, a fact which shows that the old canon of three
epistles formed the basis; whereas in the west the order varied,
the letters of Peter, the apostle of Rome, often being first.
We find this canon of seven epistles, c. A.D. 320, in Eusebius of
Cæsarea, and it spread farther in the course of the fourth
century: it reached Egypt and the west, and only then, carried

---

[1] Clem. *Alex.*, ed. Stählin, 3,203–215   [2] Eus., *H.E.*, 6,14,1
[3] Clem., *Strom.*, 2,31,2. 2,35,5   [4] *Ibid.* 4,105,1   [5] *Ibid.* 1,100,4

on the tide of the Egyptian church policy, was it victorious in the east along with the Nicene Creed.

The Book of Acts took part in this process and was elevated to the canon quietly and as of natural right: it was indeed the continuation of Luke's gospel, and at the same time the necessary complement to the apostolic letters. It was these two facts which made up for the lack of apostolic authenticity, and silenced any questions. We can understand, however, that in the earlier period this book was not held to be of the same authority as the other writings of the New Testament, and was seldom quoted: as late as the beginning of the fifth century it was practically unknown even to wide circles of the church in the capital city of Constantinople.[1] We cannot be quite sure that it was known in Africa, *c.* A.D. 200,[2] but it was usually regarded as part of the canon at this time; indeed the ancient Syrian church[3] placed it on the same footing as the Pauline letters.

The canonical character of the Apocalypses, on the other hand, was warmly disputed. As revelations given by the spirit these writings claimed the highest authority for themselves without more ado. The Revelation of John explicitly curses anyone who adds or deletes a single word. Similarly, the *Shepherd of Hermas* and the *Apocalypse of Peter* insisted on being heard, and wide circles in the church granted their request. In particular *Hermas* was much read in the west towards the end of the second century, and from Rome it reached Egypt where it maintained its place longest of all. In Rome it was thrust into the background as soon as the canon began to be defined[4] on the basis of the apostolic principle. After the third century, it was still occasionally esteemed for private reading, whereas in Egypt it was held in high respect until the fifth century, and prized as a valuable appendix to the New Testament. The *Apocalypse of Peter* was regarded as canonical by a Roman critic,[5] *c.* A.D. 200, on account of its apostolic name, but he added the note that "Many of our people are not willing that it should be read

---

[1] Joh. Chrys., *Hom.*, 1,1. *Act. Apost.* (9,1 Montf.) of the year 401
[2] Tert., *De Praescr.*, 22
[3] *Doctrina Addaei*, p. 46, edited Phillips. Zahn, *Gesch. d. neut. Kanons*, 1,1,373
[4] *Fragm. Murat*, lines 73–80   [5] *Op. cit.*, lines 71–73

aloud in church". Hence in the west it did not attain honourable rank, although it enjoyed respect in Egypt, where Clement expounded it in the *Hypotyposes*; in the fifth century, in isolated towns of Palestine, it was still read aloud in the churches on Good Friday,[1] a practice which, at this period, was really quite a rarity.

The Revelation of John quickly came to its own in the second century. Soon after A.D. 150, it was to be found in Rome,[2] a little later in Gaul, Africa, and Egypt, and thereafter its worthiness and apostolic authority were firmly rooted in the west, and on the Nile. By the nature of the case, it was also acknowledged and esteemed at an early date in the east.[3] But the same circles which repudiated the Fourth Gospel also set aside the Book of Revelation, and disputed its apostolic authorship; distrust towards all new prophecies had come to be strongly felt in the struggle with the Montanists, which we have still to describe, and operated also against this book of prophecy.[4] In the third century, the Book of Revelation was attacked by officials of the Church in Egypt: Dionysios bishop of Alexandria was struggling, *c.* A.D. 250, against crass chiliasts who looked forward to a fool's paradise enduring for a thousand years after the end of the world, and who supported this expectation by Rev. 20. In a polemic against Nepos, bishop of Arsinoë, as the leader of this movement, Dionysios subjected Revelation to a sharp criticism, and, while fully recognizing its spiritual character, denied its apostolic authorship.[5] This attitude on the part of the bishop was learned, based on sound theology, and taken up against a book still included in the Bibles of his church, where it long remained. On the other hand, Antioch and the Syrian church had not accepted Revelation, and we find the same standpoint in Palestine[6] and the hinterland of Asia Minor.[7] Even here, however, the progress of the policy which the Egyptian church carried through after Nicea

---

[1] *Sozomenus* 7,19,9   [2] Justin, *Dial.*, 81,4
[3] Presbyter in *Iren.* 5,30,1.; cf. 33,3. and Papias in Eus. 3,39,12. Theophilus in Eus. 4,24. Apollonius in Eus. 5,18,14. Melito of Sardis in Eus. 4,26,2
[4] Epiph., *Hær.*, 51,33. cf. Iren. 3,11,9; Caius in Eus. 3,28,2
[5] Eus. 7,25. *Dionys. Alex.*, edited Feltoe, p. 116 ff.
[6] Jerome in *Anecdota Maredsolana* 3,2 (1897), p. 5 f. Cyril of Jerus., *Catech.*, 4,36
[7] Gregory Naz., *Carm. Lib.*, 1, section 1, no. 12 (2,260 Ben.); cf. *ibid.* 2, section 2, no. 8, 289 ff. (2,1104 Ben.). Amphilocius of Iconium in Zahn, *op. cit.*, 2,1, p. 217

appears to have influenced the canon towards the end of the fourth century, and so to have been of advantage to Revelation, yet by no means with the same success as in the case of the seven General Epistles. The Byzantine church always regarded the book with much hesitation, and expressedly sanctioned an ambiguous verdict even at the council of Constantinople[1] in A.D. 692.

It was inevitable that a canon of the New Testament should be formed out of early Christian literature as soon as its documents were regarded as containing revelations of the Holy Spirit. This point of view was implied in the early Christian conception of the spirit; when the operations of the spirit were unbounded, so, likewise, were the possibilities of producing new writings of an authoritative character. About the middle of the second century, and even later, a New Testament was coming into being which was continually being enlarged, and gnosticism provided tools of trade appropriate to the work in hand. The church then recognized the danger that was threatening her, and called a halt to the process. The principle of apostolic authorship meant that the time limit had already been passed, and this enabled it to break the authority of the free, prophetic spirit. What took place in the sphere of church constitution was paralleled in that of literature: the Apostles became the guarantors both of episcopal authority and of the books of the New Testament—and the same thing was to happen in regard to doctrinal formulas. The foundation of the church catholic had been firmly laid.

---

[1] *Conc. Trull, can.* 2 (6,1139 Labbe)

Chapter Four

THEOLOGY AND THE RULE OF FAITH

THE RELIGIOUS ADHERENTS OF THE GREEK MYSTERIES HAD taken a certain delight in working out ritual formulas and pronouncements which had an esoteric ring, and in which the experience of the mystic, or some fundamental truth of the religion, was expressed in a manner intelligible only to an initiated person;[1] it was a way of formulating a liturgical creed of a private sort. Side by side with this, the populace sometimes used a confession of the godhead in the form of an acclamation, an address which was constantly repeated rhythmically by the people crying in chorus. Some such scene is depicted graphically in Acts 19: 34: the people of Ephesus protested against Paul's missionary preaching, "and all with one voice about the space of two hours cried out, Great is Diana of the Ephesians." A ruler's divinity was acclaimed in the same way when he entered a city.[2] So also Sarapis[3] was greeted with the formula "There is only one Zeus-Sarapis", and, in the same form, the moon or the sun was worshipped as "the one god in heaven".[4] Indeed such acclamations by masses of the people are incidentally described as an enthusiasm induced by a divine spirit.[5]

The primitive church[6] also united in the confession "Jesus is Lord", which was made by the congregation all speaking in unison when they were seized by ecstasy. This action was a counterpart of the patriotic confession that the "Emperor is Lord", a confession made in the course of the imperial cultus.[7] Amongst the pagan people of eastern cities, the confession was shouted in address to the "one Zeus-Sarapis", and was a familiar sound; similarly Paul expressed the Christian antithesis to the pagan polytheistic faith in the sentence[8] "Yet to us there

---

[1] Examples in A. Dieterich, *Mitrasliturgie*, pp. 213–19; cf. Firmicus Maternus, *de errore prof. relig.*, c. 21–26

[2] Athenæus 5, p. 213 in E. Peterson, *Heis Theos*, 141 ff.; cf. 270 ff.

[3] O. Weinreich, *Neue Urkunden zur Sarapis-religion* (1919), 24–30

[4] Peterson, *op. cit.*, 260–268   [5] *Dio Cassius* 75,4,5 f.

[6] 1 Cor. 12: 3; cf. Rom. 10: 9   [7] *Mart. Pol.* 8,2   [8] 1 Cor. 8: 6

is one God, the Father, of whom are all things, and we unto Him; and one Lord, Jesus Christ, to whom are all things, and we through Him". These, in themselves, were genuine beginnings of the formulation of a Christian creed, and they were not isolated. At baptism, the initiate confessed his faith in the presence of the one who administered the baptism, and of the congregation. But the church itself put into formal language what it understood as the meaning of the death and resurrection of the Lord, i.e. its faith in His divine origin and His glorious second coming; these formulas occasionally took on a hymn-like sound. It is no accident that the much-used, Old Testament word for "confess" also conveys the sense of "extol", and the prayer of thanks, when the Eucharist was celebrated, was frequently transformed into a solemn confession of God's saving act done on behalf of Christian believers in Him.

The starting-point of the evolution of every creed is the confession of Jesus as Messiah, a confession which is expressed when He is given the very title of Christ,[1] and is accordingly named "Jesus Christ". This formula, however, quickly lost its original force and significance when it was transferred to Greek soil, and "Christ" hardly meant more, even to the readers of Paul's letters, than the surname of Jesus. Instead, two other formulas[2] came into the foreground: Jesus is "the Lord" and the "Son of God", various additions being made at an early date to these basic assertions. When the formula was produced: "Jesus Christ, the Son of God is the Saviour", the initials of the five words of this creed in Greek produced the Greek word *Ichthys*, i.e. "fish", and therefore, probably at a very early date, a fish was chosen as a graphic symbol of Christian faith. No painted examples and no *graffiti* have survived from earlier than the third century, but the symbol is quite common in writers *c*. A.D. 200,[3] and consequently was probably an ancient tradition. Indeed it was extended, and the mystic letters were combined with a T, which reproduced the form of a cross,[4]

---

[1] Matt. 27: 17, 22; John 1: 41; Acts 9: 22; 1 John 5: 1

[2] "Lord": 1 Cor 12: 3; Rom. 10: 9; "Son of God": 1 John 4: 15; cf. 5: 5, 10; Heb. 4: 14. Acts 8: 37 as a baptismal creed.

[3] Tert., *de bapt.*, 1, perhaps also Clem., *Paed.*, 3,59,2. Origen, *Commentary on Mt.* tom. 13,10 (3,230 Lom.);'Inscription of Aberkios (in Dölger, *Ichthys*, 2,457. 486–490) with the acrostic

[4] *ZNW*. 22,263. *Or. Sib.* 8,217–250

and thus produced the creed, "Jesus Christ, the Son of God, the crucified Saviour".

Side by side with these private formularies, there was, from the first, an evolution of expressions of faith which took place quite in the open. Paul himself, at the beginning of Romans, formulated the gospel of God as the message of "His Son, who was born of the seed of David according to the flesh, who was declared to be the Son of God with power, according to the spirit of holiness, by the Resurrection from the dead; even Jesus Christ our Lord." Here he depicts the secret of the person of Jesus from the standpoint of his sonship to David and to God; but in another passage he describes the work of redemption as a process of humiliation and exaltation: "Christ Jesus who, being in the form of God counted it not a prize to be on an equality with God, but emptied himself, taking the form of a servant, being made in the likeness of man; and being found in fashion as a man, he humbled himself, becoming obedient even unto death, yea, the death of the cross. Wherefore also God highly exalted Him and gave unto him the name which is above every name; that in the name of Jesus every knee should bow, of things in heaven and things on earth and things under the earth, and that every tongue should confess that Jesus Christ is Lord, to the glory of God the Father." Both these expressions of faith in Christ have a formal character,[1] the first being conceived more didactically, the second being modelled similarly to a hymn; and we meet with both types again in the further history of the Church. The first was frequent in the course of instruction intended for catechumens, the second bore a liturgical character, and was employed especially in working out the form of eucharistic prayer used at the Lord's Supper, when the assembled church expressed its thanks, through the lips of the priest, for Christ's incarnation and act of redemption.

It is not improbable that we ought to regard the numerous and varied formulations of faith in early Christian literature as echoes of a custom in active use in the churches in their teaching and liturgy, and that we ought to value them accordingly. The custom continued to be quite active, as is proved by

[1] Rom. 1: 3 f.; Phil. 2: 5-11

the many new forms with which it expressed both the whole and the details of the gospel of Christ. In addition to the confessions of faith which we have already mentioned, Paul added the early church's tradition of the Resurrection; he regarded this tradition as one of the principal elements of instruction about Christ, and enriched it out of his own knowledge.[1] In the writings subsequent to Paul, we can see the confession of Christ developing ever richer forms. To the simple expressions of the earliest period there were added the further clauses: birth from the Virgin Mary and the Holy Spirit,[2] genuine humanity with eating and drinking,[3] baptism by John,[4] suffering under Pontius Pilate,[5] preaching in hell and ascent to heaven,[6] sitting at the right hand of God,[7] also the Second Advent and the judgment of the living and the dead.[8]

We see, then, that all the doctrinal articles to be found in the Apostles' Creed appear about the end of the first century in the formularies of the Church, giving them fullness and an impressive definiteness. They were evolved, however, because the Church felt a need for formulating its belief, and not because some special form of attack had to be met. But Ignatius emphasizes the fact that Christ was truly born, truly persecuted, truly crucified, and he adds that Christ ate and drank; here we can say with confidence that Ignatius is repudiating docetic views which denied altogether Christ's genuine humanity.[9] Other confessions of Christ have survived from the following period, and their connection with the earliest pronouncements is very plain.[10] The most important is contained in the earliest surviving eucharistic prayer, which the liturgy of Hippolytus gives as the introduction to the words of institution at the Lord's Supper: it shows what place, and, in all probability, what a crucial place, in the life of the church was occupied by the confession of Christ properly so-called.[11]

Contemporaneously with this confession, a form arose which contained two parts and expressed the indivisible unity of

---

[1] 1 Cor. 15,3–8   [2] Ign., *Eph.*, 18,2. *Smyr.* 1,1   [3] Ign., *Trall.*, 9
[4] Ign., *Eph.*, 18,2. *Smyr.* 1,1   [5] Ign., *Trall.*, 9. *Magn.* 11. *Smyr.* 1,2; cf. 1 Tim. 3: 16.
[6] 1 Pet. 3: 19, 22 in the confession 3: 18–22; cf. 1 Tim. 3: 16   [7] 1 Pet. 3: 22
[8] 2 Tim. 4: 1   [9] Cf. Vol. 1, pp. 245 f.
[10] *Didascalia* 6,23,8; *Const. Apost.* 7,36,6; Justin, *Dial.*, 85, 132; cf. *ZNW.* 22,266 f.
[11] *Infra*, pp. 165 f. gives the text

faith in God and in Christ. As against the polytheism of pagan belief, Paul expressed with perfect explicitness what it was that a Christian confessed: "One God, the Father, of whom are all things, and we unto him; and one Lord, Jesus Christ, through whom are all things, and we through him."[1] Such two-fold forms in two sentences recur continually in the early period, in the Pastoral Epistles, in Irenæus, and in the Acts of the Martyrs.[2] The confession which Justin made before his judges ran: "We worship the God of the Christians, the one God, whom we hold to be the original creator of the entire world, of things visible and invisible; and the Lord Jesus Christ the servant of God who was predicted by the prophets as the future prophet of salvation for mankind and as a teacher of noble knowledge." In Smyrna c. A.D. 200, a theological conflict broke out with Noëtos, and the presbyters of the church expressed their faith in the following manner:[3] "We also know in truth one God; we know Christ, we know the Son, suffering as He suffered, dying as He died, and risen on the third day, and abiding at the right hand of the Father, and coming to judge the living and the dead. And in saying this we say what has been handed down to us."

The dominant form, however, had become the threefold confession of Father, Son, and Spirit. Even the church at Corinth in Paul's time was acquainted with the three-fold formula, as is proved by the concluding greeting of 2 Corinthians, and Matthew's gospel gives it a liturgical form when prescribing baptism in the name of the Father, and of the Son, and of the Holy Ghost.[4] In the course of centuries, this root gave rise to the innumerable multitude of trinitarian creeds. The basis could be extended in a two-fold manner: either by giving greater detail to the separate parts, or by adding new parts. Both methods were employed, and also both were combined. At the end of the first century Clement of Rome wrote:[5] "Have we not one God and one Christ and one Spirit of grace which has been poured out upon us, and one calling in

---

[1] I Cor. 8: 6
[2] I Tim. 6: 13; 2 Tim. 4: I. *Pol. Phil.* 2. *Iren.* 3,1,2. 3,4,1. 3,16,6. *Acta Justin* 2,5. *Mart. des Hl. Schapur*, in Braun, *Ausgw. Akten Pers. Märtyrer*, p. 2.
[3] Hippolytus, *Contra Noëtum I*   [4] 2 Cor. 13: 13; Matt. 28: 19
[5] I Clem. 46: 6

Christ?" In the second century a certain writer[1] regarded the five loaves at the feeding of the 5,000 as a symbol of the five-fold Christian faith "in the Ruler of the entire world and in Jesus Christ and in the Holy Spirit, and in the holy Church, and in forgiveness of sins". In this case, the trinitarian confession has been expanded by additions until it is a formula of five parts. About the middle of the second century, Justin Martyr frequently mentions a baptismal confession which may well have been expressed in the following words:[2] "I believe in God the Father and Lord of all, and in our Saviour Jesus Christ, who was crucified under Pontius Pilate, and in the Holy Spirit who prophesied through the prophets." In this case, the three-fold form has been preserved although each part has been expanded by additional pronouncements, and this method of extension was the one of which the most use was made during the whole evolution of the creeds.

A whole series of detailed confessions of this kind is to be found in Irenæus towards the end of the second century,[3] in Tertullian[4] c. A.D. 200, and his contemporary, Hippolytus of Rome;[5] it is as plain as the day that they were particularly given to extending the second article, and of doing so by transferring here, more or less completely, the early and, originally, independent[6] confession of Christ. All this can be studied most illuminatingly in Rome. In this city there was an early trinitarian confession, with each article in three parts, and thus with nine parts altogether; it spread to Egypt, and has survived there in numerous sources. It ran:

> I believe in God, the Father, the Almighty;
> And in Jesus Christ, his only begotten Son, our Lord,
> And in the Holy Ghost, the holy church, the resurrection of
>   the flesh.

This formula has been given three separate and distinct clauses; a confession of Christ was soon introduced into the second article at the same time as the third was extended by

[1] *Epist. Apost.* 5 (16)
[2] Justin, *Apol.*, 13,3. 61,3. 10. 13. Hahn, *Bibl. d. Symbole*, 3rd edit., pp. 4 f.; cf. *ZNW*. 21,31 f.
[3] Hahn, *op. cit.*, pp. 6–8. *ZNW*. 22,272 f. 26,93 f.
[4] Hahn, *op. cit.*, pp. 9–11; cf. *ZNW*. 21,25–27
[5] *ZNW*. 26,76–83   [6] *Supra*, pp. 105 ff.

introducing the clause on the forgiveness of sins. The result is what is known as the early Roman creed, which lies at the basis of all the western creeds, and therefore also of our Apostles' Creed:

> I believe in God the Father Almighty;
> And in Jesus Christ his only begotten Son, our Lord,
>> Who was born of the Holy Ghost, and the Virgin Mary,
>> Who was crucified under Pontius Pilate and buried:
>>> on the third day he rose from the dead,
>>> ascended into heaven,
>>> sat down at the right hand of the Father;
>>> from whence he will come to judge the living and
>>> the dead;
> And in the Holy Ghost, the holy church, the forgiveness
> of sins, the resurrection of the flesh.

The arrangement of the sentences brings out clearly the Christological addition, but at the same time it also shows a further fact: there are now two different clauses making assertions about Christ, and both beginning with the pronoun "Who". The first mentions the birth from the Holy Ghost and the Virgin, and is therefore apparently intended to explain more exactly, on the basis of Luke 1: 35, how Jesus could be described in the first line of the article as "the only begotten Son of God". The second clause combines assertions about events from the Passion to the Ascension, and the future Advent for the Last Judgment. There is no particular difficulty in combining it with the description of Jesus as Son in the introductory line of the article: according to Phil. 2: 5–11 Jesus was exalted on account of His obedience as proved by His suffering, and given the title of "Lord", the heavenly *kurios*. In this way, it becomes plain that the whole Christological addition is a Biblical and theological explanation of the early form, which was a simple confession of "Jesus Christ, the only begotten Son of God, our Lord".[1]

It is possible to observe an entirely similar process in the eastern churches. From the numerous forms of confession of faith of the fourth century, an archetype can be worked out[2] which was probably worded as follows:

[1] K. Holl, *Ges. Aufsätze*, 2,115–122   [2] *ZNW.* 21,1–24

I believe in one God, the Father, the Almighty,
   the creator of everything visible and invisible;
And in one Lord Jesus Christ, the only begotten Son of God,
   Who was born from the Father before all the Aeons,
      through whom everything came into being,
   Who became man, suffered, and rose on the third day,
      and ascended into heaven,
      and who will come in glory,
      to judge the living and the dead;
And in the Holy Ghost.

This creed, too, was welded by introducing Christological pronouncements into a simpler trinitarian confession which can
be recognized as having an essentially different previous
history. Its basis is Paul's two-fold confession[1] of the

   one God, the Father, of whom are all things, and we
      unto him;
   and one Lord, Jesus Christ, through whom are all things,
      and we through him.

This is proved not only by the "one", duplicated in the first
and second articles, but also by the formula "through whom
everything came into being" in the Christological part; and,
finally, by the lack of a "one" in the third article, which itself
appears to be a subsequent appendix. From the original form in
Paul, a trinitarian confession developed in the orient which was
worded somewhat as follows:

   I believe in one God, the Father, the Almighty,
      of whom everything is,
   and in one Lord, Jesus Christ, the only begotten Son of God,
      through whom everything is,
   and in the Holy Ghost.

From this creed there developed in Rome, by deletions,
additions, and rigid systematic arrangement, the nine-fold
form which we have already discussed. In the east, the first
article was transformed so as to express more definitely a clear
confession of the Creator of the world, a process of transformation in which perhaps traditional Jewish formulas exercised

[1] I Cor. 8: 6

influence.[1] In any case, we cannot be certain that the creed
was extended in this manner just to rebut the gnostic separation
of the highest God from the creator of the world: although it is
probable that at a later date this extension served as a token
of orthodox Christianity in the struggle with gnosticism. It is
also uncertain whether, in the second article, the description of
Christ as the "only begotten" (*monogenes*) was introduced
with a polemical purpose. It goes back to John's gospel[2] and
was hardly ever used in the early period; but amongst the
Valentinians[3] it was used to describe the first emanation from
the highest pair of deities, which emanation was distinguished
from Christ. The confession of faith in the identity of Christ and
Monogenes might have been asserted against this.[4] In any case,
it is still worth noticing that the two earliest creeds of the west
do not use the term *monogenes*,[5] from which fact it follows that
the term does not belong to the very earliest stratum in the
structure of the Creed.

On the other hand, the extensions in the second article
operated in exactly the same way as in Rome: they were
concerned to explain the two predicates "Son of God" and
"Lord", and probably the Roman creed was the instigation.
From the theological standpoint, however, the east moved
along other paths. Rome explained the divine Sonship by
simply linking it up with the idea of the Virgin birth, an idea
which could be understood by the people; but the orient went
back to the process of birth before the world began, a process
which separated the Son from every creature conditioned by
time. Only at a later date did forms of the creed refer directly
to the Johannine conception of the logos. The difference in the
explanation of the name of the Son is maintained throughout,
and permanently distinguishes the eastern creeds from the
western forms determined by Rome. The second extension of
the basic form, by introducing the references to the Passion and
Ascension, survives in a shorter form than in Rome. In particular, it omits the sitting at the right hand, thereby obscuring the

---

[1] Cf. Col. 1: 16. Ps. 146: 6. Josephus, *c. Apion*, 2,121. Hermas, *Mand.*, 1,1 and
ZNW. 21,8 f.
[2] John 1: 14, 18; 3: 16, 18   [3] Cf. Vol. 1, pp. 287 ff.
[4] *ZNW.* 22,277 f. 26, 90 f. *Iren.* 1,10,3. Kattenbusch, *Apost. Symbol.*, 2,581–596
[5] *ZNW.* 21,11

reference to Phil. 2, and consequently also the explanation of the title of "Lord". The two additions are very clear and definite in Rome; but, in the east, only in a weakened form, and in general terms. Instead, during the following period, a very much ranker growth of new forms developed out of this root in the eastern church, whereas the west everywhere accepted the Roman confession, and indeed in its Latin translation,[1] and developed it further with relative restraint.

The simplest form of the third article has been preserved in the orient. Even in this article, however, extensions were introduced at an early date, partly in the form that described the Holy Ghost as the promised paraclete,[2] or else as the spirit active in the prophets and pointing towards Christ;[3] partly also by adding other dogmas like church, forgiveness of sins, resurrection, and eternal life: we have already discussed these formulas.[4] Naturally the purpose of these additions is to emphasize the faith that the matters mentioned are due to the activity of the Holy Spirit.

As was the case with the episcopal office and the New Testament canon, so also the confession of faith arose from needs felt entirely within the Church: only in quite isolated cases is it possible to suppose that the efficient cause of any particular formula was hostility towards gnostics or other heretics. The formulas, while in process of gradual extension, only took the fundamental doctrines of the Old Testament and the most important dogmas of Christendom, and made of them a series of titles for the separate sections in which the catechumens were to be instructed. The words of the creed are brief and epigrammatic, and are to be explained by the teacher; and, vice versa, the needs felt in the course of teaching the faith, introduced new words or phrases into the text of the creed. Moreover, the Creed after the second century was not a stiff formula, but a living and changeable form of expressing the church's doctrine; and it retained this character—in the east more definitely than in the west—for several centuries more. The illusion that there was an ancient creed, formulated in a

[1] *ZNW.* 21,4 f.   [2] Tert., *Adv. Prax.*, 2

[3] Justin, *Apol.*, 13,3. 61,13. *Iren.* 1,10,1. *Vide supra*, p. 110; cf. *ZNW.* 26,93

[4] *Supra*, pp. 109 f.

fixed manner, has long led scholars astray. As a matter of fact, in the whole of the ancient church there are not two writers who quote one and the same creed, and even one and the same church father formulates his "creed" differently on different occasions: hence the numerous forms of creed which meet us in the ancient sources,[1] and which are constantly being increased by new discoveries. The confession of faith was from top to bottom part of the liturgy of the Church, and it shared in the spiritual freedom of a living liturgy as long as this freedom existed[2]—i.e. until the Middle Ages: only then did it crystallize out into the unalterable fixed form which afforded no more room for new expressions of life.

The confession of the "Rule of Faith", therefore, signified much more for the Church than what is conveyed by the mere words: in every sentence the baptized Christian heard an echo of the Church's explanation which he had received in the process of instruction as a catechumen. Only when we take full account of this fact are we able to grasp how this simple and unphilosophical declaration could act as a protection against the dazzling speculations of gnostic thinkers. Irenæus and Tertullian give us some conception of what could be deduced by penetrating exegesis from the simple "Rule of Faith" as "the canon of truth". They show also how this rule, together with its explanation, was honoured, carefully protected, and handed down by the Church as a legacy from the Apostles;[3] indeed, they traced it back to Christ himself, and described it as the teaching of the Holy Spirit who had brought together all truth in this "Christian oath of fidelity to the colours".[4] Even if the Apostles had left no writings, i.e. even if we had no canon of the New Testament, this tradition alone would be sufficient to guarantee the faith of the church: that was the view of Irenæus.[5]

Hence we may regard the creed as a compendium of the theology of the Church, and we may gather from it what propositions were regarded at that time as the crucial principal doctrines of Christianity. From the various ways in which the

---

[1] Brought together in Hahn, *op. cit.*, and Lietzmann, *Symbole* (*Kl. Texte*, 17–18)
[2] *ZNW.* 26,84 f.   [3] *Iren.* 1,10,1 f. 3,4,1
[4] Tert., *de praescr. haer.* 13; *adv. Praxeam*, 2. 30   [5] *Iren.* 3,4,1

first article was formulated, we gather, first of all, that faith was confessed in a strict monotheism consciously shared with the Jews. The confession of faith in God as the creator of the world was similarly shared with the synagogue, and also as a rule the invisible spiritual world was expressly mentioned side by side with the material world; this form of creed proved to be a practicable bulwark against the doctrines of Marcion and the gnostics, who preferred to separate the creator of the world from the highest God. But the deduction was also made that the creator God was identical with the God of the Old Testament, and thus gnostic speculations about the pleroma were warded off;[1] in particular the second article was felt to guarantee the activity of the Son in the prophets before the preaching of the gospel.[2]

It is significant that the two earliest pronouncements of the creed about God were scarcely the subject of debate. His omnipotence appeared as the obvious presupposition of His creative activity[3] and, for this reason, was not expressly discussed: it was simply a predicate of majesty.[4] And when God is described as "Father" as a rule the implication is not that Jesus was His Son, but rather the point in mind is His relation to the entire world: He is the Father of the whole,[5] and is called Father on account of His love, Lord on account of His power, our Creator and Maker on account of His wisdom.[6] To call the creator of the world Father was common to Christianity, Hellenistic Judaism,[7] and the philosophic enlightened religion which warranted men tracing back the term to the Homeric "father of gods and men".[8] Therefore this article came to be understood in the sense of a general monotheism, and the churches then no longer felt any connection with the popular Jewish belief which described God as the Father of Israel.[9]

Nowadays, more than ever, is it felt to be strange that the second article is so completely silent about the life and teaching of Jesus, and that it concentrates all our attention on the birth,

---

[1] *Iren.* 1,22,1; cf. 2,1,1. 2,9,1   [2] *Iren.* 3,10,6–11,1. 3,12,9
[3] Justin, *Dial.*, 16,4. 38,2   [4] *Ibid.* 83,4. 96,3. 142,2. *Iren.* 2,6,2
[5] Justin, *Apol.*, 13,1. 45,1. 61,3. 10. *App.* 6,2. 9.2
[6] *Iren.* 5,17,1 (2,369); cf. 2,35,3 (1,387)
[7] *III Macc.* 2,21. 5,7. Philo frequently; cf. index Vol. 7, 636 f.
[8] *Epictet.* 1,3,1. 1,9,7. 1,19,12. 3,24,15 f. Cf. Justin, *Ap.*, 22,1
[9] Bousset, *Judentum*, 3rd edit., 377 f.

death, and second advent of the Lord. To the mind of the early
Church, however, that concentration was entirely necessary.
The life and teaching of the Master was for the Christian the
model of, and pointer to, the Christian life, and the teaching
given to the catechumen made him sufficiently acquainted
with it. But the acts and sayings of Jesus only received their
authority and their real meaning on the metaphysical basis of
His person and its place in the divine plan of redemption—the
"economy of salvation": this above all else had to be made
impregnably firm, and then everything else would follow as a
matter of course. It would be a very bad mistake, if we were to
conclude from its absence in the passages just mentioned, that
ethics was regarded as of lesser value; we may notice that the
"Rule of Faith" is equally silent about the sacraments, the
decisive significance of which no one would venture to deny;
but all their efficacy was derived from a right understanding
of the person of the Lord. It was this fact, therefore, which had
to be established in the first place.

Hence the second article begins with the confession that the
Lord Jesus Christ is the Son of God. The title of "Christ" had
long become a proper noun in the Church, and only those who
were versed in the Scriptures could explain it from the Old
Testament; the name "Lord" had also faded, and lost its
original power. The imagery clearly conveyed, however,
by the term "Son of God", withstood the dulling effect of use,
and inspired men ever anew to build up speculative theological
systems. It would appear as if the genealogy of Jesus in Luke
3: 23–38 has preserved a naïve attempt at such a theology when
it attempts to trace the ancestry to Adam, the "son of God";
thus it facilitates the ascription of divine sonship to Jesus,
by taking the round-about way to Adam, who, indeed, is His
prototype. The doctrine that the birth of Jesus was effected by
God from the Virgin Mary enjoyed, on the other hand, the very
widest acceptance. Matthew and Luke presented it to their
readers, Ignatius spoke with emphasis of the secret,[1] and, in the
Roman baptismal creed, the clause "born of the Holy Ghost
and the Virgin Mary" is the authoritative explanation of the
title, Son.

[1] Ign., *ad Eph.*, 19,1.; *ad Smyrn.* 1,1

The ancient world was familiar with the practice of explaining an incomprehensibly exalted personality by ascribing divine fatherhood; it was the universal custom amongst the people even in the time of the Empire.[1] Plutarch claimed to know a teaching of the Egyptians, according to which the spirit of a god was in a position to approach a woman and plant in her the nucleus of growth.[2] That a woman who had been blessed in this way by the godhead was a virgin would be the natural assumption as a rule, so long as a married woman was not expressly named as the mother of the miraculous child: it must remain an open question, however, to what extent this series of ideas had been influenced by a myth, for which there are evidences in Egypt and Arabia, to the effect that at the winter solstice the goddess, Kore (the maiden), or Parthenos (the virgin), bore the sun-god.[3] In any case, the pagan world of those days was probably familiar with the idea of virgin births due to divine causation.

Moreover, ideas of this sort were not strange even to the Jews. Granted that they cannot be found among the rabbis of Palestine, yet the Hellenistic Judaism of the diaspora was familiar with miraculous propagation by God's direct intervention. Philo[4] tells his readers a great secret, and then records, of four women in Biblical history, that God impregnated them miraculously: Sarah, Leah, Rebecca, and Zipporah; in the last-mentioned case he says emphatically that "when Moses took her to himself, he discovered she was pregnant, but not by a mortal man"—the parallel to the story of Joseph in Matt. 1: 18, is unmistakable. From this standpoint, what Paul has to say in Gal. 4: 21–31 receives a new light, and shows us that even he held that, as distinct from the "natural" birth of Ishmael, Isaac was begotten miraculously, by divine operation. It follows that Paul was acquainted with the same tradition of the Hellenistic rabbis as lies at the basis of Philo's discussions;[5] and when, in this connection, Philo asserts that God would grant His miraculous gift only to a pure virgin, we are at once

[1] H. Usener, *Das Weihnachtsfest*, 2nd edit., 71–77
[2] Plutarch, *Numa*, 4; *Quaest. conv.* 8,1 p. 718*b*. Cf. E. Norden, *Geburt des Kindes*, 78
[3] Epiphan., *Hær.*, 51,22,8–11 (2,285–7 Holl). Cf. Holl, *Ges. Aufs.*, 2,144–46
[4] Philo, *Cher.*, 45–50 (1,181 f.)
[5] M. Dibelius, *Jungfrauensohn und Krippenkind*, 27–37. 42 f.

reminded of the pagan conceptions mentioned in the preceding paragraph.

In reality, these ideas belong to an ancient religion of nature, probably of Egypt origin,[1] and we find them applied to the Bible by Hellenized Jews. This fact, however, at once makes it clear how a Christian man who came from such circles must have understood the prophecy in Isa. 7: 14. His Greek text read: "Therefore the Lord himself will give you a sign: lo, a virgin (*parthenos*) will conceive and bear a son, and thou shalt call his name Emmanuel." To him, that was the prophetic announcement of the miraculous birth of Jesus the Son of God from the Virgin Mary. The doctrine of the virgin birth of Jesus was, therefore, in those days, felt to be, not only of the most graphic simplicity, but was also founded on the New Testament; as a result it rapidly and inevitably became universal. The narratives of Matthew and Luke plainly show that they refer to the passage in Isaiah,[2] and in this way they brought to the Church the happy consciousness of the harmony between the prophecy and its fulfilment. Justin the apologist demonstrates that fact with obvious satisfaction, and expounds it to the Jew Trypho with a detailed discussion of all problems of scripture.[3]

Side by side with this doctrine of the physically divine son-ship of Jesus, was another theory which it is usual to call "adoptionist". In its simplest form, the theory declared that the man Jesus was made into the Son of God by the descent of the Holy Spirit at His baptism, and that, at the end of His life, He was raised from the dead as a reward for His good works, and exalted to the right hand of God. This doctrine has not been actually preserved in its pure form: but the western text of Luke's gospel,[4] giving in all probability the genuine, original wording, records, in 3: 22, that, when Jesus was baptized in the Jordan, a voice from heaven was heard saying: "Thou art my Son, this day have I begotten thee." That is unmistakably a divine testimony, modelled on the basis of Ps. 2:7, and bearing witness to the "adoption" of the man, Jesus, as Son of God. The same view is clearly expressed in the interpolations found in the

[1] Dibelius 44, Norden 79   [2] Matt. 1: 23; Luke 1: 31
[3] Justin, *Apol.*, 33; *Dial.* 66–85   [4] Usener, *op. cit.*, 40–52

Jewish *Testaments of the Twelve Patriarchs*,[1] whereas in the best known representative of adoptionist Christology, Hermas,[2] who wrote in Rome *c.* A.D. 150, the original form has undergone a certain transformation. According to Hermas, Jesus was a man of virtue to the extent of being sinless, and He had won God's good pleasure. The Holy Spirit of God united with Jesus, and since, during His work on earth, He served with a pure heart and laboured together with the Spirit, God rewarded Jesus and exalted Him to the heavenly throne where, with the Holy Spirit and the high angels, He became His counsellor.

In content, the earlier Adoptionism has been preserved here, and it may well be an accident that the Baptism is not mentioned. But the Holy Spirit is described by Hermas as the "Son of God", both in this connection and also elsewhere, i.e. the Holy Spirit is regarded as the pre-existent divine being who had formerly created the world, and who, after the Resurrection, separately from the risen Jesus, asserted His own original dignity as Son. In this case, therefore, the earlier Adoptionism has been combined with another, i.e. a pneumatic, conception of the Son. Somewhat similarly, Paul, in Phil. 2, takes a conception which is really Adoptionist in character, and originally applies only to man, because it consists of an exaltation granted as reward for obedient service; Paul combines this idea with that of the descent of a pre-existent divine being: this view brings us face to face with the same thing the other way round.

A "pneumatic" Christology became dominant in the Church. This Christology held that the "Son of God" was a spiritual being existing from the beginning with God, and that He appeared on earth at a pre-appointed time, in human form; He lived, taught, and worked miracles in Palestine as Jesus Christ; finally, after having suffered death on the cross, He rose again and ascended to heaven in order to reassume there His appropriate place. The conception is to be found in Paul and in John's doctrine of the logos, and through them it became normative for the future. The oriental forms of the baptismal creed expressly emphasized the doctrine of sonship in the

---

[1] *Test. Judæ* 24,1 f.; cf. *Zabulon* 9,8   [2] Hermas, *Sim.*, 5,6,4–8. 9,1,1. 9,12,1–8

form of the logos instead of the doctrine of the Virgin Birth: not in the sense of denying the Virgin Birth so much as in that of accepting the logos sonship as primary. This doctrine says nothing as to the way in which the logos became incarnate. A naïve docetism came to be based on the logos Christology, and a merely apparent body ascribed to the divine being while on earth; on the other hand, the spirit could be conceived as the divine companion dwelling with the man Jesus who was destined for adoption; this is the view held by Hermas. But the solution of the problem which became most usual in the Church was the one in which the pneumatic Christology was combined with the doctrine of the miraculous birth in such a way that the divine spirit, or the logos, entered into the Virgin Mary, and through her became a genuine man. In the world of ideas of the early Church and its theologians, all these ways of thought intermingled, or were to be found unco-ordinated side by side: what modern logical analysis separates neatly, stood closely together in the life and thought of the early Christians, and did so for the most part without any sign of clash; but, in the course of time, theologians became aware of hidden incongruities, and attempted to find a genuine agreement: this work of theirs led to the evolution of dogma within the Church.

The pronouncement made in the second half of the second article, both in Rome and the orient, constituted a connected series of assertions: Passion, Resurrection, Ascension, and Second Advent in order to judge the world, i.e. the drama of redemption as found in the "economy of salvation" past and future. These were the works of the Son of God, Jesus Christ, in which His divine power as Redeemer stood revealed: the first decisive act took place in the realm of history: the cruci-fixion "under Pontius Pilate". Thereupon Jesus left the scene of earth: the work of redemption became illumined by eschat-ology, and was to be completed in the Last Judgment. What, however, was the purpose of the economy of salvation? It was conceived from the standpoint of warfare between God and the devil: Jesus had broken the chains of the devil, trodden hell down, freed mankind from death,[1] and had shown that the way

---

[1] The prayer in the Church Order of Hippolytus (Lietzm., *Messe u. Herrenm.*, 42)

to resurrection lay in following in His steps.[1] This victory was made possible by outwitting antagonists who had attacked Jesus without suspecting that they had no claim on this sinless man, but were to meet with the unconquerable power of God in him. This theology is popular and graphic; it was given a simple, vivid form, and was very much alive in the churches. It formed part of the earliest tradition of doctrine, was accepted by gnostics as well as by thinkers within the Church, and was developed further.[2]

The third article opens with confessing the Holy Spirit revealed in the churches, a confession which, in the course of time, was given manifold and various theological explanations in proportion as the original Christian view of the operation of the spirit fell into the background behind the regular ordinances of the Church. The spirit was identified with the divine being operative in Christ—such as we have just discussed in the case of Hermas,[3] corresponding to the adoptionist view as well as to the conception of Jesus's miraculous procreation; Paul could be called in as support, particularly 2 Cor. 3: 17. On the other hand, the spirit was conceived as an independent divine being side by side with the Father and the logos in a manner deduced from the Johannine conception of the paraclete,[4] a conception which also corresponded to the three-fold structure of the creed: in this way the spirit became a third divine person. In the context of the creed, on the one hand, the function of the Holy Spirit was described as strengthening the life and faith of the Church[5]—this corresponded to the Johannine doctrine and the earliest meaning of the formula. On the other hand, emphasis was laid upon the activity of the spirit in the prophets, an activity which pointed towards Christ.[6]

[1] Ign., Trall., 9; Smyrn. 1,2; Iren. 1,10,1 (1,91) and Iren. Armen., Epideixis (p. 4 Harnack, cf. ZNW. 26,93). Didasc. Syr. 6,23,8 in Funk, p. 382

[2] Paul, 1 Cor.,2: 7f.; Col. 2: 15. Ign., Eph., 19,1; cf. Justin, Apol., 54. 55. Basilides in Iren. 1,24,4 (1,200). Origen, in Mt., tom. 16,8 (4,27 Lo) and frequently

[3] Cf. also 2 Clem. 14: 4

[4] Vol. 1, 231 f.

[5] Tert., praescr. haer., 13. adv. Praxeam 2. Iren. 4,33,7 (2,262). 4. Antiochene creed, 1. Creed of Epiph., cf. Lietzmann, Symbole (Kl. Texte 17 and 18), 6.19.31 and ZNW. 21,20 f.

[6] Justin, Apol., 13,3. 61,13. Iren. 1,10,1 (1,90). Epideixis 6 (p. 4, ed. Harnack, ZNW. 26,93). Creeds of Jerusalem, Epiph., 1 and 2, etc.; cf. ZNW. 21,20 f.

The remaining parts of the article came in at a later date and in a varied selection; first, perhaps the Church as the organ and the product of the activity of the spirit. On one occasion in Hermas,[1] the Holy Spirit appears in the form of an old lady, viz. the Church, and in *2 Clem.* the preacher takes up the parable of marriage in Paul's epistle to the Ephesians, and calls the Church the feminine element beside the masculine of Christ; he also calls the Church the body which forms a unity with Christ as Spirit.[2] The resurrection of the flesh is mentioned in the same article in the nine-sectioned creed of Rome and Egypt:[3] i.e. the resurrection is the eschatological consequence of the possession of the spirit; it takes place in the individual believer, and is what he hoped to gain by following in the train of Christ in the Church. The creed of the *Epistula Apostolorum*[4] places the forgiveness of sins, instead of the resurrection of the body, after the mention of the Church. Naturally the forgiveness referred to is that which is granted in baptism; and in the baptismal creed, there is good reason for saying that it was a subject of faith. The final form of the Roman creed combined all these elements: no further additions were made to the third article in the early period—which is quite striking, especially when we think of the Lord's Supper.

[1] Hermas, *Sim.*, 9,1,1; cf. *Visions* 3. Dibelius in *Handb.* exc. on *Vis.* 2,3,4
[2] *2 Clem.* 14; cf. Eph. 1: 23, 5: 32   [3] *Supra*, p. 110   [4] *Supra*, pp. 92 f.

Chapter Five

WORLD SHIP

WORSHIP

THE HEART OF THE CHRISTIAN LIFE IS TO BE FOUND IN THE act of public worship. This is the occasion when the powers of the world beyond flow into Christian people, and transform them into the new children of God; they are no longer of this world, but even here live in a supernatural fellowship with the heavenly citizens of the kingdom of God. The principal element in its worship is the celebration of the Lord's Supper. We have already discussed its earliest form in the original Church; it was a community meal, and Paul ascribed to it the significance of a memorial feast of the death of Christ.[1] On the threshold of the second century, the Church Order of the *Didache*[2] preserves the earliest formulated liturgy of the Lord's Supper. The sacred rite was still always combined with a genuine meal in common, although the two acts, of eating and drinking, were no longer separated by the course of the entire meal, but were placed together at the beginning of the rite. The leader blessed the cup, then the bread, with brief prayers which obviously owed their origin to the forms used in the Greek synagogues, although they had received a content showing Christian influence. Then the leader cried: "Grace is coming and this world is passing away." "Hosanna to the Son of David" was the response of the church. Then came the admonition: "If any is holy let him enter, if he is not let him repent. Marana tha (Come, O Lord)." "Amen", responded the Church, and thereupon those who were baptized, and believed themselves holy, i.e. free from serious sin, attended the communion service conducted by the leader of the liturgy. Whoever had a quarrel with his neighbour first came to agreement with him. Then the Church came to table, and the common meal began. At its end, the leader offered a longer prayer of thanks for the spiritual food which they had enjoyed, and for eternal life granted through Christ: the prayer ended with a petition on behalf of the

[1] Vol. 1, pp. 63,124,150 f.
[2] *Did.*, 9–10. 14. Lietzmann, *Messe u. Herrenm.*, pp. 230–8.

Church scattered far and wide in the world, but patiently waiting for its reunion in the Kingdom of God. No word was uttered about remembering the death of the Lord; no reminder of the Lord's Last Supper on the night when He was betrayed.

This liturgy is entirely confined to the tradition which had grown up from the very earliest period, and is unaffected by Pauline influence. Nevertheless it did not last much longer in the Church. Two matters brought about a crucial change. On the one hand, Paul's authority became so overwhelming that his words determined the meaning and the content of the rite. On the other hand, the connection broke down between the sacramental meal and a common repast of the church. The former was separated from its proximity with the daily, evening meal, which appeared in some way to be mundane; it was transferred to the morning, and united with the preaching service. This change was complete in Rome c. A.D. 150, as we see from Justin the apologist.[1]

The earlier, evening celebrations were not abolished, but they lost their old meaning, and became love-feasts of a semi-liturgical character, as formalized acts of personal goodwill. A few descriptions[2] of this kind of "Agapē" have survived. Tertullian describes them[3] as forms of social meeting of which the church was fond, and in which a modest meal of food and drink was followed by a general discussion, the reading of Biblical passages, singing of psalms, or unfettered speech. In Rome,[4] about the same time, needy members of the church received meals in some well-to-do house. A cleric conducted the proceedings, offered prayer, and broke the bread at the beginning: this was described as the "Eulogia", and was distinguished from partaking of the Lord's Supper, the "Eucharistia". Then came the common meal. On the other hand, the entire rite might be dispensed with; instead, the person officiating gave small packets of food into the hands of those who had been invited, and who then took the packets gratefully away. In this modest form, the Agapē lived for

---

[1] Justin, Apol., 67,3–5

[2] Material is given in Lietzmann, op. cit., 197–202. English trans. The Mass and the Lord's Supper

[3] Tert., Apol., 39,16   [4] Didasc. apost., ed. Hauler, pp. 113 f.

centuries apart from the formal liturgy and worship of the Church.

It is in the writings of the same Justin, who tells of the combination of the two elements to form the principal public service on Sundays, that we find the earliest description of the method followed: the church assembled on Sunday and heard readings, first from the gospel, then from the prophets "for as long as there was time": a hortatory sermon followed. That was the extent of the first part, i.e. the preaching-service, according to this very brief record—but even the accounts given in the Church Orders of the fourth century[1] are no fuller. By this time, the service was rather more divided up, and, in particular, psalms were sung between the two readings from the Bible; otherwise, however, we have no further information. We notice, especially, that no liturgical prayer is mentioned in the first part of the service. On the other hand, it is clear that, by now, there had been a change from the service customary in the synagogues, where readings of Scripture were combined with teaching in the manner which is graphically described in Luke 4: 16–30. On that occasion, Jesus read on the Sabbath the prophetic passage Isa. 61: 1 f. and preached about it. Similarly, Acts 13: 14–16 speaks of reading on the Sabbath from the Law and the prophets, followed by an address: the Mishna[2] fills out these notices by saying that the reading from the prophets took place only at the morning service on the Sabbath, and followed on the readings from the Law. We know so little of anything else in this part of the service in the synagogue, and, in particular, have no information at all as to its form on Hellenistic soil, that it is scarcely possible for us to go beyond the few notices which we have just remarked.

All the members of the church shared in the first part of divine service,[3] and, indeed, strangers were admitted in order that they might be converted to Christianity; on the other hand, the second part was confined to those who had been baptized, for they alone were permitted to partake in the Lord's Supper which constituted the centre of the rite. It follows that, at an early period, a more or less clearly-marked departure of

---

[1] *Const. Apost.* 2,57,5–9. 8,5,11 f.

[2] *Mishna Megilla* 4,2; cf. Elbogen, *Jüd. Gottesdienst*, 176   [3] *Const. Apost.* 8,6,2

catechumens and unbelievers concluded the first part of the service. When the congregation of the baptized were quite in private, they began to offer general prayer, and afterwards greeted one another with the kiss of peace. Then bread and a cup of mixed wine and water was brought to the leader, who pronounced over them the "Eucharist prayer". The people responded with "Amen", and then received Communion from the hands of the deacons. The central point of this service, however, was not really the meal, the partaking of the consecrated elements, but the act of consecration itself which was brought about by the Eucharist prayer. From the Roman church, c. A.D. 200, there has been preserved the actual wording of one of these formularies,[1] and everything essential can be clearly inferred from it:

Bishop: The Lord be with you.
Church: And with thy spirit.
Bishop: Lift up your hearts.
Church: We have them in the Lord.
Bishop: Let us give thanks to the Lord.
Church: That is proper and right.
Bishop: We thank Thee God through Thy beloved servant Jesus Christ whom Thou hast sent in the latter times to be our Saviour and Redeemer and the messenger of Thy counsel, the Logos who went out from Thee, through whom Thou hast created all things, whom Thou wast pleased to send out from heaven into the womb of the Virgin, and in her body He became incarnate and shown to be Thy Son born of the Holy Ghost and of the Virgin. In order to fulfil Thy will and to make ready for Thee a holy people, He spread out his hands when He suffered in order that He might free from sufferings those who have reached faith in Thee.
        And when He gave Himself over to voluntary suffering, in order to destroy death, and to break the bonds of the devil, and to tread down hell, and to illuminate the righteous, and to set up the boundary stone, and to reveal the Resurrection, He took bread, gave thanks, and said: "Take, eat, this is My body which is broken for you." In the same manner also the cup, and said:

[1] Hipp., *Church Order* in *Didascalia lat.* ed. Hauler, pp. 106 f.

"This is My blood which is poured out for you. As often as you do this you keep My memory."

When we remember His death and His resurrection in this way, we bring to Thee the bread and the cup, and give thanks to Thee, because Thou hast thought us worthy to stand before Thee and to serve Thee as priests.

And we beseech Thee that Thou wouldst send down Thy Holy Spirit on the sacrifice of the church. Unite it, and grant to all the saints who partake in the sacrifice, that they may be filled with the Holy Spirit, that they may be strengthened in faith in the truth, in order that we may praise and laud Thee through Thy servant, Jesus Christ, through whom praise and honour be to Thee in Thy holy church now and forever more, Amen.

This formulary begins with the "Eucharistia", i.e. thanks, not, as in the case of the early prayers at table, for material food, but for the incarnation of the divine logos in Jesus who had instituted this sacred meal on the eve of His Passion, as is re-echoed in the words of Paul and of Matthew. The words of institution end with the admonition: "As often as you do this, you keep My memory." The following words take up this phrase, and more exactly define the death and resurrection of the Lord as the subjects of such memorial. Bread and wine are described as the sacrificial gifts, which are brought in a priestly manner, and offered to God. In addition, it is in a thoroughly ancient manner, even making use of Old Testament forms, that the priest beseeches the Lord to let His Spirit descend upon the sacrifice, in order that it may serve as spiritual food for those who partake. The elements of the Lord's Supper are like the flesh of the sacrificial animal which was eaten in a feast by those who offered it, and by the priest after the act of worship had taken place. In the prayer of the liturgy, this conception received a spiritual transformation, but from Justin's explanation we see how much earthly reality was combined with it in the religious feelings of the people: Justin speaks of the transformation of our flesh and blood when we partake of this food which has been blessed by invoking the logos.[1] It is the same

[1] Justin, *Apol.*, 66,2; cf. *Dial.* 41,1–3. 70,4. 117,1–5

conception as we find, c. A.D. 110, in Ignatius, and as had already been expounded by Paul to the Corinthian church.[1]

The Lord's Supper was the act of sacrifice in the worship offered by Christians: in the first place, because it was Eucharistia, thanksgiving, and because prayers were the peculiarly Christian sacrifices;[2] in the second place, because bread and wine, and frequently also many other gifts, were brought by the church to the leader at the altar, and thereby sacrificed to God; in the third place, because the leader consecrated the elements to God by his prayers, and God accepted the gift, sent his Holy Spirit upon and in it, and in this way transformed it into miracle-working, sacrificial food for the church.[3] This, again, is a conception whose roots can be traced back to the parallel and the contrast, which Paul drew between the Lord's Supper and Jewish and pagan sacrificial meals.[4] Thus there are three points in which it is comprehensible why the rite of the Lord's Supper was described as the Christian act of sacrifice.[5]

The Christians quite consciously took the conception of the true Israel, and carried it further: they no longer set against the Old Testament sacrifice merely the single offering on Golgotha, as in Hebrews, but worked out their own regularly-repeated act of worship in the Eucharistic sacrifice. In the sequel, we shall discuss how, at a later date, accommodation was effected with the conception found in Hebrews, a conception which laid the basis for the classical theory of sacrifice in the Roman Catholic church. In the second century, meanwhile, we can only trace the three conceptions of sacrifice which we have just discussed. Since a priest was necessary to make a sacrifice, the person who led the liturgy of the church was described with the Old Testament title of priest. Even Clement of Rome drew the parallel between the bishop and deacons on the one hand, and the high-priests, priests, and Levites on the other; the *Didache* describes the prophets as the Christian high-priests.[6] About A.D. 200, there are passages comparing the bishop with the high-priest, and the presbyters with the

---

[1] Cf. Vol. 1, 124 f., 238   [2] Justin, *Dial.*, 117,2
[3] *Messe u. Herrenm.* 176–86   [4] 1 Cor. 10: 18–21
[5] *Didache* 14,1. Justin, *Dial.*, 117,1 f.; cf. 1 *Clem.* 40,2 44,4, and Ign., *Eph.*, 5,2
[6] 1 *Clem.* 40: 5. *Did.* 13,3

priests; shortly afterwards, the deacons are equated with the Levites.[1]

This act of worship bound the Church ever more closely together into a spiritual unity: that unity was reflected also in the custom of bringing the consecrated food home to absent members, lest any be excluded. After the rite, the leader collected the gifts made to meet the needs of charity, their distribution being under his oversight. It was also a frequent custom to bring food of all sorts, and indeed flowers, place them as offerings upon the altar, and have them blessed by the laying on of hands, and the prayer of the priest: in the Church Order of Hippolytus[2] the corresponding forms of prayer have been preserved, and the Mosaic floor of the oldest-surviving basilica gives us a pictorial representation of a procession bringing such gifts as sacrifices.[3]

It was one and the same loaf of which they all ate, one wine of which they all drank; these foods were a counterpart— "antitypus"—of the body and the blood of the Lord, and thus united participants "with the body of Christ". Because the elements now bore a supernatural character, they must be treated with respect: no unbeliever must share in them, no crumb must fall to the ground lest it be destroyed, or a mouse eat it; no drop must be spilt: an intrusive spirit might lick it up and so obtain heavenly powers.[4]

During the period when a fixed form was being given to the liturgy of the Lord's Supper, the initiatory sacrament of baptism reached maturity. Out of the simple act which was sometimes performed without an intermediary, there grew up a series of solemn actions following a definite plan. In the first place, the time was closely determined. In Bithynia, c. A.D. 100, and in Rome, even c. A.D. 200, it was usual to prescribe night-time between Saturday and Sunday for the baptismal cere-mony, the particular reason being that it was the weekly recurrence of the night in which the Lord rose again.[5] Then

[1] Tert., de bapt., 17 Hippol., Elenchos 1 preface. Didascalia Apostolorum,ed.Connolly, p. 86,12–19. p. 87,10–17
[2] Hipp., Church Order, c. 53, p. 114, ed. Funk
[3] The basilica of Aquileia which was built about A.D. 310. For illustrations see Vorträge der Bibl. Warburg, 1925–26, p. 59, and plate 5
[4] Hipp., Church Order, c. 60, p. 116, ed. Funk
[5] Pliny, Epist., 10,96. Hippolytus, Church Order, can. 45 f., p. 109, Funk

the limits were made still narrower, and Easter night was chosen as the time for baptism, and as an annual memorial of the night of our redemption by Christ: if there were not sufficient time or space, the whole of the period of rejoicing in the fifty days till Whitsuntide could be used for baptism. Tertullian[1] says that that was the usual custom, c. A.D. 200, in the African church. We have no information of similar limitations in the orient, about this time, but they must necessarily have been introduced as soon as it became a settled custom to give detailed instruction to those who sought baptism, and when catechumens were no longer taught individually, but general instruction was given to all the candidates in common. The *Didache* describes a very brief course of instruction in ethics as sufficient teaching; according to Justin, it is probable that a more detailed Christian teaching was presupposed, but he utters not a single word about a regular syllabus. This also applies to the Church Order of Hippolytus, in which we find that the probationary period for catechumens was prescribed as fully three years: the thing to be tested during this period was the manner of life and the moral firmness of the candidate.[2]

The baptismal rite itself was fully developed as early as c. A.D. 200, and was accompanied by a number of ceremonies reflecting nature religion, ceremonies which must have had numerous parallels in the surrounding mystery religions. The candidate for baptism was made ready by a fast which lasted one or two days, and which was shared by certain friends.[3] Then the baptismal water was purified by exorcizing the elemental spirits which dwelt in it, and was prepared for the sacred ceremony.[4] Side by side with this view, however, was the belief that the candidate himself was the dwelling-place of the unseen spirits of paganism, and that he must be freed from them before the spirit of Christ could dwell in him. The simplest view was that the baptism itself effected the purification,[5] but,

[1] Tert., *de baptismo*, 19
[2] *Did.* 1–6; cf. 7 at the beginning. Justin, *Apol.*, 61,1. Funk, *op. cit.*, c. 42, p. 107
[3] *Did.* 7,4. Justin, *Apol.*, 61,2; cf. Funk, *op. cit.*, 45,7. 10. p. 109; cf. Clem. Alex., *excerpt.*, 84
[4] Clem. Alex., *loc. cit.*, 82. Cyprian, *ep.*, 70,1. Funk, *op. cit.*, 46,1. p. 109; cf. Dölger, *Exorzismus*, p. 160–67
[5] Tert., *de bapt.*, 9. p. 208, 11 f.; cf. 5. p. 205,26 f. Reifferscheid.

in the third century, a special rite of exorcism was drawn up, by means of which the daemons were driven out of the baptismal candidate in advance. The priest placed his hand upon him, blew on him, anointed his forehead, ears, and nose: this was followed by a renewed fast for the night.[1] Early in the morning, at cock-crow, the baptism began; "living," i.e. flowing, water was necessary, a prescription which corresponded to the general requirements of ancient cults. Only in case of necessity might cistern water be used.[2]

In Rome, c. A.D. 200, after the candidate for baptism had undressed, he was required first of all solemnly to abjure Satan and all his service and works, to which hitherto he had been subject; thereupon he was once more anointed with the exorcizing oil. Then he went down into the water, and gave the new oath of service, the "sacramentum", to his new Lord by uttering the three-fold baptismal creed, whereupon he was plunged three times beneath the water by the accompanying deacon. He rose from the water, was anointed by the presbyter, and then re-clothed himself. Afterwards, all passed from the place of baptism into the church, where the bishop transferred the gift of the Holy Spirit to the newly baptized by laying on of hands, anointing, making the sign of the cross, and a kiss: in this way the bishop received them into the fellowship of the church of Christ.[3] The church immediately celebrated the Lord's Supper with them: but, in addition to the bread and wine, a cup of milk and honey was given to those who had been newly-born in baptism—they were to regard it as a foretaste of the heavenly food which was assured to the glorified in the promised land of the Kingdom of God. We have testimonies showing that this rite was practised, c. A.D. 200, in Egypt, and Africa; it may have been taken over in gnostic circles on the Nile from the ancient usage in the mysteries, and thence have penetrated into the Church.[4]

[1] Funk, *op. cit.*, 45,9 f. p. 109
[2] *Did.* 7,1 f. Justin, *Apol.*, 61,3. Funk, *op. cit.*, 46,2. p. 109. P. Stengel, *Griech, Kultusaltertümer*, 3rd edit., p. 162, note 9
[3] Hippolytus, *Church Order*, c. 46, pp. 109–12. Tert., *de. bapt.*, 7 f. *carnis resurr.*, 8, p. 36 f. Kroymann
[4] Hippolytus, *Church Order* lat. pp. 111–113 Hauler, c. 46, 1–27, p. 110–112 Funk. Clem. Alex., *Paedag.*, 1,6,45. *Strom.* 7,75,2. Tert. *corona mil.* 3. *adv. Marc.* 1,14, p. 308, 21. Kroymann. H. Usener, *Kleine Schriften*, 4.404–17

From the very beginning, the day for worship in the week was Sunday, and on this day the Eucharistic service was held. Side by side with this, we know that, at an early date, there were two fast days during the week, Wednesday and Friday;[1] in Africa, it was usual to fast until the "ninth hour", i.e. till 3 p.m., whereas the zealous continued their fast until the evening.[2] Fasting was felt to be an important enhancement of the Christian way of life, a "guard duty", and for this reason the military name, *Statio*, was applied to it in the west.[3] The Christian stood "on guard" in order to give the Lord a worthy reception when He returned. But the *Statio* was not regarded as compulsory everywhere. The Roman church in the time of Hippolytus still fasted, as a rule, according to private desire, and fasting was obligatory only on Good Friday and the following day.[4]

In accordance with its respect for the Law, the first church naturally celebrated the Jewish Passover and the festive period of fifty days until Whitsuntide;[5] these festivals were accepted not only by the Jewish-Christian church which was her successor, but also by the gentile church. In itself, that was not remarkable when we remember how close was the connection between the church which "was free from the Law" and the Greek synagogue,[6] but it is remarkable that this custom was by no means universal. In the middle of the second century, Polycarp, bishop of Smyrna, celebrated the feast of the Passover "according to the custom of the Apostles", but only learnt when he visited Rome that it was unknown there, nor was he successful in converting the Romans to this feast.[7] In Smyrna and the rest of Asia Minor, the Passover was celebrated "on the fourteenth", i.e. exactly on the same day as it began among the Jews, viz. when the moon was fourteen days old, or, in other words, on the night of the full moon, and, in particular, on that after Spring had begun.

Moreover, in the east, there was a large variety of calendars,

[1] Vol. 1, 68 ff. *Did.* 8,1

[2] Tert., *de ieiun.*, 1 p. 275,3 f. 2 p. 275,26–28. 10 p. 287,8. Wissowa

[3] Hermas, *Sim.*, 5,1. Tert., *de oratione*, 19 p. 192,11 Wissowa; cf. Svennung, *ZNW.*, 32,294–308. Holl., *Ges. Schr.*, 2,213

[4] Funk, *op. cit.*, c. 47,2 p. 112. c. 55 p. 115

[5] *Acts* 2,1; cf. *Lev.* 23,15–21   [6] Vol. 1, 199 ff.   [7] Iren. in Eus., *H.E.*, 5,24,16

and, as we now know,[1] the Jews adopted the calendar which
was customary in each particular country; as a consequence,
the beginnings of the month were very different, and accordingly the Passover was not celebrated everywhere at the same
full moon. That disturbed neither Jews nor Christians. But
when the question was raised as to the meaning which both
religious communities attached to the observance, there was a
sharp contradiction about the very rite. The Jews observed a
joyous feast in proud memory of their deliverance from
Egyptian bondage, the Christians observed the Passover by
fasting. This must be explained by the parallel instance of
fasting on Friday every week. According to the gospel tradition,
Jesus' Passion took place in connection with the Passover, and,
with this in mind, the Church celebrated Passover Eve in
sorrow with fasting and prayer.[2] When night began to pass
away at cock-crow, and the joyous feast of the Jews was at an
end, then also the Christian fast, together with its sorrow, came
to an end, and the church assembled for the Eucharistic love-
feast with the Lord abiding in their midst.[3] The content of the
Christian Passover celebration, therefore, consisted of a memorial of the death of the Lord, and, later, the Church described
this mode as "the Passover of the Cross", and those who
observed it, as the "quartodecimanians", according to the
date of the feast, i.e. as adherents of the "fourteenth".

As distinct from this practice, another arose which combined
the annual memorial of the death of Jesus with the weekly
memorial of the same content; for this reason, the observance
of the night of Christ's death was made to begin on Saturday,
and as a consequence the end of the fasting and the beginning
of the Eucharistic festival meal fell at dawn on Sunday, i.e. at
the time of Christ's resurrection; in this case, what was really
celebrated was the Resurrection, and the previous fasting on
Saturday, with its memorial of Christ's death, appeared rather
as a preparation for the Sunday festival. Those who carried
the analogy of the Passion still further began to fast on Friday,
and so celebrated with sorrow the day of Christ's death and also
the day when He lay in the grave, but with joy the day of the

---

[1] E. Schwartz, *Christl. u. jüd Ostertafeln* (*Abh. Götting. Ges. N.F.*, 8,1905), pp. 126 f.
[2] Mark 2: 20   [3] *Epist. apost.* c. 15 (26). M. R. James, *op. cit.*, 489 f.

resurrection. The form of celebration found in Asia Minor joined the Passover to the night of the full moon, and accordingly the Passover fell in turn on each of the days of the week. But the new practice transferred the feast to the Sunday which followed the night of the full moon of the Jewish Passover. We do not know when or where this mode arose; our evidence only shows that, after the middle of the second century, it was widespread in the Christian church.

In particular, about this period, there was a serious dispute as to the proper method of celebrating the Passover, and from Palestine, which agreed with Egypt, from Pontus, from Osroëne, Corinth, Rome, and Gaul, synods wrote officially in favour of the Sunday celebration—what we now call the festival of Easter.[1] Victor, bishop of Rome, then required the churches of Asia Minor to abandon their "quartodecimanian" practice, and threatened them with cessation of church fellowship in case of refusal. But the leading speaker on the other side, Polycrates, bishop of Ephesus, defended himself energetically.[2] He adduced the apostolic tradition of Asia Minor, which was witnessed by the grave of John the beloved disciple, of Philip the evangelist[3]—whom he raised to the rank of an apostle—and his daughters; he also appealed to quite a large number of important men in the church of his land as having observed the same tradition.

Even elsewhere Rome's abrupt conduct occasioned displeasure,[4] and Irenæus of Lyons, although he agreed with Victor in subject-matter, wrote a letter in which he was at pains to make his position quite clear. He laid great emphasis on the fact that, even amongst the friends of the Sunday Passover, there were still many differences in detail without this fact disturbing the peace; and that at one time, in the days of Polycarp, the contrast between Rome and Asia Minor had been very much greater. At that time, no one in Rome had celebrated the Passover, a fact that had been peaceably agreed. Why not the same now, when the point at issue was only a difference as to the day? Indeed, Bishop Soter, Victor's predecessor, had been the first to introduce the Easter celebrations

[1] Eus., *H.E.*, 5,23,2–4   [2] Polycrates' Letter in Eus., *H.E.*, 5,24,2–8
[3] Cf. Vol. 1, p. 189   [4] Eus., *H.E.*, 5,24,10

on a Sunday.[1] We hear nothing of the further stages of the dispute, but, in any case, the churches of Asia Minor did not abandon their custom. Where the new Easter usage was adopted, it sometimes exercised an effect also on the practice of fasting every week, and it added Saturday to the Friday which had long been observed as a fast day. The custom of fasting on Saturday is testified, c. A.D. 200, in the west, as a custom which was warmly contested;[2] indeed, the dispute lasted 200 years, but the custom was eventually victorious in this province of the church. The east fell into a similar dispute somewhat later, but decided the matter in the opposite direction: after the fourth century Sabbath fasting was forbidden.[3]

From the very beginning, Whitsuntide depended upon Easter. Consequently, the fifty days which followed upon Easter were celebrated in the church as a period of rejoicing in memory of the appearances of the Risen Lord and the out-pouring of the Holy Spirit; in particular it was expected that the promised return of the Lord who had ascended to heaven would take place during these weeks.[4]

At this early period, the Church had no other annual festivals. Amongst the followers of Basilides in Egypt in the second century, a feast of the baptism of Christ was observed with a celebration during the preceding night; the date was either January 10 or 6.[5] At a later date, this gave rise to the feast of the Epiphany in the church catholic, but even in the third century, we can discover no sign that it had yet appeared.

Nevertheless, it is probable that annual feasts were instituted in individual churches, particularly those that celebrated the memory of their martyrs on the anniversary of their death: at bottom, this was a development of the annual tribute which every family was accustomed to offer to the memory of its own departed. It was not without purpose that many gravestones in every century gave particulars of the day of death, whereas the year was mentioned only in the very rarest cases. On this

---

[1] Letter of Irenæus in Eus., *H.E.*, 5,24,12–17. In addition Holl, *op. cit.*, 2,114–19. E. Schwartz, *ZNW.*, 7,1–22

[2] Tert., *de ieiunio*, 14 p. 293,5. 15 p. 293,19 Wissowa. Hippolytus, *in Danielem* 4,20,3. p. 236,5 Bonwetsch

[3] Holl, *op. cit.*, 2,373–6

[4] Tert., *de bapt.*, 19 p. 217,6–12 Wissowa   [5] Clem., *Strom*, 1,146,1 f.

day, the family gathered at the grave and paid tribute to the memory of the departed in a form regulated in some way by their cult: unfortunately no details are extant in regard to this early period. A later reference shows that Christians made use of the ancient custom of observing the third, ninth, and thirtieth day after the death, by some act of remembrance: on these days, they showed their attachment to the departed by singing psalms, Bible readings, and prayers, in particular by giving alms to the poor, and also probably by a memorial meal,[1] which was naturally celebrated as a Christian agapē, and which gradually was transformed, like the agapē, into acts of charity.[2] It is not quite clear why the thirtieth day was, in the majority of cases, replaced by the fortieth, but possibly the change was based on the local differences beneath the ancient custom.

An account of such a memorial feast held on the third day has been accidentally preserved from the second century: the relatives entered into the vault in order "to break bread"[3] at the grave. Tertullian[4] frequently mentions a custom observed on the anniversary of a person's death: it was usual "to offer sacrifice for him and to pray for his soul". In this case, the ancient sacrifice, which used to be offered to the dead, had been transformed into a Christian charitable offering that is brought to God, in the name of the dead, at the Eucharist; it was placed upon the bishop's table as if upon the altar,[5] and accompanied by intercessory prayers.

This kind of worship, in connection with the dead, developed considerably in the case of martyrs, in so far as it was not limited to the circle of family and friends, but was observed by the whole church. How greatly the churches celebrated the martyrs as their heroes, to whom they looked up with pride, is seen from the letters which the churches wrote about Polycarp's death, and about the group of people belonging to Lyons: the letters give a very vivid picture. We are expressly

---

[1] *Const. Apost.* 8,42,1–5; 44,1–4. Ambrose, *de obitu Theodosii*, 3 (2,1198a Bened.). E. Rohde, *Psyche*, 1,232 ff.

[2] *Canones Hippol.* 33

[3] *Acta Joh.* 72

[4] Tert., *de corona*, 3; *exhort. cast.* 11; *monogamia*, 10

[5] Cf. Hippol., *Church Order*, c. 53

assured, in the case of Polycarp, that many wished to secure the corpse and "to have fellowship with his holy flesh"; but the devil prevented it, and brought it about that the body was burnt. As a result, only the ashes were collected and laid aside in a convenient place, and there the church celebrated the anniversary of his martyrdom with joy and gladness.[1] On this day it was also the intention "to remember the earlier martyrs"; the phrase makes it clear that, when the Church instituted a festival for Polycarp, something new was established, and that hitherto the memory of martyrs had not been officially celebrated on behalf of the church. As a matter of fact, it is possible for us to prove, on a documentary basis, that the cult of the martyrs began to be a feast of the church here in Smyrna in the year A.D. 156.

A calendar of martyrs, which has survived from the year A.D. 354, enables us to reach exact conclusions as to the situation in Rome: this list of official memorial-days mentions no martyrs belonging to the first two centuries. The first martyrs whose names are mentioned are the African ladies, Perpetua and Felicitas, who died A.D. 202, and the Roman bishops Callistus (died A.D. 222), Pontïanus, and Hippolytus (died after A.D. 235). The African calendar mentions the Scillitans of A.D. 180 as the earliest martyrs; the Syrian martyrology, which drew on various eastern sources, preserves the memory not only of Polycarp, but of Karpos and his fellows, who were martyred, in Pergamon, probably about the same time; and also Ignatius the early bishop of Antioch.[2] Thus it would appear that the church became accustomed to celebrate martyrdoms officially on their anniversary, in the east and also in Africa at a considerably earlier period than was the case in Rome; here it became an established custom only shortly before the middle of the third century.

The rites and customs in connection with the dead were also the sphere where—as far as we are able to see—the Church first began seriously to practise fine art. The decorated graves which have survived provide us with the earliest and, for a long

---

[1] *Mart. Pol.* 17 f.

[2] H. Achelis, *Die Martyrologien*, pp. 17 f. Texts in Lietzmann *Die drei ältesten Martyrologien* (*Kl. Texte* 2)

time, also the most important examples of Christian art: these are indeed only rare for the second century, but during the third century they gradually increase, and do so very differently in different places. Taken on the whole, the Christians appear always to have adopted the customs of the country, wherever these did not clash with their own views. That fact can be easily proved in the later centuries, and the deduction is probable on internal evidence, for the earlier centuries. On the other hand, Christians unanimously repudiated cremation, which was customary in the time of the early Empire in Rome, and soon afterwards in the rest of the occident.

The inference is that, in Rome, the Christians followed the custom of the Jews who lived there, and prepared sepulchral chambers underground, with square-cornered recesses (*loculi*) in the walls as burial places. Also, in accordance with Jewish custom, the corpses were laid here wound in wrappings, without coffin, and the openings were closed with tiles of brick or marble.[1] Shortly afterwards, several of such chambers were united by connecting them with a vertical gallery, whose walls were provided with *loculi* in rows one above another. These passages multiplied and were inter-connected at different points. Thus from what was a small place in the beginning, there developed an ever-growing system of criss-crossing galleries and chambers, which sometimes lay in several stories one above another, and in this manner could be extended in all three dimensions. The chambers were the privileged places. Here the members of eminent families found their common resting-place; here were laid the dignitaries of the church, and soon also the martyrs. For such persons, the form of grave that was preferred was known as the *arcosolium*: in a semi-circular recess hollowed out in the wall, a space shaped like a coffin was chiselled out to receive the corpse, and was then closed from above by a horizontal slab.

Every visitor to the Roman catacombs is acquainted with these graves, galleries, and chambers; they are to be found, with many variations of form, wherever there are underground cemeteries of that kind, and this was the case in almost every

---

[1] Hipp., *Church Order*, c. 61, uses the Greek word *Keramos* (Horner, *Statutes of the Apostles*, p. 327,19)

land of ancient times.[1] The earliest of these places which can be dated have been preserved in Rome. Here we also meet with the oldest examples of the artistic decoration of chambers and separate graves. Since, at the same date, we find, in Rome, the analogous phenomenon of Jewish catacombs, the connection between the modes of burial of the two religious communities becomes obvious; and, on the other hand, the numerous memorials belonging to the ancient worship of the dead show us plainly a dependence on Roman customs in art.

For these reasons, Rome has become the classical locus of Christian archæology, and, on account of its series of memorials, which extend unbroken from one century to the next, it offers an impressive and a self-contained record of the development of Christian art in a manner with which no other place can compete. The pre-eminence of Rome in this respect has necessarily led scholars to universalize the information obtained there, and it is one of the most important, if also most difficult, problems of modern research to discover the independent artistic life of other countries, in particular those of the orient. Memorials providing the relevant evidence are gradually becoming more numerous, either by being excavated, or because MSS. keep coming to the light of day out of the darkness of oblivion.

Nevertheless the circumstances obtaining in Rome may well be typical of the first beginnings of Christian art. They correspond to what Clement of Alexandria gave as a doctrinal opinion, c. A.D. 200, that no Christian ought to use for his signet ring any pagan image of a god, or any symbol of either war or eroticism, but rather, e.g., a dove, a fish, a ship, a lyre, an anchor, or a fisherman, i.e. seals which would permit a Christian interpretation.[2] Here, as elsewhere, Clement showed that he was not hostile to ancient culture as long as it did not endanger his faith or moral principles. Quite in harmony with this standpoint, and wherever the materials permitted, everywhere in the Roman catacombs, unrestrained use was made of carved decorations, on a ground of white stucco, for ornamenting the bald calcareous tufa. A framework of lines gives the

[1] Lists till A.D. 1900 are given by N. Müller in Hauck, *Realenc.* 3rd edit., 10,804–813. Cabrol-Leclercq, *Dict. d'archéol. chrét.*, 2,2441–47
[2] Clem., *Paed.*, 3,59,2

impression of an arbour made of reed stems or wooden laths, and flower tendrils, coloured ribbons, and wreaths wind from post to post. In between, marvellous flowers shoot out of fantastic vases, masks grin, ornamental heads laugh, dolphins leap gracefully over a trident, and fluttering butterflies flit from flower to flower.

In the chambers of the Christian catacombs, we are greeted by the whole gladsome world of Hellenistic decorative art, such as we may admire in Pompeii, and such as we may find again in the pagan burial-chambers of the Roman Campagna and Isola Sacra. The only things lacking, quite as Clement wished and as is quite natural, are erotic sketches and pagan images of gods. Scrupulousness in this respect was not excessive: the pretty winged creatures representative of Alexandrian art, known as *Erotes* or *Amoretti*, flit unmolested along with their brethren, the birds and the butterflies, between the coloured tendrils; and even Amor and Psyche[1] are not entirely banished from the world of the catacombs. Clement would have frowned at the sight, but, in general estimation, such figures had long become purely decorative elements: who was there that still knew that these little persons with wings were really figures of departed souls, and were intended to provide the dead with friendly society in the grave?

Amongst the traditional elements of Hellenistic origin, we find, after the second century, the picture of a veiled lady with hands uplifted in prayer, and the figure of a shepherd with a lamb on his shoulders and round the back of his neck. Neither is novel to us, but is to be met in many varieties amongst ancient formal figures; here, on Christian soil, they stand forth markedly from the crowd of decorative *motifs*: they have a meaning, and are symbols. The person carrying the lamb must have reminded every Christian onlooker of the parable of the "Good Shepherd" who carried back the lost sheep to the fold, and who was no other than Christ Himself.[2] Moreover, certain later liturgies preserve the conception which led to the painting of this picture in the tombs. In the Latin liturgies,[3] we read: "Lord, let these who are asleep, when they are redeemed from

[1] Wilpert, *Malereien d. Katakomben*, plate 52 [2] Luke 15: 4–7; John 10: 11–16
[3] *The Gelasian Sacramentary*, edited Wilson, pp. 298 f.

death, freed from guilt, reconciled to the Father, and brought home on the shoulders of the Good Shepherd, enjoy eternal salvation in the train of the heavenly king and in the company of the saints"; the Greeks[1] still pray, in the course of the office for the dead: "I am the lost sheep: call me back, O Saviour, and save me." Pictures in the catacombs, from the fourth century, confirm this interpretation of the Good Shepherd.[2] The ladies offering prayer appear continually on the Christian memorials of the second and third centuries until, just as in the case of the Shepherd carrying the lamb, they appear no more after the fourth century. Occasionally, the names of the departed are written near the figures, and the figures themselves are draped round with coloured flowery stems from the Garden of Eden:[3] this fact shows that they were understood as a symbolical representation of the blessed, who offered prayer to God in the kingdom of heaven.

We find similar figures in the left side-aisle of the enigmatic cult chamber of the Porta Maggiore in Rome. Here, also, it is very possible that the women offering prayer have a symbolical significance, especially as the majority of the other figures suggest an allegorical meaning drawn from Orphic and Pythagorean modes of thought. Is it possible that, in this case also, they are the souls of the departed?[4] If so, we are face to face, in the earliest period of the Empire, with the forerunners of the Christian figures.

Side by side with these figures, which were borrowed from amongst those usual in ancient times, and which were only Christianized by being given a symbolical meaning, there was to be found, as early as the second century, a number of Biblical scenes borrowed from the Old Testament, all depicting cases of deliverance from death: the sacrifice of Isaac, Noah in the ark, Daniel in the lions' den, the three men in the fiery furnace, Susannah. In addition, there was the story of Jonah in three scenes: thrown into the sea and swallowed by the whale, vomited forth on to the land, resting in safety under his

[1] Greek *Euchologion* (Athens, 1899), p. 427 [2] Wilpert, *op. cit.*, 190. 222. 236
[3] *Ibid.* 110 ff. C. M. Kaufmann, *Handbuch d. altchr. Epigraphik*, pp. 19. 34. 54. 55. 73. 74. 82
[4] Bendinelli, *Il Monumento sotterraneo di Porto Maggiore* (*Monumenti Antichi*, 31,1927), p. 747

shelter. In this case also, the liturgies, of both the west and the east, give hints as to the meaning of the pictures. Even to-day, a Roman Catholic priest, attending at the bed of the dying, prays that, amongst other things, God will deliver his soul as he delivered Noah from the deluge, Isaac from sacrifice, Daniel out of the lion's den, the three youths from the fiery furnace, and Susannah from false accusation. This prayer can be traced back to its earliest roots, and is paralleled in both Greek and oriental formulas.[1] The choice of examples proves its Jewish origin; moreover, the Mishna actually preserves a prayer of repentance during fasting, of the same type.[2]

Thus the question arises whether the Christians possibly borrowed, not only these prayers, but also the pictorial representations, from the Jews. The recent and more exact knowledge of the paintings found in the Jewish catacombs in Rome and in the eastern synagogues, but especially the excavation of the synagogue in Dura, the fortress on the Euphrates, have made it plain that the Jews practised the art of painting and sculpture; as a consequence the question that we have just raised is by no means so much of a side issue as it would have seemed a short time ago. We know that, c. A.D. 200, the city of Apamea in Phrygia, influenced by the colony of Jews there, minted coins depicting Noah and the ark, and did so in a manner which shows the closest relation with Christian representations of Noah.[3] In a Palestinian synagogue which has been dated in the third century, the Mosaic floor gives the well-known picture of Daniel between the lions.[4] In Dura at about the same time, we find the sacrifice of Isaac as a wall-painting;[5] and the same in a Palestinian synagogue.[6] These facts strengthen the probability of the hypothesis that the Christian representations of the Old Testament cycle of deliverances, together with the prayers in the liturgy for the dead, go back to Jewish exemplars, or rather were taken over

[1] Rituale romanum: Commendatio animae; cf. Ps. Cyprian, *oratio II* (3,147 Hartel), also Schermann, *Oriens christianus*, 3,303–323. Baumstark, *ibid.*, *NS.*, 4,298–305
[2] *Mishna Taanith* 2,4
[3] Head, *Historia Numorum*, 2nd edit., 667. Cabrol-Leclercq, *Diction.*, 1,2515
[4] *Revue biblique N.S.* 16 (1919), 535, and 30 (1921), 442
[5] *Illustrated London News* 1933, July 23, p. 189, fig. 10
[6] Sukenik, *The ancient synagogue of Beth Alpha*, plate 19

without significant changes from the synagogue, and were given a Christian interpretation.

A favourite picture in the early period was that of Moses striking water from the rock: this also was based on Jewish exemplars, even if it cannot be said with certainty that it belonged to the cycle of deliverances. It is possible that Christians were reminded by it of the baptismal water which saved the soul, and possibly also the ancient idea was not far away, according to which the water of life welled up in the Garden of Eden: this metaphor is to be found in the Fourth Gospel.[1] The significance of a group composed of Adam and Eve with the tree of life and the serpent is still uncertain; it appeared in the third century, and remained a favourite for a long time: it may have been intended only as a symbol of paradise, and to beckon the departed.

As early as the second century, we find, associated with the subjects drawn from the Old Testament, a number of New Testament pictures similarly employed to symbolize redemption, and, in particular, to call to mind the death-conquering power of the sacraments. In the foreground is the representation of Christ's baptism, since it was the original of Christian baptism. There is also a fisherman drawing a fish on a hook from the water; in special circumstances, e.g. if other symbolical pictures are near, he may be an apostolic "fisher of men"; similarly, following on a passage in Tertullian, the Christians are born as little fishes in the water in accordance with the exemplar of their Master, the "fish" Jesus Christ.[2] The fish, representing Christ, appears on the wall of one of the earliest Roman vaults in San Callisto, in combination with a little basket full of loaves among which can be seen a glass of red wine: the symbolism of the Lord's Supper is unmistakable.

About the same period also, the Lord's Supper was represented in the form of the feeding of the Five Thousand. This Biblical narrative was regarded as the archetype of the Lord's Supper on account of the interpretation given to it in the Fourth Gospel, and ending in the words:[3] "He that eateth my flesh and drinketh my blood hath eternal life; and I will raise him up

---

[1] John 4: 14, 7: 38, 19: 34; cf. 1 John 5: 6
[2] Tert., de Baptismo, 1; cf. also supra, p. 138   [3] John 6: 54

at the last day." As a rule the painters let seven persons represent the Five Thousand, and they paint them lying on a semi-circular cushion round a table on which are to be found the five loaves and the two fishes mentioned in the gospels.[1] In order to assist beholders to understand the picture, they group the twelve baskets filled with fragments at the end of the meal, and paint them all, or suggest their presence near the table. In San Sebastiano on the Via Appia, another and apparently earlier type has survived, even if the picture itself was painted only after A.D. 200. Here a larger number of people are represented at the meal, as is described in the gospel narrative, while Jesus walks with his disciples among the rows, and dispenses the loaves; at the lower edge of the picture we see a servant hurrying forward with the baskets.[2]

A reference to the sacrament is also to be found in the representations of the woman of Samaria at the well; this was intended to suggest Christ's living water.[3] A similar reference was intended in the very frequent pictures of the man sick of the palsy now carrying his bed on his shoulder: this man shows plainly that the Son of Man has power to forgive sins on earth,[4] especially in the sacrament of baptism. The Feeding of the Five Thousand also contains, in accordance with the doctrine of the Lord's Supper in the early church, a reference to the resurrection: but the classical promise of resurrection was given, in ancient art, by the scene representing the raising of Lazarus. With a magician's wand in his hand, Jesus stands before a grave which looks like a temple, and in the doors of which Lazarus appears, though still swathed in wrappings.

The pictures that we have discussed so far are all based on the Bible, and were intended to instruct and inspire beholders by their symbolic meaning; and we have grounds for assuming that the same motive operated in the paintings in Hellenistic Judaism. On the other hand, we must be clear that, even at this early date, New Testament scenes were composed such as it is difficult to bring into line with any of the theological trains of thought already mentioned, and which are better understood

[1] Mark 6: 38 and parallels; John 6: 9

[2] Lietzmann, *Petrus u. Paulus*, 2nd edit., plate 9 and pp. 310 f.

[3] John 4: 14; cf. *supra*, pp. 187 f.   [4] Mark 2: 10 and parallels

as pictures with a purely objective interest. In these cases, the painters only wished to depict some Biblical story, and they left it to the beholder to make his own religious response. That holds good in regard to the miracle of healing the blind man, and of the woman with the issue, both of which were probably suggested by the resurrection of Lazarus. In this way, they opened up a cycle of healing miracles, and this cycle was much favoured in the following centuries.

Along a very different line, we find the favourite group of the magi from the east doing homage to the Holy Child and His mother. This is the earliest representation of the Madonna; there were variations, it is true, in the immediately following period, but no important further developments. It is only worth remarking that there is another type of Madonna[1] where the prophet Balaam[2] is painted standing before the mother, who holds the Divine Child on her lap. The prophet predicts the "star which shall arise from Jacob"—his hand points to a star shining on Mary's head. As far as is known this *motif* disappeared, and was only taken up again at a considerably later date. In this period, there is only an isolated trace of the Passion. A picture, in the Prætextat catacomb,[3] perhaps shows Jesus crowned with thorns, and being struck by two soldiers with reeds.

Taken on the whole, this exhausts the Biblical scenes made use of by Christian artists during the second and at the beginning of the third centuries. Quite clearly, the first principle in choosing the subjects was that they should be of a symbolic and didactic character; but it is equally clear that an effort was made to break the theological fetters, and to make free use of any material that lent itself to artistic representation. The painters tried to depict a Biblical story for its own sake. This characteristic extended further, and gave rise in the next century to series of pictures. Symbolism, however, was not set aside, but only took on other forms, since it is simply inseparable from religious art of every kind. We have seen that symbolism pertained to Jewish art. To our surprise, the basilica of the Porta Maggiore in Rome[4] shows to what an immense extent

---

[1] Wilpert, *op. cit.*, plate 22   [2] Num. 24: 17   [3] Wilpert, *op. cit.*, plate 18
[4] G. Bendinelli, *Il Monumento sotterraneo . . . (in Monumenti Antichi*, vol. 31, 1927)

allegorical interpretation of Greek myths inspired the entirely ancient forms of decoration in this place of worship. We do not yet know to which sect of persons affecting a philosophy of religion the men belonged who built this beautiful place in the first decades of our era: it is not enough to refer to Orphism and Pythagoreanism. It is generally recognized, however, that in order to understand the figures we must take account of allegory and symbolical interpretation.

The same holds good in regard to the vault of the Aureliani, on the Viale Manzoni, dating soon after A.D. 200.[1] It is the burial place of a gnostic sect, and is decorated artistically; its walls depict all sorts of enigmatic scenes of its cult and doctrine; but we also find here Adam and Eve with the serpent, the Good Shepherd with the lamb upon his shoulders; and a large picture appears to symbolize the Sermon on the Mount. A bearded man sits on a hill reading aloud from a roll, while sheep graze on the hillside around and below him; a similar person of the shepherd type is to be found at a later date amongst pictures in churches. In this case, therefore, we have a monument inspired by two religions; the same use of ornamental art, approximately the same subjects, and an analogous significance. All this teaches us that the members of the early Church took pleasure in art, in the first instance as a decoration that made few pretensions. Later on, they came to practise it in earnest, and used it in accordance with the atmosphere of the time to express their religious feelings. In this way, Christians discovered in art a new and powerful means of teaching the people; in a critical age, art was presented with a new content, and this gradually developed, and continues to breathe an inexhaustible life to the present day.

[1] G. Bendinelli, *Il Monumento sepolcrale degli Aureli*, 1923 (in *Monumenti Antichi*, vol. 28, 1922); cf. p. 30 fig. 12, pp. 51–56 figs. 20. 21. 22, plate 9

Chapter Six

CHRISTIANITY FACE TO FACE WITH THE WORLD

THE SANDS OF EGYPT HAVE ALREADY PROVIDED MUCH NEW and instructive material for the benefit of science, and it is to be hoped that some day a few private letters may be discovered in which men from various classes of society have described to their relatives the reasons which moved them to join the Christian Church. These documents would afford us reliable means of testing what attraction Christianity exercised on the men of the second and third centuries.[1] During the whole of this early period, the Church spread without exercising any outer pressure, or any mass suggestion, but simply by a total of purely individual conversions, and these must have taken place by no means all from the same motives. We have a few bare pieces of information about such converts belonging to the educated classes,[2] but what is entirely lacking, and what is indeed the most important factor, is knowledge of the reactions of the lower classes who went over to the new religion, and enormously increased the number of its adherents. Thus we have no other recourse than to begin with our general knowledge of the spiritual environment, and to dissect out those traits in Christianity which might have exercised a special attraction.

The new faith had separated from Judaism: for a long time now the synagogues had not served its missionaries as the starting points of their propaganda, and the Jews diligently endeavoured to make plain to all the world the distinction between themselves and the Christians.[3] This very separation, however, in all probability exercised an attraction which recruited pagans. Much that had made Judaism very attractive, had been adopted by the Christians: e.g. monotheism, pure ethical doctrine, very ancient sacred writings; the objectionable peculiarities as found in the food taboos and rules for ceremonial

---

[1] The problem is excellently discussed by A. D. Nock in *Conversion* (Oxford, 1933), especially pp. 187–271
[2] Cf. Nock, *op. cit.*, pp. 254 ff.
[3] *Mart. Pol.* 2,2. 13,1. 17,2. 18,1. *Mart. Pionii* 3,6. 4,8

purity, in Sabbath observance, and circumcision had been abandoned. The Christians were able to set their religion forth even more legitimately as the purest and most trustworthy revelation of a reasonable knowledge of God and the world; this, indeed, was what the "Apologists" diligently sought to do. The educated were attracted. Very much more was done, however, than this. The writings of the prophets were proved to have been fulfilled in the life of Jesus, and the facts of the gospel message were shown to the pagans as necessary events willed by God. In this way, an element of the esoteric and supernatural was introduced into Christian preaching in a manner which could be comprehended by the understanding, and it considerably strengthened the convincing power of the message. What was reported of the miracles of Jesus made Him appear to pagan hearers as one of those celebrated great men of whom Apollonius of Tyana may be regarded as typical. Jesus' divine sonship was as easily a matter of course to men who had grown up in the ancient world of ideas as His ascent to heaven and His elevation to the right hand of the Father. This would appear to them as a heroization, and be understood similarly to Hercules, as a case of admission into the circle of divine beings.[1] His shameful death by crucifixion was more difficult to grasp and was, as it continues to be, an objection: but even in this case understanding came about in the period when many philosophers paid with their lives the price of giving free expression to their convictions. The brave martyr-doms amongst the Christians showed that the spirit continued to dwell in Christ's disciples, and showed it, indeed, to a world which had become accustomed to admire those strong-minded persons who despised death.[2]

Even a man like the Emperor Marcus Aurelius could only avoid the impression made by the death of Christian martyrs by refusing to regard it as a parallel case, and by setting it down as the result of a mere spirit of opposition and a theatrical gesture.[3] However, that was not the opinion of the people, and they were impressively affected by this kind of death. Lucian employed similar tactics and poured scorn on Peregrinus the

---

[1] Cf. Celsus in Origen, c. Celsum, 3,42
[2] Nock, ibid., pp. 193–197   [3] Marcus Aurel. 11,3,2

Cynic preacher. When the object of his contempt mounted the funeral pyre in the sight of the Greeks, who had streamed together for the Olympic games, and let himself be burnt in order to give them an example of the way in which a philosopher despised life, Lucian saw nothing in it except mere folly and play-acting. Nevertheless, in the same writing he records an episode from the life of Peregrinus which deserves our most serious attention. This restless man had, at one time, joined the Christians: and Lucian now goes on in this connection to characterize the Christians in a very significant manner.[1] To him they were a hopeless society of people who imagined themselves to be immortal and to possess eternal life;[2] for this reason they even despised death, and frequently accepted it voluntarily. Moreover, they worshipped that crucified Sophist, and lived after his laws which they accepted "without cogent proof". These laws influenced them to set little value upon any earthly goods, and they held their possessions in common—for this reason a man of business instincts could quickly become rich among them. Lucian takes a delight in telling how Peregrinus was honoured, given gifts, looked after while he was a martyr in prison, and, indeed, supported by members of other churches, and, "out of a thirst for notoriety", was really prepared to die. The wily governor, however, set the fool free, and he continued to play his part among the Christians until he was caught in the act of eating forbidden food: then he was cast out from among them.[3]

Even from a one-sided picture like this it is clear what features among the Christians struck the surrounding world: they died in their faith and for their faith,[4] they really did live in accordance with the commandments of their Lord in a comprehensive spirit of brotherly love, and they excluded sinners from their fellowship. They hoped for immortality and eternal life, and the founder of their religion was a philosophical teacher who died on the cross, but who was worshipped by them as a god. From these few hints, it is possible for us to perceive what was the attraction that Christianity must have had for the people of that time. Here was religious faith strong enough to

---

[1] Lucian, *de morte Peregrini*, 13   [2] Cf. also *Mart. Justini* 5,1,3
[3] Cf. *supra*, p. 55   [4] So also Celsus in Origen 2,45. 1,2. 8,54

overcome death and to transform life; it was combined with an esoteric age-old wisdom and an enduring miraculous power. The moral earnestness, which agreed with the requirements of the philosophy, became a tangible fact in a thousand different ways. A brotherly spirit, which recognized no social limitations, welded the members of the separate churches together, and softened poverty and illness; it also threw a net over the whole world, and thus united cities and lands into a mighty, organized, spiritual fellowship offering mutual aid in all the necessities of the present life.[1]

It was not difficult to find entry into this fellowship, although it is certain that no public means of proselytization was adopted: this last was due to personal contact with Christians met in the course of daily life, who gave promising accounts of their inner and outer experiences. This aroused curiosity and awakened desire for closer acquaintance with the strange religion. A visit to a service of worship, at least as regards its first part, was not impossible for a stranger who was well introduced.[2] If he were converted, he reported himself to the "teachers" of the church as a catechumen. Then there came a serious testing; he had to declare what moved him to make the change and become a Christian, and his Christian friends had to give a sort of guarantee for him. Then his outer relationships in life were tested, and the first requirement laid upon him was that he should avoid every form of non-conjugal intercourse. If he were the slave of a Christian master, he must be recommended by that master as worthy of reception; if he served a pagan, faithful labour became a duty for him for the sake of the good reputation of the Christians.

A number of callings were not reconcilable with Christianity, and had to be given up when application was made. Here were included not only the unclean trade of prostitution, but also the disreputable arts of the actor, the gladiator,[3] the racing chariot driver, together with everything closely connected with these callings. Naturally the priest of a pagan temple, an astrologer, or other soothsayer, was inadmissible. A sculptor or

---

[1] Harnack, *Mission*, 4th edit., pp. 170–220
[2] *Const. Apost.* 8,6,2; cf. *re* synagogues Tert., *apol.*, 18,9
[3] Cf. also Tert., *idol.*, 11 (pp. 42,9 ff. Wissowa)

a painter had to undertake not to depict gods, and a school-master was recommended to abandon his calling because he was required to deal with pagan mythology in the course of giving instruction. But it is characteristic of the attitude of the Church towards ancient literature that here she was prepared to exercise[1] mild caution, particularly if an indigent teacher had no other means of gaining an honest livelihood. A soldier had to undertake not to kill and not to swear oaths—a dubious thing from the military point of view; anyone already Christian was altogether forbidden to become a soldier. Quite in the same spirit, a Christian was not permitted to hold any office in the government of the state or of the city, the reason being that the power of the sword, and worship of pagan gods, were inseparable from such an office.[2] It was certainly not easy to carry out strictly the repudiation of so many and, at times, such very attractive callings, but on the whole these regulations were observed. There was small danger that Christians would subsequently take up the interdicted means of livelihood.

Nevertheless it was very difficult for the Church, as it became more at home in this world, to prevent its members from going to all kinds of public shows, whether of the amusing or the sanguinary sort. And these were not only morally dubious, but they brought members of the audience ever and again into new contacts with pagan life: the attractions of these amusements in ancient times were occasionally stronger than Christian conviction.[3] The Church had doubts also about visiting the public baths, but they were places of recrea-tion for all classes of the population, and at the same time the centres of a voluntary, social intercourse. As a consequence, they were as a rule permitted, and only mixed bathing was prohibited—although even this restriction could not be punctiliously carried out.[4]

In other respects, the Christian manner of life was not essentially different outwardly from that of any contempor-ary with sound moral feelings; the rules for life and behaviour, which Clement of Alexandria prescribed for Christians,

---

[1] See also Tert., *idol.*, 10 (pp. 39 f. Wissowa)   [2] Hippol., *Church Order*, c. 40 f.
[3] Min. Felix, *Oct.*, 12,5. 37,11 f. Tert., *spectac.*, 26. *Didascalia* 13 p. 127,20 ff. Connolly. Cyprian, *ad Donatum*, 7 f. Clem., *Paed.*, 3,76,3–77,4
[4] *Didascalia* 2 p. 14,23 ff. 3 p. 26,7 ff. Connolly. Clem., *Paed.*, 3,31–3. 46–8

c. A.D. 200, correspond largely to what we are accustomed to read in Stoic textbooks on ethics. The Stoics had the same attitude of abnegation towards everything unnatural in bodily hygiene, clothing, and manner of life, refusal of every form of growing luxuriousness, together with the recommendation of a healthy simplicity in all directions. What was characteristically Christian was shown only in details, e.g. in the emphatic refusal to wear garlands,[1] or when it was forbidden to use signet rings with pagan figures, and when men were admonished to avoid barbers' shops and bazaars, and to cease playing dice. Moreover it was forbidden to praise goods fraudulently, or to swear falsely in order to do business.[2] Indeed swearing pagan oaths was altogether forbidden and, naturally also, cursing.[3] Reluctance to express the names of pagan gods might go as far as forbidding the reciting of verses from Homer,[4] but that seems to have been regarded as a narrowness from which the educated classes of Christians withheld, and, in the case of a man like Clement, the poets and philosophers of old were held in high honour.

Our sources give us everywhere the impression that when the Christians held back from this world, the attitude was essentially inward and nothing particularly striking was to be seen outwardly. An acceptable social event in the form of a festive meal was not denied to a Christian; it linked him with his fellow believers and also with pagan "society", but it was expected that on such occasions he should do honour to the Church by his behaviour.[5] "We are neither Brahmins nor Indian fakirs, nor do we live remote in the woods", cries Tertullian with rhetorical passion.[6] "We despise none of God's gifts, but we use them with discretion and understanding. Moreover in living in this world, we make use of your forum, your meat market, your baths, shops and workshops, your inns and weekly markets, and whatever else belongs to your economic life. We go with you by sea, we are soldiers or farmers,

---

[1] Clem., *Paed.*, 2,70–3. Tert., *corona*, 1. *apol.* 42,6. Min. Felix 12,6. 38,2. *Martyr. Pionii* 18,4
[2] Clem., *Paed.*, 3,59,2. 75,1 f. 79,1 f.
[3] Tert., *apol.*, 32, *idol.* 11 (p. 41,13 Wissowa). *Didascalia* 21 p. 179,22. 15 p. 144,25 Connolly; cf. Achelis, *Christentum i. d. ersten 3. Jh.* (1912), 2 p. 426
[4] *Didascalia* 21 pp. 179,7 ff. Connolly
[5] Clem., *Paed.*, 2,4,4. 10,1. 11,1   [6] Tert., *apol.*, 42

we exchange goods with you, and whatever we make as a work of art or for use serves your purposes. But we do not join in your festivals to the gods, we do not press wreaths upon our heads, we do not go to plays, and we buy no incense from you. It is true that your temple dues are continually becoming smaller: we prefer to give to the poor in the streets rather than to the treasuries of the gods. Other dues, however, are conscientiously met by Christians, and, if in the above case there is a decrease, it is made up for abundantly to the state when the state takes into account on the opposite side your fraudulent declarations and dishonest shifts." This passage gives a clear description and a substantially correct account of the actual attitude taken up by Christians to civic life. It is by no means an idealized picture.

Disturbances of this peaceful relation with the surrounding world may have taken place occasionally in the narrower circle of the family, if the new faith had been accepted by only some of its members: suggestions of the kind are to be found at least in connection with general warnings against mixed marriages.[1] Such cases of incompatibility would of course occur just the same if one of the couple joined the cult of Isis or some other god of the mysteries; and the Roman world was used to tolerance. There were cases where a Christian soldier came into conflict with his duties: occasioned by some such circumstance, Tertullian published an apologetic writing;[2] but the problem only became urgent in the time of Diocletian. Isolated matters of this kind were not the roots out of which grew the opposition to "this world", but rather vice versa: the individual cases were the consequence of the total attitude of Christians towards the Imperium Romanum,[3] and the crucial battle-ground was religion. We have already seen that emperor worship constituted an ideological bond of unity;[4] it made the vast multiplicity of peoples conscious that they belonged to one another; anyone who denied emperor worship placed himself outside the pale of society in the civilized world. Jews alone had gained the privilege of tolerance for their special national religion—and they had to defend the privilege

---

[1] Tert., uxor., 2,4; cf. apol., 3,4   [2] Tert., de corona militis
[3] Supra, pp. 51 f.   [4] Vol. 1, p. 167

repeatedly by bloody sufferings. The privilege was refused, and it was unavoidable that it should continue to be refused, to the Christians, for they had cast off all national bonds. The antithesis between the world and the Christian community came to a head on this issue.

The Jews were hated because they withheld themselves, and because they emphasized their peculiar characteristics, but the Christians were hated still more; and at an early date they were supposed to hide evil practices behind their exclusiveness. At first they seemed to be a Jewish sect, and thus they shared with Jews the accusation of atheism. Soon even the fables told about the Jews were transferred to them. It was said that they worshipped an ass's head or something similar,[1] and that they murdered little children ritually in order to eat their flesh.[2] Indeed at a very early date there was a widespread conviction that, in their "love feasts", reserved to themselves, the Christians ate children's flesh and practised incest. If anyone with evil imagination heard that at the Lord's Supper the Christians partook of the flesh and blood of the Son of Man,[3] and that Christian "brothers" married their Christian "sisters", such a person might come finally to the above conclusions: the educated public gave the names "Thyestic meals" and "Oedipodean love" to the crimes which they inferred Christians committed.[4] Those who did not join in this nonsense were nevertheless convinced that Christians were enemies of the human race, maintained a dangerous superstition,[5] and nursed contempt of law and custom in secret associations.[6] It can occasion no surprise that from time to time they became the object of an excitement which had been whipped up amongst the people, especially if the Jews cunningly pointed the way for the raging mobs to take;[7] or if, under torture, confessions were made which seemed to support the dreadful reports.[8] Even Nero was quick to make use of this attitude in order to shift blame from himself,[9] and more than a century later we hear the complaint of a Christian[10] that whenever there was

---

[1] Tert., apol., 16; cf. Vol. 1, pp. 84 f. [2] Acta Lugdun. in Eus., H.E., 5,1,26
[3] John 6: 53 [4] Athenagoras Suppl. 3. Acta Lugdun., op. cit., 5,1,14
[5] Tacitus, ann., 15,44. Sueton., Nero, 16 [6] Celsus in Origen 1,1
[7] Mart. Pol. 12,2. 13,1. 17,2. 18,1. Tert., Scorp., 10 (pp. 168,12 Wissowa)
[8] Mart. Lugdun. in Eus., H.E., 5,1,14 [9] Vol. 1, p. 191 [10] Tert., apol., 40,1-2

a public misfortune, flood, or drought, earthquake, pestilence or famine, excited mobs roared out demanding the death of the Christians: away with them to the lions. This general attitude must be taken into account if we are to understand the strange shape in which the unavoidable conflict developed in regard to emperor worship.

Much research has been done in regard to the legal presuppositions that lay at the base of the trials of Christians, but so far without any quite clear result. This disappointment is not by any means surprising, since the younger Pliny was in the same difficulty in the year A.D. 112. At that time he was the imperial governor of the province of Bithynia; he wrote to the Emperor Trajan[1] about his difficulty, and asked for instructions: he had never yet been present at a legal inquiry in the courts against the Christians, and, as a consequence, did not know, in particular, whether the proof of adherence to Christianity was culpable, or whether the inquiry was to be directed towards illegal actions connected with this adherence. Hitherto, on account of his uncertainty, he had waived formal legal process; in the case of persons who had been denounced as Christians, he had confined himself to asking whether they were indeed Christians. When an affirmative answer was given, he had required them to abandon their allegiance, to do honour to the statues of the gods and the Emperor, which were set up in the tribunal, and to curse Christ. Those who had acted accordingly, and who had thereby obviously abandoned their Christian connection, had been set free unpunished; but those who had remained firm in refusal in spite of repeated admonition he had condemned, and had done so from the point of view that, altogether apart from their belief, this obstinacy and unbending perversity ought to be punished in any case. Roman citizens he had handed over to the imperial assize in Rome. Moreover he had sometimes instituted exact hearings about the peculiarities of Christian worship, and had done so indeed with the use of torture, but had found nothing more than a pernicious and immeasurable superstition. As a consequence, he had abandoned further use of this method, and now appealed for a decision on the part of the Emperor. The subject

[1] *Epist. ad Traian.* 96. 97

was important on account of the large number of Christians who were in this very uncertain legal position. The movement had not only laid hold of the towns but had already overflowed into the villages and the countryside; for the present it was still possible to dam it up and bring it to a stand, because it must be said, on the other side, there had also been an unmistakable increase of the worship hitherto usual in the temples, and at the sacrifices.

Trajan answered briefly and clearly that no general regulations could be given, or drawn up in simple form. Christians were not to be officially sought out. But if they had been notified to the authorities, the accused must be punished; yet everyone was to be pardoned who repudiated his Christianity and confirmed his assertion by offering sacrifice to "our gods". Anonymous notifications were to go unheeded, because they furnished highly pernicious precedent, and contradicted the spirit of the times.

This correspondence makes it clear that neither the counsellors of the highest court in Bithynia, nor the officials of the imperial secretariat in Rome,[1] possessed any juristic material which would provide an answer to the legal question proposed by Pliny, and, therefore, that there was no such material. It is also clear that even Trajan had no desire to lay down any theoretic principle, possibly because he feared unforeseen consequences. The veteran officials of the civil service were able to suggest to their chief only the customary administrative practice in accordance with which Pliny had acted; this was what even the Emperor had confirmed, although he explicitly repudiated anonymous informers. It follows that the governors did not concern themselves at all about the faith and conduct of Christians, but required any accused persons to make known the correctness of their attitude to the state by offering sacrifice before the images of the gods and the Emperor. Every inhabitant of the Roman empire had to fulfil this requirement: anyone who refused was punished with death for an offence against the respect due to the majesty of the empire, the emperor, and their guardian deities. Thus the matter remained. All the *Acts of the Martyrs*[2] portray the same circumstances; they

[1] W. Weber in *Festgabe für Karl Müller*, 1922, pp. 26 ff.
[2] Texts brought together by O. von Gebhardt, *Acta martyrum selecta*, 1902 and R. Knopf, *Ausgewählte Märtyrerakten*, 3rd edit., 1929

show that the judge instituted no judicial inquiries, and that there were neither accusations put forward nor defences made, on grounds of the general bearing of the law, or of special legal prescriptions. The only thing to be proved was adherence to Christianity, whereupon the defendant was ordered to swear by the genius of the Emperor and to offer sacrifice before the images. Frequently a long discussion then arose, in which the judge attempted to persuade the defendant to offer sacrifice, and pointed out the consequences of refusal. A definite refusal to conform to the requirement was then followed by the death sentence.

The Christian apologists constantly complained that the name of Christ was sufficient to bring about condemnation. They constantly demanded that their manner of life should be inquired into, and they repudiated the popular fables of their crimes. They constantly described the moral purity of the life of the Church, and protested their loyalty to the state and the sincerity of their prayers on behalf of the Emperor and the Empire. All this, however, was useless, and could not be anything else than useless, because the state refused to discuss these very matters. The state had no desire for religious trials with theoretic discussions, but its governors acted on the basis of the powers inherent in their position. They acted by making use of the police force against public offence, which, in each case, they first officially provoked in order to be able to punish it. Moreover, each case of refusing to sacrifice, when proved in this manner, offered further justification of official doubt as to the Christian attitude towards the state. The whole procedure assumed that it required no proof that the Christians were at bottom enemies of the state, and expressions used by contemporaries show that no real doubt existed as to the general correctness of this opinion. The attitude of the governing officials resulted from this view: they did not institute any "trials" but they took action in compliance with administrative orders.

Tertullian sometimes[1] speaks as if laws had been formulated forbidding people to become Christian, and a martyrology from the year A.D. 180[2] mentions a senatorial decision to this effect.

---

[1] Tert., apol., 4,3–5. 10–11. 37,2   [2] Acta Apollonii 13. 23

In several of these *Acts of the Martyrs*, the official administering the law expressly quotes an imperial edict which required Christians to offer the sacrifices,[1] and the whole of the persecution under Decius rested upon an edict of that kind. Its wording in regard to the crucial point may be deduced from the numerous surviving *Libelli*.[2] Those who were accused of Christianity had to make an attestation that "in accordance with the law they had offered smoke and drink sacrifices, and had eaten sacrificial meat in the presence of the appropriate officials". The edicts, of which the earlier *Acts of the Martyrs* speak, must have been expressed in very similar terms. The decision reached by the senate, as already mentioned, may have had its analogy in the numerous laws[3] which the state promulgated at a later time, when it had itself become Christian, and in which Manichees, Arians, and other heretics, were forbidden to exercise their worship; here also it is assumed that these sects were known to be hostile to the state, and that the matter needed no further inquiry. The laws were simply instructions to the governors as to the mode in which they should employ the police force against the sects. But the continual repetition of the same prescription, in decrees constantly being issued, shows that the officials responsible for the internal policy adapted the carrying out of these edicts to the temporary circumstances of the time and place, and that they frequently omitted them altogether because serious doubts stood in the way.

Exactly the same case must have held good in regard to the edicts against the Christians in the earlier period. Decrees of that kind were construed as political guiding lines, and their carrying out was left to the discretion of the governors of individual provinces. There was a single main line leading from Trajan's edict to that of Decius, and it extended beyond these two fixed points in both directions. Under Caracalla, i.e. *c.* A.D. 215, the celebrated jurist, Ulpian, wrote a work on provincial government; he listed the imperial edicts against the Christians, and reduced the penalties imposed to a system.[4]

---

[1] *Acta Carpi, Papylae*, etc., 4.45. *Acta Justini* 5,8. *Acta Apollonii* 45. *Acta Pionii* 3,2; cf. *Acta Maximi* 1,8. Melito in Eus., *H.E.* 4,26,5. 10
[2] Cf. von Gebhardt, *op. cit.*, pp. 182 f.   [3] e.g. *Cod. Theod.* 16,5,3. 5,11, etc.
[4] Lactantius, *Instit.*, 5,11,19

The Christian Apologists quote verbatim[1] two edicts, one of the emperor Hadrian, and the other of Antoninus Pius; these edicts digress from the main line in so far as they require proof of the separate crimes of the Christians, or else indeed offer protection to the Christians, but this contradicts the consistent attitude of the state as testified by all the other witnesses. Hence it follows that these edicts have been simply invented, or else the texts have since been "corrected" with a special purpose.

Formerly, scholars used to distinguish the attitude of the different emperors towards Christianity,[2] and to bring out into relief a number of separate persecutions of Christians; indeed scholars used to follow the example of Eusebius and characterize them by means of ordinal numbers. The presuppositions for such a point of view cannot be maintained. Apart from the special circumstances which held good in the city of Rome itself, the personal inclination of the respective rulers had hardly any influence upon the course of events: the most that happened was that the Emperor, moved by general political considerations or in response to an inquiry on the part of a governor, issued a decree in regard to the Christians. The "persecutions of Christians" were always of limited extent, and their outbreak was dependent on local conditions and the character of the governor. Domitian caused his cousin Flavius Clemens to be put to death, and banished his consort Flavia Domitilla to an island, "on account of atheism"—and it is highly probable that Christianity was meant.[3] Perhaps also Acilius Glabrio, who was executed on account of revolutionary intrigues, paid the price of his Christian faith: at any rate it can be proved that his family was Christian as early as the second century.[4] That Domitian took measures against the Christians also in other respects is told us by writers only in the most general terms.[5] It is true that about this time 1 Clement speaks of an imminent persecution, and the Revelation of John, which is contemporaneous, declares that Rome is drunk with the blood of the

[1] In Eus., *H.E.*, 4,9 and 13

[2] Series of texts Preuschen, *Analecta*, 2nd edit., 1909–10

[3] Dio Cassius, *epit.*, 67,14. *Prosopogr. imp. Rom.* 2 p. 66 no. 170, p. 81 no. 279

[4] Suetonius, *Domitian*, 10; cf. Leclercq, *Dict.*, 6,1259–1274

[5] Eus., *H.E.*, 3,17. Jerome, *Chron. Olymp.*, 218,2–4 and footnote p. 569 together with Dio Cass., *epit.*, 67,14

saints and martyrs of Jesus; the seer saw under the altar the souls of the witnesses who had been slain.[1] While Trajan was emperor, Ignatius was sent from Antioch to Rome, and there put to death.[2] We are without more exact knowledge of any of these early martyrdoms. A great persecution took place during which, on February 22, A.D. 156, Polycarp bishop of Smyrna was burnt alive at eighty years of age; the Church sent a detailed account of the event to Philomelion in the interior of Asia Minor, and at the same time sent round the news in an open letter. Thereby the attention of Christian people generally was drawn to such documents, and they became eager to receive them: indeed Polycarp was a man whose name was closely connected with the tradition of the highly esteemed letters of Ignatius.[3]

In the year A.D. 177 a similar persecution broke out in Lyons and Vienne owing to popular passion, and these churches also wrote a letter about it to Asia Minor.[4] The vivid descriptions in this letter arouse the deepest emotions in every new generation of readers. In this case, the Christians were genuinely hunted out: we can see the alarmed confusion in the churches; the first instances of torture spread terror abroad, a few recanted, the majority kept themselves timidly in the background, pagan slaves said what was required of them. Then the passion of the populace broke loose, the prison was filled with those who confessed themselves Christians, and all the torments of a brutal, murderous blood-lust broke upon the heads of the unfortunates. Then those who had at first recanted were once more arrested, and gained new courage when brought face to face with death. Pictures painted in blood glower dreadfully before our eyes. Bishop Potheinos at ninety years of age lay in prison, beaten by the fists and trampled by the feet of the mob, until death mercifully released him after two days. The slave girl, Blandina, hung on a cross, her body mangled and her bones broken, as food for wild beasts: to no purpose, for the beasts did not touch her, and so she ended her life on the funeral pyre. In the middle of the arena stood a chair glowing red hot holding the Christians in its Moloch-like arms: the

[1] 1 *Clem.* 7: 1. Rev. 7: 6, 6: 9; cf. 2: 13, 12: 11, 20: 4
[2] Jerome, *op. cit..* 221,4   [3] Vol. 1, p. 236   [4] Eus., *H.E.*, 5,1,3-3,3.

smoke of the burning bodies rose to the sky, and unceasingly from all the places where the martyrs stood, the death cry sounded: I am a Christian, I am a Christian. In the prison, they lay in rows fixed helplessly in stocks, and died a silent death: their bodies provided useful food for the dogs. The executioner piled the pitiable remains into a heap, crowned by the heads of the decapitated Roman citizens: finally, the flames flared up and reduced everything to ashes, and these were thrown into the Rhone with scoffing laughter in order that the Christian hope of resurrection, too, might be destroyed.

In all these bloody terrors, however, the reflection of another world gleamed with light. Heaven opened for the Christians in their agony, Christ descended from His throne at the right hand of God where Stephen had seen Him at the moment of his own death, and spoke encouragement to them; all earthly torments paled before the blessedness of the vision of God. No more pain touched the souls of the blessed: their enraptured faces reflected the glory of the Lord as they left their human condition behind, and became like the angels.[1] Hitherto they had bravely confessed their faith, but their entry into the other world conferred on them the dignity of "martyrs", "witnesses of God", who had warranted the truth of their testimony with their lives—just as had been done by Christ, the "genuine and true witness", and their example.[2] The Church of the earliest period insisted on reserving the title of martyr entirely for those who had suffered death for Christ: only by suffering thus was their witness made perfect. It was a common view in the ancient world, and one found also in late Judaism, that a genuine prophet sealed the truth of his testimony with death,[3] but also that, when he suffered death in this way, he was endowed with supramundane powers which vanquished the martyr's pain.[4] Hence we can understand the view of the early Christians that, only by carrying it through to the death, was their testimony made perfect and complete. Moreover from this standpoint, the death of Jesus gained a new meaning, and

[1] K. Holl., *op. cit.*, 2,72 f. *Mart. Pol.* 2,2–4. Eus., *H.E.*, 5,1,51. 55. *Acta Carpi* 39 and oft
[2] Rev. 1: 5, 3: 14. Eus., *H.E.*, 5,2,2 f. *Mart. Pol.* 1,2. 17,3. Ign., *ad Rom.*, 6,3
[3] Cf. Rev. 14: 7; Matt. 23: 30, 35, 37; 4 Macc. 7: 15
[4] *Ascensio Isaiae* 5,7. 14. 4 Macc. 6: 5–7, 13 f. 9: 21–22

thus the divine revelation made by Him to mankind was confirmed by an ever-increasing number of "witnesses" who, while still on earth, had passed at the moment of death from faith to sight.[1]

A very characteristic piece of writing has survived from Africa, which gives an impressive and graphic sketch of these early martyrdoms, and their character of "enthusiasm" in the full sense of the word. In the year A.D. 202, a young woman of the higher classes, Vibia Perpetua by name, together with several slaves, was thrown into prison on account of her Christian faith. She described her experiences and impressions, and Saturus, her companion in suffering, did the same. The Church added a detailed narrative to these pages, and gave an account of the further course of events. It set forth the whole in a form which could be read aloud in church as a genuine witness to the power of the Holy Spirit. That spirit was also revealed in prophecies, visions, and miracles.[2] As a matter of fact the *Acts of the Martyrs in Africa* were read aloud in the churches for several centuries, and were imitated by the composition of other *Acts*. In these writings, it is plain that the martyrs were conscious of being under the influence of a special act of God's grace from the moment when they were flung into prison; they yearned for visionary revelations, and received what they desired. They had power to redeem the dead by their prayers; in visions seen in dreams, their sight penetrated heaven, and they conversed with the Lord. No wonder that they acted as authoritative mediators, and showed the bishop of their church and his learned presbyter the way towards reconciliation. Pneumatic prophets, subject to no rules, had been found in early Christianity, but had come to rank second to the regulated office of bishop in the course of the second century, and were on the point of disappearing—their place was now taken, however, by the confessors as heroes chosen by the Spirit. These exercised extraordinary authority, occasionally making not inconsiderable difficulties for the normal leaders of a church. In particular they arrogated to themselves[3] the pardoning of fallen brothers,

---

[1] Pauly-Wissowa 14,2044–2052
[2] *Acta Perpetuae et Felicitatis:* sketches of Perpetua, chapters 3–10, Saturus chapters 11–13
[3] Cf. Eus., *H.E.*, 5,2,5

a feature which led, as we shall see later on, to conflicts of considerable importance within the Church.

About the same time as that in which the epistolary accounts of the martyrdoms came to be given, a second type of *Acts of Martyrs* was already being written, a type which became normative in subsequent history, viz. the record of the judiciary proceedings. The account is extant of the trial of Justin in Rome (*c.* A.D. 165); about the same time, the martyrdom of Karpos and Papylas was described in Pergamon, and in the year A.D. 180, in Africa, there is the lapidary text of the martyrs of Scilli. These records are not copies of official proceedings which the church may have obtained privately in some way, but original literary compositions based on the personal recollections of those who had seen and heard what had taken place, possibly supported also by a few notes. The purpose of these writings was to give the reader a description of the trial in a kind of official record in order to increase the impression of trustworthiness by means of the documentary form. Philosophers, in the other camp, had proceeded in a similar fashion when describing the courage of their comrades before the judgment seat of tyrannical emperors. They, too, cast their reports into an official form, which, at bottom, depended upon notes of the speeches, notes which enabled the proceedings to be written up in good literary fashion; in particular, the speeches of the accused were turned into effective apologies of the good cause.[1] The authors of the records of Christian martyrs followed this example, and in their case, too, the speeches of those who were to testify with their blood, provided the most fertile field for the activity of their rhetoric. To an increasing degree the records contained theological statements; these showed the influence of a learned apologetic, which grew to the point of offering detailed and penetrating proofs of the vanity of idol worship, and even issued in a hope for the conversion of the officiating judge.[2] Only for a short time were the requirements of readers who sought edification satisfied with the simple type of the earlier period, as in the *Acts of Justin* and of the *Scillitans*: the various redactions of the *Acts of the Scillitans*[3]

---

[1] Lietzmann, *Griech. Papyri*, 2nd edit. (*Kl. Texte* 14), nos. 20, 21
[2] e.g., *Acta Apollonii*, 14–45. *Acta Pionii* 4. 8. 13 f.
[3] J. A. Robinson in *Texts and Studies*, Vol. 1 (1891), pp. 112–121

plainly reveal the way in which the material assumed shape.

Although the literary principles were only adopted by Christians incidentally, yet they continued to operate for about two centuries. The literature which has come down to us, has been preserved on account of so many different accidental conditions, that it is not really possible to say whether the rise and fall of the waves of persecution were connected with changes in the inner, or the outer, policy of the Empire. The only thing that can be asserted is that, in the latter part of the reign of the Antonines and until the time of Septimius Severus, we have an increasing number of items of information about persecutions, i.e. at the time when the economic and military crisis of the imperium was beginning to crystallize out. A legend upon which little confidence can be placed, but telling of Alexander Severus, speaks of various friendly acts towards Christians. We must remember, however, that the oriental syncretism of the Syrian dynasty could not have fostered any marked tendency towards persecuting Christians; the Queen Mother, Julia Mamæa, really ruled both the empire and the weak Alexander, and, during one of the most serious war-periods, she commanded to her court in Antioch the most celebrated Christian scholar, Origen,[1] in order to be able to enjoy spiritual intercourse with him.

When Maximinus, the Thracian soldier, in A.D. 235, was preparing to bring this oriental dynasty to a bloody end, there was no further opportunity for æsthetic and religious sentimentality of that kind. The new emperor ruled with brutal force, and slew everyone suspected of clinging to the earlier ways. These included apparently even Christian clerics. He banished the two Roman bishops, and in Palestine a persecution was explicitly directed against the heads of the Church, a persecution which Origen met with an exhortation to stand firm.[2] In Cappadocia and Pontus, severe earthquakes laid whole towns in ruins; and in their excitement the masses remembered sayings which had been almost forgotten for a long period, sayings which demanded that the Christian scapegoats should be thrown to the lions: the Cappadocian legate, Licinius

[1] Eus., *H.E.*, 6,21,3 f.
[2] Eus., *H.E.*, 6,28. Origen, *De Martyr.*, 10, cf. chap. 7. 33, ed. Koetschau

Serenianus, eagerly complied with the demand.[1] During the following years of confusion, a genuine oriental, Philip the Arab (A.D. 244–249), once more mounted the throne. Origen wrote letters to him and his consort, Otacilia Severa, and, according to later Christian tradition, he was a Christian.[2] That did not make it impossible, however, that in Alexandria, in A.D. 249, Christians should be hunted out; four paid the sacrifice of death, numerous Christians were compelled to flee, and their houses were plundered in the wildest manner.[3]

All these persecutions were little more than phenomena of purely local significance, exactly the same as in preceding cases. When Decius came to the throne, the outlook was completely transformed. This soldier emperor, of considerable practical genius, recognized the need of the Empire in all its seriousness, and knew that all its resources would require to be organized if catastrophe were to be averted: perhaps also he really believed he had discovered a causal connection between the decline of the imperium and lack of due reverence to the gods. Hence, as early as the end of A.D. 249, he gave orders that, everywhere throughout the Empire, all the inhabitants should come before special officers concerned with the sacrifices, and formally declare their firm allegiance to the gods, and prove it by an act of sacrifice.[4]

It is obvious that this regulation really had a negative purpose, viz. to ascertain who were the intractable Christians in the entire empire, and to render them harmless; it was also hoped that the greater majority would be induced by threats to return to the state religion. Numerous documents have been preserved in Egypt in the form of a notice (*libellus*) issued by the local officers of sacrifice. The notices are written on papyrus and deal with the religious inquisition; they say that the owner of the paper had duly performed the sacrifice. These documents, which include one belonging to a pagan priestess, make it safe to assume what had already been extremely probable, viz.

---

[1] Firmilian of Cæsarea in Cyprian *Ep.* 75,10. Origen *in Mt. Comm. ser.* 39 p. 75,7 Klostermann

[2] Eus., *H.E.*, 6,34. 36,3; cf. J. Chrys., *de St. Babyla*, 6 (2,544 f. Montf.). Jerome, *Chron. Olymp.*, 256,1

[3] Dionys. Al. in Eus., *H.E.*, 6,41,1–9

[4] Wittig in Pauly-W. 15,1279–1284. Leclercq, *Dict. d'arch.*, 4,309–339

that really all the inhabitants, and not simply those accused of Christianity, had to appear before the governors.[1] It was an extraordinary form of worshipping the gods, viz. a formal act of petition on the part of the whole people for the safety of the emperor and Empire which was seriously threatened, but at the same time it had a cruel practical side in a bloody action on the part of the police. The change of the times can be seen even more clearly, if Augustus's[2] attempts at the restoration of religion are called in as parallels. The Emperor Decius everywhere followed the lines advocated by the adversaries of Christianity.

It follows that the persecution under Decius in fact comprised the entire Empire, and its purpose was to reconvert the Christians to the state cult, thereby destroying the dangerous religion from within: that the stubborn should be wiped out by force was only a secondary means towards this end. This fact was in agreement also with the cautious grading of the rules for the exercise of force, a policy intended to weaken and wear down the hostile attitude, and prescribe death only as an extreme penalty in special cases. Even so, the effect of this terrible attack was extremely serious.

It was quite in accordance with the policy of the state that the first of all to be seized were the higher clergy, in order to render the Church leaderless: but the objective was only partly attained. Fabian, bishop of Rome, was the first to die a martyr's death; this was on January 20, A.D. 250; on January 24 he was followed by Babylas, bishop of Antioch, and also Alexander, the aged bishop of Jerusalem, died in prison in Cæsarea.[3] On the other hand, Dionysios of Alexandria was rescued by his faithful supporters from the clutches of the police, and kept safe in a secret place in Libya;[4] Cyprian of Carthage was also successful in hiding himself: from his place of refuge, he entered into correspondence[5] with his church, and gave rules of conduct to the clergy. We also possess evidence that Gregory, bishop of Neocæsarea in Pontus, took flight successfully.[6] In all the churches which had been rendered

---

[1] Wilcken, *Chrestomathie*, no. 125 Pauly-W. 15,1280 f.   [2] Vol. 1, p. 155
[3] Eus., *H.E.*, 6,39,1–4. Lietzmann, *Martyrol.*, p. 3. 8,29
[4] Eus., *H.E.*, 6,40. 7,11,22 f.   [5] Cyprian, *epist.*, 5–7. 10–19
[6] Gregory of Nyssa, *vita St. Greg. Thaum.* (*opera* 3,569 ed. Paris, 1638)

leaderless, clergy remained behind who attended to the cure of souls, a work which was now particularly necessary, and helped to hold the faithful members together.[1]

On the whole, it would appear that the force exercised by the state caused multitudes to recant. The long period of peace had produced a sense of security, and a strong inclination towards "this world"; already a conventional Christianity had arisen which could not withstand serious molestation; this point is unanimously emphasized by men belonging to the Church in Africa, Egypt, and Palestine.[2] In Spain, two bishops fell away, similarly in Africa; Euktemon, bishop of Smyrna, even made the sacrifices with a garland in his hair, and abjured Christianity.[3] We do not know how many other heads of churches recanted: no one had any interest in preserving the information. Laymen streamed in multitudes to the places of sacrifice, led by the eminent and the prosperous: they felt they, at least, must save life and property! Others stole out of the town into the country, the mountains, and the waste places, in order to escape being compelled to sacrifice. Of course that implied abandoning house and goods, and not a few died of suffering in the wilderness, or were taken prisoners by bands of robbers, and made into slaves.[4] A favourite means of escape was bribery, whereby a certificate of sacrifice was obtained without the sacrifice having actually been offered: in this way it was believed one kept one's conscience uncontaminated by the sin of denial. The Church did not recognize this device, however, and dealt with such *libellatici* as backsliders even if not as serious offenders.[5] Strong-minded believers were not lacking who withstood all forms of oppression, imprisonment, and torture, and who won the martyr's crown, but it is surprising that scarcely any trustworthy *Acts of the Martyrs* have come down from the persecution under Decius: the *Acts of Pionius* exist in lonely state: no record has been preserved even of the martyrdom of Fabian, bishop of Rome, although such was sent to

[1] Dionys. Al. in Eus., *H.E.*, 7,11,24
[2] Cyprian, *de lapsis*, 5 f. Dion. Al. in Eus., *H.E.*, 6,41,11–13. Origen, *hom. in Jer.*, 4,3 p. 25 f. Klostermann
[3] Cyprian, *epist.*, 59,10.65,1. 67,1. *Mart. Pionii* 15,2. 18,12 f.
[4] Cyprian, *de lapsis*, 8. 11. 13. Dionys. in Eus., *H.E.*, 6,41,11–13. 42,2–4. Gregory of Nyssa, *op. cit.* (*op.* 3,569 also in Preuschen, *Analecta*, 2nd edit., 1,61)
[5] Cyprian, *epist.*, 55,11. 30,3. *de lapsis* 27

Cyprian.[1] Hence we must be content with imperfect sources of information.

In his letter to Fabius of Antioch, Bishop Dionysios tells the glorious story of numerous Egyptian heroes of the faith.[2] The *Acts of Pionius* of Smyrna give graphic descriptions, and in so doing link up consciously with the tradition of Polycarp's martyrdom; they also tell of a Marcionite presbyter, Metrodoros, who had been martyred. We have only quite general notices in regard to the persecution in Pontus,[3] and from the letters of Cyprian[4] we can only deduce, in broad outline and with incidental details, what happened in Rome and Carthage. We are frequently told that imprisoned Christians were not killed, but eventually set free, and, in the record of the tortures suffered by the great teacher Origen, Eusebius expressly asserts that care was taken not to kill him.[5] That agrees with the general policy of this particular persecution whose object was to destroy Christians inwardly and not outwardly.

This serious attack on Christianity lasted for a year, when it became apparent that it could not end victoriously. At the close of March, A.D. 251, Cyprian returned to Carthage from his asylum. About the same time, the unoccupied Roman see was filled by Cornelius, and the emperor, who was at war on the frontier fighting against the Goths, was unable to prevent it.[6] When he died in an unsuccessful battle at the beginning of July, the persecution ended automatically, and Cyprian spoke of the divine retribution which had re-established assurance as well as peace.[7] If the temper of the Christians had been as uncompromising as ever, the state would have brought about a considerable reduction in their numbers. But the Church robbed the state even of this advantage when she recognized that the courage to confess in face of the danger of death was a special and therefore highly prized attainment which, for that very reason, could not be reached by everyone. It was decided to take account of the weakness of the flesh,

[1] Cyprian, *epist.*, 9,1   [2] Preserved in Eus., *H.E.*, 6,41,1–42,6; cf. 7,11,20–5
[3] Gregory Nyssa, *vita St. Greg. Thaum.* (*opera* 3,567)   [4] Cf. Cyprian, *epist.*, 22.40
[5] Eus., *H.E.*, 6,41,20. Cyprian, *epist.*, 13,4. 6. 14,2. 21,4. 39,1 f. *Acta Achatii* 5,6. Eus., *H.E.*, 6,39,5
[6] Cyprian, *epist.*, 55,6. 8 f. Harnack, *Chronologie*, 2,351
[7] Cyprian, *de lapsis*, 1; cf. *ad Demetr.* 17

and to lay open to those who had fallen away the possibility
of being again accepted into the fellowship of the Church;
it was promised, in doing so, that reasonable regard would be
paid to the seriousness of individual cases. As we shall see,
though this attitude did not remain unchallenged, it was
maintained; and as a consequence, soon after A.D. 251, everything was, on the whole, as it had been previously, except that
the Church was immensely strengthened in her self-consciousness by the heroic example of brave martyrdoms, and by the
victory which was gained in the end. Attempts at persecution,
which frequently flared up again in the immediately following
period, effected no change in the situation; they all seemed to
be weak imitations of what had happened under Decius.
Gallus re-promulgated the edict about sacrifice, and banished
a number of clergy including Cornelius bishop of Rome,[1]
who died in exile in A.D. 253. Whether the plague which had
recently broken out provided the occasion for this inconsequent
action is a question that cannot be settled. We are expressly
told that Christians were still regarded as responsible for such
catastrophes,[2] an opinion which held good for another century
and a half.

The Emperor Valerian was throughout well-disposed to the
Christians; he permitted them even at court and in his immediate entourage until the increasing distress of the Empire
clouded the clarity of his judgment. When Macrianus,[3] his
best general, wanted regulations against the Christians whose
prayers appeared to hinder the effectiveness of his magical
sorceries, the emperor gave way[4] and, in the summer A.D.
257, published an edict which ordered the Christians, if they
preferred not to accept the religion of the state, at least to join
in the ceremonies—the way in which the edict is formulated
suggests that an agreeable compromise had been intended.
The churches were forbidden to assemble, and in particular,
they were prohibited from entering the catacombs where
refuge had hitherto been found in periods of persecution.
Moreover, the clergy were once again expressly described as

[1] Cyprian, *epist.*, 60,1. 61,3. Eus., *H.E.*, 7,1. *Catal. Liberianus Chron. min.* 1,75
[2] Cyprian, *ad Demetr.*, 3. *de mortal.* 1. 8. 17
[3] *Prosop. imp. Rom.* 2,95 no. 374. Stein in Pauly-W. 7,259–262
[4] Dion. Al. in Eus., *H.E.*, 7,10,3 f.

the crucially important persons[1] to whom the authorities should give their attention.

In addition, Dionysios of Alexandria, together with his presbyter and three deacons, was deported to a place in Libya, and on 30 August, A.D. 257, Cyprian was condemned to banishment to Curubis, a small town nearby on the coast. A short time afterwards, however, the authorities became stricter. Dionysios went to a lonely place which, however, lay nearer Alexandria, and, as a consequence, he was able to continue conducting divine services in secret. On the other hand, Cyprian was recalled and beheaded on September 14, A.D. 258. A short time previously, on August 6, Xystus, bishop of Rome, with four deacons, was taken by surprise in a catacomb, and killed. Four days later, Laurentius his archdeacon followed him in death, and every day saw further martyrdoms.[2] Just lately, the grave has been found of a certain Novatian who was martyred about this time.[3] The intensification was the effect of a new edict which prescribed stern measures against clergy and, a very significant clause, against Christian senators, knights, and other eminent persons; persons of the slave class belonging to the imperial household were threatened with compulsory labour.[4] The persecution brought about a whole series of martyrdoms in Africa, and reliable accounts have survived telling what happened.[5] Most of these martyrs were clergy of various ranks, but, in isolated cases, laymen were executed. One narrator bewails the fact that the arrested laymen were purposely separated from the clergy, in the hope that they would more easily be made to recant.[6] We hear from Spain that Fructuosus, bishop of Tarragona, and two deacons were burnt to death;[7] and Eusebius describes three martyrs in Palestine, as well as a woman who belonged to the Marcionite church.[8]

Meanwhile, in more than one region in the west, rebellions flared up in the army, and, in the east the Persians were

---

[1] *Acta Cypriani* 1,1. 5–8; cf. *Acta Dionysii* in Eus., *H.E.*, 7,11,7. 10

[2] Cyprian, *Epist.*, 80,1. *Lib. pontif.* 25 mentions seven deacons

[3] *Rivista di archeologia cristiana* 10 (1933), 217

[4] Cyprian, *epist.*, 80,1

[5] *Acta Montani et Lucii* and *Acta Mariani et Jacobi*

[6] *Acta Mariani et Jacobi* 10,2   [7] *Acta Fructuosi* (Knopf p. 83)   [8] Eus., *H.E.*, 7,12

threatening: Valerian marched out against them in semi-force, and was taken prisoner in some unexplained manner: after a short time he died in captivity. Macrianus now made an attempt to gain the throne, less for himself than for his sons, and ordered his troops to march from Edessa to Illyria, but there the enterprise collapsed at the end of A.D. 261. This fact is sufficient in itself to explain that Gallienus, Valerian's active and wary son, co-regent, and successor, put an end to that persecution of Christians which Macrianus had brought about. He immediately annulled his father's orders, and published a kind of edict of tolerance[1] in which Christians were again permitted to use their places of worship including their cemeteries, and orders were given that they were "not to be interfered with". This was more than any emperor hitherto had granted, because it included an implied recognition of Christianity as a permitted religious society. The time had passed when an attitude of impartiality could be artificially maintained. The state was now compelled to say a clear Yes or No to Christianity, because it was a force which, in spite of two bloody persecutions, had become stronger than formerly. Gallienus's decision was the equivalent of a whispered Yes, and signified that the Christians had won.

[1] Eus., *H.E.*, 7,13

Chapter Seven

THE APOLOGISTS

W E HAVE SEEN THAT THE STATE DID NOT ENTER INTO LEGAL discussions with the Christians, and similarly for a long time there was no literary examination of Christian problems, or learned argument about its doctrines. Public opinion in regard to it remained fixed so unconditionally that no one took the trouble to examine it more closely. Whether mentioned by Tacitus or Suetonius, Pliny or Fronto, Epictetus or Marcus Aurelius, Lucian or Galen the physician[1]—this was always done incidentally and in a contemptuous tone which did not alter at all even when they had to acknowledge that Christians faced death with a strange courage. But of course there must have been all sorts of discussions which were not recorded, and, in process of time, a number of anti-Christian conclusions must have found common acceptance.[2] Moreover, there is no doubt that the persecutions did not take place unaccompanied by fanfares of rhetoric. Granted that the speeches of the martyrs before their judges have mostly been interpolated, and handed down in the *Acts* in a style that has been purposely shaped to suit a special purpose, nevertheless, not infrequently, instead of the bureaucratic formulas, there must have been an actual controversy with passionate accusation and equally firm repudiation in which the vital issues were debated. Occasionally a Cynic philosopher[3] made a special point of attacking Christian preaching. Celsus is the first whom we know to have composed a regular polemic against Christians. He may possibly have written in the last years of Marcus Aurelius, but we know nothing more about the circumstances of his life than was familiar to his great opponent Origen, in whose work the polemic has been preserved.[4] Celsus really took trouble to

---

[1] Tacitus, *Ann.*, 15,44. Suetonius, *Nero*, 16. Pliny, *epist. ad Traian.*, 96, 97, Fronto in Minucius Felix, *Oct.*, 9,6. 31,2. Epictetus 4,7,6. Marcus. Aurelius 11.3 Lucian, *de morte Peregrini*, 11–16. *Pseudo-mantis* 25. 38. Galen, *de puls. diff.*, 2,4. 3,3 (8,579. 657 ed. Kühn)
[2] Geffcken, *Zwei griech. Apologeten*, 240 f.
[3] Crescens in Rome, cf. Justin, *Apol. App.*, 3 and Tatian 19
[4] Restored by R. Bader (Stuttgart, 1940)

understand Christianity; he knew the Bible, and had definite acquaintance with church doctrines, and the arguments employed by Christians; indeed he had already had discussions with educated defenders of Christianity. He shows as clearly as possible the kind of closed minds with which antagonists confronted the Christians.

Even if the fictitious crimes already mentioned be left on one side there still remained plenty, and more than plenty, of points of attack. Sometimes the Christians were regarded as belonging to the same class as the despised Jews, and contempt was expressed about the disputes between these two groups; they were held to have everything in common, especially the ridiculous belief in the Messiah, and they boasted a special relation to God whereas in fact they only seemed to be miserable vermin similar to a multitude of bats, ants, frogs, or worms.[1] The authority they recognized in common was Moses who had really borrowed his knowledge from the earlier sages, and had given his people their faith in their god, together with angel-worship and sorcery.[2] Jesus followed in his footprints: for He also was a deceptive sorcerer, and His supposed miracles corresponded to the sort of thing that the conjurors still performed in the market place—admittedly, however, the latter did not give themselves out on this account to be sons of God.[3] The stories told by Moses, about the primeval period and the patriarchs, were so foolish and scandalous that self-respecting Jews and Christians were ashamed of them and attempted to make them unexceptionable by allegorical explanation— though without success.[4] It was one and the same god whom the Jews and the Christians worshipped,[5] but He was subject to human passions, was angry, and issued threats; and, in the end, was not strong enough to assist His son in the hour of suffering, nor to avenge his death.[6] He could no more protect His chosen people, Israel, from being scattered throughout the world than He could guard Christians everywhere from bloody persecution.[7]

Nevertheless, the Jews might be granted their indigenous,

[1] Celsus in Origen 3,1. 5. 4,2. 22 f. 6,50   [2] Ibid. 1,17–26
[3] Ibid., 1,6. 26. 68. 2,7. 32. Justin, Apol., 1,30   [4] Ibid. 4,36–51; cf. 1,18
[7] Ibid. 5,59   [6] Ibid. 4,72. 1,54. 2,34
[5] Ibid. 8,69; cf. 39. Justin, Apol., 5,1. Minuc., Oct., 12,2

ancestral religion: in any case, those proselytes were to be condemned who joined them because they despised their own ways; all this applied particularly to the Christians, who were a split from the Jews, and who now existed in the world without root, and without national tradition. They pursued their crazy illusion of a universal religion which was to unite under one law all the peoples of Europe, Asia, and Africa.[1] Their doctrine of the incarnation of God served no purpose; it was inconceivable since it ascribed to the unchangeable Being a transformation into something on a lower plane;[2] and they told fables about the miraculous birth of Jesus, the Son of God, from a virgin, in order to conceal the fact that an adulteress had been seduced, and had borne him to a soldier named Panthera. Moreover, whatever else was reported about His Baptism, the wise men from the east, the flight to Egypt, and His miracles, all this was just as incredible as His resurrection, which, indeed, took place in suspicious secret.[3] His lowly origin and His shameful death, on the other hand, sufficiently proved that He was not a son of God, but a deceiver who paid the due penalty on the cross.[4]

Hence it was not surprising that his adherents wished for no acquaintance with human wisdom, that they regarded it as foolishness in God's sight, and that they always demanded faith alone, and faith on top of faith, as the pre-supposition of salvation. Of course their recruits consisted always of the uneducated and simple. Over and above this whatever they possessed that was good or reasonable they had borrowed from the Greeks, although mostly in a perverse manner.[5] Their whole mode of life was self-contradictory and foolish; and the best thing that could happen would be for them to draw the last consequences from their attitude, which was hostile to life, and simply disappear from the world without leaving any descendants, in order that such a society might vanish from the face of the earth altogether.[6]

Such was the spiritual background of the persecutions of Christians. That was what the yelling and baying masses felt

---

[1] *Ibid.* 5,25. 41. 51. 33. 8,72   [2] *Ibid.* 4,3. 14; cf. 6,69. 72
[3] *Ibid.* 1,28. 41. 58. 62. 68. 2,55. 63. 70   [4] *Ibid.* 1,69. 70, 71. 2,5. 6,74
[5] *Ibid.* 1,9. 6,11. 12. 15. 16. 19, cf. 2,5
[6] *Ibid.* 8,55. Justin, *Apol.*, 4,1. Minuc., *Oct.*, 9,1. Tert., *Scapul.*, 5

when aroused to hunt them out, and while they sated their eager
eyes in the arena with the blood of the martyrs; that was also
the opinion of the educated classes, and of the high officials
who pronounced sentence of death upon them from the
tribunal. It was a bold and difficult undertaking to struggle
against such a confirmed and universal conviction; nevertheless the appeal to public opinion, the conversion of the educated,
and, in the last analysis, the conversion of the emperor, were the
only means by which one could hope to ameliorate the situation.
It was for this reason that, after the first half of the second
century, Christian writers set themselves the difficult task.
After an otherwise unknown Quadratus[1] had sent the Emperor
Hadrian a writing in defence of the Christians, apologies were
composed ever afresh, and dedicated to the rulers. Whether
any of these pamphlets actually reached the imperial chamber
at that time, or came to the hands of the ruler, is an open
question, and, indeed, scarcely that. It is plain, however, that
the attempt was made to spread these works amongst the
educated classes, and therefore to distribute them through the
usual channels of the book-shops, apparently without success.[2]

Nevertheless, even if the first purpose was not attained, the
whole enterprise was of the greatest significance for the
evolution of Christianity. Christianity now issued quite consciously from the narrow limits in which it had been shut
away from the world, and spread its treasures out before the
eyes of those who represented culture in the Roman empire.
Every effort was made to show that the new religion did not
stand in insoluble contradiction with the recognized ideals of
culture, especially with the best achievements of philosophy,
but was in a large measure of agreement; and that it brought to
a perfect and vital actuality what was seen to exist there only in
an inchoate form and as a theoretical matter. In this way,
those tendencies were appropriately valued which, streaming
from Pythagorean and Platonic sources, managed to overcome, by mystic speculation, the intellectualism which had
hardened into scepticism, tendencies which were struggling
towards neoplatonism as the final philosophy of the ancient
world. The purpose of the Apologists in writing was to

[1] Eus., *H.E.*, 4,3,1 f.   [2] Tert., *test. anim.*, 1 (p. 135,10 Wissowa)

contribute towards the kind of literature that was recognized in the world of culture. It is not surprising that they were not immediately successful, but they pursued their way un-discouraged and created the conditions within which, scarcely a century later, a man like Origen could act as an apologist and systematizer of Christian thought, stand side by side with Plotinus the neoplatonist, and, in his own person, represent the highest culture of the age. The Apologists took the final and crucial step towards the conquest of the world by Christianity: they won the spirit of Greek science for the message of the Church.

The earliest of the apologies which have survived bears the name of a certain Aristides of Athens, and may date from *c.* A.D. 140: it is dedicated to the Emperor, Antoninus Pius. It is possible to reproduce it with some difficulty from a Syrian translation, Armenian fragments, and Greek quotations.[1] Here a man of mediocre culture employs a superficial learning in order to prove that the ancient civilized peoples, the Chal-deans, the Greeks, and the Egyptians, had had no genuine knowledge of God; that the Jews corrupted monotheism and sound moral teaching by angel-worship and various rituals; and that the Christians alone possessed the truth and lived according to their commandments. All this is put forward in a clumsy style and with an artless arrangement; it cannot have made much impression upon an educated reader of the time. Nevertheless we ought to consider its contents. Aristides begins by declaring that, after gazing at the miraculous con-stitution of the world, he had learned to recognize God as the mover of the whole; the negative formulas, which he uses elsewhere about God, were familiar in Stoic lecture rooms, and were also to be found among the philosophical representatives of Judaism.[2] At this point, he begins to say, paradoxically, that the Christians alone, "the third race" in the world, possess the truth; the other two races, Jews and Gentiles, have gone astray. The Gentiles fail by worshipping the creature instead of the creator, and by their unethical polytheism. In this connec-tion the author is making use of arguments which had already been brought together for the same purpose in Jewish apologetic,

[1] Geffcken, *op. cit.*, pp. 3–27. Goodspeed, *Apologeten*, pp. 3–23
[2] Geffcken, *op. cit.*, pp. 31–41

and which he obtained partly from the preaching of the Old Testament prophets and partly from the anti-religious speeches of the Sceptics and the Epicureans. But both streams flow in the same direction, and the entire argumentation could have been put forward in almost the same terms as early as Cicero's time. The discussion about the worthlessness of polytheism consists of purely academic declamations lacking contact with contemporaneous living religious feeling, and slaying once more an opponent already long dead. If it was desired to make any fresh impression with this sort of thing it would have to be served up piquantly in Lucian's manner: in itself the subject-matter was boring.

We remark that so far there is no single word of anything characteristically Christian; even Jewish ritualism and angel worship are repudiated without any particular proof. The positive recommendation of Christianity only comes in at the end. Here again there is no discussion, nothing repudiated or proved, but simply something recounted. Christians originate from Jesus Christ: He descended from heaven as the Son of God and became incarnate from a virgin. He chose twelve disciples in order to proclaim His teaching, and, after His death and resurrection, they spread the truth in the entire world, the truth, in particular, that it was right to offer prayer only to the Creator of the world, and to fulfil only the commandments of Christ. He who did so would win eternal life after the resurrection of the dead. What is then given as the essence of the commandments of Christ corresponds to the doctrine of the catechism, which we have already discussed in connection with the *Didache*, the *Epistle of Barnabas*, the *Epistle to Diognetus*, and other Apologists. The reader is frequently encouraged to draw information for himself from the Holy Scriptures, and he is left with the assurance that the continuance of the world is due only to the prayers of Christians: hence it was hoped that the pagans would be converted immediately, lest the Last Judgment come. In this early example of apologetic, the various elements exist to a certain extent in an immature state: they are set before the reader without being worked over: they are disconnected, and lacking in spiritual penetration. It is not surprising that they are not attractive.

Only a decade later Justin, who came from Palestine, wrote an *Apology* in Rome addressed to Antoninus Pius and his philosopher son, Marcus Aurelius. After another decade, he followed this pamphlet by a religious dialogue with a Jew, Trypho by name, and conceived it on broad lines. Justin was not a stylist nor skilled in arranging his material; nevertheless he wielded a ready pen, and he was as good a philosopher as many of his contemporaries. The fact that he had these qualifications, that he had become a Christian, and found the true philosophy in Christianity, is what gives him his real significance and makes him the classic Apologist. Even in his case, we find the traditional polemic against polytheism and the corresponding mythology, and it is drawn from the familiar sources. All these things, however, are put forward in a new light, because faith, mythology, and worship, as found in paganism, are represented as the fraudulent invention of daemons. Even as early as Paul,[1] daemons were represented as the recipients of pagan sacrifices; similarly Justin, who was influenced by the newly awakening Platonism, accorded ample scope to these beings, who were intermediate between God and the world. As early as Plutarch they had been regarded as intermediaries between gods and men, and it was their voice which was heard in the oracles. According to Justin, they had acted throughout the whole course of history as self-seeking enemies of divine truth, as creators of lies, fraud, and all such illusions as were intended to sate the senses with an alluring legerdemain. God had given predictions through the prophets: by means of strange myths and cults, and by acting in conjunction with human passions, the daemons had cheated them of fulfilment in advance in order to deprive God's genuine revelation of its power of proof. Their false game had now been discovered, and the truth brought clearly to light by the coming of Christ. For over a millennium in advance, all the details had been predicted in regard to the act of salvation, the life, suffering, resurrection, and ascension of Christ up to the destruction of Jerusalem: all of the predictions had been fulfilled promptly to time, and the certainty, that the prophets spoke the truth, left no room for doubt that the remaining prophecies of Christ's second advent

[1] i Cor. 10: 20 f.

and the Last Judgment would be fulfilled.[1] Thus Justin worked
out an entirely rational argument for the truth of Christianity.
Starting from this foundation, this type of argument entered
into the teaching of the Church, and into orthodox apologetics,
and is still alive at the present day. Moreover, Justin uses the
same method in order to give further proofs. It is only the fulfilment of prophecies which guarantees the trustworthiness of
what Christ said about Himself when He declared Himself to
be the first born Son of God.[2] What did that mean?

Justin followed up the brief hints contained in the *Apology*
with the more exact claims advanced in the *Dialogue*. To him,
as to Aristides—and similarly to the other apologists—God was
the final cause of the world, a supernatural Being, eternally
unchangeable, and only recognizable to the eye of reason.[3]
No name is truly His name for we are only able to speak in
praise of Him on the basis of His works.[4] No space, not even the
entire universe, comprehends Him who existed before the whole
world: it is inconceivable that He could ever cross the gulf in
order to become visible on earth and speak to man.[5] He exists
beyond all being, as Plato said, and Justin agrees with him and
praises philosophy.[6] The "unnameable Father and Lord of all"
sent forth from Himself "at the beginning", and before every
created thing, a power which we call the "logos", the "word" of
God, because it brought God's message to man.[7] At this point,
Justin makes use of the ambiguity in the Greek word, because
to him "logos" meant both "word" and "reason". The logos
of a man exists in him first of all as "reason" or "thought", and
then proceeds from him as the spoken "word", without the
man himself thereby suffering any loss of his inner logos, i.e.
his reason; similarly the logos of God which existed with Him
from eternity—i.e. His reason—was not diminished when He
sent forth the logos from Himself. Rather, it was as if one fire
ignited another without itself thereby becoming smaller.
Justin describes this process as the procreation of the Son of
God: and since the Son came forth from God the Father as an
independent person, we may speak of Him as a "second God"

---

[1] Justin, *Apol.*, 31–53   [2] *Ibid.* 53,2   [3] Justin, *dial.*, 3,4. 7
[4] *Apol.* 10,1. 2 app. 6,1. 2   [5] *Dial.* 127
[6] *Dial.* 4,1 (cf. Plato, *Republic*, 6 p. 509*b*). *Apol. app.* 13,2
[7] *Dial.* 127,2–4. 128,1 f.; cf. 61,1

although God's being is not divided nor are His counsel and will separated from Him.[1]

The logos is to be found in the Holy Scriptures as the Son who was begotten before all creation. When creating the world, the Father said to him "let *us* make man"; He was the divine wisdom which appeared at the beginning of God's ways, as declared in the Proverbs of Solomon 8: 22,[2] and through him God created and ordained the world;[3] in this way He was the mediator between the unapproachableness of the Father and the need felt by the world. He occasionally appeared in visible form to man, and the Old Testament often calls Him "the angel of the Lord", or even "the Lord"; He reveals Himself to men of God in word, fire, signs, and wonders, and few have been accounted worthy to see Him.[4] He spoke through the prophets, instructing, exhorting, and warning; but also beyond the people of Israel His operation was unmistakable—even the school of the Stoics spoke of a "seed of the logos" scattered among the whole of mankind. Whoever had permitted this seed-corn to germinate in his soul, and had lived according to the directions of the logos, Christians counted as one of themselves: i.e. men like Herakleitos, Socrates, and, in the most recent period, the Stoic Musonios. The world had scoffed at them and at Christians as atheists; and envious daemons had betrayed them to the hatred of the multitude, and pronounced death upon them.[5]

The final revelation, and the one that was decisive, took place when the logos, in all its fullness,[6] itself came on earth, and became man in the manner proclaimed in advance through the prophets. As a sign that a mighty act of God was taking place here, the logos caused himself to be born in a miraculous fashion from a virgin just as Isaiah (7: 14) had predicted many centuries before—and He guaranteed His mission by healings and raisings of the dead.[7] Granted that His appearance caused all the daemons to come out in array, and that they strove against Him with all their powers and brought Him to the cross; but He rose from the dead and ascended to heaven. The logos had prophesied even that in every detail.[8]

[1] *Dial.* 61,2. 128,4. 56,11   [2] *Ibid.* 62. 129,3   [3] *Apol. app.* 6,3
[4] *Dial.* 61,1. 128,1 f.   [5] *Apol.* 46,1–4. *app.* 8,1–3; cf. 10,4 f.   [6] *Apol. app.* 8,3. 10,7
[7] *Dial.* 43,3–8. 66–71. 84,1 f. *apol.* 33,2. 48   [8] *Apol.* 35–8. 45. *Dial.* 86–91

What was the purpose of the whole movement? God wished to draw mankind to Himself. For their sakes indeed, and for that alone, had He created the world in order that, by a worthy exercise in all the virtues, they might rise to Him and, when set free from suffering and mortality, might partake in His rule.[1] The logos had ceaselessly pointed out this way of approach to God, and finally, by his personal appearance on earth, had laid it most impressively upon human hearts. He became the "new law-giver", although the "new, eternal, and final" law was the old law of rational virtue long recognized by sages,[2] a law which men must obey in complete freedom of will if they would be saved. The incarnation of the logos had caused the brightest of lights to shine upon the truth that was before their eyes, a proof being the fact that the name of the crucified Jesus Christ even yet scared away all evil spirits:[3] he who now closed his eyes and blindly submitted to the fraud exercised by daemons would properly have to bear the consequences in the eternal fire.[4] Xenophon's fable of Hercules at the parting of the ways held good for the vital decision in regard to Christianity.[5]

Justin's "Christian philosophy" went so far—but no farther. Christianity of this kind was a genuinely philosophical system, constructed of familiar elements. The idea of God was borrowed from popular philosophy and, even in the expressions employed, corresponded with what we can find among the religious-minded Stoics in the first century.[6] As already said, the doctrine of daemons derives from the newly reawakened Platonism,[7] and only received from Justin a place in his apologetic argument which corresponded with his purpose: he then used the intermediate beings to explain pagan forms of worship and religion; at the same time and on the basis of Jewish models,[8] he equated them with the angels and devils of the Bible. Already in John's gospel, Jesus Christ had been described as the logos of God. Whereas, in John, this identification was meant to abrogate the historical limitations of Jesus's life, and to raise it to eternal significance, we find in Justin a tendency almost in

[1] *Apol.* 10,2
[2] *Dial.* 18,3. 11,2. 43,1. *Apol.* 23,1 f. 14,2. 16,14. *Dial.* 23,1. 30,1. 93,1–3
[3] *Dial.* 30,3. 76,6. 85,2   [4] *Apol. app.* 7,1–9   [5] *Ibid.* 11,3–8   [6] Vol. 1, pp. 172–76
[7] Geffcken, *op. cit.*, 219 f.
[8] Cf. *Handb.* on 1 Cor. 10: 20. Re Philo., see Vol. 1, p. 96

the contrary direction. The purpose was to render it impossible to reject the authority of Christ's teaching in this way, but, chiefly, to make it cast light on the examination conducted by reason. Jesus was indeed the incarnate divine reason, and consequently everything truly reasonable on this earth must in the end agree with Christianity. But the concluding proof for the identification of Jesus Christ with the logos was provided in a jejune rationalism based on the fulfilments of prophecies.

The consequence of all this was an impression, which cannot be explained away, that the life and death of Jesus did not follow their course owing to an inner necessity and a deeper meaning, but on account of purely outer reasons, viz. because they had once been prophesied like this; like this, and not otherwise, had they taken place. The "soteriological significance" of the death of Jesus, or the "work of Jesus", is not considered; and "redemption" consists, in practice, in imparting philosophically sound doctrines of God and virtue, which, moreover, each man could accept or reject freely, on his own responsibility. If mankind had seen through the daemons' deception at the right time, and taken more to heart the teachings about the logos preached by the prophets and the sound philosophers, the whole tragedy of Jesus would have been unnecessary. Justin's doctrine of the logos itself has grown out of familiar roots, roots which struck deep in Jewish and Hellenic soil, and which are already inextricably entangled in the earliest extant literature. Justin was influenced by Stoicism, and by Platonizing ways of thought, and, indeed, instructive parallels can be shown to exist in Philo,[1] without our being justified in assuming that Justin had ever had a copy of Philo in his hand. But in whatever ways this doctrine may have penetrated in detail into Justin's working ideas, and however strange it may seem when contrasted with the early Christian ideas, Justin and his fellow-warriors introduced it into speculative theology, where it immediately dominated all thought, and continued to do so triumphantly for many centuries.

We should be altogether in the wrong if, as a consequence of all this, we were to expect that the religious life of the

[1] Vol. I, pp. 93 ff.

Apologists was nothing more than a mere moralism, and that their Christianity embodied a philosophical religion of an emancipated kind such as could be equated with the philosophizing Judaism of the educated proselytes. Justin did not outline a Christian doctrine of ethics as a Stoic would have done and as, for example, Clement of Alexandria actually did, making it a transcription of rational principles; rather he presented it as the sum of Jesus' commandments arranged in systematic order under appropriate titles.[1] Thus he laid special emphasis on words like chastity, charity, benevolence, patience, gentleness, and love of truth. Aristides[2] started from the Ten Commandments and dealt with the same subject-matters without quoting words of Jesus: care for burying the dead was added by him as a specially important Christian duty. We find essentially the same case among the other Apologists.[3] It is the simple tradition of the Church unaffected by any type of theory, such as is familiar to us from the time of the *Didache*, and such as was regarded even by the Apologists as the sum of Christian rules of life. They were quite certain of the soundness of these teachings in a world which had accepted Stoic ethics. Nor did they hesitate on occasion to assert emphatically[4] that the virtues which were merely inculcated by the philosophers were actually practised by Christians, and indeed by the most unassuming of men.

The observations that we have made in regard to ethics might be repeated in all other spheres. Justin confined himself entirely to the doctrinal tradition of the Church, and made not the least attempt to bring it into organic connection with his "philosophy". After he has given the Rule of Faith, he cites the formula of the Trinity, which by that time was becoming more definitely shaped. And he speaks of faith in God the Creator, in the Son, Jesus Christ, as occupying the second place, and of faith in the "prophetic spirit" as occupying the third place—although, according to his own theory, the Son, as the logos, is identical with the spirit which revealed itself in the prophets. The doctrine of the Trinity was important to him in this

[1] *Apol.* 15–17 [2] Aristides, *apol.*, 15,4–12
[3] Athenagoras, *suppl.*, 32 f. *Resurr. mort.* 23. Theophilus, *ad Autol.*, 3,9–15
[4] Justin, *apol.*, 16,8. *app.* 10,8. Athenagoras 11. Minuc. Felix, *Oct.*, 38. Orig., *c. Cels.*, 7,44

connection, and he adds belief in the angels in order to prove to pagans how far removed were Christians from the bald monotheism which pagans derided as atheism. Moreover Justin was not the only one to adopt this attitude,[1] and he was quite unmoved by the fact that his doctrine of the Trinity was irreconcilable with his logos theology.

We hear an echo of the theology of the Church when Justin speaks of the "mystery of the cross" through which Christ had won mankind for Himself. That theology is also implied when he speaks of the redemption of the faithful by Christ's blood and death;[2] similarly when he describes the consecration of the elements of the Lord's Supper by invocation of the logos, or when he speaks of the change which comes upon our flesh and blood when we participate in the consecrated food.[3] His eschatology, together with his doctrine of Christ's second advent, keeps quite within the forms of Biblical tradition, and includes both the resurrection of the flesh and the hope of the millennial kingdom in the newly restored Jerusalem.[4] Justin is also quite content with New Testament forms of expression when he prefers to describe *aphtharsia*, incorruptibility, as the aim of the Christian life.[5] His disciple Tatian used similar language,[6] but Theophilus introduced a Hellenistic point of view when he described a Christian's reward in the words that he "receives immortality and *becomes God*".[7] That was the aim sought also by the Greek mystagogues.[8]

It is obvious that Justin's Christianity is divided into two halves; one is a philosophical religion which clothes Greek ideas and conceptions in a loose Biblical garment, and which in the end issues in man's self-redemption ethically conceived; the second aspect is that of the unreasoned faith of the Church in which words of Jesus, sacramental mysticism, and church-life combine to form an active unity. The moral code based on Judaism, and belonging to the earlier period, was outgrown; gnosticism

---

[1] Justin, *apol.*, 13,1–4. 6,1 f.; cf. Athenagoras, *op. cit.*, 10. 12. 24. Theophil., *op. cit.*, 2,15
[2] Justin, *dial.*, 134,5. 111,3
[3] Justin, *apol.*, 66,2
[4] *Apol.* 18–20. 50. 52,3. *dial.* 80,5. 81,4
[5] Justin, *apol.*, 10,3. 13,2. 19,4. 39,5. 42,4. 52,3. *dial.* 45,4
[6] Tatian 7,1. 32,1
[7] Theoph., *op. cit.*, 2,27
[8] Reitzenstein, *Hellen. Mysterienrel.*, 3rd edit., 49. 257. 290 f.

was a side-track; and even Paul and John were no longer comprehended. Nor, as yet, had Justin grasped the necessity of uniting the two parts.

In the next decades, apologetic literature developed still further. Justin's disciple, Tatian, was a Syrian by birth and he constantly emphasized the contrast between his own race and the Greeks. He hated the Greek language and culture, although he did not despise their rhetorical tinsel, nor hesitate to empty out the dustbin of the silliest of gossip on the heads of Plato and Aristotle, Herakleitos and Empedokles.[1] It is true that Christianity was for him a philosophy, yes the philosophy of barbarians,[2] and was older than all the wisdom of the Greeks. Justin had described Moses as the source of certain Platonic doctrines,[3] but Tatian went further and boldly declared that the "wisdom of the Greek sophists" had, owing to misunderstanding and conceit, been plagiarized from its Old Testament source.[4] He provided the proof of these assertions in a very rough and ready manner, in as far as he transcribed chronological tables page after page, and so proved that Moses lived before the Trojan war and the period of the Greek heroes.[5] He prefers to spend much time on the subject of the daemons, their characteristics and their activity,[6] from which latter he believes himself redeemed by Christ;[7] whereas the doctrine of the logos is only dealt with in a passage where the context requires it, and with much restraint as compared with Justin.[8] His disinclination towards the "killing of animals in order to eat meat" appears even in this writing;[9] at a later date his ascetic tendencies, in particular his rejection of marriage, made him an opponent of the Church.[10] We have already discussed his significance as the author of a Gospel-Harmony.[11]

In the case of Athenagoras of Athens, Tatian's contemporary, the daemons also played a considerable rôle, and the doctrine of the logos is still less evident. Apparently neither of these two men was willing to recognize, in the extra-Biblical world, "the seed-corn of the logos", which Justin had brought into discussion. Athenagoras, however, was not animated by

[1] Tatian 1–3   [2] *Op. cit.*, 1. 12. 29. 31. 35   [3] Justin, *apol.*, 59 f.
[4] Tatian 40,1   [5] *Ibid.* 31–41   [6] *Ibid.* 9,1. 12. 14–17   [7] *Ibid.* 29,2
[8] *Ibid.* 5,1–3. 7,1   [9] *Ibid.* 23,2
[10] Eus., *H.E.*, 4,29,1–3. Epiph., *haer.*, 46,1,1–2,3   [11] *Supra*, p. 99

Justin's passionate hatreds; he used words acknowledging the Greek sages, although only to prove in the end that they all contradicted one another because they drew the urge for research from their own souls. As distinct from this, the prophets were impelled by the spirit of God, and thereby enabled to bear unanimous testimony to the divine truth.[1] Hence, he put Christianity forward as of equal standing with philosophy, and from this standpoint he required tolerance on the part of the state:[2] yet in reality Christianity was not rational, as Justin would have his readers believe, but divine revelation of a unique kind; the enthusiasm of prophetic ecstasy was not a "human" proof, but it did provide absolute truth.[3]

It is most significant that the writings of the prophets, even apart from the question of the proof offered by prophecy, enjoyed overwhelming respect among the apologists: Justin, Tatian, and Theophilus declared that they had been converted by studying them. Even in the fourth century, when Augustine was in a state of hesitation, he was referred to the prophet Isaiah by Ambrose his confessor, although on this occasion without consequence.[4] In the case of Athenagoras, the irrational element, implied by making this reference to the prophets, is not explicitly brought out; that would have contradicted his cast of mind. He tried to hide the genuine inconsistency between his religion and all philosophy; and indeed he attempted to explain the resurrection of the flesh to the Greeks in a special writing: this writing concluded with the dictum[5] that the goal of human life was "to rejoice in the contemplation of the Creator and His counsels without ceasing"—a form of statement influenced by both the Bible and philosophy.

Theophilus, bishop of Antioch, who wrote[6] shortly after A.D. 180, introduced no new elements into the body of apologetic which we have already discussed: he wrote a more pleasing Greek, brought somewhat more of superficial learning to the front than did his predecessors, and, after acknowledging that pagan writers had some glimpses of the light, came on the

---

[1] Athenag., *suppl.*, 7,1 f.   [2] *Ibid.* 1–2   [3] *Ibid.* 9,1
[4] Justin, *dial.*, 7,1–8,1. Tatian 29. Theoph. 1,14. Augustine, *conf.*, 9,5,13
[5] Athenag., *res. mort.*, 25; cf. 13, and the reference in *suppl.* 31,3
[6] Theoph., *ad. Autol.*, 3,27

whole to an out and out rejection of all Greek wisdom. He contended that it was drawn only from recent sources, and would not bear comparison with the ancient teachings of the Old Testament prophets.

The *Letter to Diognetus*, which has come down to us anonymously, is elegant in style and cursory in content—it is possible that Diognetus is to be identified with the tutor of Marcus Aurelius. Its idyllic description of Christianity and its epigrammatic phraseology are very famous. Here also is to be found the phrase confessing that Christians are pilgrims on earth:[1] "every strange city is their home-town and every home-town is strange to them"—we must not translate with the term "native land" in a patriotic sense (motherland) since this conception was lacking in the ancient world.[2]

Patriotism, however, was intended by Caecilius the Roman when, in the graceful dialogue *Octavius*, he laid upon the heart of his Christian opponent the majesty of their common, ancestral religion, and its connection with the glorious history of Rome; and when he bespoke recognition on its behalf.[3] The only pity was that he premised the frank confession that, as a philosophical sceptic, he did not believe in these things, but only held them in respect. Octavius answered trenchantly[4] that Roman history was a sum-total of godlessness, wickedness, and violence, and had nothing to do with gods. He did not regard this history as his affair, he, no more than the other millions in the Empire. Only when rhetorical effect required it did one speak patriotically—and it is significant that the entire discussion on religion was based on the kiss which Caecilius the patriot threw with his hand, not to some ancient Roman religious image, but to a chapel of Sarapis. The rest of what Caecilius adduced in objection against the Christians, and what Octavius said in reply to his opponent, is confined to the familiar orbit, although it is well stated and impressively arranged. Thus the dialogue of Minucius Felix, which was written *c.* A.D. 200, becomingly opened the field of Latin apologetics.

---

[1] *Epist. ad Diog.* 5,5   [2] Celsus is instructive in Orig. 8,73 f.
[3] Min. Felix., *Oct.*, 6 f.   [4] *Ibid.* 25

Chapter Eight

ASIA MINOR AND THE MONTANIST MOVEMENT

CHRISTIANITY TOOK ROOT MOST RAPIDLY ON THE SOIL WHICH
had benefited by ancient Greek civilization in the west
of Asia Minor; from those regions it spread northwards along
the sea-washed coasts. It also penetrated inland wherever the
Greek tongue was spoken. It always began in the greater towns,
then obtained adherents in the villages, and finally in the
countryside. On the whole, however, the frontiers of its
conquests halted before regions dominated by the national
peculiarities of the innumerable peoples of Asia Minor, and
where their strange languages were still spoken: that remained
the case for many centuries.[1] Orthodox Christianity followed in
the footsteps of Greek civilization, and, in Asia Minor, this was
many-sided and had very attractive qualities. Ephesus, where
the Christian mission had been founded by Paul, constituted the
headquarters. From thence the message was carried into the
Lycus valley and into Phrygia, where apparently it spread
rapidly. At an early date, Smyrna became a second point
which radiated Christian influence; the Revelation of John
shows that Sardes and Pergamon were already known as
Christian cities, and, in the course of the second century,
churches were to be found in the coastal cities of Byzantium,
Nicomedia, Amastris, and Sinope, and in the chief cities of the
inland provinces of Galatia (Ancyra) and Cappadocia
(Cæsarea).[2] The Christian churches of Asia Minor were proud
of their special tradition: they could not only lay claim to Paul,
but they were connected with Jerusalem by Philip the Evangelist; and the Johannine circle had given the Church the Fourth
Gospel, round about which at an early date gathered the legend
of John of Ephesus. Powerful forces of many kinds operated
in that region; the Christians of Asia Minor were awake to the
facts, and spared no effort to let the rest of Christendom share
in their advantages.

[1] Holl., *op. cit.*, 2,238–248
[2] Details brought together by Harnack, *Mission*, 4th edit., 2,732–785

We have already seen how the dispute about Easter set these churches in strong opposition to opinion in Rome. The theologians who discussed the Christological problem started from Asia when they began their triumphant march to Rome, and thus to the rest of the occident. The first to come to our notice is a tanner of Byzantium, Theodotos by name, who, towards the end of the second century, removed to the capital of the empire and there developed the "dynamist" doctrine. This doctrine held that the spirit of God (= Christ) dwelt in the human Jesus as an inspiring power;[1] the school worked this theology out further with the aid of philosophy, and even after their master broke with the church, the school continued to grow considerably.[2] A short time later, Noëtos of Smyrna appeared in Rome with the "Monarchian" doctrine that God Himself had become flesh, had walked on earth in the figure of Jesus Christ, had been martyred, and had died: the Invisible had become visible, the Unbegotten had been born, the Immortal had been put to death.[3] He stated the secret of the person of Jesus in these paradoxes, and thereby gained the allegiance of many hearts and minds.

Praxeas was a contemporary of Theodotos, and came from Asia Minor to Rome, where he laboured for some time and then went to Carthage; here Tertullian attacked him passionately and, as he claims, vanquished him.[4] Praxeas, too, regarded it as crucial to emphasize the unity of the godhead. "I and the Father are one"; "he who hath seen me hath seen the Father also"; "I am in the Father, and the Father in me": these he regarded as Jesus' decisive pronouncements about Himself.[5] It followed that the Father had experienced birth and passion. Praxeas taught that Almighty God was, Himself, Jesus Christ, God had made Himself into His own Son; the Lord had said "I am God and beside me there is no God".[6] Thus Praxeas firmly repudiated all forms of the logos speculation which attempted to assert a divine Son as an independent being side by side with God the Father; what led to this repudiation of the trinitarian explanation of the Rule of Faith was the "plain

---

[1] Hippol., *Refut.*, 7,35. Epiph., *Haer.*, 54,1,3. 3,1. 5. cf. *supra*, 175 f.
[2] Hippol., In Eus., *H.E.* 5,28,8–12
[3] Hippol., *Refut.*, 10,27. *c. Noetum* 1 p. 43,10. Lagarde   [4] Tert., *adv. Prax.*, 1
[5] *Ibid.* 20. John 10: 30, 14: 9, 11   [6] Tert., *op. cit.*, 2. 10. 20; cf. Is. 45: 5

man's" fear of polytheism.[1] Nevertheless even Praxeas recognized the Biblical distinction between Father and Son, except that he did not look for the hall-marks in the sphere of the godhead. The fact that he had a body was characteristic of the Son; the sufferings took place in the body, and thus the godhead, which was identical with the Father, did not actually suffer, although it shared in the sufferings which the body underwent.[2] In this manner, Praxeas avoided the objection which made the godhead capable of suffering and therefore "changeable", and which would have been philosophically impossible. Praxeas sought to escape the paradoxes which Noëtos had emphasized, and, in so doing, had given the discussion a broader basis.

The disputes which were fought out in Rome and Africa, and of which we have records, had already been the subject of theological inquiry in Asia Minor, but without a decision having been arrived at. We only learn that the presbyters of Smyrna had opposed Noëtos's doctrine of unity, and had taught the duality of God and Christ as given in the Rule of Faith; and they excommunicated him.[3] This was not a theological solution, and Monarchianism continued to be the popular view; we shall have to take notice of its influence in the following centuries. It gave rise to ever-new forms based on a devout, naïve belief in redemption through the sacraments, a belief which regarded the incarnation of the godhead as the guarantee of the future apotheosis of mankind, and was satisfied with any theological formulas leaving room for this fundamental conception. If, however, the incarnate Christ was distinguished from God as a separate being, this belief was attacked, and could not be saved by any attempts at compromise. For naïve thought, there was only one God— the monotheistic dogma stood impregnably firm—and He had become man in Christ. A divine logos side by side with God was a second God, as even Justin had recognized:[4] the effect of such a doctrine was, firstly, to destroy monotheism, and, secondly, to break the logical sequence of a belief in apotheosis which could not be satisfied with any substitute for God. Thus

---

[1] Tert., *op. cit.*, 3   [2] *Ibid.* 27
[3] Hippol., *c. Noet.*, 1 p. 43 Lagarde; Epiph., *haers.*, 57,1   [4] *Supra*, pp. 180 f.

Monarchianism came inevitably into conflict both with the logos doctrine of the Apologists on philosophical grounds, and also with the formula of the Trinity which had grown out of the Rule of Faith. Monarchianism had to fight for its right to live, and this fact conditioned at bottom the great controversies of the fourth and fifth centuries. While, among the people, the original views remained unchanged, and continued to dominate their form of religion and thought, the leaders entered into the fighting line of the theories which led to theological dispute and hence to the history of dogma.

To what extent the popular religion of the people of Asia Minor was determined by a sacramental faith is plainly shown by the celebrated epitaph of Aberkios of Hieropolis,[1] a small Phrygian town between Eumenia and Synnada—not to be confused with Hieropolis in the Lycus valley. It cannot be determined whether Aberkios was a bishop, but it may be regarded as entirely probable that he was identical with the Avircius Marcellus to whom an anti-montanist writing was dedicated in that region *c.* A.D. 183. In any case, the inscription dates from the end of the second century. At 72 years of age, Aberkios himself composed this epitaph and told of the greatest event of his life: a visit to Rome from which he had, at last, returned home by way of Syria and Mesopotamia. He makes use of poetic forms and phrases, and is fond of esoteric similes, which he expects Christian readers to understand.[2] He claims to be a disciple of the holy Shepherd who had taught him the nature of Christian wisdom. The shepherd had sent him to Rome—i.e. he had been sent there on church business—"in order to see the imperial majesty and to behold the queen clad and shod in gold." By this phraseology he means the city of Rome, the polite language used by a loyal Christian in the enlightened period of the Antonines: under Domitian, Christians spoke of the Babylonian harlot on the seven hills.[3] There he saw the people with the shining seal, i.e. the Christian Church: but everywhere throughout Syria and on the Euphrates, he had found fellow believers, for Paul had travelled in

[1] The best commentary is that of F. J. Dölger, *Ichthys*, 2,454–507. A pagan explanation of the inscription is no longer worth discussion
[2] Verse 19, "Every fellow believer who understands is asked to pray for Aberkios"
[3] *Rev.* 17:3, 5, 9 18

the same coach with him—he is using poetic language to say that he had carried with him a copy of the Pauline letters as an invaluable book of devotion. Faith went on in advance of him, and everywhere prepared for him the feast, i.e. the fish from the source, the fish which the Holy Virgin had caught, i.e. wine and bread for the brethren everywhere.

This is not the place to explain in detail the phrases employed in the poem. The crucial point is quite certain, viz. that, to the author, the eucharistic meal brings about the unity of Christians throughout the world. To those who partake, it gives the divine nourishment of the "fish from the source", i.e.[1] "Jesus Christ, the Son of God, the Saviour". The fish and the shepherd represent the symbolism of the period round about A.D. 200, which we have already discussed; and the pictures of the Lord's Supper, as found in the Roman "Chapels of the Sacrament",[2] prove that Aberkios was entirely right when he recognized the principles of his faith as the same amongst all the brethren. Moreover, he found that Paul was revered everywhere; but, for his own type of religion, the vital factor was fellowship in the heavenly food provided by the sacrament. We shall do well to keep this manner of thinking and feeling steadily in mind: its roots can be plainly seen even in the faith of the Pauline and Johannine churches, and in many respects those roots go deeply down into the soil of nature religion.[3]

Taken as a whole, the Church was developing a strong life of its own, based on recognized officials, a canon of scripture, and a creed; it built up guarantees against gnostic speculations and the caprices of enthusiasm. Meanwhile, throughout its entire conduct of life, it sought peaceful association with the surrounding world. While this was taking place, the driving forces of the earlier period continued to be active in the isolated regions of the mountain valleys in Asia Minor, and, soon after the middle of the second century, gave rise to the movement of "the new prophecy" which, at a later period, was known as the heresy of Montanism. We have seen with what reluctance the free operation of those, who possessed the spirit of enthusiasm in the earliest period, came into opposition with efforts to gain order in the Church, and with efforts to

[1] *Supra*, p. 106   [2] *Supra*, pp. 144 f.   [3] Vol. I, pp. 124 f., 140, 244

present a clear didactic message; similarly we have seen how the churches mistrusted false prophets and their fraudulent devices. Nevertheless the Church had no desire, and was not able, to "quench" the spirit, but was prepared to recognize it if revealed with unexceptionable clarity—it must be admitted that all responsible persons regarded such events with anxiety, and were always inclined to prefer a healthy pedestrianism to "proofs of the spirit and of the power". By their very nature, bishop and prophet were opposites in this respect, and could not be otherwise; in this matter, no change has taken place up to the present day. Owing to this fact, the Roman Catholic Church has developed its wonderful organic hierarchy, and this operates as an abiding ever-present vehicle and mediator of the Holy Spirit by combining office and sacrament. Side by side with this hierarchy, new vehicles of the spirit have continued to arise in their own right, and, either alone, or evolving into movements and organizations, they have compelled recognition of their genuine "spirituality". The two lines of development are, by nature, mutually contradictory—and frequently in history this has meant mutual exclusion—but the consciousness of possessing a common root in genuine, early Christianity has, on the whole, been stronger than the feeling of opposition to any particular form of the phenomenon.

The first new flame of the early vehemence of the spirit took place _c._ A.D. 156 in Ardabau, a village on the borders of Mysia and Phrygia;[1] its situation cannot now be determined. Here Montanus, newly baptized, was suddenly seized by the spirit; he fell into ecstasy, and showed all the manifestations of glossolalia; this soon changed into rational speech, and revealed the speaker as a prophet of the Holy Spirit. Two women, Prisca and Maximilla, became his disciples, and they also, when in an unconscious state, uttered strange things, and spoke in the name of the divine Spirit. Doubt and faith struggled with one another amongst those who were present, but faith conquered; and, throughout the land of Phrygia, the news spread rapidly of a new, and now quite final, revelation of God through these His new prophets. Their pronouncements were written

[1] Eus., _H.E._, 5,16,7. Epiph., _haer._, 48,1,2. The most important sources collected in N. Bonwetsch, _Texte z. Gesch. d Montanismus_ (_Kl. Teste_ 129), 1914. Greater detail in Labriolle, _Les sources de l'histoire du Montanisme_ 1913

down and gathered together as sacred documents similar to the words of the Old Testament prophets, the sayings of Jesus, and the letters of his Apostles.

A few citations from such books of sayings have survived, plainly showing the ecstatic and enthusiastic character of this form of prophecy. As in the case of the ecstatic referred to by Celsus,[1] neither did Montanus speak in his own name as man; rather the spirit of God was the speaker:[2] "Lo, man is like a lyre, and I strike that lyre as the plectron would strike it. Man sleeps and I wake. Lo, it is the Lord who takes away men's heart and gives them another", or "No angel, no messenger is here, but I, the Lord, God the Father, have come Myself", "I am the Lord God almighty, transformed into a man". In sentences like these, the Monarchian theology maintains its place in unbroken continuity and naïve form; hence the formula of inspiration might have a trinitarian sound:[3] "I am the Father and the Son and the paraclete"— there was only the one Almighty God and Father, who had revealed Himself in Christ, His Son, and who now proclaimed Himself through the mouth of Montanus as the paraclete prophesied in John's gospel:[4] three names for the one being. The new enthusiasm possessed all the quality of that experienced among the early Christians. Montanists interpreted it as an invasion of the divine, which irresistibly overpowered one's own human nature. The prophetess, Maximilla,[5] was compelled to proclaim the wisdom of the Lord: she was "forced to do so with or without her own consent"; that was genuine prophecy, and it included the bitter complaint: "I am pursued like a wolf out of the sheep fold; I am no wolf: I am word and spirit and power".

Yet what was taking place in Phrygia was not a re-vitalization of the general enthusiasm of the primitive period. At first, we hear nothing of the phenomena of ecstasy spreading among the crowd, nor of a contagious glossolalia such as is occasionally to be observed, ever and again, in the course of the Church's history, and such as flames up even to-day in Methodist gatherings. Only quite gradually did the movement again set

---

[1] *Supra*, p. 55   [2] Epiph., *haer.*, 44,4,1. 11,9. 11,1   [3] Didymus, *de trin.*, 3,41,1
[4] Vol. I, p. 231   [5] Epiph., *haer.*, 48,13,1. Eus., *H.E.*, 5,16,17

the old fires alight in individual churches, and, side by side with, or else after, the great three, only gradually were all sorts of minor prophets called forth into the open. Originally there were but three persons who were seized by the spirit and who laboured as prophets, and they were conscious of their uniqueness: "After me," said Maximilla,[1] "no other prophet will come, but only the final End." This prophecy was not meant to be imitated, but to be recognized as God's concluding revelation.

What was its content? In the first place, expectation of the immediate end of the world as proclaimed by wars and rebellions.[2] The severe distresses, occasioned by the wars of Marcus Aurelius and the dreadful years of epidemic,[3] were really quite fitted to pass as heralds of the final age, and reveal the four apocalyptic horsemen riding over the earth.[4] In other regions, also about this time, there was a feeling that the world would soon end. In the province of Pontus, a bishop was tortured by visions in dreams which revealed the future to him. He prophesied to his church that the Last Judgement would come within two years: thereupon the members of the church got rid of house and goods, cultivated the fields no longer, but, in fear and trembling and with tearful prayers, waited for the last day. In Syria, a bishop led his whole church, including the children, into the wilderness to meet Christ at His second advent: they wandered about, and were saved from dying of starvation by a none too friendly intervention on the part of the police.[5]

Similarly the "Phrygian" prophets lived in expectation of the imminent end of the world; and the Revelation of John (21: 1–10) had stamped on their souls the picture of the holy city of Jerusalem as it would descend from heaven upon the reborn earth. Pepuza, a country-town which lay between Peltai and Dionysopolis, is recorded as the place where the future New Jerusalem would come. Here Christ, in the form of a shining female figure, appeared in a dream to Prisca when she was asleep;[6] He "caused wisdom to sink into her heart and had

---

[1] Epiph., *haer.*, 48,2,4   [2] Eus., *H.E.*, 5,16,18   [3] *Supra*, pp. 18 f.
[4] Matt. 24: 7 and parallels; Rev. 6: 2–8   [5] Hippol. on Dan. 4: 18 f.
[6] Epiph., *haer.*, 49,1,3. 48,14,1

revealed to her that this was a holy place, and here would Jerusalem descend out of heaven". In another passage, the neighbouring place of Tymion is mentioned side by side with Pepuza as the locus of the eschatological expectation; thither all believers were to gather to await the Lord. In the following period, however, we hear only of Pepuza as the holy site, and here at a later date the central authorities of the Montanist church made their headquarters.[1] Epiphanius heard[2] that, until his own day, men and women used to practise sleeping in the temple there, in the hope that Christ would appear to them just as he had done to Prisca; but these were only later forms of Montanism, and we must beware of predicating them of the earlier period.

On the basis of these clearly defined "chiliastic" eschatological expectations, the new prophecy led to a very rigorous code. Marriage was an earthly bond which prevented full consecration to God—Paul had already taught that much in a similar situation. Hence, the prophetesses abandoned their husbands in order to live entirely for their calling as preachers. Possibly they recommended others to follow their example;[3] certainly they advised against new marriages, as was also done by the bishop of Pontus already mentioned.[4] It is possible that Prisca, even at an earlier date, had been inclined to asceticism, and had lived with her husband in "spiritual marriage",[5] before she left him: at least, she permitted herself to be described by the church as virgin, and, in one speech, she laid emphasis upon the value of continence for the reception of revelations.[6] The earliest notices, at any rate, are quite definite in saying that the Phrygians had prohibited marriage altogether: only in Tertullian's writings, and at a still later time, was the prohibition of a second marriage remarked as a peculiarity of theirs.[7] That ascetic tendencies conformed to popular ideas is proved by the various apocryphal *Acts of the Apostles* of that period, among which at least the *Acts of Paul* originated in Asia Minor. Here celibacy appeared as a mark of genuine

---

[1] Eus., *H.E.*, 5,18,2. Jer., *epist.*, 41,3,2   [2] Epiph., *haer.*, 49,1,2. 4
[3] Eus., *H.E.*, 5,18,2   [4] Hippol., *loc. cit.*   [5] Vol. 1, p. 136
[6] Eus., *H.E.*, 5,18,3. Tert., *exh. castit.*, 10
[7] Cf. also Origen, *de principiis*, 2,7,3 p. 151,2. Koetschau, in *epist. ad Titum*, 5,291. Lommatzsch

Christianity,[1] and this view was reflected in the earliest forms of Montanism.

Fasting was a spiritual exercise by which the early Christians prepared themselves to welcome the second advent of the Lord: by fasting they stood "on the watch" (guard-duty fasting).[2] When the new prophecy infused life again into the expectation of the parousia, a new emphasis on fasting was a closely parallel phenomenon. We are told of regulations for fasting which went beyond the custom of the Church, and Tertullian tells us more exactly what were the rules prevailing in his time and district. The guard-duty fastings, universally practised on Wednesday and Friday, were not only observed until the early afternoon (3 p.m.), but continued until the evening; there were a few additional fast days, and, twice in the year, a week of abstinence (*Xerophagia*) during which succulent foods, meat, and wine[3] were not used.

These matters were precisely prescribed because Montanus had a penchant for organization, and, consequently, they created, in orthodox circles, a stronger feeling of being novelties. He organized the distribution of the sacrificial offerings within the churches, and the prophetess, Prisca, demanded the delivery of gold and silver and valuable clothing. Special officials were instituted to care for the collected moneys; itinerant preachers of the new prophecy were supported from the central funds, and were not dependent on the goodwill of the churches they visited, goodwill which was frequently quite uncertain.[4] This sort of thing gives the impression of a strong and purposeful will controlling the entire movement, and continuing to be effective after the death of the founder. In the fourth century, we find that the sect possessed a patriarch resident in Pepuza, under him being the *koinonoi*, i.e. partakers, associates, whose functions it is impossible to guess; and in addition, in isolated places, were bishops, presbyters, and deacons.[5]

Hence, it would not be correct to evaluate Montanism as essentially a reaction to an early Christian type of vehicle of

[1] *Supra*, pp. 82, 86   [2] *Supra*, p. 133
[3] Tert., *ieiun.*, 1. 2. 10; cf. Jer., *epist.*, 41,3. Hippol., *Elenchos*, 8,19,2
[4] Eus., *H.E.*, 5,18,1–4   [5] Jerome, *epist.*, 41,3; cf. *Cod. Justin* 1,5,20,3

the spirit, a reaction directed against a growing official organization: the movement agreed in organizing the leadership
of the Church by means of the familiar "elected offices" of
bishops, presbyters, and deacons; or at least they adopted this
form of leadership at a later date, without regarding it as a
declension from their first principles. Moreover, women were
admitted to these offices after having received proof, in Prisca
and Maximilla, that even the female sex was able to receive
the Holy Spirit: a feature offensive to the regular Church.[1]
Epiphanius also tells of a procession of seven virgins clad in
white, who solemnly entered the church, with lights in their
hands, in order to speak to the people, and deliver prophetic
utterances calling to repentance.[2] This again was probably a
later development. The earliest form of the movement in
Phrygia restricted prophecy to the three known principal
persons: no other prophets were to arise after them; but the
End was to come, and for this the call to repentance prepared
the way. The parousia, however, once more delayed arrival,
opponents lustily scoffed about it[3]—but the only result was a
further operation of the spirit in numerous men and women in
several churches; these persons accepted the tradition coming
down from the beginning of the movement, and passed it on
to the following generation. It was now that Montanism
cultivated enthusiasm to the extent known during the early
Christian era. It is to this period that the virgins belong, of
whom Epiphanius tells, and here also the prophetic "sister" at
Carthage.[4]

It is easy to understand that a Christianity of this kind, which
lived in the world of the future, was opposed emphatically to
the kingdoms of this world: genuine Christians who belonged
to these churches did not avoid persecution by taking to flight,
but met them with defiance; and sometimes temperament
even drove them to the attack. The *Acts of the Martyrs* recount
more than one case of voluntary surrender on the part of a

---

[1] Epiph., *haer.*, 49,2,5; cf. Firmilian in Cyprian, *epist.*, 75,10. A Gallic writing
in Labriolle, *op. cit.*, 227,8

[2] Epiph., *haer.*, 49,2,3

[3] Eus., *H.E.*, 5,19. Epiph., *haer.*, 48,2,4–7

[4] Epiph., *haer.*, 49,2,3. Tert., *de anima*, 9; cf. also *Mart. Pol.* 4, *Mart. Vienne* in
Eus., *H.E.*, 5, 1,49; cf. *Acta Pionii* 11,2; cf. *Acta Carpi* 42–44

"Phrygian", and Tertullian[1] bears witness to a stern, prophetic saying: "Do not desire death on a sick-bed, in childbirth, or by a mild fever, but by martyrdom to the honour of Him who suffered for you." The faithful, indeed, actually preferred martyrdom.

From the very beginning, the Phrygian prophecy greatly excited men's minds. What took place here was in line with the ancient tradition; indeed it could be regarded throughout as the fulfilment of the promise in John's gospel, that a paraclete would come and lead Christian believers into all truth. That is how these prophets desired their work to be understood, and they met with considerable acceptance. But in the normative regions, where the Church was already far advanced, there was hesitation. We have already seen the various kinds of defence that had been laboriously built up to protect the Church against gnosticism and arbitrary caprices. The regular officials of the Church, who stood in the apostolic succession, refused to recognize this form of prophecy although it put forward the highest claims; and, in the New Testament canon of apostolic writings, which was at that time just beginning to take definite shape, no suitable place could be found for the records of the new prophets. The problem was, however, to know how to deal with the novelty. In content, Montanist preaching apparently offered nothing that could be seized on as contrary to the doctrine of the Church, and to the canon of Scripture; hence it was not possible to refute it from this stand-point—in the way that one could deal with gnosticism.

Therefore, the only remaining recourse was to attack the persons, i.e. to raise doubts about the genuineness of the prophetic movement itself on the ground of a "proving of the spirit" by the deeds of its instruments. This method was then diligently employed, and we are told of commissions[2] sent out in order to expose Maximilla as a fraud: but the adherents "stopped the mouths" of these critics. Thereupon their moral conduct was tested, and all sorts of objections were brought against them, and finally also against their adherents; to the extent of circulating stories that Montanus had committed suicide, and that their patron, Theodotos, threw himself over a

[1] Tert., *fuga*, 9; *anima*, 55   [2] Eus., *H.E.*, 5,16,17. 18,13

precipice—stories which our informant himself did not believe.[1] Later, we are told of the horrors of mysteries in which the blood of a slaughtered child played a part.[2] Here we have got down to the level of the usual gossip about heretics.

On the other hand, in the earliest period, there was criticism of the martyrdoms. On one side it was said: you have no martyrs, hence you lack the spirit which you pretend to possess. On the other side, however, the existence of numerous martyrs was acknowledged, but attention was drawn to the fact that the true martyrs, as recognized by the Church, refused to be associated with the Phrygian martyrs already in prison.[3] Since, in the general view, martyrs in prison were vehicles of the spirit, the refusal to recognize the imprisoned Phrygians was an authoritative pronouncement of the spirit, and held good in regard to the whole movement.

There was considerable literary activity against the new prophecy: the detailed account in Eusebius rests on several works written during the struggle, and even Epiphanius had sources of that kind at his disposal. Moreover the dispute provided the occasion, for the first time, on which the leaders of the churches in Asia Minor were called together into a common synod;[4] at various places and on different occasions they discussed ways of effecting a genuine defence, and they decided to exclude the adherents of the movement from the Church. Thus, in spite of itself, Montanism became a sect; nevertheless it spread extensively. It was soon to be found in Rome; c. A.D. 200 it laid hold on Africa, where Tertullian became an enthusiastic advocate of it; and, even at an early date, it found friends in Southern Gaul, a region which was closely connected with Asia Minor. Irenæus of Lyons[5] spoke in very earnest tones of sin against the Holy Ghost in the case of those who refused to recognize the new revelations of the paraclete. The Gallic churches of Lyons and Vienne not only sent to the churches of Asia and Phrygia their well-known account of the sufferings of their martyrs, together with their view in matters relating to Montanism, but they also included several writings in which the authoritative persons expressed

---

[1] *Ibid.* 5,16,13–15   [2] Epiph., *haer.*, 48,14,6. Philastrius, *haer.*, 49,5
[3] Eus., *H.E.*, 5,16,12. 20–22   [4] Eus., *H.E.*, 5,16,10   [5] Iren. 3,11,9 (2,51 Harvey)

themselves on behalf of peace in the Church: they even wrote to
Eleutheros, bishop of Rome, in the same sense.[1] Obviously this
was an act of intermediation occasioned by the condemnation
pronounced by the synod in Asia Minor.

Nevertheless the unity which was sought, was not reached.
The dissensions which came to the light of day in the east,
broke out also in the west; Rome and Carthage became the
focal points of further disputes about Montanism.[2] In the
course of the persecution under Decius, opinions as to the way
of dealing with backsliders began to differ widely, and the
Montanists took the side of a rigorous radicalism, thereby
increasing the sense of hostility towards the church catholic.
The struggle went further in Asia Minor, and Firmilian, bishop
of Cæsarea, tells us not only of a new prophetess who appeared
in the year A.D. 236, but, in particular, of a great synod at
Iconium which went as far as refusing to recognize Montanist
baptism.[3] We lack later documentary evidence.

The inscriptions found in Asia Minor have been examined
with a view to determining the fate of Montanist churches,
but very little material affording any answer has yet been
discovered: only a few inscriptions can be declared genuinely
Montanist.[4] About A.D. 370, Epiphanius heard a great deal
about Montanist churches still flourishing in Asia Minor, and
a little later Jerome testified, from personal experience, to the
continued existence of the sect in its ancient highland fortress of
Ancyra.[5] A historian of the fifth century asserted that, by his
time, they continued to exist only in Phrygia and the immediate
neighbourhood, but otherwise had been eradicated.[6] Imperial
laws promulgated after the days of Constantine continued to
order their destruction: the name "Phrygian" constantly recurs
in the lists of heretics found in the regulations of the Christian
state Church.[7] A repudiated sect, they disappeared less than 200

[1] Eus., *H.E.*, 5,1,3. 3,4
[2] Gaius *vs* Proklos. Eus. *H.E.*, 2,25,6. 6,20,3 and oft.
[3] Firmilian in Cyprian, *epist.*, 75,10.19
[4] Schepelern, *D. Montanismus u. d. phryg. Kulte* (1929), pp. 81 f., Grégoire, *Byzantion* 8 (1933), 58 ff.
[5] Epiph., *haer.*, 48,14,2. Jerome, *comm. in Gal. lib.*, 2, Praef. cf. Eus., *H.E.*, 5,16,4
[6] Sozomenos 2,32,5
[7] *Ibid.* 2,32,2: The laws are brought together in Labriolle, *op. cit.*, 196–203. 230–35

years after their first appearance. Nevertheless their characteristics continued to live in the Church under other forms and
names: faith in the continued renewal of revelations of the
Holy Spirit given to men and women specially endowed by
grace; passionate contempt for this world, and an all-consuming
expectation of the second advent of the Lord.

Chapter Nine

GAUL

QUITE EARLY IN THE SECOND CENTURY, CHRISTIANITY MUST have penetrated the strip of coast which had been colonized from early times by Greeks, and which was dominated by the two ports of Arles and Marseilles. Nevertheless no direct evidence has survived: records begin only in the second half of the third century, and become numerous at the beginning of the fourth.[1] The circumstances are scarcely doubtful, because, as early as A.D. 180, churches existed in the Rhône valley, and in A.D. 177 the persecution of Christians which we have already described,[2] fell upon the churches at Vienne and Lyons. Vienne belonged to the old Roman province in the republican period; Lyons lay about 20 miles farther north, and Augustus raised it to the capital of Gaul soon after the country had been conquered by Cæsar: the bishop of the capital was also responsible for the church at Vienne,[3] and presumably also the small scattered churches in the Rhône valley.[4] Although the colony of citizens at Lyons was composed of Italians, and had a thoroughly Roman character, nevertheless the Celtic population of Gaul, as well as the Greeks round about the mouth of the Rhône, were represented in the Church.

Here, as in Rome, Christianity was preached in the Greek language, and for a long time Greek remained the speech of the educated class. Among the martyrs of A.D. 177, however, there were already numerous Latin names,[5] and Bishop Irenæus asserts that he frequently had to speak Celtic:[6] unfortunately he does not say whether he did so only in everyday intercourse, or also when preaching, especially in seeking to make missionary converts. The latter would appear to be the case, for he occasionally refers to the conversion of uneducated, indigenous people among Celts and Teutons.[7] Particularly close relations existed between the church at Lyons and the Christians o.

---

[1] Harnack, *Mission*, 4th edit., 2,872–880   [2] *Supra*, pp. 161 f.   [3] *Supra*, p. 65
[4] Iren. 1,13,7 (1,126)   [5] *Martyrol. Hieron.* on June 2
[6] Iren., *praef.* (p. 1,6 ed. Harvey)   [7] Iren. 3,4,1 (2,16). 1,10,2 (1,92 f.)

Asia Minor. Yet it is scarcely an accident that only in two cases amongst the martyrs was attention expressly directed to their foreign origin, and both came from Asia Minor: Attalos from Pergamon, and Alexander from Phrygia, the latter being a doctor who "had been settled in Gaul already for many years". Further there was the slave Pontikos, whose native land is indicated by his name;[1] above all, there was Irenæus who at a later date stepped into the office of Potheinos, the martyr bishop; Irenæus was born in Smyrna, and his childhood recollections still connected him with the aged bishop Polycarp.[2]

These personal relations naturally had spiritual consequences of their own, and the young missionary churches of the west in Gaul adopted ways of thought and manners of life characteristic of Asia Minor, the early homeland of Hellenistic Christianity. We have already seen how the Montanist movement was strongly re-echoed in Gaul; the Lyonese record of the martyrs boasts, among others, of the eminent Alexander the Phrygian physician, whom we have just mentioned, and declares that he was endowed with "apostolic charisma". This is a notice from which we may deduce that he was representative of the secondary type of Montanist prophecy. The attitude of Irenæus to the problem of the new prophecy is everywhere positive, a fact which shows that, in his case, he was not dealing with an exceptional phenomenon, but that its occurrence was joyfully welcomed by the whole Church. The martyrs, even when in prison, took active part in the dispute in the Church as to the recognition of Montanism, and did not dissemble their opinion to Eleutheros bishop of Rome.[3] Montanism offers the clearest example of the inner connection between Gaul and Asia Minor; but a closer inspection shows that there were also other threads which linked the Christianity of the two regions. This observation holds true in particular as regards the theology of Irenæus, the episcopal spokesman of the province.

It has just been observed above that Irenæus came from Smyrna, and was born probably *c.* A.D. 140. He went through the persecution in Lyons as presbyter of the church there:

---

[1] Eus., *H.E.*, 5,1,17. 49. 53
[2] Iren. in Eus., *H.E.*, 5,20,5 f. Iren. 3,3,4 (2,12)   [3] Eus., *H.E.*, 5,3,4–4,2

he conveyed to Rome what the martyrs had written about
Montanist questions. After his return he succeeded bishop
Potheinos who had succumbed to torture,[1] probably in A.D.
178. We then learn that he took part in the Easter dispute, and
spoke on behalf of the independence of Asia Minor as against
Rome[2]—after which we have no further evidence about his
doings, or his end. However, we possess more exact knowledge
about his theology which, indeed, he wrote in two works; the
original text has been lost (as is the case with all the other
writings of Irenæus), but has been preserved in reliable
translations.

Much the more significant of the two is the *Elenchos*, a
"Refutation and Repudiation of False Gnosis" in five books.
The Fathers who fought against heretics in the next centuries
frequently copied out this primary document, and as a consequence have preserved numerous passages in the original
wording. It was then forgotten by the Greek church, with the
result that no manuscript containing the whole has survived.
In the west, the work continued to be prized. At an early date,
perhaps while the author was still alive, it was translated into
Latin; this translation was very frequently copied, with the
result that more than a dozen manuscripts have survived to our
day. Moreover, even the Armenians made a translation, and
of this we possess the last two books; an Armenian translation
provides us with a substitute for the lost, original text of
Irenæus's second writing which was still extant in Eusebius's
time,[3] and which bore the title, *Record of the Apostolic Preaching*
(*Epideixis*).[4]

This work is a brief compendium of Christian doctrine, and
follows closely the lines of the *Elenchos*; perhaps it was conceived
as a text-book for the instruction of catechumens, and it
presents no new ideas, although in many passages it employs
felicitous phraseology.

Irenæus's *Elenchos* is the oldest surviving work in which the
Church repudiated heresy, because the *Syntagma* of Justin, the
Apologist, which was composed previously, has been lost.
Irenæus dedicated the book to a friend (who is now otherwise

---

[1] Eus., *H.E.*, 5,1,1 f. 8   [2] *Supra*, pp. 176 f.   [3] Eus., *H.E.*, 5,26
[4] Engl. Trans. by J. Armitage Robinson (S.P.C.K., 1920)

unknown) "and to all who belong to him", i.e. probably a bishop and his church. The book was intended as an aid in the struggle against heretics, in order that the bishop might have an answer for them, but it was also intended to lead wanderers back to the Church, and to strengthen the faith of the newly converted.[1] The inference is that the book is the first comprehensive work belonging purely to the literature of the Church itself. In the first book, the teachings of the Valentinians are described, followed by those of the other gnostics. With the second book, the refutation begins, and, in the following books, gradually becomes a positive account of the true doctrine of the Church. Nowhere is there any particular plan, or any general train of thought; and the range of what is said, and the crowd of repetitions, make it less attractive to read than the subject-matter promises. Nevertheless, on account of its content, the whole is extremely important; at the same time, it shows us what degree of education prevailed in those Christian circles where representatives of gnostic speculation were attempting to make converts.

It was the same people who read the writings of the Apologists and the tractates of the gnostics: they belonged to a middle-class which was proud of its education, but was nevertheless rather maladroit; yet they were now providing the leadership in Christendom. They were very much attracted by the gnostics' esoteric doctrines of wisdom, based ultimately on doctrines which Jesus was held to have taught in confidence to the disciples of His most intimate circle, and that were only intended to suit a small group of the elect as a special privilege. Irenæus, however, passionately repudiated the whole of the artificial speculations, and the extraordinary explanations of Biblical passages; and not seldom did he succeed in firing a bullet which found its billet in the inconsequences of their method. He recalls his readers to a sound common sense; he endeavours to make clear the eternal and fundamental truth that God has placed bounds to our knowledge; and that the problem of scientific inquiry consists in examining the area which is open to our powers of understanding. These are the things of this world as they lie before our eyes; and over and

[1] Iren. 1 *praef.*, 5 *praef.* (1,5. 2,313)

above them are the plain and obvious pronouncements of Holy Scripture. He who exercises unrestrained imagination on the gospel parables, and expounds them as he pleases, will of course come to dazzling results; but these results will appear different to every student and disappear in the light of truth. The starting point must be the simple and unambiguous testimonies of Scripture. These are numerous enough to provide firm ground for the whole of Christian knowledge, and to lead Christians into any depths which are necessary for them.[1] As distinct from those who practised gnostic speculations and arrogant intellectualism, Irenæus maintained that it was better and more useful to be simple, and unlearned, and to come near to God in love, than to be puffed up with knowledge, and walk in the ways that blasphemed God.[2] This point of view has been repeatedly stressed by Church Fathers and scholastics, and argued in a variety of ways.

What God did before He created the world He had hidden from us. The knowledge, which came from Scripture, was sufficient, viz. that He had created it, and every attempt to answer the other question led to foolish and culpable perversions of the idea of God.[3] Nor were we able to understand the cause of evil in the world: why some beings had fallen away from God, why others had remained faithful, God had not explained to us and we must be content. It was impossible for us ever to analyse God.[4] But, alternatively, God had given to our hand everything that it was necessary for us to know. His revelation was made plain in Holy Scripture, in the pronouncements of the prophets, the Apostles, and the Lord Himself.[5]

Irenæus's New Testament canon comprised, besides the four gospels and the Pauline letters, the Acts of the Apostles, the Johannine Epistles, and the Revelation of John; in addition there was 1 Peter and—as the only departure from the apostolic principle—the recent prophetic writing of the *Shepherd of Hermas*.[6] The sum of the knowledge contained in these writings was put together in the "Rule of Faith", and this was proclaimed by the Church as the guiding line of truth in the whole

---

[1] Iren. 2,27, 1–3 (1,347 f.)   [2] *Ibid.* 2,26,1 (1,345)   [3] *Ibid.* 2,28,3 (1,352 f.)
[4] *Ibid.* 2,28,7 (1,356 f.)   [5] *Ibid.* 2,27,2. 28,7 (1,348. 357)
[6] *Supra*, pp. 98 ff. Iren. 4,20,2 (2,213). Bonwetsch, *Theol..d. Iren.*, 40

world.[1] Lessing's celebrated question in the *Axiomata* 8, whether one could be a Christian without a Bible, would have been answered by Irenæus with an unmistakable Yes, and indeed Lessing did not fail to quote Irenæus's view. If the Apostles had transmitted nothing to us in writing, the tradition which had been continued in the Church would have been sufficient to mediate the whole truth to believers: people in the surrounding districts, who had no Bible, confessed the articles of the Creed.[2]

The original source of Christian preaching was the teaching of the Apostles; this was to be found in the New Testament writings, and also in the tradition of the Church. Irenæus frequently quotes items of information from the "ancients" who had had intercourse with the Apostles. But he felt that the broad current of tradition flowed in the living channels which had been guarded by the succession in office of the presbyters instituted by the Apostles, i.e. by the bishops. The charism of truth, which had been granted by God to the episcopal office, guaranteed the purity of the doctrine which had been transmitted in this way,[3] and this charism was to be identified with the operation of the Holy Spirit in the Church.[4] As the most eminent, the oldest, and the best known example of such a traditional series of bishops, Irenæus cites the Roman Church, which had been founded by the Apostles, Peter and Paul; on account of its overwhelming pre-eminence, every other church must agree with its teaching—hence, also, it was superfluous to adduce any other series of successive bishops.[5] The word "must" was of course not a legal prescription, but a logical consequence from the universal validity of the principle of tradition as guaranteed by the Holy Spirit.

If we now inquire what was the Church's doctrine about God, the answer would be the familiar monotheism of the early Church in both its Biblical and philosophical shape: reference would also be made to our innate, rational knowledge of the one God.[6] But when Irenæus repudiated gnostic theories of emanation, he became mistrustful towards the logos theology

---

[1] *Supra*, p. 110 f. Iren. 1,10,1 and oft. Iren., *Epideixis*, par. 6
[2] Iren. 3,4,1 (2,15 f.) 5,20,1   [3] *Ibid.* 4,26,2 (2,236)   [4] *Ibid.* 3,24,1 (2,131)
[5] *Ibid.* 3,3,1 (2,9)   [6] *Ibid.* 2,6,1 (1,263 f.)

of the Apologists. He would have nothing to do with any essential separation of the logos, or *nous*, from the Father: God was entirely *nous*, entirely logos, entirely operative spirit, and entirely light, and anyone who separated one of these from God would make Him a composite being.[1] Irenæus had a good deal to say about the logos, and made frequent use of this Biblical term occurring ever and anon among the Apologists, but his type of conception was determined by the Monarchianism of his native land; and when he spoke of the incarnation of the logos, he readily employed the favourite paradoxes about the Invisible becoming visible, the Impassible undergoing suffering, and so forth.[2] We do not hear much among the Apologists about the Holy Spirit, which sometimes appears to be identified with the Son:[3] they regarded the logos as identical with the Old Testament Wisdom, "Sophia"; Irenæus makes an exact distinction between the logos, or Son, and Sophia, which is the Holy Spirit:[4] nevertheless both are only forms of activity of the one God: he calls them significantly on occasion[5] "the hands of the Father", without, however, entering more deeply into a question which he regarded, not only as beyond the limit of the knowable, but also beyond what was worth knowing.

His thought starts from practical questions of the Christian life. What does the Church confer on mankind? Redemption. Why is redemption necessary? Because men by their sinful lives are subject to death and so pass away, whereas their real desire is for "incorruptibility" (*aphtharsia*). But why does God redeem men? Not because He has need of them, but because it is His will to show them kindness.[6] Therefore He created Adam, furnished him with body and soul, and endowed him with a will free to do good or evil. As a consequence, at the beginning, Adam possessed a similarity to God which was meant to lead him into fellowship with the spirit of God by living in a manner pleasing to God, and thereby at last make him the perfect image of God endowed with *aphtharsia*.[7] The Fall destroyed God's plan, and handed Adam and his descendants over to the power of the devil, who was now continually

---

[1] Iren. 2,28,4 f. (1,354 f.)   [2] *Ibid.* 3,16,6 (2,87 f.)   [3] *Supra*, p. 184
[4] Iren. 4,20,3 (2,214 f.)   [5] Iren. 5,1,3 (2,317). 5,6,1 (2,333)
[6] Iren. 4,14,1 (2,184)   [7] Iren. 4,37,1–4 (2,285 ff.). 38,3–4 (296 f.). 5,12,2 (351)

successful in turning mankind aside from obedience towards God, and consigning them to death and destruction. Irenæus says nothing, it must be granted, about a natural transmission of inherited sin, nor about any loss of the freedom of the will. Man could still will the good and turn to God: indeed apart from this ability, the exhortations of the prophets would have been quite incomprehensible.[1] And why should God have given the Law?

There were, in the first place, "natural laws", obedience to which made man righteous—Irenæus held this view in full earnest in spite of Paul—and upon the chosen, but disobedient, people of the Jews God had laid the ritual law, and this afforded a special training when men served it.[2] Both kinds of laws had been useless. God had then decided upon the act of redemption which was fitted to save the whole of mankind. He reaffirmed the process, begun by Adam but interrupted by the Fall, and sent His Son, the logos, as a life-giving power to mankind. From the Virgin Mary, who was the opposite of disobedient Eve, he took the elements of mankind which descended from Adam, namely body and soul, and by the inner combination of godhead and mankind brought about what our redemption pre-supposed.[3] As the second Adam, Christ the god-man, did what the first Adam had failed to do: He fulfilled God's commandments as a genuine man, and in this way vanquished in all forms of righteousness the sinful and seductive devices of the devil.[4] In His person He united our flesh and blood, i.e. our body and our soul, with the redemptive power of the godhead, and carried them to incorruptibility, as His resurrection proved. In this way, He perfected the image of God as should have been done by Adam. He became man that we might become gods, i.e. immortal men in the image of God, and "sons of God", who beheld God face to face, and thereby possessed eternal life.[5]

The work of "recapitulation" which had been completed

---

[1] Iren. 4,7,2 (2,286 f.)   [2] Iren. 4,13,1–4 (2,180–83). 15,1 (187)

[3] Iren. 3,18,1–2 (2,95). 21,10 (120). 22,1–3 (121 ff.). 4,38,1 (2,292 f.). 5,1,2 f. (2,316). 5,14,1–3 (2,360–62)

[4] Iren. 3,18,6 f. (2,100 f.). 5,21,1 f. (2,380–83)

[5] Iren. 4,20,4. 7. (2,216. 219). 5,7,1 (2,336 f.). 4,33,4 (2,259). 4,38,4 (2,297). 5 praef. (2,314). 5,36,2 (2,429)

once for all in Christ, i.e. the rehabilitation of the original, divine plan for the salvation of mankind, was now intermediated in the Church to the individual through the operation of the Holy Spirit. By its sacraments, the Church handed to mortal man the "medicine of life" which united them most intimately with the godhead.[1] In baptism, our bodies received a union with God which brought about incorruptibility, and our souls received the Holy Spirit, which endowed them with the vital and effective power of eternal life.[2] Man had sinned with body and soul, wherefore both required redemptive deification, without which they were destined to destruction. The philosophical doctrine of the natural immortality of the incorporeal soul, Irenæus definitely set aside: *all* immortality found in a creature was due to a gift of God's grace, and, on account of the close mutual operation of body and soul, *aphtharsia* must comprehend both together.[3]

The Lord's Supper was the second sacrament which mediated to mankind the redemptive operation of the incarnation of God. In the rite the eucharistic elements of bread and wine received the logos of God and became the flesh and blood of Christ: he who partook fed his body with the flesh and blood of the heavenly Lord, and thereby made it a member of the body of Christ, which now also took part in the eternal life of Christ. It is true that the Christian's body would be laid in the earth and would decompose after death. But, at the right time, he would rise again through the power with which he was endowed by the divine logos, for, in the Lord's Supper, God had endowed what was mortal with immortality.[4] He who had become a member of the Christian Church by means of the sacrament, i.e. miraculously united with Christ, to such a one earlier sins were forgiven and, having been endowed with the power of the Holy Spirit, he was able to behold God in Christ, and so to obtain a share in the divine life. Moreover, in virtue of this newly-given power, he was in a position to fulfil, in complete and genuine freedom, the "natural" commandments of God as represented in the Ten Commandments and their exposition

---

[1] Iren. 3,19,1 (2,102 f.)   [2] Iren. 3,17,2 (2,93)
[3] Iren. 2,34,1–3 (1,381–83). 3,18,7 (2,100 f.). 5,6,1 (2,333–35). 5.8.2. (2,340)
[4] Iren. 5,2,2 f. (2,319–323). 4,18,5 (2,207 f.)

by Christ. He was now a "spiritual man", and joyfully followed the example of Christ, His teachings and works, in thought, word, and deed.[1]

By this act of redemption, the "recapitulation" at the "end of the age" of which Paul spoke in Eph. 1: 10 had become fact. Adam's failure stood at the beginning of the history of the world; and similarly at its end, the restoration and continuation of God's work would take place, a work which had been so precipitately interrupted. Mankind renewed, righteous, and even here on earth united with God, marched forward into a new era in the world, a mankind which was fitted for the millennial kingdom of Christ on earth after the conquest of much distress, and after many struggles as recounted in John's Revelation; it was also fitted for an eternal life in a new heaven and on a new earth. Here the goal was reached which God had intended for Adam at his creation, viz. to be the image of God, and to behold God.[2]

Whereas the Apologists provide us with the theological constructions of a speculative philosophy, which systems reflected the views of educated men, in the case of Irenæus we find a theology of a fundamentally opposite kind. It is based on a type of religious life determined by the nature of the Church. Christians felt themselves to be a community which owed unconditional obedience to God's will, a community which had been liberated by the operation of divine miracle from the dominance of the devil and of sin, and which felt itself to possess power to live, on a superhuman level, a life of moral purity. The goal of this new life lay in the future kingdom of glory, which would impart to each individual, beyond death and the grave, both immortality and a perfect salvation consisting in the vision of God. The entire interest of theologians was dedicated to the question of how the redeemed might come to reach this form of life. The ecclesiastical phraseology and points of view, which remained unworked out by the Apologists, and which were only mentioned in passing as articles of faith,[3] stood now in the foreground, and the work of Christ

---

[1] Iren. 4,16,4 (2,192). 4,20,4–7 (2,216–219). 5,1,1 (2,314 f.). 5,8,2 (2,340). 5,9,2 (2,342 f.). *Epideixis* 96

[2] Eschatology in detail cf. Iren. 5,26–36   [3] *Supra*, pp. 182–86

received a clear and illuminating explanation. The fundamental question raised by Anselm of Canterbury, why God
became man, was propounded and answered: in order that
men might become God, in accordance with their original
condition. That was the answer provided by the Greek sense of
religion, and Irenæus gave classic expression to this common
conviction. Christians were the beings endowed with free will,
who were newly created and made God-like by means of the
sacramental miracle.

On this unremovable foundation, which was always present
even where it did not appear to sight, were built the theological
systems and the dogmatic edifices of the following centuries;
from this standpoint, the right light falls on the disputes about
the Trinity and Christology. Irenæus meant to be a Biblicist,
and the main outlines of his theology were sketched by Paul.
Both the antithesis between Adam and Christ, and the doctrine
of the identity of the conquest of sin in Christ and in
Christians, are to be found in the Pauline letters,[1] and a number
of discussions of single issues refer back to Paul's own words.

What is lacking, however, is the absoluteness of the antithesis
which was crucial for Paul. Original sin, together with the
impossibility of man's own righteousness, i.e. at bottom Paul's
doctrine of justification, was entirely and necessarily passed
over. Moreover, the theology of the Cross and the doctrine of
the expiatory sacrifice of Christ were also omitted, or only
employed incidentally and were not essential to the thought.
The vital act of redemption was the incarnation of Christ and
not His death, and the faith which made men righteous was the
acceptance of the Church's message of the miraculous power
of the sacrament. Irenæus's theology, it may be granted, made
use of Pauline conceptions: but its own contribution was the
further development of a faith proper to the Church, a faith
which had been evolved out of the Pauline ideas, and which can
be recognized in a simpler form as early as the letters of
Ignatius.[2] Behind all the discussions put forward by these
theologians, was to be found the simple faith of the churches of
Syria and Asia Minor, churches which were as yet undisturbed
by discussions of the philosophical problem of the forgiveness of

---

[1] Vol. 1, pp. 117–23　　　　　[2] Vol. 1, pp. 237 ff., 240 f., 244 f.

sins, and which, practising the naïve rigorousness of the first Church, represented the community of the saints. Irenæus's title to fame is that his "system" grew out of a religious life which was found in church people, and which was faithful to its roots. Educated people in the orient, however, made higher claims of a philosophical sort, and thus it came about that the work of the bishop of Lyons seemed to them unsatisfactory: the occident proved more grateful.

Chapter Ten

AFRICA

THE CHURCH IN NORTH AFRICA ENTERED THE LIGHT OF history at the same time as the Church in Gaul; but, whereas immediately after Irenæus, the latter once more fell back into a long period of obscurity, the former continually increased in significance for the entire Church. During the course of her history, from Tertullian to Cyprian and then to Augustine, she was the teacher of the entire Christian Church in the west. Similarly to South Gaul, Africa was the seat of an ancient Roman colony. The indigenous fair-haired, and blue-eyed Berbers had been kept in subjection by the Phœnicians; the Punic colonists enjoyed a culture predominantly of the city kind, but it fell before the power of the Roman sword. Both the conquered races continued to live in the Roman province of Africa, the Phœnicians more especially in Carthage, when rebuilt, but also elsewhere in the small towns of the country-side. Rome and its language dominated the prevailing culture. The educated classes spoke and wrote Greek until after the beginning of the third century,[1] but it was not used in daily life like Latin and Punic. The inscriptions make that fact quite clear. The province enjoyed considerable economic prosperity; after Rome, Carthage was the second metropolis of the west, and, until the present day, the numerous and beautiful Roman buildings, which are scattered over the whole of North Africa, bear testimony to the wide extent of the region which came under the sway of Roman city culture.

In the west, just as was the case in the east, the second century was the period of the greatest prosperity, and when the spirit-ually productive power of Italy began to decline, Africa started to bring forth new fruits in Latin literature from its own soils We may grant that, in this respect, the only successful person. were the archaistic orator Fronto, the philologist Sulpicius Apollinaris, and his disciple Gellius, together with Apuleius, the Roman philosophical and mystical writer;[2] but even this was more than Italy was able to rival, and the Romans sat at

[1] Greek instruction: Dessau, *Inscr. lat.*, 2937   [2] *Supra*, p. 25

these men's feet. Christianity was the power which first enabled natives of Africa to contribute towards permanent literature.

We have no information as to how the new religion penetrated into Africa. It may be taken as probable that it arrived there from Rome; the connection between Rome and Carthage was always close, and in the African Church there was a consciousness of a certain dependence on the capital of the Empire.[1] The first emissaries probably spoke Greek, as did the Roman Church. Testimonies have survived as to the use of this language in Christian circles[2] of Africa *c.* A.D. 200, and Tertullian occasionally wrote Greek, as was also the case with Apuleius, his slightly older fellow-countryman.

Latin, however, rapidly came to its own in the Church, and we can demonstrate that, towards the end of the second century, Africa already possessed a Latin Bible which contained not only the Old but also the New Testament: Tertullian frequently quotes from this Bible. In view of the fragmentary character of the surviving remains, we must leave the questions unanswered whether this translation was complete, and whether it came into being in Africa as a single work. Probably these questions must be answered differently in regard to separate parts, and we have good ground for assuming that, at the end of the Antonine period, a Latin translation of the Bible was at hand in Rome, a translation markedly different from its African compeers. When Marcion's disciples transferred their propaganda from Rome to Africa, they carried with them their master's New Testament canon in a Latin form of its own.[3] In any case, the fact of a Latin Bible in Africa before A.D. 200 testifies to a very considerable dispersion of Romanized Christians in this area. Moreover Latin was in fact the language of the Church here before this was the case in Rome.

The growing adherence of believers of Punic race brought about no change; the accession can be proved by the fourth century, and it probably began considerably earlier. Their own language was used in preaching to the people,[4] but they were

---

[1] Tert., *praescr.*, 36
[2] *Acta Perpetuae* 12,2. 13,4; cf. the Greek translation of *Acta Perpetuae* and *Acta Scillitanorum*
[3] H. von Soden in *Festg. für Jülicher* (1927), 273 f. Harnack, *Chronol.*, 2,296
[4] Zahn, *Gesch. d. neutest. Kanons*, 1,40–42

not provided with a Punic Bible nor a Punic liturgy, any more
than was done in the native language in Gaul for the benefit
of the Celts. The subject peoples were content, whereas, in the
course of time, those in the orient everywhere broke through the
fetters of the Greek language, and used Syriac instead. In
the third century, we have only occasional traces, and later
only sparing information, about the Berber Christians: but
we can say with confidence that they were as remote as possible
from contact with city culture, and here as everywhere else,
the cities were the starting-points of Christianity.

From Tertullian we learn that, in his time, i.e. c. A.D. 200,
there were Christians in Carthage and the neighbouring city
of Utica; in the small town of Uthina (to-day Odna) which lay
to the south, in the seaport Hadrumetum (to-day Sousse);
in Thysdrus (El Djem) where a mighty amphitheatre still bears
testimony to the whilom significance of the place, and in the
great garrison of Lambæsis, the military headquarters of the
district of Numidia, to-day known as Algeria. A few places
should be added, on the basis of other testimonies, but that
exhausts our knowledge of the geographical distribution of
Christianity c. A.D. 200.[1] It is but little, yet considerably more
than we know about Gaul at the same period.

The history of the Church in Africa begins for our purposes
with the martyrdom of the Christians of Scilli, a small place in
Numidia whose situation remains unknown. On August 1,
A.D. 180, they were condemned and executed by the pro-
consul in Carthage: two of the names have a Berber sound, and
therefore show that, even at this early date, a successful mission
had taken place amongst the indigenous population.

At this point Tertullian came upon the stage, and the great
contest began in full earnest: Tertullian had come into conflict
with the Church, and had become a Montanist. He had
entered into a sharp engagement with the Roman bishop—
nevertheless his writings were eagerly read, in ancient days, by
young and old, and were preserved in several manuscripts
throughout the Middle Ages: so great was the influence of his
personality. He was born in Carthage, the son of a centurion
in the command at the service of the civil authorities;[2] he

---

[1] Harnack, *Mission*, 2,902–04   [2] Jerome, *vir. inl.*, 53

made a reputation for himself as a jurist in Rome, and at a later date returned to Carthage.[1] We do not know when or where he was converted to Christianity, but that he had previously been pagan is testified by his own words.[2] In the digests of the *corpus juris* there are a few citations of a jurist Tertullian who lived about the same time: it is not impossible that he should be identified with the Church Father.

Jerome asserts that Tertullian had been a presbyter in Carthage, a statement probably in accordance with the facts, because his overwhelming activity as a writer could scarcely have taken place while he was a layman: yet in the writings which have survived, he never refers to his clerical status. The years of both his birth and death are unknown, and can scarcely be indicated even approximately; nevertheless a few of his writings give hints as to the time when they were written, and make it possible for us to say that his work as a writer took place between the years A.D. 195—220; and the writings can, with difficulty, be arranged in chronological order. He became a Montanist at latest in A.D. 207.[3] Tertullian is known to us only as a writer; we have no knowledge of him as a man of affairs. But his literary activity was a genuinely great achievement.[4]

He has been called the creator of ecclesiastical Latin, and appropriately so. He was the first who wrote fluently in Latin, and in a stylish manner, on Christian subjects; and he himself created an appropriate religious and ecclesiastical terminology without previous examples: his Latin Bible could not be used for that purpose, and he says so explicitly more than once. Moreover the terminology he created remained to a large extent normative; it was taken over by Cyprian and carried further, and was afterwards regarded without question as the accepted terminology of the west. He gave his speech an artistic form, naturally corresponding to the taste of his time, but with marked personal characteristics.[5] He never used long periods, but short sentences and phrases usually set in parallel, and with an antithetic content; he made use of puns and sometimes of an echoing rhyme; he piled up questions, gave pointed answers in a staccato style, sometimes in such a twisted

---

[1] Eus., *H.E.*, 2,2,4. Tert., *cult. fem.*, 1,7   [2] Tert., *apol.*, 18,4. *resurr.* 59 (3,120,3)
[3] Harnack, *Chronol.*, 2,256–296   [4] K. Holl., *op. cit.*, 3,1–12
[5] Norden, *Antike Kunstprosa*, 606–15

form of expression that the meaning becomes enigmatic. Nevertheless, there is always intensity, always movement, always content. It is true that that was the "Asianic" manner of the Greek orators from whose school it was introduced into Africa. Apuleius makes use of the same mode; but in the case of Tertullian a stronger dose of Tacitus's terse style is operative; Roman seriousness flows into Greek journalese, and the temperament of the man, which despised all rules and bounds, was successful in giving a unified effect to the whole.

Tertullian is the first instance of a Christian author who rose, even on formal grounds, far above his contemporaries, and proved himself a master of his own language and style: it would be interesting to know what the pagan readers said about his works. It was for such readers that he consciously wrote: his little writing *de pallio*, in which he justified himself in the eyes of a Carthaginian public for his garb as a Greek philosopher, would only have significance if it were to come into the hands of this very public. And in the case of Tertullian we may assume that even his apologetic writings were also read by others than Christians, as was not the case with the writings of his colleagues, and as he himself assures us with satisfaction.[1] He offered so much that was pleasing to literary palates, and also the content of his writing was too rich to be neglected.

Firstly, in regard to learning, Tertullian's pages are crowded with illustrations and quotations drawn from all spheres of knowledge and from the history of all eras and peoples. The above mentioned writing *de pallio* gives a good idea of the taste of the readers of the period. Tertullian discusses tunics and togas in talking about the downfall of Carthage; change as a principle of evolution in nature and history; fashion and hygiene of both sexes, and the luxury of spendthrifts. Naturally, he drew the incredibly varied fullness of his material from the usual books of reference from which every writer at that time was accustomed to quote, but he polished everything up cleverly, mixed it with the fruits of his own gift of keen observation, and made it all very delightful reading. His work may be compared and contrasted with the *Attic Nights* of Aulus Gellius. This is an alluring title, but it covers the work of a mere bookish,

[1] *Supra*, p. 176, note 2

and dry-as-dust schoolmaster copying out excerpts from authors whom he had himself read, from lexicons of all sorts, and from poetic anthologies: yet that sort of thing passed contemporaneously for learning.

The feature which immediately impresses every reader is Tertullian's passionate temperament. The purpose of his argument is plain from the opening sentence, and he sets out towards his goal with brilliant sequence of thought. All his works are occasional writings, all attack some opponent, and all end with total destruction of the enemy. The opponent is always and completely in the wrong: Tertullian makes that clear point by point in a cogent demonstration well thought out. Philosophy, academic logic, and simple daily common sense, are called in to help if they are appropriate to down his opponent; but sometimes he leaves them on one side and appeals to the written word of Scripture if it serves his purpose better to do so. He is skilled in developing the principles of a sound exegesis according to the verbal meaning and the context, and he can use all this effectively; on the other hand, he sometimes disowns these principles completely, and sets to work with boundless conceits and playful allegories, if this is the only way in which he can vanquish his foe. The purpose completely dominates the means, and any idea of objective relevance is miles distant. Tertullian is an advocate who concentrates all his powers on winning his case; but an advocate who fights with twice the passion because it is also his own case that he is advocating.

That was the way in which he contended with heretics like Valentine and Marcion; similarly he fought the gnosticizing painter, Hermogenes, as well as Praxeas, with both of whom he had had severe personal quarrels. He had already given a neat, juristic proof in a writing of his own,[1] that there was no need to discuss main principles with heretics, because the burden of proof lay upon *them*. He wrote passionately against those who persecuted Christians, and he continually cried out loud for genuinely legal standards, and for justice. Indeed he went so far as to proffer a divine test:[2] bring a possessed person before the tribunal and let any Christian whatsoever exorcize him;

[1] Tert., *de praescr. haer.*   [2] *Apol.* 23,4–6

immediately the evil spirit will confess himself as a daemon in accordance with the truth. Place there an enthusiast who has drawn into himself, from the sacrificial smoke, the godhead of Tanit or of Eshmun; and if these godheads do not confess themselves as daemons when conjured by the Christian, there and then let the Christian pay for his temerity with his life.

Tertullian wore a simple mantle and defended it against the prevailing fashion; similarly he combatted rich clothing, rouge and hair dressing, on the part of Christian ladies; and fought against attending stage-plays which many would have agreed to as a permissible pleasure for Christians. He always drew the practical consequences of the plain Christian principles, and did it trenchantly and regardless of results. In this spirit, he dedicated to his wife a writing in which he prescribed permanent widowhood in case of his own death. A second marriage was, from his standpoint, not out and out forbidden, but was nevertheless a surrender to evil among Christians: the second marriage was sinful if contracted with a pagan.

Shortly after A.D. 200, Montanism gained a foothold in Africa, although it was now only a movement of a modified enthusiasm—"the new prophecy" of the paraclete had already been transformed into the written word—but it was very much alive in maintaining the rigour of the early Christian, eschatological, moral code. It is not surprising that Tertullian became a Montanist, nor that he used the sharpest criticism to lash the weak-minded worldliness of the Church when it would have nothing to do with the new spirit. He therefore began to regard the church catholic as an adversary, and, as he had formerly done in the case of heretics, he fell upon it with the same means and with the fanatical hatred proper to a new-baked orthodoxy. Closer inspection shows that the points in dispute were of very varied importance. The Montanists insisted on the practice of fasting; required not only married women, but even young girls, to be veiled, and forbade second marriages; they took up an unaccommodating attitude in the struggle with the state, and were inflexibly hard towards backsliders.

Tertullian increased the sharpness of his tone, not in accordance with the significance of the subject, but with the duration of the struggle, and in the end he did not hesitate to fling

vituperation at the Church's agapēs which he had formerly
praised so finely to pagans.[1] He was merciful towards backsliders, but he insisted that the question of receiving them
back should be decided by the vehicles of the spirit, i.e. the
prophets; not by "the Church as a collection of bishops";
least of all by the martyrs sitting in prison, about whom
Tertullian, when orthodox, had used the most beautiful of
language, and whom now he despised and grossly vilified.[2]
His greatest indignation was aroused by the decision of the
bishop of Rome,[3] when the latter declared officially that he was
prepared to forgive a repentant sinner even the sin of sexual
immorality: with all the arts of proof from the multitude of
Biblical passages, and also by referring to the authority of the
paraclete, Tertullian struggled to maintain the uncompromising temper of the early Christians against a Church which,
he said, had become worse than a den of thieves.[4]

In spite of this exaggerated change of front, the single, straight
line of his development is unmistakable. Tertullian believed
himself to have been morally reborn through Christianity:
in this regard, he felt, every day, the difference from his pagan
past. He defended his faith passionately against persecutors,
and as a consequence he was always prepared to take up any
movement which seemed to promise an increase of moral
strenuousness, itself a divine commandment. For this reason
also, he was always inclined to regard the points of view of his
opponents as signs of lack of morals, and attacked them
accordingly.

He had no theological system, but isolated opinions took
shape in him in the course of his struggle with opponents. He
regarded the essence of Christianity as the unfolding of a
fundamental religious knowledge, which slumbered in every
human soul. It came to light in the commonplace sayings that
there was only one God, that He was both good and righteous,
that daemons were in the world and infect us with evil, that
souls lived after death, and would come up for a judgment
which would either punish or reward them eternally.[5] He never

---

[1] *Apol.* 39,16–21. *Ieiun.* 17 (1,296,25 Wissowa); cf. *Pudic.* 22 (1,271,14. 17)

[2] Tert., *ad mart. pudic.*, 22 (1,271). *Ieiun.* 12 (1,290)

[3] *Infra*, p. 247   [4] *pudic.* 1 (1,220)   [5] Tert., *test. anim.*, 1–4 (1,134 ff.)

attempted, however, to work out a system of doctrine for the
Church, and give a clear account of redemption through
Christ. For this he lacked the ability. He did, once on a day,
write a theoretic work *On the Soul*; it grew into a learned and
acute monograph, and on this account is attractive; nevertheless it is without any particular point and is not closely
knit. It is not a polemic and as a consequence only a half of
Tertullian is really in action. He discusses the question of
original sin,[1] but in a manner which lacks complete clarity,
and is without insight into the implications.

Taken on the whole, his doctrines are those universal in the
Church, but without very great penetration; and he makes sly
digs at the gnostics whenever he finds an opportunity[2] for
sharp attacks upon any form of Christianity which tended to
an alliance with philosophy. Perhaps it is for this very reason
that he so often devised appropriate phraseology. The speculative problems of the Greeks never gave him a headache, and as
a consequence he airily pre-empted the results of centuries of
dispute when he spoke of the divine *Trinitas*—he devised the
word by way of translating the Greek *trias*; the Trinity was
of one substance, one essence, and one power, and, at the same
time, it signified the Son and the Holy Spirit as the second and
third "persons" of the triad.[3] He defended the logos doctrine,
in the sense of the Apologists, against Praxeas, and taught a
strict subordination of the Son to the Father.[4]

With the same happy neatness, he also devised the formula,
made use of by later orthodoxy, to express the relation of the
divine and the human in Christ: he was God and man, one
person in two substances, preserving their own qualities,
uncompounded, side by side, and yet combined.[5] He liked to
present readers with formulas of this kind, although they did
not proceed from any logical necessity as felt by him, and were
not bound up with his religious life in any way. For him, they
were a kind of commentary on the Rule of Faith, but had no
organic connection among themselves, nor with the other
articles of Church doctrine. In Tertullian, the only self-
consistent and united thing was his will or intention; his

---

[1] Tert., *de anim.*, 39–41 (1,366–9)   [2] Tert., *praescr.*, 7
[3] Tert., *adv. Prax.*, 2 (3,229 f. Kroymann), 6 (234,22). 11 244,13. 16)
[4] *Ibid.* 9 (3,239,24) 14 (250,24)   [5] *Ibid.* 27 (3,281,21. 27)

writings were disparate. Augustine asserted[1] that he was a changeable person, that at a later date he seceded to the Montanists, and, in the end, gathered a church of his own about himself: an assertion which seems quite credible in the case of a man of his character. But we have no actual further knowledge of him after he ceased to employ his pen: hence, he disappears from sight c. A.D. 220.

Round about this period, Christianity in Africa must have extended very greatly, for c. A.D. 250 it had spread everywhere in all parts of the province, the oversight being in the hands of numerous bishops—estimated sometimes at almost two hundred.[2] The Church grew not only by the accession of newly-converted pagans, but also numerous members found their way back from schismatic and heretical communities.[3] Hence arose the question of the validity of a baptism administered in a heretical Church, a question which Tertullian had answered in the negative.[4] The Carthaginian bishop, Agrippinus—the first of whom we have any trustworthy information—assembled a synod of seventy bishops. They decided that heretics who came back should be baptized afresh, because there was no valid baptism outside the Church.[5] Agrippinus was succeeded by Donatus, of whom a notice has been preserved incidentally, that he agreed with the verdict of a council of ninety bishops meeting for consultation in Lambæsis: it is possible that he was president.[6]

The first great bishop of the African church now appeared in the person of Cyprian. No information has survived in regard to his early years: but he himself tells us that he was not born in a Christian household, but had had to be converted to the faith.[7] He had received a careful education in rhetoric, and obviously grew up in well-to-do circumstances; he therefore must have belonged to one of the eminent families of Carthage: his name, Cæcilius Cyprianus with the cognomen Thascius, unfortunately provides us with no further exact information.[8]

---

[1] de haeres. 86 (8,25b Bened.)   [2] Harnack, Mission, 4th edit., 2,898
[3] Cypr., ep., 73,3   [4] Tert., bapt., 15. (1,213 W.)
[5] Cypr., ep., 71,4. 73,3. August., de unico bapt., 22 (p. 21 Petschenig)
[6] Cypr., ep., 59,10; cf. 36,4
[7] Cypr., ep., 7,1. ad Don. 3,4. Jer., vir. inl., 67 comes from the valueless Vita of Pontius
[8] Cypr., ep., 66, tit. 4

What converted him to Christianity, he tells us in the little writing dedicated to a friend, Donatus by name. He was disgusted with the prevailing immorality of public and private life, in which he felt himself entangled; disgusted with the ostentation of the wealthy, the corruption of justice, and with all the bloodthirstiness and cruelty. This disgust aroused in him a longing to be free from everything of the sort, but he never dared to hope that his longing would be satisfied. Now, however, he had found by experience that baptism liberated and cleansed him from the old life, gave him new birth, and armed him with the heavenly gift of the Holy Spirit, a gift which endowed him with the power to live a moral life without sin. His prayer re-echoes with gratitude when he asks that God would guard His gracious gift to him. For him, Christianity meant moral liberation.

We do not know when he was baptized, nor how long he served as a deacon or presbyter, because the notices in the early biography can scarcely claim historical reliability. However, in A.D. 248 or the beginning of A.D. 249, he was chosen "pope" —the title of the bishops of Rome, Carthage, and Alexandria —of Carthage, "by the voice of the people and the verdict of God", but against the wishes of a small group of elderly and eminent presbyters, including a certain Novatus;[1] these men were to give Cyprian much anxiety.

He had not been in office a year when the Decian persecution broke out,[2] and made an immediate attack on the bishops of the chief cities. Cyprian was successful in finding a safe place of refuge which afforded him protection during the entire persecution. His absence, however, did not prevent his maintaining charge of the Church, and giving by letter the more critical directives; he also received visitors and, in a certain Tertullus, had a confidential friend who kept him in touch with everything important. The presbyters and deacons conducting the oversight of the Roman church in place of bishop Fabian, who had died in a glorious manner, sent news of the martyrdom to Carthage, and, at the same time, wrote a letter which clearly expressed their surprise at the flight of the Carthaginian

[1] Cypr., *ep.*, 43,1. 3. 4. 14,1. 52,2; cf. 59,6
[2] *Supra*, pp. 166–70

shepherd of souls. Cyprian felt the letter to be so insulting that he sent it back, and asked whether it was genuine.[1]

He gave them, too, a detailed account of his activities, sent, as proof, his letters addressed to the church at Carthage, and explained that he only kept himself in hiding because his presence in Carthage served to provoke the authorities, and would have aggravated the persecutions.[2] He had consigned the care of the churches to his clergy but had not omitted to advise even them to be cautious and to avoid drawing attention to themselves.[3] In particular he had exercised concern for strengthening the imprisoned, wrote them frequent encouraging and admonitory letters, and sent them money from his own pocket. It follows from all this, that the explicit and official confiscations, consequent on his flight, had not robbed him of all his property.[4] The bishop, however, was not as yet so intimate with his flock that his authority was fully able to act from a distance, and prevent the appearance of unhealthy symptoms; and, in his place of hiding, he was troubled by ominous visions, seen in dreams, of disharmony and splits in the Church.[5]

The question which had given the Romans concern, and which they had touched upon in their letter, soon required an answer also in Carthage: What was to be done with the backsliders (*lapsi*)? They were far too many simply to be written off as lost, in accordance with the stern practice of the early Church; the Church must exercise its cure of souls upon them and proffer them some sort of hope. But what sort? The Roman letter, mentioned above, only stated in general terms[6] how to bring backsliders to remorse and repentance in order that they be not lost, but forgiven by God: perhaps they would then have courage, if arrested again, to make a brave confession. If however they fell ill, communion was to be administered to them. Cyprian also adopted this standpoint, and gave it more precise expression: pastoral care was to be given to the *lapsi* while persecution was still in progress, although he strictly forbade coming to any decision about receiving them back into the fellowship of the Church. Any man

---

[1] Cypr., *ep.*, 9,2. Similarly Jer., *ep.*, 102   [2] Cypr., *ep.*, 8,9. 20,1 f.; cf. 7. 14,1
[3] *Ibid.* 5. 7. 14,2   [4] *Ibid.* 7; cf. 66,4   [5] *Ibid.* 11,3 f.   [6] *Ibid.* 8,2 f.

who urged that he should be received back, had the opportunity every day of appearing before the rulers of the state and becoming a martyr; in this way he could reverse his backsliding. As soon as peace was restored, a synod of bishops and other clerics, including also confessors and trustworthy laymen, were to lay down the fundamental principles and to judge the different cases according to their varied seriousness.[1] Only in a case of impending death was communion to be granted to one seriously ill, and that on the recommendation of a martyr or confessor.[2]

This prescription of Cyprian's was quite clear, but did not find general acceptance: opposition came from two sides. In the first place, the confessors who were suffering in prison, claimed it as their valid and ancient right, by virtue of the spirit operating in them, to send letters of recommendation (*libelli pacis*) on behalf of the backsliders. They claimed the highest authority for the *libelli*, and they desired that the bishop and his clergy should again accept into the fellowship of the Church those who were mentioned in such a writing, that they should accept them at once, and in particular without public repentance or other recantation. There was also a further point. Granted that they were in a state of war with the authorities, the confessors were by no means in other respects praiseworthy examples of the Christian life, and, when they were permitted to leave prison, many of them evilly misused their newly-won freedom. Moreover, they sometimes wrote *libelli* without a careful examination of the particular case, which was, perhaps, not even guaranteed by personal acquaintance; sometimes, indeed, the *libelli* were issued in the form of a blank cheque.[3]

When now Cyprian politely but firmly repudiated these presumptuous and irrelevant cases, his old opponents in the college of presbyters perceived an opportunity of undermining his episcopal authority, and acceded to the request of the confessors in full: they agreed that all backsliders should be admitted to communion if the latter brought a letter of recommendation of this kind; nor should the backsliders be subjected

---

[1] Cypr., *ep.*, 17,3. 19,2. 20,3. 30,5. 31,6. 43,3 [2] *Ibid.* 18. 19. 20,3
[3] *Ibid.* 13,4 f. 14,3. 15,3 f.; *de unit.* 20. *de laps.* 20

to further examination, or required to show their repentance in public; and they urged the bishop to approve the action.[1] But he stood his ground, and thereby provoked the confessors to repeated acts of presumption: in the end the latter granted a general pardon to all the backsliders who came within Cyprian's jurisdiction, and requested the bishop to provide an official notification of the facts to all his fellow-bishops.[2] Cyprian quietly set aside all monstrous demands of this character. His action inflamed the passion of his opponents. His fundamentally cautious attitude, and his requirement of examination in individual cases, were explained as contempt for the honour of the confessors—which was indeed the case—and, in a few cities of the province, the excited multitude compelled their bishops to accept the backsliders.[3] Cyprian remained throughout in constant touch with the college of presbyters at Rome, continued to give information about his regulations and written pronouncements, and found in the agreement of the Roman church a valuable defence at his back.[4]

After being set free from prison, a great number of the Carthaginian confessors left the country and fled to Rome: relations were opened with the Roman brethren who pined in prison there.[5] These were unwilling to agree to the extreme desires of the Carthaginians, but held firm to the leadership of their home church. In this sense also, they wrote letters and uttered warnings to Africa, receiving in return a warm letter of thanks from Cyprian, to which in turn they responded heartily.[6] In Carthage, however, all restraint was abandoned. The antagonistic presbyters had already dispensed themselves of obedience to Cyprian, to such an extent that Novatus, their leader, appointed as deacon a highly respected person, Felicissimus by name, and thus the control of the relief funds of the Church passed into his hands. Cyprian's directions for dispensing the money were no longer respected, and indeed, notice to terminate fellowship with him was given in so many words, and in the hearing of the Church. Anyone who now desired monetary help had to join those who were against the bishop—and many followed this line.[7] That was the situation

---

[1] *ep.* 14,4. 15,1. 16,1–3. 17,2   [2] *Ibid.* 23; cf. 22,2. 27,2   [3] *Ibid.* 27,1–3
[4] *Ibid.* 27. 30. 35   [5] *Ibid.* 21. 22   [6] *Ibid.* 30,4. 28. 31   [7] *Ibid.* 41. 42. 43. 52,2

in the Church in the spring of A.D. 251;[1] and when Cyprian returned after Easter (March 23), although he had solemnly excommunicated Felicissimus and his adherents, he nevertheless found them maintaining their place, and in firm opposition to himself.

In order to clarify the situation, Cyprian published two writings outlining his proposals.[2] The first dealt with the backsliders, and explained in detail his view of the varied character of the cases. The most blameworthy were those who had made the sacrifices without outer compulsion, in order, if at all possible, to preserve their house and property from confiscation. To receive these back lightly would be a sin against the clear prescription of the gospel, and no genuine martyr would come forward and guarantee such a person. Those who had recanted voluntarily in this fashion, must bear the consequences of their falling away: only God Himself could forgive them. The case was different with those the strength of whose will had been broken by the severity of their sufferings as martyrs: they would be met with sympathy, and no very long period of penitence would be required of them. But backsliders were also to be found among the *libellatici* who had used bribery in order to purchase a certificate of sacrifice without having actually sacrificed. Such persons had submitted to orders promulgated by the state, and hostile to Christians; they had indirectly denied Christ; hence they also must do penance. Really, of course, any who had seriously entertained the idea of sacrificing, ought to do penance.[3] This was the first time that Cyprian explicitly declared that he did not intend to receive back any apostates in the full sense of the word: they were to remain all their lives in the status of repentance. The question of admission to the Church only arose in the case of less serious sinners. Thus, in practice, he refused to recognize any validity in the letters of reconciliation granted by the confessors.

His second writing dealt with *The Unity of the Catholic Church*, and discussed with great penetration every form of separation and schism. In the course of his argument, he coined the

---

[1] Date: *ep.* 43,1. 4. 7 (p. 591,6. 593,4. 596,21 Hartel)

[2] H. Koch, *Cypr. Untersuchungen (Arb. z. Kirchengesch.* no. 4, 1926), 79–131

[3] *de lapsis* 17. 13. 27 (*ep.* 30,3). 28

classical phrase, which has since echoed throughout the centuries: "It is impossible to have God as Father without having the Church as mother." Outside the Church there was no life, no salvation. Moreover the Church was a unity, and this unity was expressed in the episcopacy, and this again had sprung from a single, apostolic root. Whoever separated himself from the bishop, separated himself from the Church, and, as a consequence, from truth and salvation. All this was impossible for a genuine Christian. The principle held good for everyone, including martyrs and confessors, who themselves were not beyond being tempted by the devil, and who had only reached a stage in, and not the final end of, salvation: even among these persons, there were regrettable cases of backsliding. Schism in the Church was an even greater sin than denial, since it negated the unity of the Church which a repentant backslider recognized.[1]

These two writings clearly indicate Cyprian's place in the history of the Church. He decidedly extended the line which had previously been drawn by Ignatius: the Church and the authority of the Monarchical bishop were identical, and all claims of persons of charismatic eminence, i.e. in this case the martyrs and confessors, were repudiated *in toto* by Cyprian; and so, too, the claim to independence advanced by the members of the college of presbyters. No politeness in form[2] could, or should, deceive us in regard to the fact that Cyprian did not look on the presbyters as colleagues, but as subordinates.

The synod which had frequently been projected was now held, probably in May, A.D. 251: not indeed as an assembly of clerics, confessors, and laymen, as hitherto had always been proclaimed, but as a normal council of the African bishops,[3] and, after a penetrating discussion of the question of backsliders, it confirmed the principles laid down by Cyprian. The synod also supported Cyprian's action in excluding Felicissimus and the antagonistic presbyters; and when a Roman synod[4] supported the Carthaginian resolutions, Cyprian might say that he had accomplished everything that was possible at the

---

[1] *de unitate* 4–6. 9. 19–21; cf. *ep*. 73,21. 74,7   [2] *ep*. 38,1 is instructive on this point
[3] Record in *ep*. 55,6. 17–23. 59,9   [4] *ep*. 55,6. Eus., *H.E.*, 6,43,3 f.

moment. This certainly included a considerable strengthening
of his authority, but it did not bring peace. In the next year, the
opposition attempted an attack, in the first place at the synod
of May 15, A.D. 252; however this was promptly nipped in the bud,
whereupon Fortunatus the presbyter was chosen as opposition
bishop. The split in the Church—the "schism"—was complete.
There were even bishops who recognized Fortunatus—their
number being given as twenty-five although the figure was
vigorously disputed by Cyprian—and, in Carthage, the Church
of the schismatic bishops was supported by the elderly presbyters.

Fortunatus now sent a delegation to Rome in order to win the
recognition of bishop Cornelius.[1] After more than a year's
interregnum, the latter had been elected in March A.D. 251.[2]
In this case also, the voting was not unanimous, and soon an
opposition bishop was instituted in the person of Novatian,
hitherto the leader of the college of presbyters.[3] Cyprian
kept silence in the first instance, prevented a hasty recognition
of Cornelius,[4] and, only after having received more exact
accounts, began to associate with him, and acknowledge his
status as bishop by transmitting to him the resolutions of the
council.[5] Cornelius was not greatly pleased with this caution,
and expressed himself clearly to that effect: hence it did not
appear useless to Fortunatus to seek to be recognized by
Cornelius. In the middle of A.D. 252, he sent Felicissimus, with
other friends, as his agent to Rome. Thereupon Cornelius, who
at first had set great value on friendship with Cyprian, became
uncertain. Meanwhile, the messengers from Carthage hinted
that, if their wishes were denied, they would make certain
scandals public. Cyprian then became seriously angry, and
wrote Cornelius a letter[6] which dealt in detail with all the
relevant points. But at the beginning he made it clear to his
junior colleague that all was over with the dignity of the
episcopal office if he let himself be cowed by threats: a bishop
must be able to tolerate abuse; all the aggrieved had already
been condemned by the appropriate judges in Carthage, and

[1] *ep.* 59,10 f. 14–19   [2] Harnack, *Chronologie*, 2,351
[3] Cyprian, *ep.*, 55,5 (p. 627,7 Hartel)
[4] *ep.* 44,1. 45,3. 48. H. Koch, *op. cit.*, 117–31
[5] *ep.* 48,3. 55,6   [6] *Ibid.* 59; cf. par. 2. 3. 14

they had no business to be in Rome. The tone of this lecture to his "dear brother" shows what Cyprian thought about him. But it was effective.

About the same time, representatives of Novatian agitated in Carthage for his recognition by the church there. The first delegation appeared soon after the divisive election made in Rome in A.D. 251, but did not meet with a good reception by Cyprian and his synod.[1] Nevertheless, a movement took place in the province to grant recognition to Novatian, whose rigorism, which excluded all the backsliders from repentance, necessarily found support among the elderly Montanists. In any case, a meeting was at last brought together in Carthage which honoured Novatian as the rightful Roman bishop, and welcomed his delegate, the presbyter Maximus, whom he had instituted as bishop.[2] The result was that Carthage now had three bishops: the "lenient" Fortunatus, the "strict" Maximus, and the "catholic" Cyprian. Cyprian's old enemy, Novatus, played a part in these changes; it was he who persuaded a number of confessors in Rome temporarily to Novatian's side, and, in the late summer of A.D. 251, headed a new delegation of Novatian's adherents when they were sent to Carthage.[3] We have no exact information as to the events, because Cyprian speaks only contemptuously about them, and records the continual crumbling of the hostile front.[4] It is clear, however, that he regarded it as necessary to send Cornelius a list of the names of all the African bishops in order that he might know with whom he might associate.[5] We cannot discern the attitude of the opposite side. It is impossible to say how many bishops actually opposed Cyprian, and, equally impossible, how far these contending factions had penetrated among the people. There can be no doubt that much personal passion was manifested, but there was certainly also considerable spiritual anxiety and inward distress, accompanied by much religious eccentricity and fanaticism. Taken all together, these facts undermined the unity of the African church more seriously than Cyprian's letters really indicate. All the disputes which had taken place since the days of Montanism show us that, in this region, the opposing elements increased in passion, and

[1] *ep.* 44   [2] *ep.* 44,3. 55,24. 59,9   [3] *ep.* 50. 52,2   [4] *ep.* 59,15   [5] *ep.* 59,9

went from bad to worse; this led to an inner unrest which resulted in Donatism in the fourth century.

In the meantime, it must be granted that Cyprian showed masterly skill in confirming his own position. He had secured recognition for his own fundamental principles: those who had voluntarily recanted were excluded for life. Then in the spring of A.D. 253, there appeared the first heralds of a persecution newly planned by the emperor Gallus; and the council held in May immediately interpreted the signs of the times.[1] The stern decision of life-long exclusion was rescinded, and all backsliders who had submitted to the censure of the Church were assured of reception, this plan being adopted in order to strengthen them for the impending struggle. In this way the practical question at issue with the Fortunatus party was obviated at the vital point. The danger passed Africa by—in Rome, Cornelius was banished[2]—but a way had been found of dealing with backsliders, and the struggle had resulted in advantage to the Church.

As regards Rome, Cyprian had had the good fortune of maintaining his authority, and, in regard to Cornelius in particular, that had not been a difficult matter. We hear nothing of any contacts with his successor, Lucius, who held office for scarcely a year. In A.D. 254, Stephen became pope of Rome; and then some remarkable discussions took place. In the Spanish towns of Leon (in Asturia) and Merida (in Estremadura), the bishops had been deposed as *libellatici*, and their successors had been chosen in accordance with all the rules. Suddenly one of the deposed bishops appeared in Rome, swore the innocence of himself and his colleagues before Stephen, and was told that he ought to be reinstated into his office. Thereupon the two successors in Spain set out with all the necessary records, not to Rome but to Carthage, and received attestation of the legality of their position from Cyprian and his council. In regard to the verdict in Rome, the attestation, issued by the synod, only said incidentally that Stephen had not been informed of the true circumstances, and hence had been deceived; this however was not his fault, but that of the cunning deceivers. The synod reached their verdict

[1] *ep.* 57   [2] *Supra*, p. 170

on the principle accepted by the whole world, and, in particular, also by Cornelius, that a backsliding cleric, after due
repentance, might be received again as a layman, but could
never reassume a position among the clergy.[1]

In another matter the convictions of Cyprian the Carthaginian pope, came even more strongly to the light of day.
Faustinus, bishop of Lyons, acting in the name of the bishops of
Gaul, had turned to Rome and Carthage in a difficulty
concerning Marcianus of Arles, who, as a strict disciple of
Novatian, was unwilling to offer backsliders any prospect of
being received again. Stephen had not answered, and Faustinus
wrote Cyprian for a second time. Thereupon the latter sat down
and wrote very privately to his colleague in Rome as to the
reply he should send to Lyons. Marcianus ought to be deposed
and a successor chosen—and Cyprian asked Stephen to be so
kind as to suggest a name to Carthage.[2] We have no information as to how the two matters ended, nor how Stephen replied
to his colleague's letter: but, in reference to a third question,
we possess definite particulars on both points.

The return of followers of Novatian to fellowship in the
church catholic after they had repented raised the question
everywhere whether baptism administered in that schismatic
Church ought to be recognized or not. The traditional practice
of the Church was logical: it refused recognition, and required
the re-baptism of those who came back. In the present circumstances, however, much was to be said for recognizing Novatian's baptism: the difference between the two churches was
only in outer matters, and had nothing to do with differences of
doctrine. The question was laid before Cyprian by one of his
bishops, and he refused without hesitation. He had always
branded the followers of Novatian, together with other
opponents, as outside the pale of the Church, and had conducted the struggle against them from this standpoint. What he
had so firmly maintained before, gave a lead in the present
situation, viz. outside the Church there was no salvation,
and therefore also no sacraments. It was a fundamental
impossibility to recognize the baptism of outsiders.[3] A few
Numidian bishops were in doubt: Cyprian consequently caused

[1] *ep.* 67,5 f.   [2] *ep.* 68   [3] *ep.* 69

this principle to be solemnly reiterated at a council in A.D. 255.[1] He described it as altogether incomprehensible that any colleague should have judged otherwise.[2] Since the most important of these incomprehensible persons occupied the episcopal chair in Rome, the council wrote to Stephen and informed him of its conclusions[3] "in the expectation that, as a genuinely religious and truth-loving man, he would agree with what was both devout and true. As to the rest, it was not intended to exercise constraint on, or issue prescriptions for, anybody, since, in the leadership of the Church, each bishop was free to reach his own decision, and was under obligation to give an account of his conduct of affairs only to God."

Stephen's answer was given in unexpectedly sharp tones: he advised the African bishops not to introduce novelties against tradition, and not to re-baptize returning heretics, because the baptism administered by the church catholic was recognized by the other side.[4] That was an open declaration of war, and Cyprian responded with his strongest weapon. On September 1, A.D. 256, he assembled a special synod in Carthage, attended by eighty-seven bishops. In the introductory speech, he referred only to his correspondence with an African colleague, and requested the members of the synod to express their opinion in regard to the question of baptizing heretics, "without thereby expressing a verdict about others who thought differently, and without intending to exclude them from their fellowship. Because none of us sets himself up as a bishop of bishops, or exercises the terrors of a tyrant in order to bring his colleagues to compulsory obedience." It was perfectly clear to whom he was referring even if no name was mentioned, and no letter read aloud. The official minutes of this synod have been preserved.[5] It is very impressive to note here how one bishop after another gives a shorter or longer reason for his opinion and pronounces in favour of Cyprian, and how the latter finally closes the subject; there is no doubt that the entire action had been carefully prepared down to the smallest detail.

Meanwhile, as far as Stephen was concerned, the matter

---

[1] *ep.* 70   [2] *ep.* 71,1   [3] *ep.* 72,3   [4] *ep.* 74,1
[5] *Sententiae episcoporum* 87. *de haer. bapt.* 1,435–461 Hartel; von Soden, *Gött. nachr.,* 1909, 247–307

had become a question of the authority of Rome. He therefore decided to break off church-fellowship with all those who held different opinions from his own. The African delegates, who were to carry to him the conclusions reached by the council, were not only not received but were left without lodgings: they were to feel in their own persons what it meant to be excommunicated from Rome. Moreover, in accordance with 2 Cor. 11: 13, Stephen vilified Cyprian as a pseudo-Christian, a pseudo-prophet, and a deceitful worker. Unfortunately, the churches of Asia Minor came under this pronouncement, and the Cappadocian bishop, Firmilian of Cæsarea, wrote Cyprian an indignant letter about this presumption of Stephen's.[1] We shall háve to discuss in another connection the doctrinal disputes about the authority of Rome which flared up as a consequence. It is sufficient for the moment to point out that all who took part remained in battle array, and that Dionysios, bishop of Alexandria, vainly attempted to act as mediator.[2]

Secular politics now began to play a part, and they effected a solution. The Emperor Valerian promulgated an edict against the Christians,[3] and Stephen died as a martyr on August 2, A.D. 256. Dionysios took the dispute up again with Xystus, his successor, that peace might be made;[4] and he was right in expecting success, for Xystus was not obliged personally to maintain the position of his predecessor Stephen. However, further details are unknown. On August 6, A.D. 258, Xystus was slain in a catacomb. Cyprian regarded the event as a sign of the coming storm and informed the African bishops accordingly, but without using any affectionate tone suggesting fraternal peace. Then he himself died, not unexpectedly; for years his letters had spoken of "these latter days", whose distresses had been prophesied in the Bible. He expected his end.

On August 30, A.D. 257, he was banished by the pro-consul, Paternus, to Curubis (now Kurba). A short time afterwards, he was permitted to return on condition that he remained always in his garden-villa in the suburbs. He complied, until he heard that the newly arrived pro-consul, Galerius Maximus,

---

[1] ep. 75,25. Eus., H.E., 7,5,4   [2] Eus., H.E., 7,4. 5,5
[3] Supra, p. 170 ,   [4] Eus., H.E., 7,5,4–6

wished to try his case in Utica. Thereupon he went into hiding again, because he wished to die, not in Utica, but near his church in Carthage: the wonderful letter in which he took leave of his clergy[1] expresses that desire in quite simple and moving terms. As expected, the pro-consul returned to Carthage and caused the obstinate pope, Cyprian, to be arrested by two officers, and brought to a suburb. The entire church streamed out there, and waited at the gate throughout the night. On the next day, September 14, A.D. 258, the case was brought forward and after a brief hearing ended with the sentence of death. "And we wish to die with him," cried the people, and preceded him to the place of execution. There on an open piece of ground, Cyprian laid aside his mantle, knelt down, and prayed. Then he took off his upper garment, the white sleeved dalmatica, and stood only in a linen shirt awaiting the executioner. When the latter arrived, he ordered him to be given twenty-five pieces of gold, while those who stood round threw linen cloths and handkerchiefs in front of him in order to receive the precious blood. Two clerics blindfolded his eyes—then his head fell. The body was carried away, and watch was kept with candles and torches during the night.[2] The pope of Africa had become a martyr.

[1] ep. 81
[2] *Acta St. Cypriani*; cf. Reitzenstein, *d. Nachr. über d. Tod. Cyprians, Heidelb. S. Ber.* 1913, no. 14

Chapter Eleven

ROME

DURING THE SECOND CENTURY THE CAPITAL OF THE EMPIRE reflected the prosperity of the broad imperium in magnificent buildings erected at the reigning emperor's will; even at the beginning of the third century, in spite of all the dangers and all the economic crises, no diminution was to be observed in the building activities of the city of Rome. The immense forum of Trajan, Hadrian's temple of Venus and Roma, the palace of Septimius Severus on the Palatine, the Thermae of Caracalla, still survive as impressive testimonies to the facts. Although literature was drying up, the plastic arts enjoyed thousands of commissions and maintained their own vitality even if, to a large extent, the result was only pedestrian in character, and on coarse lines. The population continued to be a varied mixture drawn from all the provinces of the Empire, but even in the Antonine period it did not increase in numbers. The continuous fall in the birthrate, the years of epidemic, and, what was in the end of the greatest consequence, the cessation of immigration from the provinces, caused the population of the city to fall ever more rapidly during the second half of the century: c. A.D. 150 it stood at one million, two hundred and fifty thousand; about A.D. 200 it may be estimated at one million, and c. A.D. 300 at half a million.[1] Nevertheless, Rome still remained a city of magnificence and luxury, in which the social problem, e.g. that of satisfying the propertyless masses, was solved by distributing bread and providing circuses. Moreover, about the same period, Christianity grew up in Rome from inconspicuous beginnings to be of dominating power.

We have already had occasion to bewail the poverty of our knowledge in regard to the early stages of this Church. We could only infer, on the basis of its own documentary and other remains, that it originated from the missionary activity of converted Hellenistic Jews.[2] Attention has been drawn to the

[1] Kahrstedt in Friedländer, *Sittengeschichte*, 10th edit., 4,21   [2] Vol. 1, p. 191, 199

supposed parallels among the Jews in Rome, and scholars have tried to make valid deductions from this source: but in vain. Under Augustus, the Jews had their quarter in Trastevere. Shortly afterwards, they also lived in other regions of the city according as it suited newcomers, or if they formed part of a larger group of slaves, that fact would have settled where they lived. Inscriptions in the Jewish catacombs show us that there were communities in the Subura and on the Campus Martius. In addition to these, mention is made of eleven other Jewish communities, including four described as groups of slaves in eminent families. The graves belonging to these communities are to be found, in an arrangement which can only be understood with difficulty, in a number of cemeteries outside the city. We hear nothing of any organized community of the Jews in Rome.[1]

On the other hand, the Christian community there was a unity from the beginning. This assertion may appear self-apparent in regard to the earliest period of all, but soon, on account of the same reasons as were operative amongst the Jews, the Christians were separated in different groups throughout the city: the case was similar in the great oriental cities of Antioch and Ephesus. Everywhere, "house-churches" were constituted among such groups, and were composed of those who had a common dwelling or occupation: even in Jerusalem that was the case.[2] But these small circles were never independent units, but always parts of the church universal in that locality: and their unity was seen in the fact that they were all under the leadership of one college of presbyters or bishops, and the unity was the more obvious when all the groups came under the leadership of a monarchic bishop. This development was lacking in Judaism: it was the consequence of the Christian conception of the Church, a conception which grew as a result of continual striving for visible unity, even in outer forms. Rome was suited for combining all these features into one: but it required centuries in order to reach its goal.

In Rome, the change from collegiate to monarchical leadership of the Church was completed by the middle of the second

---

[1] Frey in *Recherches de science religieuse* 20 (1930), 295 ff. 21 (1931), 165 f.
[2] Acts 2: 46

century:[1] a time when, after severe crises had been overcome, the principles of early catholicism as founded on the apostolic tradition had triumphed. Marcion had come to Rome, but, c. A.D. 140, the Church had managed to exclude him. Twenty years later, Valentine the gnostic laboured in the city, and in the end was compelled to depart without having met with better success.[2] About this time, the Apologist Justin was the Church's theologian, and he wrote against the heretics;[3] his work has not survived, but churchmen in the succeeding period frequently copied it out.

Soon after A.D. 150, Polycarp, bishop of Smyrna, visited Rome, and came to an understanding with Bishop Anicetus in regard to Church problems. But he was not successful in convincing the Romans of the necessity of celebrating the Passover as was customary in Asia Minor. Anicetus pointed out that his predecessors had never observed the festival, and he was unwilling to depart from this tradition. However, Rome was tolerant: Christians from Asia Minor, temporarily or permanently staying in Rome, might always observe their Passover undisturbed, and would nevertheless be recognized as members of the Roman communion: and this in spite of the fact that their rite could have been branded and definitely repudiated as Jewish in character. It follows that the difference in worship on this point had given rise to no hostility between Anicetus and Polycarp, and the Roman bishop had permitted his respected guest to officiate in his place when the Eucharist was celebrated.[4] We must note, nevertheless, that the celebration of Easter continued to spread in the Church, and Anicetus's successor, Soter, introduced it even into Rome; not however in the form usual in Asia Minor, but in that practised in the majority of cases, as a Sunday festival of the Resurrection.[5]

About twenty years later, a conflict arose on this issue when a certain Blastus, who is now otherwise unknown, began to work in Rome on behalf of the "quartodecimanian", i.e. Asia Minor, Passover rite, and to defend it on Biblical grounds;[6] for internal

---

[1] *Supra*, pp. 60 f.   [2] Vol. 1, pp. 249, 287
[3] Justin, *apol.*, 26,8. Iren. 4,6,2; cf. 5,26,2
[4] *Supra*, p. 133. Iren. in Eus., *H.E.*, 5,24,14–17   [5] *Supra*, pp. 134 f.
[6] Eus., *H.E.*, 5,15.Ps. Tert., *adv. omnes. haer.*, 8 (Hippolytus ap. *Chron. pasch.* pp. 12,21–13,7); E.T. in *Ante N. Chr. Lib.*, Vol. IX. 2, p. 94

reasons it is entirely probable that he was the spokesman of a group of Christians from Asia Minor resident in the city.[1] In any case, Victor, bishop of Rome, wished to settle the problem. He called a synod together in Rome and requested also all other church centres to call similar synods to end the question.[2] We have already shown[3] that all the others adopted the Roman practice, and that only Asia Minor, led by Polycrates of Ephesus, held firmly to its old view: this caused Victor to break with that church, an action which was universally disapproved.

It could not be said on formal grounds that Victor had gained the day, but, on material grounds, his action was of the greatest significance. For the first time, the unity of the church catholic had been exhibited in a number of decisions reached by different synods, which agreed with what the Roman Church had declared the right course. Whether on this occasion Victor had referred to his own apostolic tradition is not clear in the paucity of our sources: the representatives of Palestine made reference to, and those of Asia Minor adduced, the testimony of their own Apostles.[4] In any case, it was incontestable that Rome had raised, and taken the lead in, the whole matter, and that Rome had been judged in the right. That was a gain for the future. About this period the Church lived in a fair degree of peace with the state. Marcia, the favourite of the Emperor Commodus, was a Christian, and was even able to liberate condemned fellow-believers from the quarries of Sardinia.[5] Nevertheless there was much disquietude in the Church.

Blastus was not the only one who caused difficulty to Bishop Victor. Eusebius mentions, side by side with him, a presbyter, Florinus, who held gnostic views, not very different from Valentinism: Irenæus frequently wrote against him.[6] In addition there were the theologians of Asia Minor whom we have already mentioned; they found response in, and were possibly supported by the same communities as had favoured Blastus. Theodotos the "dynamist" was excommunicated by Victor,

---

[1] La Piana, *Harv. Theol. Rev.*, 1925, 218   [2] Polycrates in Eus., *H.E.*, 5,24,8
[3] *Supra*, pp. 135 f.   [4] Eus., *H.E.*, 5,25. 5,24,2 f.   [5] Hipp., *Refut.*, 9,12,11
[6] Eus., *H.E.*, 5,15. 20,1. Iren., *fragm. syr.*, 28 (2,457). Baumstark, *ZNW.*, 1912, 306 ff.

but he had a following, and his disciples formed a church of their own under a certain bishop Natalis who submitted again, however, to Zephyrinus, Victor's successor.[1] If we take various facts into account, viz., that even under Eleutheros, Victor's predecessor, Montanism had been favourably judged in Rome, and that it was only the influence of Praxeas which occasioned a change in the bishop's attitude;[2] that at a later date, and similarly to Praxeas, Noëtos of Smyrna had preached "Monarchian" theology to the Romans;[3] then it will become clear that the strong influence coming from Asia Minor might occasion anxiety, and that, in a certain sense, the life of the Church was faced with a "problem of Asia Minor" which was significant enough to explain the firmness of Victor's action in regard to Easter.

In any case, it was the Church of Asia Minor which provoked a theological movement in the Roman Church. Justin had stood for a logos Christology, Theodotos taught Adoptionism, Noëtos and Praxeas were Monarchians; these inconsistences roused the Church, and eventually compelled the bishop to attempt a settlement. His first action was purely negative: Theodotos's excommunication, already mentioned. We have no information as to the grounds, and it is probable that there was no discussion of the actual problem, but that the reasons were confined to branding as blasphemous the language which declared that Jesus was "a mere man".[4] Hence we remain uncertain whether Theodotos had used this very terminology, or whether these words were placed on his lips as a deduction from his teaching: there are plenty of analogies in the theological disputes of a later period.

The Monarchical doctrine of Noëtos and his disciple, Cleomenes, appeared unexceptionable for a long time, and was regarded as an appropriate expression of the religious feelings of the Church, until the representatives of the logos theology began to announce their claims. The head of this group in Rome was the learned presbyter, Hippolytus, whereas the opposite side gained a new and important protagonist in Sabellios of Libya.[5] Finally, Zephyrinus decided to put an end to the

[1] Hipp. in Eus., *H.E.*, 5,28,6 8–12   [2] Tert., *adv. Prax.*, 1; cf. Eus., *H.E.*, 5,1,2. 3,4
[3] *Supra*, p. 190   [4] Hipp. in Eus., *H.E.*, 5,28,6; cf. *Refut.* 10,23,1
[5] Caspari, *Quellen*, 3,326

dispute. He promulgated an official declaration:[1] "I know only one God, Christ Jesus, and no other in addition to Him; He was born and He suffered." This accorded with the naïve modalism of the Church's faith, a modalism which consciously avoided the theological phraseology of Noëtos or Sabellios, and inevitably appeared unsatisfactory to Hippolytus: the latter raised objections, and consequently had to suffer reproaches as a ditheist, the charges not being entirely without reason.[2]

The contest spread further, and, when Callistus became bishop after the death of Zephyrinus, a division broke out in the Church.[3] We do not know what provided the occasion, but the outcome is clear enough. Callistus excommunicated Sabellios on grounds of heresy, and published a theological statement which accepted the conception of the logos repudiated by the Monarchians, and which made the logos equal with God who was Spirit; the Spirit was called Father and had united himself in the Son with human nature. Of course this theological compromise also met with no sympathy. Indeed war was now declared on Sabellios, and even Hippolytus remained unappeased, but it is still unknown whether he had already declared himself to have broken with Callistus, or whether he only now said farewell in company with Sabellios. What is certain is that he did it in connection with the present affair. Acting together with those whom he regarded as orthodox, Hippolytus separated himself from the "heretic" Callistus, and himself became their bishop.[4] He dealt with Callistus and his adherents as schismatic heretics, and expressed contempt for their claim to belong to the church catholic; nevertheless he had to admit that they were in the majority.[5]

Naturally, Hippolytus did not regard either Zephyrinus or Callistus as opponents equal to himself: both were practical men, and neither had the mind for Greek speculations, which they must have regarded as a purposeless logomachy that endangered unity. Hippolytus declared the first to be intellectually of little consequence; and the second, with whom he quarrelled violently, he called morally shallow. In his

---

[1] Hipp., *Refut.*, 9,11,3. Harnack, *Sitz. Akad. Berl.*, 1923, 51–57

[2] Hipp., *ibid.*, 9,11,3. 12,16; cf. *supra*, pp. 237 and 252 f.   [3] Hipp., *ibid.*, 9,12,15–18

[4] K. Müller, *ZNW.*, 1924, 234   [5] Hipp., *ibid.*, 9,12,19–21. 25; cf. *praef.* 6

book about the heresies, he deals with these disputes in the city of Rome,[1] and gives a sketch of Callistus, a sketch which describes him as having originally been a slave, and which is otherwise extremely startling. Bankruptcy, attempted suicide, brawling in a Jewish service of worship, condemnation to compulsory labour in a quarry, liberation by patronage in high quarters, these were the principal events of his life before becoming a cleric. Then he had been made a deacon by Zephyrinus, and, by clever use of his bishop's weaknesses, he had attained power and become his successor. In the leading position which he had been lucky enough to reach, he had ruined the Roman Church theologically and morally. There is no doubt that personal hatred lent gall to Hippolytus's pen, and that justice would pronounce a very different verdict on Callistus.

Hippolytus lived in another world than that of his enemy. Though influenced by Irenæus, he was more in sympathy with the Greek manner of thought; he continued the line begun by Justin. That is seen most plainly in his principal work, *Refutation of all Heresies*, which is in large part extant; it is not limited to the gnostics and those of similar view, but begins with a description and criticism of ancient doctrines of the philosophers, and also deals with astrology and magic arts. The Roman dispute about Easter led him to draw up a table for calculating Easter Sundays. The real reason here was the desire to make the Church independent of the Jews in regard to these important questions of worship, and to calculate, on independent knowledge and authority, the first full moon in Spring, and the first Sunday thereafter.

Hippolytus calculated a cycle of one hundred and twelve years beginning with A.D. 222, and his is the first attempt of the sort; from a scientific point of view it is a poor performance, but it impressed his contemporaries and led to further results.[2] His friends held the tables in such high esteem that they engraved them, together with a list of all his writings, on the back of his statue. That such a statue should have been carved at all is as remarkable as the fact that it has survived.

His *Chronicle* was of greater influence; like the table for finding

---

[1] Hipp., *ibid.*, 9,6–7. 11–12   [2] E. Schwartz, *Ostertafeln*, pp. 29–40

Easter, it probably depended upon Alexandrian models, and consisted of a loosely connected body of material from the Bible and scientific sources. Finally, it tried to prove that at the present time, i.e. in A.D. 234, five thousand seven hundred and thirty eight years had passed since the creation of the world;[1] hence, before the year of the world six thousand, when the expected Last Day would be reached, there still remained a considerable time. Such a discussion was in place at a time when the sufferings brought about by new persecutions caused many people to think about the end of the world. Fear and hope gave vitality to the expectation of the parousia, as in later times, and indeed in our own age. Hippolytus considered these popular ideas to be lacking in discipline, and met them with a scholarly Scriptural exegesis. As early as A.D. 204, he had calculated the course of history from the book of Daniel, putting the birth of Christ in the world year five thousand five hundred, and placing the Last Day in the year six thousand.[2] Similar reckonings were made in Alexandria.

Eschatology claimed Hippolytus's attention pre-eminently: for this reason he annotated the book of Daniel, and wrote a monograph on the Anti-Christ. The question of prophecy and its fulfilment dominated his theological thought, and all his explanations of Biblical books made use of allegory based on this standpoint. Much of his work is extant in fragments and translations, and constitutes some of our earliest Christian commentaries on the Bible; but the remains do not reflect a mind of the first quality, even granted that their author was held in high esteem in Rome as a scholar. Origen had attended Hippolytus's lectures,[3] and the latter was permitted to dedicate to the empress mother, Julia Mamæa, a tractate on the Resurrection.[4] Nevertheless he was a dry compiler of an unpretentious kind, with a narrow range of thought; this fact partly explains his attitude in the dispute in the Roman church. The most valuable of his literary remains is a work which scarcely offers anything of his own material, viz. his *Church Order*. Here, in the form of a series of regulations, he gives a sketch of a Christian church as it should be ideally. He wrote it in order to

---

[1] A. Bauer's edition pp. 196. 200 f.; cf. 360–67   [2] Vol. 1, p. 219
[3] Jerome, *Vir .Inl.*, 61; cf. Photios, *eod.*, 121   [4] Hipp., *Werke*, ed. Achelis 1,2,251

distinguish his own views from the arbitrary ideas of Callistus, and to explain what he himself understood as Apostolic tradition.[1] He looks to the past, and on this account he is to us an important source. On the other hand, his opponent had a forward look, and grasped what the living church needed. The very points that aroused the indignation of Hippolytus show, when considered calmly, that Callistus was a capable pastor of his people.[2]

The Roman church at the beginning of the third century had already developed far in its contacts with the world. Montanism had not seriously damaged it, because, otherwise than in Africa, it obviously had no point of entry. The radical character of the moral strenuousness found in early Christianity had been tacitly modified as the church grew. Even Hermas had preached that forgiveness was possible for deadly sins once after baptism—although only once. Callistus now proclaimed the fundamental right of the bishop to grant forgiveness to those who had committed deadly sin (the subject was sexual sin), and to admit them again to church fellowship; naturally after having performed penitence as required by the church. Tertullian greeted this claim with shame and woe, and spoke of ill-timed indulgence towards adulterers.[3] It is clear, however, that Callistus was faced with the question whether he should exercise clemency, bring the sinners back, and maintain the church's cure of souls, or whether, by acting strictly, he should drive them back into paganism. He chose the former alternative, and this became normal for the entire future, because this way alone conducted the church out of the straits of separation from the world to a conquest of the world.

Hippolytus perceived quite rightly that a fundamental question was being dealt with in this matter, and therefore he objected: but Tertullian recognized far more clearly the extent of the implications contained in the decision. He would have consigned the world to perdition, and have saved a small number of the elect; Callistus wanted to save the world, and was therefore compelled to educate it, an attitude which required compromises. The church was at the parting of the

[1] E. Schwartz, *Pseudapost. Kirchenordnungen* (*Sch. d. wiss. Ges. Strassburg* 6), p. 39
[2] Hipp., *Refut.*, 9,12,20–26   [3] Tert., *pudic.*, 1; cf. *supra*, pp. 222 f.

ways: she was at the point of passing from the era of the primitive church into that of the church catholic. With considerable perspicacity, Callistus was careful to see to it that the bishop was the leader. When he cited the parable of the Tares among the Wheat, and Noah's Ark, with its many different kinds of animals, in support of his argument against the ideal of the "church of the saints" as unbiblical, he thereby parted company with the primitive church, but gave new life to the evangelical conception of the Jesus who sought out sinners.

Callistus's marriage-decree is to be judged similarly. For more than one reason, it was not easy for a Christian lady of senatorial rank to find a husband of her own class. Marriage with a freedman was forbidden to her,[1] with a slave it was juristically quite impossible: and yet it was in men of these classes that she might easily meet with a fellow-believer fitted to be a life's companion. In practice, indeed not infrequently, such "marriages of conscience" actually took place: Callistus officially recognized these unions as Christian marriages.

The schismatic church of Hippolytus continued under Callistus's successors, Urbanus and Pontianus, but in A.D. 235 a long-expected persecution broke even on the Roman church. The Emperor Maximinus[2] banished the two bishops to Sardinia, the "island of death", where neither survived very long. On September 28, A.D. 235, Pontianus resigned his office in order to facilitate the choice of his successor. On November 21, Anteros was ordained. Apparently Hippolytus took no part in instituting his own successor, but made peace for himself and his church with the other section. Pope Fabian brought the bodies of "Bishop" Pontianus and Hippolytus and buried them in Rome, the latter having been again recognized as "presbyter". The church treasured the memory of both, and revered them as martyrs,[3] but, as a writer, Hippolytus was soon quite forgotten in the west. The east made use of his writings, but, after a very short time, all knowledge of his personal doings was forgotten. About the

---

[1] *Corp. iur. dig.* 23,2,16 pr.   [2] *Supra*, p. 165
[3] *Lib. pontif.* 19 (24 f. Mommsen and *Catal. Liberianus* (*ibid.*)) cf. also *Kl. Texte* 2, p. 4

middle of the third century, Rome abandoned its Greek tradition and became a Latin-speaking church; Hippolytus's Greek writings lost their value to it.

With the advent of Bishop Fabian, greater emphasis was suddenly laid, expressly and concretely, on the high position of the Roman bishop. Beginning from his date, an unbroken series of written evidences is at the disposal of the student. The days of enthronement are noted and solemnized, a list of popes, giving exact dates, is begun, a common vault for the deceased holders of the high office was prepared in the Church's burying place in the catacomb of Callistus, the first to find a resting place here being Pontianus the martyr bishop.[1] Even in his own day Zephyrinus had taken pains with the organization of the clergy, and, in so doing, had given his deacon Callistus a position near to himself, placing under his care, about the same time, the control of the catacomb which was named after him at a later date.[2] As distinct from most others, which were in private hands, this burial place seems to have been the property of the church. Fabian enlarged it; but of greater significance is the fact that he took an important step in the organization of the clergy.

In the metropolis of Rome, care for the poor was, by the nature of the case, a problem which the church found as important as it was difficult. It became such an essential duty of the deacons that, in the course of time, they were deprived of the liturgical functions which were regarded as obviously theirs in other districts. Whereas in other places the number of deacons might be increased at will according to the requirements of the church, it remained in Rome at the number seven sanctified by Acts 6: 5. The college of deacons stood next to the bishop, and constituted his executive,[3] and the papal throne was usually filled from one of its members. Up to this period, the activity of the deacons had not been limited according to the quarters of the city, but Fabian divided the city into seven districts, setting a deacon over each: these "regions" of the church, which, we may note in passing, in no way coincided with Augustus's fourteen regions, were maintained until

[1] *Supra*, p. 61   [2] Hipp., *Refut.*, 9,12,14
[3] Cf. the directions for ordination in Hipp., *Church Order*, 33, 2–4 (2,103 Funk)

the Middle Ages.[1] At the same time, Fabian decreed that seven additional persons should be set as adjutants alongside the seven deacons: these were called sub-deacons, and they entered the diaconate as and when places became vacant. This arrangement guaranteed that the official leadership would continue, unbroken, in the same form.

A notice[2] has survived from a slightly later time; it comes from pope Cornelius and deals with the constitution of the Roman clergy: it mentions one bishop, forty-six presbyters, seven deacons, seven sub-deacons, forty-two acolytes, fifty-two exorcists, readers, and doorkeepers—it also mentions more than fifteen hundred widows and sick as being regularly in receipt of charity. The presbyters were the real pastors of the parish which surrounded their own church. The churches frequently began in private buildings transferred to the church for purposes of public worship, later being replaced by new buildings. For centuries they were described with the name (titulus) of the former owner, i.e. founder, and on this account are still known as "title churches". Recent systematic excavations have left no room for doubt on this matter, although it had long been an assumption.[3] Of the twenty-five title churches now known, fourteen are earlier than Constantine: hence we may assume that the majority were there in the days of Fabian and Cornelius, and therefore that two or three presbyters filled the pastoral office in one church.

Cornelius's notice, however, now goes on to give us all the "lower" clerical officers (*ordines minores*). We have already mentioned the sub-deacons. As the name signifies, the acolytes were the "followers" of the bishop, "orderlies" whom he employed for all sorts of purposes and errands.[4] The exorcists represented what was left of the old charismatics: viz. those members of the church who possessed the gift of exorcising daemons; we may note that Tertullian ascribed this gift to every Christian.[5] The readers were skilled in the difficult art

---

[1] *Lib. pontif.* 21 according to *Catal. liber.* (p. 27 Mommsen). Graffunder. "Regiones" in *Pauly-W.*, 2nd series, 1,485 f. Harnack, *Mission*, 2,836–866
[2] Bishop Cornelius in Eus., *H.E.*, 6,43,11
[3] J.P. Kirsch, *D. Röm. Titelkirchen*, 1918. E. Junyent, *Il titolo di s. Clemente in Roma*, 1932
[4] Cyprian, *epist.*, 7 (p. 485,13). 45,4 (p. 603,15). 49,3 (p. 612,6). 52,1 (p. 616,8). 59,9 (p. 677,7). 77,3 (p. 835,20). 78,1 (p. 836,14).   [5] *Supra*, p. 222

of using a melodious voice and the correct rhythm in reading passages aloud from the Biblical codices, which, at that time, were written without spaces between the words and without punctuation marks. The *ostiarii* or doorkeepers were the caretakers of the places of worship and other church buildings. These lower orders had similar names in Carthage about the same time, a fact which once more proves, both the close relation of the two cities, and also Rome's leading status: the names appear for the first time further east only at a considerably later date.

Fabian's practical activity, which was so significant for the future, came to an end during Decius' persecution: he was one of the first to die under it on January 20, A.D. 250. His place was left unfilled because the hand of the persecutors would immediately have fallen upon the new pope; the church was conducted for the time being by the combined colleges of presbyters and deacons: both in common conducted the correspondence with Carthage which we have already described,[1] and both opened it by transmitting an account of Fabian's martyrdom. But only the deacons were entrusted with the doubtful task of judging Cyprian's attitude, and they did so in a letter which lacked polish.[2]

On the question of the *lapsi*, the Romans really agreed with Cyprian in holding that it was fundamentally possible to readmit to the church those who had repented. After this mild attitude had already been shown in both Rome and Africa at an earlier date towards persons guilty of sex immorality,[3] the uncompromising practice of the early church being thereby abandoned, any other attitude to the *lapsi* was scarcely conceivable in the prevailing hard times. It was also agreed to prescribe a period of penance for them, and that it was the prerogative of the bishop, as distinct from the confessors, to decide about readmission. Since there was no bishop in Rome, and the bishop was absent from Carthage, it was agreed that during a period of persecution the Eucharist should only be administered in special cases of mortal illness but, as a rule,

[1] *Supra*, p. 226
[2] Cyp., *epist.*, 8,3 (p. 488,10 f.) and also *ep.* 9 tit. also pars. 1 and 2 (p. 489,1. 12); cf. Caspar, *Ges. d. Papsttums*, 1,62, against Harnack, *Mission*, 2,850
[3] *Supra*, p. 247, and Cyprian, *ep.*, 55,20 f.

the cases of those who repented were deferred. The co-operation
between Cyprian and Rome, upon which emphasis was laid,
was highly praised by the presbyter Novatian who carried on
the correspondence, not without a faint echo of Rome's
consciousness of superiority.[1] In contrast with their Carthaginian fellow-sufferers, the Roman confessors avoided a struggle
with the regular officials of the church; they agreed with and
joined in the conclusions reached by those who were leaders of
the church in Rome for the time being, and with Cyprian's
rules and regulations.[2]

In this way, the situation in the capital appeared, both
inwarldy and outwardly, to be altogether satisfying, when, in
March, A.D. 251, it was decided[3] to proceed with the deferred
choosing of a bishop. The leading person in the Roman college
of presbyters was Novatian. He had maintained his position in
the critical year which had just passed, and was not only a
skilful writer but also a learned theologian: moreover, he
had the reputation of being the first Roman who possessed
both these qualifications in the Latin language. In his writing[4]
On the Trinity he had already been more successful than
Hippolytus in repudiating both the Marcionite and the
Monarchian theology, in as far as he had given a bird's eye
view, and had proved, by means of the Rule of Faith, the
correctness of Tertullian's ideas and statements. All this agreed
with western thought, and affected the following period. At the
moment, it led the author to hope that he would be chosen as
bishop—a position which, we may note, was both honourable
and dangerous in a period of persecution. His expectation was
not fulfilled: he was passed over, as had formerly been the case
with the learned Hippolytus. An overwhelming majority of the
clergy united in favour of the presbyter Cornelius, and he was
consecrated in the presence of sixteen bishops.[5] Novatian and
five of his friends in the college of presbyters[6] were indignant,
and refused their assent.

At this point a question of principle was conjoined to the
personal antagonisms, and divided the church to a large

[1] Cyp., *ep.*, 30, 1. 36,1. 4   [2] *Ibid.* 28. 31. 30,4   [3] Harnack, *Chronologie*, 2,351
[4] Novatian, *de trinitate*, ed. Fausset 1909; cf. especially chaps. 29–31 and 21. 24.
Jerome, *vir. inl.*, 70
[5] Cypr., *epist.*, 55,8. 24   [6] Cornelius in Eus., *H.E.*, 6,43,20

extent. It may be regarded as a natural accompaniment of such a split that all sorts of gossip made various charges against both men, and from opposite sides. The only significant accusation was that Cornelius had lightly agreed to receiving backsliders again. The defence put forward by Cyprian in one case[1] shows clearly that Cornelius had made a concession in order to win the masses; and it is probable that he had been chosen in the very expectation of such a concession. On the other hand, Novatian took the radical view, refused to recognize the lines which had hitherto been followed, and now set aside altogether the readmission of backsliders. In this way he became the leader of the strict group, which was not lacking even in Rome, and they chose him as bishop,[2] a course which implied refusing to recognize the lax Cornelius. In addition they were joined by the Roman confessors who had hitherto supported Cyprian and his similar policy.

The opposition was very awkward for Cornelius, and we can understand why Cyprian at first delayed recognizing this new colleague.[3] However, that was soon changed. Cyprian felt that radicalism was impracticable, and the confessors soon changed over to Cornelius.[4] The latter called a great synod in Rome which was attended by sixty bishops and many other clerics and laymen; it supported his practice in regard to confession, and excommunicated Novatian.[5] However, the stern attitude adopted on the other side was attractive to all who were not inclined to depart from the requirements usual in the early church: and Novatian soon gained adherents under this slogan. In Africa he received more support than Cyprian is inclined to acknowledge.[6] In the east, whole provinces of the Church came to his side, and Fabius of Antioch was already preparing a great synod which was to express itself in this sense: only his sudden death prevented that outcome. Dionysios of Alexandria fought valiantly for Cornelius and wrote letters to all parties in order to prevent a general disclaimer in the east: after considerable effort, he was eventually successful.[7] Nevertheless,

---

[1] Cypr., *ep.*, 55,11
[2] *Ibid.*, 44,1. Eus., *H.E.*, 6,43,1 *re* Cornelius, *loc. cit.*, 6,43,7–10 [3] *Supra*, pp. 232 f.
[4] Cypr., *ep.*, 46. 53. 54. exaggerating Cornelius in Eus., *H.E.*, 6,43,6; cf. 6,46,5
[5] Eus., *H.E.*, 6,43,2. Cypr., *ep.*, 55,6 [6] *Supra*, p. 233
[7] Eus., *H.E.*, 6,45–6,5. 7,5,1

Novatian churches were constituted in wide regions both in the west and in the east, and they were to be found alive even in the fifth century: in Constantinople at that time they had three churches of their own, in Rome still more,[1] and numerous notices tell of their continued existence in other districts.[2] Such a state of affairs offers a clear proof of the early operation of the law that divisions in the church, unless overcome very quickly, are intractable, and will continue to exist even when the original causes of divison have lost meaning.

The letter addressed to Fabius, bishop of Antioch, in which Cornelius defends himself against Novatian,[3] does not convey the happy impression that the writer possessed outstanding personal qualities—and it is comprehensible that sometimes Cyprian adopted a very arrogant attitude towards him.[4] However, he died soon afterwards in exile ordered by Gallus, and this fact placed the halo of martyrdom around his head. He was buried in the catacomb of Callistus in a special place, outside the papal vault, and hence probably only at a later time; his epitaph is the first in Latin to be dedicated to a pope.[5] His successor, Lucius, was eight months in office, when, in the spring of A.D. 254, Stephen was elected pope. Cyprian had no hesitation in continuing to associate with him in the same way as he had been accustomed to do with Cornelius: he felt himself to be the senior, and the more experienced of two equal colleagues. When, however, Stephen began to deal with the question of the baptism of heretics in the same way, matters came to a break which showed plainly the fundamental difference between the conceptions held by the two princes of the church about their status.

We have already discussed the subject and the course of the dispute.[6] Stephen contested the African church's right to settle the question at its own discretion, and wrote as to how it ought to proceed. He described the re-baptism of returning heretics as an innovation contrary to tradition—which was undoubtedly incorrect in principle if one understood by tradition the

---

[1] Socrates 2,38,26. 7,9. 11   [2] Harnack in Hauck's *R.E.*, 14,241
[3] In Eus., *H.E.*, 43,5–22   [4] *Supra*, p. 233
[5] Diehl, *Inscr. Lat.*, no 956a. Cabrol-Leclerq, *Dict.*, 3,2969. *Catal. Liber. im. Lib. pont.* 22 p. 28
[6] *Supra*, pp. 235 f.

universal practice of the churches. What Stephen meant, however, was the practice of the Roman church, which practice he traced back to Peter. Moreover, since Christ had instituted Peter as the first Apostle, and had declared him to be the rock upon which he would build his church, Matt. 16: 18, his primacy must be recognized, and his tradition followed, in every quarter. But the one to exercise the Petrine authority was no other than his successor the bishop of Rome.[1] He then logically extended his claim, and declared that his verdict on the question of baptizing heretics ought to be accepted in the east; thereby he raised a violent storm of indignation.

Stephen was no more successful than Victor had formerly been in maintaining his claim. Nevertheless what he wanted was the same: on this occasion we have records of the official argument, a fact that enables us to see quite clearly the thread which continues through the centuries to the Vatican dogma of A.D. 1870. The churches of the east opposed the Roman tradition with their own, and this went back to Christ and the Apostles;[2] i.e. they took up the same attitude as that adopted by the churches of Asia Minor in regard to the Easter dispute. Cyprian alone opposed the Roman proof on the basis of theory, proposing one of his own in which the constitution of the early church catholic is clearly reflected. Moreover this theory of his was not first put forward in the struggle against Stephen— nor was it adapted for this purpose—but was developed in connection with his doctrine of the unity of the church; and its essential ideas had been stated as early as A.D. 251.

The church was a unity which was seen outwardly in the unanimous co-operation of the bishops: just as there was only a single church although incarnated in several individual churches, so there was only a single episcopal office embodied in its individual vehicles.[3] Any bishop who separated himself from the unanimous circle of bishops, thereby separated himself from the church, because he cut himself off from the unity. This unity was regarded by Cyprian as a mystical reality brought about by the operation of the spirit: if the church were an earthly institution, the thousand bishops might have a

---

[1] Cypr., *ep.*, 74,1. 71,1. 71,3. 75,17   [2] Firmilian of Cæsarea in Cypr., *ep.*, 75,19
[3] Cypr., *de eccl. unit.*, 5 (p. 214,1–7). *ep.* 55,24 (p. 642,12–15)

hundred different opinions, and all be in a state of dispute with one another. It was by divine miracle that they were always unanimous, and that they always regulated variations of opinion in a friendly way. For this very reason, it was clear that a bishop who disturbed this unity had been abandoned by God, and was following the promptings of evil, i.e. he was departing from the church.

The basis of the unity lay in the fact that the bishops were the successors of the Apostles, and these constituted a single body of men with equal authority and equal rank. But there was more: Christ wished to express the unity at the root of the church quite unambiguously, and therefore, in the first instance, had called a single apostle, Peter, and had declared him to be the foundation stone of the edifice of his church. However, no legal pre-eminence had been given to Peter, but all the apostles were equal: his call was a symbol of the unity of the basis upon which the church stood, and it set forth the nature of the church through all the ages.[1] That was the reason for the similar authority of all who occupied episcopal office, an authority which was uncontested over wide regions as late as the third century; each of these bishops was a successor of the Apostles, a fact which implied a total denial of all claims for primacy, no matter from what side they might come. The rejection of the "bishop of bishops" was to them an obvious duty, and Cyprian maintained this point throughout, with complete firmness: he was not driven to the final consequences, however, before Stephen died, and he himself was martyred. But Rome's claim to primacy had been plainly foreshadowed—and we may ask, What would have happened to Cyprian's theory if once the visible unanimity of the bishops had been broken in considerable degree? The answer was provided in the fourth century.

The dispute about heretics fell into abeyance. Xystus of Rome and Cyprian of Carthage died about the same time. The Romans were again compelled to leave the episcopal chair vacant for a long time. Not until July 22, A.D. 260, was it possible to install Dionysios, hitherto a presbyter. Under

[1] Cypr., ep., 45,3 (pp. 602,18 f.), de eccl. unit. 4 (pp. 212 f.) Excellent discussion in Hugo Koch, Cathedra Petri (Beiheft z. ZNW no. 11, 1930)

Stephen he had already taken an active part in the transactions regarding the baptism of heretics, and had corresponded with Dionysios, bishop of Alexandria.[1] For that reason he was now drawn into the strife which had arisen in Egypt on account of the conduct of their bishop, and in the course of events he was able to bring to the Roman church advantages which were to bear fruit at a later period. In particular the theological discussions became, what at that time no one could have dreamt, a prelude to the great Arian controversy, which shook the entire church, at the beginning of the fourth century. Consequently it will be convenient to consider the affairs of the two Dionysii in that context.

[1] Eus., *H.E.*, 7,5,6

Chapter Twelve

SYRIA AND BEYOND

THE GREAT CITY OF ANTIOCH WAS THE MILITARY AND political headquarters of Syria; it had seen many emperors and pretenders to the crown within its walls, and had experienced on its own body the various blows of fate which helped to shape the history of the world. It had been the point of departure of Hellenized Christianity, and the significance of the city had continually increased the influence of its Christian church. The abounding fertility of the soil and the favourable situation, in both commercial and political respects, brought much wealth to the province of Syria. All this flowed together in Antioch, the capital, creating there architectural beauty, and a luxurious way of living, to an extent with which not even Alexandria could compete. The upper classes of manufacturers and merchants, the thousands who belonged to the demimonde of the theatre, of the life of pleasure and of vice, the innumerable hosts of workers and workless, constituted a population which was indeed unified at bottom, and which was held together by boundless self-confidence, unrestrained search for pleasure, and unlimited love of banter. What they lacked was a noble seriousness, and a creative mentality. Ethnologically, the city was a mixture. There was a Macedonian leading class, which spoke Greek, and which since the days of the Seleucids had become highly diversified by the immigration of Hellenic and Hellenized families of varied origin. On the other hand, there was the Syriac-speaking, indigenous populace, with whom were mingled slaves and the lowest classes from every country.

Here, as elsewhere, the Jews kept closely together.[1] We have seen how the Christians separated themselves from them as a group. We have already discussed the fate and the theology characteristic of Bishop Ignatius, who died in Rome as a martyr, under Trajan.[2] We have no information, however, as to the outlook of his church at that time, nor as to events in the

[1] C. H. Kraeling in *Journ. Bibl. Lit.* 1932, 130–60   [2] Vol. 1, pp. 236–48

church of Antioch in the following decades. The mere names contained in the traditional lists of bishops tell us nothing; all we hear is that Antioch was the starting-point of a series of important men in the gnostic movement, and we may therefore conclude, at least, that there were gnostic conventicles, perhaps there were larger churches, which competed with the orthodox group, and endeavoured to influence its inner development.[1] In the neighbouring town of Rhossos, the gnostic *Gospel of Peter* was made use of unsuspectingly in the church until Serapion, bishop of Antioch, drew towards the right, and forbade the book: but his attitude in the whole affair makes it clear, at the same time, that he was not able to master the problems of the period.[2] His predecessor, Theophilus, had been a writer: we have already discussed him as an Apologist, and mentioned his Gospel-Harmony[3] (which perhaps should be regarded as an orthodox rival to Tatian's *Diatessaron*), and the latter was beginning to be accepted in Antioch. He had also written against Marcion, and against the Hermogenes whom Hippolytus and Clement of Alexandria knew, and to whom Tertullian had dedicated a polemic.[4] What is extant of the writings of Theophilus shows that he was a man with a quite moderate power of judgment: since he wrote so much, the needs of his church must have made him a polemist against the numerous influences which were active at that time among the Christians in Antioch.

Possibly the recent assertion is correct,[5] to the effect that the uncertainty of the inner situation is the reason why, after Ignatius and during the whole of the second century, Antioch never comes to our notice: its bishop is not mentioned amongst those who took part against Victor in the pronouncement of the eastern churches on the question of Easter. In any case, however, this weakness was overcome shortly afterwards. In A.D. 251 Bishop Fabius of Antioch called the entire east to his city in order to lend support to Novatian in his affairs, and subsequently Antioch always took a leading part in movements affecting church policy. Twenty years later, Bishop Paul

---

[1] W. Bauer, *Rechtgläubigkeit u. Ketzerei i. ält. Christentum* (1934) 70

[2] *Supra*, pp. 73, 98. Eus., *H.E.*, 6,12   [3] *Supra*, pp. 99, 187

[4] *Supra*, p. 221 and Hilgenfeld, *Ketzergeschichte*, 553–60   [5] Bauer, *op. cit.*, 67

was already a grandseigneur of immense influence, even in mundane matters. As a consequence, it is not surprising that, in the second century, there are few extant records of Christianity in the region round about Antioch. In the third century, it is plain that the church was meeting with increased success, and about A.D. 300 we find bishops in nearly all the important towns of Syria and far beyond in the countryside.[1] The Christianity grouped round about Antioch was Greek in language and mode of thought.

In Syria, and probably here for the first time, Christianity began to develop a national cast: and in the first instance there appear to have been two starting-points, Arbela and Edessa. Edessa lay closer to Antioch, and here, during the storms of the wars of Rome with Parthia, a family of native princes had retained the throne; about A.D. 250, a person called Abgar IX was wearing the crown, and he attracted Christian scholars to his court, being described by them as a "saintly man" who had "become a believer".[2] At that time also, there was a "temple of the Christian church" in Edessa, which, we are told, was destroyed by a flood in September, A.D. 201.[3] The importance of these notices must not be exaggerated to mean that Abgar had made Christianity the state religion of his little kingdom. Nevertheless they are not without significance.

About this period,[4] Christianity took root in Edessa, its pioneer teacher being Bardesanes. He was born in the city, and became an eminent person living at the court of the prince, and well experienced in secular arts: an eye-witness tells, with astonishment, of his skill in archery.[4] He was also the first Syrian of whom we know that he wrote learned treatises in his mother tongue, and that he composed poems: he was the founder of Syriac literature, which was primarily Christian. Eusebius speaks of him with great respect, calls him an outstanding man, and praises him as a fighter against

[1] Harnack, Mission, 2,672 f.
[2] Julius Africanus in the Kestoi (in Syncellus, Chronogr., 1,676, 13 ed. Bonn) Bardesanes p. 607 11 ed. Nau. In addition, however, Bauer, op. cit., 10 Felix Haase, Altchr. Kirchengesch. (1925) 85 f.
[3] Chron. Edessenum 86 = 1,465 ed. Hallier. Erroneously questioned by Bauer, op. cit. 18, Haase, op. cit., 89
[4] I shall neglect the legend of Abgar; cf. supra, p. 76

Marcion and other heretics, and also declares 'that his polemic
writings had been translated into Greek.[1] The Syrians of the
following period, on the other hand, decry him heartily, and
reckon him among the gnostic heretics: that is his place up to
the present day. The polemic caused many impressions to be
spread about him, which were partially or entirely false, and
which sketched him in such a way that it required penetrating
research before the main lines of his Christianity could be
brought to the light of day on the basis of unobjectionable
sources: but, recently, everything has become clear.[2]

A few fragments in Greek are extant, together with the
original text of the *Dialogue on Fate* as used by Eusebius: in
addition there is also the fragment of a poem on the Creation;
the missing parts can be supplied from a good version in prose,
and important deductions can be made from the poem.
Firstly, it is not superfluous to say that Bardesanes did not feel
himself to be the leader of a sect, but rather to belong un-
questionably to the church universal existing everywhere.
"What shall we say about ourselves, the 'new race' of Christians
whom Christ has raised in all cities and in all countries by
His own coming? We are all called Christians, by the one name
of Christ, wherever we may be found. On the one day of
Sunday, we come together, and, on the appointed days, we
fast"—and then he proceeds to speak of the brethren in Gaul,
Parthia, Judea, Persia, and Mesopotamia, without making any
kind of distinction.[3] He contrasts the unity of Christian
custom, which is obedient to the law of Christ, with the
manifold national laws which spring from human freedom.
Bardesanes does not deny the significance of "fate"; its signs
are to be found in the courses of the stars; but he limits their
significance to corporeal things and to outer circumstances of
life: all ethical action is due to the will, which decides for good
or evil. It is possible for man to free himself from the compulsion
of fate and attain freedom to obey God's good commandments;
these correspond to man's nature and are gladly laid hold of
by him.[4]

[1] Eus., *H.E.*, 4,30
[2] The basis was laid by H. H. Schaeder in *ZKG.*, 1932, 21–74. The text has
been edited by F. Nau in *Patrologia Syriaca* 2 (1907), 492–675
[3] Nau, *op. cit.*, par. 46 p. 607 f.   [4] *Ibid.* par. 11–12, pp. 550–53

Here we have an ethical optimism on Greek lines, and corresponding to the enduring attitude of the Greek Church. It was only in the west, and in the person of Augustine, that Paul's denial of all human power for good was once more brought to life as a Christian conviction. According to Bardesanes's *Dialogue*, Christianity was a new way of life which subordinated to itself all differences of a national character, and to which men of goodwill gladly submitted: that had been the theme of the Apologists, and Bardesanes's doctrine agrees entirely on this point with the universal Christian view, in spite of the fact that the majority of theologians (but not the laity) shook their heads, as in duty bound, at his recognition of some of the workings of "fate". However, there was no serious opposition to his doctrine of the church catholic, and Eusebius gave hearty approval to his *Dialogue*.

Nevertheless, we must recognize that there was a speculative basis for his conception of the moral freedom of the will as aimed at the liberation of mankind from the compulsion of earthly bonds, and the restitution of man's true being; the basis is made clear in the poem on Creation. According to this poem, there were, in the beginning, five elements: the ether of light, fire, wind, water, and darkness, which last was equated with the sombre earth; their original balance was upset by an accident, and all became intermingled; "and they began to bite one another like ravening animals". God then sent down His logos, through whom He quieted the raging elements, and banished darkness into the deeps. The four other elements then returned to their own places. After the strife, a new order of things came into existence, the Kosmos; it no longer corresponded, however, to the original circumstances, but represented a mixture of elements as the outcome of the former struggle. In particular, the shining clarity of the higher elements was clouded by a remnant of darkness, viz. matter. "Therefore all nature and created things hasten to cleanse themselves and to eradicate whatever evil has been mixed in with them." Hence, elimination of the remaining "darkness" was the purpose of Creation, and the goal of history and evolution—and darkness was, as we may now remark, the evil element. According to the wording of the *Dialogue*, its elimination resulted from an ethical process which restored mankind, and, along with him, the Kosmos, to its shining and pure original condition.

Like the gnostic conceptions of a similar sort which we have already described, this piece of mythology is only a pictorial garb for a speculative view of the universe. To the question about the origin of evil, Bardesanes replied that evil was hostility towards God, and was also what disturbed His ordination; it arose from causes which lay in the nature of the world, in any case beyond the reach of human will and obligation, but also beyond the divine volition, because the elements were not created by God, but were as eternal as He. Nevertheless, God dominated them by His logos, and showed mankind the way to liberation from evil by means of a virtuous will obedient to the logos. All was proved by skilful exegesis of the Old and New Testaments; Bardesanes found the proof there, and called himself a Christian in good faith. He freed the idea of God from the standing objection that the Almighty had not prevented the coming of evil, and as a consequence was responsible for it. He reached this point, however, by conceiving God merely as an organizer of the world, without being the Creator. The church could not let such a doctrine pass unchallenged.

Marcion had attempted to solve the same problem, but did not avoid the accusation of ditheism. His system, as such, implied a denial of the world: Creation was regarded in a purely negative manner as the work of a demiurge of a lower, not to say, an evil, character, and the way of redemption from it was that of a rigorous asceticism.[1] According to Bardesanes, however, Creation was the important act of God making redemption possible: he affirmed the world, with its light and splendour, and discovered in the human soul ethical powers which freed it from the might of darkness. As a consequence he wrote against the Marcionites, who, we may therefore gather, had already been active in Edessa. When, however, we remember that, c. A.D. 180, Theophilus the bishop of Antioch had written against the heretic, Hermogenes, who is also mentioned, with disapproval, in other sources; and when we also remember that the latter attempted to solve the problem

[1] Vol. I, pp. 251 ff.

of evil in the world by the doctrine of the eternity of matter, it is possible that we have reached one source of Bardesanes's speculations. Hermogenes speaks of matter as a mass without order and form, similar in its erratic movements to a pot boiling over, until God calmed it by His logos, and separated the ordered Kosmos from unordered matter.[1] All this harmonizes so well with the doctrines of Bardesanes that a connection seems very probable; and Hermogenes must have exercised an important influence in Syria, otherwise the bishops of Antioch would scarcely have written against him. However, Hermogenes speaks in the abstract language of philosophers, whereas Bardesanes, as a poet, gave plastic form to the philosophical conceptions of his theology.

It follows that the doctrine of the eternity of matter had reached Antioch, and the dangers of the doctrine had been foreseen; it is very probable that Bardesanes's heretical character was recognized in this city more quickly than elsewhere. A document originating in Edessa about A.D. 400,[2] although it has a legendary cast, asserts that Serapion, bishop of Antioch, had instituted a certain Palût as bishop of Edessa. This is probable. Serapion was bishop of Antioch c. A.D. 200, and, if he rightly recognized the significance of Bardesanes, it may have appeared important to him to assemble the orthodox in Edessa; and it is even possible that they had asked for Serapion's help. He consecrated a bishop for them in the person of Palût, and sent him to the threatened place with the appropriate commission. The new church was formed, but it was a small minority compared with the multitudes who held to Bardesanes, and who successfully claimed the name of Christians for themselves. Nay, here as elsewhere, the "catholic" church was regarded as a sect, and had to call itself the "Palûtians", after its leader and founder: that continued to be the case until into the fourth century;[3] and the facts suggest that Palût was really the first catholic bishop of the city.

The surviving records are not sufficient to permit us to follow the effect of Bardesanes's theology on church life and practice,

[1] Hipp., *Refut.*, 8,17,2. Tert., *adv. Hermog.*, 39. 41. 44
[2] *Doctrina Addai* ed. Phillips, p. 15,10 = 50; cf. F. C. Burkitt, *op. cit.*, pp. 11 ff.
[3] Ephraem Syrus, trans. by von Rücker (*Bibl. d. Kirchenväter*, vol. 61) 2,81 f. (2,485 f. ed. Rom)

on worship and custom: he wrote 150 hymns of importance, the number corresponding to the Psalter.[1] We are told that his son, Harmonios, diligently continued the poetic work of his father, and developed his metre further under Greek influence. This poetry was popular among the people and by it the ideas of the poet were spread.[2] The son did not retain his father's simplicity, but gave play to the fantasy of the gnostics; in this way all sorts of gnostic ideas were introduced into the church at Edessa. Moreover, about the same time, the independence of the royal house of Edessa came to an end. In A.D. 216, Caracalla marched against the Parthians and *en route* deposed Abgar IX, attaching the city to the province of Mesopotamia as a Roman colony.

Christians were to be found in the district of Osroëne outside the city of Edessa—letters were sent to Rome from many cities in this district in regard to the Easter dispute[3]—but we find no considerable traces of them in the immediately following period. Edessa remained their headquarters. Churches in Mesopotamia[4] were known *c.* A.D. 250 to Dionysios of Alexandria:[5] it is probable that there were Christians in Nisibis, certainly in Hatra;[6] in the little frontier fortress of Dura, a house with a Christian chapel has recently been excavated, and appears to have been built *c.* A.D. 230; a leaf of parchment found at the same place proves that Tatian's *Diatessaron* was in use in the Greek original as the Gospel.[7] Thus contemporary documents, recently discovered, prove, what many literary testimonies assert, that the *Diatessaron* was used as the Gospel in the Syrian east. We may also infer, therefore, that his ascetic views as to the nature of Christianity were widespread in that region.[8] As a matter of fact, even in the fourth century, certain groups of orthodox Syrians regarded celibacy as the genuine form of Christianity, and administered baptism only to such as had decided on continence.[9] That was the old tradition of the second century, and at best one can only argue whether Tatian

---

[1] Ephraem 2,554 ed. Rom.; cf. 2,66 ed. Lamy = 2,181 f. Rücker.
[2] Sozomenos 3,16,5–7; cf. Schaeder, *ZKG.*, 1932, 57. 61 f. and Nau, *op. cit.*, pp. 504 f.
[3] Eus., *H.E.*, 5,23,4   [4] Harnack, *Mission*, 2,678–98   [5] Eus., *H.E.*, 7,5,2
[6] Nau, *op. cit.*, p. 608,8
[7] *Excavations at Dura-Europos*, Report V, 238 ff.; Kraeling, *vide supra*, p. 99, footnote 3
[8] *Supra*, p. 99   [9] Burkitt, *op. cit.*, p. 62 ff.

or Marcion was the more responsible for the wide acceptance of this attitude.

Christianity had also spread over the Tigris into the region of Adiabene, striking root first in Arbela, and then penetrating far and wide. A chronicle of this city is extant[1] composed in c. A.D. 550, which, in spite of much legendary material, preserves an uncommonly sound, historical tradition from an earlier period. Addai is mentioned as missionary in Arbela, and his name also occurs in the legendary early history of the church at Edessa. The name is Jewish, and is an abbreviation of Adonijah; hence the "Apostle Addai" was of Jewish origin. The Jewish section of Arbela was particularly influential, and, under Claudius, the royal house had gone over to Judaism.[2] The chronicle fixes the founding of the Christian church in Trajan's time. The question has been raised whether the Jewish community in this district provided the starting-point for the Christian missionaries, and we must grant it as extremely probable.[3]

In the *Tractates* of Aphrahat, we possess detailed evidence as to the circumstances of Christianity in Syria c. A.D. 340, from which circumstances it is possible to draw inferences in regard to the earlier period. Christians lived here in the closest association with the Jews, were vilified and persecuted by them; but they argued with them, and defended their doctrines with Biblical proofs. Closer inspection of Syrian Christianity shows that it possessed characteristic elements which demonstrate not only its great age, but also its relation with Jewish ways. Nothing is said in regard to philosophical speculations, nor the logos theology. The fundamental dogmas are stated in a few words; they include a confession[4] of God, as Creator of the world and of men; He gave the Law to Moses. The next article confesses Christ, and His holy spirit enters man at baptism, and assists him to attain resurrection. But in order to retain the spirit, the Christian virtues must be exercised, a

[1] E. Sachau, *d. Chronik v. Arbela. Abh. Akad. Berlin*, 1915, no. 6, 17 ff. 61 f. with plan. F. Haase, *Altchr. Kirckengesch*, 1925, pp. 94–109

[2] Jos., *Ant.*, 20,17 ff. Schürer, *Gesch.*, 3,169

[3] Sachau, *D. Chronik v. Arbela.*, 1915, no. 6, 30. 42. Also Sachau, *Ƶ. Ausbr. d. Christentums in Asien (Abh. Akad. Berlin*, 1919, no. 1, 5 f.)

[4] Aphraates, *hom.*, 1,19 ed. Parisot pp. 44 f.

special place being occupied by asceticism. Christianity of this kind must not be simply equated with the moralism of the Hellenistic synagogues as, say, in 1 *Clem.*, although in its fundamentally legalistic attitude, which receives much emphasis, it differs only slightly; it contains many quotations from Paul, but not a breath of his spirit: indeed the emphasis placed on asceticism carries one still farther away from Judaism. The only thing showing a Hellenistic element and a Pauline view is the doctrine of the spirit. Whereas in regions enjoying a Greek civilization, the entire problem dealt with in speculations on the Trinity was enlivened by efforts to attain immortality, in Syria there was a primitive doctrine of the resurrection: this doctrine being based on ideas originating in rabbinic theology, and on religious motives that did not go beyond the moral sphere.[1] Aphrahat himself was not unacquainted with rabbinic learning, and, moreover, the Bible used in the Syrian churches preserved a text which was dependent upon Jewish tradition. These facts justify the supposition that, in these eastern regions and in the second and third centuries, Judaism helped, unwillingly, the work of Christian missionary propaganda, as also did the Judaism of the Mediterranean world, in the first and second centuries. Nevertheless, Syrian Christianity was not mediated from Jerusalem, nor from the Jewish Christians who set out thence; rather, it bore the stamp of Antioch from the beginning.

The Christians also spread in a very remarkable manner further to the east. The *Chronicle* of Arbela gives a list of seventeen bishoprics which lay on the left bank of the Tigris, and were in existence in A.D. 225, when the Sassanid rule was established. The list begins high among the mountains in the neighbourhood of present-day Diarbekr, and descends to the Persian gulf. A supplementary note says that Nisibis and Seleucia-Ctesiphon had no bishops in the Parthian period, "on account of fear of the pagans", but that this lack was supplied under the Persian rule. From Bardesanes[2] we learn that there were Christians, *c.* A.D. 220, in the regions of the Parthians, in Media, Persia, and Bactria; and the notices contained in the *Chronicle* of Arbela support that assertion in regard to the eastern

---

[1] *Ibid.*, 6,14 pp. 292 ff. [2] Bardesanes, Nau, pp. 607 f.

bank of the Tigris. Presumably, Christianity penetrated from that district further towards the east: a trustworthy notice in another chronicle[1] says that the Persian king Shapur, after capturing Valerian the Roman emperor (A.D. 260), permitted he bishops banned by the emperor to return to the frontier districts, and that he settled Roman prisoners in Babylonia, Susiana, and Persis: through these people Christianity became extremely widespread. Soon afterwards, in Rew-Ardashir, the seat of the archbishop of Persis (north of the Persian Gulf), two churches were built, one for Greek-speaking Christians and the other for Syrian Christians. This shows that there was a mixture of cultural traditions; these developed, and became of outstanding significance in the following period.

Side by side with the indigenous religions of the Syrians and the Iranians at the beginning of the third century, Judaism and Christianity were spreading far towards the east. Judaism had reached a critical stage, and was compelled to draw a line between itself and Hellenism. Once more this mighty western force was giving impressive evidence of its vitality. The synagogue of Dura, with its beautifully painted walls, shows to what extent the local Jews were ready to sacrifice their own tradition to the attraction of Hellenic culture. Moreover in this district, this was a new phenomenon: beneath the building erected in A.D. 245, there had been an earlier synagogue which had carefully followed national custom in the many coloured decorations.[2] That fact makes it plain that even in these lands there was a struggle between the Greek tradition and the Talmud; details have been lost to history, but they constitute part of the tragic lot of the people of Israel. The Babylonian Talmud was victorious, and it gave the spiritual direction later followed by the Jews. We may infer that Christianity gained from the contest, and attracted the malcontents to itself. Side by side with the church catholic, which was gradually confirming its position, Marcionite churches flourished, and also circles of gnostics both within and without the Church—the east was not less stirred by religious forces than was the west.

---

[1] *Chronicle of Seert*, ed. Scher (*Patrol. orient*, 4), p. 222. Sachau, *Sitz. Akad. Berlin*, 1916, 961 f.
[2] Rostovtzeff in *Röm. Quartalschrift*, 1934, 206. *Excavations at Dura-Europos*, Report VI, 332 ff.

It was in this many-sided life that a new world-religion was born. Its founder was Mani, a youth in whose veins ran the blood of the Iranian royal family; he had grown up in south Babylonia, where his father had joined a sect of Baptists who practised an ascetic type of life. Here the son must have met with all sorts of gnostic doctrines with a Christian name, and these must have combined with the basic ideas of his ancestral Persian religion: when, at 24 years of age, he set out to convert the world, his doctrine was already complete in principle. He travelled, in the first instance, to India, and there founded a church. If he had not known it previously, he learned there who Buddha was, and that Buddhism was a great religion: but obviously India taught him nothing new.[1] When Shapur I mounted the throne, in A.D. 241, Mani appeared once more in his native land and, after being graciously received by the king, began the important part of his missionary work. He laboured in the Sassanid empire undisturbed for more than thirty years, and was able to send his disciples out to all the ends of the earth. Then the anger of a new king fell upon him, and the hatred of the Parsee priests brought about his crucifixion: he died in this way A.D. 276.

He drew up his doctrines in a series of writings, of which embarrassingly numerous quotations have been preserved, and also fragments of which have lately been discovered in caves and rubbish heaps. Moreover, disciples wrote sequels to, and commented on, the master's works; the liturgical books of their churches continued to be produced, and so Mani's teaching continued to expand. Generations of modern scholars laboured fruitlessly on it until discoveries, made in our own day, put the key into our hands.[2] Earlier, it was sometimes thought that Mani was possibly a Christian heretic, and that he ought to be included among the gnostics: the view is correct to the extent that his doctrine has the characteristic marks of gnosticism. If preferred, Mani can be described as the historically most significant of all the gnostics. He himself, however,

[1] C. Schmidt, *Sitz. Akad. Berlin*, 1933, 47 f. Schaeder, *Urf. u Fortb. d. manich. Syst.*, 87 (in *Vorträge d. Bibliothek Warburg*, 1924–25)
[2] See previous note and further the summary by Polotsky in Pauly-W. suppl. 6,240–271. H. H. Schaeder, *Manich. u spätantike Religion* (Zeits. f. Missionskunde 50 (1935), 65–85)

aimed at being more than merely another gnostic, and in fact
was more.

He intended to found a religious community which would
comprehend the entire world for the first time. All religions
hitherto had been confined in space:[1] "Those which have
spread in the west (i.e. Christianity) have not reached the east,
and those which have spread in the east (Parseeism and
Buddhism) have not reached the west. My hope, however,
will extend to the west, and will also extend to the east, and
its preaching will be heard in every language, and it will be
preached in every city. My church is superior to earlier churches
in this, its prime characteristic." His programme of world-wide
missionary activity became fact. Manichæism penetrated into
north Africa in the west, and into China in the east; and was
preached in a multitude of languages. Granted that it quickly
came to an end in the west, nevertheless it endured about a
thousand years in Central Asia. The attention which the master
paid to the national characteristics of the different peoples
gave rise to a corresponding modulation of doctrinal form:
Iranians heard names sounded in their ears which were familiar
to them in the Avesta: in Hellenistic regions, philosophical
conceptions took the place of mythological description, whereas
New Testament elements were emphasized among Christians.
He did not reject the earlier religions outright, but recognized
them as preparatory stages, and he appraised Buddha,
Zoroaster, and Jesus, as divinely-sent forerunners. He described himself as the paraclete prophesied by Jesus, and thus
claimed a place among the number of men of God regarded as
holy by Christians.[2]

As in the case of Bardesanes, the starting-point of his theological thought was the problem of evil in the world. He did
not solve it, like the Syrian, in a mediating and optimistic
sense, but by the dogma of an absolute evil, eternally opposed
to the absolute good. This dualism was the fundamental
dogma on which all understanding of the world must be
based, and was seen in the opposition of light and darkness,
of God and matter. Quite on gnostic lines, Mani taught, further,
that this world was the result of a catastrophe. Darkness strove

Schmidt, p. 45   [2] *Ibid.* 56 f.

to reach the light, and, out of the struggle between the two mutually opposed powers, a mixed universe came into being in which the substance of light was imprisoned in the chains of darkness. Moreover, man was himself a mixed creature. But God made use of him in order to liberate the light. He sent His envoy on earth to teach man his worth, and to show him the way in which he might liberate his own divine substance of light, and be able to bring it back to its original condition. This way was that of asceticism, the breaking of the material bonds of the kingdom of darkness: it was particularly important to refrain from the propagation of children, as that would bind new souls of light ever afresh in new bodies.

Moreover, no animal was to be hurt or killed, no plants uprooted, and no fixed dwelling established in any place in this world. The "elect", the perfect disciple of the master, must wander about and preach the new gospel: his food, which was to be entirely vegetarian, would be provided by another group of Mani's adherents, the "catechumens", who would remain in the present world, and, by their "alms", make the way of redemption possible for the elect. The catechumens would be satisfied with intellectual agreement with, and active support of, the faith to which the "elect" would dedicate their practical life. The members of the Church confined their acts of worship properly so called to offering prescribed prayers, and carrying out prescribed fasts, together with the confession of sins. Such confession exercised its own redemptive power on their natures since it was an act in which the soul became aware of itself. There were no sacraments nor mysticism of any kind in Manichæism, points on which it differed from both Hellenistic gnosticism and Christianity.

The principles of this doctrine of redemption were clear and simple, but Manichæism gave them a mythological form which left earlier gnosticism far behind. Its structure was involved, and had a multiplicity of parts borrowed from every sphere. The kingdom of light was governed by the highest god, "father of greatness", whose nature exhibited a series of five conceptions: opposed to him was the land of darkness, with the five "sombre" elements, smoke, fire, wind, water, darkness. The entire material world was similarly divided into pentads, a world ceaselessly at war with itself, and so only able to organize its powers when it looked beyond its own frontier, saw the glory of the kingdom of light, and decided to conquer it. God sent His personified powers in defence, particularly the "primordial" man with the five "light" elements, air, wind, light, water, fire. In the course of the struggle, primordial man abandoned the elements of light: they were swallowed up by darkness, and became so mixed with it that they grew to a living unity with the foreign elements, and forgot their home. Moreover, primordial man fell for a time into this unconscious condition but was rescued by the "living spirit" which was sent down from above; at the same time the *nous*, heavenly reason, which dwelt in him, was also rescued. Thereupon the world was created for the purpose of redeeming the imprisoned light elements: a highly developed mythology depicts the judgment which the living spirit pronounced on the daemons (archons) of the world of darkness, from whose skin, flesh, and bones, the Kosmos was constructed. From the parts of light which had remained uncontaminated, the sun and moon were created as the "ships of light"; in these, all other light elements that became free, were to gather in order to voyage home to the kingdom. The increase of the incoming multitudes of light can be observed each month as the moon increases in size.

At this point, the "third envoy" descends in order to begin the work of redemption, the first act being the sexual seduction of the daemon-archons by attractive light beings: great multitudes of light are thereby set free and give darkness concern about the rest of its booty. The latter, therefore, creates the human pair, Adam and Eve, in a fantastically extravagant manner. They are ordained to take the germs of light which dwell in them and, by sexual reproduction, bind them ever anew to the flesh, i.e., the material of darkness, and thereby make further liberation impossible. But even this plan of defence fails. A new figure in the mythological drama now came down to Adam in the person of the "Jesus of glory", and taught him to recognize the character of light which his soul possessed, and which had a divine origin. Man thus rebelled against the bonds of matter, and made to long for freedom. Jesus brought *nous*, the divine reason, as an operative factor to mankind—somewhat the same as the Christian apologists mean by the term logos—and created in human hearts five "members of the soul"—i.e. elements in the understanding—and the five virtues, love, faith, perfection, patience, and wisdom: those were the weapons which the soul could use in its fight for freedom.

In the course of time, however, the operations of *nous* are forgotten; messengers are continually being sent to earth to advise men and direct them in the right way: these were the founders of the great religions, recognized by Mani as his forerunners, the last of them being Jesus. In this mythology, Jesus can, of course, only be a preacher of *nous*, but He is frequently identified with primordial man, or described as his son; and He is also set side by side with the third envoy, or put in his place—His sufferings and death are not regarded as historical events, nor as genuine experiences on the part of Jesus. For the Manicheans, the Passion is a mythological event, and Jesus on the Cross means the soul chained and bound to matter. In his letters, Mani regularly follows the example of Paul, and describes himself as "apostle of Jesus Christ"; in this way, he consciously claims his place in the long series of the divinely sent envoys of *nous*, the last and final herald of redemption by light. All that now remained was the end of this world as predicted and depicted already in the New Testament, and the triumph of light over darkness.

The outlines have only been reproduced quite roughly in the above discussion, but if we take the mythological elements exhibiting innumerable details and applications, and follow them in their rhythm as shaped by the numbers five and twelve, we shall obtain some conception of the variety in the Manichean view of the world; over and above all this, it contains numerous cross currents, illogical interpolations, parallels, and changes of images, names, and ideas, all confused together in such a manner that no conspectus is possible. Moreover, whereas the principles of the new religion remained unchanged for centuries, yet even during the master's lifetime, the fantasy of his school took forcible possession of the mythological images, developed them further in some respects, simplified them in others, and introduced new colours until the ground tints totally disappeared. As far as we can tell, that is a characteristic phenomenon found among all gnostic schools, but in Manichæism it is particularly plain, and has contributed more than a little towards our difficulty in understanding its original form. Nevertheless, even in Mani's own thought, the visionary figures of gnostic fantasy were dominant, and drew him aside from simple observation and unsophisticated knowledge.

His religion was a development of both Christianity and gnosticism, and he was quite conscious of both: but the Greek spirit, which demanded rational clarity, had departed, and the mythological redeemers had silenced the voice of the Galilean preacher. The roots of religion as found in history have been lost, the incomprehensible godhead alone surviving; sparks of whom abide in the human soul and await redemption—and man, who, by negating this world, redeems both himself and God. This religion was not capable of a genuine growth. For a millennium it retained a mummified form, almost unnoticed in Europe, and lost its soul. Christianity entered the living stream of spiritual growth in the west, and, in the course of centuries, changed with it: in every age, however, in the Christian churches, the ancient, simple words of the gospel re-echoed unchanged.

Chapter Thirteen

EGYPT

IT HAS ALWAYS BEEN A STRIKING FACT THAT DURING THE
first hundred years of Christian preaching, and indeed
for a considerably longer period, Egypt never comes within
our horizon; as a consequence when scholars attempted at a
later date to write the history of the Church, they tried, though
clumsily, to fill the blanks of knowledge from a fictitious list of
bishops of Alexandria, and a legend that Mark founded the
Church. Nevertheless Egypt enjoyed the liveliest intercourse
with the east and Rome, both of which were already strongly
penetrated by Christianity. There must be special grounds for the
absence of information, and, recently,[1] a theory has been
advanced that, at the earliest period in Egypt, a Christianity
flourished which was, later, felt to differ too widely from the
ways of the Church in the following period; in other words it
was heretical. On this theory, the orthodox writers of history
would have had every reason for silence; and, in fact, we must
admit that all the notices about Christians in Egypt during the
first three-quarters of the second century have to do with heretics.

Basilides first appears as a teacher during the reign of
Hadrian, and Valentine similarly in the early Antonine period.
These great gnostics were soon surrounded by a swarm of
disciples and rivals; we even find Apelles the Marcionite
present for a short time.[2] Moreover, although the Church repudiated the gnosticism which surrounded it in the Mediterranean
world, that heresy continued to reverberate for centuries,
particularly in literature translated into Coptic, as well as on
papyrus in the Greek original. In addition, a thoroughly
gnostic product, the *Gospel of the Egyptians*,[3] is shown by its
name to have been the one that was quite customary in Egypt,
and was used rather than our four gospels. It follows that "the
Egyptians", or, more precisely, the Egyptian Christians, were

---

[1] W. Bauer, *Rechtgläubigkeit u. Ketzerei*, 49–64   [2] Vol. 1, 262. 280
[3] Klostermann, *Apokrypha II* (*Kl. Texte* 8, 2nd edit. p. 12 f.); cf. *ZNW.* 1936,
pp. 24 ff. M. R. James, *op. cit.*, pp. 10 ff.

gnostics. The *Gospel of the Hebrews*, which was also current in Egypt, was not less gnostic; it was cited by Clement and Origen, and is probably to be differentiated from the text used by the Jewish Christians of Syria:[1] it is possible that it was used by groups of Jewish-Christian gnostics. All these facts support the presumption that in Egypt—similarly to Syria—Christianity took root at first in gnostic forms, and that the church catholic was victorious in this region only at a late date, and after a severe struggle with gnosticism; possibly Rome gave help of vital significance. It is also possible that the remarkable independence of what might be called the parish churches of Alexandria, and the late development of the episcopacy, were alike connected with these facts.[2]

In any case, the earliest signs of the church catholic are found in the person, and at the time, of Bishop Demetrius (A.D. 189–231), and the first great representative of the church catholic was Clement of Alexandria. In all probability he was born in Athens, and his writings give the impression that he was a genuine Greek. His family came to possess Roman citizenship by the aid of Flavian, as is shown by his full name, Titus Flavius Clemens: it has been suggested[3] that his patron was the consular Flavius Clemens[4] executed by Domitian. Like the Apologist Justin[5] he travelled throughout the world in search of wisdom, and learned much from teachers in Hellas, lower Italy, and the orient; but all his longings were satisfied by Pantainos whom he found in Egypt.[6]

The latter belongs to the not very small number of extraordinary teachers whose memory has been preserved to history only by the grateful recollections of their eminent pupils. Over and above all this, Eusebius mentions the rumour that Pantainos had been a Stoic, and had made a missionary journey to India.[7] Modern attempts to reconstruct his lectures from the writings of Clement may be regarded as failures.[8] We must reckon Pantainos as belonging to a group of "presbyters" often quoted by Clement, i.e. to those of an older

[1] Vol. 1, 186, Klostermann, *op. cit.*, p. 5 f., no. 5. 27   [2] *Supra*, pp. 64 f.
[3] O. Stählin in the excellent introduction to his translation: *Bibl. d. Kirchenväter*, 2nd series, vol. 7, p. 10
[4] *Supra*, p. 160   [5] Justin, *dial.*, 2   [6] Clem., *Strom.*, 1,11,1 f.
[7] All the notices have been assembled by Harnack, *Altchr. Lit.*, 1 291–96
[8] J. Munck, *Unters. über Klemens v. Alex.* (1933) 173–204

generation, who taught him only by word of mouth, and whom he regarded as trustworthy vehicles of early Christian tradition. Irenæus, too, felt himself dependent on a quite similar group of "presbyters". Pantainos, however, was the most influential among them, because he was the head of the "Alexandrian catechumen school".[1] Only at a later date do we learn fuller particulars about the school: under Origen it was a centre of Christian scholarship, employing the methods of ancient science and learning; it was attended by adherents of all religions and philosophies. The early stages of the Christian school were also probably characterized by the breadth of horizon corresponding to the spirit of Greek learning which had been at home in Alexandria from early in the Ptolemaic period; it is likely that the school was interested in philosophy and Biblical study as found in Egyptian gnosticism, with interests which served to link the school with the growing church catholic.

Whatever the beginnings may have been, Clement succeeded Pantainos, stamped his personality upon the school, and gave it a character which can be clearly and unambiguously expressed in the formula of "a Christian gnosis of a consciously catholic type". All we know of the rest of Clement's life can be said in a few words. He first became well known under the emperor Commodus (A.D. 180–192).[2] The persecution under Septimius Severus (A.D. 202–03) scattered the Christian teachers of the town,[3] and, in the year A.D. 211, we meet again with Clement carrying an episcopal communication from Cappadocian Cæsarea to Antioch. About five years later, he was mourned as dead.[4]

The notices in regard to his work as a writer are more detailed and provide valuable information which extends our knowledge beyond the extant works: in his *Church History*, Eusebius lists those with which he was acquainted, and the Constantinoplitan scholar, Photios, caused Clement's works to be read aloud (c. A.D. 850) while he dictated copious notes to his secretary

[1] Eus., *H.E.*, 5,10,1. 4
[2] Eus., *H.E.*, 5,11,1; also E. Schwartz in Eus., *H.E.*, vol. 3,29. Julius Africanus fragm. 52 (Routh, *Reliquiae Sacrae*, 2nd edit. 2,307)
[3] *Supra*, p. 165. Eus., *H.E.*, 6,3,1
[4] Eus., *H.E.*, 6,11,6. 14,9. Harnack, *Chronologie*, 2,6

on every paragraph.[1] Three large works and a small tractate
are extant, but only short notices and fragments of other
writings.[2] The three principal writings are connected in
substance with each other, and, in spite of all the hesitation
which has been felt about the term, they may confidently be
described as a trilogy. The first was intended to convert the
reader to Christianity, the second to instruct in the Christian
manner of life, the third to describe the ideal of a complete
Christian as initiated into the deep things of knowledge.
Clement fixed his plan at quite an early date, but, in carrying
out the third part, his mind oscillated, and after many delays
he was finally obliged to leave it unfinished.[3]

Clement lived in the midst of the lively mental activity of
his time, and his eyes were open to the crowd of ideas which
were nowhere else developed in such varied ways as in Alexandria. Here exact science was quite at home, and for a long
time the reflection of a fading glory shone over it. When
Clement first came to the city, the astronomer, Claudius
Ptolemaios, who was responsible for the cosmology which was
to be normative for the next millennium, had died shortly
before. Philology still maintained its tradition, and Apollonios
Duskolos wrote on Greek accidence and syntax. Athenaios
lived in Naukratis close by, and prepared a Platonic feast
from the content of several handbooks and numerous pigeon
holes, as Aulus Gellius had already done in the west: and the
educated public accepted his invitation gladly. By that time the
great gnostics had already passed away, but their schools
remained, and influenced both Christians' and pagans. Those
who pursued philosophical inquiries, held Plato to be the most
important force, and Ammonios, who was to be his prophet,
was still undiscovered, and still carrying bales into the ware-
houses at the harbour.

Clement felt himself at home in a world of this kind; he wrote
for it, and enjoyed a wide public, because he was already one
of themselves, and had no need to struggle for recognition as

---

[1] Eus., *H.E.*, 6,13,1–7. Photios, *Bibl. cod.*, 109–11
[2] Ed. by O. Stählin, 1905–09 translation of the *Protr. Paedag.* and *Strom.*, I–III
in *Bibl. d. Kirchenväter*, 2nd series, vol. 7. 8. 17 (1934–36); Engl. transl. by
W. Wilson in the Ante-Nicene Christ. Library, Vol. 4. 12. 22. 24 (1867–72)
[3] Clem., *Paed.*, 1,1 f. *Strom.* 4,3

was the case, e.g., with Justin and his fellow Apologists. In Alexandria, mental life and culture had developed more rapidly than elsewhere, a fact which signified a better pathway for Christianity. Clement was a philosopher and a gnostic, a philosopher at the beginning, a gnostic at the end, but both as a Christian: and he tried to prove to the world that it was in this very combination that the solution of its problems was to be found; at the same time it afforded complete insight into the apparently simple and broadly outlined doctrines of the church catholic. He expressed these opinions to his readers in a vocabulary and a style expected of a writer of belles-lettres.

He took trouble to write Attic Greek, and, where it seemed to him appropriate, he made use of the optative mood although it was already dying out in living speech. Occasionally, he interwove elegant acrostics, and other grammatical tit-bits. He constructed rhetorical sentences effectively, and his balanced clauses in twos and threes or longer series, frequently even with a rhythmic movement, made pleasant reading. Then again, artistic periods rolled musically along, filled with the vocabulary of impassioned language. The modes, which were usual at the time as effective oratory, were applied by Clement to attain his purpose, nor did he refrain here and there from contrasting the "unsophisticated" and "simple language" which he used "merely to serve his purpose", with the ornamental "cooing of doves", usual in the "ear-ticklings of the Sophists": these very phrases are quoted from his *Handbook*.[1] Like Tertullian in the west, so Clement in the east (where it was more difficult) was the first Christian whom the literary world was compelled to recognize as a modern writer in the full sense of the term. It regarded Clement as a sophist equally with Aristides or Philostratos, and felt that it was possible to take up his writings, with their special content, without spoiling one's good taste.

First of all, there was a *Protreptikos*, an "address aiming at conversion": this was a customary title for rhetorical documents intended to encourage men to come to a certain decision, and was employed both in political rhetoric and among philosophers and moralists: Aristotle wrote a *Protreptikos*; so did Epicurus,

---

[1] Clem., *Strom.*, 1,22,4 f. 2,3,1 and frequently

and a considerable number of Stoics, including Kleanthes, Chrysippos, and Poseidonios. Clement chose a similar title in order to show the reader that it was intended to convert him to Christianity, but, both here and in his other writings, he was right in avoiding the dryness of a philosophical schoolmaster, and in using the language of an elegant and modern Sophist: the subject-matter would show that his actual purpose was serious.

In this work, he reproduces the bewitching songs of Amphion, Arion, and Orpheus, and the cicada alights helpfully on the lyre of Eunomos—but what is the significance of these ancient sages? Error and Bacchic madness, slavery and the tyranny of daemons. Soon, however, the voice of eternal truth can be heard in the new song of the divine logos, "which banishes worry and ill will, and causes us to forget suffering". This pure song of harmony will be heard to the ends of the world and weave everything closely together according to God's fatherly will. The lyre and the zither are mindless instruments which the logos contemns. His instrument of many notes ´is the great universe, and mankind the microcosm; its harmonious music, produced by the spirit, is his accompaniment when he sings the praises of God. Thus the meaning of the new song is that the logos, who was in the beginning and who had created the world, has become visible and has appeared to us as Christ the Saviour, the teacher of the right life, the life which leads to immortality.

Such words reflect the beginning of a Christian sense of life such as we have not hitherto met. It is no longer the defiant, polemical tone of the Apologists condemning wrong and insisting on righteousness; it is not the fanatical hatred and the forensic skill seen in Tertullian; rather, superior conviction and calm assurance help Clement to express his ideas in poetic language, and produce a hymn of triumph to Christ as the herald of the final and eternal truth.

The very first sections of the book lead the reader up to the heights: the subject-matter is to be the logos of the world, and this logos has appeared as Christ, after being prophesied in the Bible and preached by John the Baptist. Then the reader experiences a sense of great disquietude as the argument deteriorates, and Clement discusses the long-silent oraçles of forgotten gods, and the shameless features of obscure mysteries. True, Clement soon enters on the customary polemic against ancient forms of worship; the unavoidable themes are handled in detail. The Sibyl is made to bear witness on behalf of the truth. Philosophers are cross-examined, and Plato, who stands close to the gateway which leads to a final knowledge of God, is compelled to confess that the Hebrews were his tutors. Even Xenophon, Kleanthes, and, in particular, Pythagoras are called in as preachers of a true doctrine of God. Then follows a multitude of quotations selected from the poets, some of the quotations being taken from anthologies known to us elsewhere; then with an impressive independence, the prophets of the Old Testament follow on, accompanied by the Sibyl, as if anything else were impossible. This intentional blotting out of the boundary between Hellenic and Biblical writings raises the unity of the divine revelation in the entire world to the point of being an implicit conviction, with which, in the sequel, the doctrines of the New Testament writings are harmonious. Later a thousand voices from all regions of the world combine in a unity of divine harmony, a single chorus rises, which the logos conducts as choirmaster, concluding with the theme of the final truth expressed as "Abba, dear Father".[1]

Thus far Clement has been sketching in broad lines. The doubts of the hearers now come to expression, and he piles up urgent exhortations, in earnest and in satire, against these doubts in order to compel hesitating hearts to make the decision that would mean salvation: as a pastor of souls, he is always finding fresh reasons, winding up with brilliant images. The sirens sit on cliffs dangerous to life, and sing the seductive song of worldly pleasure. But you must remain in the ship which the logos steers, and bind yourself like Odysseus to the mast: then you are certain of voyaging to the heavenly harbour; you shall celebrate the mysteries of the logos on God's holy mountain, and dance in the circle of the righteous and of the angels round about the uncreated and eternal God, who is truly one. Jesus addresses mankind, all who possess reason, barbarian and Hellene, the entire human race whom he

[1] Clem., *Protr.*, 88,3

created according to the Father's will: "Listen, you thousand tribes, come to me"—and then follows a rhetorical finale of exceptional artistry: the words of Jesus echo ever more mightily, shorter sentences strike on the attention of listeners like hammers on the anvil; immortality, *aphtharsia*, and gnosis flare up and re-echo in the Saviour's call, "Come unto me, all ye that labour and are heavy laden, and I will give you rest."

We now come to Clement's peroration; he begins in a tempestuous mood, then, becoming more leisurely, he takes up Christ's warning and faces philosophic hearers with the choice of "the truth of the logos or the illusion of the masses". The logos makes you the friend of God, and everything will be yours just as everything is God's, for what friends possess they possess in common. Indeed, it may even be claimed that the Christian alone is devout, and rich, and nobly born, the image of God; we believe that he who is in harmony with reason, and has become holy through Christ Jesus, is already to that extent like God. This blessing is spoken of in the prophetic word, "I said ye are gods and all of you children of the most high." That is the final word that Clement has to say to the Greeks: his purpose is to show them the way to deification; Christ's promise is the fulfilment of the deepest human longing. The *Protreptikos* then closes.

Clement's second book follows immediately on the first, and develops before the reader's eye the plan of a trilogy. The logos has inspired man to moral endeavour—the *Protreptikos* was intended to prove that point—and it now comes forward as tutor in order to edify his soul with advice and encouragement: hence the theme of the work, upon which we are entering, is Christ as tutor (*Paidagogos*). The description of Christ as teacher (*Didascalos*) is reserved for future treatment when theological doctrine and revelation will form the subject-matter. In the first work, Clement had really had pagans in mind, and had taken account of their views and prejudices, but now, in the *Paidagogos*, he clearly draws the line between his own doctrine and those gnostic theories in which a gulf separates faith and knowledge. According to these theories, the psychics and the average writings of the church catholic stand on one side of the gulf, make shift with blind faith, and understand the Bible literally; on the other side are the pneumatics to whom the Spirit reveals the knowledge of divine secrets, and who pierce through the letter of scriptural words to a deeper sense. They and they alone are complete Christians.

Clement refuses to recognize anything of this sort of thing. He who has been baptized has thereby become a complete Christian, illuminated, son of God, perfected, immortal—just as Christ gave us an example by His baptism. Baptism takes the Christian, at one stroke, out of the kingdom of darkness, and puts him into the shining light of the knowledge of God; sin falls from him like a dark cloud; and, with the pure eyes of the Spirit, he looks towards heaven to behold the divine. All who have been baptized have set aside earthly passions, and are spiritual men, pneumatics, before the Lord. Faith is the essence of the Christian life in the present world; it seizes in advance what will be in the future, and therefore it is comprehensive and perfect—for what can stand higher than eternal life as seized by faith, a life which only becomes actual after the resurrection? Gnosis is not essentially different from faith, but is the new light now come to awareness.[1] The *Paidagogos* gives no hint how Clement was, later, to construe the term gnosis.

We have seen how the question of the origin of evil, or of sin, frequently disturbed the minds of Christian thinkers. With occasional side-glances at gnostic opinions, Clement reduces the problem to a discussion whether, in God's case, righteousness harmonizes with goodness, anger and punishment with kindly promises; and in the context of his argument, he reaches an easy solution by the theory of the divine tutelage: he refers not only to Biblical passages but quotes Plato's *Gorgias*, and he opposes the conception of a righteous God to false ideas of the divine wrath; "The one who exercises choice is guilty; God is innocent", says Plato, and Paul agrees. The cause of sin is to be found in human free will[2]—but in the breath of the spirit of God, which man received at Creation, lies the worth of man whom God loves; here, too, is the reason why He sends on earth His only begotten son.[3] At this point Clement touches upon the

---

[1] Clem., *Paed.*, 1,25-31; cf. 32-52
[2] *Op. cit.*, 1,62-70; cf. Plato, *Rep.*, 10 p. 617e   [3] Clem., *Paed.*, 1,7 f.

gnostic view of the spark of light, or the nucleus of *pneuma*, which rests in man, and which would constrain God to give redemption.[1]

Man whom He had made from dust, God brings to a new birth by water, makes him grow by means of the spirit, trains him by the Word, brings him by His commandments to sonship and salvation; in order that, by His help the earth-born might be transformed into a holy and heavenly man, and thus fill the scriptural word: "Let us make man in our image after our likeness." What God then said is completely fulfilled in Christ, whereas all the rest of mankind remain at the stage of "likeness". But we desire to fulfil the Father's will, to hear the word of the logos-paidagogos, and in our lives to imitate the redemptive life of our Saviour. He gives us the commandments and describes their nature in order that we may be able to fulfil them. This kind of life is simple and makes no claims; it is self-sufficient, and moves, without a burden of cares, towards eternity. The logos guides it with his instructions, which are in accordance with reason.

What is contrary to right reason is sin, and leads to sufferings. Obedience to the reason of the logos is what we Christians call faith, and that leads automatically to the fulfilment of what the Stoic philosophers call "duties". The Christian life, to which the *Paidagogos* now directs us, is a sum of reasonable actions which are covered by the Lord's commandments, divine principles which have been written down in Holy Scripture to provide us with spiritual guidance.[2] In this way the basis of a Christian doctrine of ethics is provided: Christ the logos, the world principle of reason, has himself undertaken the upbringing of the immature Christian race. He has written down His commandments in the Bible of the Old and New Testaments. He brings about their fulfilment in individual Christians by His holy spirit, but also determines all other obligatory actions round about in the world, because "duty" is always the consequence of a rational principle, which therefore proceeds from the logos. It is not surprising, but due to an inner necessity, that Christian and Stoic ethics are in agreement. All this becomes clear in the last chapter of the

[1] *Supra*, pp. 273 f., and vol. 1, pp. 290 f.   [2] Clem., *Paed.*, 1,98–103

first book of the *Paidagogos*, and it is prominent at every turn in the two following books, which set out the practical consequences of the basic principles. Clement is a disciple of the Stoics, also, in so far as he constructs his ethics not only in the form of general principles, but also discusses systematically the various spheres of life, and makes his teaching clear in individual cases—what we should call casuistry.

Hence, with the beginning of the second book, the writing deals immediately with problems of daily life. It discusses one after the other the questions of eating, drinking, expensive furniture, music, dancing and other forms of amusement, banquets, laughter, ribaldry, gentlemanly behaviour, anointings, and wreaths, sleep, sexual intercourse, luxurious clothing, footwear, costly ornament—such are the subjects of the first book. It is significant that ethical exhortation and rules of politeness go hand in hand here, that Biblical proofs are to be found in closest combination with philosophical considerations and with typical Stoic references to what is in accordance with nature, and therefore to what is reasonable.

Simple foods are healthy, over-eating and drinking spoil digestion and make a man ill. The gluttony of rich epicures is contemptible, as also their insatiable search for new tit-bits. And if such a banquet, with its redolent meats and tasty ragouts, should be called a Christian agapē, that would be blasphemy against the logos. A distinction must be made between the feast of agapē and every other social meal, although such was instituted and esteemed by Christ Himself. We must use the gifts of food as if we were their masters, and not like slaves dependent on them. If we accept an invitation, we must partake of the foods that are offered, but always in moderation, without undue eagerness, and wait until it is our turn to be served. It is impolite and unreasonable to stand up and hold one's nose above the dishes in order to smell the odours, or to stir the foods with the hands, or to chew with the mouth full so that one's veins stand out in the head and sweat rolls down. One should also be careful not to soil the hands, the table-cloth, or the beard, not to speak with the mouth full, nor to eat and drink at the same time. Foods are also an evil in so far as their purpose is to tickle the appetite. A simple meal can

itself provide an attractive change. The middle way in all
things is good, and not least in matters of the table: extremes
are dangerous, the mean is good, but the mean is present where
nothing essential is lacking, for the natural appetites find their
limits in a satisfying moderation. In this doctrine, Moses and
Plato are agreed.[1]

Such examples enable us to perceive the style in which
Clement wrote his Christian ethics: at the same time, it also
shows for whom he was writing. Obviously it was not for
Christians as such, but for the wealthy and educated amongst
them, to whom luxuries of the table, of clothing, and of
ornaments, provided daily seductions, and who associated with
people to whom the style of living of the upper ten thousand
in the rich commercial city of Alexandria, was an everyday
matter. These were the same groups as those for whom he
wrote his tractate on the rich young man, groups in whose
ears the saying about the camel and the needle's eye had a
sharp sound; they wished indeed to follow the Lord, but, to no
greater extent than the rich young man, did they desire to sell
their goods and give to the poor. Clement comforted them with
the assurance that that was not to be understood literally. The
Lord did not command them actually to dispose of their
property, but not to let considerations of property dominate
their hearts. He really commanded us to break the bonds
forged by greed or anxiety in all their phases. Poverty
itself did not bring one to God, and to give away one's goods
made no one into a Christian. The decisive matter was the
attitude of the soul. He who gave away his property but
afterwards missed it regretfully and longed for it, had only
suffered by his action. It was much better to possess enough for
one's self, so as to be able not to worry, and to be in a position
to help others. How could human society survive if no one had
any property? Wealth rightly used was an aid to righteousness.[2]

In all the greater towns at the end of the second century,
Christianity had penetrated into the upper classes; in Alexandria, this fact necessitated formulating a theology to deal
with the question of the relationship between culture and
Christianity: Clement did not hesitate to answer this question

[1] Clem., *Paed.*, 2,1–18   [2] Clem. *Quis dives salvetur*, 11–14

in a positive sense. The gnostics had acted similarly in various ways, but Clement was not at all inclined to modify the ethical requirements of religion in order to purchase the friendship of cultured people. Similarly, he gave away no ground to fanatical hatred of this world, nor to the cruder forms of asceticism which sometimes produced that hatred. Philosophers of the Stoic and Cynic schools had not seldom adopted drastic forms of denial of the world, and Clement had examples of this kind in mind. He affirmed the world and the forms of society as a field for the operation of Christian neighbourly love,[1] and felt it only desirable that the world, as an object of desire, should be banished from the soul: thereby, he came, as a Christian, to the same attitude as we have already noted in the most eminent Stoics. The only difference was that the coolness which formed the undertone of the latter's philosophy gave place to a warm-hearted love and a readiness to help in the service of God: and that difference was of critical importance. Thus the idea of a Christianization of the world was transferred from the spheres of apocalyptic fantasy, and brought into the region where historical forces were in operation.

The first two writings of the trilogy are exhortations, of which one is addressed to pagans and the other to Christians. The third was intended to be of didactic content dealing with Christian knowledge, and revelation. Clement had not the gifts adequate to writing such a work as this. He would have had to lay out his material quite logically, expound his leading ideas as to Christian doctrines in a systematic interconnection, and give a lucid account, down to the details. This he was unable to do, as he was not a systematic theologian. Proof of this is seen quite clearly in the two previous works. Splendid discussions of details, appropriate statements of the case, surprising connections, noble feelings voiced with masterly, rhetorical skill and applied to crucial points—he possessed all these accomplishments. But he was unable to bring together great masses of material in a perspicuous manner, and to arrange it with logical clarity. He delighted in the whole of the material which came his way, but he did not dominate it. For this reason, it was impossible for him to write the projected *Didaskalos*.

[1] *Ibid.*, 30–35

But in his case, necessity became a virtue. He was firmly convinced that, in the Holy Scriptures, the basic principle was carried through: the concealment of the final truths about divine things; and therefore that it was a duty of contemporary theologians to follow the same example, and to conceal the best and deepest things of knowledge, so that only the tireless searcher would be able to find them. The form of a learned compendium, such as the *Didaskalos* was intended to supply, was unsuitable for this purpose. For the extensive discussions which were to follow, he therefore chose the literary form of the *Stromateus*, i.e. "carpet", a form which was also more suited to his genius. The title was familiar amongst the sophists of the second period, and is similar to other titles usual at the time such as "The Meadow", "The Mountain of the Muses", "The Honeycomb", and the already mentioned "Banquets", and "Attic Nights". The idea conveyed was that the writing possessed a many-coloured content with most varied interests, and was presented in an attractive form and with charming variety. It was put forth in the light and entertaining style of a journalistic article, and the reader was intended to know that he was safe from the dryness of a pedantic scholar. All this was frequently the case, but, among the extant examples, some are not exactly to our taste.

This kind of writing was eminently suited, however, to Clement's literary style. It left him free from all the bonds of systematic treatment, and free to make effective use of his wide reading and his earnest type of thought, where and when and how it suited him; he passed from one thing to another, and, after long digressions, returned to the highway along which he was actually journeying. He brought confusion to a reader who, pen in hand, was endeavouring to trace the logical connection of his discussions; and he opened his heart only to one who had time to let him say all he had to say, who had patience to test the selection of material again and again, and who would search for the seeds of corn, the vein of gold, the nut kernels, and the glowing coals, which were cleverly concealed in the apparently confused medley of what Clement had to offer. His intention was to make it difficult for the reader to discover his deepest truths, and to frighten away the unelect from visiting the sacred region. He expressly declared that that was his duty, because he must not throw the pearls of Christian truth before swine.[1] When we remember that, in the preface to his *Attic Nights*, Gellius[2] had similarly warned off the unelect from entering the mysteries of his learned medley, we perceive that such forms of expression belong to the style of this kind of literature, and were not intended to be taken too seriously in themselves. In Clement's case, however, he was treating the matter theologically and in earnest. Of course, he did not really conceal any secrets, but simply mingled the theological ideas, which were very dear to his heart, with a thousand other things and then handed the whole over to the reader to search them out for himself.

Moreover, these fundamental tendencies come out clearly from the crowd of discussions, when we consider the work as a whole. First, there is his defence of philosophy against the objection that it was of no value to Christians, but only endangered faith. This is the subject with which his book commences, the thesis that philosophy was given by God, and granted to the Greeks by divine providence.[3] There was indeed only one truth, and that was to be identified with the revelation of the divine logos which took place through Christ: this truth could be grasped by faith without philosophy, indeed without any education. But, just as one and the same coin can be used, according to its economic purpose, both for paying a fare, or a tax, or rent, or a debt, or for buying an article, so truth could appear in the form of mathematics, or music, or philosophy. Hence, no individual case has room to exhibit all the functions of truth, any more than a single way of spending shows the whole function of a coinage; nevertheless the coin is good money, and, similarly, the truth is always genuine. Greek philosophy can therefore render important service to the Christian if he is anxious to use rational means to attain knowledge of the content of faith. Philosophy does not make Christian truth more true, but reveals the lack of content of the attacks directed against it on the part of sophists; it erects a protective wall for the vineyard of the Lord. The truth

---

[1] *Strom.* 1,18. 20 f. 55 f. 2,3,3–5. 4,4,1–3. 6,2,1. 7,110—111
[2] Gellius, *Noct. attic.*, Praef. 19–21   [3] *Strom.* 1,18,4. 20,2

comprised in faith is bread necessary for life: philosophy is the jam which renders it more tasteful, and makes eating a pleasure. Its clarity helps in passing on the truth, its dialectic is a protection against heretical invasion.[1] Either tacitly, or expressed in an endless variety of ways, this point of view is to be found in all parts of the *Stromateis*, and the practical goal becomes quite plain, viz. to repulse heretics, understood, essentially, as gnostics. An entire book, the third, discusses their views of marriage, and their attitude to martyrdom is attacked in detail in the following book.

Two other purposes are most closely connected with those just mentioned: in attacking gnosticism, Clement defended the Old Testament, and brought the familiar thesis before philosophers that their wisdom was really borrowed from the Old Testament prophets. It follows naturally that he explained the sacred books in an allegorical manner, such as was practised by the Church from the first; and Clement possessed earlier commentaries on the Scriptures which he occasionally consulted. His surviving writings therefore contain numerous extracts explaining separate passages of the Bible, including some from a commentary on Pss. 17–19,[2] and, in more than one passage of the *Stromateis*, it is possible to detect the influence of this traditional scholarship. The very gnostics whom he attacked, preferred to make use of allegorical exegesis, and in particular they applied it, as usual, to the New Testament. Consequently, Clement was compelled to fight them with their own weapons, and, against their incalculable, arbitrary exegesis, he set his criterion of sound exegetical method, viz. the "Church's canon", the agreement of Law and prophets, combined with the legacy handed down to us by the appearance of Christ on earth.[3] Hence, he approximated to the gnostic practice by recognizing allegory even for the New Testament: it was authoritatively justified by Christ's parables. Moreover, in the discussion in the gospels about the purpose of speaking in parables (Matt. 13: 10–17), he found the basis of his favourite thesis, viz. that it was necessary to conceal the secrets of Christian knowledge from profane eyes. He liked to argue that, in both pagan cults and pagan philosophers, the same attitude

---

[1] *Strom.* 1,97–100; cf. 6,156   [2] Clement, *Eclog.*, 42–64   [3] *Strom.* 6,5,3 12

of secrecy was maintained in regard to final knowledge about the divine.[1]

On almost every page, the *Stromateis* bears witness to his principles of scriptural exegesis: all his discussions are supported as much as possible by Bible passages, and allegory plays an important part in the process. Clement composed a special work of an exegetical character, the *Hypotyposes*; it still survived at the time of Photios,[2] who indignantly asserted that, in addition to many justifiable views, it expressed doubtful and indeed blasphemous opinions, of which he reproduces a few. Most of the heresies which he regrets, appear to be exaggerations of genuine Clementine speculation, and, possibly, the book should be ascribed to the author's early period. Nevertheless, on account of its theological defects, the work was consigned to oblivion by the orthodox of a later date. Only tiny fragments of the original text have survived, together with an abbreviated and expurgated Latin translation of the commentary on the General Epistles.[3] Here we find, on every page, that Clement is handing on numerous excerpts from the "presbyters", frequently in the form of anecdotes. In spite of occasional allegory, his exegesis was such that he brought out splendid religious teachings from the text; moreover, in so doing, he was frequently acting in a genuinely scientific manner. All this only confirms what the *Stromateis* abundantly testifies.

Nevertheless the *Stromateis*, at bottom and in main outline, describes the true gnostic—not the true gnosis. Clement readily accepts the slogan of the time and of his opponents, and is willing to become a gnostic himself and teach gnosticism, but a gnosticism proper to the Church[4] and drawn from the Bible. We have already seen that, in the *Paidagogos*, he attacked the essential distinction between psychics who are only acquainted with faith, and pneumatics who possess knowledge. All baptized Christians possess the Holy Spirit. Nevertheless there is a difference between them which, however, is not based upon material differences but on the degree of effort one chose to make for higher perfection, i.e. differences of moral strenuousness. A pagan turns to Christianity and gains faith,

[1] *Ibid.* 5,32–66   [2] *Supra*, p. 727   [3] *Clement* ed. Stählin 3,195–215   [4] *Strom.* 7,41,3.

i.e. a "concise knowledge of what is most necessary". But the believer strives for gnosis, i.e. "an assured and trustworthy account of what is contained in faith, an account which is built on faith as derived from Christ's teaching, and which leads to an irrefragable and rational kind of understanding". This gnosis reaches its perfection in love, and leads towards the final completion in the promised vision of God, and this makes us similar to the angels.[1]

As far as content goes, gnosis is nothing else than knowledge of God and, in Clement, has nothing to do with the fantastic speculations of a curiosity trying to find out details about all the secrets of the macrocosm or the microcosm. On the other hand and in particular, gnosticism is not rational comprehension of theological theses or exegetical truths. To possess gnosis implies an attitude to life, and to teach gnosis means to exhibit an example of Christian life. If philosophy had put the exemplar of the "sage" before mankind as the symbol of its work as educator, Clement worked out a new ideal of culture in the figure of a Christian gnostic, an ideal which he based on the Bible and philosophy. Gnosis was not a part of speculative philosophy or magical mysticism; rather it was ethics.

The Christian who had been conducted from an astonished admiration of nature to faith in God and His providence, would strive for a deeper understanding; and every step of progress increased his longing in as far as he "was successful in tasting the will of God". That experience raised him above the simple understanding of the plain believer, and he understood ever more perfectly what was the real meaning of the Ten Commandments in the deepest sense.[2] The prescriptions of the Law were completed by knowledge of the gospel.[3] It was not sufficient to keep one's self far from evil—that was a matter of course for everyone—but also to keep one's self free from motives too dominant among simple believers,[4] fear of punishment and hope of reward. The true gnostic had set aside all self-seeking and lived only in love for God as the clue to knowledge of Him. If it were possible to separate knowledge of God from eternal salvation and to permit the gnostic to choose between the two, he would choose knowledge of God without

[1] *Strom.* 7,55,1–7. 57,1–5. 149,8   [2] *Ibid.* 7,60,1–4   [3] *Ibid.* 4,130,4   [4] *Ibid.* 7,21,2. 69,8

hesitation.[1] In this final surrender to God, he attained insight into the deepest connections between the world and the nature of man, between man's virtues and vices; and thereby he comprehended the absolute truth to which all Greek philosophy provided only the preparatory schooling.[2]

His objective was "to become like God" (he is fond of using this phrase which was current among the other Platonists), i.e. to re-attain the image of God proper to the Garden of Eden, or "to become God": i.e., in accordance with Ps. 82: 6, become equal with the angels who behold God's face; in other words, to share in the vision of God for which the gnostics yearned.[3] This is brought into harmony with Pauline doctrine when we also find union with Christ mentioned as the goal, and when we learn that Christ as the image of God impresses his stamp on a gnostic in such a way that the latter now becomes the "third image" of God.[4] By means of his knowledge, the gnostic opens heaven wide, marches among all the spiritual beings and hosts of angels, and reaches God's throne: Christ as high priest conducts him thither, and he speaks with God.[5]

The estrangement from the world, which is connected with progressive gnosis, is not necessarily expressed in an outer asceticism; not even celibacy is a necessary form of self-denial, although it is to be recommended in accordance with the Apostolic saying (1 Cor. 7: 38): the important matter is that the soul should abandon the tangible, and turn to the theoretic, i.e., to the spiritual values and the divine essence.[6] The gnostic lives in an abiding fellowship with God, his life is a continual prayer, an endless festival day.[7] Moreover, the reflection of this blessedness shines back on the earthly brethren in lasting kindliness, friendliness, and benevolence; and these convert the gnostic into a helper in all cases of bodily or spiritual need. At home and among friends, at Church and in one's calling, in joy and in sorrow, he sets the example of a noble conduct of life,[8] and, in words reminiscent of Paul, Clement says[9]

[1] *Ibid.* 4,135 f.   [2] *Ibid.* 7,17,1–20,2
[3] *Ibid.* 2,131,2–133,3; cf. Plato, *Laws*, 4 p. 716d. *Theaet.* p. 176a Clement, *Strom.*, 4,149,8. 148,1. 7,13,2–4. 56,6–57,1
[4] *Strom.* 7,13,2. 16,6   [5] *Ibid.* 7,82,5. 13,2
[6] *Ibid.* 4,146,2–147,1. 7,36. 69,8–70,8   [7] *Ibid.* 7,35–40. 49,3–8
[8] *Ibid.* 7,16,4. 19,1. 36. 66,1. 67,4. 69 f.
[9] *Hypotyp.* on *I John* 2,3. p. 212. Stählin, *Strom.*, 7,82,7

"The gnostic discharges all the unconditionally necessary duties: although a man who does such works is not a gnostic on that account. Nevertheless the works follow on gnosis like one's own shadow." Outwardly the difference between a faith-Christian and a Christian gnostic is but small and scarcely noticeable. The decisive advance made by the gnostic consists in his inner attitude, and, finally, in the conquest of self-seeking by means of a pure love of God.

Thus Clement had found the road which, in its further reaches, led to a mysticism based on Johannine conceptions: but he did not take it. He adopted the Apologists' conception of the logos without developing it further. In the *Hypotyposes* expressions are to be found which suggest speculative formulas,[1] but they are incidental, and do not modify the general conceptions which meet our eyes in the principal extant works. In these, the logos is simply God in the act of revealing Himself; the logos has appeared in human form as Jesus Christ, and, even before his earthly life, had brought all truth to effect amongst Greeks and barbarians in the teachings of the philosophers and in the Old Testament; the logos was the principle of universal reason and, at the same time, the object of Christian faith. Clement gives us no theory of the relation of the logos to the Father or to the Holy Spirit, nor any doctrine in regard to the nature of Christ's humanity: Clement was not impelled by any necessity to attack these problems, because he had recognized more important matters which he then proceeded to discuss. He had no need to go into the other questions, because he did not acknowledge any real redemption by means of a sacramental transformation of mankind. The world of ideas as found in Irenæus remained altogether remote from him, as remote as the popular form of piety based on nature religion. He regarded redemption as belonging to the sphere of the ethical will, and the effective power was the logos as the leader, and as the giver of spiritual gifts.

Succeeding ages have not done justice to Clement, and the Church has paid him only small thanks for his outstanding contribution. It was his lot to be only the forerunner of a greater man who completely overshadowed him: the greater man was

---

[1] Clem., *Hypotyp.*, p. 210,5. 211,15 Stählin

Origen, the most outstanding teacher known in the Church of the east. For two centuries, the Church loved and honoured him fervently, but only to condemn him as a heretic a century later. When he was condemned by the Church, his influence was shattered, and, as a consequence it came about that, of the almost unbelievable multitude of his writings, only very few have survived in the original, and somewhat more in translation. His letters have disappeared, although these would have been most valuable for enabling us to understand his personality, but we must be grateful that at least a sketch of his life has been preserved in the sixth book of Eusebius's *History of the Church*.[1] Eusebius had collected the letters, and he was fond of making use of them along with other trustworthy sources.

It would appear that Origen was born A.D. 185; he was the eldest son in a large and probably prosperous Christian family; he was carefully educated, and, at an early date, showed uncommon gifts. When his father, Leonidas, was imprisoned during Severus's persecution, A.D. 202, the son, who was scarcely a full-grown man, conceived a passionate desire for martyrdom. His mother, in her concern, hid his clothes so that he could not leave the house. All he could do was to write and tell his father what she had done; he then exhorted him bravely to confess himself a Christian. Leonidas died as a Roman citizen, for he was executed by the sword: his possessions were confiscated. Thereupon an eminent lady took care of the highly gifted youth, and as a consequence he entered a house which vividly reflected the religious spirituality of the city. The lady had adopted as son, a gnostic named Paul who had been born in Antioch, who, on account of his recognized and outstanding talents, had many attentive hearers, whether gnostic or orthodox. Contact with this person greatly influenced Origen; at any rate he began to show himself actively opposed to what gnosticism stood for.

His excellent academic education now availed him for tutorial purposes, and he soon became financially independent. Since the Christian catechumen school had been broken up under pressure of the persecution, he acceded to the request of pagans who were anxious to learn, and gave instruction

---

[1] Eus., *H.E.*, 6,1–8,6. 14,10–19,19. 23,1–2. 23,4–33. 36 f. 39,5. 7,1

in Christianity. He continued this work in spite of all hostile attacks, and all threats on the part of the police, and enjoyed increasing success. The school, conducted by the youth of scarcely eighteen years, was officially recognized by the bishop, and soon attended by such numbers that he was no longer in a position to continue both to give instruction in Christianity and to conduct the secular courses by which hitherto he had made his living. He abandoned the latter lectures and sold the library, which it had given him much pleasure to collect, in exchange for a current income of four obols a day, i.e. one denarius per week.[1] That was literally starvation pay, and during the next years Origen actually lived a life of strictest asceticism, carrying it through to the last extremes of need in regard to food and clothing, and by allowing himself insufficient sleep. This "philosophy" of his made a deep impression and gained imitators; it also converted educated pagans, who regarded Origen as combining the ideal of Cynicism with a living faith in God. Moreover Eusebius, our informant,[2] records, with justifiable pride, that six martyrs belonged to this stern school of the young teacher, martyrs who testified to their faith with their life. During this period of thorough-going asceticism, Origen followed literally the saying in Matt. 19: 12 and emasculated himself, an act which, in spite of all his care, did not remain secret in the end. Bishop Demetrius forgave him at the time but did not forget.

Eusebius also asserts that Origen had been a disciple of Clement who, on his part, had followed Pantainos as leader of the catechumen school. Whether the relationship of teacher and pupil, asserted by Eusebius, ever really existed is, however, by no means certain.[3] In spite of all theological similarities Origen never mentions Clement, not even in passages where one might expect it. Origen may have attended Clement's lectures but did not enter into closer relationship with him. On the other hand, he remembered Pantainos with respect, and mentioned Ammonios Sakkas as his teacher in philosophy.[4]

We must not regard the famous "catechumen school" in any

---

[1] *Supra*, p. 22, and Wilcken, *Grundzüge*, 1, 1, LXVI   [2] Eus., *H.E.*, 6,4
[3] J. Munck, *Unters. über Klemens*, 224 f. Alexander of Jerusalem in Eus., *H.E.*, 6,14,9
[4] *Origen* in Eus., *H.E.*, 6,19,13 (cf. 19,5 f.)

way as a formally organized, teaching institution with appointed professors, but rather as voluntary lectures given by men who felt themselves called to do so, and who were willing to introduce others into the secrets of Christianity without being paid in cash. If the Church liked their work they would be officially recognized and recommended by the bishop. Origen was the first to begin something in the nature of an organization, in as far as he divided up the instruction, and handed over the introductory course to his friend Heraklas,[1] in order that he might be able to deal with the increasing crowds of pupils. Origen had made the acquaintance of Heraklas at the lectures of Ammonios, lectures which he had already been attending for five years when Origen first came. Ammonios, who had developed from a porter into a philosopher, dominated men's minds at that time with his doctrine based on Plato; and he founded a school which produced the two greatest thinkers of late Greek antiquity: Origen the Christian and Plotinus the classical exponent of Neoplatonism.

Origen was the first Christian of whom any record has survived that he had a close personal contact with the known head of a philosophical school, and the philosophers did not overlook the matter. Porphyry records that as a young man he had met the famous Origen, the pupil of Ammonios; that Ammonios had abandoned the Christianity inherited from his parents; that Origen, although a Christian in his mode of life, became a Greek in his doctrine about God and material things; and that his studies were continually applied to Plato, the Neoplatonists, and the Pythagoreans.[2] Origen's writings confirm these notices. His studies under Ammonios were actually of the greatest importance to him because they gave him a scholarly knowledge of the methods, and the entire mode of feeling and thought, which passed as modern learning at the beginning of the third century. A good idea of this is given by an excerpt which has fortunately been preserved from the Platonizing dogmatics of Albinos,[3] an excerpt in the form of a

---

[1] Eus., *H.E.*, 6,15   [2] Porphyry in Eus., *H.E.*, 6,19,5–8
[3] Albinos, *Eisagoge in Plato*, *opera*, ed. C. F. Hermann, 6,152–189. Also Hal Koch, *Pronoia u. Paideusis*, p. 243–68

simple compendium and of systematic definitions; it shows how
Plato was understood in the Antonine period. If, in addition,
we take note of scattered records in regard to Numenios, "the
Neopythagorean", a Syrian of Apamea, we shall find a valuable
supplement on the religious side. This last had been so influenced by Jewish philosophy of religion, probably by Philo in
the first instance, that he even found it possible to accept and
teach the thesis that Plato was a "Moses speaking Attic Greek".
This thesis greatly influenced Christian thought.[1]

As early as Plutarch, it is possible to detect most of the
characteristic signs of this "middle Platonism": the increased
elevation of God above the present world and its material
character, and, in connexion therewith, an inclination to
fantastic developments of the conceptions of daemonic intermediate beings, conceptions already present in Plato; detailed
discussion of the problem of divine providence and divine
righteousness; the assertion of the immortality and personal
responsibility of the soul; the doctrine of its share in the divine
being, and occasional traces of a mystical tendency. Ethics are
developed under Platonic influences: "to become as similar as
possible to God." Allegorical exegesis was frequently employed
to support one's own philosophical ideas by Plato's words, and
especially by religious myths and sayings of poets and thinkers
of the earlier ages. Side by side with every effort made to
develop a pure, Platonic tradition, the methods and the
doctrinal principles of Aristotelians and Stoics were adopted
indifferently, because these schools were felt to be on the
same side against the negatives of the Sceptics and the atheism
of Epicurus. We have already noted that the Apologists were
bound by this type of ideas. Thanks to his higher education,
Clement was strongly under the same influence and he increased it by a diligent study of Plato. Nevertheless, Origen
was the first to enter into the genuine tradition of the Platonic
school, and both his intake and his output fully reflect the
Platonic heritage which was alive in his day, and which was
of increasing influence.[2]

The fame of Origen, as a scholar who was mastering all

---

[1] Clement, *Strom.*, 1,150,4. Eus., *Praep. ev.*, 11,10,14 (7)
[2] Hal Koch, *op. cit.*, pp. 163–304

departments of learning, spread far and wide, and attracted even heretics and pagan philosophers to the scene of his labours. The conversion of Ambrosius, a Valentinian, had some personal importance for him. Ambrosius was a wealthy man and possessed means to enable Origen, whom he honoured enthusiastically, to enter on literary activity without any essential change of his methods of work. To the scholars round about Alexandria the writing of books was by no means a natural consequence of their calling: their duty was to deliver oral lectures, and men like Ammonias Sakkas, Plotinus, and Epictetus, left no writings of their own. This state of affairs was sanctified by the classical instance of Socrates, and it is only due to the subsequent writings of Arrian and Porphyry that we have any detailed information in regard to the teachings of Epictetus and of Plotinus. Ambrosius placed seven or more stenographers, writing in rotation, in Origen's lecture room. His lectures were thus given written form, and eventually published as books.[1] Ambrosius was in fact successful in giving permanence to Origen's life-work in an almost unbelievable number of writings.

Before we proceed to discuss them, however, let us first take note of the further details of his outer life as recorded in Eusebius. During the time of pope Zephyrinus, he was in Rome for a short stay, and afterwards visited the imperial governor of Arabia at the latter's request. The fearful massacres in Alexandria, ordered in his pathological conceit by Caracalla in A.D. 215, caused Origen to leave the city. He went to Cæsarea, and, at the request of Theoktistos, bishop of the city, and of Alexander, bishop of Jerusalem, he gave Biblical lectures for the benefit of the Church. This leaving of the sphere of scholarship and entering into that of church life was, however, displeasing to the bishop of Alexandria, who advised him urgently to return home at once. Origen obeyed.

Fifteen years later, when he touched at Cæsarea while on a journey to Greece, his two episcopal friends there ordained him as presbyter. Such a consecration in a strange diocese was unusual, and the ordination of a eunuch offended widespread opinions. At an Alexandrian synod, Demetrius refused to

[1] Eus., *H.E.*, 6,18,1. 23,1 f.

recognize his status as presbyter, and expelled him from the city. The office of teacher was taken from him and transferred to his colleague, Heraklas, who shortly afterwards became Demetrius's successor in the diocese. Origen removed in the year 230–31 to Cæsarea, where he continued his customary teaching work with undiminished success.[1] From that centre, he made many journeys, and on two occasions was invited to Arabia as theological arbitrator. Here he held a debate with Beryllos, bishop of Bostra, who was inclined to Monarchianism, and was successful in "leading him back to the sound views which he had formerly held". When the persecution broke out under Decius the fatal hour struck in which Origen, the teacher and panegyrist of martyrdom, was to make his own confession. He was cruelly tortured, and, in letters which he wrote from prison, but which are not extant, he showed his unquenchable courage and the soul-stirring witness which he bore. Every attempt was made to avoid killing such a celebrated person; but his physical strength failed, and soon afterwards, in A.D. 253–54, Origen died at Tyre at the age of 69. His grave was pointed out to visitors there for many years afterwards.[2]

Origen's literary remains were taken care of by admiring friends from an early date. We have already spoken of Ambrosius. Towards the end of the century, Pamphilus the presbyter, who had been a teacher at the school in Cæsarea, collected Origen's writings from all quarters, and copied them out with his own hand. His zeal preserved the lists found in Eusebius and Jerome, in regard to the works available in Cæsarea.[3] In every case, the foremost position is occupied by the scriptural commentaries, and these deal with all the books of the Old and New Testaments; they are partly in the form of scholarly exegesis splendidly planned, partly in the form of homilies, or rather Bible studies, in the church at Cæsarea— all these works having been done in the last nine years of his life.[4] The original text is extant of parts of the commentaries on Matthew and on John, together with sermons on the witch

---

[1] Eus., *H.E.*, 6,14,10. 19,15–19. 23–24. 26; cf. Photios, *Bibl. Cod.*, 118
[2] Eus., *H.E.*, 6,33,1–3. 37. 39,5. 7,1 (also Schwartz, vol. 3,38) Photios, *Cod.*, 118; Jer., *vir inl.*, 45; and Holl on Epiphan., *haer.*, 64,3,3
[3] Eus., *H.E.*, 6,24. 28. 32. Jerome, *Vir. inl.*, 75; *Epist.* 33. 34,1
[4] Eus., *H.E.*, 36,1

of Endor, and fragments on Jeremiah: to these must be added numerous small fragments relative to all the Biblical books in the Byzantine symposium known as the Catenæ. Then we must take account of the Latin translations made by Rufinus, who laboured about A.D. 400, but who unfortunately did not hesitate to transform and to "purify" numerous series of sermons on the Old Testament, commentaries on the Song of Songs and on Romans, all in Latin; Jerome has preserved for us a Latin translation of selected homilies on Luke. Origen's defence of Christianity against the attacks of Celsus the Platonist is extant complete in eight books: like the commentary on Matthew, the work was written in the last period of Origen's life.[1] The ten books of the *Stromateis*, now lost, were written in the Alexandrian period, and the title shows that he intended the work to be parallel to that of Clement. "In this work, he compared the teachings of Christians and philosophers with one another, and demonstrated all the principles of our religion from Plato, Aristotle, Numenios, and Cornutus."[2]

On the other hand, the main work of the earlier period, consisting of four books of "bases" (*Peri Archōn*), has been preserved fairly completely. Rufinus translated the whole, and expurgated dubious sayings here and there: but Jerome, his critic, put his finger on these corrections and wrote to a friend in regard to all the passages felt to be objectionable.[3] Hence it is possible to compare both texts, and to restore the sense intended by Origen. Finally large portions of the third and fourth books have been preserved in the original form. This work was the first Christian system of theology, the first bold attempt to combine Christian pronouncements about God, the world, and man, in a closely-knit, and strictly logical, system of doctrine, and it stands in majestic isolation in the history of the early Church. No theologian of the east, and none of the west, dared to attempt again this immense task. Their own scholarship was devoted to single issues, and their compositions were not more learned than was necessary for instruction appropriate to catechumens: that is the case also in

---

[1] Eus., *H.E.*, 6,36,2   [2] Jerome, *Epist.*, 70,4,3; Eus., *H.E.*, 6,24,3
[3] Jerome, *Epist.*, 124; cf. Koetschau in his edition of Origen's *de princ*. pp. lxxxviii ff.

regard to Theodoret's fifth book of *Fables of the Heretics* and
Augustine's book on Christian doctrine. John of Damascus
was the first to attempt something more ambitious than this
in his *Source of Knowledge*, and in fact he was successful: it is a
collection of the doctrinal traditions as recognized by the Greek
Church, *c.* A.D. 750, and is systematically arranged and
comprehensive, a learned museum, but not an organism born
of the stress of life.

For our purpose, we may disregard Origen's smaller writings,
but one more work must be mentioned which shows his system-
atizing cast of mind, and is of the highest significance for
understanding his methods, viz. his great work on the Bible.
When studying the Old Testament, Origen even took account
of Jewish exegesis, and sought the advice of Jewish scholars;
probably also he attempted to learn Hebrew. In this, however,
he scarcely went beyond the alphabet, since his writings
reveal no real knowledge of the language.[1] Hence he remained
uncertain whenever the wording or meaning of the original
text or its relation to the Church's translation of the Septuagint was questionable; the uncertainty was particularly great
in discussions with the Jews. He discovered another means of
approaching more closely to the original text, and compelling it
to disclose the final secrets of divine revelation. He began to
assemble all the extant Greek translations of the Old Testament,
and, by diligent search, he was successful in obtaining not only
the translations of Aquila, Symmachos, and Theodotion, which
were in widespread use, but also in discovering two other
translations of the Psalms by unknown authors. At this point
he undertook an immense task, which indeed could only be
carried out by means of Ambrosius's wealth. Using six parallel
columns, he wrote side by side: the Hebrew original text in
Hebrew, i.e. unvocalized, characters, the Hebrew original text
in Greek letters in order to fix the pronunciation, and then he
gave a column each to the translations of Aquila, Symmachos,
the Septuagint, and Theodotion. The lines were quite short: in
the Hebrew text, as a rule, the words stood under one another

---

[1] Harnack, *D. kirchengesch. Ertrag d. exeg. Arbeiten des Orig.*, 1,22–30 (*Texte u.
Unters.* 42,3). Wutz, *Onomastica sacra*, 1,36 (*Texte ;. Unters.* 41). Eus., *H.E.*.
6,16,1. Origen, *epist. ad Afric.*, 7 (17,28 Lo.); *In psalt.* (11,352 Lo.); *de princ.*
1,3,4. 4,3,14. Jerome, *adv. Rufin.*, 1,13

in a column, and the lines of the translations were arranged correspondingly: it was possible to tell at a glance how each translator had reproduced the Hebrew word. Owing to the six columns, it was called The *Hexapla*, i.e. the six-fold Bible, but in the Psalms, other columns were added for a fifth, sixth, and, in parts indeed, a seventh translation.

The whole must have been a gigantic work consisting of several dozen great folios, and it is scarcely possible that there can have been more than a single copy of the whole. Only in regard to isolated parts were copies made of selected groups of columns, and a few remains of such manuscripts have survived. For the general use of scholars, Origen edited, and the library at Cæsarea published, special editions of the text of the Septuagint, editions which contained in the margin Origen's most important results of the comparison of parallels. The verses and words lacking in the original Hebrew text were indicated by a mark (*obelos* ÷). If on the other hand the LXX omitted portions of the text which were present in the Hebrew, this was to be found in the text in its place after another translation, but indicated by a preceding star (*asteriskos* *). In addition, the most important variations found in Aquila, Symmachos, and Theodotion were written in the margin at the appropriate places, so that the student quickly obtained a clear oversight of the facts. At a later date, Pamphilus, whom we have already mentioned, and his friend Eusebius were zealous in publishing these "hexapla editions" of the LXX, and libraries still preserve numerous manuscripts based on such copies.[1] Origen's gigantic number of writings must not be permitted to hide it from us that his real life's work did not consist of writing, but of oral instruction, i.e., that his books were only notes, taken down by others, of his spoken teaching. Every estimate of his personality must start with this fact. It is a very fortunate matter that we possess a detailed description of his way of teaching and of its methodological development. The description is to be found in a speech by a grateful pupil, Gregory, afterwards bishop of Neocæsarea in Pontus, a speech which he delivered before his fellow students and their teacher, when departing from the

[1] H. B. Swete, *An Introduction to the O.T. in Gk.*, 3rd edit., and thereon *Götting. Gel. Anzeigen*, 1902, 329–38

school at Cæsarea.[1] Here we find, admittedly, mighty waves
of rhetoric occasioned by his grateful thanks and genuine
emotion. Nevertheless, we can see the facts in all desirable
clarity. A regular *Protreptikos* to philosophy as the highest art
formed the commencement of study, an art which, alone and
in itself, could make the student a genuine thinker, and which
alone rendered possible the true service of God. It is significant
that Gregory acknowledges that, at first, he was rebellious,
but that he was not only overcome by the compelling arguments, but also bound in unbreakable chains by the charm and
friendliness of the great teacher. Then a preliminary course of
instruction began which employed the Socratic method in
examining the mental quality and practical ability of each
individual, and which, by continual training in the art of
thinking, rendered him apt for academic education. This
latter began with logic and dialectic, followed by natural
science with geometry and astrology. The crown of the building
erected on this foundation consisted of ethics and theology.
The study of ethics was by no means confined to a merely
rational discussion of moral problems; rather it consisted
essentially in the discipline of the soul for the practical realization of philosophic virtue—and, in this very respect again,
Origen appeared as an illuminating example because his own
way of life corresponded perfectly with the words of his
teaching.

The study of theology began with an extended review of all
accessible philosophers and poets. Their opinions about the
godhead were described, compared with one another, and
examined for their content of truth; only the atheistic writers
were excluded from the review as useless, indeed hurtful. He
taught his listeners, however, to discover the final truth in the
place where God spoke through His prophets in the Holy
Scriptures. He was a true exponent of Scripture, whether he was
explaining difficult passages or finding a deep meaning in
simple words, because he was filled with the same divine spirit
as had spoken in the prophets. Thus all wisdom came to a
climax in the knowledge of God, and this was based on the Bible.

[1] *Gregorios Thaumaturgos' Dankrede*, ed. by P. Koetschau (G. Krügers Sammlung
9); thereon A. Brinkmann in *Rhein. Museum N.F.* 56,55–76

The sketch is drawn with obvious faithfulness: the system of instruction corresponded to the traditions of philosophic schools with a modern tendency, and depicts Origen's theological quality in a manner confirmed by his writings. The intermingling of philosophy and the Bible gave rise to the system which is described in detail in the work *Peri Archōn* which Origen had written in early manhood. The title is probably intentionally ambiguous as it can be translated either "on basic principless" or "on primordial matters". He placed the greatest importance on finding Scriptural references for all the doctrinal principles he put forward, and he was successful because the forms of thought for which he sought were actually present in high degree in the late Jewish world as well as in that of the New Testament, and they only required putting together systematically. But the total picture of the constitution of the universe, a picture into which he interwove the Biblical elements, arose from the philosophy of "middle" Platonism.

In so doing, Origen was the first to accomplish the task that all the later, systematic theologians set themselves to do, viz. to present a Christian view of the world in harmony with the educated opinion of the era. Origen's system was impressively complete, and gave a clear insight into the leading principles. His foundations were the conceptions, familiar from the days of the apologists, in regard to God, the logos, providence, and freedom of the will as found in spiritual beings: the eternal drama of the world was the consequence of their interaction. God, the final unity, the original source of all existence, was incomprehensible and inconceivable to human thought alone: it was only possible for us to make negative or indirect pronouncements about Him, apart from recognizing His omnipotence. Of these pronouncements the first, and, for Origen, the most important, was the genuinely Platonic assertion of His incorporeality: an assertion which contradicted not only Stoic views, but also the vulgar ideas of the laity.[1] But the positive understanding that God was the final cause of all creation was transformed into the striking view of the absolute goodness of God, who created living things because He wished to manifest goodness to them. Moreover, since God's will was

[1] *de princ.* 1,1,1–5; cf. Hal Koch, *op. cit.* 20 f.

part of His being and therefore eternal, it followed of necessity that the created world was eternal.[1]

A peculiarity of Origen's mode of thought has now become clear, and it is indispensable for understanding his system. He taught that the conception of time was not applicable to God or the divine, and that, in addition to the horizontal division of phenomena in a temporal sequence, there was a vertical division which took account of a series of causes and effects apart from the conception of time.[2] Hence the Son of God was eternally begotten by the Father just as radiance is always produced by a light—a Platonist would say as an eternally necessary effect of the eternal cause, but Origen preferred to use Biblical language in accordance with Heb. 1: 3. The Son was therefore of the same nature as the Father, because he was born of God and not created out of nothingness.[3] He proceeded from the Father without diminishing the Father's essence, in the way that will is produced by the Spirit: but the Son was an independent person, and could be described as a "second God" subordinate to the Father.[4] Moreover, the Son was the "mediator" between God and the world. In the first place, He was mediator as regards the world, since all things were created by Him. But He was also mediator in the opposite sense, as it was only through Him that knowledge of the Father was possible to created beings: only to the extent that we know the Son do we know God, and our knowledge is therefore always merely relative, and can never be absolute.[5]

Whereas the conception of a logos who was also the Son corresponded to the current Platonic view of the world, knowledge of the third divine person, the Holy Spirit, could only be obtained from the Bible. Origen laid emphasis on this point, and then began to weave into his system a teaching appropriate to the words of Scripture. The Spirit proceeded from the Son as the Son from the Father, and so constituted the third stage in the unfoldings of the godhead. The activity of the Father comprehended the whole, that of the Son was limited to rational beings, the Holy Spirit came to effect only in the saints.

[1] de princ. 4,4,8. 1,2,10. 1,4,3. p. 65 with footnote   [2] Cf. de princ. 1,2,2. p. 29,14
[3] de princ. 1,2,4–7. p. 33 with footnote on p. 37   [4] c. Cels. 5,39. 7,57
[5] de princ. 1,2. 6 f. 13. pp. 35–37. 46 and footnote

All three persons, however, constituted the one incorporeal Godhead as distinct from the created world.[1] It is clear that Origen was endeavouring consciously to give a systematic foundation to the doctrine held by the Church, a foundation which cannot, however, be brought into organic connection with that doctrine.

On the other hand, an immediate and illuminating consequence, flowing from the fundamental, divine property of goodness and benevolence, was the necessity of creating a universe as the object of the divine love. The universe consisted, it is true, of an inconceivably large, but nevertheless not infinite, number of rational beings, the kernel of whose existence was constituted by the fact that they shared the eternal nature of the divine light. Thus, at bottom, despite all the difference between creature and creator, their nature was "of one essence" (*homoousioi*) with the godhead; in other words, it was related in a certain sense to God, and hence was immortal.[2] On this point, Origen shared the gnostic view about the divine spark in man. Nevertheless, all men had free will, and accordingly they could shape their own course of life. The result was the manifold variety of the world, with all its contradictions and degrees of development. The providence of God maintained, in perfect order and balanced equilibrium, the interaction of the whole which man could not conceive nor comprehend; and, in spite of unconditional freedom of the will in the individual, God carried out His universal plan for training everyone in preparation for returning to the Father's house. This standpoint enabled Origen to speak of God's logos as the soul of the world,[3] just as did the philosophers.

The freedom of the will was made the excuse by all created beings to turn aside from God, and to reach out towards what was anti-godly, i.e., evil, and this, again,[4] was also the "non-existent". This fall into sin was of smaller or greater degree, and decided their future fate. By their very nature, their original beauty consisted of the divine reason, *nous*. Now their fervour cooled; they became "souls"—*psyche* meaning soul, a

---

[1] *Op. cit.*, 1,3,1. 5. 8. p. 55 with footnote
[2] *de princ.* 2,9,1. 4,4,9 pp. 362 ff. with footnote
[3] *Ibid.* 2,1,3   [4] *Ibid.* 2,9,2. p. 166,2; in *John* 2.13,94 p. 69 6

word which Origen derived from *psychein,* to cool.[1] They
received bodies consisting of matter, and the further the cooling
went which estranged them from God, i.e. the more their own
will came into opposition with God, the grosser became the
material and the more repugnant the bodily form. From the
refulgent spheres of the heavenly stars, through the æthereal
figures of the spiritual realm, to mankind on earth in their
varied races and multitudinous circumstances, finally down to
the daemons and devils of the underworld, we see or guess the
manifold variety of bodily forms. On the other hand, according
to its degree of moral development, an individual soul either
makes its way upward to finer shapes, or is condemned to
punishment even in an animal body. For redeemed inhabitants
of hell, our earth is a heaven, but to beings who have fallen
from heaven it must appear a hell. Origen succeeded in
providing a Biblical basis for this Platonic and Pythagorean
doctrine of metempsychosis.[2]

The ascent and descent made by human souls was not due to
the play of blind chance, no matter how often it might appear
like it from the earthly point of view; but was governed throughout by God's providence, and moved towards a definite goal.
That could not happen compulsorily, because souls were by
nature free. Hence God chose the method of training by
teaching, and, since the inmost kernel of all rational beings was
divine, He was assured of the final effectiveness of His appeal
to their original ethical goodness. Wherever God's might and
providence became visible in the world-process and in the
laws of nature, the logos called the human soul to recognize
God, and, to a large extent, the philosophers had obeyed this
call. Nevertheless, all including Plato, who was the best amongst
them, had come to a halt before the last gate. None had shaken
off the remnants of polytheism, and confessed a pure worship
of God.[3] Nor were all combined able to deliver men from their
sins, and to convert them to a virtuous life: and that is what was
important in the end.[4] On the other hand, God had granted the
Jewish race a special revelation, in as far as he trained them by

[1] *de princ.* 2,8,3 p. 157 with footnote
[2] *Ibid.* 1,4,1 (p. 64 with footnote). 1,7,1. 1,8,4 (pp. 102 ff. with footnote). 2,9,3.
3,5,4. 4,3,11 (pp. 273 ff., p. 339 with footnote)
[3] *Contra Celsum* 6,3–5. *de princ.* 4,1,1   [4] *c. Cels.* 3,60 f.

the legal prescriptions of Moses and the preaching of the prophets, and placed before their eyes prophecies which promised bliss. At the same time, the writings of these men, as brought together in the Old Testament, concealed a deeper sense, which, though occasionally glimpsed at an earlier date, became increasingly plain to the student who was a seeker after God, and who lived in days when prophecy had been fulfilled.[1]

The incarnation of the logos was the decisive act in the redemption of groaning creatures (cf. Rom. 8: 22). The Son of God appeared on earth by uniting Himself with a human soul, which, as distinct from all others, never swerved in its complete self-giving to God. This soul was the mediating link between the godhead and the corporeal nature of mankind, and its unchangeable harmony with the divine will brought about the unity of the person of the God-man. In this union with the logos, however, the humanity of Jesus became ever more divine, until, after the Resurrection, the material corporeality disappeared, and the soul became one with the logos in a manner which we are not able to imagine. Thus the way was opened up, along which all rational creatures, including mankind in particular, would find redemption. Christians were men whose souls were possessed by the same pure love of God, as the soul of their Master; and who, filled by the same power of the logos, strove to attain the same dematerialization and deification as had been actualized in Christ: new companies of Christs were continually being formed, and they followed the one Christ from this earth to heaven.[2]

It is clear that, according to this view, no real soteriological significance can be ascribed to Christ's death on the cross; and, as a matter of fact, Origen often explicitly declares that, for perfect Christians, only the logos, who imparted knowledge, was relevant. At this point, however, he made use of an idea familiar from the time of Clement, an idea in which a difference was concealed between a lower but thoroughly legitimate stage of faith, as found in simple members of the Church on the one hand, and, on the other, the knowledge possessed by those

---

[1] *Ibid.* 5,31. 7,7. *de princ.* 4,3,9–14

[2] *de princ.* 2,6,3; *in Matt. comm. ser.* 33 p. 61,7. *Hom. in Jer.* 15,6 p. 130,15 ff.; *c. Cels.* 3,41 p. 237,7 ff.; *de princ.* 2,3,3 p. 117. 3,5,6 p. 277; *c. Cels.* 6,79 p. 150

who had reached an advanced stage. Sinners required the physician. But it was plain that, when Jesus was crucified, He had defeated the daemons. This victory helped the man who lingered at the stage of naïve faith, because it gave him the tangible certainty of a newly-gained salvation and a real forgiveness of sins;[1] the reason was in the vicarious sacrificial death of the Lord for the sins of the world, and particularly in His outwitting of the devil. In this way, Origen introduced the historical event and its Biblical presentation into his system, without transforming the main outline of the latter. He used this device ever and again, both in large matters and in detail. He also made room for the sacraments—but the path he took always led unerringly towards the goal of deification through the logos. No matter how frequently or profoundly he examined ecclesiastical doctrines, Biblical questions, and philosophical problems, he did it as a scholar with clear understanding, calm judgment, and objective interest.

Most deeply of all, however, there glowed a fire, like the yearning of a man who could no longer tolerate a mediocre life confined to the valleys, but who was irresistibly drawn towards the pure and calm stillness of the snow-capped mountain-tops, where one forgets to look at the earth, but stretches one's hands towards the stars. Thus the present earth, the present time, the present world, sank away from Origen the thinker. The man who had gained Christ was freed from matter and sin; he had no need to fear that, after death, he would fall into the pains of Hell, premonitions of which already burned in his conscience. He would rise again out of the grave with a spiritual body composed of heavenly glory, and a soul fired by the logos, a soul which thirsted for ever higher knowledge. A "heavenly Jerusalem" was granted to such persons even on the present earth, a "school for souls" where they would comprehend the connection of all earthly things: the enigma of mankind, his soul, and his *nous*, would be solved there, and men would understand the work of the spirit, and penetrate into the secrets of the Mosaic law. Moreover, the secret powers of medicinal plants would become plain to them, as plain as the

[1] *c. Cels.* 3,62 p. 256,8; *comm. in John* 1,107. 124 pp. 23, 25. Hal Koch. *op. cit.*, 87 f.

authority of the fallen angels to seduce mankind. What seemed like coincidence here on earth would appear as a just decree of divine providence, and men would learn how God numbered the hairs of every human head, and cared for the two sparrows which cost only a farthing, as in the gospel.

The soul did not remain here below. It mounted into the upper air, and searched out the secrets thereof. Then the heavens opened before it, and it moved towards Jesus by passing from sphere to sphere. The nature of the stars, their constellations, their paths, and the heavenly equilibrium, now became open to its gaze. The way led higher up into the regions of the invisible: the soul became more and more spiritualized, and grew to perfect knowledge until at last it was no longer soul, but wholly *nous* and spirit, and was able to behold "face to face", the world of intelligible being and essence. That was the way towards likeness to God which was dreamed of by philosophers as the highest good, but granted to Christians in order that they might rise from their present bodily condition, and reach pure *nous*, the "glory of the sons of God when God is all in all", for purified beings no longer feel or conceive anything else than God alone.[1]

Only a few elect souls reach this, the highest goal. The millions on earth struggle with error and evil, and the spirits in Hell strive against God. But since all formerly proceeded from God, none can finally be abandoned by God. His call will sound ever anew in their ears; they will trace His guidance in their lives, feel His parental hand in their suffering and need, a hand which will not abandon even the last creatures of all in the deepest regions of Hell. One after the other will be seized, accept conversion, mount slowly upwards joined by increasing numbers, and, after inconceivable periods of time, the day will come when none will remain outside, and when even the prince of Hell will return to God.[2] Then the "return of the whole" will be completed, the purpose and meaning of the historical process fulfilled, death abolished, and Christ will place everything, in himself and with himself, at God's feet "in order that God might be all in all".

Even yet Origen was not content: his eye sought to see

[1] *de princ.* 2,10,4. 11,3–7. 3,6,1. 3   [2] *Ibid.* 1,6,3 p. 83 with footnote

eternity beyond the mere infinitude of this world and its
temporality. The present course of history, from the first Fall
of man through the immense periods of time to the return home
of the lost, and until the blessed final perfection, was nevertheless only one event among many, one period of the universe
which had been preceded by others, and would be similarly
followed. The will of individual creatures remained eternally
free, and always lured to another Fall, and this automatically
brought about the further consequences, and introduced a new
period of decline towards what was material. But the love of
God also remained eternal, and gave rise in Him to merciful
compassion, and thus to watching over and educating the
world. Once more there would arise the duel between the
obstinacy of the creature and the redemptive work of the logos,
until even this drama reached its conclusion, and God once
more gathered all to Himself, for nothing could be eternally
lost.[1] Thus Origen the seer sees, in the light of eternity, the
endless series of God's worlds.

It is clear that this "system" presents a Christian gnosticism
approximating to perfection, and that, like Clement, it was
influenced by gnostic views outside the Church. It is also clear
that it made large use of material and forms of thought current
in contemporary philosophy. Nevertheless it would be a
grievous mistake to regard Origen as a philosopher with a
purely intellectual orientation. The philosophers of the time
were only seldom men of pure intellect; the gnostics were never
of that kind, and Origen felt himself to be a Christian, and
philosophy was, to him, only a means to that end. In his great
apology against Celsus the Platonist, he made quite plain how
much he had in common with the philosophy of his opponent—
no small amount[2]—and he showed where the important
differences were to be found: that was the crucial matter to
him. The differences were determined by his adherence to the
Bible and to the doctrine of the Church, and by the manner
of his life as thus determined for him.

Moreover, it must be granted that the simple faith, found in
popular and crude forms in the Church, was often abandoned,

[1] *de princ.* 3,5,3–5 pp. 273–76 with footnote
[2] A. Miura-Stange, *Celsus u. Origenes (Beih. z. ZNW.,* no. 4, 1926)

and the only conception of Christianity that remained alive, was one which developed into gnosticism. This corresponded in other respects, however, to Origen's view of the relation between faith and knowledge. To him, the superiority of the completely spiritualized form of his religion was so obvious that he rarely discussed the subject.[1] He regarded faith by no means as a simple antithesis to knowledge. He used to speak also of a "genuine faith" which was a gift of God's grace, which grasped the truth with a more certain judgment, and which understood the deeper sense placed within the Bible by the Holy Spirit.[2] Even Gregory, in his farewell speech, stressed the fact that all the scholarly labour of Origen's school issued in Bible study, a pronouncement confirmed by Origen's life's work as seen in the multitude of commentaries, homilies, and scholia. Even the last book of the *Peri Archōn* contains theoretic discussions on the necessity of allegorical methods.

Anyone who seeks to understand Origen's heart must watch him as a Bible student. It was in the Bible and here alone, that the way to knowledge opened out for a Christian; here spoke the Lord through His holy spirit to the spirit which had taken up a dwelling in man: and, without the revelation of the logos, it was simply impossible to enter into God's presence. Origen used to lift his hands in prayer when he was struggling to find a right meaning, and he felt the kiss of the lips of the logos when a divine secret was revealed to him apart from worldly learning;[3] but he always worked on the basis of academic principles and, as is shown by the case of the Hexapla, he carried out serious philological work in a most extensive measure, and developed a method of allegorical exegesis carefully thought out, and based on the Alexandrian tradition.[4] His commentary on the Gospel of John proves how his methods of work could maintain their place in face of the gnostic methods of Herakleon the Valentinian. His work became the model for Biblical exegesis as practised in the entire Greek Church. Copied out and imitated, it held good from century to century,

[1] W. Völker, *D. Vollkommenheitsideal d. Orig. (Beiträge z. histor. Theol.* 7,1931) pp. 77 ff.
[2] *Comm. in John.* 10,43,298–300 p. 221. 20,32,284–86 p. 369
[3] *Comm. in Cant.* prol. p. 63,26 lib. I p. 91 f.; cf. *Comm. in Matt.* 15,30 (3,392 Lo.)
[4] *de princ.* 4,3,3–9

long after his theology had been condemned. His Bible commentaries still reveal, therefore, many aspects of his religious life and theological thought, aspects re-appearing in his principal, systematic works: we have already taken the opportunity of making the same observation when discussing his Christology.

We mount step by step in our knowledge of God, but each step is Christ: we first understand Him as man, then as angel and heavenly being; first as way, then as door; first as Lord and shepherd, then as king; first is He the lamb who takes away our sin, then His flesh becomes our real food: but in this way, and only in this way, do we come to knowledge of the Father.[1] In the Commentary on Canticles, we hear of three stages: on the first, we exercise ourselves in keeping the Commandments and in the moral life; on the second, we deny the world and its vanity; the third is characterized by longing for the sight of the invisible and the eternal: this yearning is satisfied when God's mercy fires the soul to love the beauty of the logos, and when the logos responds to this love.[2] We find a detailed description of the ascent towards knowledge in the exegesis of Israel's wanderings in the wilderness;[3] and, when explaining the names of places, Origen endeavours to find an indication of the way by which the soul moves towards God, "whether it is the journey out of this world into the future æon, or whether the soul's conversion from the errors of life to virtue and the knowledge of God."

It follows that Origen held that the education of the human race conducted by God's providence only proceeded slowly and step by step, and that he made use of metaphors, and, occasionally, even of terms, which were taken over by mystics of a later date and filled with a new content. We must beware, however, of understanding Origen himself in a mystic sense: the idea of a dissolution of the soul in God was as foreign to him as that of the union of God with a creature. Moreover, a right understanding of the relevant passages proves that visions and ecstasy were never elements of his personal religion.[4]

[1] *Comm. in John.* 19,6,35–39 p. 305   [2] *Comm. in Cant.* prol. p. 79,12 ff.
[3] *Hom. in Numeri* 27,9 ff. p. 268
[4] Hal Koch, *op. cit.*, 333–39 as against W. Völker, *op. cit.*, 62–144

His soul walked along a path to God illuminated by the light of the logos, and he drank open-eyed the more than earthly glory of continually renewed revelations: his soul retained its ego even in feeling the blessedness of God's merciful love.

In his commentary on Canticles he speaks of the gradual ascent of his soul to God, but this is not connected with a technical education in meditation, nor dependent on the production of special sensibilities, but reflects, simply and clearly, a logical, inner development.

The important matter for him, as even his pupil Gregory had felt profoundly, was the complete unity of thought and action. Hence education leading towards moral conduct, towards keeping the Commandments, was placed at the beginning, and, particularly in his sermons, he used to warn hearers continually against self-confidence; he called them to a tireless warfare against sin and the temptations due to daemons. In accordance with the words of the Sermon on the Mount, he opposed the opinion of the average man, set forth a profound conception of sin, and inquired into the matter of evil thoughts. It sounds harsh when he refused those who continue to live in sin the right to share in the "communion of saints", i.e., of genuine Christians.[1] He also taught, however, that perfect righteousness before God could never be attained, and that man's righteousness was always a relative conception: it depended on the criterion employed. It was always possible, and always essential, that a Christian should maintain a higher level than a pagan. He could and should keep God's Commandments. In so doing he earned no dessert: it was his unconditional duty—the first stage of religious training. The conception of merit would only be in place where more was accomplished than the Commandments required; i.e. by asceticism, and for Origen the essential moment in asceticism was sexual continence:[2] what he himself had done in this respect in his youth is recorded by Eusebius.[3] Only the ascetic who had trodden the path to perfection was permitted to enter on the third stage, a life enabling one to conceive the logos gnostically.

[1] Hom. in Lev. 4,4 p. 320 W. Völker, op. cit., p. 31 f.
[2] Comm. in Rom. lib. 3,2 f. (6,178–182 Lo.) lib. 10,14 (7,423 Lo.). Comm. in Matt. 15,13 f. (3,352–54 Lo.). c. Cels. 7,48
[3] Supra, p. 296

The idea, however, of this path, with its ascent from an earnest, moral struggle against the passions to asceticism and so to perfect knowledge, did not arise from a point of view peculiarly Christian, but corresponded to current opinion, and in particular was preached by Platonists. Here we see, not only in theory but also in Origen's practical conduct of life, the influence of Ammonios Sakkas. When we remember that, in Origen's entire system, remoteness from God is reflected in the very creation, and existence, of matter; and that the ascent of the soul implies, at the same time, redemption from the present body; then the parallel between his teaching and the philosophy of Ammonios Sakkas becomes the more illuminating. Nevertheless, even in this regard, Origen had no intention of playing the philosopher; he was a Christian, and was altogether right in feeling the harmony between his opinions and the Bible: he needed no allegory in order to discover the constituent elements of his teaching in Paul and the Gospels, and when he made use of philosophy in order to weld these elements to a unity, he had every right to do so as a systematic thinker. We must admit that he did not come to terms with the entire Paul, the entire John, the entire Gospel, but in this respect who has been his superior? What theologian to the present day is able to boast that he has laid hold of everything which the New Testament sources have given to the world? Origen lived in the Bible to an extent which perhaps no one else has rivalled, except Luther. What knowledge he gained he owed to this book. Here stood the Commandments which regulated his moral life, here echoed the instruction which pointed the way to perfection, here he perceived the voice of the logos which satisfied his Greek thirst for knowledge, and which promised future life to his soul. He read this book like a philosopher, but nevertheless learnt from it something that was higher than any kind of reason, viz. that the way to God did not open out as a reward, but was given by grace. A gifted teacher, for more than fifty years, he marched along this way and offered a practical example to multitudes of his pupils; finally, he testified to the truth of his teaching by dying a martyr's death. The marks left by the life of this Greek Christian are ineradicable, and can be seen in the life and thought of the Greek

Church, by anyone acquainted with the facts. The contest between Christianity and the syncretistic gnosticism ended, even in the sphere of knowledge, with victory for the Ecclesia Catholica: her greatest thinker had created Biblical gnosticism for her use.